O9-BTN-172

THE LION
ENCYCLOPEDIA
OF THE
BIBLE

A LION BOOK
Tring · Batavia · Sydney

Published by The Reader's Digest Association, Inc.,
with permission of Lion Publishing Corporation

Copyright © 1978 Lion Publishing
New Revised Edition copyright © 1986 Lion Publishing

Published by
Lion Publishing plc
Icknield Way, Tring, Herts, England
ISBN 0 7459 1113 7
ISBN 0 7459 1425 X (export edition)
Lion Publishing Corporation
1705 Hubbard Avenue, Batavia, Illinois 60510, USA
ISBN 0 7459 1113 7
ISBN 0 7459 1425 X (export edition)
Albatross Books Pty Ltd
PO Box 320, Sutherland, NSW 2232, Australia
ISBN 0 86760 824 2

First Edition 1978
Reprinted 1981, 1982, 1983, 1985
New Revised Edition 1986
This edition 1987

The original edition of *The Lion
Encyclopedia of the Bible* was
previously published in the USA
by Wm. B. Eerdmans Publishing Co.
under the title *Eerdmans Family
Encyclopedia of the Bible*

British Library Cataloguing in Publication Data

The Lion Encyclopedia of the Bible.—
    New rev. ed.
    1. Bible—Dictionaries
    220.3'21   BS440
    ISBN 0-7459-1113-7

Library of Congress Cataloging-in-Publication Data

The Lion Encyclopedia of the Bible
    "A Lion book."
    Includes index.
    1. Bible—Criticism, interpretation, etc.
    I. Alexander, Pat, 1937–
    BS510.2.L56   1986   220.6'1   86–7226
    ISBN 0-7459-1113-7

PREFACE

For almost 2,000 years the Bible has guided, inspired, helped and comforted countless people the world over. Its attraction is as great today as ever and with the help of modern translations many are reading it for the first time.

Yet, for most readers, the Bible is set in a foreign country, against an unfamiliar background and lifestyle. It is not in fact one book, but a basic collection of sixty-six books (plus the Deutero-canonical writings), written by many different authors. And it spans nearly 2,000 years of history.

All these things can make the Bible difficult to understand and interpret. Questions inevitably arise, and here good reference and background material can be invaluable. Who are the people referred to in a particular passage? When did they live? Where did these events take place? Is anything known about the writer?

The Lion Encyclopedia of the Bible was designed to answer questions like these. At the time this new revision was prepared well over half a million copies were in circulation worldwide, in twelve languages apart from English – a tribute to the help this book has given readers to get into the Bible and understand it.

Information is given, not just in words, but also visually wherever possible. In each of the twelve parts, facts are arranged in the way which best suits the subject and is most helpful to the reader. So sections on people, places and Bible words are in easy reference A–Z order. In other sections information is grouped by theme, with special photo-features. An index to these non-alphabetical sections gives instant access to both text and pictures on a particular subject.

The emphasis is on sheer information – accurate, up-to-date and factual – presented in an interesting and visually exciting way. The text is the work of an experienced and well-qualified team of contributors. Difficult, technical language has been avoided. Photographs and drawings – there are 500 in the book – are factual rather than imaginative. Every effort has been made to ensure their accuracy.

The revision has given the opportunity to update information where that was necessary, to rearrange and supplement material for the maximum benefit of the reader. Above all it has provided more space for larger, clearer text and to liberate the pictures, which have also been added to and improved.

It is the hope of all who have shared in the original creation and the revision of this book that it will give pleasure and enjoyment, and that it will open up the Bible in a new way, making its meaning and message clear.

CONTENTS

CONTRIBUTORS

David Clines MA, Professor of Biblical Studies, Sheffield University: Part 5, *Religion and Worship in the Bible*.

John W. Drane MA, PhD, Lecturer in Religious Studies, Stirling University: *Introducing the Bible* and *Biblical Criticism*, in Part 4, *Understanding the Bible*.

Margaret Embry BA, BD: Part 8, *Work and Society in the Bible* (except *Government* and *Travel*).

David Gillett BA, MPhil: all entries on Bible words in Part 6, *Key Teaching and Events of the Bible*.

Ralph Gower MEd, BD, Staff Inspector for Religious Education, County Hall, London: Part 7, *Home and Family Life in the Bible*.

Colin Hemer MA, PhD, Research Fellow, Tyndale Library for Biblical Research: *Greeks* and *Romans* in Part 11, *Nations and Peoples of the Bible*; co-author of Part 10, *Places of the Bible*.

Kenneth Kitchen BA, PhD, Reader in Egyptian and Coptic, School of Archaeology and Oriental Studies, Liverpool University: *Egyptians* in Part 11, *Nations and Peoples of the Bible*.

Robin Keeley BA: *The Books of the Bible* in Part 4, *Understanding the Bible*.

Alan Millard MA, MPhil, FSA, Rankin Reader in Hebrew and Ancient Semitic Languages, Liverpool University: Part 2, *Archaeology and the Bible*; Part 11, *Nations and Peoples of the Bible* (except *Greeks*, *Romans* and *Egyptians*).

Margaret Moore BA, BD: research material for Part 12, *Atlas of the Bible*.

Stephen Parish Dip Th: *Government* and *Travel* in Part 9, *Work and Society in the Bible*.

John Paterson MA, Emeritus Professor of Geography in the University of Leicester: *The Geography of the Land of Israel* in Part 1, *Land of the Bible*.

Canon R. W. F. Wootton MBE, MA: *Translations and Translators*, in Part 3, *The Story of the Bible*.

Vines grow on the terraced slopes of the Judean hills. After their years of desert wandering, God brought his people to a fertile land where grapes and olives grew in abundance.

1

Land of the Bible

The Geography of the Land of Israel

The Bible claims to be a record of the way God showed himself to man – at a particular time and in a particular place.

The fact that the events happened in one particular area creates problems of understanding for people living in a totally different environment. But it has the great advantage of giving the Bible story a real location. A real history needs a real setting. It says, more clearly than any words, that the Bible is not a series of folk myths that relate only to some legendary country. The land and the people were real, and so, says the Bible, the coming of God to that particular place was real, too.

But why did God select the land of Israel for his 'chosen people'? It was a small, unimportant corridor-land. The national capital, Jerusalem, was a third-rate trade centre in a world which already, even then, possessed some great cities. But the very fact that Israel was a land to pass through, rather than to stop in, made it an ideal place from which new ideas – or new revelations – could spread. It lay between two of the great cultural centres of the early world, Egypt and Mesopotamia. It was a land through which many people passed on the great trade-routes.

It also provided a good environment in which to learn lessons about God, the Creator and Provider. The land depended on him sending the all-important rains, and keeping away locusts and famine. And the landscape quickly showed up any folly or greed on the part of the people who occupied it. Soil erosion, the loss of trees and shrubs,

wells drying up, or fields losing their fertility, all showed that things were going wrong among the people in a land that was supposed to 'flow with milk and honey'. Whatever the reasons for God's choice, the geography of the land of Israel is always relevant to the story of the Bible.

The structure of the land

Most of the Bible story takes place in a very small area at the eastern end of the Mediterranean Sea, in the narrow coastlands that lie between the sea and the vast Arabian deserts. The two worlds of the sea and the desert are separated by the 'Fertile Crescent'. This is the name given to a belt of well-watered lands extending from Egypt in the south (with its civilization based on the flow of the River Nile), through an area of natural rainfall on the east Mediterranean coast, to the fertile irrigated lands of Mesopotamia with their great rivers, the Tigris and the Euphrates.

The crescent forms an attractive feature of the Middle East. It has always appealed to desert peoples from the south and mountain peoples from the north. This is why it has been invaded, or overrun, or changed hands, so many times during its history. The Jewish people themselves never took to the sea – they left that to the Phoenicians. But certainly the desert is never far away in the Bible story. And in the south of Israel it reaches westwards almost to the coast.

☐ A hill country

The 'Promised Land' is very small. From north to south – 'from Dan to Beersheba' as the

Bible puts it – it is less than 150 miles, barely 230km, long. The northern end of the Dead Sea is only 50 miles/80km from the coast (though about 1,300ft/400 metres below sea level). The land is, in fact, rather like the roof of a house. It rises gently from the Mediterranean to about 3,200ft/ 1,000 metres above sea level, and then plunges steeply down to the great gash of the Jordan rift valley. There the earth's surface has cracked and dropped to form a trench which we can trace south all the way into East Africa. East of the Jordan and north of Galilee the mountains rise to greater heights – to nearly 6,500ft/2,000 metres in Edom on the eastern desert fringe, and over 9,800ft/3,000 metres in Lebanon and Mt Hermon to the north.

To surrounding nations, therefore, the people of Israel in their land seemed like hill tribes. 'The gods of Israel are mountain gods,' say King Benhadad's officials. The heart of their kingdoms lay along the mountain spine between the coast and the Jordan rift. In these mountains, they could hold off attacks from the Philistines on the coast. But they themselves never really conquered the coastlands. From time to time (especially under King David) they expanded north into Syria or east beyond the Jordan where, at different times, they took control of Moab and Edom. But the Judean hills were their first base – and their last.

☐ Geology

Geologically, most of the materials making up these lands are young. Limestones or chalk occupy a large part of the surface. The structure is important in helping us understand the Bible.

There are certain characteristic landscape features wherever limestones occur. Water sinks through them (they are permeable), and there is little surface drainage. But they usually develop underground streams and the water can be tapped by sinking wells. Limestones contain many caves. And on the surface they often develop a kind of stony pavement which makes cultivation difficult and yields only a patchy soil. All these features are found in the hills of Palestine and all of them figure in the Bible story.

The desert climate also has its effects on the landscape and its structures. In the desert, regardless of rock type, there is usually a surface covering of sand, flintstone or salt. Much of the southern part of the land is covered by these infertile deposits. Wind and water are the forces which shape the desert rock. The wind scours the desert rocks into fantastic shapes. The force of water, made all the more powerful and dramatic because it is so rare, gouges out steep-sided valleys and overhanging crags. Occasional 'flash' floods can fill a dry valley several metres deep with water in a few minutes.

□ The rift
The long, straight gash of the Jordan Valley, deepening at the Dead Sea, is one of several signs that the earth's surface is unstable. Volcanic activity and changes in the structure are still going on. The Jordan rift has slipped down between two parallel 'faults' to produce the deepest natural depression in the world. The shore of the Sea of Galilee is 660ft/200 metres below sea level. The deepest point of the Dead Sea is more than 2,600ft/800 metres below sea level, despite the deposits brought down by the River Jordan for thousands of years. Hot springs and mineral-stained rocks along the sides

of the rift show that the area is still geologically active.

Climate
The lands on the Mediterranean coast have a climate which is midway between temperate and tropical. The winters are wet, like those of northern countries. The summers are hot and dry, influenced by the tropical deserts that lie beyond the sea's southern rim. Thanks to this seasonal contrast, snow will lie on the coastal mountains but tropical fruits will ripen in the plain.

The climate varies a good deal in the different areas of the Middle East. But there are a few general factors.

□ Rainfall
The amount of rainfall generally depends upon height above sea level. The mountains attract more rain than the lowlands. They also tend to cut off rain-bearing winds and prevent them reaching inland. In Israel/Syria, the result is more rain in the high mountains north of Galilee (29–60in/750–1,500mm each year) than in the hills of Judea (20–29in/500–750mm). The rainfall total lessens rapidly going south. By the time we reach Beersheba it is less than 8in/200mm. South again, desert conditions apply all the way into the Sinai peninsula.

The fall-off in rainfall going *both* inland *and* downhill to the Jordan Valley is even more rapid. The average rainfall for Jerusalem is about 20in/500mm, whereas at Jericho, 15 miles/25km to the east but 3,200ft/1,000 metres lower, it is barely 4in/100mm. It then rises again on the east side of the Jordan, so that there is a

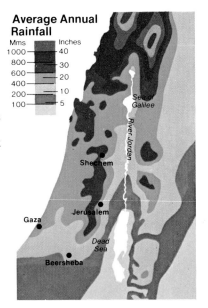

Average Annual Rainfall

Mms		Inches
1000		40
800		30
600		20
400		
200		10
100		5

Sea of Galilee

River Jordan

Shechem

Gaza

Jerusalem

Dead Sea

Beersheba

tongue of desert extending north up the Jordan Valley from the Dead Sea, but a tongue of well-watered hill country extending south on the east side of the Jordan all the way from Lebanon to Edom.

No wonder that two and a half of the original twelve tribes decided that the land on the east side of the Jordan Valley was as good for their cattle as the land on the west, and asked if they could settle there rather than across the river in the land God promised (Numbers 32). In later years, this land – the land of Gilead – became famous for its fertility. Its hills brought as much rain as that of the hills of Judea, which are nearer the coast but not as high.

Although the northern part of Palestine seems to have a good amount of rainfall (similar to that of southern Britain, for example) the average is very deceptive. There are in fact great

Cross-section of the land

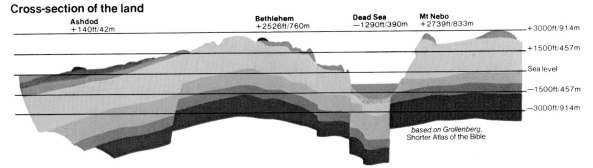

Ashdod +140ft/42m

Bethlehem +2526ft/760m

Dead Sea −1290ft/390m

Mt Nebo +2739ft/833m

+3000ft/914m

+1500ft/457m

Sea level

−1500ft/457m

−3000ft/914m

based on Grollenberg,
Shorter Atlas of the Bible

variations in the total from year to year. In Jerusalem, where the average is 20in/500mm, there have been years with as little as 10in/250mm and as much as 42in/1,075mm during the past century. This means that the margin of the desert is not fixed. In some years the margin withdraws east and south. In other years it overruns the area and there is drought and famine. These exceptionally wet and exceptionally dry years play a great part in the Bible story. They constantly remind God's people that they depend on him.

☐ Dew
In places where there is not much rain, the dew may play an important part in watering the land. Most of the areas with heavy dews are on the coast. The moisture comes in from the Mediterranean during the summer days, then falls to the ground as dew when it is cooled at night.

Some coastal areas may have dew on 200 nights each year, and it can give them as much as a quarter of their moisture. So it is not difficult to see why the dew plays so large a part in the life of Bible peoples. Elijah the prophet, for example, predicting a drought, says 'there will be no dew or rain' (1 Kings 17:1).

☐ Winter rains
In the Near East and northern Africa most of the rain for the year comes in the winter season. Between the middle of June and September, rain is unlikely to fall. The weather conditions are stable and predictable, dominated by a flow of air from the east. For example, for thirty years Tel Aviv, on the coast, has never recorded rain in June, July or August.

After such a dry summer, the coming of the rains is especially important for the farmer. They should begin in mid-September, but the start of the rainy season is sometimes delayed. This gives the farmer

less time for ploughing, and there is also less time for the wells to fill up again after the summer's use. So the Bible pictures the farmer watching and waiting for the autumn rain (James 5:7), to begin work.

Once the rains really start, the winter months are wet. December, or January, has most rain. The rain blows in from the Mediterranean for two to three days at a time, followed by drier and brighter conditions. This pattern continues until, in late March or early April, drier weather sets in. But this is a very important time for the farmer. Plants are beginning to grow after the winter cold. It is vital that the rains continue for long enough into the spring for his crops to be watered during their growing period. He therefore looks for the 'later' rain in April, as well as the 'early' rain in October.

☐ Temperature
The temperature range in lands with seasonal rainfall is often very large. There are great contrasts – for example between a summer's day by the Dead Sea, with temperatures reaching 40°C as a matter of course, and a wet winter's day a hundred miles away in Upper Galilee, where a freezing rain is falling. Winter weather on the uplands can be very unpleasant. There are 45–60 days of rain, and snow often falls in winter in Jerusalem. The daily changes can be trying in low-lying areas, too. Jericho has a January average temperature of 15°C. But this is made up of high daytime temperatures and freezing nights.

Temperatures in summer on the coast and in the uplands average a pleasant 22–25°C. They are affected generally by height above sea level and, from time to time, by the winds. In the daytime, in summer, cooling breezes blow in from the Mediterranean to make the heat less intense. But the effect of the *hamsin* is

Vegetation in Bible times

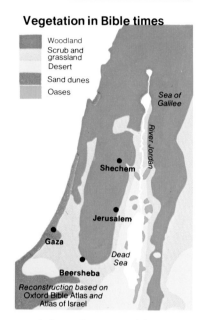

Woodland
Scrub and grassland
Desert
Sand dunes
Oases

Sea of Galilee

River Jordan

Shechem

Jerusalem

Gaza

Dead Sea

Beersheba

Reconstruction based on Oxford Bible Atlas and Atlas of Israel

much less pleasant. This fiercely hot and dry wind blows from the south, out of Arabia, bringing a breath from the desert which can sometimes be felt even near the coast. It is well known to the people who live in Israel. 'When you feel the south wind blowing,' Jesus said, 'you say that it is going to get hot – and it does' (Luke 12:55).

The climate today does not seem to be very different from the time when Israel occupied the Promised Land, or when Jesus lived there. The landscape has certainly changed (see below) but this is not because of a change in climate.

Vegetation
In an area with this sort of climate we would expect to find the following kinds of vegetation – starting in the heart of the desert and moving outwards to the coast and the mountains: desert scrub – steppeland with shrubs and grasses – grassland – transitional woodland – forest at higher levels. We would also expect many of the plants to be specially adapted to store water from the wet to the dry season – plants with shiny, smooth,

continued on page 22

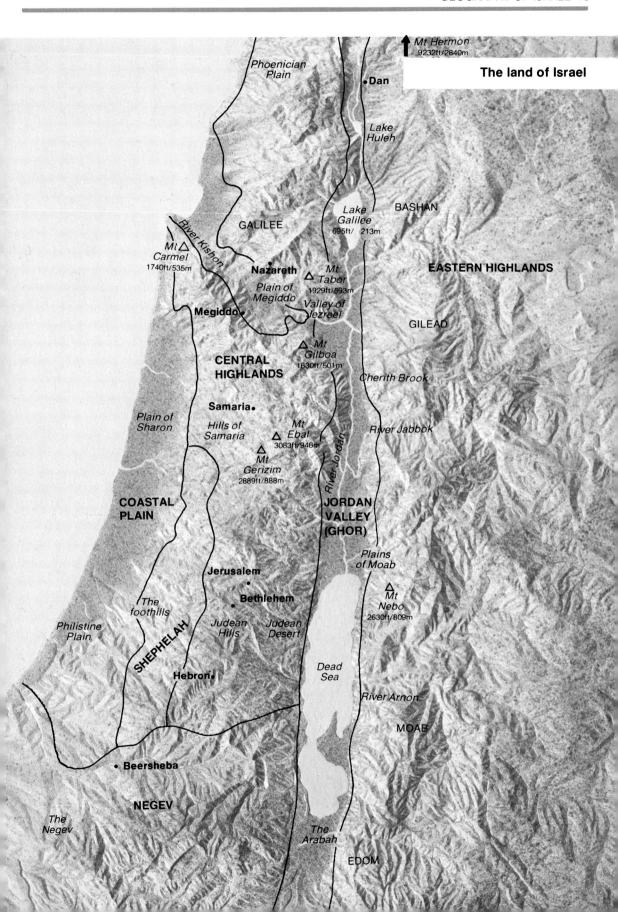

Mt Hermon
9232ft/2840m

The land of Israel

• Dan

Phoenician Plain

Lake Huleh

BASHAN

Lake Galilee
695ft/ 213m

GALILEE

River Kishon

Mt △
Carmel
1740ft/535m

Nazareth

△ Mt
Tabor
1929ft/593m

EASTERN HIGHLANDS

Plain of Megiddo

Megiddo•

Valley of Jezreel

GILEAD

△ Mt
Gilboa
1630ft/501m

Cherith Brook

CENTRAL HIGHLANDS

Samaria•

Plain of Sharon

Hills of Samaria

△ Mt
Ebal
3083ft/948m

River Jabbok

△ Mt
Gerizim
2889ft/888m

River Jordan

COASTAL PLAIN

JORDAN VALLEY (GHOR)

Plains of Moab

Jerusalem
•

△ Mt
Nebo
2630ft/809m

The foothills

Bethlehem
•

Philistine Plain

Judean Hills

Judean Desert

SHEPHELAH

Hebron•

Dead Sea

River Arnon

Beersheba

MOAB

NEGEV

The Negev

The Arabah

EDOM

Plants of the Bible

The Bible mentions many different plants. Some are well known; others are hard to identify. This page shows some of the most interesting and important ones. Herbs and spices were used in seasoning food, preparing medicines, and as sweet-smelling incense in the tabernacle and temple worship.

Staple crops and plants

Beans and lentils Broad beans can be cooked as a vegetable, or dried and ground into flour. The lentil grows in a small flat pod, like a pea. It is red-coloured and is usually made into soups and stews (such as Jacob made for Esau), but can also be dried and ground into flour.
2 Samuel 17:28; Ezekiel 4:9; Genesis 25:34

Cereals: barley, wheat, millet and spelt These were a major part of the normal diet in ancient Israel. Wheat made the best flour and bread; it was used to make the bread the priests offered to God. Barley, which ripens before wheat and is harvested in early summer, was the food of the poorer peasants. When Egypt's barley crop was ruined by the plague of hailstorms, the wheat, which came up later, was saved. Spelt is a poor kind of wheat; and millet, which is rather like rye, makes the worst bread of all. It is mentioned in Ezekiel as food fit for a time of famine.
Exodus 9:31–32; Ezekiel 4:9

Flax Linen cloth is made from this pretty blue-flowered plant which grows about 1½ft (45cm) high. After the plants are pulled up, the stem fibres are separated by steeping them in water (retting). They can then be combed and woven like threads. The fibres are also used for string nets and lamp-wicks. Linen was used for sails. It was also wrapped round dead bodies, and made into fine clothes, in Egypt and Israel.
Exodus 26:1; Joshua 2:1, 6; Proverbs 31:13; Ezekiel 27:7; Mark 15:46

Papyrus A sedge which grew in the marsh areas of the Nile Delta (and still grows in northern Israel), from which the paper of the ancient world was made. Its mop-like flower-heads are 10ft (3m) high or more. The three-cornered stems were cut into thin strips. Two layers, one at right-angles to the other, were laid out on a hard wooden surface and hammered together. These sheets of paper were then pasted end to end to form a roll. Much of the Bible would have been written on papyrus. It was also used to make boats and baskets (like the one in which Moses' mother put her baby son), ropes and sandals.

Flavourings and seasonings

Cinnamon Oil distilled from the bark of the cinnamon tree, and used to flavour food and wine.
Song of Solomon 4:14; 8:2

Ointments, medicines and perfumes

Frankincense Gum collected by peeling back the bark of the frankincense-tree (*Boswellia*) and cutting into the trunk. The resin gives off a sweet scent when warmed or burned, and was used as incense in Bible times. Frankincense was one of the gifts brought to Jesus by the three wise men.
Exodus 30:34–38; Leviticus 2:1, 15–16; Matthew 2:11

Wild flowers and weeds

'Lily of the field' In the Old Testament the lily may have been the wild blue hyacinth, or the madonna lily (the bulb was also considered a delicacy to eat). When Jesus spoke of the lilies of the field he was probably thinking of wild flowers in general, rather than one in particular. In spring the hillsides of Galilee are ablaze with brightly coloured flowers: anemone, crocus, poppy, narcissus and yellow chrysanthemum.
Song of Solomon 5:13; 6:2; Matthew 6:28

Plants of the Bible

Cummin and dill Cummin seeds were used to spice meat, also in eye medicine. Dill (or anise) seed flavours bread or cakes. The Pharisees gave God a tenth of everything, even their seasoning herbs – mint, cummin and dill – but Jesus said they neglected more important things: honesty, justice and mercy.
Isaiah 28:25 – 27; Matthew 23:23

Hyssop On the cross, Jesus was given vinegar in a sponge passed to him on a bunch of hyssop. In the Old Testament it was used in sprinkling the blood of the sacrifice, and on the eve of the Passover. It was obviously a bushy plant, and must therefore have been different from the herb we call by the same name today, and may have been either marjoram (pictured here) or caper.
Exodus 12:21 – 22; John 19:29

Mustard God's kingdom, Jesus said, is like the tiny mustard seed, which grows into a great plant. He was probably talking about the black mustard, whose seeds were grown for oil as well as flavouring. Usually about 4ft (120cm) high, these plants can grow to 15ft (460cm).
Matthew 13:31 – 32

Myrrh Pale yellow gum from a shrub which grows in Somalia, Ethiopia and Arabia. Used as a spice and a medicine, and in making the holy oil for the tabernacle and temple. Myrrh was brought to Jesus by the wise men. It was mixed with the drink offered to him on the cross as a pain-killer. And Joseph and Nicodemus later embalmed Jesus' body with myrrh and aloes.
Exodus 30:23 – 24; Matthew 2:11; Mark 15:23; John 19:39 – 40

Spikenard (nard) A sweet-smelling ointment was made from this plant which grows in India. It was imported to Israel in sealed alabaster jars to preserve the perfume. This was the costly gift that Mary lavished on Jesus.
Song of Solomon 4:13; Mark 14:3; John 12:3

Wormwood and gall Wormwood is the bitter-tasting absinthe, used in the Bible as a symbol of sorrow and bitterness. Gall may be the juice of the opium poppy.

'Rose' The word often translated 'rose' in the Bible is not the rose as we know it, but probably the narcissus in Isaiah 35:1, and a mountain tulip in the Song of Solomon 2:1.

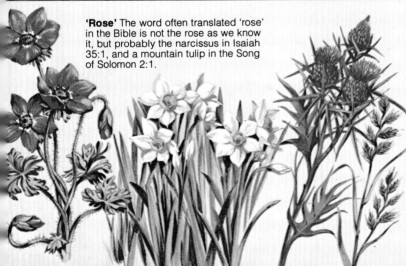

Thistles, thorns and tares Thistles and thorns abound in dry lands like Israel – over 120 kinds, some growing to over 6ft/2m. Some, such as the milk-thistle, have beautiful flowers, but can quickly suffocate young plants at the edges of fields (as in Jesus' story of the sower and the soils). Thorns like those pictured here were plaited into a mock-crown for Jesus at his trial. The 'tares' in the story of the wheat and the weeds are darnel, which looks exactly like wheat in its early stages.
Genesis 3:18; Matthew 13:7; Mark 15:15, 17 – 18; Matthew 13:24 – 30

Trees and Shrubs

Trees are very important to any country's economy. They affect climate and prevent soil erosion, quite apart from their practical uses. Before industrialization, people depended on trees for food and shelter, fuel and most building projects. In Solomon's day the wealth of Lebanon lay in its great forests of cedar and other valuable woods. Some of the more important trees for the people of the Bible are illustrated on this page.

Gourd The plant which grew up overnight to shade Jonah from the burning sun may have been the fast-growing castor-oil bush.
Jonah 4:6

Trees and shrubs for fruit

Almond The almond was the first fruit-tree to blossom in Israel, sometimes as early as January. As well as being a favourite food, the nut also produced oil. The most famous Bible reference is Aaron's almond rod which flowered and produced fruit overnight.
Numbers 17:8

Fig and sycomore fig The fig was an important fruit in Bible times. The ideal of peace and prosperity was summed up as 'everyone able to sit down under his own vine and fig-tree'. Figs are slow-growing trees, bearing fruit for about ten months of the year. The large leaves make useful wrappings. Cakes of dried figs made excellent food – compact 'iron rations' which were easy to carry. Amos the herds-man and prophet also 'took care of fig-trees'. The tree Zacchaeus climbed to get a better view of Jesus was a sycomore — another kind of fig-tree.
Amos 7:14; Luke 19:4

Olive One of the main tree-crops of ancient Israel. The berries were harvested in about November, by shaking or beating the branches with poles. Some olives were eaten pickled, but most were taken in baskets to the presses, where the valuable oil was crushed out. Olive oil was used for cooking, as fuel for lamps, and as a soothing lotion for the skin. In ancient Israel it was also used to anoint kings and priests. It was the way a person was set apart for special work. The trees themselves can live to an age of several hundred years. The wood can also be carved and polished for fine work, as in Solomon's temple.
Deuteronomy 24:20; Judges 9:8; 1 Kings 17:12–16; 1 Samuel 10:1; 1 Kings 6:23

Non-fruiting trees and shrubs

Acacia (*shittim*) The wood from which the Covenant Box (ark) was made for the tabernacle. The acacia is one of the few trees to grow in the Sinai desert.
Exodus 25:10

Cedar The beautiful, giant cedar of Lebanon, which once grew in great forests. Although the cedar is still the national symbol of Lebanon only a few of these trees remain, high in the mountains. In Solomon's day King Hiram of Tyre exported vast quantities of cedar. The wood is a warm red colour, and long-lasting. It could be carved and decorated, and was used to panel Solomon's temple and palace.
1 Kings 6:15–7:12

Myrtle An evergreen with fragrant leaves and sweet-scented white flowers which were used as perfume.

Fir and pine The wood from these evergreens which grew on the mountains and hills was used in building the temple, for ships' decks and making musical instruments.
1 Kings 5:8; Ezekiel 27:5

Trees and shrubs

Palm (date) A tall tree with a straight trunk topped by a tuft of huge 6ft (2m) leaves, amongst which the clusters of dates grow to provide valuable food. The palm became a national symbol of Israel, standing for victory. The people waved palm leaves when Jesus rode in triumph into Jerusalem. The shape of the palm was often copied for decoration in stone carving.
John 12:13

Pomegranate Scarlet flowers contrast with deep-green leaves on this large shrub. The yellowy-brown edible fruits are the size of an orange. Inside the hard rind is a juicy pulp, full of seeds. The shape was copied in embroidery round the edge of the high priest's robe, and carved on the pillars in Solomon's temple.
Exodus 28:33; 1 Kings 7:20

Vine A trailing shrub producing grapes, one of the most important of all fruit-crops. Moses' spies brought back huge clusters of grapes as a sign of the richness of the Promised Land. Vines were planted in rows in carefully prepared vineyards on the sunny hill slopes. Each spring the vines were pruned, and as the grapes ripened the owner kept a sharp look-out for intruders – animal or human – from a special watch-tower. At harvest time the grapes were picked and taken to be trodden out at the wine-press. Some were also made into raisin-cakes. The fermenting wine was stored in new skins or pottery jars to mature. The vine was a national emblem in Israel, a symbol of peace and prosperity. Jesus used it in five of his parables, and described himself as the true vine on which the branches (his followers) depend.
Numbers 13:20, 24; Matthew 9:17; 20:1–6; 21:28–32, 33; Luke 13:6–9; John 15:1

Oak There are many kinds of oaks in Israel, some of them evergreen. They are strong trees growing for many years. The wood was used for oars and for carving statues. Absalom was caught in an oak when he fled from King David.
2 Samuel 18: 9–10; 1 Kings 13:14; Isaiah 2:13

Terebinth A spreading tree, less than 25ft (7m) high, common in warm, dry hilly places in and around Israel.

Poplar Jacob peeled poplar shoots when he tricked Laban. The white poplar has fast-growing shoots and gives a dense shade. The 'willows' of Babylon, where the exiles mourned, were probably a kind of poplar.
Genesis 30:37; Psalm 137:2

Willow The willows of Israel are shrubs or small trees, often found in thickets beside streams. See also *Poplar*.

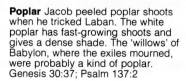

Animals of the Bible

The animals pictured and listed on this page are those most often mentioned in the Bible, and the most important ones. You will find more information in Part 5: *Religion and Worship in the Bible* and in Part 7: *Home and Family Life in the Bible.*

Wild animals: hunters and hunted

Bear The Syrian brown bear was quite common in the hilly and wooded parts of Israel in Bible times. Bears will eat almost anything. They usually live on fruit, roots, eggs, bees' and ants' nests. But when they are hungry they may take a lamb from the flock. David, as a shepherd, had to protect his flock against them; and the Bible tells how bears attacked a mob who were jeering at the prophet Elisha. The Syrian brown bear still lives in the Middle East, but not in Israel. 1 Samuel 17:34–36; 2 Samuel 17:8; 2 Kings 2:24

Leopard Isaiah and Jeremiah both mention the leopard, which was well known in Israel in Bible times. Its spotted coat helps it to creep up on its kill unseen, even in the open. Isaiah 11:6; Jeremiah 13:23

Fox and jackal These are smaller cousins of the wolf. The fox, who hunts alone, likes fruit and often damages the low vines. Jackals go about in packs, scavenging at night. The foxes in the story of Samson were probably jackals. Judges 15:4

Beasts of burden

Ass (donkey) and mule The most common of all pack animals, used for carrying heavy loads, and also for riding by rich and poor alike. The donkey is a descendant of the North African wild ass. The mule is cross-bred from a donkey (male) and a horse. Both ass and mule are sure-footed and can live in much rougher country than horses. The ass is the 'hero' of the story of Balaam. Lost asses led Saul to a vital meeting with Samuel. And it was an ass which Jesus rode into Jerusalem on Palm Sunday, as a king coming in peace. Numbers 22; 1 Samuel 9 and 10; Zechariah 9:9; Matthew 21:1–11

Camel In the Old Testament, usually the one-humped Arabian camel, invaluable to desert nomads. It can live on poor food and go for several days without drinking. In ordinary use it can carry a load of about 400lb/180kg, as well as its rider. Camels are mentioned in the stories of Abraham, Jacob and Job. The Israelites were not allowed to eat camel-meat. Genesis 12:16; 30:43; Job 1:3

Horse In Bible times horses were owned only by the rich. They were not kept in Israel until David's day. The country's geographical position made Solomon a convenient middleman, trading in chariots from Egypt and horses from Turkey (Cilicia). The horse was a 'weapon' of war and stood for power. Exodus 14:23; Joshua 11:4; Esther 6:8, 10, 11

Animals of the Bible

Lion The lion is mentioned many times in the Bible – although by New Testament times it was rare in Israel. Assyrian kings kept lions in pits, and enjoyed lion-hunts with their nobles. Lions lived in the thickets of the Jordan Valley and could be a danger to flocks and to humans. The strength and courage of the lion made him a symbol of power, so that Jesus himself is called 'lion of the tribe of Judah'. Daniel 6:16–24; Revelation 5:5

Deer and gazelle These graceful animals provide the Bible writers with a picture of swiftness and gentleness. Fallow and roe deer, gazelles and ibex, whose sandy colouring makes them difficult to spot, were a major source of meat. Deuteronomy 12:15; Song of Solomon 2:8–9

Wolf Fierce and dangerous hunters which usually feed on smaller animals, but will also attack and kill deer, sheep and even cattle. The Bible speaks of cruel and evil leaders as 'wolves' and Jesus described his followers as 'sheep among wolves'. Matthew 7:15; Luke 10:3

Rock hyrax (Authorized Version, 'coney', Revised Standard Version, 'badger'.) A small, shy animal about the size of a rabbit, with neat ears and no tail. The hyrax lives in colonies in rocky places. Proverbs 30:26

Farm animals: flocks and herds

Sheep and goats From very early times, before there was settled farming, nomads depended on their flocks of sheep and goats for milk, cheese, meat and clothes. Goatskins were the standard water-bottle. Black goat-hair was woven into strong cloth for tents. Wool from the sheep was spun and woven into warm cloaks and tunics. Both sheep and goats were killed in the tabernacle and temple sacrifices. They were well suited to rough hill pasture. Shepherds often looked after mixed flocks of sheep and goats, protecting them from wild animals and leading them to fresh grazing and watering-places. Genesis 27:9; 4:2; Exodus 26:7; Leviticus 1:10; Matthew 25:32; John 10:1–12

Cattle Long before Abraham came to Canaan, herds of cattle were kept to provide milk and meat, and leather from skins. The ox pulled the farmer's plough and his threshing-sledge, and was harnessed to wagons and carts. Cattle were killed in the tabernacle and temple sacrifices. A man's wealth was reckoned by the numbers of cattle and sheep he owned. Bashan, to the east of the Jordan, was famous for its cattle. Genesis 1:24; 13:2; Leviticus 1:2

Birds of the Bible

The Bible names about 50 kinds of birds, and it is difficult to be sure of the exact identity of many of them. Some of the more common ones are pictured and listed here. You will find more information in Part 5: *Religion and Worship in the Bible* and in Part 7: *Home and Family Life in the Bible.*

Birds of prey

Eagles and vultures The word usually translated 'eagle' also includes the Griffon-Vulture. From a distance both look alike. Isaiah and the Psalmist both speak of the eagle's strength and vigour. The 'eagle' was the badge of the Roman legions. Matthew probably had that in mind when he described the eagles waiting for Jerusalem to fall.
Isaiah 40:31; Psalm 103:5; Matthew 24:28

Owl Owls are night-time hunters, flying on almost silent wings to swoop down on the small creatures they eat. The Eagle Owl (the largest), Tawny Owl, Barn Owl and Scops Owl (the smallest) are all known in Israel. In the Bible the owl is pictured as the inhabitant of ruined and desolate places.
Leviticus 11:16; Isaiah 34:15

Raven The name probably includes crows and rooks as well as ravens. All are large, black, flesh-eating birds. After the flood, Noah sent out a raven to see if the land was dry. Ravens are also said to have fed Elijah in a time of famine.
Genesis 8:7; 1 Kings 17:4

Birds for food and sacrifice

Doves and pigeons The most common and important of all the Bible birds. Several kinds are native to Israel; others come as winter visitors. They were widely kept as domestic birds, for food. Poor people who could not afford to sacrifice a sheep or goat would offer two pigeons – which they could buy in the temple courts – instead. It was a dove that brought back to Noah the first green leaf after the flood.
Genesis 8:8–12; Psalm 55:6; Matthew 3:16; 21:12

Partridge The name probably includes three kinds of partridge: the Rock Partridge, the Desert Partridge and the Black Partridge. All are game birds whose flesh and eggs can make a good meal. The Rock Partridge hides itself so well that it is more often heard than seen.
1 Samuel 26:20

Birds of the Bible

Migrants and visitors

Quail Quails provided the Israelites with meat as they journeyed from Egypt at the time of the exodus. Twice a year vast numbers of quails fly across this region, migrating north in summer, south in winter. Exhausted by the long flight, they fly low above the ground and are easily caught.
Exodus 16:13; Numbers 11:31-35

Crane A regular migrant and winter visitor to Israel. A large grey bird with a wing-span of 8ft/2.5 metres, the crane feeds mostly on seeds and leaves.

Sparrow The word is often used to mean any small bird suitable for eating, but in some places refers specifically to the Hedge Sparrow. Larks and finches as well as sparrows have often been trapped or shot to be cooked and eaten. Jesus used the sparrow to emphasize how much God loves his creatures. If he cares even for the smallest birds, how much more will he care for people.
Matthew 10:29-31; Luke 12:6-7

Peacock A native of India and Sri Lanka (Ceylon), the peacock was imported into Israel by King Solomon and kept as an ornamental bird, suiting the splendour of the royal palace.

Stork Both White and Black Storks pass through Israel every year, flying north from their wintering-places in Arabia and Africa. The larger and more numerous White Stork is seen most often. Storks live mostly on small animal life – snakes, fish, mice, worms and insects.
Jeremiah 8:7

non-evaporating surfaces. All these types of vegetation are, in fact, found in the land of the Bible and its surroundings, the forests in Lebanon to the north, and the desert scrub to the south. The steppe and grassland forms just a narrow band around the uplands of Judea and east of the Jordan at middle levels. However, on the coastal slopes most of the original grassland has long since been ploughed and sown. And some of the desert was cultivated by irrigation agri-culture in Roman times just as it is in modern Israel.

☐ **Changes**
But there have been great changes over the centuries. When Israel entered the Promised Land, most of the upland area was covered by woods. Even in the time of Jesus there seems to have been considerable tree cover. Many kinds of hardwoods and softwoods are referred to in the Old Testament, and the Romans laid out forest plantations. Today, the landscape is quite different, and almost all the forest and woodland has disappeared.

Felling trees for building and firewood and to clear land for ploughing led to soil erosion. This meant that new trees could not grow, and the woods were gradually replaced by the kind of thorny scrub (*maquis*) which is so common in long-settled Mediterranean lands. This scrub clutters the ground and is quite useless (for example, for building). It contains few trees of any size, is a serious fire risk in summer and today may represent all that remains of once-splendid forests. In Israel there has also been deliberate destruction of trees in war after war and destructive grazing by goats. The same has happened on the now-bare hills of Moab, east of the Jordan, which was once a densely-settled woodland area.

Only in the past half-century have we begun to reverse this process of deforestation. This was just in time to save a few of the famous cedars of Lebanon and some of the mountain forest of the north. Landscape changes over the same time have been even more dramatic, because they have happened so much more quickly than those taking place in the long and dreadful period of destruction. Marshes have been drained and cultivated. Groves of fruit trees have been planted in place of the old oak woodlands. And irrigation has been extended into the desert, in some cases to the same areas once farmed under Roman rule in the time of Jesus. It is well known that some desert soils are fertile when watered. And the southern fringe, together with the lower Jordan Valley, is an area of oasis agriculture – for example at Jericho and Engedi.

The resources of the land
☐ **Water**
Israel has the desert at its door and the rain comes only in winter. It is a land where it has always been important to save and store water. The Jordan is the only river of any size, and that empties uselessly (from the point of view of conserving water) into the Dead Sea – where water evaporates from the surface at a rate of 60in/1,500mm a year. The Jordan flows all the year round, fed by snow from Mt Hermon. But this is exceptional. Most streams flow in sudden spates, followed by months when their beds are dry.

So, from earliest times, the towns and villages of Israel have relied on wells and springs for their water supply. The right of access to a well was a valuable privilege. If the wells in an area were blocked up, the inhabitants were left to die of thirst. As cities grew bigger, the problem of keeping them supplied with water became acute. Jerusalem, high in the porous limestone hills, needed a whole system of waterworks. King Hezekiah 'built a reservoir and dug a tunnel to bring water into the city' to safeguard the supply of water if the city was besieged (2 Kings 20:20).

The Romans built aqueducts and irrigation canals to cope with the problem. But after they left, the works fell into disrepair. Only in the twentieth century have they been restored or replaced. However, the modern state of Israel was not content to watch its main water resource – the Jordan – run untapped into the Dead Sea. A project has been developed in recent years for diverting Galilee water to other uses. Part of the problem is, of course, that both the Sea of Galilee and the Jordan are far below sea level and, if their waters are to be used anywhere outside the rift valley, it is necessary to pump water up over the 'spine' of Israel. This has now been done, and the water is taken south down the coastal plain in a series of canals and tunnels. These go as far as the Tekuma reservoir, near Gaza. They have made town supply schemes and irrigation possible as far south as the fringe of the desert.

☐ **Minerals**
God promised Israel a fertile land. In addition 'its rocks have iron in them, and from its hills you can mine copper' (Deuteronomy 8:9). Copper has been mined from very early times. Mining for iron came later, after the Hittites had discovered how to smelt it. The Philistines brought the secret with them. But not until the time of David and Solomon were the Israelites able to make their own iron tools. The copper mines just north of the Gulf of Aqaba were in full production in Solomon's time.

The country's other main resources are building stones, pitch, sands and clays, with a variety of chemical salts in the Dead Sea area where evapor-ation has left them bedded in thick layers. Today phosphate rock is extensively worked, and the waters of the Dead Sea themselves yield potash, bromine and magnesium.

Many other materials have to be imported but there is nothing new about this. The enormous wealth of Solomon came from trade with Israel's neighbours. The fleet which sailed with the ships of Tyre brought back 'gold, silver, ivory, apes and monkeys' (1 Kings 10:22). Spices were brought from Arabia. The fine timber and jewels for the temple were imported through King Hiram of Tyre.

☐ Fisheries
Fishing, which plays so large a part in the New Testament Gospels, was a natural food resource of Israel. Almost all the fishing was on the Sea of Galilee (also called Chinnereth or Chinneroth, the Lake of Gennesaret or Sea of Tiberias). This inland freshwater lake is 12 miles/20km long and 6 miles/10km broad. The River Jordan flows through it. The fishing industry supported whole communities in the shore-line villages. It was here that Jesus chose his first disciples, from among the fishermen. Some of the fish was dried and kept for eating in the winter.

Rather surprisingly, these were the *only* fisheries the Jewish people had. They never really controlled the Mediterranean coastlands, and they certainly never took to the sea, either as merchants or as deep-sea fishermen. The fish sold in Jerusalem was supplied by non-Jewish merchants, for example from Tyre.

Nothing can live in Israel's other great reservoir of water

the Dead Sea. So what might otherwise have been a larger and busier lake than Galilee had empty shores. The prophet Ezekiel had a vision of fishermen lining the shores of the Dead Sea and spreading out their nets to dry (Ezekiel 47:10). But this has yet to be, at some future time when living fresh water flows to replace the dead salt water.

The land of the Bible and its regions
The Jews in the time of Jesus had a very precise idea of what was, and what was not, 'the land'. Their 'regional geography' was based on a scale which worked from the most sacred to the least sacred area.

The Holy of Holies in Jerusalem came highest on the scale and, at the other end, the very touch of the dust of areas outside 'the land' was considered defiling.

The heart of the country consisted of Judea and Galilee on the west side of the Jordan, separated by Samaria (which did not belong to it) but linked on the east bank by Peraea. The approved route from north to south without leaving 'the land' (avoiding Samaria) involved crossing the Jordan twice.

Surrounding this core area was a kind of inner belt of lands which had once belonged to Israel. They were thought to be not quite as defiling as the heathen lands that were completely outside the boundaries.

The more usual regional geography, however, recog-

The Lake of Galilee, ringed around by hills.

nizes seven major natural divisions in the land.

☐ The central highlands
The core area of the Jewish kingdoms lay in the 'hill country' along the watershed – with the land sloping away to the coast on one side, and away to the Jordan Valley on the other. This upland rises to just over 3,280ft/1,000 metres at its highest points, near Hebron. The western slope is gentle, the eastern abrupt. The forest cover has long since gone and it has become a region of bare limestone slabs and poor soils. Cultivation is on terraces and in very small fields; much of the area is used for raising stock. The fortified

The hills and valleys of Samaria.

towns of this hill-country made good defence points. The capitals of the southern and northern kingdoms (Judah and Israel) were both in this area. The northern kings of Israel used several different strong-points before building the capital at Samaria.

At the northern end of this region a number of isolated hills look down on the neighbouring region, the Plain of Esdraelon. But the hill country continues north-westwards to the coast in the jutting promontory of Mt Carmel. The 1,970ft/600-metre ridge cuts the coastal plain in

Vines and olives grow on the terraced slopes of the Judean hills. Many famous Bible places – Hebron (Abraham's eventual home), Bethlehem (birthplace of Jesus), Jerusalem – lie in this area.

two, breaking the general north-south pattern of the regions. On the northern edge of Carmel lies the modern port-city of Haifa.

Even today the 'hill country' has few roads apart from the main Hebron–Jerusalem–Nablus (ancient Shechem) highway. The main highways of both the ancient and modern worlds pass north of the hills or run parallel with them along the coast. So, although this region contains Jerusalem, it has always stood a little apart from the everyday comings and goings through the land.

☐ The Plain of Esdraelon

Some distance back from the Mediterranean coast, mountain ranges run in a continuous line from Lebanon to Sinai. But there is one important break where a fault in the underlying rock has caused a section of mountain to drop to a height of 300ft/100 metres or less. This break divides the central highlands from Galilee and the northern mountains. It extends from Haifa Bay, north of Mt Carmel, to the valley of the Harod, a tributary of the Jordan. The watershed itself is cut through by the Valley of Jezreel.

The central plain forms a rough triangle, with each side about 15 miles/24km long. Originally, the floor of the valley was marshy. It was here that Sisera lost his chariots and had to escape on foot – Judges 4:15. But it has been drained and today forms the most fertile agricultural area in the modern state of Israel.

Although the plain was infertile for many centuries before Jewish settlers began to reclaim it in 1911, it has always had great strategic importance. The principal north-south route of the ancient world (which the

In the foreground is the Negev Desert, scene of Israel's wilderness wanderings. On the far side of the dry Arabah Valley is the mountainous land of Edom.

Galilee is a region of dry hills and fertile valleys to the west and north of Lake Galilee. Jesus grew up at Nazareth in Galilee. When he began his public work, he spent much of his time teaching and healing here. Many of his closest friends earned their living as fishermen on the lake.

Romans called *Via Maris*, 'the way of the sea') cut through it on the way from Egypt to Damascus and Mesopotamia. It was an obvious route for trade – or for invasion. This may account for the long list of battles which have been fought in the plain, right up to modern times, in the Israeli War of Independence (1948). Megiddo lies at the western edge of the plain so the Hill of Megiddo, or 'Armageddon', became a symbol of the great battle in Revelation 16.

☐ Galilee

North of the Plain of Esdraelon, the upland ranges begin again. They stretch away northwards, gradually rising as they come nearer to the high mountains of Lebanon. They rise in a series of steps, with scarp edges facing generally south or south-east. The lower steps in the 'staircase' were and are fertile basin lands, separated from each other by the barren limestone edges. In the time of Jesus, these basins were known for their grain, fruit and olives. They formed a prosperous, well-populated area. But the higher steps rise to a bleak and windswept upland. This is isolated and infertile, and lacks the forests of the higher mountain slopes further north.

This whole area forms the region of Galilee, sometimes divided into Lower and Upper Galilee. The southern and eastern edges of the region are clearly drawn, but to the north, it merges into the mountains. In the past this northern boundary area was always the part of 'the land' where foreign influences were strongest. The Israelites seldom really had it under control. And the great trade routes which passed across it brought in many strangers.

This was the region where Jesus spent his childhood years. It was a busy area, full of coming and going, with a very mixed community. Along its trade routes it was in touch with the outside world and aware of non-Jewish ideas. It lived off its fertile farmlands and its lake fisheries. And it was far more alert to the realities of life in the Roman Empire than the aloof Jews of Jerusalem – who despised their northern cousins as country bumpkins and because they were racially mixed.

The coastal plain
When Israel occupied the Promised Land, they captured the central highlands and then made sporadic attempts to spread their control down to the Mediterranean coast. But this region was occupied by the powerful nation of the Philistines. And although, under David, Israel was able to gain control for a while, more often in Israel's history the Philistines were exerting pressure from their five cities on the coastlands up into the hills.

The coastlands were not, at this time, a particularly attractive area. They consisted of a belt of coastal sand dunes backed by forest, lagoons and swamp. There were no large natural harbours south of Carmel. The Philistines were not seafarers, and the first major port on this coast was the artificial harbour at Caesarea, built by King Herod the Great, not long before Jesus was born.

South of Mt Carmel, the plain was known as the Plain of Philistia and the Plain of Sharon. North of Carmel, it became the Plain of Asher. Going north, it narrows, but is much better provided with natural harbours. It was from here that the sea-going Phoenicians traded.

The 'Shephelah' or Piedmont
Between the coastlands and the upland is an area of low foothills formerly covered by forests of sycamores. When the Philistines fought the Israelites the hills formed a kind of no-man's-land, where there were constant skirmishes. For either side to attack the other, it was necessary to pass through the Shephelah. Most of the routes through it were therefore fortified or guarded. Today, much of it is cultivated.

The Jordan Valley
The River Jordan rises near Mt Hermon and flows south through Lake Huleh (now largely drained) and into the Sea of Galilee. At the southern end of the Sea it enters a deep valley known as the Ghor. Not only is the valley itself steep-sided but the river has cut into the floor and has created a winding, cliff-lined 'valley within a valley', filled with dense, jungle-like vegetation. This made crossing the river very difficult before the first modern bridges were built.

The Jordan valley is a geo-logical rift. The sides follow parallel faults in the earth's crust. These faults carry on the line of the valley down to the Dead Sea and beyond it, through the depression known as the Arabah, which even-tually leads to the Gulf of Aqaba. The faults are the

The desert or wilderness of Judea, where Jesus faced temptation after his baptism.

The River Jordan, bordered by dense green scrub, winds its way from Lake Galilee to the Dead Sea. It features in many Bible stories: Joshua's crossing into Canaan, the healing of Naaman, and the life of John the Baptist who baptized Jesus in the river.

reason why the valley is so deep. The shore of the Dead Sea is 1,270ft/388 metres below sea level. The distance from the mountain rim on one side of the valley to that on the other is 9–12 miles/15–20km. But no major road follows the valley. One reason for this is the broken and difficult ground created by the Jordan and its tributaries. Another is the fact that inside the Ghor, the summer temperatures are so high that travellers are glad to cross as quickly as they can from the heights on one side to the heights on the other.

□ **The land east of the Jordan (Transjordan)**
Here there are uplands, like those to the west, but higher. They are well-watered and provide good pasture for the huge flocks of sheep and herds of cattle formerly raised in Moab. At one time the king of Moab paid 100,000 lambs and the wool from 100,000 sheep every year to Israel as tribute (2 Kings 3:4). The mountains here rise from 1,900–2,300ft/ 600–700 metres east of Galilee to almost 6,560ft/2,000 metres south and east of the Dead Sea. They attract a rainfall which increases with their height and makes them a fertile belt between the dry valley on one side and the Arabian Desert on the other.

The fertility of parts of the region, such as Bashan and Gilead, the prosperity of the sheep raisers of Moab, and the success of the traders of Edom made all these areas powerful rivals of the Israelites west of the Jordan. It was, perhaps, just as well for Israel that the Jordan made it so difficult for these people to move into their land from the east. It almost completely separated two similar regions which lay within sight of each other across the valley.

This, then, was the land in which God chose to place his people, and to which he chose to send his Son. It is not very rich or very important. All its importance stems from the fact that he chose it. It is a small land – a barren, eroded, hilly piece of the earth's surface. Yet it has been more coveted and fought for than perhaps any other country in the world.

This aerial view of Tell Beersheba in the south of Israel clearly shows the work of the archaeologists in excavation.

2

Archaeology and the Bible

Digging up the Past

The Bible is a collection of ancient books. The cultures in which those books were written have perished long ago. Much of the information about the New Testament period has come down to us in Greek and Latin books which, like the Bible, have been copied and re-copied over the centuries. But hardly anything has come down to us in this way on the Old Testament period, apart from the Bible itself.

Of course, it is possible to read the Bible and understand its message with very little knowledge of the world in which it was written. What the Bible has to say to men and women is timeless. Its message is for everybody. Yet the Bible records events which are firmly tied to people and places.

Much of its teaching is based on things that happened to particular people, their nations, and the part God played in the events. Although the Bible may look like a book of theology, it is quite different from most modern books of theology. It does not contain a collection of abstract ideas about God. Instead it reveals God's character by recording his activities in the history of Israel and the life of the first Christians. And the history presented by the Bible is only a part of the human story in the world in which the Bible's events took place. So anything we can find out about the world of the Bible will help

Archaeologists examine finds from the Cave of Letters in the Judean Desert.

us to understand its essential message more clearly.

As we learn more of the background to the Bible, we begin to see how the Bible blends with it or stands in contrast to it. By uncovering ruined towns of the ninth century BC we may discover the type of house that the prophet Elisha visited, or the style of lamp his hostess is likely to have placed by his bed (2 Kings 4:8–10).

Occasionally a discovery may relate directly to a Bible verse. We may find an object or building mentioned in the text.

The most valuable of all our finds are ancient writings that name men or women who are also mentioned in the Bible, or that describe the same events.

Discoveries like this are not often made – and when they are made, we need to be careful how we interpret them. If we are to find out anything about the Old Testament world, and much about the New Testament world, we must turn to archaeology.

Curiosity about the past

People have always been curious about their past. Even in Old Testament times, Babylonian kings rescued and preserved pieces of old statues and foundation stones uncovered in the course of their own building work. At a later period, wealthy Romans had antique statues brought from Greece to decorate their villas. In their turn, princes at the time of the Renaissance took many of these statues to grace their own palaces. Collecting ancient works of art became fashionable then, and has been so ever since.

In the nineteenth century, with easier travel and wider education, public interest in ancient and strange things grew rapidly. For a long time most of the effort went into filling museums and galleries. Statues, jewellery, tools and pottery were dug from ruins or tombs by local people and visitors, and sold to the highest bidder. Fine drawings of these objects were published in expensive books, often with imaginative captions describing their possible meaning or use.

Eventually scholars realized that the value of any ancient object was much greater if a proper record was kept of where it was found, what was found with it, and other details. An old vase may look attractive in a showcase, displayed for all to see. But it adds a great deal to its meaning if the label can state that it stood originally in the bedroom of a palace – or the kitchen of a cottage! If the vase is seen in its original position it may help to date the use of the place it belonged to; the building cannot have been ruined before the vase was made.

Napoleon and after

The first notable steps in learning about the ancient world were taken in 1798 when Napoleon's invasion of Egypt included a survey of monuments there. During this invasion the Rosetta Stone was discovered. This is a stone block on which the same text was engraved in Greek and Egyptian writing. It helped the

Sir Charles Warren was in at the beginning of archaeological work in Palestine itself. In 1867–70 he traced the foundations of Herod's temple wall in Jerusalem.

One of the great nineteenth-century archaeologists was the explorer/politician, Sir Henry Layard. He is famous for his excavations in Iraq, particularly at Nineveh. The picture shows him directing operations at the Assyrian city of Nimrud (1845–48).

Frenchman Champollion to decipher ancient Egyptian hieroglyphs for the first time (1824). Within a few years, a British diplomat in Baghdad, *Claudius James Rich*, had made the first accurate surveys of the sites of ancient Babylon and Nineveh. He also made the first representative collection of Assyrian and Babylonian seals and inscriptions.

Places in Israel were better known, because pilgrims had visited the 'Holy Land' for centuries. In 1838 *Edward Robinson*, an American professor of biblical literature, undertook the first careful study of the country. From its geography and the way in which place-names survived, he was able to identify many of the towns named in the Bible. Most of his identifications remain satisfactory even today.

☐ Egypt and Assyria

In Egypt the task of clearing mounds of sand and tumbled stone from tombs and temples continued throughout the nineteenth century, and during this period a great many stone sculptures were taken out of the country.

Excavations began in Assyria when the French consul, *Paul-Emile Botta*, opened trenches in the mound of rubble that was ancient Nineveh. His work there was unrewarding, but nearby he discovered an Assyrian palace whose walls were lined with carved stone slabs (1842–43).

An English traveller, *Henry Layard*, was also interested, and in 1845 he found similar carvings in Nineveh, where Botta had failed to do so. Writing cut into the stonework and impressed on small tablets of clay was deciphered by 1850. This was the Babylonian cuneiform script (see *Writing*, below). Documents written in this script have proved particularly valuable for biblical study (see the chart of the kings of Israel and Judah named in Assyrian records).

The digging in Egypt, and in Assyria and Babylonia, was carried out by British, French and Italian expeditions, quickly joined by teams from Germany and the United States. Most of the money raised for excavation came from museums, and some were intent only on acquiring spectacular exhibits for their sponsors. Others carefully noted many details and collected examples of the less exciting finds – pottery, knives, and so on. They measured buildings and drew plans on which they marked the positions of the objects they unearthed.

International expeditions still carry out this work, with permission from local departments of antiquities. Egyptian and Iraqi scholars also excavate independently. They pay special attention to preserving their national heritage. Even after a century and a half of exploration in those lands, it is clear that there is a great deal still to be found.

□ **Palestine and Syria**
The early excavators were mostly concerned to find great monuments of imperial power to impress the western public, and so the cities of Palestine and Syria were by-passed. Apart from a few isolated trenches at Jericho and other sites (1866–69), the first digging was confined to Jerusalem. There *Charles Warren* traced the foundations of King Herod's temple wall and surveyed other ancient remains (1867–70). He cut through masses of fallen stones and rubbish (sinking shafts 211ft/65m deep and burrowing along the natural rock surface) to show how the shape of the city had changed over the centuries.

Archaeology becomes a science
Near Eastern archaeology took a major step forward in 1890 when *Flinders Petrie* started to

Sir William Flinders Petrie, another famous name in biblical archaeology. His work in southern Israel led to a break-through in methods of dating discoveries.

excavate at Tell el-Hesi, near Gaza in southern Israel. He realized that, on any given site, the things he found at one height above sea-level were different from things found at another height.

This was most obviously true of the broken pottery. Taking care to separate the pieces according to their levels, he managed to work out a series of pottery styles that followed in order of time. He then gave dates to each style, by comparing them with Egyptian objects found in the same places. (The ages of the Egyptian objects were known from the discovery of similar pieces in Egypt, where inscriptions related them to the reigns of individual kings.)

Petrie's observations have become basic to all archaeological excavation. For several decades other archaeologists working in Palestine failed to realize their importance, and because of this many of their own conclusions have been proved wrong. But the basic idea of using pottery styles as a guide for dating other objects is now adopted by all archaeologists – though, of course, there have been some further important developments since.

As people's interest in the subject grew, museums and universities began to pay attention to sites in the land of Israel. Regrettably, the standard of excavation was often poor. Better techniques for observing and recording

finds were developed by *G. A. Reisner* and *C. S. Fisher* during their excavation at Samaria in 1908–11. Following Petrie's example, the American, *W. F. Albright*, established the basic system of dating Palestinian pottery (at Tell Beit Mirsim from 1926 to 1936).

British archaeology had progressed by developing 'stratigraphy', the close examination of the soil inside and underneath ancient remains. *Kathleen Kenyon*, working at Samaria, was the first to apply this approach to an excavation in Palestine (1931–35). From 1952 she used it with conspicuous success at the difficult sites of Jericho and Jerusalem. So far this method of excavation is unsurpassed, although it makes far more demands on the excavator during the digging, and afterwards in interpreting his finds.

The work of excavation
Mud is the commonest, and one of the earliest, building materials in the Near East. Walls made of mud-bricks dried in the sun will last for thirty years or so if they are plastered regularly to keep out the damp. Bricks baked in kilns were expensive in ancient times, so they were used only for important buildings. Foundations were built of stone wherever it was available, and in very stony areas entire houses were stone-built. Roofs were normally made of wooden beams with matting and mud plaster laid over them.

These buildings easily collapsed through neglect, old age, fire, earthquake, or enemy attack. When they fell, people re-used the best pieces from the heap of debris, but most of it was left where it had fallen. In the course of time, new houses were built on top of the old ones. This meant that street levels became higher, and over the centuries the level of the whole town gradually rose. The results of this process can be seen all over the Near East in the ruin-mounds called *tells*.

Cities that once surrounded an inner fortress with heavily defended palaces and temples may leave an extensive area covered with low mounds, the fortress standing up as a great hill. Or the whole city may be a single mound. These tells can be 90–130ft/30–40m high, and 540yds/500m or more in length.

The most recent remains lie at the top of the mound. They may not be the ruins of the last buildings that stood there, because winter wind and rain quickly erode the dry mud-brickwork once the site is no longer occupied. At the lowest level, on the original soil, will be traces of the first town. There are many reasons why ancient towns were abandoned. The town may have grown up around a spring or well, at a ford of a river, or at a cross-roads. If the spring dried up or the roads changed, the town may have died. Some political turn of events may have deprived a place of its influence and prosperity. Or the mound may have grown too high for people to live on top of it conveniently.

Cities like Jerusalem and Damascus, however, have never lost their importance, and they can be excavated only when buildings are demolished or areas are left undeveloped.

□ The dig

The archaeologist digs into the mound from the top or at one side. As he cuts into it, the remains of one period appear on top of another, much like the layers in a large cake sliced down the middle. Once he has disturbed the earth and the objects in it, they can never be replaced in exactly the same way. So his first job is to note where, and in what layer of soil, each item is found.

A plan of the area will show horizontal positions of walls and other things. But the re-mains are rarely in absolutely even levels. A street may slope, or a wall may stand much higher at one point than another. Very often people of a later period will have dug a pit, for storing food or for rubbish, and that will go down from their own floor level deep into earlier ruins. Recording things by absolute levels (metres above sea level) would put rubbish from the bottom of the pit with bits and pieces from the earlier periods it had broken into. So the depth of any discovery has to be linked to the layer of earth in which it was found.

When the trench has cut into the earth the layers can be clearly seen in the vertical side of the excavation. Pottery lying on the floor of a room will belong to the last period the room was lived in. Pottery found underneath the floor will be older than the floor. The archaeologist has to note how the floor joins a wall, because a later wall may have cut through an earlier floor. If he does not notice, he could produce a wrong plan of the building.

Expert knowledge is necess-ary at every stage. Before any earth is removed, a surveyor has to measure the whole site and fix points from which measurements can be made. As work goes on he will plot the edges of the trenches and any other noteworthy features. A photographer is needed to record the stages of excavation, to picture important or fragile objects in position in the soil, and afterwards to photograph them and other pieces for publication.

□ Studying the finds

Every object has a label fixed to it, or a mark written on it as soon as it is discovered, to show where it was dug up. Individual finds, such as pins, knives, jewellery, but not usually broken pottery, are listed and described. The pottery is sorted according to the place and level or layer of discovery. Someone who knows the whole range of discoveries can then choose significant pieces for detailed records.

Some pottery will need to

This golden shrine is one of many treasures recovered from the tomb of Pharaoh Tutankhamun in Egypt.

be mended, and metal things will need treatment for rust or corrosion. Woodwork and other fragile objects will require special care to ensure that they do not decay any more. Samples of all sorts of natural remains can also give us information about the ancient environment, so shells, bones, and earth containing seeds, are all carefully collected.

□ Publishing the findings

It is only when the excava-tion is finished and all the specialists have prepared their reports, that the excavator can present a final account of his work. At a small site this may be done quickly. At larger sites, when work carries on for several years, it is only possible to make a summary of each season's work. This is an en-couragement to the universities and museums that have given funds for the work. Some pre-pare a detailed account of each season's results and publish them. Others wait until their excavations are finished, then produce comprehensive reports. These may amount to several volumes if the work has been done on a large scale.

Publishing findings is an expensive and time-consuming

business. Excavators usually have other jobs as well – teaching in universities, or museum work. So many years may pass between the time excavation ends and the time the final report appears. New discoveries may have taken place in the interval; theories may have been revised. And these may raise questions about some of the results.

All objects belong to the country where they are unearthed. Outstanding pieces take their place in the national museums. Others are kept locally, near the site where they were discovered. Foreign expeditions may be allowed to take home samples for chemical and similar tests. Some countries allow them to remove representative selections of pottery and other objects found in quantity. Eventually these are divided among those who supported the excavation.

Some limits of archaeology

Archaeology is concerned with remains of human activity. People all over the world have always had similar needs to meet: finding food and shelter, protecting themselves from wild animals and invaders, and disposing of their dead. They tend to find similar ways of solving these problems. So, from what he finds in one region, the archaeologist can be fairly certain of what to expect in a similar situation somewhere else. For example, on Mt Carmel in Israel archaeologists found traces of early families making shelters and harvesting wild grains. Afterwards, scholars were able to locate similar primitive village-sites at other places in the Near East where conditions were almost the same.

On the other hand, human beings do not always behave consistently. So it is dangerous to make neat types with no room for variation, or to insist that everyone *must* have followed a certain known pattern of behaviour. That attitude is

bound to run into problems sooner or later, and in the past has distorted the evidence.

In any case, the things we find today have survived by chance. Strange geological conditions at Jericho preserved wooden furniture in tombs sealed about 1600 BC. Even hair and meat could be recognized. Before these tombs were excavated we had no evidence of what items and styles of furniture were used in Middle Bronze Age Canaan. Nor did we know how skilled the carpenters were.

The Jericho tombs are an isolated case. A more common example of the hazards of survival is a town that has been destroyed. If an enemy set it on fire, soldiers probably looted the valuables. But most of the ordinary household equipment will have been left in the houses. Archaeologists, working centuries later, will uncover only those things that can survive the burning, exposure to weather, and burial. Woodwork may be visible only as a black stain or powder, impossible to preserve.

The fire caught the town at one moment in time. Everything in it belongs to that time or a short while before. Unless the place was subject to many destructive attacks, the citizens will have been living there quite normally for generations. They would have moved out of old houses, leaving them to decay, and later on built over their ruins. So not many of the household goods from the earlier generations will be recovered. As a general rule, most of the finds on any site will belong to the final decades of any period of occupation. Written documents found on the site usually back this up. For these reasons excavation cannot give a complete picture of a city's history. In addition, the cost prevents anyone clearing the whole of a city-mound.

☐ Hit-and-miss

The aims of excavators vary. One may try to obtain samples of pottery and architecture

from every level. Another may concentrate on a single phase, uncovering a large area to discover the plans of the main buildings or city areas. Temples and palaces are a special attraction, holding out hopes of richer finds than private houses and city defences. But the study of these last two can be just as valuable. At some places the big buildings are easy to find because they have left a higher mound of debris. At other sites the excavation may just happen to strike them – or to miss them. And the archaeologist can never tell what he may have missed!

These rather drab-looking clay tablets represent one of the most exciting of recent finds. They come from Tell Mardikh in Syria (the ancient city of Ebla), about 2300 BC, and show that personal names known to us from the Bible were already in use.

In 1928 *John Garstang* sank trenches into the mound of ancient Hazor, north of Galilee. He concluded that the major part of the city had been deserted about 1400 BC, because he found no sign of the distinctive Mycenaean pottery imported from Cyprus and Greece after that date. But extensive excavations by *Yigael Yadin*, thirty years later, yielded large amounts of that pottery in nearby areas of the city, and it was quite clear that many people had lived there between 1400 and 1200 BC. Our knowledge of Hazor's history was radically changed by the later excavation.

Another case of an earlier trench narrowly missing

THE DIG

The dig requires a team with many skills.

When trenches have been dug and layers of earth carefully removed, the detailed work begins. Right: archaeologists are excavating the site of King David's City in Jerusalem.

Finds need delicate handling. Below: earth is carefully brushed away to reveal the skeleton.

Highly skilled work will be needed to preserve and repair objects. The best finds will be put on display in a local or national museum. The picture shows a range of Israelite pots from about 800–600 BC.

All new finds are recorded. In the case of reliefs like this one at Karnak in Egypt the experts may need ladders to examine and record inscriptions.

The Rosetta Stone, discovered in 1799, provided the 'key' which made it possible for us to read Egyptian hieroglyphs. It records a decree in honour of the Egyptian King Ptolemy V in Greek, and in Egyptian demotic and hiero-glyphic scripts. By comparing the hieroglyphs with the Greek words it was possible to work out their meaning.

important finds is at Kadesh on the Orontes, in Syria. A French expedition worked there on a large scale in 1921–22. The director died, and work stopped. A small British team re-opened the excavations in 1975. They deepened one part of the old trench work and struck mud-brick walls. In the rubble on top of them, half a metre below the bottom of the earlier digging, were Babylonian cuneiform tablets. They confirm the identity of the ruins and name a king of Kadesh who can be precisely dated, so that we now know the age of the ruins in which they lay. The previous exca-vators had not reported finding any inscribed tablets at all.

All through ancient times the whole area covered by modern Syria was rich and supported major cities. Damascus and Aleppo still thrive; Palmyra is a famous ruin from Roman days. A great city of 1800–1200 BC has been under excava-tion on the coast near Lattakiya

since 1928. It came to the attention of archaeologists when a farmer opened a stone tomb on his land there. Collections of texts written on clay tablets proved that it was ancient Ugarit.

Far away on the Euphrates another accidental discovery brought an expedition to work from 1933 onwards at a city called Mari, that flourished between 3000 and 1760 BC. About 25,000 cuneiform tablets were found in the rooms of a vast palace destroyed around 1750 BC by Hammurabi of Babylon.

Another recent discovery, the most notable since the Dead Sea Scrolls, was made by an Italian team working in north Syria. They made a survey of a region south of Aleppo, looking at several mounds before they chose to excavate one, Tell Mardikh. Nothing was known about it; but its size – a great encircling rampart with a tell in the centre – showed that it had been a prosperous place. Pieces of broken pottery scattered on the surface pointed to the years 2500–1600 BC as its life-time.

Work began in 1964. From then until 1972 buildings of the period 2000 to 1600 BC were excavated. In 1968 an inscribed statue was unearthed which implied that Tell Mardikh was ancient Ebla. Inscriptions from Babylonia had spoken of Ebla as a trading city in Syria, but no one had known where it was. Scholars had tried to locate it up to 124 miles/ 200km from Tell Mardikh!

Since 1973 the trenches have cleared several rooms of a royal palace that was destroyed by fire about 2200 BC. A small group of cuneiform tablets was found there in 1974, and then, in 1975, about 8,000 of them in two rooms, one originally lined with wooden shelves. These are the first documents of so early a date known to us from north Syria. They also contain a language previously unknown, although related to other West Semitic dialects. The texts, and other objects, show very strong

influences from Babylonia, and a wide range of trading links reaching to Egypt (see *Abraham and his family*, below).

The documents from Ebla illustrate how easy it is to reach faulty conclusions. When they were first found, the scholar responsible for translating them claimed they contained the names of many places stretching from Persia to the Mediterranean, including towns in Palestine such as Ashdod, Hazor and Megiddo. Most remarkable was his assertion that the towns of Sodom and Gomorrah were named in the tablets.

The excitement of the new discovery apparently led him to speak too hastily, and further study has brought a change of view. The business of Ebla and its king was limited to north Syria and the River Euphrates; the tablets do not mention towns in Palestine.

It should now be clear that archaeology is subject to chance. Discoveries are made by accident, and even the most carefully planned expedition can never be sure what it will find. The evidence unearthed is seldom complete. An archae-ologist's trench may reveal only one half of a house, and even when that is cleared, forces of decay may well have destroyed much beyond recovery.

The example of Hazor illustrates the risk of a mis-leading result. Ebla stresses the value of written documents. They identify the place and the age, shed light on many aspects of life, and explain many things which would otherwise be obscure or uncertain.

If there are no written texts, much of an archaeologist's interpretation of his discov-eries is speculative. He cannot be certain of dates; he may not know the purpose of a building; he can only guess at the range of its contents. Above all, he cannot get to know the people who lived in the place, and so is more likely to overlook the human side of his discoveries.

Archaeology and the study of the Bible

When we use archaeology to help us understand the Bible we must be cautious. Not only is it sometimes difficult to understand what the archaeologist has unearthed, but there are also passages where the meaning of the Bible text is uncertain: sometimes a discovery can help to clarify it. Often there is an accepted way of explaining a Bible passage, which may make no sense in the light of archaeology until a different suggestion is made. Even then it may become a matter of opinion, remaining unconfirmed until we have more evidence.

There has been a great deal of discussion among scholars about how the different books of the Bible came to us in their present form, and when they were written. As we recover ancient Egyptian, Babylonian, and other writings, we can see how other ancient peoples produced and treated books.

Occasionally, these cultures have left copies of the same book, but made several generations or centuries apart. We can compare these and see how they differ. We have examples where no changes occurred over lengthy periods, except for modernizing the spelling. In some books, later copies leave out incidents described in earlier ones; or they may add further episodes. When only one copy is available, it is impossible to be certain whether or not these changes have happened.

Our only copies of the Old Testament were made centuries after the books were first written, yet confident statements that one chapter was added long after another, or a verse or sentence inserted are commonly made. These depend entirely upon the judgement of the scholars responsible. There is no external proof. In fact the practices of other ancient scribes raise questions about drawing such conclusions.

The value of ancient writings

It is important to realize that these different opinions exist, because many archaeological discoveries are assessed in the light of one view or another. Since early in the nineteenth century western scholars have tended to treat the claims of ancient writers with disbelief.

The Greek historian Herodotus (about 450 BC) has frequently been accused of making mistakes or being inaccurate. Yet archaeological discoveries in Egypt, Babylonia and Russia again and again support his chronicles.

The same can be said for very many other writings in many languages. We are gradually learning to treat these ancient books with respect, and to value their contents. If we treat them positively these ancient writings and other archaeological material can throw light on one another.

British Museum excavations at Carchemish on the River Euphrates found traces of burning in the city, bronze and iron arrowheads, and fragments of a decorated bronze shield. They could be dated roughly to the seventh century BC. Considered in the light of ancient records, the date could be fixed as 605 BC. In that year the Babylonians defeated the Egyptians at Carchemish. The decoration on the shield is a Greek design, a Gorgon's head. In Egypt there are tombstones cut for mercenary soldiers (some of them Greek speaking) from the cities of eastern Turkey. In addition to this, a Greek poet wrote of a relative who fought in the battle. Everything agrees!

Of course it is not always possible to relate literary and material remains so neatly. From 1969 to 1976 the late Israeli archaeologist *Yohanan*

The Royal Graves at Ur have yielded a treasure-trove of beautiful objects. The golden head-dress of flowers and leaves once belonged to a queen of Ur.

EXCAVATION OF A TOWN MOUND ('TELL')

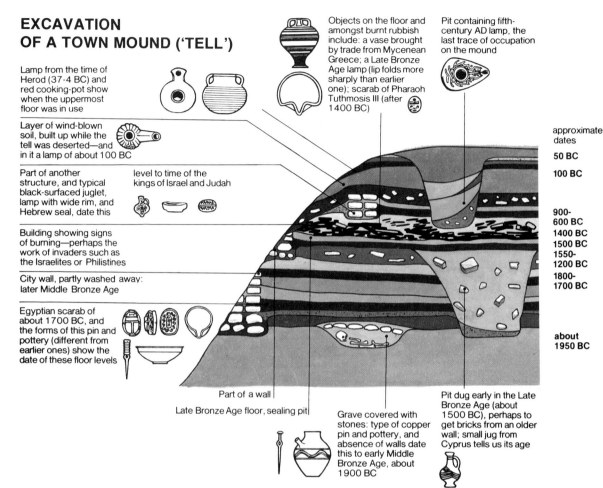

Lamp from the time of Herod (37-4 BC) and red cooking-pot show when the uppermost floor was in use

Layer of wind-blown soil, built up while the tell was deserted—and in it a lamp of about 100 BC

Part of another structure, and typical black-surfaced juglet, lamp with wide rim, and Hebrew seal, date this

level to time of the kings of Israel and Judah

Building showing signs of burning—perhaps the work of invaders such as the Israelites or Philistines

City wall, partly washed away: later Middle Bronze Age

Egyptian scarab of about 1700 BC, and the forms of this pin and pottery (different from earlier ones) show the date of these floor levels

Objects on the floor and amongst burnt rubbish include: a vase brought by trade from Mycenean Greece; a Late Bronze Age lamp (lip folds more sharply than earlier one); scarab of Pharaoh Tuthmosis III (after 1400 BC)

Pit containing fifth-century AD lamp, the last trace of occupation on the mound

approximate dates

50 BC

100 BC

900-600 BC
1400 BC
1500 BC
1550-1200 BC
1800-1700 BC

about 1950 BC

Part of a wall

Late Bronze Age floor, sealing pit

Grave covered with stones: type of copper pin and pottery, and absence of walls date this to early Middle Bronze Age, about 1900 BC

Pit dug early in the Late Bronze Age (about 1500 BC), perhaps to get bricks from an older wall; small jug from Cyprus tells us its age

---

Aharoni led the excavations at a place now called Tell Beersheba. Outside the gateway of the ancient town was a well. Some twelfth-century BC ruined houses (the oldest on the mound) probably dated from the time when the well was dug. The excavator identified the well he found with the one mentioned in Genesis (21:25; 26:15), in the stories about Abraham and Isaac. From this identification he deduced that

the stories were not composed until the twelfth century BC or later, after the exodus and conquest of Canaan.

This view cannot be disproved at present, but its assumptions can be challenged.

First of all the modern Tell Beersheba is not necessarily the ancient Beersheba; small excavations in the modern town, 3 miles/5km to the west, have found evidence of occupation there at several

periods. Some of these coincide with the existence of the town on the tell.

Secondly, even if the identification of the place is right, no one can prove that the well is the Genesis well.

Thirdly, there is no mention of a town in the Genesis stories. Abraham may have dug a well in an uninhabited area – there are still many wells like this in the Near East.

Fourthly, Aharoni claimed that Beersheba was deserted from 701 to about 530 BC, yet an inscription of about 600 BC implies it was in use then. He simply takes that reference to mean small villages near by. There is no reason why Genesis

A 'tell' is a great mound of stone and earth left by a succession of cities built on the same site. This picture shows the tell at Lachish.

references may not be treated in the same way, the name Beersheba being taken by the town long after the time of Abraham. There seems to be no compelling reason for dating the patriarchal stories in the twelfth century BC when many other clues point to a much earlier date for them (see below, *Abraham and his family*).

Unless there are specific details in a text which can be indisputably linked to objects or features unearthed, the relation of written text to archaeological evidence will be uncertain. An important example is the matter of Jericho and Ai, discussed in *The conquest of Canaan*, below.

Archaeology's main service is to illustrate the general context of the Bible and to show us what the biblical world was like. It may sometimes throw light on a particular verse; it may guide interpreters along some paths and bar others. It may appear to support historical statements in the Bible, or make it less difficult to accept them. But we must always remember two important facts.

One is that much of our knowledge of the ancient world from archaeology is tentative and subject to change. Today's 'assured results' may tomorrow be little more than a curiosity.

Then we should also remember that ultimately it is pointless to speak of archaeology either 'proving' or 'disproving' the Bible. For the Bible's message is about God and his dealings with men and women – and it is outside the scope of archaeology to say anything about that.

Writing

The most informative discoveries made by archaeologists in the Near East are the written documents. These give names of places, kings and other people. They tell of invasions and wars, of famine and inflation. They may describe social customs and behaviour, or disclose them incidentally. Some may be hymns and prayers, reflecting religious beliefs; or they may be spells, relating to magic. There may also be stories of gods and heroes of the past. In fact, once writing had been invented, any aspect of life could be recorded.

Many records have been destroyed; many have still to be discovered. Very often we have a letter, but not the reply. The victor's account of a war may survive, but not his victim's. A mass of documents may have been preserved from one century, none from the next. Consequently, the information these ancient writings give us is often lop-sided, and has to be interpreted with care.

Cuneiform
The invention of writing in Babylonia between 3500 and 3000 BC is described in Part 11: *Nations and Peoples of the Bible*, under *The Babylonians*. The first language to be written down seems to have been Sumerian. This language used picture symbols to represent words. The Semitic Akkadian language (a name used for Assyrian and Babylonian) quickly followed. That was different from Sumerian, and the Sumerian word-signs were more often used as syllable-signs to reproduce Akkadian.

Other Semitic languages in the west (Syria and Palestine) were written in cuneiform. So too were the Indo-European dialects spoken in the area of modern Turkey (generally called Hittite), and another different language, Elamite, which was spoken in Persia. Cuneiform writing continued to be used in Babylonia until as late as the first century AD.

Egyptian
The idea of writing was carried from Babylonia to Egypt soon after it was invented. Egyptian clerks made up their own system of picture word-signs, which we call hieroglyphs. Some of these were very often written for their sounds only (syllables), as in Babylonia. But they were not used without the word-signs to the extent that they were in cuneiform, and so the system was less easily adapted for other languages.

The Egyptian script kept its picture form for inscriptions on buildings and other monuments until the fifth century AD, when people stopped using hieroglyphs. For ordinary records, letters, accounts and books, a simpler handwriting, called hieratic, was developed. A sort of shorthand, now called demotic, grew out of that after 1000 BC.

Books and everyday documents in Egypt were written on paper made from the papyrus reed. Long thin strips of its pith were laid side by side, with another layer of strips pressed onto them at right angles, to produce a page of writing material. It was rather rougher than modern paper, but just as strong and flexible. Papyrus documents buried in tombs or ruined buildings in the dry sands of

THE DEVELOPMENT OF THE ALPHABET

Picture represents	Sound	Canaanite Sinai about 1500 BC	Phoenician about 1000 BC	Old Hebrew about 700 BC	Aramaic about 500 BC	Hebrew first century AD	Early Greek about 600 BC	Formal Greek 5th century BC
ox	'/A							
house	B							
throw-stick	G							
palm of hand	K							
staff	L							
water	M							
eye	'/O							
head	R							

Egypt have survived until the present day. But papyrus cost money, and unimportant matters – such as short notes or school exercises – were written on flakes of stone or pieces of broken pottery (called *ostraca*). People usually wrote with reed brushes, using black ink made from soot.

Wherever Egypt ruled or traded, the Egyptian writing system followed. Examples of Egyptian writing are found in Palestine and Syria, and far south into the Sudan.

Other systems

Between 2000 and 1000 BC other scripts were used in different parts of the Near East. In Turkey the Hittites had their own form of hieroglyphs. About seventy signs stood for simple syllables (*ta*, *ki*, etc.), with a hundred or more word-signs. A similar system was used in Crete, where three related forms have been discovered. The last of these, known as Linear B, had about eighty-five syllable-signs and some word-signs. These were scratched on clay tablets to record government affairs in an early Greek dialect. Another branch of that group of written languages was used in Cyprus, and a few examples have been found in Syria.

All these methods of writing were difficult to learn, so that only a few people, the prof-essional scribes, could read and write. Most people who wanted to send a letter, to write a will, or to keep accounts, had to call on a trained man. The scribes' services were also needed to read a letter or a legal deed, or to check accounts. Naturally, some scribes rose to high positions in the royal courts, while others sat at street corners waiting for customers.

The alphabet

The scribes' monopoly was broken when the alphabet became widely used. Archae-ology has enabled us to recover quite a lot of examples of the

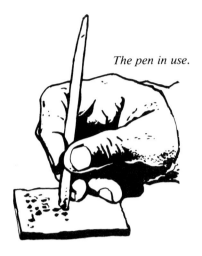

The pen in use.

An early pen: made of bone, for writing cuneiform signs. About 2000 BC.

The earliest picture writing: on a stone from Sumer, about 3500 BC.

alphabet in its early stages. But there are many aspects of its development which are not yet known. It seems that a scribe in Canaan realized that it was possible to write a language without the many signs which the Egyptians and Babylonians had. He studied his language and drew one sign for each consonant. He apparently chose the signs on the scheme 'door stands for d'. But they were used only for sounds, never as word-signs. There were no separate signs for vowels, and this creates problems in reading Hebrew and Arabic writing even now.

Examples of the early alphabet have been found in Israel. These are very short, probably men's names, written on pottery, stone and metal. Canaanites working in the Egyptian turquoise mines in south-western Sinai scratched prayers on rocks and stones. They used the letters of the alphabet, and have left us the best specimens we have of the alphabet at an early stage (about 1500 BC).

How it developed over the next five hundred years can be seen from more scattered examples. (Unfortunately for us the scribes usually wrote on papyrus, which rots when

buried in damp soil.) During that time the letters took stan-dard shapes. Scribes trained in Babylonian traditions at Ugarit in Syria saw the advantages of an alphabet over the other scripts. There they composed an alphabet of thirty letters in cuneiform and wrote their own language with it.

By 1000 BC the alphabet was firmly established. In Syria and Canaan the newly settled Aramaeans, Israelites, Moabites and Edomites adopted it. Soon afterwards the Greeks learned it from the Phoenicians. They made some adjustments to suit their own language, especially the use of distinguishing signs for vowels.

The Aramaean tribes of Syria spread into Assyria and Babylonia, and many were carried off captive by Assyrian kings. They took with them their form of the alphabet. Jewish exiles adopted it and popularized it in Jerusalem in preference to the older Phoenician-Hebrew form. Arab tribesmen (the Nab-ataeans) borrowed it too, and the modern Arabic script is descended from the letters they developed.

The alphabet brought reading and writing within the reach of everyone. The scribes did not go out of business, nor did everyone become literate, but far more people learned their letters in areas where the alphabet was used. This is made clear by the fact that in seventh-century BC Judah many people had seals with their names on them but no distinctive designs. These would have had no value if their owners and others could not read them.

The scribes in Assyria and Babylonia, and in Egypt, usually worked with great care. There were several checks to make sure that books were copied accurately. The number of lines was counted and compared with the original; any damage to the original was noted; and sometimes a second scribe checked the whole copy. The Israelite scribes no doubt followed the same conventions when they copied the books of the Old Testament.

WRITTEN LANGUAGES OF THE BIBLE LANDS

A clay tablet impressed with wedge-shaped cuneiform signs used at Ugarit in imitation of the alphabet.

Egyptian hieroglyphic writing.

Hebrew, the language of the Old Testament, with a paraphrase in Aramaic.

Aramaic as written in the Persian Empire. Later it was the language of Jesus and the apostles.

A letter in Greek – the language of the New Testament – written on papyrus.

Archaeology and the Old Testament

Creation and the flood

All over the world men tell stories of the way they and the land they occupy were made. Very similar ideas are found in quite separate places.

For example, the Chinese and the Hebrews both said they were made from earth or clay. There is no connection between the two peoples; the similarity may have arisen naturally out of the process of death, burial and decay.

There are also stories of a great flood from which a few people escaped in a boat. Floods causing widespread damage and loss of life happen quite often: the only hope of escape is by running to the highest hill or taking to a boat. So, again, there need be no connection between one flood story and another.

□ Stories from Babylonia and Assyria

When we read literature recovered from Babylonia and Assyria, we find several stories of man's creation. Their basic message is that man was made to serve the gods, that is to say, he was to supply them with food and drink through sacrifices, and to look after their temples.

One story in particular is so like the Genesis account that it is agreed they are related to each other. This story is known as the *Epic of Atrahasis* (see *Assyrian and Babylonian Religion* in Part 11 for a summary). Copies written about 1635 BC have been found, and others show that it was still studied a thousand years later.

The *Atrahasis* account of the next major event in human history, the flood, was borrowed and used in the *Epic of Gilgamesh* (see *Babylonians* in Part 11). This was the first version to be found, and it is the one usually quoted. It was translated from copies written about 650 BC for the Assyrian royal library at Nineveh.

From other documents we learn that the Babylonians knew of several cities founded before the flood. Each of the kings of these cities is said to have ruled for thousands of years. After the flood, which was a major break in history according to the Babylonians, the reigns of the kings soon shorten to a more normal length of time.

The drawing shows the partial reconstruction of the great ziggurat (temple-tower) of Ur. The tower of Babel may have been something like this.

Egypt has given us many treasures from the past. This is just one example of many lovely wall-paintings. It shows Queen Ahmes-Nefertari.

□ Comparison with the Hebrew story

The Hebrew story, like the Babylonian one, tells how God created man from the earth and put him in charge of a garden. After the creation, God rested. The human race increased in numbers, built cities and their behaviour disturbed God. The early 'fathers' in Genesis lived to a very great age. Methuselah, who lived longest of all, was 969 when he died. To punish human wickedness God decided to send the flood, from which only faithful Noah, safe in his boat with his family and some animals, would escape. As the flood storms quietened, and the boat grounded on a high mountain, Noah sent out birds to find vegetation. Then he left the boat and made sacrifices to God.

There is a counterpart for each of these points in the

Babylonian story, although often the action of several different gods makes it more complicated. But the purpose of man's creation in the two accounts is not really the same.

Genesis does not suggest that God needed to be fed: he made men and women in order to share his company. Both accounts see man's work as being to cultivate the ground. But according to Genesis the work was not arduous until after the 'fall'. There is no fall in the Babylonian texts. We do not know what lies behind the long reigns and life-times credited to early man. It is striking that this feature appears in both accounts at the same point in man's career. Obviously the long lives had some special meaning for the ancient writers.

The reason for sending the flood is clear in both cases: man had sinned against God; he had angered the gods. In the Babylonian story a trick enabled a kindly god to warn his favourite and instruct him to build a boat. He was told to deceive his fellow men about its purpose. When the survival of this man was discovered by the god who had proposed sending the flood in the first place, there was a bitter dispute among the gods. The kindly god argued that each man should bear the punishment for his own crime rather than all suffering equally.

In the *Gilgamesh Epic* three birds were sent from the boat to seek food: a dove, a swallow and a raven. (The tablet of the earlier version is damaged at this point, so we cannot be sure the episode was included.) Noah sent the stronger bird – the raven – first, then the dove. In both accounts sacrifices were made after the flood had begun to subside.

Such strong similarities point to the close relationship of the Babylonian and the Genesis stories. The over-all pattern of creation, growth, flood and many points of detail common to both can hardly be coin-

cidence. But archaeology cannot explain the connection. The memory of a great flood was evidently very strong. Polytheistic Babylonians and monotheistic Hebrews each had their own form of it. To say either is derived from the other raises difficulties. There could have been an older ancestor of both – but we are guessing. There is no archaeological evidence.

☐ **The flood at Ur**
During his excavations at Ur in 1929, *Sir Leonard Woolley* came across a layer of water-laid clay, 8–11ft/2.4–3.3m thick. He was convinced he had found silt left by the flood. At other sites similar layers were found, but these were from different dates. These findings show that Babylonia has been subject to serious flooding in the past. In fact floods remained a problem until recent times, when dams were built to control the Tigris and Euphrates rivers. We cannot claim that any one of these layers was left by *the* flood. However, the written traditions are so strong we cannot doubt that a catastrophic flood did occur early in the history of mankind in Babylonia.

The Israelites and their ancestors

Archaeology provides no direct evidence relating to the story of the Israelites and their ancestors until the people occupied their Promised Land. Abraham, Isaac, Jacob and his sons lived most of their lives in tents. Although they may have been rich and powerful, such a way of life leaves little for the archaeologist to recover.

Abraham and his early descendants had dealings with the rulers of Canaanite cities and with the pharaohs of Egypt. But it would be extraordinary to find their names in the records of those princes. In the first place we would have to unearth archives of the right years and places. And in the second, the contacts

would have had to have been reckoned worth recording at the time. As it is, not a single collection of documents of that time is known to us from Canaan. In Egypt any government records from this period have perished long ago. If they were not deliberately destroyed, they would have decayed in the damp soil of the cities near the Nile.

People are often surprised that Egyptian monuments give no hint of the exodus. Yet we could hardly expect it, unless we had a complete chronicle of the period. After all, the Israelites were a group of foreigners used as forced labour. The Old Testament says that they escaped after Egypt had been hit by a series of disasters (the plagues), and the Egyptian army had been caught in the 'Red Sea'. They marched into a sparsely populated area away from the main roads controlled by Egyptian troops, and so moved beyond Egypt's interest. It was only when they had reached Canaan, officially an Egyptian province, that they did come to Egypt's notice. Israel is listed as one of the groups conquered there when Pharaoh Merenptah tried to restore his country's rule late in the thirteenth century BC.

However, archaeological discoveries *can* supply background information for the first five books of the Bible. They can provide examples of events, customs, or ideas that shed light on the Bible's stories.

If, for example, there is clear evidence that some activity, say making coins, was not introduced until after 700 BC, but Abraham is represented as paying for a purchase with coins a thousand years or more before that date, we may suspect the account was written after 700 BC, or that an older story was revised after that date. But before we come to this conclusion every aspect of the problem has to be properly weighed. Often a text that seems to have an 'anachronism'

JERICHO: ONE OF THE WORLD'S OLDEST CITIES

Jericho's fresh-water spring makes it an oasis in the surrounding desert. A flourishing town today, its history goes back more than 6,000 years BC.

Water is channelled from the spring, making Jericho quite literally the 'city of palms'.

The work of archaeologists lays bare walls in the ancient city.

Many objects have been recovered from tombs at Jericho. This wooden box inlaid with bone dates from about 1700 BC.

This plan was made during an early excavation at Jericho.

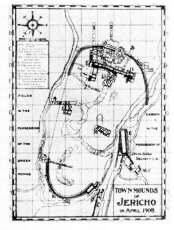

The great mound, all that is left of ancient Jericho, shows clearly from the air.

of this sort is shown by a new discovery, or better understanding of an old one, to be correct.

Abraham and his family

□ Ur of the Chaldees
Abraham's lifestyle seems to fit into a period about 2000 BC. At that time Ur of the Chaldees, his family home, was already an ancient city. Excavations made there by *Sir Leonard Woolley* from 1922 to 1934 revealed the riches of local kings about 2400 BC (see Part 11 under *The Babylonians*).

The gold dagger and sheath were found in the Royal Graves at Ur, about 2600 BC.

When Ur was at the height of its power (about 2100 BC) its king built a great temple tower (ziggurat, see page 41) for the moon-god (named Nannar or Sin) which still dominates the site. Citizens living there during the next two or three centuries had well-made houses, planned to suit the climate, and provided with adequate drains. Cuneiform tablets tell of trade with far-off places, of family affairs, and of intellectual pursuits.

Kings and others were interested in history. They copied the inscriptions of their predecessors, and the scribes wrote out stories of long-dead heroes. Some of these legends can be placed in their historical setting as a result of knowledge gained recently. Although no document of his own day mentions Gilgamesh we may be confident that he was a notable king not long before 2500 BC. Some of the deeds which legend reports he performed also make sense against the background of that period.

□ 'Uncivilized barbarians'
From this civilized city, Abraham's family travelled hundreds of miles north to Harran. This was also a centre for the worship of the moon, and Terah, Abraham's father, may have been connected with it. After living there for a time, Abraham obeyed the call of God to go west and south. Instead of being a city-dweller, he was to live in tents, moving from campsite to campsite, in search of pasture and water.

Abraham's journeys and his new way of life can be understood against a background of the Amorite people's movements about 2000 BC (see Part 11, under *The Babylonians*). The Babylonian scribes despised the people who lived in tents, ate raw meat, and did not bury their dead. They were considered uncivilized barbarians. Abraham was called to lead that kind of life. While the Amorites gradually settled in the old cities and mixed with earlier inhabitants, Abraham and his family remained nomads.

The names of the 'patriarchs' (the great ancestors of Israel) belong in general to a kind of name common at the time amongst the Amorites. Of course, some continued in use long after. It is clear that they began as personal names and not names of gods or tribes.

In fact, the naming of a tribe after its ancestor, who was an actual person, not an imaginary figure, can be observed in other ancient texts besides the account of Israel and its twelve tribes in Genesis and Exodus.

□ Cities of Canaan and Syria
When they reached Canaan the patriarchs found cities, each under its own prince, some strong, some weak. Many of them had been founded centuries earlier, had fallen into ruin and been recently rebuilt. Excavations have disclosed the houses, palaces, temples, and city walls of those very early times, but, so far, no written records of life in them.

In the palace of the north Syrian city of Ebla, however, the royal archive unearthed in 1975 proves that Babylonian writing was current there. Besides business and administrative files, the archive contained literary works from Babylonia and others of local origin. These show the wide influence of the cuneiform writing system and its related culture. This influence still continued after 2000 BC, mixing with Egyptian culture entering from the coast, especially at Byblos – where Egypt bought cedar-wood – and in Canaan itself.

□ Social customs
The patriarchs kept links with Harran, and their family arrangements seem to follow Babylonian social custom. These differ in some respects from later Israelite ways. The birth of Ishmael by the slave girl Hagar because Sarah, Abraham's wife, was childless; Abraham's reluctance to dismiss Hagar when she laughed at Sarah; and the fact that Jacob treated the sons he had by the two maids as equal with the sons of his two wives, all find parallels in various Babylonian documents of the period 2000 to 1500 BC. Canaanites may have followed similar customs but their records do not survive.

From the Bible's description it seems that the 'ark of the covenant' was rather like this wooden box with rings and carrying poles found in King Tutankhamun's tomb.

In Egypt

□ Joseph

Famine drove Abraham's descendants into Egypt. There was a constant flow of people from southern Canaan seeking food and work in Egypt. Some were taken as slaves, like Joseph, sold at the average price of twenty silver shekels. Joseph's rise to high office also has parallels. Others of Joseph's race (Semites) reached the status of vizier and even pharaoh about 1700 BC (the Hyksos dynasty). Joseph's position gave him access to the cultural heritage of Egypt which, by his day, was 1500 years old. As in Babylonia, anything one wanted could be recorded in writing, and the running of the country could be managed very efficiently.

The Israelites stayed away from the central cities on the Nile, living in the eastern parts of the Delta, where they could pasture their herds. For several generations they lived peacefully, until a pharaoh from a new dynasty came to power. He forced them to work on his new capital in the region where they had settled. If this king was Ramesses II (about 1279–1213 BC), as most scholars believe, then it is worth noting some accounts and other texts of this reign.

□ The 'Apiru'

Egyptian texts from several periods detail the quotas of mud-bricks to be made by gangs of labourers. One, from the reign of Ramesses II, mentions a group called *Apiru* (in Babylonian, *Khabire*) moving stone for a royal building in Memphis.

The Apiru may have included the Israelites. The word itself meant people who had no country or property of their own. Among them, probably, were fugitives escaping from debt or slavery, and people displaced by war or famine, from a number of different backgrounds. They hired themselves out as casual labour, and were not difficult to control when a king was strong. But they presented a threat to organized society if its rulers were weak. It is very likely that Abraham's family, who had no land of their own, took up this name to describe themselves to foreigners, so giving us the word 'Hebrew'.

□ The covenant

At Mt Sinai Moses brought his people the constitution which established them as the people of God. It was set out in the form of a covenant, a treaty, between God as the chief partner and Israel as the subject.

Dozens of ancient treaties have been translated, the majority of them treaties made in the period 2000–1000 BC. Exodus and Deuteronomy are not themselves treaty texts, they are reports of treaties made. They contain a number of the same elements found in those ancient Near Eastern treaties. What took place at Sinai was a solemn event, to be impressed upon the people.

The actual arrangement of the sections of the treaty (title, historical introduction, requirements, instructions about keeping the treaty document and making its contents known, witnesses, curses and blessings) is closely parallel to the treaties regularly made between the Hittites and their subject nations during the period 1700–1200 BC.

Laws concerning social life similar to those in Exodus are known from the law-code of Hammurabi, king of Babylon about 1750 BC (see Part 11, *The Babylonians*). However, no other collection has anything like the Ten Commandments as a basic set of rules of conduct.

On the way to the Promised Land

□ The tent-shrine

In the Sinai Desert, Israel constructed a prefabricated tent-shrine (tabernacle) for the worship of God. Careful study of the instructions shows that the method of linking wooden frames by bars, the curtains, and the cover made of cloth and skins, has parallels in Egypt.

Examples of prefabricated

Carved on a wooden shrine overlaid with gold is this portrait of Pharaoh Tutankhamun on his throne, with his wife. One of the treasures from the king's tomb, discovered in Egypt.

wooden shrines, plated all over with gold, were found in the tomb of Tutankhamun. They were put there to contain the king's coffin. A wooden chest, buried in the same tomb, was provided with wooden pole-handles for carrying. These slid neatly under the box when not in use. They were a more complex version of the kind of wooden carrying-poles made to slide through rings on the Covenant Box (ark) and other furniture in the tabernacle.

The elaborate rules about the priests and attendants in the tabernacle, and about various sacrifices, have some parallels in texts from Ugarit in Syria and from a Hittite library in Turkey of about the same date, as well as some from Babylonia. In none of those centres, by contrast with the Old Testament, has a complete set of rules been preserved.

☐ **A discovery at Amman**
During their forty years of wandering, the Israelites met various other tribes. Some, like the Moabites, already had their own cities or strongholds. But excavators have not so far identified the remains of any captured by the Israelites. A discovery made at Amman airport may shed some light on conditions at the time.

A small square building was uncovered, containing a central courtyard enclosed by small rooms. Large quantities of Mycenaean pottery imported from Crete and Cyprus, jewellery and other precious objects lay in every level. Some of these things had been burnt, together with large numbers of bones – animal and human. Reports state that the majority of the human bones were children's.

This could be a shrine where children who died of disease or famine were cremated (the infant mortality rate was certainly very high). It is equally possible that it was a site of child sacrifice, the rite of 'passing children through the fire to Molech' which the Israelites were forbidden to do (Leviticus 18:21). This is an example of a discovery where no one interpretation is certain.

The conquest of Canaan
From the time Israel became a nation with their own land (a little before 1200 BC), we could expect archaeology to provide inscriptions and other objects as evidence of their presence. The fact that it is very difficult to produce more than one piece of evidence for the period 1250–950 BC has led to great debate and widely differing opinions. Although the debate continues, it is a good illustration of the limits of archaeological evidence.

☐ **Written documents**
The single piece of evidence we have is the inscription of the Egyptian King Merenptah (no earlier than 1210 BC). Its words make it clear that Israel was present in western Palestine by the date of Merenptah's campaign there. Egypt gives us few other records about the area, and from 1160 BC was too weak to be concerned with her former province of Canaan.

The interests of Assyria reached to the Mediterranean coast in Phoenicia, but not as far south as Israel. From about 1100 to 900 BC Assyria, like Egypt, suffered a decline.

Only a handful of documents is available to us from southern Syria and Canaan, and none are of the sort that would be certain to mention the Israelites if they were already there. So we have no written evidence for the Israelite conquest of Canaan apart from the Old Testament. And we have only one other record of their presence there before 1200 BC.

☐ **Ruined cities**
Conquest usually implies looting and destruction. Joshua's campaigns are often viewed as a series of destructive raids. So many scholars have looked for signs of this in the ruined cities of late Bronze Age Canaan. In particular, they have looked for burning.

For several years it was accepted that traces of burning had been found at several places which had all been destroyed about the same time, and that this was the work of the Israelites. Some of those destructions, it is now clear, took place at other times. Others, it is argued, may have been the work, not of Israelites, but of the Philistines and their friends who were trying to invade the coastal areas at about the same time. There are also uncertainties in dating pottery and there are other aspects of these excavations which demand fresh and accurate study.

At present we cannot point to any Canaanite building and say: 'The Israelites destroyed this,' though there are some sites where they were probably responsible.

After the conquest, the Israelites settled in their Promised Land. We have already noticed that there are no known inscriptions which relate to that period, or which are clearly Israelite. But can we trace their presence in any other way? The answer, once more, is disappointing. Nothing has been found that is distinctively Israelite. Some discoveries, however, do hint at a change in the culture of the country, and perhaps of its population.

☐ **What should we expect?**
Before discussing the evidence that may relate to the conquest, some other points need to be made. In the first place, the books of Joshua and Judges relate the sacking of very few cities (Jericho, Ai, Hazor, Hormah). A country of ruined towns would have been useless to the newcomers, and Judges 1 explains how they often occupied Canaanite towns alongside the local population. So we would not expect to find signs of violent attack and destruction at many places.

Then the fact that they mixed with the Canaanites, or took over their cities, will have weakened any features which may have been characteristic of Israelite culture. In any case, the Israelites had not been living in towns before their invasion, and are unlikely to have had distinctive possessions which would survive for us to see.

Here the Israelites may be compared with the movement of the Amorites into Babylonia (see Part 11, *The Babylonians*). Cuneiform tablets reveal the time and the course of the Amorite advance into Babylonia, and in due course their control of the land. Without those texts, it would not be possible for us to tell that there were Amorites in Babylonia. Very few objects can be identified as the product of a particular ancient nation without some additional written information. (To take an example a long way off in time and place from Israel, it is worth noting that there is no clear archaeological evidence for the Norman conquest of England in AD 1066.) So there is not much real reason to hope for a clear change in archaeological material following the Israelite conquest.

☐ **Bronze gives way to iron**
The hundred years 1250–1150 BC saw great changes in the lands of the Near East.

Old states fell and new ones gradually arose, often formed on different patterns. In the north, the great Hittite Empire crumbled. In the south, Egypt lost control of Canaan, and excavations along the coast of Syria and Israel have uncovered clear signs of cities violently destroyed.

Egyptian sources imply that this was the work of invaders from the sea, among them the Philistines, a foreign people who probably came from Crete (see *The Philistines* in Part 11: *Nations and Peoples of the Bible*). They used a distinctive type of pottery, which has been found in buildings erected on top of the cities that were destroyed.

In Syria the Aramaeans were occupying some of the old cities – Damascus was one of these. And east of the Jordan Ammonites, Moabites and Edomites were beginning to settle down.

A major technical change took place as the art of iron-working spread, bringing stronger, more efficient tools. The Late Bronze Age gave way to the Iron Age.

Excavations at the sites of Bethel, Beth-shemesh, Hazor, Lachish, Tell Beit Mirsim (thought by its excavator to be Debir), and Tell el-Hesi (perhaps Eglon) have discovered that each was burnt late in the thirteenth century BC. That could have been the work of Israelite troops. Similarly, at Ashdod and Ashkelon the Late Bronze Age cities were destroyed by fire, and that could have been the work of the Philistines. But Ashkelon is one of the places Merenptah captured, so the Egyptians may bear the blame.

Afterwards some of the cities were re-occupied, though less extensively, while some were deserted. On the other hand, several places where there had

Scenes like this, a narrow, crowded shopping-street in the ancient city of Aleppo, Syria, make it easy for us to step straight back into the past.

been no Late Bronze Age buildings (Beth-zur, Ai) were now settled. And new villages were established in some parts, on both sides of the Jordan.

☐ **Jericho**
Two places which feature in the Book of Joshua cause problems: Jericho and Ai. In 1931 *John Garstang* claimed he had uncovered the walls of Jericho which fell flat at the trumpet-blast and shout of the Israelites. Excavations made from 1952 to 1958 by *Kathleen Kenyon* showed that Garstang was wrong.

Improved techniques for disentangling ruined walls and foundations, and better knowledge of pottery fashions, make this plain. The later excavations traced only a tiny area of Late Bronze Age building, and even that seems to have been deserted before about 1300 BC, according to Dr Kenyon. So there are no surviving ruins of the city mentioned in the Book of Joshua.

Some scholars have suggested that the story of the city's fall was an 'aetiological'

story, told to explain how the old ruined town fell into decay. Others have thought that Joshua's Jericho must be in a different place, not yet identified. A third possibility is that the deserted and burnt mud-brick buildings were entirely eroded by winter winds and heavy rains.

There is certainly some evidence to show that earlier buildings have disappeared in this way during Jericho's long history. A great city wall, erected about 1800 BC, had disappeared except at the highest point of the mound. There just its lowest course of stones remained. Erosion like this is known at other ancient sites in the Near East.

□ Ai
At the site known as Et-Tell, usually identified with Ai, no remains of buildings have ever been found that can be dated between 2300 and 1200 BC.

Again, some argue that the Bible's account of the two attacks on Ai is a folk-tale that explains the existence of the large ruined walls in terms related to the Israelites' ancestors. Others believe the place has been wrongly identified, and that Ai lay somewhere else. A third proposal assumes that the ancient defences at Et-Tell, which are still impressive, served as a stronghold which the people living nearby could make use of in time of trouble.

The only clear record of Israel's conquest of Canaan, then, is the account we have in the Bible. Archaeology has produced information which may be linked with it, but we cannot be certain how to interpret this at present.

David and Solomon
During King David's reign Israel finally managed to rule the whole of Canaan and control large areas of neigh-bouring lands. Wealth flowed into the kingdom through taxes. Expanding trade brought wider contacts and new ideas. At present nothing has been discovered that is definitely the work of David.

□ Three cities
But from Solomon's time (about 970–930 BC) fragments of city walls and gateways have been identified at three cities: Gezer, Hazor, and Megiddo. These are mentioned just after Jerusalem in the list of Solomon's building-works given in 1 Kings 9:15. Each of them was surrounded by two

This stone slab found at Thebes, recording the victories of Pharaoh Merenptah, clearly shows the name of Israel. It dates from the end of the thirteenth century BC and is the oldest evidence for the existence of Israel outside the Bible.

walls 6–9ft/2–3m apart, joined by crosswalls to make a series of rooms ('casemate' walls). Gates led through the walls into the cities. Two square towers guarded the entrance, either projecting from the wall (as at Hazor) or part of it (as at Gezer and Megiddo). Behind them three rooms stood on each side of the road. The whole entrance-way may have been vaulted.

At Gezer and Megiddo an outer gate was joined by walls to the main gate, but stood almost at right angles to it. This old device enabled guards to restrict entry more easily than they could do if the road ran straight to the main gate. All three of these city gateways were built to the same basic design, and their measurements are very similar.

Of course, to be *absolutely* certain that these structures were erected at Solomon's command, we would need an inscription, indisputably in its original position, and contemporary with Solomon. The style of pottery found in the ruins does support the dating.

□ **Solomon's temple**
The temple, Solomon's most famous building, was destroyed by Nebuchadnezzar's soldiers

The temple at Arad

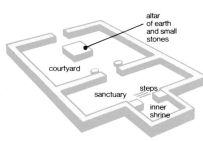

in 586 BC. A replacement was erected in about 520 BC. Then, five centuries later, King Herod rebuilt the temple on an even grander scale than Solomon's. In AD 70 this temple, the last, was destroyed by the Romans. On its site, in about AD 690, Muslims built the Dome of the Rock and, a little later, the Aqsa Mosque, which stands there today. Consequently, no trace of Solomon's temple can be seen.

1 Kings 6 and 7 describe the

The Bible says that King Solomon rebuilt the cities of Gezer, Megiddo and Hazor. Archaeologist Yigael Yadin discovered that all three cities had identical gates and casemate walls. The plan of Hazor and photograph of Megiddo clearly show the distinctive structure.

temple. Discoveries at other places show that the plan of a porch, a holy place, and an inner sanctuary was not unique. It occurs in a Canaanite temple at Hazor and in a ninth-century BC temple at Tell Tayinat in north Syria.

The rich decoration of Solomon's temple also followed ancient custom. Cedarwood had always been prized for beams and panelling. Egyptian and Assyrian records boast of temple floors paved with silver, and of walls and doors overlaid with sheets of gold. In some Egyptian buildings the holes for nails to attach these sheets still survive. Naturally, the precious metal has been stripped off long ago. On rare occasions small pieces left by the looters are found here and there.

Copper and bronze were less attractive to the raiders, and in one case the bronze plates that overlaid and sheathed the gates of an Assyrian temple built a century after Solomon's still survive. The largest of these gates had two leaves, each almost 6ft/2m wide and 18ft/6m high. The metal sheets were embossed with pictures of the Assyrian army's success in the reign of the king who built the temple.

□ **Solomon's palace**
Solomon took longer to build his palace than the temple. He used cedar and other fine woods, and further quantities of gold. The king had some of the gold beaten into shields to

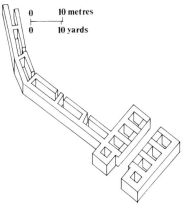

hang on the walls (1 Kings 10:16–17). When an Assyrian king captured a temple in ancient Urartu (modern Armenia), in about 710 BC, he carried off golden shields which had decorated it. Each of those was considerably heavier than the ones Solomon had made. Solomon's shields came to a similar end; they were taken as booty by invaders in his son's reign (1 Kings 14:26–27).

For state occasions, Solomon had an elaborate throne. It was made of ivory, overlaid with gold. A calf's head was carved at the back, a lion at each side, and a pair of lions on each of the six steps leading up to it (1 Kings 10:18–20). Wooden furniture, including a throne, completely overlaid with gold can be seen among the treasures of Tutankhamun's tomb in Egypt. Wooden furniture plated with ivory was part of the tribute received by Assyrian kings from Syria and Palestine. Thousands of pieces have been recovered from a royal store-house at Nimrud (ancient Calah), south of Nineveh. There is a collection of carved chair-backs, and a chair-leg carved at the end in the shape of a lion's foot.

Enough pieces were found in position in a tomb in Cyprus to make it possible for archaeologists to reconstruct an ivory throne. The ivory was often covered with gold foil. Carved or engraved pictures of thrones show the arms supported by sphinxes, an idea rather like the lions beside Solomon's throne.

□ **Pharaoh Shishak's invasion**
After Solomon had died and his kingdom had split into two smaller states, a new and powerful king of Egypt marched north. This king, Shishak, took the treasures from Jerusalem and sent his forces throughout the territories of Israel and Judah. Two verses in 1 Kings (14:25–26) and a slightly longer passage in 2 Chronicles (12:1–9) report the event from the Hebrew side.

Shishak celebrated his victory by starting work on vast temple buildings to honour his gods. Carved on the stone wall of a great courtyard at Karnak is a picture of the king striking his enemies. Beside it is a list of the places his army had visited. Some of the names are no longer readable but those that are can provide valuable information for the historical geography of the land of Israel. Several towns which are hardly mentioned in the Old Testament (for example, Adam, Penuel, Taanach) were evidently quite important.

A text like this, with a known date and specific references, gives the archaeologist a fixed point to help reconstruct the history of several sites. Burnt debris at a number of places has been related to the arrival of Shishak's men. It should be noted that Shishak's inscription is not a narrative and mentions only geographical names. Not surprisingly, it does not name either the king of Judah (Rehoboam), or the king of Israel (Jeroboam I). Nor does it mention their greater predecessors, Solomon and David.

Kings of Israel and Judah
The northern kingdom of Israel lasted for 200 years after Shishak's invasion; Judah another 140 years. The opportunity of greatness provided by David and Solomon had gone. When Solomon's empire fell to pieces there were too many other kings eager to assert themselves for Israel to rise to 'great power' status again. From then on the history of Israel and Judah was largely a history of their struggle to maintain independence, both from other states and from each other.

□ **Defences**
The kings tried to make themselves secure by rebuilding city walls on as massive a scale as they could afford. They also undertook major engineering projects to secure permanent

JERUSALEM IN THE OLD AND NEW TESTAMENTS

The ancient stronghold of Jebus, captured by King David, became the nation's capital and the site of the temple built by David's son, Solomon. As the city of God it is the focus of great events in both Old and New Testament times.

Models show city buildings, the Fort of Antonia, where Roman soldiers were garrisoned at the time of Christ, and the temple.

Jerusalem at the time of the kings

SOLOMON'S CITY
Temple
Palace
THE JEBUSITE STRONGHOLD (DAVID'S) (CITY)
Kidron Valley
Tyropoean Valley
Gihon Spring
Hezekiah's tunnel
Pool of Siloam
Valley of Hinnom

Jerusalem in Nehemiah's time

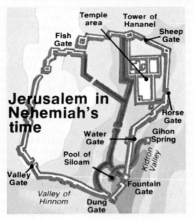

Temple area
Tower of Hananel
Fish Gate
Sheep Gate
Horse Gate
Water Gate
Gihon Spring
Pool of Siloam
Valley Gate
Kidron Valley
Fountain Gate
Valley of Hinnom
Dung Gate

When Judah was under threat from the Assyrians, King Hezekiah cut a tunnel through the rock from the Spring of Gihon to ensure a supply of water under siege. Water from the spring was brought to the Pool of Siloam, shown here.

Jerusalem in New Testament times

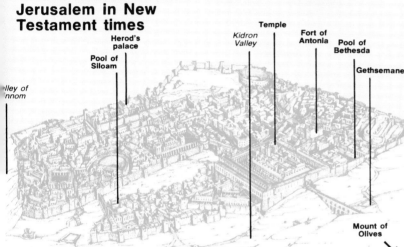

Herod's palace
Pool of Siloam
Valley of Hinnom
Kidron Valley
Temple
Fort of Antonia
Pool of Bethesda
Gethsemane
Mount of Olives

This aerial view of the city is taken from the north. It shows the medieval city walls and the ancient temple area now occupied by the Dome of the Rock.

SAMARIA: CAPITAL OF ISRAEL

Plan of Samaria

Israelite remains are shown in red, Roman buildings in blue, and work completed by King Herod in black.

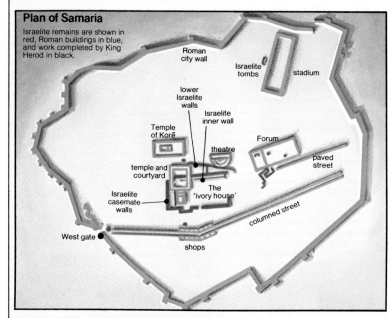

Many beautiful carved ivories have been found at Samaria from the time of King Ahab's 'ivory house'.

Looking towards the hill of Samaria, site of Israel's capital city.

water-supplies within those walls. At Hazor and Megiddo these works are attributed to King Ahab of Israel.

In Judah, too, the defences of towns like Mizpah, Tell Beit Mirsim and Tell Beersheba have been uncovered. Houses within these walls usually have

Ivories carved in the shape of calves, from the great Assyrian city of Nimrud, ninth–eighth century BC.

the same basic plan: an open courtyard with rooms on one, two, or three sides. Large oblong stones, set on end, mark the limits of the yards. Presumably they supported piers of smaller stones or mud-brick, to take the weight of the roof or of an upper storey. In some towns a row of houses was built against the city wall, making a street all round the town. Other lanes led from that street towards the town centre. Pots and pans lying in the houses, and occasional stone containers and metal tools, help to build a picture of daily life. The pottery was well made on a fast-spinning wheel. Shapes were simple, yet often elegant. Decoration was rarely used, and glaze was unknown. Dishes and small jugs were often polished before baking to make the terracotta less absorbent. Sometimes the owner's name is preserved, scratched on a pot.

☐ **Standard weights and measures**
Some large jugs were stamped with a seal. Probably this was a guarantee that they held a standard amount. The seals either belonged to private persons, perhaps holding an official post to control weights and measures, or are govern-ment marks. The latter bear a design with the word 'royal'

above and the name of an administrative centre below. About 1,000 have been discovered. This kind of standardization appears to have applied in Judah in the seventh century BC. See p. 240.

Another sign of it is the number of small stone weights, made from pebbles carefully reduced to conform with a fixed symbol. The shekel was set at 11.4 grammes. The actual weights found give this average, each one varying to a greater or lesser degree. There were larger and smaller weights.

Among the smaller weights some of those found are inscribed with the letters *pym*. Their weights show that their value was two-thirds of a shekel. In 1 Samuel 13:21 the word *payim* occurs in the description of how the Israelites were forced to go to the Philistine smiths to have their iron tools serviced. The word was not understood until study of the weights revealed that it was the price charged by the Philistines, equivalent to two-thirds of a shekel of silver. Modern translations of the Old Testament can now give a good sense for this verse, which the Authorized and Revised Versions could not do.

☐ **The Moabite Stone**
Outside the Bible, the first mention of the name of Israel's God (YHWH – widely thought to have been pronounced Yahweh) is on the Moabite Stone discovered in Trans-jordan in 1868. Mesha, king of Moab, had this monument inscribed and set up at Dibon about 840 BC. He recorded how the Moabite god 'Chemosh was angry with his land' and allowed Omri of Israel to oppress it.

In Mesha's reign Chemosh relented and enabled him to regain territory from Israelite hands. Triumphantly, Mesha brought temple prisoners and vessels which had belonged to Yahweh 'from Nebo to Chemosh'. Mesha's description of his god's behaviour is quite

similar to the Bible's descrip-tions of Israel's God in his dealings with his people, though God's anger with his people had a moral basis, whereas Chemosh's anger is unexplained.

☐ **An unorthodox shrine**
In the corner of the Judean fortress of Arad, the excavator, *Y. Aharoni*, found a structure he identified as a shrine of Yahweh. The basic plan is a roughly rectangular courtyard with an altar in it leading to a long narrow room. At one time there were benches around the walls of this room. A small room, less than 6ft/2m square, opened off the long wall opposite the doorway. Its floor was raised and on the steps leading to it stood two stone incense altars, each about 18in/0.5m high. Within the room was a paved platform (called a 'high place' by the excavator), and a smoothed stone pillar, about 3ft/1m high, painted red.

There were small pieces of pottery lying in a room beside this 'temple' and on each a man's name was written. Two of the names are those of priestly families known in the Old Testament (Meremoth, Pashhur). These potsherds seem to have been used in drawing lots to decide whose turn of duty came next.

☐ **The royal palace of Samaria**
An expedition from Harvard University dug at the site of Israel's capital, Samaria, in 1908–10. Another, led by the British School of Archaeology in Jerusalem, with support from other institutions, worked there from 1931 to 1935. Underneath the ruins of a great temple erected by King Herod in honour of Augustus the archaeologists unearthed parts of a royal palace. Foundations for the later temple had cut into it, but enough remained to enable part of the plan to be drawn. A double 'casemate' wall (with rooms in its thickness) sur-rounded the citadel. There was

a gateway at the east end. At the west end were buildings thought to be palaces of Ahab and later kings. Even where only the foundations survive, it is possible to see that the stone blocks have been cut square and fitted exactly.

At one place, among the debris on the floor of Ahab's palace, lay a piece of carved ivory and a fragment of an Egyptian stone vase. On it was the name of the pharaoh (Osorkon) who had sent it full of perfumed oil to Ahab or some other king. Its presence gave a clue to the date of other things found with it (Osorkon II ruled from about 874 to 850 BC).

A large collection of ivory carvings were found in a different area. Some 200 pieces, smashed and burnt, had served as veneer and inlay for wooden furniture. Precious objects like these would have been kept for a long time, so it is likely that some belonged to Ahab's 'ivory house' (1 Kings 22:39), and some to later days. The prophet Amos condemned the nobles a century after Ahab for lounging on expensive ivory beds (Amos 6:4).

Various designs display influences from Egypt, with lotus flowers and Egyptian religious motifs, and also from Syria. Phoenician craftsmen carved the ivory, sometimes marking individual sections with letters of the alphabet to ensure that they were correctly assembled by the cabinet-makers. The white ivory was often inlaid with blue and red glass, or covered with gold foil. As Amos reveals, luxury goods like these were paid for at the expense of the poor, and brought undesirable foreign influences into the court.

In Assyria quantities of identical ivory-carvings have been discovered, evidently tribute from kings of Israel and nearby states, or booty from their cities. One bears a Hebrew inscription and so may have come from Samaria. Another has the name of Hazael, the king of Damascus in Elisha's day.

One hundred and two pieces of pottery used as scrap paper (*ostraca*) were discovered mixed with other materials to make up the floors of a building erected late in the history of the palace. They were notes in the Hebrew dialect made by royal clerks about wine and oil delivered from crown estates to supply the court. On about half of them the ink has been rubbed, so that little can be read. The others are dated by the year of the king's reign. Unfortunately, the scribes knew who the king was and so did not write his name; whereas we do not know. Several places are mentioned which throw light on farming in the Samaria region.

Stewards in charge of the estates are mentioned by name. Their names show that some of the people of Samaria continued to revere the God of Israel, because they include shortened forms of his name, Yahweh – such as Uriah ('the Lord is my light'), or Jonatan ('the Lord has given'). But others clearly worshipped Baal, and their names include Abibaal ('Baal is my father') and Meribaal ('Baal has blessed' or 'Baal is my master').

Few traces remain of the houses of less important citizens. When the Assyrians captured the city, their inscriptions report that they took away some 27,200 people when they captured the city. It is impossible to know how accurate this figure is, and whether it accounts for the city alone or includes surrounding districts. But it does give some idea of the number of people living there after a period of foreign invasion (720 BC). The Assyrians made Samaria the capital of a province. Their king, Sargon, set up a victory monument there as he did in other places (Ashdod among them), but only shattered bits survive. At Hazor and Megiddo strongly-built fortresses probably housed Assyrian garrisons. Distinctive pottery, identical with the kind usually found in the Assyrian cities of Nineveh and Calah (now Nimrud), has also been discovered.

☐ **Judah and Jerusalem**
Judah existed for 140 years after Samaria fell. For more than half that time it was a subject kingdom of Assyria. However, the Assyrians did not interfere in the internal affairs of the state, so we would not expect any change in culture.

King Ahaz had made a pact with Tiglath-pileser III of Assyria about 735 BC, when the kings of Damascus and Samaria were threatening him (see Isaiah 7; 2 Kings 16). Assyria promised to protect Judah as long as Judah had no dealings with Assyria's enemies and paid an annual tribute. In due course both Damascus and Samaria were captured by Assyrian armies. Some of the Philistine cities were also taken (see Isaiah 20).

Judah would have remained unharmed, but when King Sargon was killed in battle (705 BC) Ahaz' son, Hezekiah, thought he could take advantage of the situation to break Assyria's hold on Judah. He took prisoner the pro-Assyrian king of Ekron, and received ambassadors from Merodach-baladan, the anti-Assyrian leader of the Babylonians. Hezekiah had been foolish. Sennacherib, the new king of Assyria, routed the Babylonian and other rebels, then turned west. He 'came down like a wolf on the fold', overran Judah, and tried to persuade Hezekiah to surrender.

A sculptured frieze from Nineveh shows the attack on Lachish, south of Jerusalem. It pictures archers shooting into the city, battering-rams trying to break the walls, and daring soldiers climbing ladders to gain entry. The defenders are depicted throwing stones and flaming torches on their enemies. The city fell, and the reliefs also show lines of sorry citizens marching into exile,

A jar-handle stamped with a seal. Some of these seals may have been government marks guaranteeing that the container held a standard amount.

their possessions packed on bullock-carts.

Sennacherib claims he removed 200,150 people from Judah. Exile like this was the normal punishment for rebels, spelt out in the pacts of alliance, and carried out by powerful kings, even from remote times. Sennacherib himself appears on the frieze, enthroned, listening to his general's report and accepting the submission of the leaders of Lachish.

In excavating the ruins of Lachish archaeologists found the crest of an Assyrian helmet, as well as arrowheads and slingstones. Violent destruction had befallen the buildings of archaeological level III, and many scholars think that this was the city destroyed by Sennacherib. A great ramp of earth and stones built outside the city will then be part of the siege-works, for wheeling battering-rams up against the walls, as shown on Sennacherib's sculptures.

☐ Hezekiah's tunnel
Jerusalem alone withstood Assyria's might. Eventually King Hezekiah sent tribute to Sennacherib, but not until he had returned to Nineveh. One of the reasons for Jerusalem's safety was the water supply apparently improved by Hezekiah. The Gihon Spring (now the Virgin's Fountain) lay outside the city wall. Obviously an enemy could quickly cause the city's collapse by preventing access to the spring. An awkward shaft, partly vertical, had been cut down through the rock from inside the city

in Canaanite times, but could only have been used in siege conditions.

Hezekiah's workmen cut a horizontal tunnel to lead water from the spring to an underground cistern 1,750ft (over 500m) away on the opposite slope of the hill. A few ventilation shafts were cut, for the tunnel nowhere comes to the surface. It is possible to walk almost the whole length of the tunnel without stooping. Its very winding course makes it more than half as long again as it need have been. The reason for this may have been to avoid royal tombs, or, more likely, to follow underground streams and cracks in the rock for some distance.

Cutting the tunnel successfully was a notable achievement. Its plan, and an inscription scratched on the rock wall by the workmen, reveal that there were two gangs of miners, one working from each end. At a vital point, a crack in the rock allowed one gang to hear the pick-axes of the other and make a turn to meet them. But for that, they might not have met at all! In later years the rock roof of the cistern broke away. The pool was surrounded by an arcade in New Testament times and known as the Pool of Siloam. (See the Jerusalem photo-feature.)

☐ Rock tombs and broken walls
Wealthy citizens of Jerusalem in Hezekiah's day and after had elaborate tomb-chambers carved in the rock around the city. Stone masons were employed to cut the rock in imitation of houses, and in some instances the owners' names were engraved at the doorway. One states, 'This is the grave of X, the royal steward. There is no gold or silver here, only his bones and his maidservant's. A curse on anyone who opens this.'

Excavations made on the Ophel Hill, where ancient Jerusalem stood, cleared parts of the city wall which was there

during the last years of Judah. Behind it *Dr Kenyon*, the excavator, was faced with a mass of tumbled stones. By close observation she established that these had originally been built as terraces along the steep hillside. Further work by Yigal Shiloh has uncovered ruins of several houses that stood on the terraces or at their foot. Many objects of daily life and fine pottery have been found, and in one house were tiny lumps of clay which had once sealed documents written on papyrus which perished long ago. Seal impressions on the lumps of clay give the names of men active in Jerusalem about the time of the prophet Jeremiah (compare Jeremiah 32:10, etc.).

In another area, to the north-west, *N. Avigad* revealed a heavy stone wall and part of a gateway. The buildings against them had been burnt and bronze arrowheads lay in the layer of burnt material. The excavator suggests that the fire and the arrows were part of Nebuchadnezzar's attack on the city in 586 BC. On other sites, too, excavators have found towns violently destroyed and deserted at that time (Gezer, Beth-shemesh, Tell Beit Mirsim). The gateway of the city of Lachish had been destroyed by fire. In the ashes on the floor of the guard-room lay messages scribbled on potsherds, perhaps the contents of the captain's in-tray. Some were sent by the commander of a smaller garrison somewhere near by. These are the 'Lachish Letters', and they deal with orders given and received and military arrangements.

After the exile
In 538 BC, Cyrus the Persian permitted any Jews who wanted to go to return to Jerusalem. The Cyrus Cylinder, a famous inscription in the British Museum, London, reflects his tolerant policy of allowing exiles to return to their original homes. Those who returned to Jerusalem

The 'Cyrus cylinder' is inscribed with Cyrus the Mede's own account of how he overthrew Babylon in 539 BC. He then returned all prisoners-of-war, including the exiled Jews, to their homelands.

lived in the city and villages around. Other towns in Judah were occupied by descendants of Jews who had not been taken into exile, and by other people who had come into the country from the east. Remains of this period of Persian rule are rare. Military buildings at Lachish, as at Hazor in the north, may have served as control points. Impressions of seals and a very few coins imply that Judah was a distinct political division within the Persian Empire. As in other lands, local aristocrats acted as governors for the great king.

□ **The second temple**
One piece of stone wall may belong to the temple in Jerusalem rebuilt by Zerubbabel and others who returned from Babylon. On the east side of the great enclosure, the outer face of Herod's stone platform can be traced from the southern corner northwards for about 32yds/30m. Then the great blocks stop at a vertical edge and the wall that continues is built of smaller stones smoothly finished only around the edges. Stonework of the same style can be seen in a number of buildings of the Persian period in the Near East, so it is likely that this is a relic of the second temple.

□ **Deeds from Samaria**
The Persian Empire eventually fell to Alexander the Great. In 331 BC he attacked Samaria because its inhabitants had killed the governor Alexander had appointed over Syria. Some of the wealthy citizens escaped and hid in caves in the Jordan Valley. Many of them were trapped there.
In 1962–64 some of their bones and possessions were found. Among the precious objects the fugitives took with them were papyrus documents which lay preserved in the completely dry soil. These proved to be legal deeds drawn up in Samaria. They were dated, and spanned a period from 375 to about 335 BC. The writing is Aramaic, but the men involved often have Hebrew names. Small lumps of clay were applied to the folded papyrus deeds and impressed with the seals of the various parties and the governor.
Two seals belonged to a son of 'Sanballat the governor'. Here is an addition to known history. Nehemiah faced a hostile governor called Sanballat about 444 BC, and the Jewish historian Josephus wrote of another a century later. Some scholars had found it difficult to believe that there were two governors with the same name. But these seals show that there was certainly one between Nehemiah's time and 330 BC, so making it more likely that there was another later, each being named after his grandfather.

□ **Greek influence**
Greek influences are apparent in sites of the Persian period. Typical painted pottery and some coins have been unearthed, although not in great quantities. From Alexander's time onwards Greek material and Greek fashions spread everywhere. Even after the Maccabean revolt and the establishment of the Jewish

KINGS OF ISRAEL AND JUDAH IN ASSYRIAN RECORDS

Kings of Israel/Judah	Named by Assyrian king	Date of reference
Ahab the Israelite	Shalmaneser III (858–824 BC)	853 BC
Jehu of the Omri-state	Shalmaneser III	841 BC
Joash the Samarian	Adad-nirari III (809–782 BC)	802 or 796 BC
Menahem the Samarian	Tiglath-pileser III (744–727 BC)	about 737 BC
Pekah deposed, **Hoshea** made king	Tiglath-pileser III	about 732 BC
Jehoahaz (Ahaz) the Judean	Tiglath-pileser III	about 728 BC
Hezekiah the Judean	Sennacherib (705–681 BC)	701 BC
Manasseh of Judah	Esarhaddon (680–669 BC)	about 676 BC
Manasseh of Judah	Ashurbanipal (668–627 BC)	about 665 BC

Babylonian chronicles
These record the capture of Samaria in 722 BC during the reign of Shalmaneser V (726–722 BC), and the capture of Jerusalem on 15–16 March, 597 BC, during the reign of Nebuchadnezzar II (604–562 BC). Four tablets recording the issue of rations to foreigners at the Babylonian court about 590 BC name Jehoiachin, captive king of Judah and his family.
These names and dates are very valuable in working out the chronology of Israel's kings. They set the kings firmly in international history.

LACHISH: A CITY UNDER SIEGE

In King Hezekiah's time Lachish was attacked and captured by the Assyrians. Arrowheads and sling-stones (pictured here) have been discovered in the ruins; the walls show signs of burning.

The Assyrian King Sennacherib recorded his victory at Lachish on his palace walls at Nineveh. The scene here shows siege-engines and battering-rams brought against the walls, the Assyrian soldiers, and captives leaving the city.

This letter, written on a broken piece of pottery, is one of a number written by a soldier to his commanding officer just before King Nebuchadnezzar of Babylon attacked the city in 587 BC.

The aerial view, taken from the east, clearly shows the great city-mound (tell) of Lachish.

kingdom under the Hasmonean rulers, Greek ideas were strong. Jewish coins of the second and first centuries BC have Hebrew letters on one side and Greek on the other. Small sketches of fortifications in Jerusalem and a series of houses and citadels at Bethzur, south of Jerusalem, witness to the material culture and abilities of people in the second and first centuries BC. A number of castles and palaces that King Herod built are now known to have been Hasmonean buildings in the first place.

Archaeology and the New Testament

International policies, wars and kings have little place in the New Testament. Its story is about ordinary men and women whose lives were affected by a great teacher. His words and deeds, and the effect they had, take up most of the New Testament books. New Testament history covers less than 100 years, so there is much less scope for archaeology to illustrate and complement the New Testament writings than there is for the Old. Despite these limits, many helpful discoveries have been made.

Herod's Jerusalem

King Herod was not a Jew. His interest in Jerusalem was to make his capital city as splendid as possible. Through his power and his links with Rome, as well as through its own religious position, Jerusalem prospered. Excavations made by Israeli scholars since 1967 have revealed some of the

Recent discoveries in Jerusalem have revealed something of the life-style of wealthy households at the time the city fell to the Romans in AD 70. Amongst the finds were the objects pictured here: mosaic pavements, stone cups and bowls, beautifully-shaped red pottery flasks, and cooking-pots.

richness of the city in New Testament times.

□ Private houses
In the old 'Jewish Quarter' of the city, well-built houses have been uncovered. They were stone buildings, with rooms opening off courtyards. All of these had been destroyed when Jerusalem fell to the Romans in AD 70. In the burnt ruins lay smashed crockery and utensils. Those made locally, as well as those imported, were fashionable. There was fine glassware for the tables of the wealthy, and stone bowls and cups which were not subject to the strict laws of ritual purification. At least one household enjoyed wine brought from Italy, as we see from pottery jars with notes scribbled on them in Latin.

Floors in some rooms were covered with mosaic pavements. Attractive geometric designs were picked out in red, black and white stones. Plaster

Archaeologists have uncovered extensive remains of the great New Testament city of Ephesus. The pictures show a paved street lined with columns and the beautiful arch at the entrance of the temple dedicated to the Emperor Hadrian.

**New Testament
city of Ephesus**

on the walls was painted to imitate marble panelling, architectural features and flowers. Houses had underground cisterns for water storage – the rain water was channelled into them from the roofs. They also had bathrooms, some of them designed for immersion according to the Jewish laws of purity. A small stone weight from one house carries its owner's name, Bar Qathros, and it is assumed that this man was the owner of the house itself. (According to later tradition, the Qathros family misused its power by giving relatives jobs in the temple service.) Some of the wealthy men mentioned in the Gospels would have lived in this kind of luxury.

☐ **Herod's temple**

'Not a single stone here will be left in its place' (Mark 13:2). Jesus' words about the temple were fulfilled when the Romans set fire to the building in AD 70. To make an area large enough for this grand temple, King Herod built an artificial platform over the south end of the temple hill, where the ground sloped away. The outer walls holding the structure still stand, although not to the level of the courtyard. The Wailing Wall is part of this platform.

Since 1967, Israeli archaeologists have cleared some of the lower courses of the stonework which have not suffered as much damage through the centuries. They found blocks which had fallen from the upper part of the wall, including parts of the top-most course and decoratively carved fragments. The stones still in position at the foot of the wall measure as much as 11yds/10m in length. At the south end of the temple area, a street paved with stone slabs led to a staircase going up

This notice, written in Greek, was once fixed to the barrier in the temple courtyard in Jerusalem. It forbids non-Jews to go beyond the barrier into the inner courtyards on pain of death.

into the Court of the Gentiles through a double gateway.

At the western side, the street passed under a great arch that carried a path from the temple across the valley dividing the temple hill from the western district of Jerusalem. The base of the arch has been visible in the temple wall for many years. Now the stones of the first pier of the viaduct have been uncovered, and its span can be calculated. A staircase ran down the pier and into the valley. With the help of these discoveries, a more accurate picture of the outside of Herod's temple can be drawn. The wall he built around Abraham's tomb at Hebron is another example of his impressive building works. That wall still stands to almost its full height.

One other valuable stone block remains from Herod's temple. It was found a century ago, and is now preserved in a museum in Istanbul because Jerusalem was then part of the Turkish Empire. On the face of it are a few lines of Greek carefully engraved. A similar piece was found more recently in Jerusalem, with the letters picked out in red paint. The inscriptions threaten death to any non-Jew who passes the boundary they mark and goes into the sanctuary.

Josephus, the first-century AD Jewish historian, and other writers explain that Herod's temple had four courtyards.

Anyone could enter the first, the Court of the Gentiles. But only Jews were allowed to walk in the inner courts. A low stone fence marked the limit of the first court, with notices in Greek and Latin warning foreigners to go no further. Obviously the stone in Istanbul is one of these.

Jesus and his disciples would have seen it when they visited the temple. The Acts of the Apostles tells of a riot provoked by Jews who thought Paul had taken a non-Jewish friend past the fence. Only the arrival of Roman soldiers saved Paul from being lynched (Acts 21:27–36). Later Paul seems to have taken this barrier as a picture of the division between God's people, the Jews, and people of other races. The work of Jesus, he said, abolished the distinction. So the notice lost its purpose: all men can gain access to God (Ephesians 2).

Roman officialdom

When he travelled to preach the gospel, Paul often came into contact with the officials of the Roman Empire. The Senate in Rome appointed some; the emperor himself others. There was a wide variety of ranks, and appropriate titles for each. Past history often lived on in special titles applied in individual cities.

We see some of this variety in Acts. At one time scholars

dismissed Luke's work as an imaginary story written a century after the time of Paul. But when the book is tested on points of detail like the official titles, it often turns out to be remarkably accurate. Of course, that no more proves the factual nature of Acts than similar tests prove the factual nature of other parts of the Bible. What it does demonstrate is the care and accuracy of the author over unimportant matters, which at least suggests that he probably reported the main events with equal care.

□ Titles
The titles occurring in inscriptions and other ancient writings with the same reference as in Acts are:
● 'Governor' (*anthupatos*) in Cyprus, from 22 BC onwards (Acts 13:7).
● 'City authorities' (*politarchai*) in Thessalonica, replaced by 'first ruler' later (Acts 17:6); this is known from several inscriptions but in no book apart from Acts.
● 'Provincial authorities' (*asiarchai*) in Ephesus, capital of the province of Asia (Acts 19:31). Other provincial capitals often had a single leading man.
● 'The Chief' (*prōtos*) of Malta, also known in one Greek and one Latin inscription (Acts 28:7).

On other technical terms of administration and custom Acts reflects the first century AD perfectly. So, too, do the Gospels. Pontius Pilate was officially Prefect of Judea; the title Procurator apparently applied to his successors after AD 54. An inscribed stone found in the Roman theatre at Caesarea styles Pilate 'Prefect of Judaea', and the Gospels and Acts represent that title, not Procurator, in Greek.

Egyptian waste paper
Probably the most important of all archaeological discoveries for New Testament study are the collections of papyrus documents from Egypt. From about 300 BC until AD 700 busy towns flourished along the Nile and in the Fayyum oasis to the west. When the canals became choked and the elaborate administration system ended with the Arab invasion, the towns were deserted. In the hot dry air the papyri lying in houses and rubbish dumps were dehydrated and so have survived. During the nineteenth century they began to be dug out and sold to museums in large numbers. Excavations made from 1895 onwards have brought countless pieces to light.

□ Letters and documents
The papyri cover every sort of written record, from tax receipts to famous books. Government papers make up a large part of them. There are letters from one official to another, instructions issued by superiors, complaints, records of taxes due or paid. Letters about private business and family affairs, legal deeds of marriage, divorce and so forth, and invitations to weddings all come from the papers of individual citizens. When a secretary ran out of fresh papyrus he might use the back of an old roll. In this way valuable books that would otherwise have been lost have been preserved for us.

Public letter-writers and secretaries did much of the actual writing. People who could write would add a greeting in their own writing at the end. An official letter had to carry the sender's writing in this way to give it authority. Paul 'guaranteed' some of his letters – 1 Corinthians, Galatians, Colossians and 2 Thessalonians – like this.

□ New Testament Greek
The Greek language and Greek alphabet were used for most of these documents. Soon after the first collections were published, scholars saw that this was a style of Greek identical with the language of the New Testament. There is a difference between this and the classical Greek of writers such as Plato or Euripides. With the help of the papyri, the New Testament use of the language can be understood much better. Words and phrases which appear only once or twice in the New Testament occur again and again in the papyri. This is one reason why Bible translations made since 1895 differ from older ones. Earlier translators could give meanings based only on classical Greek.

The way in which the word translated 'author' by the Authorized Version in Hebrews 12:2 is used shows that a translation like 'pioneer' is better. A series of orders from government to local officials tells them to prepare for the visit of the ruler. The word for the visit is *parousia*, the same word used by New Testament writers about the second coming of Christ. Readers would have recognized the picture of a royal visit.

□ Taxes and the census
Tax collectors are harshly criticized in the Gospels. They were unpopular because they could buy the right to collect taxes in a district for a fixed sum. It was their business to collect that sum and a little more as their profit. The papyri show people's hatred of this system, especially in the hands of men like Zacchaeus, who took far more than was due.

In Egypt, from the middle of the first century AD a census was taken every fourteen years. Public notices ordered citizens to go back to their family houses to be listed. Householders had to list the names and ages of everyone in the house, and declare that there were no others. At present we do not know whether exactly the same arrangements were made earlier in Palestine, although according to the Gospels Joseph and Mary were caught in a similar process that made them go to Bethlehem. These Egyptian census records illustrate Luke's account of Jesus' birth very well.

DISCOVERIES AT MASADA

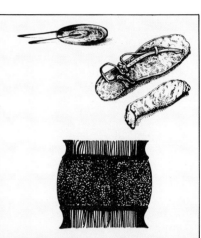

Jewish loyalists fighting the Romans in the war which led to the destruction of the temple in AD 70 took their last stand at Masada.

Masada is a natural fortress standing some 800ft/240 metres above the surrounding Judean Desert, close to the shores of the Dead Sea. King Herod made it into a fortified palace, with great storehouses and a careful system of water collection and underground storage.

The aerial photograph below shows the three terraces of Herod's amazing 'hanging villa'.

The night before the Romans took the fortress, all but a handful of the defenders, about 1,000 men, women and children, committed mass suicide rather than be taken prisoner.

Among the objects which remained from the Jewish Zealot occupation were these kohl spoons, mirror lid, sandals and a comb.

☐ Ancient books

Copies of famous Greek books such as *The Iliad* and *The Odyssey* or the *Histories* of Herodotus have been found among the papyri. Some are as much as 1,000 years older than any copies known before. Other books, that were not re-copied by later scribes, have been identified in the papyri, including a work by Aristotle. In the same way we have recovered copies of the Old Testament books in Greek (the Septuagint) and copies of New Testament books.

One tiny scrap belongs to a page of John's Gospel copied about AD 130. This is the oldest piece of a New Testament manuscript to survive. Other copies of Gospels which have come to light were made about AD 200, and we have copies of several other New Testament books from the following century. Early examples like these help in the study of the history of the New Testament text.

The Dead Sea Scrolls

The most exciting discovery from New Testament times has been the Dead Sea Scrolls. No one had expected that ancient papers would last in Palestine.

The earliest known fragment of the New Testament contains part of the eighteenth chapter of John's Gospel.

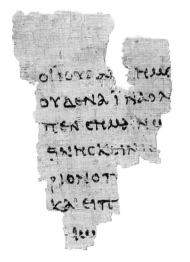

Early references to Jesus and the Christians

'Since the Jews constantly made disturbances at the instigation of Chrestus (Christ), Claudius expelled them from Rome.'
Suetonius, *Lives of the Caesars*, AD 121

'To kill the rumours, Nero charged and tortured some people hated for their evil practices – the group popularly known as "Christians". The founder of this sect, Christ, had been put to death by the governor of Judea, Pontius Pilate, when Tiberius was Emperor. Their deadly superstition had been suppressed temporarily, but was beginning to spring up again – not now just in Judea but even in Rome itself where all kinds of sordid and shameful activities are attracted and catch on.'
Tacitus (AD 51–117), *Annals* 15.44

Yet in 1947, in a cave near the north-west shore of the Dead Sea, a shepherd boy happened to find jars containing old leather rolls. He did not know what they were, and sold them for next to nothing. Eventually archaeologists heard about the find and where it had been made. Between them, shepherds and archaeologists collected pieces of over 400 rolls.

These books belonged to the library of a religious commune at Qumran on the edge of the Dead Sea. Their owners had hidden them in caves when the Roman army advanced against the rebel Jews in AD 68. The dry heat of the region preserved them. They are less valuable than the papyri for understanding the text of the New Testament. But the scrolls, mostly written in Hebrew or Aramaic, bring a mass of new information about Jewish religious life in the New Testament period.

Old Testament books were favourites in the library. Every one of them is there, except Esther. Many copies show that the traditional Hebrew text (only available in copies made about AD 900 before this discovery) was current in the first century AD, and earlier. There are also slightly different Hebrew texts of Old Testament books amongst the scrolls, though they are in a minority. These have variations, some of which are reflected in the Greek translation (the Septuagint) and in the New Testament (the quotation of Deuteronomy 32:43 given in Hebrews 1:6 is one of them).

☐ The Qumran community

Other books are commentaries on sections of the Old Testament. Commentators explained ancient names of people and places in the light of current affairs. They believed the prophets had spoken about them, not about their own days. From these remarks, and from other writings, we learn of the community's early leader, the Teacher of Righteousness. He disagreed with most Jews about the dates of major festivals and withdrew from Jerusalem to set up the strictly ruled community by the Dead Sea, during the second century BC.

Enemies were called the 'Sons of Darkness'; the people of the Dead Sea community considered themselves 'Sons of Light'. They looked forward to a day when God's Messiah would lead them to a great victory over their opponents. Then they would worship as they thought right in the temple.

Their hopes were disappointed. Their Messiah did not come, and the Romans broke up their commune. It is important to realize that the men of Qumran and the early church were very different. The owners of the scrolls were thoroughly Jewish. They had no direct connection with early Christianity. Some ideas are

THE COMMUNITY OF THE DEAD SEA SCROLLS, AT QUMRAN

The aerial photograph shows the settlement at Qumran and the hills in whose caves the scrolls were hidden.

When the Romans overran the country during the Jewish War (AD 66–73) the community at Qumran stored its library in nearby caves.

Here a scholar patiently pieces together fragments from the scrolls discovered in a cave in 1947 by Bedouin shepherds.

The Isaiah scroll, found at Qumran with many other Old Testament manuscripts, is 1,000 years older than any previously known copy of Isaiah.

These storage jars held books written on leather rolls.

shared by both – for example, contrasting good and bad, light and darkness – but these are common Jewish ideas of the time. In some cases the similarities – which have been heavily emphasized in recent books – seem striking because there is no other material from Jewish groups of the same date. A study of the attitude to the Old Testament shown in the Scrolls has given a clearer view of the way Jesus and his followers treated it.

Jesus attacked Jewish leaders for strict obedience to details of the Law without understanding its real meaning. The Scrolls reveal a Jewish sect as strict as these leaders, if not more so. The 'phylacteries' that have been found are an indication of this. In order to obey God's command to remember his laws they actually tied them to their hands and foreheads (see Exodus 13:9, 16). Passages of scripture were written on minute pieces of parchment, bound in leather cases (phylacteries), and strapped on the head and left hand at prayer time. An example from Qumran is ¾ × ½in/20 × 13mm. The parchments, unfolded, are about 1½ × 1⅛in/40 × 27mm. On one piece Deuteronomy 5:22–6:9 was written in twenty-six lines. Jesus accused the Pharisees and teachers of the Law of showing off by wearing phylacteries for others to see (Matthew 23:5).

Tombs of New Testament times

For a century or more before Jerusalem fell to the Roman

IMPORTANT EXCAVATIONS IN PALESTINE

Sites	Dates	Excavators
Jerusalem	1867–70	C. Warren
Tell el-Hesi	1890–92	W. M. F. Petrie, F. J. Bliss
Shephelah sites	1898–1900	F. J. Bliss, R. A. S. MacAlister
Gezer	1902–3, 1907–9	R. A. S. MacAlister
Taanach	1902–4	E. Sellin
Megiddo	1903–5	G. Schumacher
Shechem	1907–9	E. Sellin, C. Watzinger
Jericho	1907–8	C. Watzinger
Samaria	1908, 1910–11	G. A. Reisner, C. A. Fisher
Tell Beit Mirsim	1926–36	W. F. Albright
Beth-shan	1921–33	C. S. Fisher, A. S. Rowe
Megiddo	1925–39	C. S. Fisher, P. L. O. Guy, G. Loud
Beth-shemesh	1928–31	E. Grant
Jericho	1930–36	J. Garstang
Samaria	1931–33, 1935	J. W. Crowfoot, K. M. Kenyon
Lachish	1932–36	J. L. Starkey
Ai	1933–35	J. Marquet-Krause
Tirzah (Tell el-Far'ah)	1946–60	R. de Vaux
Qumran, Dead Sea caves	1949–67	R. de Vaux and others
Jericho	1952–58	K. M. Kenyon
Ramat Rahel	1954–63	Y. Aharoni
Hazor	1955–58, 1968	Y. Yadin
Gibeon	1956–62	J. B. Pritchard
Shechem	1956–73	G. E. Wright
Caesarea	1959–	M. Prausnitz, R. Bull
Megiddo	1960,1965–67	Y. Yadin
Jerusalem	1961–68	K. M. Kenyon
Herodium	1962–67	V. C. Corbo
Arad	1962–	Y. Aharoni, R. B. K. Amiran
Ashdod	1962–	M. Dothan
Gezer	1964–	W. G. Dever
Ai	1964–72	J. A. Callaway
Dan	1966–	A. Biran
Jerusalem	1968–71	B. Mazar, N. Avigad
	1978–	Y. Shiloh
Beersheba	1969–76	Y. Aharoni
Tell el-Hesi	1970–	G. W. van Beek
Lachish	1973–	D. Ussishkin

The low doorway into the rock-cut 'tombs of the kings', Jerusalem, first century AD.

Emperor Titus in AD 70, Jews living in the city buried their dead outside the walls. Rather than cut individual graves in the limestone, they carved large rooms in the rock to hold many bodies. A low doorway, so low you might have to crawl through it, led into a room large enough for people to stand upright inside. Around the walls, or some of them, a waist-high bench was often shaped in the rock. Above the bench, holes 5 or 6ft/2m deep were tunnelled into the rock. Sometimes one or two extra rooms opened out of the first. In front of the tomb a courtyard was cleared for funeral ceremonies and possibly for a garden.

When someone died, the body was laid on the bench or in one of the holes in the wall, anointed and wrapped. The entrance was plugged with a stone boulder, or occasionally with a round slab rolling in a shallow channel. (A secure door was needed to protect the dead from wild animals and scavengers.) When the flesh had decomposed, the bones were sometimes collected into a chest (an ossuary), and placed in one of the holes. Some of these chests, carved from stone, can still be found in the tombs. Wooden ones have long since rotted away.

If we read the resurrection story against this background, we can see that the details exactly fit this setting: the heavy stone blocking the entrance, the low doorway, the position of the grave-clothes and of the angels Jesus' followers saw.

☐ The names of the dead

Relatives often scratched or wrote the names of the dead on the burial-chests. Here is first-hand evidence of the names in use in Judah in the first century AD. They are names already familiar from the New Testament: Matthew, Judas, Simon, Elisabeth, Martha, Salome. These are all good Hebrew or Aramaic names. But foreign names, especially Greek ones like Andrew and Thaddeus also appear. Jesus is quite a common name. In fact, the New Testament mirrors many of the ordinary names of Judean citizens in the Gospel period.

These names are written in Hebrew, Aramaic, or Greek, most of them in Hebrew or Aramaic. The fact that all these languages are clearly used by Jews shows how mixed the population was. A few of Jesus' words were reported in Aramaic, which is kept in most English versions:

abba, 'father' – Mark 14:36
eloi, eloi, lama sabachthani, 'My God, my God, why did you abandon me?' – Mark 15:34
ephphatha, 'open up' – Mark 7:34
raka, 'you good for nothing' – Matthew 5:22
talitha koum, 'Little girl, get up I tell you' – Mark 5:41

Jesus would normally have spoken Aramaic. He also read the Old Testament in Hebrew, and quite probably knew Greek.

The Bible books have been faithfully copied out and handed down for thousands of years.

3

The Story of the Bible

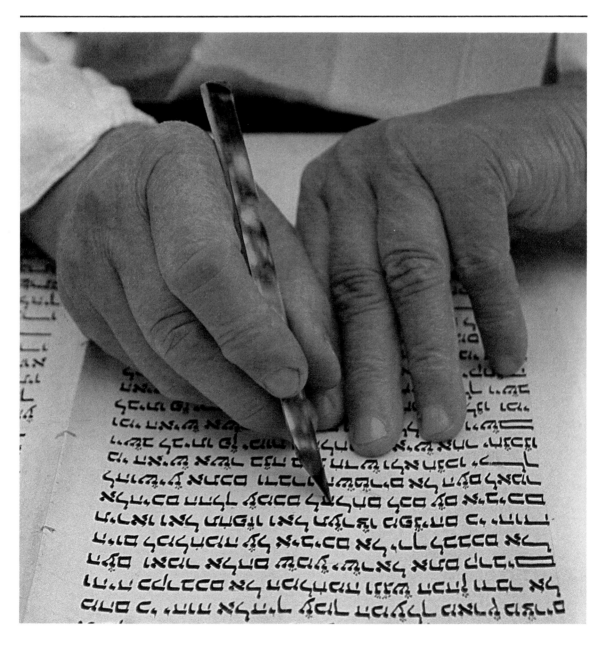

How the Bible was Written and became one Book

When we look at a Bible on a bookshelf we see a rather thick book, with almost as many pages as a dictionary. But once we take it down we can see that it is not at all like a dictionary. Indeed it is not even just one book. The Bible is made up of a whole collection of books – sixty-six of them in all. Some of these are quite long, some short; some *very* ancient, some not quite so old. They contain history, poetry, philosophy, hymns – and even personal letters and sermons.

How did these various books come to be written? Who wrote them? When? And how did they come together to make the book we now know as the Bible?

The Bible is divided into two major sections – the Old Testament and the New Testament.

The Hebrew Old Testament

The Old Testament is made up of the first thirty-nine books of the Christian Bible. These books are the holy writings – or scriptures – of the Jewish people, and their religion, Judaism. They were first written down in Hebrew and Aramaic, the ancient languages of the Jews. Many of these writings are so old that little is now known of their origins. The Jewish scribes used to make new copies of the Hebrew sacred writings from time to time. But documents did not last long in the climate of the Bible lands, and so we rarely find very old copies of the writings.

Until 1947 the oldest known Hebrew manuscripts of the Old Testament dated from the ninth and tenth centuries AD. They were copies of the first five books of the Bible – the Pentateuch. Then in 1947 came the remarkable discovery of the Dead Sea Scrolls. These were early manuscripts from the library of a Jewish religious group who flourished at Qumran, near the Dead Sea, about the time of Jesus. These manuscripts are about a thousand years earlier than the ninth-century AD documents. Amongst the Dead Sea Scrolls are copies of all the Old Testament books except Esther.

These early manuscripts from Qumran are very important because they have essentially the same text as the ninth-century manuscripts. They show that the text of the Old Testament had changed very little for a thousand years. The careful copyists had made few errors or alterations. Of course there are a few places where different words and expressions are used. And sometimes it is no longer possible to discover exactly what the Hebrew words meant.

But we can be confident that the Old Testament as we now have it is substantially the same as its authors wrote many centuries ago.

Other ancient versions of the Old Testament

The text of the Old Testament has also come down to us in other early translations. Some of these, too, confirm the accuracy of the Hebrew text of the Old Testament that we use today.

One of the most important translations is the Greek version of the Old Testament, the *Septuagint*. Greek-speaking Jews and many Christians used the *Septuagint* in the first Christian centuries. Another early document, *The Letter of Aristeas*, suggests that the *Septuagint* was compiled for Jews living in Egypt during the reign of Pharaoh Ptolemy Philadelphus (285–246 BC).

Greek was the main language of the Roman Empire, and several other Greek versions of the Old Testament were in use during the first Christian centuries. Sometimes the Greek translation helps to make clear obscure parts of the Hebrew text, but often it is not precise.

A Moroccan Jew studies the scriptures at Sefat in Israel.

The other translations can help occasionally in this way. (For examples, study the notes in any modern translation.) Later, as Christianity spread to people who spoke other languages, the Old Testament was translated into Latin (the Vulgate), Syriac (the Peshitta) and Egyptian (Coptic).

How the Old Testament came together

It is not possible to know for certain how the Old Testament came together in the collection of books we now know. But we do know which books made up the Old Testament in the period just before the birth of Jesus, and we can know which books Jesus and his apostles would have regarded as their 'Bible'.

The Jews have a strong tradition that the scribe Ezra (whose story is told in the Book of Ezra) arranged and collected the books of the Old Testament. But collections of the first five books ('the books of Moses', or the Pentateuch) and of some of the sermons of the prophets were in existence much earlier, as were the psalms and proverbs.

The Jews arranged their sacred books into three groupings: the Law, the Prophets and the Writings.

'The Law' consisted of the first five books of the Old Testament (Genesis–Deuteronomy). Although Genesis contains no 'law' as such, it was included because all five were thought to have been written by Moses.

'The Prophets' contained not only the messages of men like Amos, Jeremiah, Isaiah, and many others, but also the books of history – Joshua, Judges, 1 and 2 Samuel, and 1 and 2 Kings. These books were included in this section because they are concerned not only with the facts but also with the meaning of history as God sees it.

The Writings included the books of Wisdom (wise sayings) – Proverbs, Ecclesiastes, Job

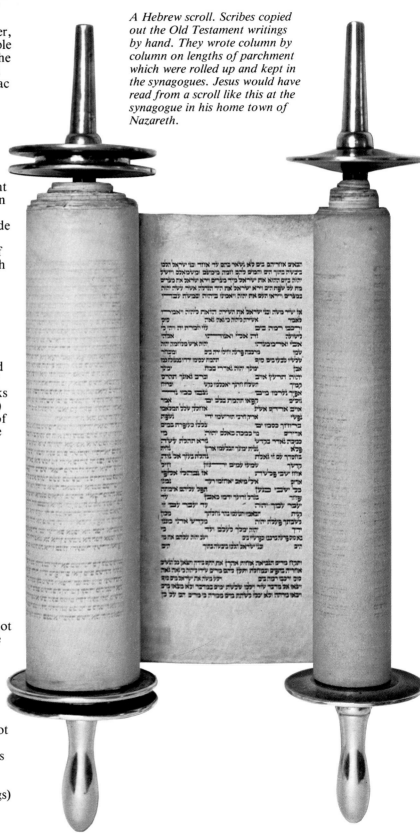

A Hebrew scroll. Scribes copied out the Old Testament writings by hand. They wrote column by column on lengths of parchment which were rolled up and kept in the synagogues. Jesus would have read from a scroll like this at the synagogue in his home town of Nazareth.

– some books of history that were written later, such as Ezra, Nehemiah and Chronicles, and one book of prophecy, Daniel.

It is clear that by the time of Jesus the Hebrew Scriptures usually consisted of the thirty-nine books we know today as the Old Testament. Most of the books of our Old Testament are quoted somewhere in the New Testament. This makes it likely that Jesus and his followers were familiar with the Old Testament as we know it.

As well as the thirty-nine books of the Old Testament, the Jews had other sacred writings. In the Greek version, these were given the same respect as the other Old Testament books. But these additional books, known as the *Apocrypha*, were not given the same recognition as the other Old Testament books in the Hebrew version.

How the New Testament text came down to us

In the case of the Old Testament we had barely enough evidence to reconstruct the story. With the New Testament we have almost too much! Scholars are faced with many thousands of different ancient manuscripts of the New Testament. They have to decide which of these are most trustworthy and which have preserved the more accurate version of the original.

The New Testament was originally written down in Greek. Scholars have many thousands of Greek manuscripts to which they can refer. In addition they possess early translations of the New Testament – in Latin, Syriac, Egyptian (Coptic) and other languages. They can also refer to quotations which some early Christian writers and theologians made from the New Testament (though these are sometimes inaccurate).

Many of the Greek manuscripts contain a text of the New Testament which was standardized in the fifth century

AD. The first printed edition of the Greek text came in 1516 – in a form prepared by the Dutch scholar Erasmus. Up until then no-one had questioned the accuracy of this text.

During the next two centuries, some Bibles included notes to indicate where certain other manuscripts varied from the standard version of the New Testament. Particularly important examples include the text of Stephanus, used in translating the King James' Version in England (1611), and the edition of Elzevir (1633), which became the standard for New Testament translations in Europe (it came to be known as the Received Text, *Textus Receptus*).

But during the eighteenth and nineteenth centuries, scholars began to delve deeper into the history of the New Testament text. They discovered that many older manuscripts of the New Testament differed from the fifth-century standard text. They showed that it was more important to ask how old a manuscript was and how good it was, than how many copies survived. Other scholars found that manuscripts could be grouped together in

St Catherine's monastery, Mt Sinai, where Codex Sinaiticus, *one of the most important Greek manuscripts of the New Testament, was discovered.*

'families' which share a similar kind of text. Older 'families' of texts such as the 'Alexandrian' and the 'Western' texts are now known to preserve a more accurate version of the original writings than the standard fifth-century text.

How the manuscripts were copied

Before the invention of printing in the West, in the fifteenth century, all writing had to be hand-copied for circulation. This was usually done by a group of scribes, each of whom wrote out his copy of the manuscript as the head scribe dictated. If a scribe did not hear clearly, or failed to concentrate, mistakes would occur. Even a single copyist working from an original manuscript sometimes misread the writing, or accidentally introduced his own mistakes. Very few private individuals could afford to own a hand-written manuscript. They

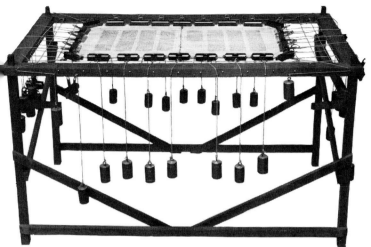

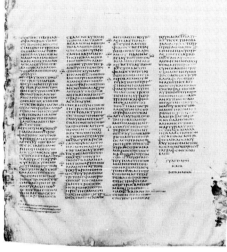

A page from Codex Sinaiticus. *The last chapter of John's Gospel.*

The first Christian writings were on papyrus scrolls. But quite early on (in the second century AD) Christians began to use the codex *(book) form, paged and bound very much like books today. These were easier to use than the long scroll.*

were expensive to make, and Christian churches would usually own manuscripts which all their members could share.

At first the New Testament books must have been written on scrolls made of papyrus, leather or parchment. But from about the second century Christians probably began to use the book form which we use today (the *Codex*). This was much easier to handle than an awkward scroll.

A reliable New Testament text

Two of the most important groups of manuscripts for our New Testament are the Bodmer Papyri (one of which dates from the late second century) and the Chester Beatty Papyri (probably from the early third century). But these contain only parts of the New Testament. The *Codex Sinaiticus*, which dates from the fourth century, contains the complete

New Testament; and the *Codex Vaticanus* has everything up to Hebrews 9:13. Both of these manuscripts were probably made by professional copyists in Alexandria, Egypt.

These two codex manuscripts were the main sources for the Greek text of the New Testament prepared in the nineteenth century by the scholars Westcott and Hort. Most scholars agree that they are more accurate than the standard fifth-century text which so many previous versions had used.

The two papyrus collections were discovered after the time of Westcott and Hort. They in turn have been used with others to achieve an even more accurate version of the New Testament text.

Since then, still more papyrus evidence has been discovered. No single manuscript is clearly the best. The evidence of each has to be weighed carefully.

Over the last 250 years many careful scholars have worked hard to make sure that we have a New Testament which is as close as possible to what its authors originally wrote. The few small areas of doubt which remain are over minor matters of wording. But none of these questions raises any doubt whatever about the basic meaning of the New Testament.

How the New Testament books were collected

Although there is little direct evidence from the earliest years, we have a good idea of how the New Testament took on its present shape. The first gatherings of Christians probably followed the practice of the Jewish synagogues and had regular readings from the Old Testament during their meetings. Since they were worshipping Jesus Christ, it was natural for them to add an account of some part of his life and teaching.

At first this may have been in the form of a first-hand account from someone who had known Jesus during his lifetime. But then, as the churches grew in numbers, and as the eye-witnesses began to die, it became necessary to write these stories down. This was the way the four Gospels (Matthew, Mark, Luke and John) came into being, and they obviously had an import-ant place in the worship and life of the early churches.

Then the apostles and other leaders had written a number of letters to various churches and individuals. Since these often gave general guidance on Christian life and beliefs, their usefulness for the whole church was soon recognized. Acts was accepted because it continued the story from Luke's Gospel. It preserved the only full account of the beginnings of Christianity.

We know that by the year AD 200 the church was offic-ially using the four Gospels – and no others, although fictitious tales about Jesus and writings by other Christian leaders who came after the apostles were in circulation. But the mainstream church clearly accepted only the Gospels of Matthew, Mark, Luke and John as their auth-ority for the life and teaching of Jesus. By this time, too, Paul's letters were generally accepted as of equal import-ance with the Gospels.

It was only later that the remaining books of the New Testament became generally accepted. Revelation, for ex-ample, was certainly read in the second century. But not until the third century was it circulating widely. Hebrews was read towards the end of the first century, but took longer to become accepted in the Western churches. It was not generally acknowledged by the church in the West until the fourth century, partly because of doubts as to whether Paul wrote it.

It took longer, too, for 2 Peter, 2 and 3 John, James and Jude to be accepted by the church as basic Scripture. Perhaps this was because of questions about the content of these books. The New Testa-ment books were mainly used at first for public reading. If they were unsuitable for this purpose, their usefulness must have seemed limited.

It is clear that no church council arbitrarily decided that certain books composed the New Testament. Rather, over a period of time, the church discovered that certain writings had a clear and general auth-ority, and were helpful and necessary for their growth. At the Council of Laodicea (AD 363) and the Council of Carthage (AD 397) the bishops agreed on a list of books identical to our New Testa-ment, except that at Laodicea Revelation was left out.

Above all, the churches were concerned to make sure that the documents they included in the 'New Testament' truly represented the witness and experience of the apostles – the men who lived closest to Jesus.

Translations and Translators

Ancient versions of the Bible

For many Christians in the first century 'the Bible' was the Greek translation of the Old Testament (the *Septuagint*) which was begun in the third century BC. Soon after the New Testament was completed, translation work began. The first translation was probably into Latin. This was the off-icial language of the Roman Empire, though Greek was the most widely spoken language among Christians, even in Italy. At first Greek was used in most churches.

☐ Jerome

From the second century on, there were many local trans-lations of the Bible. But people felt that there should be a standard text that could be recognized and used by every-one. So in about AD 384 Pope Damasus instructed his secre-tary to revise the Latin New Testament.

This man was Jerome. He is the first Bible translator whose name has come down to us (we know of earlier Jewish scholars who revised the Greek Old Testament). His Latin trans-lation, the Vulgate (or Com-mon Version), has been the standard Bible of the Roman Catholic Church ever since. Scores of other translations have been made from it, in-cluding the first English ones.

Jerome was a good scholar and he did his work well. In order to translate the Old Testament he learnt Hebrew, living for many years in Bethlehem. Through his work, copied out by hand in many lands, God's word brought hope and new life to countless people.

☐ Syriac and Coptic Bibles

In the second century, trans-lators began work in Syriac, a dialect of the Aramaic language which Jesus himself spoke. Although old Syriac is no longer spoken, the fourth-century translation (known as the Peshitta) is still used in worship by Nestorian and Syrian Christians in Syria, Iran, India and other lands.

In Egypt the church at first used the Greek language. But

as Christianity spread south, an Egyptian (or Coptic) version was needed. Translation began in the third century. The Coptic Bible is still used in worship.

☐ Fourth- and fifth-century translations

After the Roman Emperor Constantine was converted (AD 312) Christianity spread rapidly, and new translations were soon needed. The Goths, who invaded the Empire in the River Danube basin, received almost the whole Bible in their own language from the missionary translator, Ulfilas. Much of the text survives in manuscripts, although the language has long been extinct.

St Mesrop worked out an alphabet for the Armenians, the first Christian nation in the world, and gave them their Bible in the fifth century. This is still the standard version of the ancient Armenian Church, both in the Armenian SSR (part of the USSR) and in the many lands where Armenians are scattered. The Ge'ez and Georgian Bibles, used to this day in the churches of Ethiopia and Georgia (USSR), probably also date from the fifth century.

☐ Old Slavonic Bible

Later there was a translation in Old Slavonic, the language spoken in Bulgaria, Serbia and southern Russia in the ninth century, when the Slavic tribes became Christians through the work of St Cyril. He invented the Cyrillic alphabet, and before long the whole Bible had been translated. This version is still the official version of the Russian Orthodox Church.

Although not many copies could be made, these early translations of the Bible were very widely distributed. A single copy may well have cost the equivalent of several hundred pounds. Many were copied by monks as a work of Christian love. Their main use was in public worship and in private study by Christian leaders. Apart from the Latin Bible, not many were read widely by ordinary Christians. Some of them are important today because they are still used for worship in the ancient Eastern churches. And they all help build up our knowledge of the text from which they were translated.

As well as these church translations, we know of at least one 'missionary' version made *before* a church had been established. In about AD 640 a group of Nestorian missionaries, whose language was Syriac, translated the Gospels into Chinese for the Emperor Tai Tsung.

The Dark Ages

In the centuries following the break-up of the Roman Empire in the West, Christianity was spreading fast, especially in northern and eastern Europe. As the church grew, parts of the Bible were translated into many new languages.

The earliest real translation in England was Aldhelm's translation of the Psalms. Aldhelm was Bishop of Sherborne, in the south of England, AD 700.

About the same time in the north of England the great historian, Bede, was concerned about priests who knew little or no Latin and so could not read the Bible. So he began to translate the Bible into Anglo-Saxon. He died in AD 735, working on his translation of John's Gospel on his death bed. Unfortunately, neither Bede's nor Aldhelm's work has survived.

The English King Alfred (AD 871–901) was also a Bible translator, giving his people parts of Exodus, Psalms and Acts in their own language. Educated priests sometimes made their own versions, too. After the Norman conquest, various books of the Bible were translated into English, some in local dialects.

Other unofficial translations, mainly for church leaders and often in metre, were made in other languages. A translation

The opening page of Mark's Gospel in the Lindisfarne Gospels. This beautiful Bible manuscript was made by Celtic Christians at the monastery on Lindisfarne, an island off the coast of Northumbria, England. It dates from about AD 700.

of Matthew in Frankish (early German), made in AD 758, has survived. The earliest French texts date from the twelfth century; Italian from the fourteenth. The first Bible translations in Arabic probably appeared in the eighth century, though there were Christians in Arabia in the fourth century.

Forerunners of the Reformation

In the latter part of the Middle Ages a number of new Bible versions appeared. These were designed to be read by ordinary Christians and the work was supported by people who were critical of the official church leadership. About 1170, a merchant of Lyons, Peter Waldo, found new purpose in life through reading the New Testament. He arranged for the Bible to be translated into Provencal (southern French). His followers formed the Waldensian Church, which was bitterly persecuted for centuries.

Wycliffe

Nearly 200 years later, an Oxford theologian, John Wycliffe, was studying his Bible. He became convinced that it was so important that it must be available to everyone. As a result, by 1384, the Latin Vulgate Bible had been translated into English. Nicholas of Hereford, John Purvey and others were the actual translators of most of it. They followed the Latin text closely, even in its very un-English order of words! By 1395 Purvey had revised the work in better and clearer English.

Some copies carried notes expressing the controversial views of the Lollards (as Wycliffe's followers were called). In 1408 a synod of the church met at Oxford and banned the writing, circulation or study of these English versions. But the appeal of the English Bible was too great. Many hundreds of copies were still circulating when the first printed books of the Bible appeared over 100 years later.

Hus

A similar movement took place in Bohemia (Czechoslovakia). Jan Hus, Rector of the University of Prague, was influenced by Wycliffe's teaching. He was burnt at the stake in 1415, but his followers began the work of Bible translation. The Czech New Testament, printed in 1475, was the result.

Printing and the Reformation

Around 1450, at Mainz in Germany, Johann Gutenberg pioneered the process of printing from movable type. His work began a new era in the history of books, and with them, of the Bible. The first major work to emerge from the press was the Bible (1456) – in Latin. Ten years later it was printed in German at Strasbourg, from the text of an unknown fourteenth-century translator. In 1471 the first Italian Bible was printed and this was soon followed by the French New Testament. The first Dutch Scriptures appeared in 1477. Next came the whole Bible in Catalan (for Spain, 1478).

Erasmus

All these versions were based on existing manuscripts and translated from the Latin. But with the revival of learning, texts in the original languages began to be studied. Jewish

The monks who copied Bible manuscripts often also decorated ('illuminated') the first letters of each book with gold, silver and brilliant colours. Here Jean Mielot, secretary to Philip the Good, Duke of Burgundy, copies and 'illuminates' a manuscript. He is seen at work in a library, about AD 1340.

The Spread of Bible Translation up to 1850

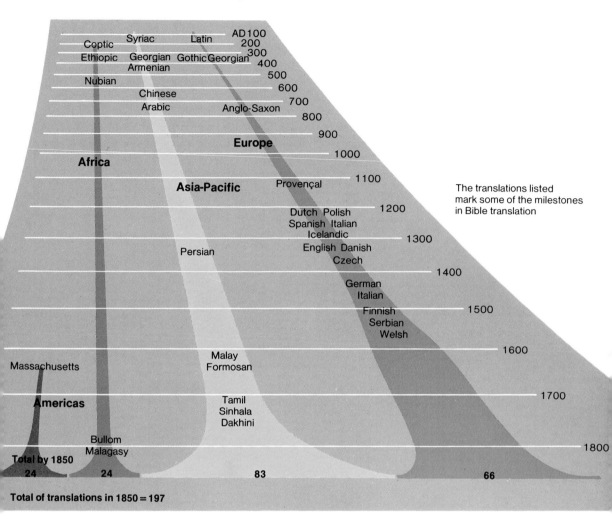

The translations listed mark some of the milestones in Bible translation

scholars had preserved the Hebrew Bible and in 1488 they printed it in Italy. The Greek New Testament was first published by the great Dutch scholar, Erasmus, in 1516. Although he was not himself a translator (except into Latin) Erasmus, unlike many others, was very much in favour of translating the Bible into ordinary speech. He wrote:

'I wish that the Scriptures might be translated into all languages, so that not only the Scots and the Irish, but also the Turk and the Saracen might read and understand them. I long that the farm-labourer might sing them as he follows the plough, the weaver hum them to the tune of his shuttle, the traveller beguile the weariness of his journey with their stories.'

□ **Luther**
Meanwhile, in Germany, a young monk called Martin Luther was anxiously studying his Latin Bible. As he read, he was especially struck by Paul's words in Romans 1:17: 'The gospel reveals how God puts people right with himself. It is through faith from beginning to end.'

He describes the great release and freedom these words brought. 'I felt completely reborn . . . My love for that sweetest word "righteousness of God" was henceforth as great as my hatred for it had been hitherto. In this way this passage of Paul was truly the gate of Paradise.'

Luther was a lecturer in the university at Wittenberg. He proclaimed this message, and made a close study of the Hebrew Old Testament and Erasmus' Greek New Testament. Then he undertook the task of making a new translation in German, in the clearest possible language. The New Testament appeared in 1522 and the task was completed in 1532. It has remained the best-known German Bible ever since.

The English Bible
□ Tyndale
About the same time, William Tyndale, who had been a scholar at Cambridge soon after Erasmus, and was influenced by his writings, began to translate the New Testament into English. The church authorities gave him no encouragement. So he went to Germany to finish his work.

The first New Testament printed in English appeared at Worms in 1526. Copies soon reached England and were eagerly studied. The authorities denounced them and the Bishop of London bought large quantities and burnt them.

Tyndale's reaction was to publish a better version! He revised it twice, and by 1566 it had been printed forty times. He went on to write other books and to translate part of the Old Testament. But the New Testament is his great legacy to the English-speaking world, for the Authorized/ King James' Version of 1611 follows it very closely.

□ Coverdale
In 1535 Myles Coverdale published the first whole Bible in English. It was printed abroad but soon found its way into England. In 1533 the clergy of the province of Canterbury had asked King Henry VIII for an official translation of the Bible. They wanted this 'delivered to the people for their instruction'. A dedication to the king was added to the Coverdale Bible. It seems that when the scholars assured him that it did not contain any heresies Henry authorized its circulation.

Coverdale did not work from the original Greek and Hebrew. He based his work on that of Tyndale, Luther and the Latin versions. His translation is still used today, in the version of the Psalms that is still printed in *The Book of Common Prayer*. Coverdale was the first to include chapter summaries, as in the Authorized/ King James' Version, and to separate the

A portrait of John Wycliffe, one of the pioneers of Bible translation into English.

Apocrypha from the Old Testament books. In the older versions the apocryphal books were set out in the same way as they are in the Greek *Septuagint*.

In 1537 came the first Bible actually printed in England. It had on it the name 'Thomas Matthew', the pen name of John Rogers, a fellow-worker of Tyndale's. It is made up mostly of Tyndale's translation, including his Joshua to Chronicles, not previously published, and contains a good deal of extra material in the form of indexes and notes. It was the first Bible to be published 'with the King's most gracious licence', a privilege

A reconstruction of the room (in Mainz, Germany) in which Gutenberg printed the first books in Europe.

granted to Coverdale's Bible in the same year.

□ The Great Bible
In 1538 an order was issued with the king's authority that the clergy must provide 'a book of the whole Bible of the largest volume in English' to be set 'in some convenient place within the church, whither your parishioners may most conveniently resort to the same and read it . . . It is the very living Word of God that every Christian person is bound to embrace, believe and follow if he look to be saved'.

The book the king intended was the Great Bible, Coverdale's revision of Matthew's version. It appeared in 1539. Its second edition contained a preface by Archbishop Cranmer, encouraging everyone to read the Bible. It also contained a note: 'This is the Bible appointed for the use of the churches.' One of the two bishops who had examined it for the king was Tonstall, who as Bishop of London had burnt Tyndale's New Testament. All controversial notes had been dropped.

Before Henry's death in 1547 Tyndale's and Coverdale's translations were forbidden and large numbers were destroyed. But the Great Bible remained in the churches throughout the reign of Edward VI and some even in the reign of the Roman Catholic Queen Mary (1553–

58), although the church services were once more in Latin.

The Geneva Bible

Meanwhile, in Geneva, scholarly English exiles were at work on a revision. This appeared in 1560, dedicated to Queen Elizabeth I. It contained the first translation of Ezra to Malachi directly from Hebrew. The Hebrew idiom was kept wherever possible, in the New as well as the Old Testament. The Apocrypha was included, with a note about its value. The Bible also contained some notes about its meaning. It became a very popular Bible. In Britain, as well as in Geneva, it was printed seventy times in Elizabeth's reign.

In Scotland this was the Bible officially read in churches, and it continued to be used for some time after the Authorized/King James' Version had appeared. It is sometimes called the Breeches Bible, because in its translation of Genesis 3:7 it says that Adam and Eve made themselves 'breeches'.

The Bishops' Bible

Meanwhile the Great Bible was being revised. This was mainly the work of the bishops, with Archbishop Parker playing a leading part. So the new version which appeared in 1568 became known as the Bishops' Bible. The revisers aimed to improve the accuracy of the text, to change expressions offensive to public taste and to avoid controversial notes and interpretations. But the result was not as good as the Geneva Bible. Although it was used in churches, it proved to be less popular.

King James' (Authorized) Version

When he came to the throne in 1603 James I of England (VI of Scotland) agreed to a new revision. He himself took a share in organizing the work, which was entrusted to six teams of scholars. After they had done their work, two scholars from each team worked over the whole Bible before it went to press.

The work was based on the Bishops' Bible, but using the original Hebrew and Greek. Names were given their familiar forms, and familiar ecclesiastical words (like 'church' and 'bishop') were to be kept. Notes in the margins explained Greek and Hebrew words and linked parallel passages. Words added to complete the sense were printed in a different type. New chapter summaries were included.

This famous translation was the King James' or Authorized Version of 1611, which in fact was never formally authorized. There was a dedication to James, and a long preface, 'The Translator to the Reader'. This is now rarely printed. It answers criticisms and states the translators' purpose 'to make a good translation better'. It stresses the great care taken in consulting other translations and commentaries. It defends the practice of giving alternative translations in the margin, where the translators could not be certain about the meaning. And it also puts the case for translating the same word in the original by different English words, even where the meaning was the same.

This version enjoyed enormous prestige for 350 years. The main reasons for this are probably the beauty and rhythm of its language. All early editions included the Apocrypha. This was not omitted from the Geneva Bible till 1640, and much later from the Authorized Version. Since the first edition the spelling has been greatly modernized, the chapter summaries reduced and marginal references expanded. In 1701 Archbishop Ussher's dates were added in the margin and continued to appear for 200 years.

The Douai version

One year before the Authorized Version, the standard Roman Catholic version, the Douai Bible, was published. This was the work of Gregory Martin and others at the English College at Douai, in France. His New Testament appeared in 1582 when the college was at Rheims. He tried to translate the Vulgate word for word, sometimes making little sense in English. Some unusual words taken over from the Latin are explained in a glossary. Full notes explain the text and points of doctrine.

Many found the language of the Douai Bible hard to understand, and so Bishop Challoner issued two revisions of the Old Testament and five of the New up to 1772, much influenced by the Authorized Version. His last revision came to replace the original Douai as the official Roman Catholic version.

In this room, in the Wartburg Castle in Germany, Luther translated the New Testament from Greek into German. Although his own life was in danger, he was determined that everyone should be able to read the Bible.

Major modern English versions

A number of private revisions of the Authorized Version and new translations were made in the following centuries. Some of them were based on much older and more reliable Greek manuscripts than the 'Received Text' from which the Authorized Version was made.

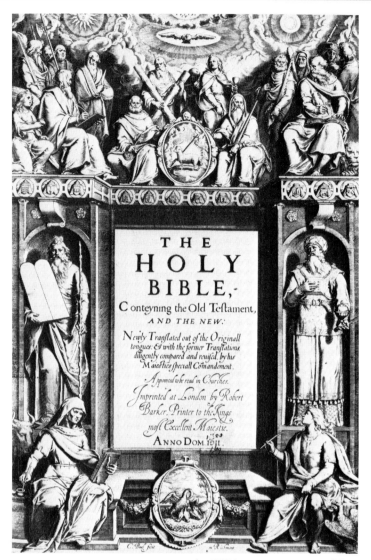

Title page of the first edition of the Authorized (King James') Version of the Bible, 1611.

☐ The Revised Version

In 1870 the Church of England passed a historic resolution, to prepare a revision of the Authorized Version, making only necessary changes. Teams of Old and New Testament scholars were appointed, and Church of Scotland and Free Church scholars were invited to join. They were to make 'as few alterations as possible' in 'the language of the Authorized Version'. No changes in the Greek and Hebrew text were to be adopted without a two-thirds majority. Two parallel groups were formed in the USA to co-operate with suggestions and criticisms.

The Revised Version New Testament, printed in 1881 and telegraphed to Chicago, aroused great interest. It was based on a far more ancient Greek text than the Authorized Version, relying chiefly on the fourth-century Vatican and Sinaitic codices (see *How the Bible was Written*). Many marginal notes referred to the sources of the original text. Quite a number of well-known words and verses in the Authorized Version were left out because there was no good manuscript authority for them. This led to strong opposition, though without good reason. The translation is often over-literal or pedantic. But the Old Testament translation (1885) was a great advance on the Authorized Version. Many meaningless passages were made clear through new knowledge of the Hebrew; poetic passages were set out as poetry; paragraphs were used; and a good reference system was introduced in 1898.

☐ The Revised Standard Version

The American scholars who had been associated with the English Revised Version produced the American Standard Version in 1901. In 1937 the council which held the copyright for this decided on a revision. The New Testament appeared in 1946 and the Old Testament in 1952. Its language is a compromise between the outdated language made familiar by the King James' Version, and modern English. Most, but not all, of the out-of-date words have gone. Quotation marks are used for speech. In some places ancient translations have been followed where the Hebrew text seems clearly wrong. And in Isaiah some changes have been introduced in the light of the Dead Sea Scrolls.

In 1973 a new edition, known as *The Common Bible*, was issued. It was authorized by Roman Catholic authorities as well as the RSV committee.

☐ The New English Bible

In 1946 the Church of Scotland approached the main British churches and suggested an entirely new translation. The idea was welcomed and soon three teams of scholars were at work, with a further group to advise on questions of style. Dr C. H. Dodd was the general director. The New Testament appeared in 1961, the Old Testament in 1970. This is the first official interchurch translation in Britain and the first major version to depart from the Tyndale/Authorized Version tradition.

The New English Bible takes all the latest research into

account. The Dead Sea Scrolls have thrown new light on the Old Testament text. Newly-discovered documents in languages related to Hebrew have revealed the meanings of some difficult words. It is intended to be in modern English without the old-fashioned 'biblical' language of the Authorized Version. But there are still frequent echoes of it. Some of the words are long and difficult and it did not capture the idiom of modern English.

□ The Jerusalem Bible

In 1966 Roman Catholic translators published the Jerusalem Bible. This was a new version made from the original languages. It was similar to the French *Bible de Jérusalem*, and included the introductions and notes from the French translation. This translation has been widely used by Protestants as well as Roman Catholics. Its language is more lively and modern than that of the Revised Standard Version.

□ The Good News Bible

The Good News Bible, produced by the American Bible Society (New Testament 1966, Old Testament 1976), has broken new ground. The aim is a reliable and accurate translation using words which make the meanings clear to everyone. This includes people who have no Christian background, people without much formal education, and people who use English as a second language. It is based on a careful study of linguistics and provides a pattern for translations in many other languages all over the world.

The basic aim is to provide in English the closest *natural* equivalent of the original language.

A second important aim concerns the level of language. Scholarly, poetical and technical religious terms are avoided. And so are all slang expressions. The result is a 'common language', which should be

clear and acceptable to all readers of English.

□ The New International Version

(1972 and 1979), a translation by a team of Protestant evangelical scholars, mainly from the USA, uses the best results of recent research to produce a dignified version in the tradition of earlier English Bibles.

Other modern English translations by groups and individuals

1902
The Twentieth Century New Testament
The thirty or so translators included ministers but not textual experts. Easy to read and understand.

1903
R. F. Weymouth, **The New Testament in Modern Speech**
Long sentences are divided, and section headings added. Uses dignified and sometimes old-fashioned language.

1913 and 1924
J. Moffatt, **A New Translation of the Bible**
A good translation, especially in the Old Testament. Rearranges and changes parts of the text, for reasons which Moffatt explains elsewhere.

1923 and 1927
E. J. Goodspeed, **The Complete Bible: an American translation**
A very readable version. The

This beautifully illuminated manuscript is in Armenian.

Old Testament was the work of four other scholars.

1941 and 1949
The Basic English Bible
A successful experiment using a vocabulary of only 1,000 words.

1941
The Confraternity Version
A Roman Catholic translation made in the USA. A revision of Challoner's New Testament. The Old Testament translation is based on the Hebrew.

1945 and 1949
Ronald Knox, **The Holy Bible**
A Roman Catholic translation based on the Latin Vulgate, by a master of English style.

1947–1957
J. B. Phillips, **The New Testament in Modern English**
A free and racy version which has been very popular.

1945 and 1959
The Berkeley Version
The New Testament by Dr G. Verkuyl; the Old Testament by a team of scholars in the USA. A conservative version.

1958
K. S. Wuest, **Expanded Translation of the New Testament**
Designed to help Bible students who do not know Greek.

1958
The Amplified New Testament
Produced in the USA. Includes alternative and additional words to bring out the meaning.

1971
K. Taylor, **The Living Bible**
A popular American paraphrase into everyday language, designed for family reading.

1971
New American Standard Version
The American Standard Version of 1901 with modernized English.

1982
New King James Version/ Revised Authorized Version
A revision to deal with changes of language and the meaning of words since the 1611 edition.

Statistics of Bible translation up to 1984

At present, a total of 5,445 languages are known to be practised. Bible translation work involves approximately 1,745 of these languages. Of these, the Bible has been translated, either in its entirety or the New Testament, into 586 languages.
Europe and the Middle East: 46 languages
Asia-Pacific: 285 languages
Africa: 249 languages
Americas and the Caribbean: 6 languages

In addition, there are 1,159 translations currently in progress or undergoing revision. Europe and the Middle East: 12 languages
Asia-Pacific: 465 languages
Africa: 402 languages
Americas and the Caribbean: 280 languages

Other European languages
The Reformation produced great Bible translations in many other languages beside English and German.

□ **Dutch**
The first complete Dutch Bible, translated partly from Luther's German version, appeared in 1525. A number of other Dutch versions were published in the following century, and in 1637 the States-General Version, the standard Protestant Bible, appeared. This remains in use today, though the Roman Catholic Bible has a separate tradition, and a number of modern versions, including a New Testament similar to the English Good News Bible, have appeared.

□ **French**
There have been many French Bibles. The *Segond* Version of 1880 and the *Synodale* of 1910 are most often used today by Protestants. Among new versions, the Roman Catholic *Bible de Jérusalem* (1956) and *La Traduction Oecumenique de la Bible* (1967–76) have broken new ground. *Le Nouveau Testament en Français Courant*, similar to the Good News Bible, has proved popular, especially in French-speaking Africa.
Similar stories could be told of all the major languages of western Europe. But in eastern Europe, under the influence of Orthodox Christianity ancient or medieval versions were used for a long time. The whole Bible was not translated into Russian until 1876. It was not translated into modern Greek until 1840. Today there is a great deal of Bible translation work being done all over Europe.
A new Polish translation was issued in 1975. The Bible is being translated into five different Yugoslavian languages. Ten new Spanish translations of the New Testament, or the whole Bible, were made between 1947 and 1968, mostly by Roman Catholics.

Pioneer missionary Bible translators
When missionary work began again after the Middle Ages, the first translations were made by Roman Catholics. They generally began with the Ten Commandments, the Lord's Prayer and selected parts of the Gospels or Bible story books, as well as the catechism. But in 1613 Jesuit missionaries published the whole New Testament in Japanese.
The first Protestant version was in Malay, and was made by employees of the Dutch East India Company.
The first whole Bible was John Eliot's 1663 version in 'Massachusetts'. This is a complex American Indian language, with some words 15–20 letters long.
Bible translation in India began in earnest with Danish Lutheran missionaries. Ziegenbalg's New Testament in Tamil appeared in 1711 and the Old Testament was added by Schultze in 1728. But a new era began when the first English missionary, William Carey, reached India in 1793. He spent forty years working at Serampore in Bengal with two colleagues and many Indian helpers. When he died, his press had produced translations of the whole Bible or New Testament in 37 different languages or dialects. These included Burmese and Chinese. He had also compiled grammars and dictionaries. It was an amazing achievement.

The Bible Societies
In 1804 the British and Foreign Bible Society was founded 'for Wales, for the kingdom, for the world'. At first it issued existing Bible versions. But its members soon took an interest in new translations. They issued the Hindustani (Urdu) New Testament, translated by the pioneer missionary, Henry Martyn, in 1812 and the first modern African translation in 1816. This was in the Bullom language for Sierra Leone.
Since then there have been translations into about 480 African languages. Christians were the first to write these languages down, using the Roman script. The first com-

THE WORK OF BIBLE TRANSLATION TODAY

Bible translation is team work. Here two translators, a missionary and a national Christian, work together on a translation into one of the languages of Mexico.

In Nigeria a group is involved in checking a new Bible translation.

When translation is completed the text is often duplicated for final checking and revision. Then it can be printed, making thousands of copies available at once.

This mobile bookshop sells Bibles and scriptures to local people.

Most important of all, the Bible is read, and lives are changed.

HOW MANY BOOKS?

All Bibles contain the same 27 New Testament books. But a comparison of the two lists of Old Testament books below shows 39 in common and nine extra books in *The Jerusalem Bible*. A selection of modern versions would reveal some other minor variations in the books added to the basic 39. These additional books are called either 'The Apocrypha' or 'The Deutero-canonical books'. The Revised Standard Version Common Bible lists the following, placing the extra material between the Old and New Testaments:

Tobit
Judith
Additions to the Book of Esther
The Wisdom of Solomon
Ecclesiasticus (or *The Wisdom of Jesus the son of Sirach*)
Baruch
The Letter of Jeremiah
The Prayer of Azariah and *The Song of the Three Young Men* (additions to Daniel)
Susanna
Bel and the Dragon
1–2 Maccabees
1–2 Esdras *
The Prayer of Manasseh *

*These books are included in the Greek canon of Scripture but are not regarded as authoritative by the Roman Catholic Church.

The historical reason for these differences is that Jerome, drawing on the Greek Septuagint Old Testament, included these extra books in his Latin Vulgate version, and this has influenced subsequent Roman Catholic versions. (The Greek Orthodox and associated churches also include an Apocrypha, but based on Greek and Slavonic originals, not the Latin Vulgate.) Protestant versions have generally gone back to the Hebrew Old Testament which includes only the basic 39.

Are the extra books a part of the Bible?

Roman Catholic Christians would accept them as a true part of the Old Testament (though the name 'Deutero-canonical' gives them a secondary position and they are certainly less-read), but most others do not.

The Old Testament in *The Revised Standard Version* (Protestant)

Genesis
Exodus
Leviticus
Numbers
Deuteronomy
Joshua
Judges
Ruth
1 Samuel
2 Samuel
1 Kings
2 Kings
1 Chronicles
2 Chronicles
Ezra
Nehemiah
Esther
Job
Psalms
Proverbs
Ecclesiastes
Song of Solomon
Isaiah
Jeremiah
Lamentations
Ezekiel
Daniel
Hosea
Joel
Amos
Obadiah
Jonah
Micah
Nahum
Habakkuk
Zephaniah
Haggai
Zechariah
Malachi

The Old Testament in *The Jerusalem Bible* (Roman Catholic)

Genesis
Exodus
Leviticus
Numbers
Deuteronomy
Joshua
Judges
Ruth
1 Samuel
2 Samuel
1 Kings
2 Kings
1 Chronicles
2 Chronicles
Ezra
Nehemiah
Tobit
Judith
Esther (including the *additions*)
1 Maccabees
2 Maccabees
Job
Psalms
Proverbs
Ecclesiastes
Song of Songs
The Book of Wisdom
Ecclesiasticus
Isaiah
Jeremiah
Lamentations
Baruch (including *The Letter of Jeremiah*)
Ezekiel
Daniel (including *The Song of the Three Young Men*, *Susanna* and *Bel and the Dragon*)
Hosea
Joel
Amos
Obadiah
Jonah
Micah
Nahum
Habakkuk
Zephaniah
Haggai
Zechariah
Malachi

plete New Testament for Africa was in Amharic, for Ethiopia, in 1829. The first whole Bible in an African language was in Malagasy in 1835.

A similar process began in the Pacific (with Tahitian in 1818) and in Latin America (with Aymara, for Bolivia, in 1829).

By this time other societies had begun work. The Netherlands Bible Society, the American Bible Society and the National Bible Society of Scotland all began the work of Bible translation. In India, Africa and the Arab lands Roman Catholic missionaries also worked on Bible translation.

The modern missionary movement grew all through the nineteenth century, and until 1939 translation went ahead at a great rate. Practically every missionary society had a part in it. The chief translators were generally missionaries, though nationals were also involved. Some played a major role. Nigerian-born Bishop Samuel Crowther, for example, worked on the Yoruba Bible (Nigeria, 1862) and Pandita Ramabai on the Bible in Marathi (1912). The Bible Societies helped set the work up. They gave money where it was needed. They had the translations printed and distributed and generally helped out with any problems. Only the Netherlands Society trained its own linguists and sent them out as translators.

Missionary Bible translation today
There have been great changes in Bible translation since World War II.

□ The Wycliffe Bible Translators
The Wycliffe Bible Translators were founded in 1934 to bring people the Bible in their own language. Thousands of languages were still without it. This group has now expanded into the largest missionary society in the world. It has over

Around the world the Bible is read by young and old, by individuals and by groups. In its pages men and women discover God's message to them.

3,000 missionaries, who carry out a carefully organized programme in about 700 languages.

Each translator is first trained in linguistics. They usually have to give the language a written form for the first time. This is no easy task, especially when it contains sounds unknown in any European language. Then the translator has to write a grammar and a complete list of words used. He is usually helped by a national who has at least some knowledge of another language known to the missionary. Years may pass before he can begin even the simplest translations. Meanwhile the tribal people have to be taught to read. And then the translation must be tested all the time, to make sure that people can understand it.

Many things mentioned in the Bible may be quite unknown to people of other cultures. The translator has to find the closest equivalent, or some other way of explaining what is meant. But he is trained to do this and has other experienced people to help him. At last he completes the translation of one of the Gospels. And his reward, when the

printed copies arrive, is to see the joy with which they are read and studied! A Christian in India, reading a Gospel for the first time, exclaimed, 'It's just like looking at the face of the Lord Jesus!'

□ The United Bible Societies
A still larger programme, covering some of the major languages of the world (Hindi, Chinese, Arabic) has been carried on by the United Bible Societies. This organization unites sixty or so national societies all over the world. Both Roman Catholics and Protestants co-operate in this work. The second Vatican Council encouraged Roman Catholics to supply their people with the Bible in their own language.

The typical translator is no longer a missionary pioneer, working under primitive conditions with one or two local helpers. More often he is himself a local, living in his own country and working in his own mother tongue. He may well be translating into a language which already has a Bible. But it may have been the work of foreigners, not as clear and idiomatic as it could be. Or it may have been too literal, or the language might have

A man studies his Bible in a hospital in Thailand.

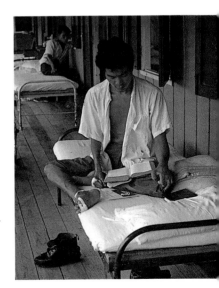

In many areas literacy work goes hand in hand with Bible translation. It may be that the first book this Brazilian woman is able to read is part of the Bible.

become out of date. Perhaps it was based on a text which modern knowledge has improved.

Consultations are held to gain wide support for the new translation. Some people are bound to resent any changes in the Bible they have known from childhood, and their views must be taken into account. If a new translation is decided on, translators will be chosen and trained. They will make the first drafts, sharing them with each other and noting criticisms. Then their agreed draft will go to a team of experts on the Bible and the language, who will send their criticisms in writing. If the translators do not accept these, they will be discussed at a meeting of the experts. Church leaders will also receive drafts, so that when the work is finished they will support it and help churches to accept it. A Bible Society translations officer will keep in close touch with a number of projects like this. He will make regular visits, offering advice and suggestions and occasionally settling disputes.

☐ **The future**
More is being done in translation work today than ever before. Besides the world-wide programme of the Wycliffe Bible Translators and the United Bible Societies there are several other missionary agencies at work. And here and there individuals and groups are making their own versions. Thousands of people are working to make the Bible clear in terms which ordinary people can understand. There are still many hundreds of language groups, mostly small ones, with no existing translation that meets their need. And languages are always changing. United Bible Society scholars reckon that, to keep up with this change, some revision, if not a new translation, will be needed in every language every thirty years. Certainly there will be enough work to keep the Bible translators busy for many years to come, bringing God's message to everyone in his own language.

'Your word is a lamp to guide me and a light for my path,' says the Psalmist, writing about God's law.

4

Understanding the Bible

Introducing the Bible

By any standards, the Bible is a great masterpiece. It begins in the Stone Age, and ends in the world of the Roman Empire. Its most recent parts are almost 2,000 years old. Yet millions of people read it regularly, and find in it a personal inspiration for their daily living. People have often been prepared to die for it – and Christians all over the world still go to extraordinary lengths to possess their own copy.

Why does such an ancient book, with stories that happened long ago and in unfamiliar places, still captivate us today? Why should space-age people trouble to read a book whose authors had not yet witnessed the invention of the bicycle? Every Bible reader will have their own favourite answer to that question. But there are at least three basic reasons why we should take it seriously.

The influence of the Bible

As soon as you start to analyse modern western civilization, you come up against the Bible. For many hundreds of years it has been a predominant in- fluence in shaping our laws, our education systems and our democratic ideals – not to mention our concept of human rights. One way and another, the Bible has had a profound influence on most of the great European political, social and religious reformers and through them on the other great western nations of the world. It is impossible to understand the modern western mentality without taking account of the Bible.

The Bible is also at the centre of many great cultural changes throughout the world today. As the people of many emerging nations search for their own identity, they are turning for guidance to – the Bible. Its distinctive message is changing the face of society in South America, in Africa, and in many parts of Asia today.

Worldwide, the Bible has an enormous influence today, and in many places people are becoming Christians in their millions as they read it and respond to its challenge. The Bible is indispensable for a proper appreciation of the cultural currents that are sweeping through the world today!

The message of the Bible

The Bible may be an ancient book but it is part of an unfinished story. Its characters no doubt had a very different lifestyle from twentieth- century people. But their story is the first instalment in our own story. Their experience of God was the same as ours, and modern Christians are united with them across the centuries in the same story of salvation.

The story begins, continues – and will end – with God's love. Wherever we look in the Bible, the message is essentially the same. The stories of creation, the great events of Old Testament history, the life, death and resurrection of Jesus, the coming of the Holy Spirit at Pentecost, and the life of the earliest churches – in all of these we see God reaching out in love to men and women and boys and girls, challenging them to respond to him in wholehearted commitment. At the centre of the story is Jesus. He not only calls into question our accepted standards of belief and behaviour. He also makes it possible for men and women to find release from the domination of evil, and be given the power to live a new quality of life which will reflect the character of God himself.

The Bible is full of remarkable and helpful insights into how people can – and do – react to the news of God's great and forgiving love. Abraham, Amos, Isaiah, Paul, Peter, and the rest – they are all our contemporaries. When people today commit their lives to God, they are joining an age-long spiritual pilgrimage – and we need the story of our predecessors for our own direction and encouragement.

The God of the Bible

The Bible could be much like any other biography of great religious leaders, but for one thing: the claims that it makes about God and about Jesus Christ. The Old Testament everywhere emphasizes that the God of the Bible makes exclusive claims. It is simply not possible for Israel to worship their own God alongside the gods of the Canaanites. For one is true, and the others are false.

Jesus repeats the same claims. He declares that his message is not just one possibility among several; it is, he asserts, the only way to know God and to have a valid relationship with him. The earliest Christians all accepted this. Some of them had been deeply religious people long before they heard of Jesus. But in the light of his perfect disclosure of God's will and character, they soon saw that even their best religiosity was not enough. To know God truly, a person must acknowledge Jesus Christ to be God's only Son, and be prepared to seek forgiveness for the past by repentance and commitment to him as Lord and Saviour.

This, above all else, explains the authority that the Bible must have for the Christian today. It is a unique book, for it opens a series of windows through which we can glimpse a unique God. Indeed, more than that. For as we read it with open minds, looking for God's instruction as we do so, we may confidently expect not only to discover what God said to heroes of the faith in the past: we will also hear God's word spoken direct to us today.

The Books of the Bible

THE LAW

This is the name (Hebrew 'Torah') the Jews gave to the first five books of the Bible – Genesis to Deuteronomy. In Greek they were called the 'Pentateuch' or 'five scrolls'.

The actual laws or rules for living which God gave his people, ancient Israel, are mainly in the books of Exodus and Deuteronomy. That is where the Ten Commandments are recorded.

Genesis 1–11 looks back to the very beginning, when God first made our world. The rest of Genesis tells the life-stories of Abraham and the founders of the nation of Israel.

Exodus to Deuteronomy focus on Moses, telling how God rescued his people from slavery in Egypt and led them during the years in the desert until they were ready to enter the new land he had promised them.

These books tell us about the religion and worship of Israel – how they should behave as God's people. The great festivals and their meaning is explained, and the special tent or tabernacle made for God is described.

Although the five books are very different, they really tell one story. They show God at work, not just in creating our world but in calling out individuals and a nation to obey him and to bring blessing to the whole world.

☐ GENESIS

This rather strange title to the first book of the Bible means 'origin'. It is a book of beginnings: the beginning of our world, the new beginning after the great flood, and the beginning of the Jewish nation.

Contents
Part 1: The Creation to Noah and after, chapters 1–11
The creation of the world and everything in it by God 1–2
The first people disobey God: death enters the world 3
From Adam to Noah 4–5
Noah and the flood 6–10
The tower of Babel (or Babylon) 11
Part 2: Abraham and his family, 12–50
Abraham, Isaac, Esau and Jacob: God's new family 12–35
Esau's descendants 36
Joseph and his brothers 37–45
Jacob and his family in Egypt 46–50

Main characters
Adam and Eve, Cain and Abel, Noah, Abraham and Sarah, Lot, Isaac and Rebecca, Jacob and Esau, Rachel and Leah, Joseph and his brothers (the twelve sons of Jacob/Israel, to whom the twelve tribes of Israel traced their origin)

Great events
The creation and 'fall' into sin 1–3
The rescue of Noah and his family 6–10
God chooses Abraham and makes him a special promise 12
The stories of Abraham (12–25), Isaac (21–28, 35), Jacob (25–50) and Joseph (30, 37–50)

The setting
The events in Genesis take place in the Middle (Near) East: Mesopotamia (Iran/Iraq), what is now Israel/Jordan/Lebanon, and Egypt

Time-span
From before 2000 BC to about 1650 BC

Meaning and message
Genesis shows God at work. He is the Maker of our world and of all humankind. What he made was good. But he gave people the freedom to choose, and they chose to disobey him. As a result we became estranged from him: the world knew suffering and death. But God did not give up. He made a new start with Noah. And he chose Abraham and his descendants to begin his plan for the rescue of the whole human race.

☐ EXODUS

The title means 'exit' or 'departure'. In this book God rescues his people from slavery in Egypt under the leadership of Moses.

Contents
Part 1: God frees the Israelites from slavery in Egypt, chapters 1–15
Slaves in Egypt 1
Moses: the early years 2–4, Aaron and the king of Egypt 5–11
Passover – and the Red Sea crossing 12–15
Part 2: The journey to Mount Sinai 16–18
Part 3: God makes a covenant with his people and gives them laws to live by 19–24
Part 4: The special tent (or tabernacle) for God, and rules for worship 25–40

Main characters
Moses, his brother Aaron and sister Miriam; Pharaoh, the king of Egypt

Great events
Rescue of the baby Moses 2
God calls Moses to be the leader of his people 3
The ten plagues 7–12
The first Passover 12
Crossing of the Red (or Reed) Sea 14
God gives his people the Ten Commandments 20
God offers to make Israel a nation and they accept his terms 23–24
The story of the golden calf 32
Building of God's special tent (or tabernacle) 36

The setting
The events of Exodus take place in Egypt (the Nile Delta) and the Sinai peninsula

Time-span
About 100 years: roughly 1325–1225 BC

Meaning and message
Exodus shows God at work in history, setting his people free from captivity and leading them out to a new life. He gives them rules to live by, telling them how to behave towards one another, how to live together, and how to please him in worship. The tent he instructs them to build shows his willingness to identify with his people: he is there at the centre of their camp.

God is with his people. He knows all that is happening. He cares – and comes to the rescue. These great facts are true today: many believers suffering oppression find particular help in Exodus.

☐ LEVITICUS

The book of rules God gave to his people through Moses at Mt Sinai. The name comes from the tribe of Levi, who with the priests led the nation's worship.

Contents

Laws about offerings and sacrifices, chapters 1 – 7
Aaron becomes High Priest; rules for priests 8 – 10
Food-laws, rules about diseases – clean and unclean 11 – 15
The Day of Atonement 16
What God requires in life and worship; the festivals 17 – 27

Main characters

Aaron – with the priests and Levites

Great events

The consecration of Aaron as the first High Priest 8
Celebration of the great annual religious festivals: Atonement, Passover, Harvest, Shelters (Booths) 23

The setting

The Sinai peninsula: God's people on their way from Egypt to the Promised Land

Famous passage

'Love your neighbour as yourself' (19:18): the words Jesus used in his summary of the Law.

Meaning and message

God expects his people – all of them, not just the priests, the professionals – to do as he tells them. Not all of the laws in Leviticus were meant for all time, though many are sensible rules for health and hygiene. But behind all the detail is the permanent truth that God is perfect goodness and purity. We are selfish and wilful and disobedient. Our sin inevitably separates us from a holy God. We need a way of becoming 'at one' with him. The Old Testament sacrifices point to that way: sin results in death, the death of an animal, pointing forward to the one perfect sacrifice of Jesus, sufficient for all time, offered in atonement for 'the sins of the whole world'.

The second half of Exodus and the books of Leviticus, Numbers and Deuteronomy are set against the background of the Sinai Desert. It was here that the Israelites lived as nomads on their way to Canaan.

☐ NUMBERS

The story of the Israelites during almost forty years living as nomads in the Sinai peninsula, after their escape from Egypt. The title comes from the two censuses recorded in the book.

Contents

Part 1: Mt Sinai – getting ready to break camp, chapters 1 – 9
A national census 1
The tribes in camp 2
Duties of the priests and Levites; various rules 3 – 8
The second Passover 9
Part 2: From Mt Sinai to Moab 10 – 21
Part 3: Events in Moab – Balaam and Balak 22 – 32
Part 4: Summary of the journey and instructions for the land 33 – 36

Setting

Mt Sinai and the Sinai peninsula

Important events

Miriam punished 12
The twelve spies and their report 13
Complaints, disobedience and God's sentence: 40 years' wandering 14
Challenge to the leadership of Moses and Aaron 16 – 17
Plague of poisonous snakes 21
Balaam and his donkey 22
Joshua chosen to lead 27

Main characters

Moses and Aaron, Caleb and Joshua, Balaam and Balak

Famous passage

'The Lord bless you and keep you; the Lord make his face to shine upon you
and be gracious to you;
the Lord turn his face toward you and give you peace' (6:24 – 26, the words God gave to Moses and Aaron as a blessing on his people).

Meaning and message

Numbers records the faithfulness of God, and the complaining disobedience of his people. God is infinitely patient. He is unfailingly loving in his care and provision for his people. But in the end disobedience is bound to be punished – to turn people back to God before it is too late.

☐ DEUTERONOMY

This book records Moses' words to God's people, after the long years of wandering, when they were about to enter the Promised Land. The name means 'a second Law': the book contains further reflections on how God's people should live.

Contents

Moses thinks back over the events since they left Mt Sinai, chapters 1 – 4
Moses reminds the people of God's laws and calls on them to obey 5 – 26
Instructions for the new land: the importance of obeying God 27 – 28
The covenant between God and his people is renewed 29 – 30
Moses hands over the leadership: last instructions 31 – 33
The death of Moses 34

Setting

The plain on the east side of the River Jordan

Time

Immediately before the entry to the Promised Land: approximately 1230 BC

Main characters

Moses and Joshua

Famous events

Account of the twelve spies 1
God's punishment: the years in the desert 2
The Ten Commandments 5
The appointment of Joshua 31
Moses' death 34

Famous passages

'Love the Lord your God with all your heart, with all your soul, and with all your strength' (6:4 – 6), the words quoted by Jesus in his summary of the Law.
'Man cannot live on bread alone, but needs every word that God speaks' (8:3). When Satan tempted him in the desert, Jesus answered with these words and with two other sentences from Deuteronomy 6: 'Do not put the Lord your God to the test' and 'Worship the Lord your God and serve only him!'

Meaning and message

Although Deuteronomy gets its name from being the second record of God's laws, the great theme of the book is obedience. Remember all that God has done for you, Moses says, and do as he tells you. When you choose to obey God you are choosing life. God rewards obedience, which comes not from fear but from love. Disobedience leads to unhappiness, punishment and death.

THE HISTORY BOOKS

The big section of books from Joshua to Esther spans about 800 years of Jewish history – roughly 1200–400 BC. They record what happened from the time the Israelites conquered and settled their land, on through the times of the Judges and the kings, to their conquest by the great nations to the north, when God's people were taken into exile.

The books of Ezra and Nehemiah describe their return. The book of Esther records the influence of one Jewish girl at the palace of the Persian king – and how she saved her people.

No history book tells everything. And those who wrote these books had a special purpose in mind – to show how God's purpose was fulfilled in the nation's life. So they faithfully record the disasters which happened when God's people chose to disobey him. And kings are 'good' or 'bad' according to whether they obeyed God, or chose to go their own way.

☐ JOSHUA

The story of the Israelite invasion of Canaan – the land God had promised them – led by Joshua, Moses' successor.

Contents
Part 1: The conquest of Canaan, chapters 1–12
Across the River Jordan 1–5
Jericho and after 6–7
Ai 8
The southern campaign 9–10
The northern campaign 11–12
Part 2: The land divided among the tribes 13–21
Part 3: The eastern tribes and Joshua's farewell 22–24

Setting
The plains on the east of the River Jordan and into Canaan

Time-span
About 1230–1200 BC

Time of writing
Probably during the lifetime of the prophet Samuel

Main characters
Joshua; also Rahab and Caleb

Famous events
The two spies 2
Crossing the Jordan 3
Battle of Jericho 6

Famous passages
God's instructions to Joshua (1:5–9), 'Be strong and courageous . . . .'
Joshua's decision for God, 'As for me and my household, we will serve the Lord' (24:15).

Main theme
Invasion of Canaan, under God's direction and led by Joshua. God has kept his promise. Joshua leads the people in renewing their allegiance to God.

☐ JUDGES

The stories of national heroes in the lawless time between Israel's invasion of Canaan and the first kings.

Contents
Fighting for the land, to the time of Joshua's death, chapters 1–2
Stories of the 'judges' or champions 2–16
Other stories from the time when there was no king 17–21

Famous people and their exploits
Deborah and Barak 4–5
Gideon and the Midianites 6–8
Jephthah and his daughter 10–12
Samson and Delilah 13–16

Time-span
Less than 150 years, from about 1200 to 1070 BC

Setting
The land of Israel/Canaan

Main theme and message
The Israelites did not carry out God's instructions to drive out all the tribes occupying the land. Some stayed, and in consequence the Israelites began to worship the local gods. They became divided and weak, an easy prey to attack. Their faith no longer held the scattered tribes together. But even though they had broken their promise to God, when they turned to him in desperation, he came to the rescue and provided champions to set them free.

☐ RUTH

The story
Famine drives Naomi and her family from Bethlehem to Moab. Her husband and two sons die there. When Naomi returns, her Moabite daughter-in-law Ruth refuses to leave her. Gleaning for grain so that they will have bread to eat, Ruth meets a distant relative, Boaz. Moved by her loyalty to Naomi, Boaz clears the way to marry Ruth. It is a foreign girl, who has chosen Naomi's people and Naomi's God, who becomes part of the family line of King David.

Time and setting
This story is set in the violent times of the Judges; the places are the land of Moab (east of the Jordan) and Bethlehem.

Theme
The theme is one of love and loyalty – and of God's care for everyone who turns to him, whatever their nationality.

☐ THE BOOKS OF SAMUEL

A history of Israel, from the last of the Judges to the final years of King David.

Contents
How Samuel became Israel's leader, under God, chapters 1–7
Saul becomes Israel's first king 8–10
Saul's early years as king; disobedience and rejection 11–15
God chooses David 16
The battle with Goliath 17
Jealous King Saul: David outlawed 18–30
The death of Saul and Jonathan 31; 2 Samuel 1
David is made king of Judah 2–4
David becomes king of all Israel; God's promise 5–7
David's wars 8–10
David and Bathsheba: God's punishment 11–12
Family troubles: Absalom's rebellion and after 13–20
The later years 21–24

Setting and time-span
Israel is now settled in the land, but it takes King David a life-time of campaigns to push back the boundaries and win peace. The period covered is roughly 100 years, about 1075–975 BC.

Time of writing
The historian wrote his account some time after the kingdom split in two. He may have used Samuel's own writings and those of the prophets who came after him. He knew, and quotes, some of David's poems.

Famous people and events
Hannah – and Samuel's birth 1 Samuel 1
Eli – and God's message to Samuel 3
Capture and return of the Ark or Covenant Box 4–6
Samuel anoints David king 16
David and Goliath 17
David and Jonathan 18–20
God's promise of a permanent dynasty – David's thanksgiving 7
David and Bathsheba 11

Famous passages
Hannah's prayer 1 Samuel 2
David's lament for Saul and Jonathan 2 Samuel 1
Story of the poor man's lamb 12
David's victory song 22

Main theme and message
The idea was that Israel should have no other king than God himself. Samuel saw this, and tried to resist the people's pressure to have a king like the surrounding nations. God gave them the king they longed for, even though he knew that trouble would follow.

Saul, the first king, began well, but pride led him to disregard God – and God rejected him.

The books of history tell how the Israelites captured the cities of Canaan, including the Jebusite stronghold of Jerusalem which eventually became their capital.

David was a man after God's own heart. His trust in God never failed. Though he often did wrong he was always ready to acknowledge his wrongdoing and ask God's forgiveness.

At the heart of these books is God's promise of a dynasty that would last for ever – a promise he fulfilled at last in the person of Jesus – born of David's family line.

□ **THE BOOKS OF KINGS**
An account of Israel's history from the death of King David, through the division that followed King Solomon's death, to the fall of Jerusalem and destruction of the temple by the Babylonians.

Contents
Part 1: Solomon succeeds King David, 1 Kings chapters 1–2
Part 2: The reign of Solomon 3–11
Solomon the wise 3–4
Building and dedication of the temple 5–8
God's promise; Solomon's trade and building projects 9
Visit of the Queen of Sheba 10
Solomon's failure and death 11
Part 3: The divided kingdom 12 – 2 Kings 17
The northern tribes rebel 12–14
Kings of Israel and Judah 14–16
Elijah the prophet and the contest with Baal 17–19
King Ahab of Israel 20–22
Jehoshaphat of Judah and Ahaziah of Israel 22 – 2 Kings 1
Elisha becomes God's prophet 2–8
Kings of Israel.and Judah 8–16
Israel's capital, Samaria, falls to the Assyrians 17
Part 4: The kingdom of Judah 18–25
King Hezekiah and the Assyrian threat 18–20
Manasseh and Amon of Judah 21
King Josiah's reforms 22–23
The last kings of Judah 24
Jerusalem falls to the Babylonians; the temple destroyed 25

Setting and time-span
The reign of Solomon, about 970–930 BC, was Israel's golden age. The events that followed in the two kingdoms of Israel and Judah took place against the background of the rise to power of first Assyria, then Babylon. The books of Kings cover about 400 years, roughly 975–586 BC.

Samaria fell in 722; Jerusalem in 586.

The books of Chronicles cover the same period. And the prophets Amos, Hosea, Isaiah, Micah, Nahum Habakkuk, Zephaniah and Jeremiah all fall within this time-span.

Time of writing
The books were finally put together in Babylon during the exile, perhaps about 550 BC. But the editors used much earlier material: court and official records, and stories about the prophets.

Famous people and events
The judgement of Solomon 1 Kings 3
The building of the temple 6
Solomon and the Queen of Sheba 10
Elijah and the drought: the widow at Zarephath 17
Elijah and the prophets of Baal 18
Elijah and the 'still, small voice' 19
Naboth's vineyard 21
Elijah and the fiery chariot 2 Kings 2
Elisha and the woman from Shunem 4
Naaman is cured 5
The siege of Samaria 6
Queen Jezebel's death 9
Queen Athaliah's pogrom 11
Fall of Samaria 17
Assyrians at the gates of Jerusalem 18
King Josiah discovers the Law-book 22
Fall of Jerusalem; destruction of the temple 25

Famous passages
Solomon's prayer for wisdom 1 Kings 3
Solomon's prayer at the temple dedication 8

Main theme and message
Each of the rulers in these books is judged according to his faithfulness and loyalty to God. When the ruler and people determine to obey God and honour him, things go well. When they deliberately choose to disobey, disaster follows. But God takes no pleasure in this. He wants the willing obedience of his people, for their own good. Again and again he warns them of the danger they are in. He sends the prophets Elijah and Elisha as his special spokesmen. But the people still refuse to listen, and disaster comes. First Samaria, then Jerusalem, fall into enemy hands. The nation of Israel, in the north, disappears for ever. And the people of Judah are taken into exile.

□ **THE BOOKS OF CHRONICLES**
These books cover the same events as those in 2 Samuel and Kings. But because they were intended for the people who returned to Jerusalem from exile in Babylon, the story concentrates on the southern kingdom of Judah and its kings.

Contents
Part 1: Family trees, from Adam to the people who returned from

Babylon, 1 Chronicles chapters 1–9
Part 2: The reign of King David 10–29
The death of King Saul 10
David's reign 11–21
David's preparations for building the temple 22–29
Part 3: The reign of King Solomon 2 Chronicles 1–9
The source of Solomon's wisdom and wealth 1
Building and dedicating the temple 2–7
Solomon's international fame 8–9
Part 4: The kings of Judah 10–36
The revolt of the northern tribes under Rehoboam 10
Rehoboam to Asa 11–16
King Jehoshaphat's reforms 17–20
Jehoram to Ahaz 21–28
King Hezekiah's reforms 29–32
Manasseh and Amon 33
King Josiah's reforms 34–35
The end of the kings and Jerusalem's fall 36

Time-span
These books, together with the books of Ezra and Nehemiah with which they are linked, narrate the history of God's people from the death of King Saul to the re-settlement of Judea after the exile. The story told in Chronicles stretches from about 1000 BC to the sack of Jerusalem by Nebuchadnezzar in 587/6.

Time of writing
After the Jews had repopulated Judea – perhaps about 400 BC.

Great events
David brings the Ark of the Covenant to Jerusalem 1 Chronicles 15–16
Solomon dedicates the newly-built temple 2 Chronicles 5–7
Hezekiah rededicates the temple after its closure 29

Famous passages
David's song of praise 1 Chronicles 16
David praises God and commends Solomon to him for the work 29
Solomon's prayer at the dedication of the temple 6–7
God's promise to Solomon for the future 7

Main theme and message
The great aim of the Chronicler is to convince the Jews, now back home in Jerusalem, that they are still God's special people. The beginning of their kingdom, in the great days of David and Solomon, was blessed by God. And their national worship – the detailed organization of temple services and of priests, Levites and musicians – was God-given. The corruption of all this, through the

disobedience of many kings, led to the fall of Jerusalem, the destruction of the temple and exile. But God's promises to Israel still hold true, and now is the time to rebuild. The restoration of true worship under kings Jehoshaphat, Hezekiah and Josiah encourage the returned exiles to renew their own faith. (The message is similar to that of the prophets Haggai and Zechariah.)

☐ EZRA
The story of how two parties of Jews returned to their homeland from exile in Babylon. They rebuilt the temple, and under the leadership of Ezra began to observe the details of the law.

Contents
Part 1: The first party returns to Jerusalem, with Zerubbabel, chapters 1–2
Part 2: The temple is rebuilt, despite opposition 3–6
The people joyfully begin to rebuild 3
Years of local opposition, and support from Persian emperors 4
The rebuilding begins again 5:1 – 6:12
The temple is rededicated and Passover held 6:13–22
Part 3: A second party returns, with Ezra 7–10
The people who come, and their journey 7–8
The problem of mixed marriages 9–10

Time-span and setting
The return from exile was not a single event. Several journeys were made, at intervals of many years, in the reigns of different Persian emperors. This account covers the time from about 538 to 428 BC. The returning exiles found a land still inhabited by Jews who had not been taken to Babylon, mixed with other nationalities opposed to them. Jerusalem was desolate, the temple in ruins and national life at a standstill.

Time of writing
Probably written to complement the books of Chronicles – around 400 BC.

Important people
Ezra, a priest descended from Aaron, and scholar in the law of God. Zerubbabel, leader of the first return; he was grandson of King Jehoiachin who had been taken into exile.
Emperor Cyrus of Persia, who overthrew the Babylonians and decreed that the Jews, and other peoples, should return home. The prophet Isaiah saw this pagan emperor's actions as the

work of God.

Great events
Cyrus' command to return and rebuild 1
Celebration of the first Passover festival in the rebuilt temple 6
Ezra and other descendants of temple officials return 7 and 8

Main theme and messages
The Chronicler, who probably wrote this book as well as Chronicles, believed strongly that the Jews were still God's special people, despite banishment into exile and the end of the kings. In the book of Ezra we see this belief working out in practice, as the returned exiles rebuild the temple and begin again their national religious life. The law of God had to be kept in detail; they were to be a people apart.

☐ NEHEMIAH
The story of how Nehemiah, a Jewish exile who became a great leader, led a third stage of the return to Jerusalem. He was made governor of Judea, and inspired the rebuilding of the city walls. His religious reforms overlapped with the work of Ezra.

Contents
Part 1: Nehemiah returns to Jerusalem and the walls are rebuilt, chapters 1–7
Nehemiah receives bad news and prays for Jerusalem 1
Nehemiah's return 2
The rebuilding of the walls, in the teeth of opposition 3:1 – 7:3
A list of the returned exiles 7:4–73
Part 2: The law, the confession and the renewed covenant 8–10
Ezra reads the law and the people repent 8
A prayer of confession 9:1–37
The people sign an agreement to keep the law 9:38 – 10:39
Part 3: The people and their reforming governor 11–13
Lists of people and officials 11:1 – 12:26
The dedication of the new walls; at last Jerusalem can be defended! 12:27–43
Nehemiah's reforms 12:44 – 13:31

Time-span and setting
Nehemiah returned to Jerusalem in 445 BC and was governor for twelve years, to 433 BC. The way this story ties in with the book of Ezra and his returning group is not always easy to sort out. Nehemiah left a highly-developed Persian royal court and came to a city that had begun to be rebuilt, but with much still in chaos. The prophet Malachi's ministry was perhaps at about this time.

Time of writing
There are close links with the books of Chronicles and with Ezra, which suggest a date around 400 BC, but the heart of the book seems to be Nehemiah's diary.

Important events
Nehemiah's return to Jerusalem 2
The finishing of the walls 6

Famous passages
Nehemiah's prayer 1
The people's great prayer of confession 9

Message and meaning
Nehemiah, a man of action, lifted the spirits of a despondent people and gave them both spiritual and practical leadership, so that they completed a difficult task against fierce opposition. He was also a man of prayer, utterly dependent on God and highly efficient. Under him, and with Ezra's specialist help, the Jews' religious life was renewed.

□ ESTHER
The story
Esther, a beautiful Jewish girl, becomes queen to the Persian Emperor Ahasuerus (Xerxes). By a diplomatic stratagem, worked out with the help of her guardian, Mordecai, she thwarts a plot to have all the Jews in the Persian Empire exterminated. In the process, Haman, prime minister and instigator of the plot, is executed, and Mordecai is promoted to high office.

The setting
The events take place in Susa, winter capital of the Persian Empire, during the years after most of the Jews had returned to Jerusalem from their exile in Babylon. Some Jews had stayed on in Persia, the empire that overthrew the Babylonians.

Theme
God is not mentioned in this book, and it is not a significantly religious story. But it is an example of how the Jewish people have been preserved through times of great danger. The Jews still read this story during the Festival of Purim.

THE WISDOM BOOKS
The books of Job, Proverbs and Ecclesiastes are collectively known as books of Wisdom. The same sort of writing appears elsewhere in the Old Testament, especially in some of the Psalms. It is found also in the literature of some of Israel's neighbours.

King Solomon had a great reputation for wisdom, and his name is linked to the wisdom of Proverbs and Ecclesiastes, much as King David's is to the poetry of the Psalms.

The three Wisdom books are very different from each other in subject. Job is a great poem about the meaning of suffering; Ecclesiastes reflects on life's apparent meaninglessness; Proverbs is a series of sayings about how to behave in everyday life.

And yet these books have many features in common. Each is concerned with behaviour and everyday life. God is all-important, and in these books we see him in the home and at work, rather than in the temple.

At the centre of the Wisdom books is the belief that God has so ordered life that we find wisdom when we respect him and follow his laws.

□ JOB
This book – a wonderful dramatic poem – deals with the age-old problem of suffering. It tells of a good man, Job, who lost everything but still believed in God.

Contents
Prologue: Satan is allowed to test Job, and Job meets with disaster, chapters 1–2
Part 1: Job's discussion with his three friends 3–31
Job complains against God 3
Job's friends tell him he must deserve his suffering, but Job denies this; he questions God 4–14
Job and his friends argue about whether wicked people prosper 15–21
The friends repeat their condemnation, but Job declares his innocence before God 22–31
Part 2: A bystander, Elihu, gives a false picture of a remote God 32–37
Part 3: God reveals his greatness to Job 38:1 – 42:6
God's power in creation 38–41
Job bows before God 42:1–6
Epilogue: Job is blessed once again 42:7–16 (the prologue and

the epilogue are the only parts not in poetry)

Time of writing
Quite unknown. There is nothing to suggest when the book was written or by whom, although it depicts a 'patriarchal' life-style.

Famous passages
The hymn in praise of wisdom 28
Job's trust in God's goodness (19:25): 'I know that my Redeemer lives . . .'

Message
Job's story raises a thorny problem. If God is just, why do good people suffer? Job is convinced that he is not suffering for any sin, but he cannot find God to argue his case before him. Then God reveals himself, and Job is satisfied – not by arguments but by meeting God himself in all his power and wisdom.

□ THE PSALMS
A collection of 150 hymns, prayers and poems expressing every kind of emotion. What unites them is deep faith in and love for God. After the exile the Psalms became Israel's hymn-book and prayer-book, and Christians, too, still use them in this way.

Contents
The Psalms are grouped into five books, each of which closes with words of praise (see the end of Psalms 41, 72, 89, 106, and the whole of Psalm 150).

But perhaps it is more helpful to group them under types of psalm. Among the largest such groupings are:
hymns in praise of God
community laments
royal psalms (linked to some occasion in the king's life)
personal thanksgivings and laments

Time-span
Collections of psalms were being made in King David's time and perhaps earlier. This process went on through much of Israel's history, though some think it came to a peak at the time when the Jews came home from exile in Babylon and rebuilt the temple.

Setting
Many psalms were used during worship in the temple. But others plainly stem from times of exile. Some express the faith of all Israel, but others are highly individual and deeply personal.

Who wrote them?
Many different people. Seventy-three of them are linked by traditional titles to King David, some being connected to particular episodes in his life.

Plainly King David's love for music and worship made him the first patron of Israel's psalms.

Favourite psalms
Everyone has a favourite psalm. Among the most widely known are:
'The heavens declare the glory of God' 19
'The Lord is my shepherd' 23
'God is our refuge and strength' 46
A plea for forgiveness 51
'Come, let us praise the Lord' 95
A psalm of God's goodness 103
God our Protector 121
'Lord, you have searched me and you know me' 139

Message
The range is tremendous – from the utmost joy to the deepest despair. The common message is that in every area of life God is present. The most searching realism about human experience is joined to an unshakeable faith in God's love. There can be few people who do not find their own feelings mirrored somewhere in the Psalms.

☐ **PROVERBS**
A collection of sayings from Israel's Wisdom teachers. The important thing is to find and to follow God-centred wisdom, and to apply it to practical everyday living.

Contents
Part 1: In praise of wisdom, chapters 1–9
Part 2: Wise sayings 10–29
Proverbs of Solomon 10:1 – 22:16
Thirty wise sayings 22:17 – 24:21
Additional sayings 24:22–33
Hezekiah's collection of sayings 25–29
Part 3: A supplement 30–31
Agur's sayings 30
Sayings of King Lemuel's mother 31:1–9
The ideal wife 31:10–31

Time-span
Two Old Testament kings are referred to: Solomon, under whose patronage Wisdom may well first have flourished, and Hezekiah, who arranged for wise sayings to be collected. The process of collecting and arranging wise sayings probably continued well after these kings, so Proverbs introduces us to the Wisdom teaching of much of the Old Testament period. Many scholars find a link, in the 'thirty wise sayings', to a document from Egyptian wisdom teachers.

Famous verses
'The fear of the Lord is the beginning of wisdom' 1:7
'Trust in the Lord with all your heart' 3:5–6

Themes
Unlike the agonies of Job and the pessimism of Ecclesiastes, Proverbs is basically optimistic. In common with the teaching of Deuteronomy, the belief is that by following God's way a person will find blessing.
The setting is home and friendship, work and business, the life of king and subject.
And the topics are wisdom and folly, the righteous and the wicked, how to speak wisely, wealth and poverty, hopes and fears, joys and sorrows, anger, hard work and idleness.
The foundation of all wisdom is fear of (respect for) God.

☐ **ECCLESIASTES**
Ecclesiastes, like the book of Job, ponders a timeless question: why does life seem so meaningless? This is one of the Wisdom books.

The writer
Qoheleth, 'the Philosopher', is described as 'a king, David's son'. Whoever he was, Qoheleth looks

'Wisdom is calling out . . . At the entrance to the city, beside the gates, she calls,' says the writer of Proverbs. The books of Wisdom set out a way of life which is wise because it begins with respect for God.

back on a lifetime of experience and study.

Famous words
'There is a time for everything' 3:1–8

The theme
However hard people strive for wisdom, success or justice, the results will only be short-term and limited. To look for anything lasting in life is like 'chasing the wind'.
This pessimistic approach stems from Qoheleth's understanding of God. He believes in God but thinks we can never know what God's intentions are. The book reflects the poverty of a life limited to purely human concerns.
'Work hard and enjoy the fruits of your work,' says the Philosopher, 'because that is all there is.'
The presence of this book in the Bible shows that God has time for the person who finds faith difficult.

☐ **THE SONG OF SONGS**
The songs
A collection of six songs, in the form of a dialogue between a young man and his bride, on the theme of their love for one another. (Modern translations make it clear who is speaking at each point.) The setting is the countryside in springtime, and many rural images are used to express the great physical delight the couple find in one another.

The writer
Solomon is mentioned several

times, but the connection with him is not clear.

The meaning
The songs are about the wonder of physical love. Such love is God-given, and it is fitting that one book in the Bible should be devoted to it. Often the Song of Songs has been interpreted as a picture of love between Christ and the church, but there is nothing in the songs to suggest this.

THE PROPHETS
The last great section of the Old Testament is known as The Prophets. The section consists of seventeen books, sixteen of which are called by the name of the prophet whose words they contain (the exception is Lamentations). Isaiah, Jeremiah, Ezekiel and Daniel are known as 'major prophets', and the other twelve named books as the 'minor prophets'.

There had been prophets in Israel since early times, Moses being the first and greatest. Then, through the period of the Judges and early kings, prophets appear regularly in the story, some fleetingly, others – Elijah and Elisha particularly – dominating their times.

Apart from Moses, we know little of what these prophets taught. But during the eighth century first Amos and then Hosea delivered messages which were written down in books which survived. For more than 300 years a succession of such prophets appeared, covering the whole period up to the people's exile in Babylon, and on through that exile into the years after the Jews had returned home.

Did any or all of these prophets actually write the books? Or were they written by people who heard and remembered their words? We do not know for certain, though Jeremiah at least had some of his teaching written down. But the essence of prophecy is something *spoken*.

The prophets were men of God who acted as God's messengers, so taken up by his message that they often spoke as if on his behalf – 'I say to you . . .' They were conscious of being called by God (see especially Isaiah 6, Jeremiah 1, Ezekiel 1–3) and were inspired by his Spirit and his word. Their messages were often very vividly expressed, using pictures, acted parables, even visions.

The word 'prophecy' today implies foretelling the future, and the Old Testament prophets certainly did make accurate predictions – particularly about the coming Messiah. But the heart of the prophets' message was about the present, not the future. Their task was to call the nation back to God's ways and to faith in him alone. So it is important for us to understand a prophet's own times in order to grasp his meaning clearly. Once this is done, the message of the Old Testament prophets speaks powerfully to every age and culture.

☐ ISAIAH
A collection of prophecies relating to events which happened over a period of some 200 years. They help us to see some key events of Israel's history in the light of God who judges, saves and restores his people.

Contents
Part 1: The threat from Assyria, chapters 1–39
God's message for Judah and Jerusalem 1–5
The prophet's vision 6
The kingdom, present and future 7–12
Judgement on the nations 13–23
God's final judgement and victory 24–27
Promises of future judgements, with blessing to follow 28–35
The contemporary crisis 36–39 (this is almost the same as 2 Kings 18–20)
Part 2: Promises to the exiles in Babylon 40–55
On the brink of freedom 40–48
God's servant and the redemption he brings 49–55
Part 3: The returned exiles 56–66
A call to Israel to repent and be restored 56–59
Glory to come 60–62
Edom will be judged 63:1–6
A prayer for God's people 63:7 – 64:12
New heavens and a new earth 65–66

The Prophet
Isaiah prophesied for over forty years in Jerusalem. Called to be a prophet in the year that King Uzziah died (see chapter 6), his ministry continued through the years of Jotham and Ahaz on into Hezekiah's reign. He was able to make kings listen to his prophecies.

Isaiah attracted a group of 'disciples' (8:16), and some think that the prophecies directed to exiles in Babylon and returned exiles in Jerusalem (40–66) were delivered by Isaiah's successors in the tradition he established. Whether or not this is so, the message of the prophecies and the vision of God are consistent throughout the book.

Time-span and setting
Isaiah was active in the last decades of the eighth century BC and perhaps on into the beginning of the seventh. Amos had prophesied in the northern kingdom in the years before Isaiah, and Hosea was active in

Samaria during Isaiah's early years. Throughout much of this time Judah was under threat from the Assyrians, and in Hezekiah's reign Jerusalem nearly fell. Then, in 586 BC, Jerusalem did fall to the Babylonians and most of its people were taken into exile: chapters 40–55 refer to this time. After some years the exiles returned and began to re-establish the nation; the final chapters probably relate to this period.

Famous passages
Isaiah's vision and God's call 6
'Immanuel' 7:13–16
'To us a child is born' 9:2–7
The coming king: the Branch from Jesse 11:2–9
'We have a strong city' 26:1–9
'The desert will rejoice . . .': God's Highway 35
'Comfort, comfort my people': the mighty God 40:1–31
'The servant of the Lord' 42:1–4, 49:1–6, 50:4–9; 'a man of sorrows' 52:13 – 53:12
The welcome messenger 52:7–12
'Come, all you who are thirsty . . .' God's free invitation 55
Messiah's deliverance: 'good news to the poor . . .' 61:1–4
New heavens and a new earth 65:17–25

Main themes
Isaiah's great vision of God (chapter 6) contains the seed of the whole message of the book. The focal point is the majesty of God, 'the Holy One'. The nation must depend on him alone. The prophet must warn of God's judgement on all who turn from God. But God loves to forgive, and the book is full of promises about the coming Messiah and future restoration.

☐ JEREMIAH
Jeremiah's prophesies belong to the reigns of Judah's last five kings: the events that led up to the fall of Jerusalem to King Nebuchadnezzar of Babylon. A sensitive man, Jeremiah hated having to prophesy God's judgement. But all that he said came true.

Contents
Prologue: Jeremiah's call to be a prophet, chapter 1
Part 1: Prophecies to Jerusalem and Judah 2:1 – 25:14
In the time of Josiah 2–6
In the time of Jehoiakim 7–20
In the time of Zedekiah 21:1 – 25:14
Part 2: Jeremiah's life and times, and God's promises 26–45
Some of Jeremiah's trials 26–28
Letters to the exiles in Babylon

and to Shemaiah 29
The promise of return from exile and a new covenant 30–31
Hope for the future 32–33
More events from Jeremiah's life 34–45
Part 3: God will judge the nations 46–51 (also 25:15–38)
Epilogue: The fall of Jerusalem 52 (NB. The chapters in the book do not follow the order in which events happened.)

The prophet
Jeremiah was born into a priestly family in Anathoth, near Jerusalem. He was called to be a prophet in 627 BC. His ministry began during good times for Judah, in Josiah's reign. But then disaster followed disaster as Babylon's power grew and Judah's kings foolishly sided with Egypt. Jerusalem fell, and Jeremiah was taken to Egypt with a group which fled the country. His consistent message that God would judge the people brought him great unpopularity and inward turmoil. One constant friend was Baruch, who wrote down many of the prophecies. Jeremiah's contemporaries included Zephaniah and Ezekiel, who was with the first group of exiles in Babylon.

The prophecies come in many different forms: some in poetry, some in prose; some using allegory, some acted parables. All are vivid and memorable.

Famous passages
Jeremiah's call 1:1–19
'Blessed is the man . . .' 17:5–8
The deceitful human heart 17:9
Jeremiah's complaint 20:7–18
The false and the true prophet 23:15–32
The new covenant 31:31–34

Main themes
The chief message is one of coming judgement: it is no use claiming God's promises of protection while continuing in sin and idolatry. Jeremiah consistently taught that Jerusalem would fall. But there is also hope for the future, both in return from exile and in a new covenant which God will write in the hearts and minds of his people. More than any other prophet, Jeremiah is concerned with personal faith and repentance. His own prayers reveal his personality more fully than the other prophets.

☐ LAMENTATIONS
The poems
The book of Lamentations consists of five poems, author unknown. The first four are written as

acrostics based on the letters of the Hebrew alphabet. They express the people's anguish at the destruction of Jerusalem by the Babylonians. Their writer seems to have witnessed the city's fall in 586 BC and to be one of those who stayed on in poverty and ruin when the exiles had gone to Babylon.

Their theme
The poems are laments. It is bad enough that Jerusalem has fallen and its people have suffered. Worse still is the reason: that God has given up his people and handed them over to suffering because of their sin. Yet there is still a ray of hope, in 3:21–27, when the writer puts his faith in God's unfailing mercy.

☐ EZEKIEL
The visions and prophecies of the prophet Ezekiel in exile in Babylon, some time after 597 BC.

Contents
Prologue: Ezekiel's vision of God and his call to be a prophet, chapters 1–3
Part 1: Prophecies concerning Jerusalem 4–24
An acted parable of Jerusalem's fall 4–5
The end has come 6–7
Jerusalem's guilt 8–1
Parables, allegories and prophecies 12–17
Individual responsibility 18
Israel's rebellion 19:1 – 20:44
Fire and sword 20:45 – 21:32
Israel's doom and Jerusalem's destruction 22–24
Part 2: Prophecies against other nations 25–32
Part 3: Hope for the future 33–39
The prophet as a watchman 33:1–20
The exiles hear of Jerusalem's fall 33:21–33
The sins of rulers and of people 34
Against Edom 35
Promises of return and of a new heart 36
The valley of dry bones 37
Against Gog 38–39
Part 4: A vision of a new temple 40–48
Plans for the temple building and worship 40–42
The Lord's glory returns to the temple 43:1–12
Rules for temple and priesthood 43:13 – 44:31
Rules for the land, the prince and the festivals 45–46
A stream flowing from the sanctuary 47:1–12
The land and the tribes 47:13 – 48:35

Time-span and setting

Ezekiel gives us a number of precise dates in his book. His call came in 592 BC, five years after his exile to Babylon. He was a younger contemporary of Jeremiah, though living in Babylon not Jerusalem. His prophecies continued after Jerusalem had fallen (586 BC) and more Jewish exiles had come to Babylon. There is one puzzle: although he was exiled in Babylon, many of Ezekiel's prophecies concern Jerusalem and show detailed knowledge of events there. This was probably a spiritual gift of second sight, though he may also have visited the city during this period.

The prophet

Ezekiel was taken captive to Babylon with King Jehoiachin and the first group of exiles (all from leading families in Judah) in 597 BC. He belonged to a family of priests, though exiled too young to become a priest himself, and he therefore had a special interest in details of worship and ritual purity. He was also given to visions and trances, and God's messages really took possession of him. He communicated these through acted parables, allegories and reports of his visions.

Famous passages

Ezekiel's call and his vision of God's glory 1–3
Personal responsibility: 'the soul who sins will die' 18
The prophet as a watchman 33:1–20
God as shepherd of his people 34:11–16
A new heart 36:22–32
The valley of dry bones 37
The life-giving river which flows from the temple 47:1–12

Main themes

The book opens with a mighty vision of God on the plains of Babylon. Many of Ezekiel's messages denounce sin and proclaim God as judge. His lofty view of God's glory makes impurity and idolatry totally unacceptable. He knows that there is no hope for Jerusalem and predicts its fall, which duly happened in 586 BC. Yet once the city has been destroyed his prophecies begin to show a strong note of hope. God will show his greatness by bringing the people back, giving them a new heart and new worship. Ezekiel's prophecies often end with the words '. . . that they may know that I am the Lord.'

VISIONS OF THE FUTURE

During the time between the end of the Old Testament and the beginning of the New, a kind of visionary literature known as 'apocalyptic' (from a Greek word meaning 'uncovering') was common among the Jews. Times were very hard and these writings were intended to encourage God's people with the assurance of God's control of history and the reality of his final victory. They use visions full of symbols and unusual images.

Visions of this kind appear occasionally in the Old Testament prophets. Ezekiel used them, especially in the vision of Gog and Magog. The second part of Daniel is in this style. So too is part of Zechariah. In the New Testament, the book of Revelation is an 'Apocalypse', and the writer takes up and re-uses many symbols from Ezekiel, Daniel and Zechariah. For him, however, there was a major change: with the coming of Christ the new age had already begun.

It is sometimes difficult to understand these visions. They all refer to events and people with whom their original readers would be familiar – but they are written in a coded language, so that only the faithful (and not their persecutors) would understand them. When they describe strange animals and grotesque human figures we need to remember that these were not meant to be understood in a matter-of-fact way. They are all colourful symbols, depicting the way the powers of evil can attack God's people, and showing how God will finally overcome them.

☐ DANIEL

The book begins with stories about Daniel. He was taken into exile in Babylon while still a boy, and triumphed by sheer courage and faithfulness to God. The second half contains visions of the future, and a memorable prayer.

Contents

Part 1: Daniel in Babylon, chapters 1–6
Daniel and friends at Nebuchadnezzar's court 1
Nebuchadnezzar's dream 2
The fiery furnace 3
Nebuchadnezzar's madness 4
Belshazzar's feast 5
Daniel escapes the lions 6
Part 2: Daniel's visions and his prayer 7–12
Visions of four empires 7–8
Daniel's prayer, and an answer 9
Visions of future conflict 10–11
The time of the end 12
(One section of the book, 2:4–7:28, is in Aramaic, the international language of the time. The rest is in Hebrew.)

The setting

Daniel lived during the sixth century BC and the visions are set during his lifetime in Babylonia. However, there is so much detail about the second century BC that many people believe that the book of Daniel reached its final form at the very end of the Old Testament period, during the time when the Seleucid king Antiochus IV Epiphanes was ruling over Judea (about 165 BC). The vision of the four empires builds to a climax that seems to describe this king's oppressive reign. Courage was needed to stay true to God, and the stories of Daniel's courage during a time of trial would inspire later generations too.

Famous passages and events

The fiery furnace 3
Belshazzar's feast 5
Daniel escapes the lions 6
Daniel's prayer 9:1–19

The message

The stories of Daniel are a lasting inspiration to all who face persecution for their faith in God. Daniel's uncompromising courage and faith were completely vindicated by God. The visions of the future show God's ultimate victory.

☐ HOSEA

It was Hosea's own experience of love and suffering, when his wife left him for another man, which enabled him to express in this beautiful book God's love for Israel and his sadness at the

people's rejection.
Contents
Part 1: Hosea's sorrow for his wife, and God's for Israel, chapters 1 – 3
Hosea's wife and children 1 – 2:1
Unfaithful Israel 2:2 – 23
Hosea gets his wife back 3
Part 2: God loves Israel but will judge her 4 – 13
Epilogue: A promise of restoration if Israel repents 14
Time-span and setting
Hosea overlapped with the first years of Isaiah. He came from the northern kingdom of Israel. His ministry began during the reign of the last important king of Israel, Jeroboam II, and continued through twenty years of rapid decline when six kings came and went before Israel's capital, Samaria, finally fell to the Assyrians in 721 BC.
The prophet
Hosea was a man of deep sensitivity, whose sad personal experience increased his compassion. His prophecies are mainly about judgement, but they are expressed in terms of enduring love and concern.
Famous passages
God's love for Israel 11:1 – 4
God's promise of blessing 14:4 – 9
The message
The people were turning back to the Canaanite fertility religion of the Baals (nature gods). The corruption of Israel's religious and civil life made the nation's overthrow inevitable. The prophet voices God's deep and intimate love for unfaithful Israel, his longing for the people to return to him and enjoy his blessing.

☐ JOEL
A ruinous plague of locusts is seen as a sign of the coming final 'day of the Lord' when God's judgement will be more devastating still. Joel calls the nation to repent, and looks forward to a time of rich blessing.
Contents
A plague of locusts, chapter 1
The day of the Lord; a call to repent 2:1 – 17
Future fertility; the universal gift of the Spirit 2:18 – 32
Against the nations 3
Time of writing
Nothing is known about Joel or when he wrote. The only indication comes in 3:2, which speaks of Israel scattered among the nations, and so suggests a time after the Jews were exiled to Babylon.
Famous passage
'I will pour out my Spirit on all

people . . .' 2:28 – 29
Message
Joel calls for a time of national repentance, not just because of the warning 'sign' of the locusts but because God will judge unrepented sin.
The passage about God's Spirit being poured out on everyone was quoted by the apostle Peter to explain the events of the Day of Pentecost.

☐ AMOS
The prophet's chief concern in a time of prosperity and corruption was for social justice – a theme taken up again and again by the prophets.
Contents
Prophecies against other nations, chapters 1:1 – 2:5
Prophecies against Israel 2:6 – 6:14
Five visions 7:1 – 9:10
A promise of restoration 9:11 – 15
Setting
Amos prophesied in the northern kingdom of Israel in the eighth century BC, probably just before Hosea and a few years before Isaiah. They were prosperous days for Israel, with Jeroboam II on the throne and enemies defeated. But Amos saw the seeds of the decline which was soon to begin.
The prophet
Amos was a country shepherd who burned with a message from God. He travelled from Tekoa in southern Judah to the northern kingdom of Israel, with its shrines at Bethel and Gilgal. His prophecies were totally uncompromising in their exposure of injustice and hypocrisy.
Famous passage
'Let justice flow . . .' 5:21 – 24
Message
Amos was adept at exposing the people's comfortable illusions. As they listened to him denouncing the sins of other nations, they would not have expected to hear 'The people of *Israel* have sinned . . .' And their hopes for a future 'day of the Lord' were confounded when the prophet foresaw a day of darkness rather than light. There could be no security when wealth was for the few and the many were denied justice. This was not God's way.

☐ OBADIAH
The shortest book in the Old Testament: a prophecy against the Edomites. This nation, who lived to the south-east of Judah in the area where the city of Petra was later built, had taken advantage of

Jerusalem's misfortune and plundered it at the time when it fell to the Babylonians (586 BC).

☐ JONAH
The story of God's most reluctant messenger, Jonah, and the lesson he had to learn: that God's mercy is not restricted to Israel.
The story
A prophet named Jonah is called by God to prophesy in Nineveh, capital of the enemy, Assyria. He tries to avoid this call, but God prevents his escape (this is where the great fish comes in!). When Jonah prophesies in Nineveh, the inhabitants repent and are spared. This irks the prophet, who sits in contemplation under a shady plant. The plant withers in the sun and Jonah is sorry for it. God points out that his compassion would be better directed towards the Ninevites.
Time of writing
This is hard to know. It is probably a story *about* Jonah rather than *by* him, so the date of the Jonah mentioned in 2 Kings 14:25 may not be relevant. Equally, it may have been written after the decline of the Assyrians, during a later generation, using the events of earlier times as an object lesson.
The message
What Jonah resisted so strongly was the idea of God's mercy reaching out beyond Israel, particularly to that nation's enemies. The central point of this riveting little story is that salvation is ultimately for the whole world. Israel's special calling is not simply for their own sake, but to be 'a light to the nations'.

☐ MICAH
Micah is the fourth of the great eighth-century prophets, alongside Amos, Hosea and Isaiah. As a hill-country farmer, he knew the injustices of social life from experience.
Contents
The sin of Judah and Israel, chapters 1 – 3
Restoration and peace 4 – 5
What God requires 6
Darkness and light 7
Time-scale and setting
Micah prophesied at much the same time as Hosea (in Israel) and Isaiah (in Judah). But his messages were to both kingdoms, though Israel and its capital, Samaria, fell to the Assyrians during his ministry. The Assyrians also attacked Judah at this time, though Micah only refers to this briefly.

Famous passages
God's reign of peace 4:1–4 (this also appears in Isaiah 2:1–4)
A king from Bethlehem 5:2–4
What God requires 6:6–8

Main themes
Like several other prophets, Micah is repelled by sacrifices and worship which are not matched by just dealing and real spirituality. His central concerns are for social justice and true religion. But he looks on to a future time of peace and blessing from God.

☐ NAHUM
This is a poem celebrating the decline and then the fall of Nineveh, capital of the cruel and powerful Assyrians. It was probably written around the time of that city's overthrow by the Babylonians and Medes in 612 BC. This is one of the few prophetic books not to include a call to repentance. Its deeper message is that God is Lord of the nations and of world history, and that national power and pride are not the ultimate reasons for what happens in politics and war.

☐ HABAKKUK
This prophet tackles a question which has troubled people throughout history. How can God allow wicked people to prosper? Specifically, how is it that the rapacious Babylonians (or 'Chaldeans') are so much stronger than other, less evil peoples?

Contents
Why do evil people prosper? chapter 1
God's answer 2
The prophet's psalm of praise 3

Time of writing
The content of the book shows that it stems from a time between the rise of Babylon to dominance – overthrowing Assyria in 612 BC and defeating Egypt at the Battle of Carchemish in 605 BC – and the first conquest of Jerusalem in 597 BC. So Habakkuk was Jeremiah's contemporary, though we know nothing else about him.

Famous passages
Living by faith 2:4 (quoted at a key point by Paul the apostle, Romans 1:17)
The supreme God: 'The Lord is in his holy Temple; let everyone on earth be silent in his presence' 2:20

Meaning
The prophet's question is real and important; it is similar to Job's problem, or that in Psalm 73. The answer is not an intellectual, philosophical one, but simply the

assurance that constant faith will never be disappointed, because God is in control and he can be trusted.

☐ ZEPHANIAH
Zephaniah foresees only doom for Jerusalem, because of the people's disobedience. But, like his predecessor Isaiah, he believes a purified remnant of the nation will survive to inherit a great future.

Contents
The day of judgement, chapters 1:1 – 2:3
Doom for the nations 2:4–15
Hope for the remnant 3:1–13
A song of joy 3:14–20

Setting
This prophet was at work during Jeremiah's early years. These prophecies probably date from the early part of King Josiah's reign, before that king's great religious reforms took place.

Message
Zephaniah focuses on a question that several prophets ask. How do prophecies of judgement and destruction for Israel fit in with messages of hope for the longer future? The answer is that judgement will purify the people, burning away their pride and complacency. Those remaining will be 'the meek and humble who trust in the name of the Lord' (3:12).

☐ HAGGAI
The last three Old Testament prophets worked in the time just after some of the Jews had returned from exile in Babylon. Like Zechariah, Haggai urged the people to get on and rebuild the temple.

Contents
A summons to rebuild the templ is obeyed, chapter 1
The splendour of the temple 2:1–9
God's blessing on the obedient 2:10–19
A word for governor, Zerubbabel 2:20–23

Time of writing
Haggai gives precise dates. He prophesied in 520 BC. He and Zechariah are mentioned in Ezra 5:1–2 and 6:14 as urging the people to rebuild. The new temple was actually finished in 516 BC.

Famous words
The danger of economic inflation 1:6

Message
Under governor Zerubbabel the returned exiles had made a start on the new temple, but got discouraged and gave up. Instead

they built good homes for themselves. Haggai challenges such false priorities. Unlike the experience of most prophets, his words found a response and the people did what he said. His universal importance is in showing that true security is found only when we put God's wishes first.

☐ ZECHARIAH
The visionary Zechariah worked alongside Haggai. His messages come in the form of vivid and arresting pictures.

Contents
Part 1: A new age is beginning, chapters 1–8
Introduction 1:1–6
Eight visions 1:7 – 8:23
Part 2: Israel and the nations 9–14
First message 9–11
Second message 12–14

Time-span and setting
Zechariah's prophecies about Jerusalem and rebuilding the temple continue for longer than Haggai's – from 520 to 518 BC. The second part of the book, chapters 9–14, is in many ways very different from the first part; some think it may be by a different author, and from a later time. What links these messages to chapters 1–8 (and also to Malachi) is their subject, the new age of blessing.

Famous verses
Victory through God's Spirit 4:6
The king is coming! 9:9

Meaning
The small community of returned Jewish exiles in Jerusalem plainly felt a keen sense of new beginnings. Things might still be hard, but they were following God's guidance. Zechariah's thought moves from this new start to a new age, not only for Jerusalem but for the whole world. Mixed in with prophecies of this new age, we also find messages about a 'Messiah', a king of love and justice who will be sent by God. This emphasis explains why Zechariah is often quoted in the New Testament, for the early Christians believed that this Messiah was Jesus.

☐ MALACHI
Malachi challenges the people about their relationship and obedience to God.

Contents
God's love for Israel, chapter 1:1–5
Worthless sacrifices 1:6 – 2:9
Broken promises 2:10–16
God's judgement 2:17 – 3:5
The payment of tithes 3:6–12
God's promise of mercy 3:13 – 4:6

Setting
It is generally thought that Malachi (the name means 'my messenger') prophesied some eighty years after Haggai and Zechariah, probably a little before Nehemiah became governor of Jerusalem, about the middle of the fifth century BC. They were difficult times, and the people had begun to relax their obedience to God's laws.

Famous verses
God's messenger 3:1
'I will open the windows of heaven . . .' 3:10
'The sun of righteousness will rise . . .' 4:2

Message
Malachi believed that the only way to know God's blessing was to keep his commandments wholeheartedly. It was taking a long time for the returned exiles to get national life going again, and they were growing disheartened. But it was their own fault, for they were paying more attention to their own inclinations than to God's will. The prophet challenged them to get their priorities right and encouraged them with the promise of God's future blessing.

NEW TESTAMENT HISTORY
THE FOUR GOSPELS
The Gospels are more than simply biographies of Jesus. They contain very little on his early years, and a great deal on the last week of his life and what happened in the days after his death. The word 'gospel' (used in Mark 1:1) means 'good news', and the Gospels concentrate on the good news of what Jesus brought to the world – teaching and healing, above all freedom through his death and resurrection.

For thirty years after Jesus died and rose, the apostles declared the good news about him by word of mouth. Meanwhile written records of his sayings and actions were being collected. Eventually these records and the word-of-mouth memories about Jesus in different centres of Christianity were brought together to make the four Gospels. These became an essential back-up to the apostles' preaching, steadily increasing in importance as time passed and eyewitnesses of Jesus' life became fewer.

Any account of a person's life is bound to be selective. And the particular concerns of the Gospel writers are clearly reflected in the selections they make. The first three Gospels have a considerable amount of material in common, whereas John's Gospel is rather different in its approach. But we can be very thankful that there are *four* Gospels, giving us a much more comprehensive picture of Jesus than if there had been only one. Each portrait has something special and important to bring to the whole.

□ MATTHEW
This has been called the 'Jewish Gospel', because it shows particular interest in the concerns of Jewish Christians. More than in the other Gospels, the stress is on Old Testament prophecies fulfilled in Jesus, who is the Messiah long expected by the Jews.

Contents
Prologue: Jesus' family tree, and his birth, chapters 1–2
Part 1: A new way of living 3–7
Jesus' baptism by John, and his temptations 3 – 4:11
Jesus begins his work 4:12–25
The Sermon on the Mount 5–7
Part 2: Being disciples 8–10
Healing and teaching 8 – 9:34
The apostles' mission 9:35 – 10:42
Part 3: The kingdom of heaven 11 – 13:52
Jesus' reply to John the Baptist's messengers 11:1–19
Teaching, and disputes with religious leaders 11:20 – 12:50
Parables of the kingdom 13:1–52
Part 4: The church, the people of Jesus 13:53 – 18:35
Teaching and miracles 13:53 – 16:12
Peter's declaration 16:13–28
The transfiguration and what follows 17
Relationships among Jesus' disciples 18
Part 5: Moving towards the crisis 19–25
Teaching, and a healing 19–20
Jesus in Jerusalem 21–22
Jesus warns the Pharisees 23
Things that will happen soon 24
Parables about judgement 25
Conclusion: The last days 26–28
The Last Supper 26:1–30
Jesus' arrest and trials 26:31 – 27:26
Jesus is crucified 27:27–56
Jesus' burial and resurrection 27:57 – 28:15
The great commission 28:16–20

Time of writing
Matthew is not thought to be the earliest Gospel: like Luke, the writer seems to use material from Mark and from other common sources. The likely date is much discussed, but is probably between AD 60 and AD 80. Early second-century Christians claimed that the writer was Matthew, a tax-collector whom Jesus called to be an apostle.

Great events
Jesus' birth 1
Jesus' baptism 3
The temptation of Jesus 4
The transfiguration 17
Jesus' entry into Jerusalem 21
Trials and crucifixion 26–27
Jesus' resurrection 28

Famous passages
Sermon on the Mount 5–7
The Beatitudes 5:3–12
Love your enemies 5:43–48
The Lord's Prayer 6:9–13
First things first 6:25–34
Ask, seek, knock 7:7–11
The narrow gate 7:13–14
The two houses 7:24–27
'Come to me and rest' 11:28–30
The parable of the sower 13
Parables of God's kingdom 13
Peter's great declaration 16:13–19
The parable of the bridesmaids 25
The parable of the last judgement 25:31–46
The great commission 28:16–20

Main themes

It is fitting that this Gospel should be placed first, because more than the others it makes the link between Old Testament and New. It portrays Jesus as the Messiah, the 'anointed one' foretold by the prophets. This may be one reason why this Gospel has always been so popular. Another is that it has a clear and organized structure, focussing on the central themes of Jesus' teaching. A distinctive theme is the church, the great community of disciples Jesus called into being.

□ MARK

Almost certainly the earliest of the Gospels to be written, Mark is short, fast-moving and action-packed. It may well have been written to help Christians convince others of the truth about Jesus.

Contents

Part 1: The events of Jesus' ministry, chapters 1 – 8:26
Preparation 1:1–13
Jesus begins to teach and heal in Galilee 1:14 – 3:6
Further ministry in Galilee 3:7 – 6:13
Jesus goes outside Galilee 6:14 – 8:26
Part 2: Jerusalem and the last days 8:27 – 16:8
Preparing for suffering and death 8:27 – 10:52
Jesus teaches in Jerusalem 11–13
Jesus is anointed; the Last Supper 14:1–31
Jesus' arrest and trials 14:32 – 15:15
Jesus is crucified 15:16–41
Jesus' burial and resurrection 15:42 – 16:8
An old ending: 16:9–19 (This does not appear in early copies of the text, and must have been added later to make the end less abrupt.)

The writer and time of writing

Early traditions associate this Gospel with John Mark, a disciple who is mentioned in Acts. He was active from the early days of the church in Jerusalem. Tradition, underlined by the stories themselves, suggests that Mark's main source was the apostle Peter, and that the Gospel was written in Rome. Mark provided material for Matthew and Luke, and was probably written between AD 60 and AD 70.

Great events

John the Baptist prepares the way 1
Jesus' baptism and temptation 1
Choosing the twelve 3
Feeding the 5,000 6

The transfiguration 9
Jesus' triumphal entry 11
The last supper 14
Jesus' arrest, trial and death 14–15
The resurrection 16

Famous passages

The good news in a nutshell 1:14–15
'I will make you fishers of men' 1:16–20
Sins forgiven: the paralysed man 2:1–12
Choosing the twelve 3:13–19
'Who is the greatest?' 9:33–37
'Let the little children come . . .' 10:13–16
The rich young man 10:17–31
'A ransom for many' 10:42–45
Casting out the moneychangers 11:15–17
The greatest commandment 12:28–34

Main themes

Whereas Matthew's Gospel centres on Jesus as a teacher, Mark's shows him as a man of action. The Gospel is made up mainly of short sections, most of which narrate something Jesus *did*. The phrase 'and immediately . . .' is frequently used. The apostles are shown as very slow to understand who Jesus was (this may be a sign of Peter's influence on Mark). Jesus is keen to keep his role as Messiah secret from the people, who would misunderstand its meaning: he frequently uses the title 'Son of man', from Daniel's vision, to refer to himself. The Gospel moves swiftly from Peter's great declaration of faith in chapter 8 to Jesus' death and resurrection. A key passage is 'the Son of man (came) to give his life as a ransom for many' (10:45).

□ LUKE

The Gospel of Luke and the Acts of the Apostles are two parts of one work. Luke sets out to recount 'the full truth' (1:4) about Jesus' life and what followed, drawing on first-hand sources. His Gospel is written specifically for non-Jewish people.

Contents

Introduction, chapter 1:1–4
Part 1: John the Baptist and Jesus 1:5 – 4:13
Birth and childhood of John and Jesus 1:5 – 2:52
John the Baptist's work 3:1–20
Jesus' baptism, family tree and temptations 3:21 – 4:13
Part 2: Jesus in Galilee 4:14 – 9:50
In Nazareth and Capernaum 4:14–41
Jesus teaches, heals and calls

disciples 4:42 – 6:16
Teaching on discipleship 6:17–49
Jesus' miracles, teaching and way with people 7:1 – 9:17
Peter's declaration and the transfiguration 9:18–50
Part 3: On the way to Jerusalem 9:51 – 19:27
The journey begins 9:51–62
Jesus sends out seventy-two disciples 10:1–24
Teaching and controversy 10:25 – 11:54
Warning and reassurance 12:1 – 13:17
Mainly parables 13:18 – 18:14
Jesus with people 18:15 – 19:10
The parable of the gold coins 19:11–27
Part 4: Jesus in Jerusalem 19:28 – 23:56
Jesus enters the city and the temple 19:28–48
Disputes with religious leaders 20:1 – 21:4
Teaching on what is to come 21:5–38
Betrayal and Last Supper 22:1–38
Jesus' arrest and trials 22:39 – 23:25
Jesus is crucified and buried 23:26–49
Part 5: Jesus raised from death 24

The writer and his purpose

From quite early on the author of Luke and Acts was believed to be Luke, a Gentile doctor who travelled with the apostle Paul on many of his journeys (see under Acts). He wrote for a man called Theophilus (1:1). Acts ends with Paul in prison at Rome, and some have thought Luke and Acts were intended partly to prepare the ground for the apostle's defence in any trial, which would mean a date around AD 64. But this cannot be certain, and any date between about AD 60 and AD 85 is possible.

Great events

The angel's message and the birth of Jesus 1–2
Jesus' baptism and temptation 3–4
The transfiguration 9:28–36
Jesus' entry into Jerusalem 20:28–40
The last supper 22:14–20
Trial and crucifixion 22–23
Jesus' resurrection 24

Famous passages

The angel's message to Mary 1:26–38
Mary's song (the Magnificat) 1:46–55
Zechariah's song 1:68–79
The shepherds and the angels 2:8–20
Simeon's song (the Nunc Dimittis) 2:29–32
'The Spirit of the Lord is upon me':

Main themes

Luke's Gospel begins and ends in Jerusalem, and many of its best-known and most distinctive stories are set within Jesus' final journey to Jerusalem from Galilee. Then Acts begins in Jerusalem and ends in Rome. This crystallizes one of Luke's great themes: Jesus came first to the Jews, heirs of God's promise of salvation, but they rejected him and now salvation comes to the whole world.

This Gospel, the fullest and most rounded of the accounts of Jesus, also has other important themes. Jesus' salvation is for the most needy – the sick, the outcast, the prodigal. Jesus relates to individuals in a personal way; he is a man of prayer, full of the Holy Spirit.

Luke gives us many unique stories, among them the prodigal son, the good Samaritan, the Pharisee and the tax-collector, Zacchaeus . . .

☐ JOHN

John's Gospel is very different from the other three, giving its own special perspective on Jesus. The author's declared intention is to draw his readers to faith: he writes '. . . that you may believe that Jesus is the Messiah, the Son of God' (20:31).

Contents

Writer and time of writing

The probable writer of this Gospel describes himself as 'the disciple whom Jesus loved'. This disciple has long been held to be John the apostle. Since John's Gospel represents a source of information about Jesus independent of the other three, there is no reason to think it must be later. Some years ago this was not realized, and a time of writing around AD 90 or AD 100 was normally accepted. But any date from about AD 60 is now reckoned to be possible.

Great events

Famous passages

Main themes

Since the very beginning of time, John says in his opening words, Jesus has been the 'Word of God' – God's way of communicating with the world. The 'Word of God' is an idea with roots both in the Old Testament and in Greek thought, an interesting mixture which is typical of the Gospel. The writer wants to show the meaning of Jesus for Jews and for those familiar with Greek thought.

John sets his account of Jesus' life in the framework of seven 'signs' (miracles) and seven sayings (the 'I am' sayings of Jesus). His leading themes are the light, the life and the love that Jesus brings.

The differences between this Gospel and the others are partly the setting – the first three Gospels are mainly in Galilee, John mainly in Jerusalem – and partly the style of teaching. There are no parables in John (unless 'the good shepherd' is a parable) and Jesus engages in longer conversations and talks than we find in Matthew, Mark and Luke. Perhaps Jesus needed a distinct method of teaching for the people of Jerusalem. Certainly this Gospel has, over the centuries, achieved its writer's objective of helping people to believe that eternal life is to be found through believing in Jesus.

☐ ACTS

Luke's Acts of the Apostles completes New Testament history. It takes the story on from Jesus' ascension into heaven and the gift of the Holy Spirit at Pentecost, and tells how the Christian movement grew from a group of under two hundred to a great community stretched around the Roman

Empire. A key verse is 1:8: 'You will be witnesses . . . in Jerusalem, in all Judea and Samaria, and to the ends of the earth.'

Contents
Introduction: Waiting for the Spirit, chapter 1
Jesus is taken from the disciples 1:1–11
A replacement for Judas Iscariot 1:12–26
Part 1: The gospel in Jerusalem 2:1 – 8:3
The Day of Pentecost 2:1–42
A snapshot of the first believers 2:43–47
The witness of Peter and John 3:1 – 4:31
The life of the early church 4:32 – 6:7
Stephen's arrest, trial and killing 6:8 – 8:3
Part 2: The gospel spreads through Palestine 8:4 – 9:31
The gospel in Samaria 8:5–25
Philip and the Ethiopian chancellor 8:26–40
Saul's conversion and contact with church leaders 9
Part 3: Peter opens the way for the Gentile mission 9:32 – 12:34
Peter in Lydda and Joppa 9:32–43
Peter's vision and its results 10:1 – 11:18
Christians in Antioch 11:19–30
Herod persecutes the Christians 12:1–24
Part 4: Paul takes the gospel to the Roman Empire 13–28
The first journey: Paul and Barnabas 13–14
A council of Christians in Jerusalem 15:1–35
The second journey: Paul, Silas and Timothy 15:36 – 18:23
The third journey: Paul (and Luke?) 18:24 – 21:16
Paul's imprisonments in Jerusalem and Caesarea 21:17 – 26:32
Paul's voyage to Rome 27:1 – 28:15
Paul in Rome 28:16–31

Writer, time-span and setting
Luke the doctor, Paul's Gentile friend, wrote both Luke and Acts. Acts has some passages where the writer suddenly switches from speaking of 'them' to using 'we'. He was obviously present at the time, and a careful analysis of Paul's travelling-companions at these times points unmistakably to Luke. He is probably the only non-Jewish writer of the Bible. His history in the Acts of the Apostles takes us right into the details of Roman imperial administration, with the touch of an accurate historian. The events cover a period of a little over thirty years,

from the Day of Pentecost around AD 30 to Paul's imprisonment in Rome in about AD 61–63. The date of writing may be any time in the twenty years or so after that.

Great events
The ascension 1
The gift of the Holy Spirit at Pentecost 2
Stephen's defence and death 7
Saul (Paul) is converted 9
Peter's vision 10
The council at Jerusalem 15
Paul's arrest and trials 21–25
The voyage to Rome 27–28

Famous passages
The heart of Peter's great sermon 2:22–24
Snapshot of the first believers 2:43–47
The believers' shared life 4:32–35
Stephen's speech in his own defence 7:1–53
The church at Antioch 11:19–26
The jailer at Philippi 16:22–34
Paul in Athens 17:22–31
Paul's farewell to the elders at Ephesus 20:17–38
Paul's defence before Agrippa 26:1–29

Main themes
Acts describes the first years of Christian expansion and persecution.

A repeated theme is that Christianity presents no threat to Roman authority: every time there is trouble, it is caused by Jewish or other opponents of the Christians. Christianity is the true fulfilment of Judaism, and the Romans should see it as such.

Luke makes it very plain that the power which made Christian expansion possible is that of God's Holy Spirit. Humanly speaking, the central characters are Peter and Paul. It is also shown that the springboard for the mission to non-Jewish people was the church at Antioch, not Jerusalem. Luke's account brings out very clearly that the gospel of Jesus Christ has the power to change people's lives. Filled with his Spirit a group of ordinary men and women are able to 'turn the world upside down'.

THE LETTERS
☐ ROMANS
Of the twenty-one New Testament letters, thirteen are thought to be by Paul the apostle. They give a penetrating insight into the faith and life of the churches in the first years of their existence. Paul's letter to the Romans has been the most influential of all, having an immense impact on leaders of Christian thought down the centuries. It contains a reasoned statement of the gospel Paul preached.

Contents
Prologue: Greeting, prayer and introduction, chapter 1:1–15
Part 1: The good news of Jesus Christ 1:16 – 8:39
Brief statement of the theme 1:16–17
Mankind's need: everyone has sinned 1:18 – 3:20
God meets our need through faith in Jesus 3:21 – 4:25
Being justified by faith 5
Our new life in Jesus Christ 6–8
Part 2: God's plan for Israel 9–11
Part 3: The Christian way of life 12:1 – 15:13
The shared Christian life 12
Duties to the state and to other people 13
Questions of Christian conscience 14:1 – 15:13
Epilogue: Closing words and greetings 15:14 – 16:27
Paul's reasons for writing 15:14–33
Greetings and instructions 16:1–24
A closing prayer of praise 16:25–27

Time of writing and setting
Paul probably wrote this letter during a second visit to Corinth in Greece, around AD 57. He planned to visit the Christians in Rome, and may have written this statement of his beliefs to prepare for that meeting. But circumstances delayed his visit, and he finally arrived as a prisoner. His letter reveals a flourishing and well-established church in the capital city of the empire.

Famous passages
The power of the gospel 1:16–17
God's grace for our need 3:23–24
Justified through faith 5:1
Wages of sin and gift of life 6:23
The new life of freedom 8:1–2
Nothing can separate us from the love of God in Christ 8:35–39
A living sacrifice – the true offering 12:1–2
The encouragement of the Bible 15:4–6

The message
Paul unfolds the central message of the gospel step by step. Everyone has sinned and so we all need God to save us; Jesus died for everyone; through Jesus God puts us right with himself, as a free gift to be received by faith. This is the good news that has changed millions of lives throughout the world, and Paul's last section shows how in practice a person's life is made different through believing the gospel.

□ 1 CORINTHIANS
Paul had founded the church at Corinth. He was saddened to hear of division, disagreement and immoral behaviour. In this letter he answers their problems and questions one by one.

Contents
Introduction: Greeting and thanksgiving, chapter 1:1–9
Part 1: Divisions in the church 1:10 – 4:21
The wisdom of God 1:10 – 2:16
Building together on the one foundation 3
True servants of Jesus Christ 4
Part 2: Sexual morality; marriage and the single state 5–7
The danger of immorality among Christians 5
Christians should keep out of the law-courts 6:1–11
The right use of our bodies 6:12–20
A question about marriage 7
Part 3: Living in a pagan society 8:1 – 11:1
Should Christians eat food sacrificed to idols? 8
Paul's own practice 9
Following Christian conscience 10 – 11:1
Part 4: True Christian worship 11:2 – 14:40
Women should cover their heads in church 11:2–16
The Lord's Supper 11:17–34
Spiritual gifts in the Christian community 12
Love comes first 13
Using spiritual gifts in public worship 14
Part 5: Resurrection, Christ's and ours 15
Conclusion: Final instructions 16
The collection of money for fellow-Christians 16:1–4
Paul's future plans 16:5–12
Personal greetings and messages 16:13–24

Time and place of writing
Paul had been in Corinth for eighteen months during AD 50–51. But it was some time later, probably while he was going through a difficult period in Ephesus, that he received the news that provoked this letter. The date is between AD 54 and AD 57.

Famous passages
The message of Christ crucified 1:18, 23–25
We are God's building 3:10–15
'I have become all things to all men' 9:19–22
'This is my body . . .': the bread and the wine 11:23–25
'You are the body of Christ, each one a part . . .' 12:27–31
'If I speak in the tongues of men and of angels, but have not love . . .': love is the greatest gift 13:1–13
The truth of Christ's resurrection 15:20–21
'Death, where is your sting?''; victory over death 15:51–57

Main themes
The Corinthian Christians were an extremely mixed group, racially and socially: the city of Corinth lay at a junction of trade routes and all kinds lived there. As often happens in such places, morality was corrupt, and this affected some of the Christians. Others succumbed to a sense of pride in their spiritual wisdom. So Paul had to deal with the difficulties of ordinary, fallible people trying to live a new kind of life together – just like Christians ever since. He draws his principles for right living in every case from all that it means to be called to follow Jesus Christ.

□ 2 CORINTHIANS
This letter more than any other reveals the heart of the apostle Paul. He expresses his deep personal concern for the young churches, the hardships he had to pass through in his Christian service, and his sense of privilege in being called to work for Christ.

Contents
Introduction: Greetings and personal explanations, chapters 1:1 – 2:13
Greetings and thanksgiving 1:1–7
Paul's movements and plans 1:8 – 2:4; 2:12–13
How to deal with an offender 2:5–11
Part 1: The privilege of serving Jesus Christ 2:14 – 6:10
True spiritual service 2:14 – 4:15
Living in the light of eternity 4:16 – 5:10
Christ's ambassadors 5:11–21
The cost of Christian service 6:1–10
Part 2: A personal message to the Corinthians 6:11 – 7:16
An appeal to the church 6:11 – 7:1
Paul's encouragement at their response 7:2–16

Part 3: Giving to the Christians in Judea 8–9
Part 4: Paul's ministry as an apostle 10:1 – 13:10
Conclusion: Final instructions and the grace 13:11–14

Date and reasons for writing
Paul seems to have written this letter somewhere in Macedonia – the northern part of Greece whose capital was Philippi – perhaps a year or two after his first letter to the Corinthians. It seems that his appeals to the church had no effect, so he made another short visit and sent another letter. At last his friend Titus reported to him that the Corinthian Christians had taken his appeals to heart, and this letter is Paul's grateful response. But he still needed to restate his right to rebuke them where necessary, so he affirms his authority in chapters 10–13.

Famous passages
'The letter kills, but the Spirit gives life' 3:5–6
Growing more like Jesus 3:17–18
'If anyone is in Christ, he is a new creation' 5:17–21
Paul's hardships 6:4–10
'God loves a cheerful giver': Christian generosity 9:6–10
The grace 13:14

Main themes
The core of this letter, and what has made it so important for Christians, is Paul's teaching on the essentials of being a minister for Jesus Christ. This has nothing to do with calling people to keep a set of laws. Its effectiveness comes from the Holy Spirit, and its goal is that people should be reconciled to God through Christ. When this happens, men and women become new people (5:17), enabled by God to live a completely new life.

□ GALATIANS
This letter was written to oppose a specific, damaging error – the idea put about by some Jewish Christians that if a person is to be saved it is necessary to be circumcised and keep the Law of Moses. Paul saw this as a threat to the whole basis of the Christian gospel.

Contents
Introduction: Greetings; the only gospel, chapter 1:1–10
Part 1: Paul's authority as an apostle 1:11 – 2:14
Paul's early Christian experience and commissioning 1:11 – 2:10
A conflict with Peter 2:11–14
Part 2: Law or faith? 2:15 – 4:31
Living by faith 2:15–21
Reasons why we cannot be saved

by the law 3:1–14
The purpose of the law 3:15–25
Children of God through faith
3:26 – 4:7
An appeal to the Galatians 4:8–20
An allegory of freedom 4:21–31
Part 3: The freedom of the gospel
5:1 – 6:10
Faith and love 5:1–15
Spirit and law 5:16–26
Practical Christian living 6:1–10
*Postscript: An appeal in Paul's own
handwriting* 6:11–18
Time of writing
Paul may have written this letter
just before the council meeting in
Jerusalem which discussed its
central point; this gives a date
around AD 47 or 48 and makes
Galatians the earliest of Paul's
letters. But it is also possible that
the problem remained acute, and
that he wrote several years later,
closer to the date of his letter to
the Romans (covering a similar
theme) around AD 54 to 57. The
province of Galatia may refer to an
area in northern Turkey (this would
require the later date: Paul had not
been there in AD 48), or otherwise
to a much wider area including
cities known from Acts such as
Pisidian Antioch and Lystra.
Famous passages
Living by faith 2:19–21
All one in Christ Jesus 3:28
God sent his Son 4:4–5
Freedom! 5:1
The fruit of the Spirit 5:22–23
Message
Paul is extremely insistent that a
person does not need to keep the
Law of Moses to be saved. Why
such great emphasis? Because in
his death for us Christ has done all
that is needed to put us right with
God. Paul uses his apostolic
authority to denounce any
teaching that undermines faith
in Christ alone.

□ EPHESIANS
This letter has a lofty theme:
God's plan is 'to bring all creation
together . . . with Christ as head'
(1:10). The focus of this unity is to
be the Christian church, whose life
together is therefore of the highest
importance.
Contents
Introduction: chapter 1:1–2
Part 1: God's great plan of unity
1:3 – 3:21
The unity of creation and the
fullness of Christ 1:3–23
Life in Christ 2:1–10
Jews and Gentiles made one
2:11–22
Paul's role in announcing God's
plan 3:1–13
A prayer for knowledge of God's

love 3:14–21
Part 2: Christians' shared lives
4:1 – 6:20
Together as the body of Christ
4:1–16
Practical Christian living
4:17 – 5:20
Husbands and wives, children
and parents, slaves and masters
5:21 – 6:9
The armour of God 6:10–20
Postscript: Final greetings 6:21–24
Time of writing and the people addressed
Ephesians is one of the four letters
written while Paul was a prisoner
in Rome in the early sixties AD.
(The others are Philippians,
Colossians and Philemon.) It
was a circular letter addressed
to a group of churches around
Ephesus, in what is now western
Turkey.
Famous passages
God's great plan 1:9–12
Saved by God's grace, through
faith 2:8–10
Paul's prayer for love 3:14–21
Reaching the stature of Christ
4:12–16
High standard for marriage
5:25–33
'Put on the full armour of God'
6:10–17
Message
The central theme in Ephesians –
the unity of all things in Christ – is
unique in Paul's letters. Perhaps it
formed in his mind during his time
of imprisonment. He uses it to
show how vital every aspect of
Christian unity is – within the
church, between Jews and
Gentiles, in marriage and the
family, in working relationships.
Such unity is the means by which
God's universal plan of love is to
be achieved.

□ PHILIPPIANS
Paul's letter to the church at
Philippi is full of deep love and joy.
Contents
Greeting, thanksgiving and prayer,
chapter 1:1–11
Paul's experience, and his hopes
1:12–26
Living the Jesus way 1:27 – 2:18
Two of Paul's friends 2:19–30
Profit and loss 3
Instructions, and thanks for their
gift 4:1–20
Final greetings 4:21–23
Time of writing and the people addressed
The church at Philippi was the first
Paul founded after he crossed into
Europe. Luke – the doctor who
accompanied Paul and compiled
the Gospel and Acts – seems to
have had close connections with

the church in this strongly Roman
city in northern Greece. Paul's
letter is normally thought to be one
of the four written during his
imprisonment in Rome in the early
sixties AD, but some prefer a date
around AD 54, during a supposed
time in prison at Ephesus.
Famous passages
God completes what he begins
1:4–6
'To live is Christ' 1:20–24
The humility and greatness of
Jesus 2:5–11
Profit and loss 3:4–11
The goal and the prize 3:12–14
God's peace 4:4–7
'Whatever is true . . .' 4:8
Strong in Christ 4:11–13
Main themes
The particular reasons why Paul
wrote this letter were the gift the
Philippians sent him and his wish
to commend Epaphroditus to
them. But he used the opportunity
to express his love for these
Christians and his delight in their
progress. Although Paul sensed
that his own death might be near
the words 'joy' and 'rejoice' occur
again and again. The possibility of
death makes him take stock of
priorities and the things he counts
most important.

□ COLOSSIANS
The central subject is the
greatness and supremacy of
Jesus Christ, which affects
everything Paul writes about.
Contents
Greeting and thanksgiving,
chapter 1:1–8
The supremacy of Christ 1:9 –
2:10
Errors in the church 2:11–19
New life in Christ 2:20 – 4:6
Final greetings 4:7–18
Time of writing and the people addressed
Colossians is almost certainly one
of the four letters Paul wrote while
a prisoner in Rome in the early
sixties AD – together with
Ephesians, Philippians and
Philemon. He had never visited
Colossae, which lies some miles
inland from Ephesus in western
Turkey. But he heard news of the
church there from its founder,
Epaphras, who probably became
a Christian while Paul was in
Ephesus.
Famous passages
The greatness of Christ 1:15–20
'You have been raised with Christ'
3:1–4
'Whatever you do, it is Christ you
are serving' 3:23–24
Main themes
During his imprisonment at Rome

Paul's mind was clearly occupied with the greatness of Christ. It is the key theme of both Ephesians and Colossians. In this letter there is a particular reason why he concentrates on that subject. Epaphras had told him of a serious error among Christians at Colossae: they thought they possessed secret knowledge – a higher philosophy which undermined the place of Jesus as the only 'mediator' between people and God – and were becoming slaves to rules and regulations. Paul does not argue over detail: he provides the positive answer. Jesus Christ is all they need, to reconcile them to God and to guide their lives, for 'in Christ all the fullness of the deity lives in bodily form' (2:9).

□ 1 THESSALONIANS
The tone of Paul's first letter to the Christians at Thessalonica is one of tremendous encouragement. Paul is encouraged by their faith, and wants to encourage them still further.

Contents
Greeting, chapter 1:1
Paul encourages the Christians 1:2 – 3:13
Practical Christian living 4:1–12
Be ready for Christ to return 4:13 – 5:11
Final instructions and greetings 5:12–28

Time of writing, and the people addressed
Paul, Silas and Timothy visited Thessalonica, capital of Macedonia in northern Greece, during the second missionary journey. It was a short visit, because they were forced out by Jewish opposition. Paul heard nothing of those who had responded to his preaching and become Christians, until Timothy brought him good news while he was in Corinth, in AD 50 or 51. He wrote immediately. This is the earliest of Paul's letters, unless an early date is proposed for Galatians.

Famous passages
A new allegiance 1:9–10
Christ's promised return 4:15–18
The blessing 5:23–24

The message
The news that the Thessalonians had made such good progress after their brief teaching renews Paul's own faith and fills him with joy. His main message to them is to carry on as they are going, only more so. One important question had arisen over just how Jesus would return to the world – one

of the basic elements in early Christian preaching. Paul repeats much of Jesus' own teaching about this, and discourages pointless speculation. Instead, he advises them to be 'free from every fault at the coming of our Lord Jesus Christ' (5:23) – whenever it might be.

□ 2 THESSALONIANS
The Thessalonian Christians misunderstood what Paul wrote in his first letter about Christ's second coming. This second letter informs them more fully about what is to come.

Contents
Greeting and commendation of the Christians, chapter 1
Days of evil will precede Christ's return 2:1–12
Paul reassures the Christians 2:13 – 3:5
Practical Christian living 3:6–15
Personal postscript 3:16–18

Message
Paul probably wrote this letter soon after 1 Thessalonians (see there for time of writing). The Christians seem to be confused about Christ's return, partly as a result of fake letters by extremists (2:2). They thought Jesus had already come back, but Paul explains that days of evil (and in particular the 'man of lawlessness') must come first. He stresses again that Christian expectation of the second coming should never distort the everyday practice of our Christian lives.

□ 1 TIMOTHY
Taken on as a colleague by Paul when still a shy young man, Timothy was given demanding responsibilities. This letter finds him leading the church in Ephesus. It advises and encourages him in his service for Jesus Christ.

Contents
Greeting, chapter 1:1–2
False teaching 1:3–11
Paul and Timothy 1:12–20
Prayer and worship 2
Leadership in the church 3
How to counter false teaching 4
Serving people of all kinds 5:1 – 6:2
Real wealth 6:3–10
Personal instructions 6:11–21

Time of writing
1 and 2 Timothy and Titus – known as 'the pastoral letters' – are closely linked in style and subject. Some of the events referred to are hard to fit into what Acts tells us of Paul's life, as they require that Paul was released

from house arrest in Rome, undertook a further journey and was then imprisoned again (the circumstance of 2 Timothy). This has led some to suggest that these letters are not by Paul, but were written later, using some pieces of Paul's writing. Their teaching is certainly consistent with what we know of Paul.

Famous passages
'Christ Jesus came into the world to save sinners' 1:15–16
'Godliness with contentment is great gain' 6:6
'The love of money is a root of all kinds of evil' 6:10

Main themes
The pastoral letters have always been specially valued by those called to lead or hold office in the churches. This letter gives close, practical attention to the character needed for Christian ministry and the best way to conduct relationships with different groups of people in the churches. The writer also points to the best way to counter false teaching in the church – by giving careful and thorough instruction in the true Christian faith.

□ 2 TIMOTHY
Expecting death at any moment, Paul encourages Timothy to persevere in his ministry, using his own life as an example.

Contents
Greeting, chapter 1:1–2
'I thank God' 1:3–18
A worker for Jesus Christ 2
Troubled times ahead 3
Final instructions and greetings 4

Time of writing
If this letter is by Paul (see 1 Timothy), it is the last he wrote. He is in prison in Rome, and tradition states that he died there, probably during the Roman Emperor Nero's persecution in AD 64.

Famous passages
The Spirit God has given 1:7
The inspired Scriptures 3:15–17
'I have fought the good fight . . .': the race and the prize 4:6–8

Message
Paul had much to contend with during his years of Christian service, but he foresaw that his successors, Timothy included, might pass through even harder times. However, he regrets nothing and is full of gratitude to God. His advice to Timothy is both deeply spiritual and thoroughly practical.

□ TITUS
A letter to the leader of the church on Crete. Much would depend on

the quality of leadership these young churches received in the years after the apostles, and Paul does all he can to advise Titus.

Contents

Greeting, chapter 1:1–4
The kind of leader the church needs 1:5–16
What to teach, and how 2
Practical Christian living, and its basis 3:1–11
Final instructions 3:12–15

Time of writing

Titus is one of·the 'pastoral letters', but is not the last of them to be written. (See 1 Timothy.)

Famous passage

The gospel in miniature 3:4–7

Message

Like 1 and 2 Timothy, this letter is deeply concerned with the character of Christian leaders and the practicalities of their ministry. At the heart of these careful instructions, we find one of the clearest and most beautiful statements of the gospel Paul preached (3:4–7).

□ PHILEMON

This short, personal letter was probably carried, along with Colossians, by Epaphras when he returned from visiting Paul under house arrest in Rome.

Philemon was a leader of the church at Colossae. Onesimus, one of his slaves, had run away to Rome, met Paul and become a Christian. Paul sent him back, carrying this warm and tactful letter, commending him to his owner's generosity as a fellow-Christian.

Nowhere in Paul's letters is slavery – which was universal in the Roman Empire – explicitly condemned. But it is certainly undermined from within, particularly in this letter.
How can one human being, let alone one fellow-Christian, own another?

□ HEBREWS

The great theme of the letter to the Hebrews is that Jesus has completed all that the Old Testament began. It is packed with references to the Old Testament scriptures.

Contents

Introduction: Jesus has completed God's revelation, chapter 1:1–3
Part 1: Jesus Christ is greater than any alternative 1:4 – 10:39
Jesus is greater than the angels 1:4–14
Jesus has opened the way for our salvation 2
Jesus is greater than Moses 3:1 – 4:13

Jesus is *the* great high priest 4:14 – 7:28
Jesus has made a greater covenant and a greater sacrifice 8–10
Part 2: Faith and perseverance 11–12
Old Testament heroes of faith 11
Endure God's discipline 12:1–11
The kingdom that cannot be shaken 12:12–29
Conclusion: Final exhortation, prayer and greetings 13

Who wrote it, when and to whom?

This is the mystery book of the New Testament. The letter is anonymous. For centuries it was thought to be by Paul, but no one thinks so now, as its style and ideas are so different from his. Despite various interesting theories, we do not know the writer.

Plainly he was writing to Jewish Christians, but where did they live? There are indications that it was not Jerusalem, and some have suggested Rome, but we cannot be sure.

One factor points to a fairly early date: there is nothing about the destruction of the temple by the Romans in AD 70 which, given the subject, would surely be mentioned if it had happened. So it was probably written before then.

Famous passages

Jesus Christ, God's final revelation 1:1–3
Our sympathetic high priest 4:14–16
Christ's one great sacrifice for all time 10:11–14
'By faith . . .' 11
Jesus, the author and perfecter of our faith 12:1–3
'Jesus Christ, the same yesterday and today and forever' 13:8
The great shepherd 13:20–21

Main themes

The Jewish Christians who received this letter were facing opposition and were tempted to turn back to Judaism. The writer uses several powerful arguments to persuade them to persevere. Jesus is greater than any of the Old Testament institutions, in fact he has fulfilled everything that they foreshadowed. The Old Testament heroes give supreme examples of faith in the face of suffering, and Jesus himself suffered more than anyone. To turn from Christ is to face the judgement of God. This great letter ties together Old and New Testaments and reminds us of the Bible's unity.

□ JAMES

A totally practical letter about the importance of a high standard of conduct. It is more like the Sermon on the Mount than any other part of the New Testament, and echoes the style of Proverbs in the Old.

Contents

Deeds not words, chapter 1
The need to avoid social prejudice 2:1–13
Faith and actions 2:14–26
Control of our speech 3:1–12
Heavenly wisdom 3:13–18
God's way, not the world's way 4:1 – 5:6
Patience and prayer 5:7–20

Who wrote it, and to whom?

The letter is addressed to 'all God's people scattered over the whole world' (1:1). Nothing can be gleaned from this about how it was originally used. Many people think it was written quite early in the first century.

The writer is James, but which James? The commonest suggestion is James, the brother of Jesus, who is mentioned in Acts as one of the leaders of the church in Jerusalem, and in 1 Corinthians as having seen the risen Jesus. But we cannot be certain.

Famous passages

Hearing and doing 1:22–25
Faith and actions 2:26
The wisdom that comes from God 3:17–18
The prayer of faith, and Christian healing 5:14–16

Main themes

The letter covers a wide area of practical Christian living. It emphasizes that commitment must relate to every area of life. The Christian should avoid double standards and show integrity – in prayer, in obeying the Bible rather than just hearing it, in actions rather than simply intellectual belief, in control of the tongue, in avoiding social or economic injustice. There is also a short and influential passage on Christian healing (5:14–16).

□ 1 PETER

A letter to prepare Christians for coming persecution. Peter is strong in hope.

Contents

Introduction, chapter 1:1–2
Faith, hope and right living 1:3 – 2:3
A chosen people 2:4–10
The example of Christ's suffering 2:11–25
Wives and husbands 3:1–7
Suffering for doing right 3:8 – 4:19
Advice for the people of God 5:1–11
Final greetings 5:12–14

The writer and time of writing

Peter was foremost among the apostles, and became leader of the first Christians. He probably wrote this letter from Rome (the 'Babylon' of 5:13), perhaps about the time of Nero's persecution of Christians in AD 64. The letter is addressed to Christians in what is now western and northern Turkey.

Main themes

Peter's letter is full of the joy of belonging to Jesus Christ, which no suffering can shake. He is full of confidence in Christ's death for us, his resurrection and his future coming. He believes that suffering can be the crucible in which faith is purified. But his concern is not only that suffering should be survived; he gives instruction too on deepening the quality of the Christians' lives together.

☐ 2 PETER

A letter written to combat some who taught that morality does not matter for Christians, and that Jesus Christ would not return.

Contents

Knowing God and his message, chapter 1
False teachers 2
The certainty of Christ's return 3

Writer and time of writing

The writer announces himself as Simon Peter. But some have doubted if it is really by Peter, and have dated it at the end of the first century or a little later: they observe that the style and ideas are very different from 1 Peter; the letter took a long time being accepted in the early church; and chapter 2 is almost the same as the letter of Jude. Yet the reference to Jesus' transfiguration (1:16–18), for example, points the other way.

Message

Concentrate on true knowledge of God, and live as those who long for Jesus Christ's return. These are the writer's antidotes to the corrupting teaching which was undermining the faith of the Christians to whom his letter is addressed.

☐ 1 JOHN

Written to Christians confused by false teaching, this letter seeks to reassure them by giving three tests of genuine Christian life.

Contents

The theme stated, chapter 1:1–4
Light and darkness: the first two tests, walking in the light and loving the brethren 1:5 – 2:17
Truth and falsehood: the third test, believing that Jesus Christ, God's

Son, was a real, human person 2:18 – 4:21
The victory of faith 5:1–12
Closing instructions 5:13–21

Writer and time of writing

The ideas and way of arguing are very close to John's Gospel, so this letter is usually assigned to the same writer (see John). But it is not certain which was written first, and the Christians who received this letter cannot be identified.

Famous passages

Walking in the light 1:5–10
God's love and ours 4:7–12
Life through God's Son 5:10–12

Main themes

John's gospel was written to bring people to faith (John 20:31); this letter is to confirm the faith of those who already believe (5:13). Wrong teaching always leads to confusion, and the writer longs to see the Christians firm and clear in heart and mind. His three tests point to the nature of the false teaching, and remain applicable to all times. Are those who claim to belong to Christ living open and honest Christian lives (e.g. 1:5–10)? Are they demonstrating true Christian love (e.g. 4:7–12)? And do they believe that Jesus was both God's Son and a real human being (e.g. 4:2–3)? Like John's Gospel, the structure is not logical and clear-cut; the writer weaves his ideas around the three tests, stating and restating them in different ways.

☐ 2 AND 3 JOHN

These tiny letters, the shortest books in the Bible, are plainly by the same person who wrote 1 John. 2 John is addressed to 'the dear lady and her children', which is a way of saying 'the church and her members'. It contains John's usual stress on love, and another reference to the same false teaching as in 1 John. 3 John is written to a church leader, Gaius, commending him and warning him against a petty local dictator.

☐ JUDE

This brief letter from Jude, the brother of James and presumably of Jesus (Mark 6:3), concentrates on strengthening Christians to resist false teachers. Closely parallel to 2 Peter chapter 2, the letter is full of references to the Old Testament and other Jewish writings. It closes with a well-loved prayer of praise (verses 24–25).

☐ THE REVELATION

This book is unique in the New Testament. Its message of the final victory of Jesus Christ over all the forces that oppose God is conveyed in a series of visions.

Contents

Introduction: A vision of Christ in glory, chapter 1
Part 1: The letters to seven churches 2–3
Part 2: Visions of judgement and victory 4–20
The heavenly council 4
Seven seals 5:1 – 8:1
Seven trumpets 8:2 – 11:19
The dragon and his kingdom 12–13
The Lamb and his coming 14
Seven plagues 15–16
The fall of Babylon 17:1 – 19:4
Christ victorious 19:5 – 20:15
Part 3: A vision of heaven 21:1 – 22:5
Conclusion: Come, Lord Jesus! 22:6–21

The writer and time of writing

Revelation was plainly composed at a time when Christians were undergoing persecution, most probably under the Roman Emperor Domitian near the end of the first century. The writer's name is John, and he was confined to the island of Patmos in the Aegean. He has often been linked to the writer of John's Gospel and letters, but there are many reasons for thinking this may not be so.

Famous passages

Christ in glory 1:12–18
Christ at the door 3:20
God enthroned 4
Hymn of the victors 15:2–4
A new heaven and a new earth 21
'The bright morning star' 22:16–17

Main themes

Revelation is an 'apocalyptic' book (see *Visions of the future*, page 96). Its theme comes through the whole pattern of visions rather than the details of each vision taken separately. The message of God's sovereign power has encouraged and sustained persecuted Christians throughout history. However much power the persecutors may seem to have, their days are ultimately numbered. The final picture is of Christ victorious, his people vindicated, and all evil destroyed. The book begins with seven letters to churches, showing Christ's continuing close relationship with his people, giving words of comfort, challenge and rebuke. The book ends with a poetic description of heaven, with God and his people wholly at one, all pain and evil gone for ever.

Understanding the Bible

Some of the stories in the Gospels are so clear that anyone can understand them. But it is not so easy to get the meaning of some other parts of the Bible. The Bible is an ancient book made up of many parts. It has many different writers, different audiences, different styles of writing and language.

When we read a passage from the Bible it is useful to ask three questions:
● What does the passage actually say?
● What does the passage mean?
● What does the passage mean for us today?

1 What does the passage actually say?

To understand what the passage says we need to ask some further, more detailed questions. For example, it is important to ask: **when** and **where** the book, or passage, was written.
● Was it before or after the birth of Christ?
● Before the exodus or after?
● When Israel was ruled by kings, or during the Roman occupation?

Where was it written?
● In exile in Babylon?
● In a prison cell in Rome?

● At the royal court as an official record?

If we find out the answers to these questions (see *Books of the Bible*) we shall discover the setting of the passage in history. This helps us to understand what the writer intended.

A second useful question is: **why** was this passage written? If we can discover the purpose of the writer, we will begin to understand better some of the things he says. For example, some of Paul's letters were written to try to correct errors among groups of Christians. He points out their mistakes, and shows them a better way for the future. Similarly, it helps to know that the writer of the Book of Revelation wanted to encourage his readers who were suffering persecution for their faith.

It also helps to ask generally: **what** is this book about? The answer to this question will help us to read the book in the right way.
● Is it the account of events in the life and death of Jesus?

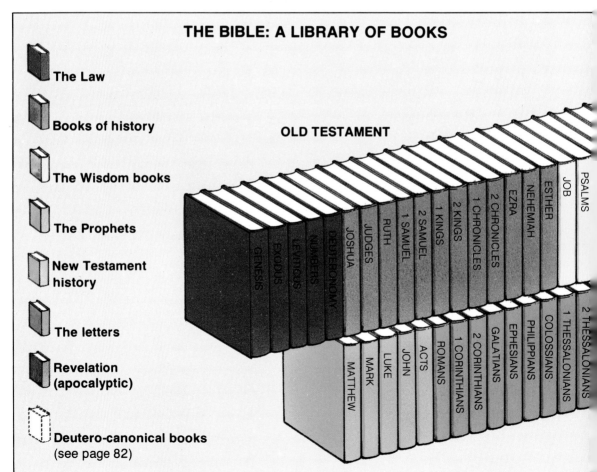

THE BIBLE: A LIBRARY OF BOOKS

The Law

Books of history

The Wisdom books

The Prophets

New Testament history

The letters

Revelation (apocalyptic)

Deutero-canonical books (see page 82)

OLD TESTAMENT

GENESIS · EXODUS · LEVITICUS · NUMBERS · DEUTERONOMY · JOSHUA · JUDGES · RUTH · 1 SAMUEL · 2 SAMUEL · 1 KINGS · 2 KINGS · 1 CHRONICLES · 2 CHRONICLES · EZRA · NEHEMIAH · ESTHER · JOB · PSALMS

MATTHEW · MARK · LUKE · JOHN · ACTS · ROMANS · 1 CORINTHIANS · 2 CORINTHIANS · GALATIANS · EPHESIANS · PHILIPPIANS · COLOSSIANS · 1 THESSALONIANS · 2 THESSALONIANS

- Is it a list of the religious duties of the Hebrew people?
- Is it a collection of religious poetry?

Sometimes it is important to ask what particular words mean. There are some special terms in the Bible – 'atonement', for example, or 'sin'. (See Part 6: *Key Teaching and Events of the Bible*.) It is important to understand their special meaning if we are to get the writer's message.

We need, especially, to ask: what *sort* of writing is this? In what form has it been written?
- Is it history?
- Is it poetry?
- Is it a letter?

Then we can go on to ask the questions that apply to that kind of writing.

If we are reading a book of history, we can ask: what actually happened? What other important events were occurring at the same period? Why has the writer chosen these events to recount? And why

does he recount them in the way he does?

But if it is a book of poetry, we should look at the writer's use of picture-language. What does he mean by his pictures? How was the poem or hymn used in worship?

It is worth looking in more detail at some of the forms of writing in the Bible.

☐ HISTORY AND BIOGRAPHY

The Old Testament has many books of history, such as Samuel and Kings, and we find New Testament history in the Gospels and Acts. If we are reading history, we need to enquire about the background to events.
- What was going on in the wider world at the time?
- What important affairs were taking place?

Then we need to look at the passage itself carefully.
- What actually happens?
- Who are the principle characters?
- Where did this all occur?

Sometimes history books are written to prove or make a particular point. So it is important to ask what the writer was trying to show.

☐ LAW

The main law-books of the Old Testament are Exodus, Leviticus, Deuteronomy and Numbers. These books contain long passages listing laws which cover many different aspects of life. It is useful to ask what part of life particular laws apply to.
- Does the law deal with matters of behaviour and morals?
- Are they state laws or social rules?
- Are the laws about hygiene or family life?
- Or are they religious laws – about worship, ritual and sacrifice?
- Are they solemn ritual blessings and cursings related to Jewish religion?

When we read passages of the law, it is important to relate them to the particular periods in Israel's history to which they applied. When we come to the New Testament, we need to understand how far Jesus' teaching overruled the law. Galatians and Hebrews, for example, show how the first Christians believed the scope of the law was altered.

☐ POETRY

Some Old Testament books are largely made up of poetry. Job, Psalms and the Song of Solomon are good examples. There are also passages of poetry in the prophets and shorter ones in the New Testament – for example Mary's song of praise, the Magnificat. We need to read these passages as poetry, not as prose.
- Is the book written rather like a play, with characters? (The Book of Job can be looked at like this.)
- Or is the writer's personal feelings, which we can sometimes share? Examples of this include some of the psalms.
- Or does the poetry have much picture-language?

Some Old Testament poetry was written for official temple worship. A psalm, for example, may retell the great events in Israel's history. Sometimes it is important to know the history behind a particular poem – for example, David's lament over the death of his friend Jonathan. There are some special

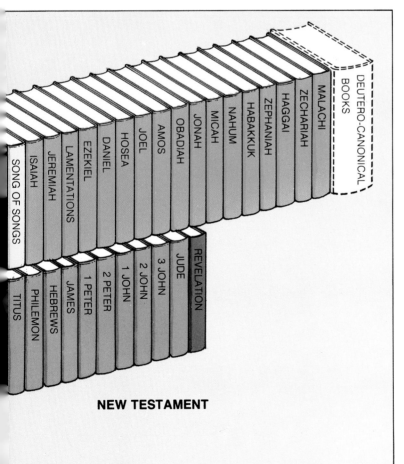

SONG OF SONGS · ISAIAH · JEREMIAH · LAMENTATIONS · EZEKIEL · DANIEL · HOSEA · JOEL · AMOS · OBADIAH · JONAH · MICAH · NAHUM · HABAKKUK · ZEPHANIAH · HAGGAI · ZECHARIAH · MALACHI · DEUTERO-CANONICAL BOOKS

TITUS · PHILEMON · HEBREWS · JAMES · 1 PETER · 2 PETER · 1 JOHN · 2 JOHN · 3 JOHN · JUDE · REVELATION

NEW TESTAMENT

effects in Hebrew poetry. The one we see most often is the way the poet makes the same point in two slightly different ways in consecutive lines.

☐ WISE SAYINGS

Some Old Testament books – particularly Proverbs and Ecclesiastes – are made up of 'wise sayings'. Some of these stand on their own: sometimes they are grouped into sayings with a common theme. Some of the sayings are common-sense comments on everyday living, often with a touch of humour. Others try to draw out general principles about human life. Some talk about life without God; others about the true source of happiness.

☐ PROPHECY

A large section of the Old Testament is made up of 'books of prophecy'. This does not necessarily mean that they foretell the future. The prophets who wrote the books were usually concerned to speak out against evils, or the disregard for God and his rules which they saw in society around them. But they also occasionally looked forward to what God had in store for the future.

When we read the prophets, we need to find out their background in history. There are other useful questions.
● Is the writer using picture-language?
● Is he writing a kind of poetry?
● What do his word-pictures mean?
● What was the prophet's purpose in speaking as he did?
● Was the prophecy understood in a special way by the New Testament writers?

☐ PARABLES

Many of Jesus' parables are written down in the Gospels. We also find parables, or picture-stories, in some of the Old Testament books of history and prophecy. We need first to find out what the main point of the parable was. Do the details of the parable have any special meaning – or are they there just to set the scene for the story? Many of Jesus' parables were told to help ordinary people understand what God's kingdom was like, and how he deals with men and women.

☐ LETTERS

Many of the later books of the New Testament are letters from apostles or other Christians in various places. When we read these letters we must ask:
● Who wrote this letter?
● To whom?
● What was his purpose in writing?
● What is the main theme of the letter?

2 What did the passage mean to its first readers?

If we have answered all the questions, and know what the passage actually says, it is not so difficult to find out what it meant to its original readers. We can try to find out what the main point of the passage is. What does it teach? If the passage was written to answer a specific need or situation, we can ask: Is there a general principle behind these events?

When we feel we know what the passage actually says, and what it meant for its original readers, we can confidently ask our final question.

3 What does the passage mean for us today?

Is there a modern situation like that of the original reader? What would the writer have to say to such a situation? If not, is there a principle that still applies? What specific teaching is there in the passage? (It is often useful to compare it with other Bible passages dealing with similar subjects. Sometimes they may set it out more clearly – or add to the meaning of the passage we are reading.) Is there something we can learn?
● About God?
● About man?
● About the world?
● About the church?
● About some other specific theme?

Can we find some example to follow? Is there a warning? Does it contain a promise that applies to us? Is there some action we should take in the light of this passage? Does it make us want to pray? Or to praise? Can we use the writer's words to express our own feelings about God? How does this passage, and its meaning, fit in with other passages we know with similar themes?

Biblical Criticism

What does the Bible say – and what does it mean?

To understand the Bible fully we must answer these two questions – and the process of doing so is called 'biblical criticism'.

'Criticism' is a slippery word. Quite often it means fault-finding. But in the context of literary studies, it refers to a thorough analysis of a particular piece of writing, examining its language, thought patterns and concepts in an effort to get to the bottom of what has been written. This is the sense in which we use it here. Biblical critics, far from trying to undermine the Bible's message, are actually trying to understand and explain it in all its possible ramifications.

What does the Bible say?

That may seem an odd question, for with the Bible in front of us it seems perfectly obvious what it says. Yet the very fact that we can read a Bible that makes sense in our own language is itself a tribute to the endeavours of past generations of biblical critics. A few facts about the Bible will help to explain why.

● The Bible was written in what to us are foreign languages: the New Testament in Greek, and the Old Testament mainly in Hebrew, with a few pages in Aramaic. To understand what the Bible says, we need to have a good grasp of these languages. To translate a modern book from, say, French into English is a fairly straightforward business, for large numbers of people speak both languages and we can readily discover what their various expressions mean. But nobody today speaks any of the Bible languages.

Languages change all the time, and the modern languages called Hebrew and Greek are both significantly different from their predecessors in Bible times. Even the New Testament's Greek is rather different from that used by classical thinkers like Plato, only a few centuries before the time of Jesus.

Discovering the exact meaning of the Bible languages is a complex affair, which includes the study of history and culture as well as strictly linguistic considerations.

● We should also remember that no modern person has ever seen the original texts that the Bible authors themselves wrote. Even our most ancient Greek and Hebrew texts are copies of yet older copies.

All the oldest copies were made long before the invention of printing. Scribes wrote them by hand, often in difficult conditions – and they occasionally made mistakes. They often wrote from dictation, and sometimes heard the words wrongly. Even when copying from other written manuscripts, an ancient scribe would occasionally miss out whole sections of text, as his eye jumped accidentally from one use of a particular word to the next, a couple of lines down.

If a previous reader had made his own comments in the margin, they might sometimes be copied into the text as if they were a part of it. Then, on top of that, groups of people with a particular message to put over might occasionally introduce deliberate changes in order to provide 'biblical' evidence in support of their point of view.

☐ **BIBLE TEXTS**

It is part of the job of the biblical critic to sort out these matters, and to discover as accurately as possible what the Bible writers actually wrote, and what they meant by the words they used. This form of investigation is often called 'textual criticism', because it is concerned with establishing the text of the Bible as accurately as possible. It is also occasionally called 'lower criticism', because it forms a foundation from which we can go on to ask other questions about the Bible's origins and

meaning ('higher criticism').

Yet in spite of the problems, we can be certain that modern translations of the Bible are based on Hebrew and Greek texts that are in all essential respects exactly what the original authors wrote. We know more about the Bible than about any other comparable ancient text.

There are literally thousands of Bible manuscripts, some of them written within a generation or two of the original authors. They are written on all sorts of materials, and vary from virtually complete Bibles to mere scraps. But when we put these alongside ancient translations of the Bible into languages like Coptic or Syriac, and then take account of the many quotations in the writings of the early Christians, our knowledge of the Bible text is really enormous.

Konstantin von Tischendorf (1815–1874) was one of the first to realise the importance of such textual study. In a monastery at the foot of Mt Sinai, he discovered what is still one of the most accurate ancient manuscripts: Codex Sinaiticus, written in Greek about AD 350, and containing the whole New Testament as well as much of the Old. Following this, he and other scholars – notably B. F. Westcott (1825–1901) and F. J. A. Hort (1828–1892) – established rules for assessing this mass of documentary material, and ensured that our modern versions of the Bible are based on the most reliable texts possible.

☐ **BIBLE LANGUAGE**

Other important discoveries are helping us to understand the exact meaning of the Bible languages.

Our knowledge of the Hebrew Old Testament has been immeasurably enriched by the discovery of the Dead Sea Scrolls, with examples of Hebrew texts several centuries older than any previously known.

Inscriptions like that found in Hezekiah's water shaft in Jerusalem have also cast light on the way the language was used during the period when much of the Old Testament was being written.

The Ras Shamra texts have shed new light on many obscure Hebrew expressions. These texts were written in Ugaritic. But like Hebrew (with Aramaic and Arabic) this is a 'Semitic' language and, since these texts concern religious topics, much of their imagery has had a direct bearing on our

knowledge of Old Testament Hebrew – particularly in poetic books like the Psalms.

Texts written in Hellenistic Greek also shed new light on the nature of the New Testament books. We now know, for instance, that Paul's letters were not literary 'epistles', but personal letters written between friends. In both language and structure, Paul's letters are strikingly similar to many letters written on papyrus sheets by ordinary people at about the same time.

All these things have expanded our understanding of the actual words of the Bible, and thanks to the work of biblical critics we now have a much better idea of what the Bible says.

What does the Bible mean?

To make useful sense out of the Bible, we need to ask this question too. Here the answers are far less certain – partly because of the nature of the question. For it is really two questions: What did it mean – then? and What does it mean – now? In theory, biblical critics have tried to keep them separate. But it is not so easy, and quite often what a particular individual thinks the Bible means now will affect the way he views its meaning in its original context. This so-called 'higher criticism' inevitably must be a good deal more subjective than 'lower criticism'.

Nevertheless, these questions are important and cannot be ignored if we are to do justice to the Bible's message.

● Every part of the Bible comes to us today as part of an alien culture. Modern people are not the same even as ancient Greeks or Romans – let alone ancient Canaanites or Egyptians! The way they thought and wrote needs to be interpreted and reformulated if it is to have the same impact on us today.

Take the earliest Christian confession: 'Jesus is Lord.' In modern British culture, that statement would seem to mean that Jesus was a member of an aristocratic family. In point of fact, nothing could be further from the truth. But what is the truth?

To Romans and Greeks in the first Christian century, to say 'Jesus is Lord' could have indicated he was a deity of the sort worshipped in the esoteric mystery religions – much like Lord Isis or Lord Serapis.

To Jews, on the other hand, the name 'Lord' (Greek *kurios*) was the personal name of the one true God of the Old Testament (Yahweh) – and to say 'Jesus is Lord' in that context had rather different connotations.

So which set of associations is right? The mere words themselves are not much help. They need to be set in their proper historical and cultural perspective – and that is the job of the higher critic.

● Then we must remember that the Bible is not just one book, but a whole library. Moreover, the Old Testament is a national archive, and its assorted parts were variously used at different periods.

The book of Psalms has many references to the king who ruled as God's agent in Jerusalem. Before the exile, these were hymns of celebration in the worship of the temple. But later, when the monarchy had disappeared, they were understood in a different way, and even in the Bible itself we can see signs of a reinterpretation of them.

The same phenomenon is present in the New Testament, though on a shorter time-scale. The Gospels inform us about the teaching and life of Jesus. But they were also part of the preaching of the earliest Christian churches – and what their teaching meant in the church was not necessarily exactly the same as it meant in Galilee at the time of Jesus.

The story of the lost sheep, for example, has two meanings given to it: referring to the work of the evangelist who goes to those who do not know God (Luke 15:1–7), and also to the work of the pastor caring for those who are already followers of Jesus (Matthew 18:10–14).

□ SOURCES

Because of such facts, biblical critics came to see that part of understanding the Bible is asking where it has come from. How were these books written? Who wrote them – and why? Knowing what an author is doing is not of course the same thing as understanding what he wants to say. But if you know how he tackled his material, then you have a better chance of appreciating what he was getting at.

A modern author – especially of history or biography – may use several sources, which he will reinterpret and incorporate into his own work. The Bible writers were just the same. Luke categorically tells us this is how he wrote his Gospel (Luke 1:1–4). And the Old Testament also has many references to sources that are either consulted or quoted (Joshua 10:13, 1 Kings 11:41, 1 Kings 14:19, etc.).

It has been the work of *source critics* to try and identify some of these materials. In 1924, B. H. Streeter expounded a view of how the first three Gospels were written that is still widely held today. Matthew and Luke, he said, copied Mark's Gospel almost word for word, supplemented with selections from another document containing Jesus' teachings (Q), together with various other materials. His theory has stood the test of time largely because we still have Mark's Gospel, and we can check whether and how Matthew and Luke used it.

The work of other source critics has been less durable. Like that of Julius Wellhausen (1844–1918), who argued that the first five books of the Old Testament were composed out of four different sources, each one more advanced in theology and morals than its predecessor: J (950–850 BC), E (850–750 BC), D (621 BC), and P (450 BC). He believed that the author of Genesis– Deuteronomy operated with scissors and paste to join together various bits of these documents to make a coherent whole.

Further knowledge about ancient methods of writing, and a general discrediting of the idea that human history has moved from savagery to sophistication, have put serious question-marks against Wellhausen's reconstruction of Old Testament history. But most biblical critics would still accept that the search for sources of many of the Bible books is a valuable way of elucidating its message.

□ CONTEXTS

Some of the Bible books existed in spoken form long before they were written down, and other critics have tried to explore these oral forms.

Form critics begin from the fact that in the ancient world the actual literary form of a piece can often indicate the way in which it was used. Careful application of this insight by Hermann Gunkel and others shed valuable light on the way the Psalms were used in Israel's worship; while people like Rudolf Bultmann and Martin Dibelius have helped us to see how the Gospel stories were used in the life of the early Christian communities.

This approach has often been associated with extreme scepticism about the historical value of some parts of the Bible. But that is not an inevitable outcome of form criticism itself: it is rather a by-product of the theological position of some of its practitioners.

□ AUTHORS

None of the Bible writers was a mere recorder of materials handed on from others. They all interpreted their materials, explaining their significance for their own readership. Like any other authors, the Bible writers had their own perspective, and the way they tell a story can often show us what that perspective was. The modern search for it is called *redaction criticism*.

In the study of the Gospels, for instance, we can often learn a good deal about the diversity of life and thinking in the early churches by comparing the different ways the four writers recorded the life and teaching of Jesus. And the same is true in the Old Testament, especially the history books and the messages of the prophets.

Biblical criticism has been with us now for a couple of centuries, and there can be no doubt that it has made a valuable contribution to our understanding of the Bible and its message. Much of it is painstaking – even tedious – and there have been many false trails and blind alleys. But it is an essential tool in biblical exposition. Whether or not we agree with the ever-changing theories of the experts, every modern reader has much to learn from them. Finding intelligible answers to the questions which biblical criticism raises will help to apply the Bible's reading more fully to our own life experience.

The shofar is blown to announce the start of a Jewish religious festival.

5

Religion and Worship in the Bible

Note: Most of the information in this whole section on the religion and worship of Israel concentrates on the outward forms (the rituals). For the basic beliefs which underlie the Jewish and Christian religions, see Part 6: *Key Teaching of the Bible.*

From earliest times, men and women have felt the need to worship, or pay respect to, someone or something greater than themselves. In every age people have tried to describe and picture a powerful 'god' or 'gods'. Although many people today think they have out-grown religion, they often un-consciously substitute a leader, the state, the individual, or even science for the 'gods' worshipped in earlier times.

For the Israelites and their neighbours religion was an essential part of life. It touched everything that happened and everything they did. Every nation believed there were powers controlling the uni-verse. The sun, storms, earth, sea and other natural elements were treated as powers in themselves, or the work of superhuman beings, the gods. Only the Israelites believed that one God held all power in his hands.

It was difficult to think of the gods as abstract 'powers'. Instead they were usually pictured as being like men or animals, with particular powers, or character, to match. Once people began to describe supernatural powers in human terms, the gods quickly became little more than large-scale versions of human beings. Leading gods and goddesses were like human kings and queens. The lesser gods were their 'families' and 'court officials'. People thought of their behaviour in human terms, too. The gods loved and cared like human beings. They grew angry, hated, and fought. They punished and rewarded one another, and the creatures under their control.

An Israeli soldier prays at the western wall in Jerusalem, wearing his phylactery and shawl over uniform and arms.

People thought of themselves as having been created by one, some, or all of their gods. The fact that they had to work to provide food for their own families made them think they had been made by the gods in order to feed them, too. So they put a helping of their own meals on one side for the god, or they prepared a special meal.

From the first, certain places were thought to be 'sacred' – this was where the god lived, or the place where people might meet him. Some of these places may have been private ones, for a particular man or family. But most were centres where many people worshipped. That being so, they needed caretakers and attendants, and these had to be fed and provided for. In large cities the offerings brought by the people might be more than enough for this, allowing the 'priests' to store up wealth for the 'temple'.

People have always felt it right to give the very best they can afford to the object of their worship. 'Offerings' might be made for many reasons. Some were almost a bribe, seeking some favour from the god. Others might be 'thank-you' presents when something good had happened (for example, the birth of a son, a good harvest or a victory).

Human experiences sug-gested that the gods could be offended and made angry. They showed their annoyance by bringing illness and mis-fortune. To avoid that, or try to stop it, people brought special sacrifices, more costly than those usually offered. Disasters and failures were put down to the fact that people had somehow failed to please the gods, or deliberately dis-obeyed them. Special sacrifices were needed to put matters right. The worshipper con-fessed his faults before his gods and asked forgiveness and pardon.

The priests often held great power as agents or spokesmen for the gods. They could say whether or not a god was pleased. They could decide what offerings were necessary. In many cases, they could influence the affairs of the nation by claiming to speak the god's mind.

The gods of ancient times were unpredictable. So people could have no certainty about the future. They were ready to listen to anyone who made out a good case for having a message from the gods. So there were prophets and for-tune tellers, as well as priests, in most societies. They often worked with witches and magi-cians who gave spells to help those in trouble. These en-abled people to escape the plots of their enemies and the evils inflicted upon them by their gods.

Most religions of the ancient Near East were designed to gain some control over the gods. The idea that a god would actually reveal his nature to man is unique to Israel.

For more about the religions of other nations, see Part 11: *Nations and Peoples of the Bible.*

The Religion of Israel

Abraham

The starting-point of Israel's religion is the day when God spoke to Abraham, telling him to leave his land and his family home and go to a new country. On that day God promised to make Abraham the founder of a great nation. Abraham took God at his word. 'He put his trust in the Lord, and because of this the Lord was pleased with him and accepted him.'

So the very first and most basic belief of the Jewish and Christian religions is the certainty that God is a real person, and that human beings – individually or as a group – can know him. Abraham, we are told, did as God said. He moved to Canaan, and in various places where he set up camp he built an altar and worshipped God.

Abraham's faith in God was at times shaky. But he knew that God had committed himself to him and to his family, that was to grow into the nation of Israel.
Genesis 15:6

Jacob

The history of Israel as a nation begins with Abraham's grandson Jacob (renamed Israel) and his twelve sons, from whom the twelve tribes were descended. 'I am the Lord, the God of Abraham and Isaac,' God said to Jacob.

'I will give to you and to your descendants this land . . . I will be with you and protect you wherever you go, and I will bring you back to this land. I will not leave you until I have done all that I have promised to you.'

Famine came. Jacob and his sons followed Joseph into Egypt. Their descendants remained there for centuries. But God's promise still held. This family and nation were his people. When the Egyptians made slaves of them and they cried out for help, God heard.

Moses was in the Sinai Desert, looking after his father-in-law's flocks when God's call came. He saw a bush which was on fire but did not burn up.

Moses

One day, in the desert, God spoke to Moses. 'I am sending you to the king of Egypt,' he said, 'so that you can lead my people out of his country.' Moses needed to know how he could describe God to the people, and so God explained more about the kind of God he was. He revealed his own personal name, Yahweh ('the Lord'), and also his mysterious name 'I am', or 'I will be who I will be'. That name showed two things. God was unchanging: he was completely reliable. But also he was always alive, active, creative. It was the knowledge of this God that Moses brought to his people.

But God did not just give information about himself. He proved by what he did that he was that kind of God.

When he rescued the Israelites from Egypt to keep the promises he had made to their ancestors, he showed his reliability. But also, when he led them through the unknown wilderness, he met their need for food and water and cared for them in spite of their rebellions. Here was the living God in action.

The Exodus and Mt Sinai

In Moses' time, God made himself known as a God who acts and speaks. At the exodus

from Egypt he proved that he was the defender of oppressed people and the enemy of the unjust. That in itself was a revelation of his character.

At Mt Sinai he revealed himself still further. He told Moses that he was 'a God who is full of compassion and pity, who is not easily angered and who shows great love and faithfulness'. He also revealed his will for his people in the commandments. The Israelites could see from what he required of them what his own character was like.
Exodus 34:6

The time of David and Solomon

In this age, Israel became an independent state for the first time. The Israelites were impressed by the pomp and splendour of kingship, but they recognized that the dignity of their earthly kings was only a shadow of the greatness of the Lord, the King of kings.

A new sense of the grandeur of God can be seen in the temple and its worship and in the psalms sung in the temple, hailing God as a 'mighty God, a mighty king over all the gods'.

Along with the solemnity of the temple worship went a strong sense of joy: 'The Lord is king! Earth, be glad! Rejoice, you islands of the seas!' Gladness and reverence went hand in hand, as many of the psalms show.

In the age of David and Solomon God also made a new promise: he would make David's kingdom a lasting one; his dynasty would never end. This kept Israel loyal to the kings of David's family line even when they did not deserve it. And it developed in the end into the hope that God would send a new David, a son of David who would rule justly. So in that promise to David lay the seeds of an expectation of a Messiah.
Psalm 95:3; 97:1; 2 Samuel 7

The prophets

The work of the prophets is more fully treated in the special section below. Their greatest contribution to Israel's faith was not a new revelation from God, but a new challenge to be faithful to what God had already made known of himself, and to return to God in repentance.

The prophets never tired of hammering home the fact that true religion is not just a matter of ritual, or even of belief, but also of behaviour. They mercilessly attacked the religion of their day, not because it did not follow the patterns laid down in the law-books like Leviticus, but because it was not matched by right behaviour.

The prophets spoke to the conscience of Israel. They gave warning of the approaching disaster of the exile. And when God's punishment had come upon Israel, they offered hope and God's promise for a new future.
Amos 5:21–24

The exile

The exile was not a gap in the history of Israel, an unhappy experience best forgotten as quickly as possible. Though it was a time of misery for many thousands of Jews, it was one of the most creative periods in Israel's history. For in it the people of Israel found again both themselves and their God. In the exile they came to recognize, in a way they had never needed to before, how much the two things were connected.

Israel had no reason for existing apart from the treasure it possessed in knowing God. Unless they saw themselves as the people of God, Israel was no different from any other nation on earth. It could be wiped off the map as easily as many nations have been in the course of history.

Many Israelites saw the exile only as a disaster. But those who saw in it God's discipline of his people could also see the exile as a time of purification.

The Jews who returned to the land, 'whose heart God had moved, got ready to go up and rebuild the Lord's Temple in Jerusalem'. They realized that they would only survive by keeping themselves separate from other nations and by insisting on obedience to the letter of God's Law. This was the only realistic attitude; and although, eventually, it led some of them into legalism, it produced a piety that is very praiseworthy. For the story of Israel's development after the exile, see *Between the Testaments*.
Ezra 1:5

The Commandments

After their escape from slavery in Egypt, God led the Israelites through the desert to Mt Sinai. They camped at the foot of the mountain, while God gave Moses the laws his people were to obey. The promise (covenant-treaty) God had previously made with individuals – Abraham, Isaac, Jacob – he now renewed with the whole nation. They were his people; he was their God. He had rescued them and he expected them to respond by obeying his laws. These were not just rules for worship or religious occasions. They covered every aspect of life. And they are summed up in the Ten Commandments.

The Ten Commandments

'God spoke, and these were his words:

I am the Lord your God who brought you out of Egypt, where you were slaves.

● Worship no god but me.

● Do not make for yourselves images of anything in heaven or on earth or in the water under the earth. Do not bow down to any idol or worship it, because I am the Lord your God and I tolerate no rivals. I bring punishment on those who hate me and on their descendants down to the third and fourth generation. But I show my love to thousands of generations of those who love me and obey my laws.

● Do not use my name for evil purposes, because I, the Lord your God, will punish anyone who misuses my name.

● Observe the Sabbath and keep it holy. You have six days in which to do your work, but the seventh day is a day of rest dedicated to me. On that day no one is to work – neither you, your children, your slaves, your animals, nor the foreigners who live in your country. In six days I, the Lord, made the earth, the sky, the sea, and everything in them, but on the seventh day I rested. That is why I, the Lord, blessed the Sabbath and made it holy.

● Respect your father and your mother, so that you may live a long time in the land that I am giving you.

● Do not commit murder.

● Do not commit adultery.

● Do not steal.

● Do not accuse anyone falsely.

● Do not desire another man's house; do not desire his wife, his slaves, his cattle, his donkeys, or anything else that he owns.'

This is the best-known collection of Israel's laws. It clearly has a special significance: in Exodus it is the first set of laws given on Mt Sinai, and in Deuteronomy it is said at the end of the Ten Commandments: 'These words the Lord spoke to all your assembly . . . and he added no more' (Deuteronomy 5:22), that is, there were no others of equal importance.

The Ten Commandments are addressed to the whole nation of Israel, not just to a particular group like the priests, and to every Israelite as an individual. All the same, though these Ten Commandments are unique as a collection, each one of them is found again in other places in the Hebrew laws.

The Ten Commandments were written on two stone tablets. This probably means two copies. The reason for having two copies of the Ten Commandments has only recently been understood. When a written covenant was made in the world of the Bible, each party making the covenant had a copy of its contents. If the covenant was between two nations, for instance the Hittites and the Egyptians, the two copies would be kept far apart, in the temple of a god of each land.

In Israel, though, the covenant was between God and his people. Both copies of the Ten Commandments were kept in the Covenant Box (ark). This was the centre of Israel and it was also the place of God's presence. So God's copy and Israel's copy could be kept together.

The Ten Commandments, then, were the terms of the covenant that God had made with his people. At Sinai, in response to all that God had done for them, the people of Israel accepted these terms.

The penalty for breaking any of the Ten Commandments is not mentioned. But if we compare these commandments with similar ones, it seems that the penalty was death (compare Exodus 20:13 with Exodus 21:12). This does not mean

In a setting like this God gave the Israelites his commandments, as they camped near Mt Sinai.

that the penalty was always carried out.

Other collections of laws

Of course in any society many more detailed rules and laws are necessary. The basic laws need to be expanded. If the commandment says that you are not to do any work on the sabbath, who is meant by 'you' and what counts as 'work'?

Already in Exodus 20:10 the simple command has to be spelled out in detail. It has to be made clear that 'you' is not just the father of the Israelite family, but also 'your children, your slaves, your animals . . . the foreigners who live in your country' (Deuteronomy 5:14). (We must assume and hope that 'your wife' was also included!)

Later, the Jewish rabbis spent much time on defining exactly what was 'work'. Jesus was criticized by some because he and his disciples healed and picked grain on the sabbath (Luke 14:3–4; Matthew 12:1–2). This was against the Pharisees' definition of 'work'.

The Ten Commandments are God's 'covenant-law' for Israel. In addition to these, Israel's law-books (Exodus to Deuteronomy) contain many 'case-laws', some of them similar to those of other nations. There are three major collections of laws.

The first follows on from the Ten Commandments, in Exodus 21–23. It is sometimes called the 'Book of the Covenant'. It contains moral, civil and religious laws. Instructions about worship are followed by laws dealing with the rights of slaves; manslaughter and injury to human life; theft and damage to property; social and religious duties; justice and human rights. At the end come instructions for the three great religious festivals: Unleavened Bread, Firstfruits and Harvest (see *Fasts and Festivals*).

The laws show God's concern that life as a whole should be just and fair. They show his concern to protect the rights of those least able to help themselves – slaves, the poor, widows and orphans, foreigners.

Leviticus 17–26 contains a second collection of laws (the

The scroll of the Law is handled with great respect in a Jewish synagogue today.

'holiness' laws). These mainly concern how the Israelites should worship God, the rituals connected with the tabernacle. But they also deal with everyday behaviour. The keynote of the teaching is the command, 'Be holy, because I, the Lord your God, am holy' (Leviticus 19:2). Israel is to be 'holy' because the nation belongs to God.

The third collection of detailed laws is set down in Deuteronomy 12–25. They cover many of the same matters dealt with in Exodus and Leviticus. But they come in the form of a sermon given by Moses to the Israelites before they went into the Promised Land. They include frequent encouragements to keep the Law, and warnings of what will happen if the people disobey. Deuteronomy 17:14–20 is the only part of the Law which spells out the duties of the king.

The purpose of the commandments

The Law was intended to be a guide to good relationships – with God and with other people. In it, God, the maker and rescuer of his people, tells them how they are to live – for their own good and well-being. The Hebrew word which is usually translated 'law' (*tōrah*) actually means 'guidance' or 'instruction'. These laws were never intended to be a long list of dos and don'ts to make life a burden.

The Law reflects God's character – his holiness, justice and goodness. It expresses his will. It gives his people the practical guidance they need in order to obey his command to 'Be holy, as I am holy.'

How far does the Old Testament Law still apply? Are Christians today bound by it as the Law of God?

On the one hand, we have the sayings of Jesus. He has not come to abolish the Law; he has come to 'fulfil' it (that is, to fill it with fuller meaning). Until heaven and

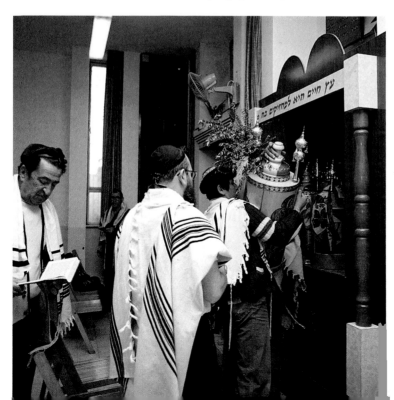

earth pass away, he says, not the least portion will pass from the Law. Whoever disobeys the least important of the commandments shall be called least in the kingdom of heaven.

On the other hand, Paul states that Christ 'has brought the law to an end'. He sees the Old Testament Law as something that was 'introduced' at a certain point in history and was intended to be valid only till the time of the coming of Christ.

How do these two attitudes fit together?

Some have thought the difficulty can be solved by distinguishing between the moral laws, which are still in force, and the ritual, ceremonial, and social laws of the Old Testament, which applied only to the Israelites. But for one thing it is impossible to say which laws are which, and, for another, although Paul acknowledges that the Law is from God and is 'holy, just, and good', he speaks of even the moral law as 'cancelled' by the work of Jesus Christ. Christians are 'free' from the Law and are not subject to it – and in these passages Paul is thinking of the law as a whole, not just the moral law.

For Christians, then, Jesus Christ has taken the place of the Law. He has not put the Law aside or rejected it, but has summed it up. When Paul says that he is under Christ's law, he does not mean that he has accepted a new set of laws. Rather, he is a follower of Jesus and is filled with his spirit. By being linked with Jesus, sharing his new life and the power of his Holy Spirit, Christians are able to follow his example and obey his law. Christ's law is not a law that enslaves people because they are unable to keep it. It is the 'perfect law that sets people free'.

Deuteronomy 6:5; Leviticus 19:18; Matthew 5:17–20; Romans 10:4; 5:20; Galatians 3:19; Romans 7:6, 12; Colossians 2:14; Galatians 5:18; 1 Corinthians 9:21; Galatians 6:2; 5:1; James 1:25

Fasts and Festivals

The sabbath and most of the great festivals of the Jewish religion were kept from the very earliest period of Israel's history. But two of the festivals described here began to be observed much later – Purim (from the time of the Persian Empire, fifth century BC) and Dedication/Lights (from the time of the Maccabees, second century BC).

Israel's main religious festivals were connected with the seasons and the farmer's year in Canaan. They were held in the spring, the early summer, and the autumn. On each occasion the men were expected to go to their local shrine and present their offerings to God.

After the seventh century BC these 'pilgrim' festivals were held only in Jerusalem. By the time of Jesus, the city's normal population of 40,000 or so was swollen to about 150,000 by the pilgrims who came for the Passover.

Festivals were times of thanksgiving to God for harvests, occasions for remembering outstanding events in Israel's history, and opportunities for great rejoicing and feasting.

Fasts

Only one day in the year is set apart for a national fast in the Old Testament laws. That is the Day of Atonement, on the 'tenth day of the seventh month' (end of September/ beginning of October). During the exile in Babylon, special fasts were also held in the fifth and seventh months to mourn the destruction of the temple and the murder of Gedaliah, governor of Judah.

After the exile two other regular fasts were held: in the tenth month, to remember the start of the siege of Jerusalem, and in the fourth month, marking the final capture of the city. Fasts were also kept by the nation and by individuals at times of special need.

Prayer and fasting often went together. People fasted as a sign of genuine repentance. During the time of fasting they did not eat or drink. Other customs were to tear their clothes, dress in coarse sackcloth, throw dust and ashes on their heads, and leave their hair uncombed and their bodies unwashed. But the prophets, and

Traditional prayers at the end of the sabbath in a Jewish home.

The Festivals

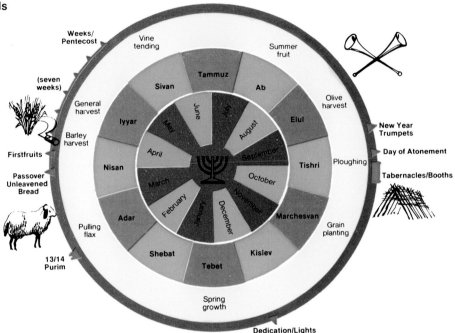

Jesus himself, made it plain that these outward signs of fasting were not enough. A real change of heart was what mattered most.
Leviticus 16:29; Zechariah 7:5; 8:19; Judges 20:26; Nehemiah 1; 2 Samuel 12:16, 20; Esther 4:16; Isaiah 58:3−5; Joel 2:13; Jonah 3:5; Matthew 6:16−18

Annual festivals
□ **Passover and Unleavened Bread**
Passover was one of the most important annual festivals. It took place the evening before the fourteenth of Nisan. On that night every family sacrificed a lamb. It was a reminder of the first such sacrifice, which took place just before God rescued the Israelites from Egypt. On that occasion God 'passed over' the Israelite houses where the blood of the lamb had been sprinkled on the door-posts and lintel, and he spared the lives of their firstborn.

Bread, made quickly and without yeast ('unleavened bread') was eaten at the Passover meal and all through the following week. This, too, was

a reminder of the hurried preparations made when Pharaoh finally allowed the Israelites to leave Egypt. It also recalled the first bread baked from new corn, four days after the Israelites entered Canaan.

At first the Passover was held in people's homes, but by New Testament times it was the main 'pilgrim' festival celebrated in Jerusalem.
It remains one of the most important Jewish festivals today.
Exodus 12; Joshua 5:10−12; Mark 14:1−2

□ **Firstfruits**
This ceremony was held on the last day of the Festival of Unleavened Bread. The first sheaf of the barley harvest was presented to God. The main harvest festival (Weeks) came later.
Leviticus 23:9−14

□ **Weeks** (later **Pentecost**)
At the end of the grain harvest the priest offered two loaves of bread made from the new flour, along with animal sacrifices. This took place fifty days (or seven weeks plus one day) after Passover and the start of the harvest. The festival later came

to be known as 'Pentecost', from the Greek word meaning 'fiftieth'. It was a time of great rejoicing and thanksgiving for God's gifts at harvest.
Exodus 23:16; Leviticus 23:15−21; Deuteronomy 16:9−12

□ **Trumpets** (later **New Year**)
The beginning of every month, as well as every festival, was signalled by a blast of trumpets. But on the first day of the seventh month the trumpets sounded for a special celebration. It was a day for rest and worship, more important even than the sabbath, judging by the offerings made. It marked out the seventh month as the most solemn month in the year. After the exile it was treated as a religious New Year festival (*Rosh Hashanah*), but the months were still counted from Nisan (March/April).
Numbers 10:10; 28:9; 29:1−2

□ **Day of Atonement**
On this day (*Yom Kippur*) the whole nation of Israel confessed their sin and asked for God's forgiveness and cleansing. The high priest, dressed in white linen, first offered a sacrifice for his own sin and the sin of the priests,

and then offered another sacrifice for the sin of the people.

It was the only day in the year when the high priest went into the 'holy of holies' – the inner, most sacred part of the tabernacle (worship tent) or temple. There he sprinkled blood from the sacrifice. Then he took a goat, known as the 'scapegoat', and, after laying his hand on its head, sent it off into the desert as a sign that the people's sins had been taken away.

See also *Priests, Levites and Sacrifices*, and Part 6: *Key Teaching of the Bible* under *Atonement*.
Leviticus 16

☐ Ingathering/Tabernacles/ Booths/Shelters

This was the most popular and joyful of all the festivals. It was held in the autumn when all the fruit crops had been harvested. The celebrations included camping out in gardens and on roof-tops in tents or huts made from the branches of trees. These tents (or 'tabernacles') were a reminder of the time when Israel had lived in tents in the desert.

This festival included a ceremony in which water was

The festival of booths, recalling life in the desert, is still celebrated today.

poured out and prayers made for good rains for the coming season. It was at this festival, perhaps following this particular ceremony, that Jesus stood up and declared: 'Whoever is thirsty should come to me and drink. As the scripture says, "Whoever believes in me, streams of life-giving water will pour out from his heart."'
Exodus 34:22; Judges 21:19–21; Nehemiah 8:14–16; Leviticus 23:39–43; John 7:37–38

☐ Dedication/Lights

This festival commemorated the cleansing and re-dedication of the second temple by Judas Maccabaeus in 165 BC, after it had been defiled by the Syrian ruler Antiochus IV Epiphanes. It was also called 'Lights', as each evening lamps were placed in houses and synagogues. This festival, called Dedication in John 10:22, is celebrated today as *Hanukkah*.
1 Maccabees 4:52–59

☐ Purim

An excited and noisy celebration, traced back to the time when Esther and her cousin Mordecai saved the Jewish people from massacre during the reign of the Persian King Xerxes ('Ahasuerus'). Purim means 'lots' and the name refers to the lots cast by Haman, the king's chief minister, to decide on which day he

The festival of Purim is an occasion for noisy celebration.

should massacre the Jews.
Esther 3; 7; 9:24, 26

Other festivals
☐ The sabbath

The sabbath was Israel's most distinctive festival. Other nations had their harvest festivals and new moon rituals. Only Israel had the sabbath, which cut across the rhythm of the seasons.

Every seventh day was set aside for rest. This was the 'sabbath' and it belonged to God. The fourth commandment instructed the people of Israel to stop work on this day. The pattern of six days' work followed by a day of rest was also traced right back to creation, when God 'rested' on the seventh day. On the sabbath people were to remember all that God had done, especially in rescuing them from slavery in Egypt.

'If you treat the Sabbath as sacred,' God said through the prophet Isaiah, 'and do not pursue your own interests on that day; if you value my holy day and honour it by not travelling, working or talking idly on that day, then you will find the joy that comes from serving me.'

By New Testament times, keeping the sabbath had become so complicated with rules

and regulations that Jesus had to remind people that 'the Sabbath was made for the good of man; man was not made for the Sabbath'.
Genesis 2:2–3; Exodus 20:8–11; 31:12–17; Deuteronomy 5:12–15; Isaiah 56; 58:13–14; Matthew 12:1–14; Mark 2:23–27

☐ **New Moon**
The day of the new moon signalled the start of each month. Trumpets were blown and special sacrifices made. The arrival of the new moon was understood as a reminder that God had created an orderly world. No work was done on this day, but there were special meals and religious teaching.
Genesis 1:16; Numbers 10:10; 28:11–15; Psalm 104:19; 1 Samuel 20:5, 24; 2 Kings 4:23

☐ **Sabbatical year**
Just as every seventh day was to be a day of rest, so every seventh ('sabbatical') year was 'to be a year of complete rest for the land, a year dedicated to the Lord'. Obviously the whole land could not lie fallow at the same time. Probably each field lay fallow every seventh year after it was first sown.

Anything which did grow in this year could be harvested free by the poor. This arrangement was a sign to the Israelites that the land was not their own. It was 'holy' (belonging to God).

Also, each seventh year all Israelite slaves were to be set free and all debts cancelled.
Leviticus 25:1–7; Exodus 23:10–11; 21:2–6; Deuteronomy 15:1–6

☐ **Jubilee year**
The law said that in every fiftieth year – the year after seven 'sabbatical' years – land and property (except for town houses) was to be returned to its original owners, Israelite slaves were to be set free, debts cancelled and the land allowed to lie fallow. The jubilee law may have proved too difficult to keep, so it was looked forward to as a time that only God could introduce. It was the 'year' promised by Isaiah, and announced by Jesus.
Leviticus 25:8–17; 23–55; Isaiah 61:1–2; Luke 4:16–21

These pictures show the celebration of Hanukkah, *the festival of lights.*

Tabernacle and Temples

The tabernacle was a large tent made by the Israelites to a design given to Moses at Mt Sinai. It was the place where they worshipped God on their journey from Egypt to Canaan. Each time they camped (see Numbers 1:50 – 2:31), the Levites set up the tabernacle. It stood at the centre of the camp, with the Levites' tents around it on all four sides. Behind them were the tents of the twelve tribes of Israel, three tribes on each side.

The tabernacle was the centre of Israel's religious life. It was a sign that God was always with them. Even though they had been kept out of the Promised Land for forty years because of their disobedience, still God was willing to protect and go with them. So the tabernacle is often called the 'tent of meeting' (between God and man) and 'the dwelling place' (of God).

The tabernacle and its furniture

The tent (**T**) was supported by a frame of acacia wood. It was about 45ft/14m long, 13½ft/4m wide, and 15ft/5m high. Four types of coverings were draped over this frame. First came linen curtains, decorated with blue, purple and scarlet tapestry which could be seen inside the tabernacle.

Next came a set of curtains made of goats' hair. These were a little longer than the linen ones, and one of them formed the door of the tent.

On top of these curtains went a weatherproof covering, made of rams' skins, dyed red.

Finally, there was another waterproof covering made from the skin of some other animal (translated 'badger', 'porpoise' or simply 'fine leather').

Inside, the tent was divided into two rooms. The smaller one, furthest from the door,

was called the 'holy of holies' or 'the most holy place'. Only the high priest, once a year, was allowed to enter the 'holy of holies'. A linen curtain separated this from the larger room, which was called 'the holy place'. The entrance to it was covered by another embroidered linen curtain. Exodus 25 – 27; 30:1–10, 17–21

□ The Covenant Box/Ark of the Covenant (AC)

This was a rectangular box (about $4 \times 2\frac{1}{2} \times 2\frac{1}{2}$ft/$115 \times 70 \times 70$cm). Like the framework of the tabernacle, it was made of acacia wood, a very durable timber which grows in the Sinai Desert. The wood of the box was overlaid with gold. The box was carried by poles pushed through rings at the four lower corners. It contained the two tablets of the Ten Commandments, a golden pot of manna, and Aaron's rod that blossomed overnight. The lid was of solid gold and at both ends were the figures of two creatures (cherubim) with wings spread out as a sign of God's protection.

The Covenant Box stood in the 'holy of holies'. It was thought of as the place where God was invisibly enthroned because he said, 'I will meet you there, and from above the lid between the two winged creatures I will give you all my laws for the people of Israel.' It was sometimes carried into battle, as a symbol of God's protection. The fact that on one occasion it was captured by the Philistines showed it had no power of its own. Exodus 25:10–22; Deuteronomy 10:1–5; Hebrews 9:4–5; Joshua 6:6, 8; 1 Samuel 4:3

□ The incense altar (I)

In the holy place, in front of the curtain which screened the holy of holies, stood a small altar on which incense was burnt each morning and evening. It was made out of acacia wood, overlaid with gold. It had a horn at each corner, and

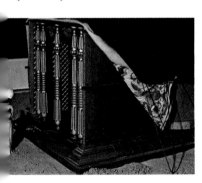

A model of the tabernacle showing the carrying-poles and layers of coverings.

The tabernacle

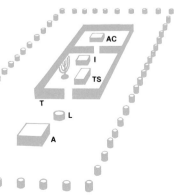

For key to initials, see text

rings were attached to two of the sides to make it easy to carry.
Exodus 30:1–10

☐ The golden lampstand (GL)
The seven-branched lampstand was hammered out of one piece of gold, weighing 66lb/30kg or more and decorated with flowers and buds like almond blossom. It was the only source of light in the tabernacle.
Exodus 25:31–39

Inside the tabernacle and the temple stood a golden seven-branched lampstand.

☐ Table of showbread/Bread of Presence (TS)
Each sabbath, twelve new loaves, one for each tribe, were placed as an offering on the gold-overlaid table that stood in the holy place.
Exodus 25:23–30

☐ Courtyard (C)
The tabernacle itself stood in the western part of a courtyard about 150×75ft/50×25m. The courtyard itself was enclosed by a screen of linen curtains. There was an entrance on

A reconstruction of the altar in the tabernacle courtyard.

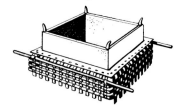

one side, with a curtain of embroidered linen drawn across it.
Exodus 27:9–19

☐ Laver (L)
The laver was a huge bronze basin on a bronze base. It was used by the priests for washing their hands and feet each time they were about to enter the tabernacle or offer a sacrifice.
Exodus 30:17–21

☐ Altar of burnt offering (A)
Here sacrifices of lambs, bulls, goats, and other animals were made. (See *Priests, Levites and Sacrifices*.) This altar, like several objects in the tabernacle, was made of wood overlaid with bronze. It was about 7½ft/2.5m square and 4½ft/1.5m high. Halfway up the altar was a ledge on which it seems the priests stood to make their sacrifices. The altar may have been filled with earth, or empty and used like an incinerator.
Exodus 27:1–8

Solomon's temple
When the Israelites conquered Canaan the tabernacle was no longer carried about with them. For a long time it remained at Shiloh. The Covenant Box was taken into battle and captured by the Philistines. But it brought them trouble and they sent it back.

Eventually King David brought it to Jerusalem. He had bought a piece of land just north of the city, and planned to build a permanent temple there for God. But although he longed to do this he was unable

to do so. As he explained to his people, it was because 'I am a soldier and have shed too much blood'. So he had to be content with getting materials together. Solomon, his son, became the builder of the first temple in Jerusalem.

This temple was not large by today's standards, but it must have been the largest building the Israelites had constructed up to this time. It measured about 30×87ft/9×27m, and was 43ft/13.5m high. No other temple quite like it in plan has been found, though a Canaanite one recently excavated at Hazor, and a ninth-century BC shrine found in Syria have the same basic three-room design. The temple was very similar in layout to the pattern of the tabernacle.

The priests entered the temple through a large porch. Then came the main room, the 'holy place'. In it stood the incense altar, the table for showbread, and five pairs of lampstands.

The inner room, as in the tabernacle, was the 'holy of holies' (the most sacred part

A model of the first temple at Jerusalem, built by King Solomon.

Solomon's temple

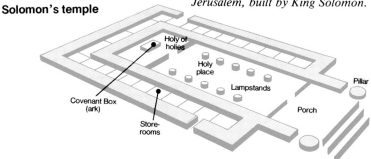

Holy of holies

Holy place

Lampstands

Pillar

Porch

Covenant Box (ark)

Store-rooms

of all). It was probably approached by steps from the holy place. It contained two cherubim made of olivewood and covered with gold. They were the symbols of God's protection of the most important object in the holy of holies: the Covenant Box (ark; see above).

The walls of each room were panelled with cedar, carved with flowers, palm-trees and cherubim, and overlaid with gold. No stonework could be seen from inside the building.

*A model of
the table of showbread.*

The holy place was dimly lit by high windows and by the lampstands. But the holy of holies – the place of God's presence – had no windows and so was completely dark.

Incense was burnt in the temple itself, but the sacrifices took place in the courtyard outside. Only priests and Levites were allowed inside the temple building.

A full account of how the temple was built and furnished is given in 1 Kings 5–7. All the skill and resources King Solomon could muster went into the construction and decoration of the temple. It was God's temple. Even the stones were prepared at the quarry 'so that there was no noise made by hammers, axes or any other iron tools as the temple was being built'.

When it was finished, Solomon held a great dedication service. The cloud of

God's presence filled the temple and King Solomon himself led the worship:
'You, Lord, have placed the sun in the sky,
yet you have chosen to live in clouds and darkness.
Now I have built a majestic temple for you,
a place for you to live in for ever.'

From this time on the centre of worship was the temple at Jerusalem, though the ten tribes who later broke away to form the northern kingdom of Israel set up their own temples in other places.

King Solomon's temple was finally destroyed by King Nebuchadnezzar of Babylon when he captured the city of Jerusalem in 587 BC. Its remaining bronze and gold and silver furnishings were taken to Babylon.
2 Samuel 6; 7; 24:18–25;
1 Chronicles 28:2–3;
1 Kings 5–8; 12;
2 Kings 16:5–9; 24:10–13;
25:8–17

This bronze stand recalls the 'lavers' in Solomon's temple – cauldrons on wheeled stands for carrying water.

Zerubbabel's temple (the second temple)

When the Persian King Cyrus allowed the Jews to return from Babylon to Jerusalem in 538 BC, he commanded them to rebuild the temple. He also gave them back all the gold and silver objects which Nebuchadnezzar had taken from Solomon's temple. They began work straight away, but soon became discouraged. Only after the prophets Haggai and Zechariah had spurred them on was the temple completed in 515 BC.

Although it stood for 500 years we know very little about this temple. It almost certainly followed the plan of Solomon's temple, but was not nearly so splendid.

When the Syrian ruler Antiochus IV banned sacrifices in the temple in 168 BC and defiled it by offering a pagan sacrifice, a revolt broke out (the Maccabean revolt). Three years later the temple was re-dedicated – the event still remembered at the Jewish festival of *Hanukkah*. (See *Fasts and Festivals*, under *Dedication*.) It was destroyed by the Roman general Pompey in 63 BC.
2 Chronicles 36:22–23;
Ezra 1; 3–6

Herod's temple

In 19 BC King Herod the Great began work on a new temple at Jerusalem. He wanted to win favour with his subjects and to impress the Roman world with his splendid building. The main building was finished by about 9 BC, but work continued for many years afterwards. Built on the same plan as Solomon's temple, this third temple was by far the grandest. It was twice as high as Solomon's temple, and covered with so much gold that it was a dazzling sight in the bright sun.

The most impressive feature was the great temple 'platform', still in existence today, where

A 'horned' altar from Megiddo, Israel.

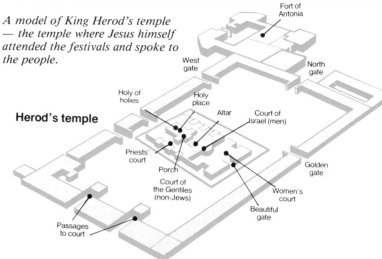

A model of King Herod's temple — the temple where Jesus himself attended the festivals and spoke to the people.

Herod's temple

Fort of Antonia

West gate

North gate

Holy of holies

Holy place

Altar

Court of Israel (men)

Priests' court

Porch

Court of the Gentiles (non-Jews)

Golden gate

Women's court

Beautiful gate

Passages to court

pilgrims gathered and sacrifices were offered. The walls of this platform extended beyond the summit of the hill to enclose an area of 35 acres. At its southern end, it stood 100–150ft/30–45m above ground level. One of the southern corners of the platform is probably the 'pinnacle' from which the devil tempted Jesus to throw himself down.

A covered cloister (where Peter and John taught the people) ran right round the outer courtyards. The main entrance was from the south, and led to the Court of the Gentiles. Anyone could enter this part of the temple. But notices in Greek and Latin forbade non-Jews to enter the inner court of the temple. The result of breaking this rule was likely to be death. Acts 21, describing Paul's arrest, gives an idea of the intense feelings aroused by the suggestion that a non-Jew had 'defiled the holy place'.

The next court was the Court of the Women. This was as far as women were allowed to go into the temple itself. Men could go further, into the Court of Israel, and they could even enter the Priests' Court for a procession round the altar at the Festival of Tabernacles.

The temple was destroyed by the Romans at the time of the Jewish rebellion in AD 70, and its treasures taken back to Rome.
Matthew 4:5–6; Mark 13:1; Acts 3:11

Priests, Levites and the Sacrifices

Priests and Levites
The Levites were originally just one of the twelve tribes of Israel, descended from Levi, one of the sons of Jacob. But they were given a special position among God's people, because they defended his honour at the time when the rest of the people worshipped the golden calf. So they were dedicated to serve God. They became his own tribe in a special way.

They were set apart from the other tribes for religious duties. As they did not own any land, they had to be supported by the other tribes. To do this the people gave a 'tithe' (a tenth) of all their harvests and live-stock to God. In Israel forty-eight towns were set aside for the use of the Levites.

Levi had three sons (Kohath, Gershon, and Merari) and their descendants formed the three clans of Levites. During the time in the desert the Kohath-ites were responsible for carry-ing the tabernacle furniture; the Gershonites carried its cur-tains and coverings; and the

Merarites carried and set up the tabernacle itself.

One family, belonging to the Kohathite clan, was set apart for special service. This was the family of Aaron, the brother of Moses. He and his descen-dants were appointed priests. Only priests could offer sacri-fices. The other Levite families did the more menial jobs, and were virtually servants of the priests. So the priests were the most 'holy' group within Israel.

That does not mean, of course, that they were the most godly; many were not (for example, Eli's sons, who are described in 1 Samuel 2:22–25). 'Holy' is used in the special sense of 'belonging to God'.

These men were the profes-sional officials of the tabernacle and temple. Because of their special position they were subject to strict rules. A man of this family became a priest at the age of thirty.

The man in charge of the priests was the chief or 'high priest'. He had one privilege allowed to no one else. He could enter the 'holy of holies'

once a year, on the Day of Atonement.
Levites: Exodus 32:25–29; Numbers 3:12–13; 18:21–24; 35:2–8
Priests: Exodus 28–29; Leviticus 8–10; 16; 21–22

Duties of the priests and Levites

The duties of the priests and Levites are mostly connected with the tabernacle and temple sacrifices and worship. But they also had a number of other duties. A group of men from each of the three Levite clans formed the temple choirs, and they may have composed several of the psalms (for example, Psalms 85 and 87).

This model shows priests and Levites carrying out sacrifices in the tabernacle courtyard.

The priests and Levites also had to give answers in God's name to questions that could not otherwise be decided (for example, whether it was the right time to go out to battle). For this purpose they used the sacred stones called Urim and Thummim, which were kept in a pouch worn on the high priest's chest. If the priest pulled out the Urim stone, the answer was 'no', but if it was the Thummim stone, the answer was 'yes'.

More important, they were also responsible for teaching the people the Law of God. When Moses blessed the tribes of Israel he said that the Levites will first 'teach your children to obey your Law'; and, secondly, 'offer sacrifices on your altar'. The Book of Nehemiah describes one occasion when Ezra and the Levites held a reading of the Law to all the people. The prophet Malachi sums up their role: 'It is the duty of the priests to teach the true knowledge of God. People should go to them to learn my will, because they are the messengers of the Lord Almighty.' Sadly, the prophets often had to call the priests and Levites to task for failing in these duties.
1 Chronicles 6:31–48; Leviticus 13; Deuteronomy 33:8–11; Nehemiah 8:1–12; Malachi 2:7; Jeremiah 23:11–32; Ezekiel 34

The sacrifices

The practice of animal sacrifice goes back to very early times. Genesis 4 tells how Abel killed one of his lambs and gave the best parts as an offering to God. Noah made a sacrifice of animals and birds after his escape from the flood. The agreement between God and Abraham was sealed with a sacrifice.

The details of the sacrifices are described in the Book of Leviticus. There we learn certain basic facts about their meaning.

● **Sacrifice is always made to God himself.** So only the best is good enough. Sacrifice was also a way of setting apart for God something belonging to a man.

● **Sacrifice is a way of approach given by God.** He gave the rules for sacrifice. It is not simply man's own attempt to earn favour with God, it is God's way for men to make their peace with him. All the same, a person must freely wish to make use of the ritual which God has laid down.

● **Sacrifices are for everyone.** In most religions, rituals like these are the secret of the priests. The fact that they alone know how to approach the god helps them to keep their special position in the community. But in Israel, the laws of sacrifice (that is, the Book of Leviticus) are part of the Scriptures that belong to everyone. And in fact in Israel most sacrifices were actually carried out by the worshipper, and not by the priest.

● **There are limits to the effectiveness of sacrifice.** In most cases, the sacrifices could only compensate for accidental or 'unwitting' sins. For deliberate disobedience sacrifice could only express repentance. If a sinner is to be pardoned, he must seek pardon directly from God. The New Testament also makes it clear that the blood of bulls and goats could not take away sin.

● **Sacrifice as a substitution.** Sometimes, the death of the sacrificed animal was seen as taking the place of the person who brought the sacrifice. Sin that deserved death could not be atoned for by sacrifice, but a person who had repented of his sin and had been forgiven by God, would often bring a sacrifice as a sign of his sorrow for sin.

In the New Testament, the death of Jesus is understood as a sacrifice which *did* take the place of the sinner.
Genesis 4; 8:20; 15; Leviticus 1–7; 16–17; 4:2, 13, 22, 27; Psalm 51:16–17; Hebrews 10:4; 9:11–12; 10:12

Types of sacrifice
☐ **Burnt-offering**
The whole animal, except for the skin, which went to the priests, was sacrificed to God. The worshipper placed his hands on the animal to show that it was a sacrifice for his own shortcomings. The animal had to be in perfect condition (only the best is good enough for God). The blood of the animal was sprinkled on the altar as a further sign that the life of the animal given in

death had been dedicated to God.
Leviticus 1

☐ Grain-offering
This was an offering of flour, baked cakes, or raw grain, together with oil and frankincense. It was a good-will offering to God. Part of it – 'a memorial portion' – was burnt on the altar. So it was a way of asking God to 'remember' the worshipper for good. It was also a contribution to the upkeep of the priests. Again, it was a sacrifice of the best the worshipper could give.
Leviticus 2

☐ Peace (fellowship)-offering
The ritual was similar to that for the burnt-offering, except that here only the fat – which the Israelites considered the best portion – was burnt on the altar, and the meat was shared by the worshipper and his family. Since God also shared in the sacrifice, it was thought of as a friendship meal with God too.
Leviticus 3

Present-day Samaritans sacrifice sheep for the Passover Festival, according to the Jewish Law.

☐ Sin-offerings
These sacrifices were offered when a person had sinned against someone else or against God. This sin 'defiled' (contaminated) the holy place of tabernacle or temple, and so it needed to be cleansed. The blood of the sacrifice was sprinkled as a sign that the defilement had been removed through the death that had taken place. Some of the sacrifice was taken as food for the priest. When the worshipper saw the priest eat the meat without being harmed he knew that God had accepted his act of repentance.
Leviticus 4; 5; 7

The ritual of sacrifice on the Day of Atonement (Leviticus 16) is somewhat different. Here, as well as other sacrifices, two goats were used. One was killed as in the usual sin-offering, but the other was sent into the wilderness as a symbol that the sins were being removed. (See *Fasts and Festivals*, and Part 6: *Key Teaching of the Bible*, under *Atonement*.)

The Prophets

The work of the priests continued throughout the history of Israel. But the great prophets whose messages we have in the Old Testament appeared on the scene only at times of crisis in the nation's history. They were God's men for the moment and their messages were generally concerned with particular times and places. They remain valid and helpful because the same kind of situations have recurred again and again in history.

The early prophets
The prophets first emerged as a group in the time of *Samuel*, who is often described as 'the last of the Judges and first of the prophets in Israel'. The Philistines were a great threat to Israel at the time. These early prophets, with their enthusiasm for Israel's God, strengthened the Israelites' determination to be free and independent. When the young Saul met them he was overcome by their sense of God's dynamic energy. He joined in excited prophesying as God's power took control of him.

Samuel himself does not seem to have been caught up in the ecstasies of these prophetic groups. He played an important role as a judge of the people. He also reproved them for worshipping foreign gods, and prayed to God on their behalf for forgiveness. (These were also important aspects of the work of later prophets.) Samuel obviously also had other, supernatural, gifts. When Saul was out looking for his father's lost asses Samuel could tell him they were found – and also predict what would happen to him on his way. But these are comparatively trivial matters.

Samuel is best remembered for the fact that he, like many of the prophets, was the one through whom God's choice of a king was made known. He anointed Saul, and later David, as God's chosen rulers.

While David was still king, the prophet *Nathan* was similarly involved in king-

The prophet Amos called for justice: no false scales to cheat the customer.

Jeremiah declared God's right to remake his spoilt people, like a potter moulding a pot.

The prophet Joel used the picture of a locust-plague to describe God's judgement.

making. But it was not until the middle of the ninth century BC that prophecy came to the fore with the work of *Elijah* and *Elisha*.

A crisis in the northern kingdom of Israel formed the backcloth to the work of these prophets. Foreign gods had been imported into the worship of Israel by Jezebel, wife of King Ahab. She had brought from her home city of Tyre 850 prophets of Baal and Asherah, a Canaanite god and goddess. Elijah realized that he must challenge this false religion and uphold faith in Israel's God.

So Elijah challenged the Canaanite prophets to a contest on Mt Carmel where God proved by fire that 'The Lord is God; the Lord alone is God!' Elisha continued Elijah's mission. He performed miracles of healing and later in his life had Jehu anointed king of Israel. He gathered a number of disciples – 'sons of the prophets' – who preserved the memory of his deeds.
1 Samuel 7:3–17; 9–10; 2 Samuel 7; 1 Kings 1:11–40; 17–19; 2 Kings 1–9

Later prophets
None of the 'older' prophets have left us any books of their prophecies, though we do know a little of what they said and did. But in the 'classical'

period of prophecy, from the eighth to the fifth centuries BC, many of the prophets' messages were written down and compiled into the Old Testament books we now have: Isaiah, Jeremiah, Ezekiel, and the Book of the Twelve Prophets (the 'minor' prophets – Hosea to Malachi), plus the Book of Daniel.

The crisis behind this new period of prophecy was the changing political scene that led first to the exile of Israel (the northern kingdom) after its capital, Samaria, was captured in 721 BC, and then to the exile of Judah (the southern kingdom) after Jerusalem had been destroyed in 586 BC.

The message of these prophets centres on the exile. Some looked ahead to it. Others reflected on its meaning. And the later prophets encouraged the nation to rebuild itself out of the disaster.

□ Before the exile
The prophets warned that judgement was inevitable. Amos and Hosea did so in the northern kingdom in the eighth century; Jeremiah in the southern kingdom in the late seventh century. They called on the people to repent. It was not yet too late for God to change his mind. But the prophets

were forced to realize that the people were in no mood to repent. They had been given many chances, but they refused to take them. At this point Amos speaks for all the prophets. This is God's message: 'Get ready to face my judgement!'

What had Israel done to make God so angry? Different prophets exposed different aspects of Israel's sin. Amos attacks social injustice; Hosea Israel's unfaithfulness to God; Micah the sins of Israel's rulers; Jeremiah the false gods and the unchecked corruption in Judah. For these sins, the righteous God must punish his people, even though it pained him to the heart to do so.
Amos 9:1–4; Hosea 11:5–7; Jeremiah 25:8–11; Amos 5:14–15; 4:6–12

□ The exile and after
Once Judah as well as Israel had gone into exile, some, at least, began to realize that they had deserved this punishment. From this time on, the prophets were able to stir up hope. Ezekiel foresaw a day when the nation, lifeless as a heap of dead bones, would begin to live again as the Spirit of God breathed new life into the people. He looked forward to the rebuilding of the temple and a new settlement of the land. The prophecies of Isaiah

40–55 also brought a message of assurance to the people. God was about to bring the exiles back across the desert from Babylonia to Jerusalem.

Then, after the first exiles had returned, and the excitement of the beginning of temple rebuilding had worn off, a new generation of prophets was needed to meet the crisis of disillusionment and despair. If Haggai and Zechariah had not encouraged the people to work on the temple, it would never have been completed. The return from Exile would have been a failure if the worship of God had not been properly restored. Ezekiel 37; 40–48; Isaiah 40:1, 9–10

The role of the prophets

The prophets are best understood as messengers. Their speeches (or 'oracles') often begin with the words 'God says' or 'God spoke'. This is the way a messenger in the ancient world would begin a message he was bringing by word of mouth. The prophets were called by God to hear his plans and his messages. Then they were sent by him to bring this message to Israel and the nations. Sometimes they saw visions; sometimes they preached sermons; sometimes they used parable or poetry or drama to speak to the people. They tell us little about how they actually received their messages. But they were completely convinced that what they said came from God.

The prophets were usually against the mainstream of opinion. When all seemed well, they attacked the evils of their society and predicted its doom. When their people were pessimistic, they prophesied hope. They brought these disturbing, challenging words from God because God's call had broken into their own lives and changed them drastically.

The prophets were also teachers calling Israel back to obey God's laws. They were not preaching a new religion,

'I will climb my watch-tower,' writes the prophet Habakkuk, 'to see what the Lord will tell me to say.' This stone watch-tower is at Bethlehem.

but applying the word of God to their own day.

The Old Testament owes a great deal to the prophets. Not just the books of the prophets, but many of the history-books, especially those from Joshua to 2 Kings, were written either by prophets or by men who had learned much from the prophets' teaching. They wrote history as God sees it. Jeremiah 23:18, 21–22; Amos 7:1–2; Zechariah 1:7–21; Jeremiah 7; 18; 19; Isaiah 1; Ezekiel 5:17; 1 Kings 18:19; Amos 7:14–16; Isaiah 6; Jeremiah 1

☐ False prophets

All through Israel's history there were false prophets who claimed that their messages came from God, when in fact they did not. A prophet might begin his preaching with 'God says', but that was no guarantee at all that it really was a word from God. It needed spiritual insight to decide, in a particular case, what actually came from God. The Law in Deuteronomy recognized the problem and gave two helpful rules. If a prophet predicted something and it did not happen, he was a false prophet. And if his message led people away from God and his laws, it was false. 1 Kings 22; Jeremiah 28; Micah 3:5–7; Jeremiah 23:13–32; Deuteronomy 13; 18:21–22

☐ The message of the prophets

Jeremiah saw that the exile meant the end of God's covenant with Israel: 'Both Israel and Judah have broken

the covenant that I made with their ancestors.'

Yet the prophets believed that God would not desert Israel even though they no longer had any claim upon God. That is why even those prophets who pictured a dreadful future for the people could still look beyond the tragedy to a time of hope. In Amos it is promised that the family of David will be restored to the throne; in Hosea that God will heal Israel's faithlessness; in Jeremiah that God will remake the covenant.

So the prophets' message looked to the past, recalling Israel to obedience; to the present, dealing with the crisis of faith in which the people found themselves; and to the future, because they believed that God had committed himself to Israel. The commitment might mean the destruction of Israel for a time but it would end in rebuilding.

The time when Israel would be destroyed and rebuilt was sometimes called the 'Day of the Lord'. The hope of a Messiah who would bring about a restoration has its roots in the Old Testament, but it became important only in the last centuries before Christ (see next section). For the prophets, it was God who would step in to restore Israel. Jeremiah 11:10; Amos 9:11–12; Hosea 14:4; Jeremiah 31:31–34; Amos 9:9; Zechariah 13:8–9; Isaiah 2:12–17; Zephaniah

Between the Testaments

During the exile in Babylonia prophets such as Ezekiel, and historians such as the unknown author of 1 and 2 Kings, had shown how the exile was God's punishment for Israel's disobedience to God. So those who returned to Israel were determined that in future they would not neglect God's Law.

They wanted to be faithful to it in all its details. They had no king, but the high priest became their natural leader, assisted by a new class of 'scribes' who were able to explain the Bible's laws. The lesson had been learnt so well that after the exile the prophets never had to rebuke the Jews for worshipping foreign gods, though they did protest at their laziness in rebuilding the temple and their reluctance to pay their tithes.

The Jewish community of returned exiles was a small one, probably less than 75,000 people. It was very aware of being different from the surrounding nations. Three things which stressed this 'difference' were specially emphasized at this time: strict observance of the sabbath, of the rite of circumcision, and of the Jewish food laws.
Haggai 1; Malachi 3:7–11; Nehemiah 13:15–27; Isaiah 56:6–7; Genesis 17; Leviticus 11 (see also Daniel 1)

Jewish history after the exile
☐ Phase 1
In the first phase of Jewish history after the exile, the Jewish state formed a province of the Persian Empire, founded in 539 BC, when Cyrus the Great captured Babylon and became heir to the Babylonian Empire and its rich civilization. Unlike the Babylonians, the Persians encouraged the growth of local loyalties and national religions within their empire. They even provided for the upkeep of the Jerusalem temple on a lavish scale.
Ezra 1; 6:1–12

☐ Phase 2
The second phase came with the overthrow of the Persian Empire by Alexander the Great, the general from Macedonia (northern Greece). When he conquered Persia in 331 BC, his dream of spreading Greek culture and language throughout a world empire began to be fulfilled. But he did not live to see it. A few years later he died, and his empire was divided among his generals.

Palestine was a bone of contention for centuries. During the third century it was controlled from Alexandria by the kings of Egypt, Ptolemy and his descendants. But throughout the second century BC the Seleucid kings, with their capital at Antioch in Syria, determined its destiny. Whichever group held the country, the effect was the same. Greek culture (hellenism), with all its attractions, made its impact on the Jewish religion (Judaism).

By the second century BC it became necessary to have the Old Testament translated into Greek for the benefit of those Jews, mostly outside Palestine, who now spoke only Greek. But Greek culture brought with it Greek religion, which the Jewish faith was utterly against. So two parties grew up amongst the Jews: those who favoured the foreign ways (the Hellenists), and the more conservative Jews (the Hasidim) who believed that hellenism and Judaism were incompatible.

The conflict came to a head in the reign of Antiochus IV Epiphanes. With the support of some leading Jewish families he transformed Jerusalem into a Greek city. Antiochus eventually decided to root out the Jewish religion altogether, and forbade them to offer sacrifices, to circumcise or to read the Law. When the Jews resisted, he took the final step of placing a statue of the Greek god Zeus in the Jerusalem temple, and sacrificing pigs on the altar. In the eyes of all pious Jews the temple was contaminated and could no longer be used for worship.

☐ Phase 3
The third phase was brought about by the revolt led by Judas Maccabaeus. After a long struggle, he drove Antiochus' followers out of the temple, built a new altar to replace the one defiled by Antiochus, and rededicated the temple in December 165/4 BC (1 Maccabees 1–4). From then until 63 BC, Judea remained an independent state, ruled by a succession of priest-kings – the Hasmoneans.

☐ Phase 4
The fourth phase of Jewish history 'between the Testaments' began with the Roman conquest of what was left of the Seleucid Empire in Syria and Palestine. The Roman general, Pompey, took Jerusalem in 63 BC, and from then until the fall of the Roman Empire several centuries later, Judea was governed directly or indirectly by the Romans. For one important period Judea again had a king. This was from 37–4 BC, the reign of Herod the Great.

Herod was appointed king by the Roman Senate, and was responsible to Rome. On his death his son Archelaus was made ethnarch ('ruler of the people') by the Romans. But in AD 6 he was deposed by the Romans, and Judea became a Roman province.

Changing ideas

More important than the changes in history and politics that took place between the return from exile and the time of Christ were the developments in Jewish belief.

☐ The coming of the new world

Hopes for the future were very much alive in the time of Christ. Several centuries before, the prophets had predicted the end of Israel as a nation-state, and those prophecies had been fulfilled by the exile. Some of their prophecies seemed, though, to reach beyond the near future into a distant future when God would, as Haggai put it, 'shake heaven and earth' and a totally new age would dawn.

From the second century BC on, a new type of writing called apocalyptic (meaning 'revelation') was produced. The writers of these apocalyptic books were sure that the end of the world was close. God was about to step in, destroy the foreign rulers, whether Greeks or Romans, and begin a new era in history. One apocalyptic group was the community of the Dead Sea Scrolls (see *Essenes*, in the next section).

☐ The Messiah

Many of the hopes for the new age centred on the Messiah. In the Old Testament the Hebrew word 'Messiah' meant simply 'someone who has been anointed' and could be applied to kings, priests, or prophets. Some prophets, such as Isaiah, spoke of a future king descended from David who would 'reign in righteousness' and upon whom God's Spirit would rest.

In the century and a half before the coming of Christ, many people began eagerly to look forward to such a ruler. The men of the Dead Sea sect looked for two 'Messiahs': one would be a priest, the other a king. The collection of hymns from the first century BC called the *Psalms of Solomon* was one of the first writings to use the phrase 'the Lord Christ (that is, Messiah)' (or, 'the Lord's Christ') for this coming ruler (compare Luke 2:11).

Most often the Messiah was expected to be a warrior who would rid the Jews of hated foreign rulers. It is not surprising that Jesus, whose kingdom 'does not belong to this world' was reluctant to let himself be called 'Messiah'. It created the wrong impression. But the disciples, who in the end understood what kind of a king he was, often used this title for him: 'Jesus the Christ'. Isaiah 9:1–7; 11:1–9; John 18:36; Mark 8:29–30; Luke 22:67

☐ Resurrection

Another hope had also developed: for personal resurrection. In Old Testament times the Israelites generally believed that after death good and bad people alike entered the land of *Sheol*. This was a kind of underworld existence which was only a shadow of real life, and from which no one could return. Occasionally the prophets expressed hope for the resurrection of the nation – as in Ezekiel's vision of skeletons which became men again. But the nearest the Old Testament comes to a hope of resurrection of individuals is in Daniel 12:2, 'many of those who have already died will live again'.

But by the time of Jesus, most Jews (except the *Sadducees*; see next section) probably believed in a resurrection for everyone. The righteous would 'rise again into life eternal' (*Psalms of Solomon* 3:16) in 'the garden of life' (1 *Enoch* 61:12), or 'Abraham's bosom'. The wicked would be thrown into Gehenna, the underworld equivalent of the Valley of

The time 'between the Testaments' was marked by a new determination to obey the Law in all its details. Scribes not only copied the Law with great care – as they still do today – but explained the laws to the people.

Hinnom, the rubbish dump of Jerusalem, where fires always burnt.
Job 7:9–10; Ezekiel 37; Daniel 12:2; Luke 16:22

☐ **Belief in angels and demons**
Israelites had always pictured God as a king surrounded by his courtiers, the angels. God's decisions were made in his council-room, and the prophets thought of themselves as listening in. Not much attention was paid to 'bad' angels. But when they are mentioned, they are clearly under God's control.

In the time between the Old and New Testaments there was great debate about the names and duties of the angels and demons.

The evil angels were sometimes identified with the 'sons of God' or 'supernatural beings' mentioned in Genesis 6:1–4. They and their assistants, the demons or unclean spirits, were held responsible for evil in the world. In the Old Testament Satan was 'the tester', trying to find grounds to accuse man before God. But now he was regarded as a demon prince opposed to God. He was also called Belial and Beelzebub.
Job 1–2; Jeremiah 23:18, 21–22; 1 Samuel 16:14; Daniel 10:13; 8:16; Matthew 12:24; 1 Peter 5:8

As well as these changes in belief, there were two other important developments in the last centuries before Christ. It was a time when the Law was studied, and extended, as never before (see *Pharisees* in the next section). And during this time various religious and political groups sprang up. We meet some of them – Pharisees, Sadducees, scribes – in the New Testament. But even those not named had an effect on the Jewish religious 'climate' of New Testament times. The main groups are described on the following pages.

Jewish Religion: New Testament Times

In order to understand the religious 'climate' in Palestine at the time of Jesus we need to know something about a number of Jewish groups or sects which developed in the last centuries before Christ. Some, but not all, are mentioned by name in the New Testament. Most Jews did not belong to any sect, though the Pharisees were most highly respected by the ordinary people.

Developing groups
☐ **The Hasidim** (the 'pious ones')
This group was not an organized sect. It is the name given to those Jews who resisted the inroads of Greek culture (hellenism) into Jewish life and culture. In the second century BC some of them joined the Maccabees in the armed struggle against the Greek rulers (*1 Maccabees* 2:42). Others were pacifists. All certainly were faithful followers of the Law, and many of them joined the sects of the Pharisees and the Essenes.

☐ **The Pharisees** (a word which may mean the 'separated ones')
The Pharisees were a strict, religious sect, probably beginning in the second century BC. They were mostly ordinary Jews – not priests – who kept closely to the Jewish Law. They often extended the way the laws applied, so that they became very hard to keep. The forbidding of work on the sabbath is an extreme example. Pharisees counted as 'work': walking more than ³/₅ mile (about 1km) from one's town; carrying any kind of load; lighting a fire in the home.
Strict rulings like this often

led to people being so concerned to keep the law in every detail that they lost sight of the 'spirit' behind it. But the motive was good. Pharisees believed that their rules 'built a fence around the Law'. By keeping these other rules people would be in less danger of disobeying the actual Law of God.

Although the Pharisees were the largest Jewish sect in the time of Jesus, there were only about 6,000 of them. Many Pharisees were very godly men. But they tended to despise those who did not, or could not, keep their burdensome laws, and referred to them as 'sinners'.

Jesus frequently argued with the Pharisees. He condemned their self-righteousness and legalism. And he identified himself with the common people whom the Pharisees, as religious leaders, had written off. Nicodemus, who became a secret follower of Jesus, was a Pharisee. So too was Paul.
Matthew 12:1–42; 22:34 – 23:36; Mark 7:1–23; Luke 18:9–14; John 18:3; Acts 23:6–10

☐ **The Sadducees**
This group was smaller than the Pharisees, but more influential. Most Sadducees were members of the families of priests. They supported the Hasmonean high-priest kings (see *Between the Testaments*) and later the Roman rulers. We have little reliable information about the Sadducees, since most of it comes from their opponents. But we do know that they did not accept the Pharisees' extensions of the Law (the oral law, as distinct from the Old Testament written law). That is why they could not believe in resurrec-

tion, for it is not clearly taught in the Old Testament Law (Genesis to Deuteronomy). Matthew 16:1–12; Mark 12:18–27; Acts 4:1–2; 5:17–19; 23:6–10

Pilgrims throng into Jerusalem today, just as they did for the great festivals in New Testament times.

□ The Essenes

The Essenes were a smaller and more exclusive sect than the Pharisees, never numbering more than a few thousand. They had grown up in the second century BC as a protest movement – against Greek influence on the Jewish religion; against corrupt kings; and against the growing carelessness among Jewish people about keeping the Law. They were even stricter than the Pharisees, whom they denounced as 'givers of easy interpretations'! They were so disgusted with Jewish society that many of them opted out of it and went to live in monastic communities.

The community at Qumran, the people who wrote the Dead Sea Scrolls, probably belonged to the Essene movement. See Part 2: *Archaeology and the Bible*.

□ The Zealots (or Nationalists) This was the group that

kept alive the spirit of Judas Maccabaeus – the guerrilla leader who had succeeded in regaining the temple from the Syrians in the second century BC. They refused to pay taxes to the Romans and held themselves ready for the war that would bring in God's kingdom. They engineered several revolts. One of these was ended only by the Roman destruction of Jerusalem in AD 70. At least one of Jesus' disciples, Simon (not Simon Peter), had been a Zealot. Luke 6:15

□ The scribes

They were not a sect or a political party. They were the experts in the Law and are also called lawyers or teachers (rabbis). They interpreted the Law and applied it to everyday life. Jesus had not been to one of the schools for rabbis, but his own disciples called him 'teacher' (rabbi). So too did many of the professional rabbis. They were greatly impressed by his understanding of the Law. Later, Paul came to Jerusalem as a student of Rabbi Gamaliel. Mark 7:28–29, Luke 2:41–47; Acts 4:5–7, 18–21; 6:12–14; 22:3

Jewish worship
□ In the temple

In New Testament times the temple was still at the heart of Israel's religious life. Crowds of pilgrims went there for the great annual festivals (see *Fasts and Festivals*). It was also a centre for religious teaching. And, as in Old Testament times, the priests serving in the temple carried out the rites and sacrifices of the law.

Each day began with the recitation of Bible passages and prayers. The chief rituals were the morning and evening sacrifices. Then the priests would address the worshippers with the words of the ancient blessing:

> 'May the Lord bless you and take care of you;
> May the Lord be kind and gracious to you;
> May the Lord look on you with favour and give you peace.'

Hymns were sung by the temple choirs of Levites, but sometimes the people joined in,

The meeting-place for every Jewish community was the local synagogue. It was a simple hall with seats and a raised reading-desk. Next to it there might be a room used as a school or library.

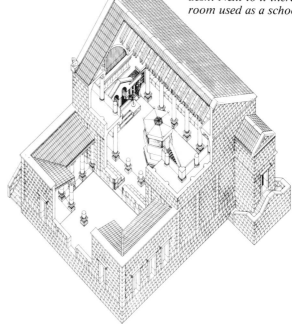

especially in the torchlight procession at the Festival of Tabernacles.

The Gospel of Luke describes Jesus' first visit as a boy to the temple, for the Passover Festival. John's Gospel records that when he grew up, Jesus often went to Jerusalem for the festivals, and much of the teaching in that Gospel was given in Jerusalem, in the temple courtyards. After Jesus' ascension his followers met and taught there, too. Luke 2:41–49; John 2:13–25; 5:7–8; 10:22–38; 12:12 and following; Acts 2:46; 3; Mark 14:58

□ **In the synagogue**
Synagogues probably first began during the exile, when there was no temple and the people were far away from Jerusalem. By the time of Jesus, most Jews outside Jerusalem normally met together on the sabbath at the local synagogue. The service at the synagogue was mainly for readings from the Bible (usually a passage from the Law and one from the Prophets) and prayers.

The service began with the *Shema*: 'Hear, O Israel, the Lord our God is one Lord; and you shall love the Lord your God with all your heart, and with all your soul, and with all your might.' The Bible passages were read in Hebrew. But since most Jews in Palestine at the time of Christ spoke Aramaic, an interpreter gave a verse-by-verse translation and explanation (a *targum*). Sometimes there was also a sermon.

Every synagogue had a chest ('ark') in which the scrolls of the Law were kept. The leaders sat in front of the ark, facing the people. Men and women sat separately.

Jesus went regularly to the synagogue, and read and taught there. Paul, on his missionary journeys, went first to the synagogue in each town, and spoke there.

The synagogue served as the local school and as the centre

for local government as well as worship.
Deuteronomy 6:4–5; Luke 4:16–30; 6:6; Acts 13:14–18; 14:1, and other references in Acts

□ **In the home**
At home every Jew was expected to pray the 'Eighteen Benedictions' every morning, afternoon and evening. Each benediction begins, 'Blessed art thou, O Lord, king of the universe'. They all praise God – for the promise of a redeemer, or the resurrection of the dead, or the gift of repentance, or healing the sick, and so on.

Before every meal the father of the household said a blessing: 'Blessed art thou, our God, king of the universe, who createst the fruit of the vine' (or, 'who bringest forth food from the earth'; or, 'who createst the fruit of the tree').

Jewish religious life
Festivals, sacrifices, synagogue services, prayer and fasting were basic to Jewish religious life, although not all Jews observed them. The Jewish religion also affected other aspects of daily life:

● **Tithing** Each year a 'tithe' (a tenth of one's produce) was given to God for the upkeep of the priests. A second tax was used for a sacrificial meal, in which the worshipper and his family shared at one of the

The Jewish Passover, a family celebration, is a focal point in the religious year.

festivals. A third tax was used to help the poor.
Leviticus 27:30–33; Numbers 18:21; Deuteronomy 14:22–29; Matthew 23:23

● **Food laws** A wide range of animals were, by God's command, not to be used for food. There were also strict laws about how animals for food should be killed so as to avoid eating blood. Meat produced according to this Jewish law is known as *kosher*.
Leviticus 11; 17:10–16

● **Uncleanness** Many things made a person ritually 'unclean' and so unable to take part in worship, among them touching a dead body or a grave and eating meat with blood in it. If this happened a person had to follow the Law's instructions to become 'clean' again.

● **Education** Many Jewish boys were educated at synagogue schools from the age of six. See Part 9: *Work and Society in the Bible*.

The Teaching of Jesus

Many people today think of Jesus' teaching as basically the Sermon on the Mount, summed up in the 'Golden Rule': 'Do for others what you want them to do for you' (Matthew 7:12). But the centre of Jesus' message was his announcement that the 'kingdom of God' had arrived.

(For more information about the meaning of some of the special words mentioned here see Part 6: *Key Teaching of the Bible*.)

The message of Jesus
☐ The kingdom of God

The 'kingdom of God' meant the rule of God in people's lives. That happens when people realize that God is the ruler of the world. It also meant the 'realm' or community of people where God's rule is obeyed.

For a long time Jews had looked forward to the time when God would come in power to be their King. He would set his people free and judge the nations. 'No king but God' was in fact the slogan of the fanatical Zealots (see above), who hoped to drive the Romans out of their land by force. But the kingdom that Jesus announced and brought with him did not 'belong to this world'. It would not be brought about by brute force.

The kingdom of God had in fact already arrived with the coming of Christ – for he was the first who fully obeyed the will of God. So he could say to the Pharisees: 'The kingdom of God is among you.' It was present in the words and works of Jesus.

Yet there is another sense in which the kingdom of God has not come, even yet. 'May your kingdom come', Jesus taught his followers to pray in the Lord's Prayer. So far the kingdom of God is still only partly in operation. In the future it will come 'with power'. Yet the future coming of the kingdom will not be a joyful event for everyone. For all who believe the good Jews of the kingdom there is 'salvation', a new life. But for many the coming of God's rule will be a judgement.

Jesus often used parables to explain what the kingdom of God is like. The kingdom turns the world's values upside down. It is the humble, the poor and those who mourn who are really happy. God's kingdom belongs to them. Rich people cannot buy their way in. For the first time in their lives they may find their riches a hindrance. Beggars are invited

One of Jesus' best-known parables is the story of the seed (God's message) and the soils: some seed falls onto the path, some amongst stones and weeds, some into good soil where it can grow.

in – and they accept God's invitation when respectable people refuse and find themselves shut out.

Jesus' parables show God at work in the world, quietly, almost secretly. Yet 'the kingdom' goes on growing and spreading from small beginnings. It is like the tiny mustard seed which becomes a tree, or the yeast which makes a great batch of dough rise.

The 'Sower' goes out, making God's message known to people everywhere. Much of the 'seed' is wasted. People close their minds to what they hear. Or other things crowd in and they forget. But some listen, and their lives are changed. The seed comes to harvest.
John 18:36; Luke 17:21; Matthew 3:2; Mark 1:15; Matthew 6:10; Mark 9:1; 14:25; Luke 13:23–30; 14:15–24; Matthew 20:1–16; 19:23–24; 13:31–33; Mark 4:3–8

☐ 'Repent and believe'

'The kingdom of God is near!' said Jesus. 'Turn away from your sins and believe the Good News!' People must 'repent', have a total change of heart, if they are to accept the rule of God in their lives. They must believe the good news Jesus came to bring.

God offers new life to all who believe, who will leave their old way of life and follow him. This is worth everything anyone has. Finding it is like finding treasure hidden in a field – and selling everything to buy the field. It means

Jesus gave us many pictures of God's kingdom. It is like a pearl which we sell everything to buy.

Jesus pictured God as a shepherd going in search of the lost sheep.

It is what we are like on the inside that counts. Jesus had harsh words for religious leaders who thought only of outward show. 'You are like whitewashed tombs,' he said.

the vital life of God that can be shared by human beings also – is to believe in (put our trust in) Jesus the Son of God. That is the same as true belief in the Father who sent him. It brings a person from 'death' to 'life'. John 10:30; 14:1; 14:6; 5:19–20, 30; 6:32–33; 3:16, 18, 36; 5:24

□ **Joy**
A note of joy runs all through the teaching of Jesus. The kingdom of God frees people and releases them to live a full life. Even when Jesus' disciples fast, he tells them they must make a festival out of it, anointing themselves with oil, not going about with dismal faces like most people. Among the Jews of Jesus' day, being good and obeying God's law was often a gloomy business.

The religious leaders grumbled because Jesus enjoyed himself, and became angry when he was greeted with shouts of joy in Jerusalem. They were like the bitter elder brother in the parable of the lost son. But the boy's father says: 'We had to celebrate and be happy, because your brother was dead, but now he is alive; he was lost, but now he has been found.' God himself rejoices over every man and woman who comes back home to him, every 'sinner who repents'.
John 10:10; Matthew 6:16–18; 11:19; 21:15; Luke 15:11–32

□ **The 'Beatitudes'**
Jesus pronounced blessings ('beatitudes') on the 'humble' – those who realized that spiritually they were 'poor'. In fact all those mentioned in the Beatitudes are 'poor' and 'humble' in one way or another. ('Blessed' means 'happy'.) These are the people God declares 'happy'. They will receive what God has promised. His kingdom belongs to them. They have nothing in the world, but they can expect everything from God.

Those who are 'hungry and thirsty for righteousness',

giving up all we have clung to for security, and trusting God. It also means being sorry for our sins.

This is not something we can manage just by trying hard enough. God actually comes to find the sinner. In the parables of the lost sheep and the lost son Jesus emphasizes the joy of being found by God.
Mark 1:15; Matthew 13:44–46; Luke 15:1–7, 11–32

□ **Jesus' teaching about himself**
Jesus knew that he was very close to God. He encouraged his disciples to call God their father, but he was God's Son in a unique way. John's Gospel especially presents us with this aspect of Jesus' teaching. He even said 'the Father and I are one'.

So believing in God means believing in Jesus also. He is so close to God that people may rely on him as they do on God. But he said nothing to make himself more prominent than God. He was the 'way' to God. He did nothing of his own accord, but only as the Father directed him. He was mankind's 'bread' that the Father had sent from heaven.

The way to 'eternal life' –

'whose greatest desire is to do what God requires', have their lives centred on God. They know they cannot survive without him. The 'merciful' are dealing with other people in the way God deals with them. Those who work for peace have no worldly power. They depend on the love of God which can change two enemies into friends. The persecuted are hunted out of the world of men.

It is to people like this that God's 'kingdom' belongs. They are the ones God will reward. All these are praised by Jesus. And so the Beatitudes turn the world's idea of 'happiness' upside down. They also set a standard. They represent a challenge, the demand the kingdom makes upon God's people.
Matthew 5:1–12; Luke 6:20–26

□ **Jesus' followers**
To be a 'disciple' of Jesus, one of his students, was a great privilege. Unlike other teachers he did not lay great burdens on his followers. 'The yoke I will give you is easy,' he said, 'and the load I will put on you is light.' Yet he taught that 'the gate to life is narrow and the way that leads to it is hard'. His disciples must be like their master, ready to put themselves

and their own interests last. Even family ties must not stand in the way of whole-hearted obedience to him.

Jesus told his disciples to expect persecution. But they need not be anxious. God would give them the words they needed when they were on trial. Jesus called his followers to a life of service for others, yet he treated them as friends. They shared his confidences. They shared his sufferings. They would also share his life, his joy and his future glory. Matthew 13:16–17; 11:30; 7:13–14; Mark 8:34; Luke 9:57–62; Matthew 10:16–25; John 13:4–17; 14–17

☐ God and worship

Jesus spoke of God as 'Father' in a new, more personal way than anyone before him. He taught that God was, in a special way, his own Father. But he also taught his followers to pray: 'Our Father in heaven'. He taught them to come to God as children to a loving, forgiving and wise Father. He gave his followers 'the right to become God's children'.

This teaching was new and revolutionary to many people. 'Religion' for many was a burdensome system of rules and ceremonies. Jesus showed that the basis of religion was a loving relationship with God himself. God, as Father, was concerned about every detail of life. He cared. This changed people's attitude to prayer.

As a result of what Jesus said and did, greater changes were to come. When the woman at the well asked where people should worship God, Jesus answered: 'The time will come when people will not worship the Father either on this mountain or in Jerusalem . . . by the power of God's Spirit people will worship the Father as he really is, offering him the worship that he really wants.' In the Book of Acts we see this beginning to happen, as the 'good news' is preached to non-Jewish as well as to Jewish people.

Jesus himself went regularly

to the local synagogue and attended the festivals in Jerusalem. He did not set up a new system of religious ceremonies. He expected his disciples to follow his example, to meet to study the Bible, to pray and to fast. And he commanded them to baptize new believers and remember his death for them by sharing bread and wine together, as he had done with his disciples at the last supper. Matthew 6:6–18, 31–32; 7:7–11; John 1:12–13; Matthew 9:14–17; John 4:19–24; Matthew 28:19; 1 Corinthians 11:23–25

This section has concentrated on Jesus as a teacher, but he is far more than that. He was a prophet sent by God, with a new message of hope. Even more than that, he came to the world to be its saviour.

Christian Worship in the New Testament

Jewish background

The earliest Christians were Jewish, so it is not at all surprising that they drew very much on their Jewish background for their forms of worship. Acts 2:46 tells us: 'Day after day they met as a group in the Temple, and they had their meals together in their homes, eating with glad and humble hearts.' They continued to worship at the Jewish temple, and added a special Christian meal.

But Christians came to see that the temple sacrifices were no longer necessary, since Jesus' death had been the final, once-for-all sacrifice for sin. So Christians tended to break away from temple worship, especially when there began to be conflict between Jews and Christians. But for several decades many Jewish Christians continued to attend the synagogues. Paul usually began his preaching in any town in the synagogue, and continued worshipping there until he was forced out.

Two aspects of Jewish worship especially influenced Christian worship. The Passover ritual is reflected in the Lord's Supper. And the synagogue service, with its Bible reading, prayer and sermon, formed a model for early Christian services. Hebrews 7:23–27; Acts 17:1–8

The Lord's Supper

Jesus instituted this communal meal at Passover time, at the last supper with his disciples before his death. At the Passover Festival people looked back to the deliverance from Egypt, and forward to the coming kingdom of God. The Lord's Supper, too, looks back. It reminds us, by the bread and wine, of the past event of Jesus' death. And it looks forward to the time when Jesus will come again. 'You proclaim the Lord's death until he comes,' says Paul.

The Passover meal began with a blessing – thanking God for the bread. Then pieces of

This wall-painting from a third-century AD catacomb in Rome shows Christians sharing bread at the Lord's Supper.

the loaf were passed round to the guests. The same action in the Christian service was a reminder of the fact that Jesus' body had been 'given for you'. The meal ended with a shared cup of wine.

The bread and wine of the Lord's Supper. At first Christians shared these as part of an actual meal.

In the Christian ceremony the wine was a token of the blood (the death) of Christ. His death was a sacrifice that sealed the new covenant-agreement between God and man, just as the old covenant was sealed by the blood of sacrificial oxen (Exodus 24:5–8). So Jesus says, 'This is my blood . . . which seals God's covenant.'

Those who share in this sacred meal declare their loyalty to the Lord who has created the new covenant. The wine also points to the future

A report about the Christian religion from the Roman governor, Pliny, to the Emperor Trajan, about AD 113

'They were in the habit of meeting on a certain fixed day before it was light, when they sang an anthem to Christ as God, and bound themselves by a solemn oath not to commit any wicked deed, but to abstain from all fraud, theft and adultery, never to break their word, or deny a trust when called upon to honour it; after which it was their custom to separate and then meet again to partake of food, but food of an ordinary and innocent kind.'
Pliny, *Letters* X.96

kingdom of God, pictured as a banquet. Jesus said, 'I will never again drink this wine until the day I drink the new wine in the Kingdom of God.'

In Acts, the Lord's Supper is called 'the breaking of bread' ('fellowship meal'). This was the name used by the Jews for the blessing said over the bread. Originally it was part of an actual meal. The Christians at Corinth brought their own provisions for just such a meal together. Paul saw a further meaning in sharing the loaf. Christians share in Christ as they share the bread, and they also share in the 'body of Christ', the church. Division and disunity in the church denies the truth for which the one loaf stands.

Eventually the Lord's Supper moved from the homes of individual Christians to a special building, and was no longer part of an actual meal.

Christian prayers and praises that had developed from the synagogue services were added to the ceremony. The earliest account we have of the prayers at the Lord's Supper (or Eucharist) come from the *Didache* ('The Teaching') written late in the first or early in the second century AD.
Matthew 26:26–30; Mark 14:22–26; Luke 22:14–20; Acts 2:46; 20:7; 1 Corinthians 11:20–34; 10:16–17

It was in the context of a Passover meal that Jesus gave his followers the remembrance meal they continued as the Lord's Supper.

Baptism

The second rite which Jesus commanded his followers to keep was the baptism of Christian converts. This also had a Jewish background. In the time between the Old and New Testaments, people who became converts (proselytes) to the Jewish religion were baptized, or immersed in water, usually a nearby river, as a sign of cleansing. John the Baptist also baptized many people as a sign of their repentance and their inner cleansing by God.

But Christian baptism was not usually regarded as a 'washing' from sin. Paul explains that when the person being baptized disappears beneath the water and then re-appears, he or she has undergone a symbolic death, burial, and resurrection. Christians share in the death and resurrection of Jesus by the act of baptism: 'By our baptism, we were buried with him and shared his death, in order that, just as Christ was raised from death . . . we might live a new life.'

The fullest account of a baptism in the New Testament is in the story of Philip and the Ethiopian. Acts 8:37 shows one form of words that the early Christians would have used. The preacher says: 'If you believe with all your heart you may be baptized.' The person being baptized replies: 'I believe that Jesus Christ is the Son of God.' People were baptized sometimes 'in the name of Jesus Christ', sometimes 'in the name of the Father, Son, and Holy Spirit'. Matthew 28:19; Mark 1:4–11; Romans 6:3–4; Acts 8:26–39; 2:38; 19:5

Prayer

As well as the private prayers of individuals, the New Testament often mentions groups of Christians praying together. From the very beginning Christians shared in 'the fellowship meals and . . . the prayers'. They prayed for courage when the Jewish Council banned Peter and John from preaching. They prayed for Peter when he was imprisoned. They prayed for the success of the missionary work of Barnabas and Paul. These prayers were spontaneous, but they are full of the spirit and language of the Old Testament.

Some of the actual words of early Christian prayer are still known.

● **Marana tha** (1 Corinthians 16:22). These are two Aramaic words, meaning 'Our Lord, come!' They were addressed to Jesus, calling him by the same name, 'Lord', that Jews had reserved for God alone. *Marana tha* comes again in the last prayer of the Bible: 'So be it. Come, Lord Jesus!'

● The word **abba** (Mark 14:36) was used by Jesus himself in addressing God. It is an Aramaic word meaning 'dear father' or 'dad'. A child would use it to speak to his own father. Jews would have thought it an irreverent way to speak to God. They used the word *abinu*, 'our father', instead. But Jesus' relationship with God was so close that he could use this family word, and encourage his disciples to do the same. The word comes twice in Paul's letters: 'When we cry out to God, "Abba, my Father!", God's Spirit . . . declare(s) that we are God's children.' And: 'To show that you are his sons, God sent the Spirit of his Son into our hearts, the Spirit who cries out, "Father, my Father".'

● **Amen** This is a Hebrew word used in the temple and synagogue services at the end of prayers. It means, 'It is sure', or even, 'There is no doubt about that.' So, in the worship in heaven described in Revelation 5, when the cry goes up, 'The lamb who was killed is worthy to receive power, wealth, wisdom, and strength' the prayer is concluded with a great 'Amen'. 'Amen' ends a prayer in Romans 15:33, a blessing on God in Romans 9:5, an expression of praise in Galatians 1:5, and a blessing upon fellow Christians in Galatians 6:18.
Acts 2:42; 4:24–30; 12:5; 13:3; Revelation 22:20; Romans 8:15; Galatians 4:6; Revelation 5:12–14; 1 Corinthians 14:16

Creeds and hymns

The New Testament church was a community which believed certain basic truths – 'the apostles' teaching', or 'the true teaching', or 'true words'. These beliefs were expressed not only in the New Testament writings, but also in worship, often sung as hymns.

Some of the early Christian creeds were very simple and short. 'Jesus is Lord' was the basic one. These were probably words each new convert spoke. Some creeds contain two or three statements of faith. 'There is one God, and there is one mediator between God and men, the man Christ Jesus'; 'one Lord, one faith, one baptism'.

At times, New Testament writers clearly quote early Christian statements of faith. 1 Timothy 3:16 is a creed in the form of a hymn (like the *Te Deum* in later Christian worship):

'He appeared in human form,
was shown to be right by the Spirit
and was seen by angels.
He was preached among the nations,
was believed in throughout the world,
and was taken up to heaven.'

An even more detailed confession of the person and work of Christ was used by Paul in Philippians 2:6–11. The hymn ends with the confession of the new convert: 'all will openly proclaim that Jesus Christ is Lord'. It may have been sung at a baptism service. Acts 2:42; 1 Timothy 4:6; 2 Timothy 1:13; 1 Corinthians 12:3; 1 Timothy 2:5; Ephesians 4:5

After the flood God promised Noah that he would never again destroy the earth by flood. The rainbow was the sign that God would always remember his covenant promise.

6

Key Teaching of the Bible

Note: This section explains some of the important words in the Bible's teaching. Part 5: *Religion and Worship in the Bible* provides further information on the beliefs, and particularly the practice of the Jewish and Christian faiths.

Angel The word means 'a messenger'. In the Bible it is used of the supernatural beings who surround the throne of God. Jesus tells us that they share in God's joy 'over one sinner who repents'.

Angels are also referred to as 'sons of God' or 'heavenly beings' and 'heavenly powers', the 'servants of God'. Their work is to serve God. In heaven they worship God and on earth they act as God's messengers, bringing his word to men and women. They also help people. They took care of Jesus after his temptations and they care for his followers.

The Jews believed there was a complex hierarchy of angels, all of whom had their own names. The Bible has no clear reference to such a system. It names only two angels – Gabriel and Michael. It was Gabriel who brought news of the birth of Jesus.

The phrase 'the angel of the Lord' is often used in the Old Testament as a way of describing how God sometimes came to people in human form, to give them a special message. The 'angel of the Lord' is also God's agent of judgement.

See also *Heaven*.
Luke 15:10; Job 1:6; 1 Kings 22:19; Psalm 103:20–21; Daniel 12:1; Luke 1:26–38; Matthew 1:20; 4:11; Hebrews 1:14; Genesis 16:7–14; 22:11–12; 31:11; Judges 6:11–21; 13:3–21, and many other places

Apostle The word means 'a person who is sent' – a messenger or representative. In the New Testament it is mainly used to refer to Jesus' twelve disciples, to Paul, and to other Christians who were involved in missionary outreach.

Jesus chose twelve apostles to be with him, to preach and to heal. After he rose from the dead Jesus told them to go and tell the whole world what they had learnt about him.

When the disciples were looking for an apostle to replace Judas Iscariot, Peter told them that they must choose someone who had been with Jesus from the very start of his ministry, and who had seen him after he rose from the dead.

Paul claimed that he was an apostle, because he believed that his experience on the Damascus road was not just a vision but a meeting with the living Jesus. He had been chosen by Jesus as his special messenger, particularly to bring his message to the non-Jewish world (the 'Gentiles').
Luke 6:12–16; Acts 1:12–26; 14:1–4; 1 Corinthians 15:5, 7; Galatians 1:1; 2:7, 8

Ascension For forty days after Jesus rose from the dead he often visited his disciples. Then he returned to heaven. The disciples were with him on the Mount of Olives when Jesus gave them his final message. As they watched, they saw him 'taken up to heaven . . . and a cloud hid him from their sight'. This is what we call the 'ascension'.

Although the ascension was the end of Jesus' ministry on earth, it was not the end of his work. As the disciples watched Jesus being taken from them two heavenly messengers asked them, 'Galileans, why are you standing there looking up at the sky? This Jesus, who was taken from you into heaven, will come back in the same way that you saw him go to heaven.' The rest of the New Testament makes it clear that between Jesus' ascension and his return at the end of time he is with God, his father, in the glory of heaven. He reigns over the whole universe. He represents his followers before God and sends the Holy Spirit to help them.
Luke 24:50–53; Acts 1:6–11; Hebrews 1:3; 4:14–16; 7:24–26; John 16:5–15

Atonement The people who wrote the Bible were concerned with one problem above all others. How can men and women enjoy friendship with God? Because of sin they are separated from God, and their basic need is to be made 'at one' with him. This is what the word 'atonement' means.

However hard people try they can never make themselves acceptable to a holy God. We always fall short of God's standards.

In Old Testament times, sacrifices were offered in order to atone for sin. But this system could not be the final answer. A number of Old Testament writers saw that God himself would have to deal with the problem of sin. Isaiah wrote of the coming of God's servant to solve this problem: 'All of us were like sheep that were lost, each of us going his own way. But the Lord made the punishment fall on him, the punishment all of us deserved.'

The New Testament describes how God sent Jesus, his Son, to do just this. His death was the complete sacrifice for all men. When Jesus died on the cross he died in our place and suffered the death-penalty due for our sin. On the cross he became acutely aware of the agony of separation from God, and cried, 'My God, my God, why did you abandon me?' Matthew goes on to tell us that the curtain hanging in the temple was torn from top to bottom. The fact that the curtain was torn in two announced in a dramatic way that we need no longer be cut off from God. Jesus had atoned for the sin of the world.

See also *Cross, Reconciliation, Redemption*.
Genesis 3; Leviticus 16; Isaiah 53; John 3:14–17; Mark 10:45; 15:34, 38; 2 Corinthians 5:14–21; Ephesians 2:14; Hebrews 7:26 – 9:28; 10:19–20

Baptism In New Testament times people were 'baptized' when they became Christians. They publicly declared their new faith by going through a simple ceremony of 'washing in water'. Paul explains this by saying it was a picture of how the Christian could share in Jesus' death, and be raised with him to new life. It meant a complete break with the past, a removal of sin, and the start of a new life lived in the power given by Jesus Christ himself.

A few years earlier, John the Baptist had begun to prepare people for Jesus' coming. 'Turn away from your sins and be baptized,' he told them. Many obeyed and were baptized in the River Jordan.

But on the Day of Pentecost Peter made it clear that Christian baptism means more than just a change of heart. 'Each one of you must turn away from his sins and be baptized in the name of Jesus Christ,' he said, 'so that your sins will be forgiven; and you will receive God's gift, the Holy Spirit.'
Mark 1:1–8; Matthew 29:19–20; Acts 2:38–41; Romans 6:3–11

Blood The New Testament often describes the death of Jesus by the phrase 'the blood of Christ (or Jesus)'. The background to this unusual phrase is in the Old Testament, where the word 'blood' is used in a number of distinctive ways:
• When blood is shed a person's life is over: 'The life is in the blood.'
• Life is the gift of God, so no one must shed another's blood.
• The blood of animals was shed in sacrifice. It represents the animal's life poured out in death. Since life is the gift of God, this blood must not be used for food (this ruling applied to every animal killed, not only in sacrifice).

So when the New Testament uses the phrase 'the blood of Christ' it refers to the violent death of Jesus on the cross. Indeed, some modern versions simply translate the phrase as 'the death of Christ'.

See also *Atonement, Cross, Redemption*.
Genesis 9:4–6; Deuteronomy 12:15–16, 20–28; Ephesians 1:7; 1 Peter 1:18–19; Hebrews 10:19–22

Body In the Bible the word 'body' is often used to stand for the whole person. So it can sometimes be translated as 'self'. For instance: 'Offer your bodies (your selves) as a living sacrifice.' The New Testament speaks of the 'resurrection body', the new form we will have when God raises us from death. This means a full, continued life for the whole person, not merely some disembodied existence as a spirit.

Paul uses the idea of the body – in which different parts have different functions – as a picture of the church. Christians are like the different parts which make up a body. Each has a different part to play in the church, working under the direction of Jesus.

The New Testament places great importance on the physical body. It is 'the body' which is the temple of the Holy Spirit, and our 'bodies' which are to be used for God's glory. Romans 12:1; 1 Corinthians 15:35–49; Romans 12:4–5; 1 Corinthians 12:12–30; Ephesians 4:15–16; 1 Corinthians 6:15–20

Call The God of the Bible is a God who calls people and speaks directly to them.

In the Old Testament the story of the nation of Israel begins with the call of Abraham, and shows how the Israelites were God's people, not because they had earned the right to be his children, but because God himself decided to 'call' them.

It is the same in the New Testament. Jesus called people to follow him, to respond to his teaching about his new kingdom, and the early church did the same. Christians are 'called' to salvation, to eternal life, to a life of endurance, to a life of peace, to go on being changed by the Holy Spirit.

In both Old and New Testaments the personal nature of God's call to his people is often emphasized. God calls men and women to specific tasks: Abraham, Moses, Samuel, David, Isaiah, Jeremiah, Ezekiel and many others. In the New Testament Paul was 'called to be an apostle', and to travel abroad to preach the gospel.

See also *Election, Grace*.
Genesis 12:1; Hosea 11:1; Matthew 11:28–30; Mark 1:20; 2:14; Acts 2:39; 2 Thessalonians 2:13–14; 1 Timothy 6:12; 1 Peter 2:21; 1 Corinthians 7:15; 1 Thessalonians 4:7; Exodus 3; 1 Samuel 3; 16; Isaiah 6; Jeremiah 1:4–10;

Ezekiel 1–3; Romans 1:1; Acts 9; 13:1

Church The church is the community of those who believe in Jesus. In the New Testament the word always refers to people, never, as it often does today, to a building. In fact for several generations Christians had no purpose-built meeting-places.

Jesus promised Peter that he would establish the church, and it was Peter's sermon on the Day of Pentecost that led to the first 3,000 people being baptized and joining the Christian group. In the Old Testament God had chosen the Israelites to be his special people. The New Testament states that all those who believe in Jesus – whatever their race – are now God's chosen people, his 'church'. They are being prepared for the day when he returns – the great 'wedding-day' of Jesus and his people.

In the New Testament, the word for church refers both to a local group of Christians and to all Christians throughout the world. Paul teaches that Jesus Christ is head of the church, and that no Christian stands alone but is part of the whole: 'Though we are many, we are one body in union with Christ, and we are all joined to each other as different parts of one body.'

In New Testament times there was no organization of the local church comparable with what we know today. (See Part 5: *Religion and Worship in the Bible*.) Some churches had leaders, sometimes called 'elders' or 'bishops', who taught and looked after the members. But many others had no 'official' leaders, and special gifts, such as preaching or healing or caring for others, were exercised by different members. There must have been great variety in the gatherings of these churches, as different people took part.
Matthew 16:18; Acts 2; 13:1; 1 Corinthians 12:12–28; Romans 12:5; Colossians 1:18; Ephesians 4:11–16; 1 Corinthians 12:1–11; Acts 2:42–47; 4:23–25; 1 Corinthians 11:13–34; 1 Timothy 2–3; Titus

1:5–9; Revelation 19:5–9
Circumcision
Circumcision is a minor operation to cut away the loose skin covering the end of the penis. It is widely practised by primitive peoples, and was carried out on every Israelite baby boy on the eighth day after his birth.

When God promised Abraham that he would be the founder of a great nation, the nation of Israel, he commanded that all his male descendants should be circumcised. This was to be the physical sign that they belonged to the people of God.

As time went on, the sign came to be more important than what it represented, and the prophets often had to remind the people that the outward sign on its own was not enough. It should be matched by love of other people and obedience to God.

The New Testament makes a similar point. 'True circumcision', or membership of the people of God, is really a matter of what we believe and how we behave. Therefore non-Jews (Gentiles) who become Christians do not need to be physically circumcised. Christians are sometimes called the true circumcision, for they have come into a right relationship with God and are now the heirs to the promises of God alongside the believing people of Old Testament times.
Genesis 17; Luke 2:21; Jeremiah 9:25–26; Romans 2:25–29; Galatians 5:2–6; Philippians 3:2–3; Colossians 2:11–15

Commandments See *Law*
Covenant The basic meaning of 'covenant' in the Bible is summed up in the words of Jeremiah 31:33: 'I will be their God, and they will be my people.' God enters into a special relationship with men and women. He commits himself to protect his people, and in return he expects obedience from them. Most covenants mentioned in the Bible are between God and man, but there are also 'man-to-man' covenants in the Old Testament.

The Bible itself is arranged into two major 'covenants', the Old and the New. They are more

often called the Old and New 'Testaments' (which means the same thing). The old covenant is the one made with Moses on Mt Sinai, when the Ten Commandments were given to God's people as the basic rules for living. This covenant forms the basis of Israel's religion. Some archaeological discoveries suggest that the way the covenant is set out may be based on the pattern of treaties made between certain Near Eastern nations at that time.

There are also other covenants in the Old Testament. There is the one made with Noah after the flood, when God promised never again to destroy the earth with a flood. This is God's general covenant with all people.

Then there is the covenant with Abraham, in which God promised his descendants a land of their own, and urged them to share their blessings with the other nations of the earth. This is God's covenant with his special people, renewed in the covenant with Moses on Mt Sinai.

The New Testament writers show that the new covenant between God and men, to which the Old Testament looks forward, rests on the death of Jesus. Jesus himself spoke of this at the last supper: 'This cup is God's new covenant, sealed with my blood.' The letter to the Hebrews compares the old and new covenants. The new covenant offers something the old covenant could never secure – release from the power of sin; the freedom to obey God.

See also *Election*.
Exodus 19:3–6; 20:1–17; Genesis 9:1–17; 12:1–3; 15:7–21; Jeremiah 31:31–34; 1 Corinthians 11:25; Hebrews 8:13; 10:4
Creation The Bible teaches that everything was made by God. He was the Creator in the very beginning, and his work continues as he maintains, and occasionally intervenes in, his creation. The Bible has nothing to say about which scientific theory of creation is most likely to be true. This is not surprising, since it was never intended to be a

book of science. Its purpose is to tell us about God, and his dealings with men and women and the world they live in.

In Genesis 1 we learn that God created the world perfect. He created plants and animals, able to reproduce themselves. And he placed man and woman at the centre of creation to take care of it. According to Genesis 2 the world as God created it was a delightful place in which to live, especially since the man and his wife enjoyed a free and open relationship with God.

The first perfection of creation is now gone, because people chose to disobey God. But the Bible continues to speak of God as Creator. Again and again it reminds us of his greatness, and the smallness of man in comparison. Yet he cares for people and provides for all his creation. So:
'Fear the Lord, all the earth!
Honour him, all peoples of the world!
When he spoke, the world was created;
At his command everything appeared.'
Paul also speaks of a 'new creation'. By Jesus' death and resurrection God made it possible for people to be forgiven and to share in the new life of the new creation. Christians already know something of this new creation and one day they will be fully part of it, when the universe spoilt by sin exists no more and all things are made new.
Genesis 1–3;
Job 38 – 42:6; Psalms 8; 33:6–22; 104; Isaiah 40:21–26; Matthew 6:25–33; Acts 14:15–18; Romans 1: 18–23; 8:18–23; Colossians 1:15–20; Hebrews 1:1–3; Revelation 21–22

The Bible says that God created our world and everything in it. In the beginning, all that he created was good.

Cross The cross has come to be the universal symbol of the Christian faith, because it reminds us of the most astonishing and important event in the story of Jesus of Nazareth.

It was astonishing because Jesus the Messiah (God's chosen one) was executed like a common criminal. The Jews found it impossible to accept that such a person could really be the Son of God – and many ordinary people just could not understand how the world could be saved by a person who had met such a bizarre end.

Yet to the early Christians the cross had a deep meaning. It was at the heart of all that God had planned for his people. Paul was quite sure that the cross was all-important – so much so that he wrote to the Corinthian Christians: 'While I was with you, I made up my mind to forget everything except Jesus Christ and especially his death on the cross'.

The New Testament makes it clear that Jesus died on the cross, not because of his own wrong-doing (the charges against him were false), but in the place of ordinary sinful men and women. He experienced the separation from God which they deserved, and so made possible forgiveness and new life for all who will trust their lives to Jesus as the one who died for our sins and rose again from death.

In Jesus' death on the cross we see the depths of God's love. As a result of this, men and women can be reconciled both to God and to each other. In the cross God defeated all the powers of evil.

The cross is also a dramatic symbol of the sort of life Christians ought to live. Jesus called people to 'take up their cross' and follow him. He called them to a life of self-sacrifice. They must give up their own claims over their lives, and live in the power of the new life which God gives them. And Paul understood what this meant in his own experience: 'I have been put to death with Christ on his cross, so that it is no longer I who live, but it is Christ who lives in me.'

See also *Atonement, Reconciliation, Redemption.*
1 Corinthians 1:18 – 2:5;
Romans 5:6 – 11;
Ephesians 2:16 – 18;
Colossians 2:14 – 15;
Galatians 2:20;
1 John 4:7 – 10

Death Man 'is like a puff of wind; his days are like a passing shadow'. The Bible faces the fact that death comes to everyone. On the other hand, death is seen as something evil that strikes a note of terror in all our minds.

Throughout the Bible there is a close link between death and sin. Death is part of the judgement that comes to Adam after his disobedience. Paul regards death as the inevitable consequence of the presence of sin in the world. For God is 'holy', and cannot tolerate evil. If we die with sin unforgiven, our death is not only physical but spiritual: it is separation from God. The New Testament often speaks of non-Christians as being physically alive, but 'spiritually dead because of disobedience and sins'.

When Jesus died on the cross he took the ultimate consequences of sin on himself. His resurrection showed that he had defeated death. So although our human fate is to die, by faith in Christ we can have 'eternal life'. The Christian is already lifted out of spiritual death to new life and looks forward to the end of the age when physical death, 'the last enemy', will also be overcome.

See also *Heaven, Hell, Judgement, Life, Resurrection, Second coming of Jesus.*
Psalm 144:4; Deuteronomy 30:15, 19; Psalm 55:4; Genesis 3:19; Romans 6:23; Matthew 7:23; Ephesians 2:1; Hebrews 2:14 – 15; 1 Corinthians 15:21, 26; 2 Corinthians 5:1 – 10

Election 'You did not choose me; I chose you', said Jesus. These words sum up the Bible's teaching on election (choice). Because God is the all-powerful Creator he is the one who makes the ultimate decisions – not man.

The Old Testament records how God chose people. He chose Abel and not Cain; Isaac and not Ishmael; Jacob and not Esau; Joseph and not his brothers. They were not chosen for their own goodness or greatness. Moses tells the people of Israel: 'The Lord did not love you and choose you because you outnumbered other peoples . . . But the Lord loved you'. 'Do not say to yourselves that he brought you in to possess this land because you deserved it.' The reason for God's choice is hidden within his own mind and no human being can understand it.

It is clear, however, that those who accept the challenge of God's choice are expected to obey him and give their lives in his service. This was so for Abraham and the people of Israel. It is now true of Christians: 'You are the chosen race, the king's priests, the holy nation, God's own people, chosen to proclaim the wonderful acts of God, who called you out of darkness into his own marvellous light.'

For God's choice of individuals, see *Call*; see also *Covenant, Grace.*
John 15:16;
Deuteronomy 7:7 – 8; 9:4 – 5;
Romans 9:18 – 29;
1 Peter 2:9

Faith Paul carefully explains in his letters to the Christians in both Rome and Galatia that a person can find a right relationship with God, not through his own good deeds (as people often think), but only through faith or believing.

'Faith' means having confidence and trust in God. It is not a 'leap in the dark' which a man must take without thinking. It is trust in a God whom we believe to be trustworthy. Confident in this knowledge, a person can believe and entrust his life to Jesus Christ. As sinful people we can do absolutely nothing to save ourselves. We have to depend totally on what God has already done for us through Jesus.

This is the start of a 'life of faith'. No one can be certain of living aright by his own efforts. We need to continue to trust wholly in Jesus and the Spirit he gives to help us live in a way that pleases God. This life of dependence on God goes right back to the beginning of God's dealings with man, as Paul shows when he traces it back to Abraham.

The New Testament also refers to 'the faith', meaning the basic teaching about Jesus on which our trust is grounded.
1 John 5:1 – 5; John 1:12; 3:16; 5:24; Romans 1:17; 5:1; 10:9 – 10; Galatians 3; Ephesians 2:8 – 9. See also Genesis 15:6; Psalm 37:3 – 9; Proverbs 3:5 – 6; Jeremiah 17:7 – 8; Habakkuk 2:4; Hebrews 11; James 2; 1 Timothy 3:9; 5:8

Fall Sin is present in the world because mankind has rebelled against God. There has never been a person (except Jesus) who was not a sinner. The Bible traces this back to the very beginning of history. The story of Adam and Eve depicts the dramatic 'fall' of men and women from the high place they once had as friends of God and the crown of his creation.

Adam and Eve originally lived in full and open fellowship with God and each other. There was no sin to spoil their lives. This was how God meant it to be. But in Genesis 3 we learn that all this changed drastically. The couple listened to the serpent and decided to rebel against God by doing what he had forbidden. As a result of this disobedience Adam and Eve were banished from God's presence. They were told that from then on life would be hard work. They would know sorrow, and life would end in death.

Since the fall of Adam and Eve the whole creation has been affected by their rebellion against God. 'Sin came into the world through one man, and his sin brought death with it. As a result, death has spread to the whole human race because everyone has sinned.'

Every part of the universe is affected by sin – both people and the natural world in which we live. Although we still have much of the original nature God gave us, and we still know and search for God, yet we have an inbuilt bias towards sin.

See also *Death, Judgement.*
Genesis 1 – 3; Romans 1:18 – 32; 5:12 – 19; 7:14 – 25

Fellowship The 'sharing' companionship which is at the heart of Christian experience. Man was made to live in 'fellowship' with God. Man's disobedience broke this friendship. Jesus came to restore it by dying to deal with the sin which separates us from God.

So Christians can begin to know the companionship with God for which every man and woman was created. A Christian shares, with Jesus, in the love of God himself, 'the fellowship that we have with the Father and with his Son Jesus Christ'. Jesus pictures the closest possible 'sharing' between himself and his followers. 'I am the vine,' he said, 'and you are the branches.'

Just as we share Jesus' life, so we share in the lives of our fellow-Christians. The Christian is not just an individual joined to Christ, he also shares a new life with fellow-Christians and with Christ himself. 'We are all joined to each other', and the hallmark of this Christian 'fellowship' is love.

This sharing and love which characterizes the Christian church shows itself in action. The early church in Jerusalem showed their oneness by sharing all their possessions with one another. The non-Jewish churches showed their love for the needy church in Jerusalem by sending money.

See also *Body, Church.*
1 John 1:3; John 15:1 – 17; Romans 12:4 – 13; John 13:34 – 35; Acts 2:44 – 47; 4:32 – 37; Romans 15:25 – 27

Flesh The word 'flesh' in the Bible is often used to refer to people as physical beings – 'mortal flesh'. In this sense it can be used to show the weakness of man, who is 'only human', in contrast with the strength of God. When Jesus' disciples fell asleep in the Garden of Gethsemane he told them to watch and pray: 'the spirit is willing, but the flesh is weak'.

Paul used the word 'flesh' ('lower nature' or 'human nature' in some recent translations) to refer to the life non-Christians live under sin's domination.

The Christian, on the other hand, is both 'in the flesh' and 'in the Spirit'. He is caught in a battle between his own inborn bias to sin and the presence of God's Spirit in his life, working to make him more like Christ. He has to say 'no' to the sinful desires which are part of his fallen nature, and allow the 'fruit' of the Spirit to grow in his life.

See also *Body*. Psalm 78:39; Isaiah 40:5; Mark 14:38; Romans 7:13–25; 8; Galatians 5:16–24

Forgiveness It is one of the most extraordinary things that God loves sinful human beings and delights to forgive them.

'If you kept a record of our sins,
    who could escape being condemned?
But you forgive us,
    so that we should stand in awe of you.'

Yet from start to finish the Bible makes it clear that when we repent and turn from our sinful past to God, he will forgive us.

As Christians we enter a new life; we become children of God; we have been forgiven. Christians will forgive others because they have been forgiven, and although there may still be times when they fall into sin, they have only to turn to God in repentance and God will forgive and restore them.

See also *Repentance*. Exodus 34:6–7; Psalm 51; Psalm 130:3, 4; Isaiah 1:18; 55:6–7; Hosea 14; Matthew 6:12–15; 26:26–28; Luke 7:36–50; Acts 2:38; Ephesians 4:32; 1 John 1:9

Freedom In any society where some men rule harshly over others one of man's greatest longings is for physical freedom. So it is not surprising that this idea has a large place in the Bible. Freedom is the central theme in the quotation from Isaiah which Jesus used to describe his own work. 'The Spirit of the Lord is upon me . . . he has sent me to proclaim liberty to the captives.'

Many hoped that Jesus had come to set Israel free from the Romans. But he made it plain that his first concern was to deal with a far more cruel slavery. He had come to set men free from the power of evil, and he demonstrated this by releasing people from the grip of evil spirits, and healing the sick.

In his letters to Rome and Galatia Paul is anxious to show how important this freedom is. It is freedom from the penalty of our sin, and freedom from the effort of trying, and failing, to please God. The Christian knows he is saved by God's grace, not by anything he can do himself.

Paul saw two main ways in which Christians abused this precious gift of freedom. Some hankered after the rules and regulations of the old Jewish religion. This was happening in the churches at Galatia, and Paul wrote his letter to them to show how Christian faith was entirely different from a religion of rules. Others thought that because Jesus had set them free they could do what they liked, even sin as much as they wanted. This was quite wrong: they were freed *from* sin, not to go on sinning. They gladly serve a new master – Jesus Christ. True freedom is found in serving God and in serving others. Luke 4:18; John 8:31–36, 41–44; Mark 3:22–27; 5:1–13; Luke 13:10–16; Romans 6:16–23; 8:2, 21; Galatians 3:28; 5:1, 13; Romans 1:1; 6; Matthew 11:28; James 1:25; 2:12; 1 Peter 2:16

Future destiny Apart from the certainty of judgement at the second coming of Jesus, the Bible says very little about what happens after death.

The Old Testament writers generally expected a continued existence in *Sheol*. This was simply a place of rest and silence when the blessing of life had been taken away. But as time went on people began to understand more clearly that God had a glorious future in store for them beyond *Sheol*. God does not abandon his people in *Sheol* but will lead them into life and joy. Job and Daniel both express confidence about the future. Job is certain he will see God. And Daniel speaks of the dead living again.

Hades is the New Testament equivalent of *Sheol*. Peter, speaking of the death of Jesus, said that David 'spoke about the resurrection of the Messiah when he said, "he was not abandoned in the world of the dead (*Hades*); his body did not rot in the grave" '. In another context Peter says that Jesus went to preach to the dead, 'the imprisoned spirits', presumably in the time between his crucifixion and his resurrection.

The New Testament often talks of death as a sleep. 'Paradise' is the word used by Jesus to describe the pleasant existence of those who die at peace with God. And Paul was confident that when a Christian dies he is in the presence of Jesus. It is impossible for us to imagine an existence outside time; but the New Testament writers were confident that Christian believers, whether dead or living, would meet with Jesus, and enter into the glory of heaven, being given new 'resurrection' bodies no longer subject to death.

See also *Death, Heaven, Hell, Judgement, Second coming of Jesus*. Psalms 94:17; 16:9–11; Job 19:25–27; Daniel 12:2, 3; Acts 2:31; 1 Peter 3:19–20; Matthew 9:24; 1 Corinthians 15:20, 35–58; Luke 23:43; 1 Thessalonians 4:13–17; Revelation 20:11 – 22:5

Glory When the word 'glory' is applied to people in the Bible, it usually refers to their wealth or position. But the 'glory of God' refers to his unique power and greatness: 'the King of kings and the Lord of lords. He who alone is immortal; he lives in the light that no one can approach. No one has ever seen him; no one can ever see him.' Though people cannot see God, they are sometimes allowed to catch a glimpse of his 'glory'.

In the Old Testament God's glory is seen in history, especially perhaps in the two major events of the exodus and exile. The Israelites were led through the desert by the glory of God seen in the cloud and fire which guided them on their journey. When Moses went up the mountain to receive the law of God the cloud of God's glory covered the mountain. Again, during the exile the prophet Ezekiel saw some amazing visions which showed the 'glory' of God.

The New Testament suggests that Jesus was the glory of God made visible on earth. God's glory was seen by the shepherds when they heard that Jesus was born. And those who saw Jesus recognized God's glory in him. 'We saw his glory,' writes the apostle John (see also *Transfiguration*). Jesus' way of life and his miracles 'revealed his glory'. But the glory of God was seen above all in Jesus' death on the cross. Jesus went to the cross, not as a defeated man but as the conqueror of sin and Saviour of the world. His resurrection was the living proof. Because of this there is a 'future glory' promised to all God's people as they share in the glory with which he will return to earth. 1 Timothy 6:15–16; Exodus 16:7, 10; 24:15–18; 40:34–38; 2 Chronicles 7:1–3; Ezekiel 1:26–28 and other passages; Luke 2:8–14; 9:28–36; John 1:14; 2:11; 17; Romans 8:18–30; Mark 8:38; 13:26

God In the Bible, God is the all-powerful, personal, spiritual being who is beyond our understanding, but who has revealed himself to mankind in his work of creation and in his continuing activity in history. He created all life – and he is the one who keeps it going. We see him at work time and again in the Old Testament as he helps his people Israel. In the New Testament we see him at work especially in the life, death and resurrection of Jesus. He also continues to work in a personal way in the lives of Jesus' followers.

The Bible tells us what God is like by telling us what he does. It does not give us abstract philosophical descriptions of God's nature. But it is clear that he is all-seeing and all-knowing, present everywhere. His nature is both holy and just, loving and forgiving. The Bible takes the existence of God as a fact which needs no proof. It begins with the simple statement, 'In the beginning God created . .

People have always had many ideas about God. They have worshipped many different gods. One of the concerns of the Old Testament is to show that *Yahweh* (the Hebrews' name for God) is the only true God. He is the Creator, and King over all there is; the one who is 'light', who is utterly holy – and at the same time, utterly loving.

The word *Yahweh*, the personal name for God in the Old Testament, is sometimes spelt Jehovah in English, and in many translations of the Bible is written LORD. The ordinary Hebrew word for 'God' is *Elohim*. The name *Yahweh* means 'the one who exists eternally', though the Jews have always referred to him by the Hebrew word *Adonai*, which means 'my Lord'.

In the Old Testament God was sometimes referred to as the 'father' of the people of Israel. Jesus gave this a new importance. God has made us for a parent-child relationship, made possible through faith in Jesus. God delights to work in the world through the people he has made for friendship with himself. He works with them through their prayer and action so that the whole world might come to know him.

See also *Trinity* and the many words which describe what God does.
The 'otherness' of God: the eternal spirit; the Creator: Genesis 1; Deuteronomy 33:26–27; 1 Kings 8:27; Job 38ff.; Psalms 8; 100; 104; Isaiah 40: 12–28; 55:9; John 4:23–24; Romans 1:19–20; Revelation 1:8
The power of God: Genesis 17:1; Exodus 32:11; Numbers 24:4; Job 40 – 42:2; Isaiah 9:6; 45–46; Daniel 3:17; Matthew 26:53; John 19:10–11; Acts 12; Revelation 19:1–16
– his knowledge: Genesis 4:10; Job 28:20–27; Psalm 139:1–6; Daniel 2:17–23; Matthew 6:7–8; John 2:23–25; 4:25–29; Ephesians 1:3–12
– his presence everywhere: Genesis 28:10–17; Psalm 139:7–12; Jeremiah 23:23–24; Acts 17:26–28
The character of God – his holiness and

righteousness: Exodus 20; Leviticus 11:44–45; Joshua 24:19–28; Psalms 7; 25:8–10; 99; Isaiah 1:12ff.; 6:1–5; John 17:25–26; Romans 1:18 – 3:26; Ephesians 4:17–24; Hebrews 12:7–14; 1 Peter 1:13–16; 1 John 1:5–10
– his love and mercy: Deuteronomy 7:6–13; Psalms, e.g., 23; 25; 36:5–12; 103; Isaiah 40:1–2, 27–31; 41:8–20; 43; Jeremiah 31:2–4; Hosea 6; 11; 14; John 3:16–17; 10:7–18; 13:1; 14:15–31; 15:9, 12ff.; Romans 8:35–38; Galatians 2:20; Ephesians 2:4–10; 1 John 4:7–21
God the 'father': 1 Chronicles 25:10; Psalms 68:5; 103:13; Matthew 5:48; 6:1–14; 28:19; Romans 8:14–15

Gospel The word 'gospel' means 'good news'. This good news, as far as the Bible is concerned, is the fact that we need not be cut off from God because of sins, for Jesus has come to bring forgiveness.

Mark's Gospel describes itself as 'the good news of Jesus Christ', and at its simplest Jesus himself *is* the good news, the 'gospel'. The facts of the gospel are simple: 'That Christ died for our sins, as written in the Scriptures; that he was buried, and that he was raised to life three days later, as written in the Scriptures.' We can have forgiveness and new life because of the death and resurrection of Jesus.

In fact the gospel is so simple that some sneered at it. It was not as complex as they thought it should be. Paul made it clear that it is never difficult to find God. The good news of Jesus Christ was not a system of philosophy, but the plan of God himself. Paul had proved in his own experience that it was 'God's power to save *all* who believe'.
Luke 2:10–11; Mark 1:1, 14; Luke 4:18–21; 1 Corinthians 15:3–4; 1:17–23; Ephesians 1:6–13; Romans 1:16–17

Government The Bible does not put forward any one form of government as the right way to organize society. In fact the Bible reflects many different forms. The 'patriarchs', Abraham, Isaac and Jacob, lived in family clans. The nation of Israel

was at first ruled by Judges, then by kings. And Christians in the New Testament accepted the Roman system of government under which they lived.

From the beginning Israel was meant to be a 'theocracy' – a nation with God as its king. But because of the sinful nature of men and women, it was soon clear that society also needed its human rulers to make laws and enforce them. The nation of Israel discovered this during the period of the Judges when there was no central government. 'There was no king in Israel at that time. Everyone did just as he pleased.'

God delegates authority to governments to uphold justice. 'Everyone must obey the state authorities, because no authority exists without God's permission, and the existing authorities have been put there by God.' God's people should pray for the government and support it as it tries to rule justly.

At the same time, the Bible shows that God expects rulers to uphold justice, not to pervert it. The Old Testament prophets – especially Amos – spoke out plainly against the injustices and tyrannical rule of many of the kings of Israel and Judah. And when governments oppress their subjects, the people of God must stand up fearlessly and condemn them. If it comes to a straight choice between what the government says and doing God's will, Christians 'must obey God'.
Judges 21:25; Romans 13:1–7; 1 Timothy 2:2; 1 Peter 2:11–25; Isaiah 56:9–12; Jeremiah 21:11 – 22:19; Daniel 3; Amos and many other passages from the prophets; Matthew 22:15–21; Acts 5:27–29

Grace Both the Old and New Testaments teach that God is good and kind to men and women. There is no need for God to be like this. We certainly do not deserve it. God is good to us because he loves us – this is the 'grace' of God.

The Old Testament is full of reminders of God's

goodness, his constant love. But the grace of God is seen most clearly in the coming of Jesus. In the cross God has shown us how much he loves us – it was 'while we were still sinners that Christ died for us'. The human race did not deserve salvation, but God freely gave it. This is what the New Testament means by 'the grace of our Lord Jesus'.

But the New Testament also suggests that the Christian life, from start to finish, depends on God's grace. We obey God out of gratitude for his 'grace'. 'My grace', God says in answer to Paul's prayer for healing, 'is all you need, for my power is strongest when you are weak.' Paul's letters often begin or end with a prayer for God's grace.

See also *Covenant, Justification.*
Deuteronomy 7:6–9; Psalms 23:6; 25:6–10; 51:1; Jeremiah 31:2–3; Romans 5:8; 16:20; 3:19–24; 6:14; Ephesians 2:8–9; 2 Corinthians 12:9; 1 Timothy 1:2; 1 Peter 5:5–7; 2 Peter 3:18

Healing One of the results of evil in the world is illness. People become sick, age and die as a result of the 'fall', the coming of sin into the world.

This does not mean to say that a person is ill because he has sinned. This idea was commonly held in Jesus' day, but he did not agree.

Jesus came to announce a whole new creation in which sin and sickness and death would be no more. The new creation has already begun, with the resurrection of Jesus, but it remains to be completed in the future. Those who believe in him will share in it.

So the power of Jesus to heal sickness as well as to forgive sins was a way of showing what the new kingdom was like, and that it was real. He applied to himself the prophecy of Isaiah: 'The spirit of the Lord is upon me, because he has chosen me to bring good news to the poor. He has sent me to proclaim liberty to the captives and recovery of sight to the blind.' His healing of the sick in mind and body was a sample, a foretaste, of the coming age.

Christ's healing work has been continued by his disciples ever since. Paul describes a gift of healing given to every church. James considers it natural to call in the elders of the church to pray for a sick person. He advises Christians: 'Confess your sins to one another, so that you will be healed.' The salvation Jesus brings is for the whole person.

But until 'all things are made new' at the end of time, the church cannot reverse the whole process of sickness, ageing and death. People will continue to be sick, grow old and die, but God intends the church to carry on the healing ministry of Jesus until he returns. Then the kingdom of God will be fully established and there will be no more tears, pain or death.

Genesis 3:14 – 19. *Some Old Testament healings:* Numbers 21:4 – 9; 1 Kings 17:17 – 24; Deuteronomy 7:12 – 15; 28:20 – 23; 2 Kings 4:18 – 37; 5. *Some of Jesus' healings:* Matthew 8:5 – 13, 28 – 34; 9:32 – 33; 17:14 – 18; Mark 7:31 – 37; 10:46 – 52; Luke 4:18 – 19; 7:11 – 15; 8:41 – 42, 49 – 56; 17:11 – 19; John 9; 11; Acts 3:1 – 10 and other passages; 1 Corinthians 15; James 5:14 – 16; Revelation 21:1 – 5; 22:1 – 2

Heaven The Hebrews used the word 'heaven' to refer to the sky. The phrase 'the heaven and the earth' means the same as our word 'universe'.

Heaven can also refer to where God is. So Jesus taught his disciples to pray, 'Our Father in heaven . . .' God is not alone in 'heaven'. He is surrounded by the 'angels of heaven' who serve him. Christians are promised a place 'in heaven' after this life. Jesus promised his disciples that he was going there to prepare a place for them. So 'heaven' is the experience in which all the angels and all the believers who once lived on earth join in unending worship of God.

What is heaven like? We are told that it will be 'home', where there will be rest, but also a share in God's work. In 'heaven' we shall be safe and happy in God's presence, with nothing to spoil things. In 'heaven' we shall meet all who have trusted Jesus in life – and we shall know them, as Jesus' disciples recognized him after the resurrection. 'Heaven' is a 'treasure-house', where more important things than money are kept for us. In heaven there are no tears, there is no pain, no weakness, no night or need for sleep. In God's presence there is joy for ever.

See also *Angel, Future destiny, Resurrection, Second coming of Jesus*. Matthew 6:9; Nehemiah 9:6; Mark 13:32; Luke 6:21 – 23; 1 Peter 1:4; John 14:2; Romans 8; 1 Corinthians 15; Philippians 1:21 – 23; 3:12 – 21; 1 Peter 1:3 – 5; Revelation 4; 21 – 22

Hell The teaching of Jesus is clear about the fact of hell as an eternal punishment for those who do evil. Jesus uses very vivid imagery to describe it – a rubbish tip; outer darkness; fire which never goes out; a fiery furnace where people will cry and grind their teeth; and the place where God destroys both body and soul.

These phrases are not to be taken as a literal description. They are meant as warnings. They emphasize the absolute and final nature of God's judgement and it is a mistake to draw exact meanings out of them. But it is also a mistake to dismiss the idea of hell as some medieval idea about little devils with pitchforks. Hell is an essential part of Jesus' own stern warnings about sin and its power. In fact Jesus said that he himself will pronounce sentence on the day of judgement – 'Away from me, you that are under God's curse! Away to the eternal fire which has been prepared for the Devil and his angels!'

In English (for example in the Apostles' Creed) the word 'hell' has sometimes been used with a different meaning to describe the Hebrew word *Sheol* (Greek *Hades*). In this case it means, not the place of eternal punishment but the place of the dead.

See also *Death, Future destiny, Judgement*. Matthew 18:8 – 9; 3:12; 13:42; Mark 9:48; Matthew 10:38; 25:41; Revelation 20:10 – 15

Holiness The basic idea of holiness is 'separate (set apart) for God'. In the Old Testament, places, things, people and seasons were called holy when they were set apart for God. For that reason the seventh day, the sabbath, was holy.

The character of God himself shows what holiness is. He is different. He is the one who is absolutely separate from creation, and from all that is evil. Nothing compares with him. His very nature is different from our own: he is 'holy'. Because of this we should stand in awe of him. When someone realizes how holy God is, as Isaiah did, he is intensely conscious of his own sin that separates him from God.

The people of God have always been expected to reflect the holiness which they see in God. God wants his people to share his holiness. So in the New Testament the common word for Christians is 'saints'. This did not then mean an especially devout Christian. It meant 'the holy ones', those who are set apart and dedicated to God's service. And 'saints' are meant to grow in holiness and likeness to God – a process sometimes called 'sanctification'.

Genesis 2:3; Exodus 20:8; 30:22 – 33; Leviticus 19:1; Isaiah 6:1 – 5; 40:18 – 28; 10:20; Psalm 33:21; Isaiah 8:13; 6; Hebrews 12:10; Ephesians 5:25 – 27

Holy Spirit The Spirit of God is one with God the Father and Jesus Christ (see *Trinity*). He is active throughout the history of God's work and God's people. But it is not until the New Testament and the 'age of the spirit' that we see the details of his work.

The Spirit of God was active in the creation of the world. As God, he is present everywhere – there is nowhere in the whole of creation outside his domain. Again and again we read of the Spirit of God giving people the power needed for special service. The Spirit of God gave the prophets their inspiration and communicated the word of God through them. But the Old Testament looked forward to the day when the Spirit of God would be poured out on all people.

When Jesus came, he was born by the power of the Holy Spirit. The Holy Spirit descended upon him at his baptism in the River Jordan. He was led by the Spirit into the desert where he was tempted by the devil. And at the beginning of his public work Jesus declared that he would carry it out through the power of the Spirit. John the Baptist declared that Jesus would baptize people with the Holy Spirit. And Jesus himself promised his disciples that after he had left them he would send the Holy Spirit to be with them all the time. After Jesus had returned to his Father, the Holy Spirit would teach and guide the followers of Jesus and give them power. 'He will give me glory,' Jesus said, 'because he will take what I say and tell it to you.'

The disciples were baptized with the Holy Spirit, as Jesus promised, on the Day of Pentecost. This was obvious to everyone because of a new note of praise and boldness, because they spoke in other languages, and because of their powerful preaching. As Peter told his listeners on the Day of Pentecost, the prophecy of Joel had come true. God had poured out his Spirit on all believers.

When someone becomes a Christian he or she receives the 'gift' of the Holy Spirit. The Holy Spirit lives within the Christian giving new understanding and direction, and making him aware that he really is a child of God. The Spirit is a guarantee of a future with God in heaven.

The Holy Spirit helps Christians to realize their oneness in Jesus Christ. He works to reproduce the character of Jesus in the life of every Christian – the qualities of 'love, joy, peace, patience, kindness, goodness, faithfulness, humility and self-control'. And he gives Christians the power and gifts needed to serve God.

See also *Trinity, Church*. Genesis 1:2; Psalm 139:7 – 12; Judges 3:10; 14:6, and many other passages; Isaiah 11:1 – 3; 2 Samuel 23:2 – 5; Ezekiel

36:26–27; Joel 2:28–29; Micah 3:8; Luke 1:35; 3:22; 4:1–18; 3:16; John 14:16–17; 16:7–15; Acts 2; Romans 8; 1 Corinthians 12; Galatians 5:22–23

Hope The Christian's hope is a confident looking forward to a future beyond this world, promised by God. It is something that keeps him joyful in troubles.

He has learned that God's promises can be trusted, and so he is confident about the future. 'I alone know the plans I have for you,' says God to Jeremiah, in the dark days of exile, 'plans to bring you prosperity and not disaster, plans to bring about the future you hope for.'

The resurrection of Jesus is the great foundation of the Christian's hope. 'Because of (God's) great mercy he gave us new life by raising Jesus from death,' wrote Peter. 'This fills us with a living hope.' This is confirmed by the gift of the Holy Spirit, who is the guarantee of the Christian's own future resurrection.

See also *Future destiny*. Romans 4:18; 5:1–5; 8:24–25; 12:12; 15:4; Jeremiah 29:11; 1 Corinthians 15:19–20; Colossians 1:15; 1 Peter 1:3–6; 2 Corinthians 5:1–5

Jesus Christ 'Jesus' is the personal name given to the Son of God who became man; it means 'Saviour'. (See Part 6: *People of the Bible* for an outline of Jesus' life.) The word 'Christ' is the Greek word for 'Messiah', the promised deliverer for whom the Jews had long been waiting. It is a title, rather than a surname. The Bible's teaching about Jesus is summed up in these other titles:

Jesus, the 'Servant of God'. Matthew gives Jesus this title, which comes from the prophecies of Isaiah. The character of the lowly, gentle servant of God who comes to bring justice was perfectly lived out in the

It was in Jerusalem that the great events of Jesus' life took place: here he died, and here God raised him to life again, fulfilling the words of the Old Testament prophets.

person of Jesus. When Jesus said that he 'came to serve and to give his life to redeem many people', he was living out the work of the Servant of God, suffering to bear the sins of mankind, just as Isaiah describes him.
Matthew 12:15–21; Isaiah 42:1–4; 52:13–53; 12 and other passages; Mark 10:45

Jesus, the 'Son of David'. The angel who announced his birth told Jesus' mother that God would make her son a king 'as his ancestor David was'. By human birth Jesus was a descendant of King David. This title shows Jesus as the fulfilment of the hopes of the Jewish nation. It is the one used to describe Jesus in the opening sentence of Matthew, the most Jewish of all the Gospels. It was the title that the Jews used when they acknowledged Jesus as the Messiah. 'Praise to David's Son! God bless him who comes in the name of the Lord! Praise God!'
Luke 1:32; John 7:42; Matthew 1:1; 21:9

Jesus, the 'Son of man'. This is the title Jesus most often used of himself, and it tells us much about him. He borrowed the phrase from Daniel's vision of someone who 'looked like a human being', yet had God's authority for ever. 'His kingdom,' Daniel says would 'never end'. The Bible teaches clearly that Jesus was a real man. He identified himself completely with mankind. As the 'Son of man' he came to serve men and women and to give his life to save them. 'The Son of man must suffer . . . He will be put to death, but three days later he will be raised to life.' As the Son of man Jesus defeated sin and death and will come again 'with great power and glory'.
Daniel 7:13–14; Mark 10:45; 9:21–22; 21:25–28

Jesus, the 'Son of God'. At Jesus' baptism at the River Jordan a voice from heaven declared, 'You are my own dear Son. I am pleased with you.' Again, on the mountain, when Jesus' glory was seen, the voice came, 'This is my Son, whom I have chosen – listen to him.' John's Gospel explains what this

phrase means. Jesus is God's 'only Son'. His whole life and purpose is to carry out the Father's work. 'The Father and I are one,' Jesus says. He was with the Father before the world was made. They are one for ever. Because Jesus shares God's nature and is free from sin, he was able to pay in full for the sins of the whole world for all time. And we now 'have someone who pleads with the Father on our behalf – Jesus Christ, the righteous one'.
Mark 1:11; Luke 9:35; John 1:14; 10:30; 17; Romans 1:3–4; Hebrews 1; 1 John 1 – 2:2

Jesus, the 'Lord'. In the Gospels Jesus is often called 'Lord' in the everyday sense of 'master'. But after the resurrection the word took on a new meaning. 'My Lord and my God,' declared Thomas when he saw the risen Jesus with his own eyes. This was the way in which Jews often referred to God, and the first Christians publicly declared their faith in the words, 'Jesus Christ is Lord.' Paul, in his letter to the Philippians, looks forward to the time when Jesus will return as Lord, when 'all beings in heaven, on earth, and in the world below will fall on their knees, and all will openly proclaim that Jesus Christ is Lord, to the glory of God the Father'.
Luke 5:8; John 20:28; 1 Corinthians 12:3; Philippians 2:6–11

See also *Trinity, Judgement, Justification, Kingdom of God, Messiah, Redemption, Salvation,* and the events of Jesus' life: *Resurrection, Second coming of Jesus, Transfiguration*.

Joy Joy in the Bible is not an occasional emotional experience; it is a basic part of a personal relationship with God. As the Scottish *Shorter (Westminster) Catechism* says, 'The chief end of man is to glorify God and to enjoy him for ever.'

Living with the presence of God in one's life is a continuous experience of joy. And as this joy is a gift of God, it is possible for Christians to rejoice even in times of persecution. 'Rejoice in the Lord always,' wrote Paul to his readers at Philippi.

Psalms 16:11; 30:5; 43:4; 51:12; 126:5–6; Ecclesiastes 2:26; Isaiah 61:7; Jeremiah 15:16; Luke 15:7; John 15:11; 16:22; Romans 14:17; 15:13; Galatians 5:22; Philippians 1:4; 1 Thessalonians 2:20; 3:9; Hebrews 12:2; James 1:2; 1 Peter 1:8; Jude 24

Judgement Because God is Ruler of the universe he is also the Judge. The ruler makes laws and carries them out. This is what the Bible means by judgement.

Judgement in the Old Testament often meant 'good government'. The 'Judges' were national leaders before Israel had a king. God was the supreme Judge, the Ruler of all things.

So the 'last' judgement, as taught by Jesus, will be the final sorting out of good from evil. Because the Judge is God himself there will be no injustice. We can be confident that the Judge of all the earth will act fairly. God has given to Jesus the actual task of judgement.

Everyone will be judged according to what they know. Those who have never heard the written laws of God will be judged by what they know of God from creation, and what their own conscience tells them about right and wrong. But it is a fact that we all fail to live up to what we know of God and his standards, and we all stand condemned on the basis of the life we have led.

On the great day of judgement everything will depend on a person's relationship to Christ. Jesus himself said so. The early Christians were certain that the only way to be sure of life on the day of judgement was by believing in Christ. 'Whoever believes in the Son has eternal life,' wrote John, 'whoever disobeys the Son will not have life, but will remain under God's punishment.'

See also *Future destiny, Heaven, Hell, Second coming of Jesus*.
Psalm 96:10; Genesis 18:25; Romans 3:3–4; 1:18 – 2:16; 3:9–12; Matthew 10:32–33; John 3:18; 5:24–30; Acts 4:12; 10:42; 2 Corinthians 3:10–15; 5:10; 2 Thessalonians 1:5–10;

Hebrews 12:22–27; Revelation 20:12–15

Justification There is nothing a person can do to get right (be justified) with God. Sin cuts us off from a holy God. However 'good' we try to be, we cannot escape its grip.

Therefore if a person is to be made right with God it can only come about by God's own action: by 'grace'. This is the point made by the doctrine of 'justification'. God accepts us as his children because of Jesus' death on the cross. 'Christ was without sin, but for our sake God made him share our sin in order that in union with him we might share the righteousness of God.' Christ took on himself the sentence on sin so that we could be acquitted. God now looks upon the Christian as 'in Christ' – a new person acquitted because of Jesus' obedience, and given the power to be obedient himself.

The Christian is therefore put right with God ('justified') by 'grace' on the basis of the death of Jesus. And his acquittal comes through faith in Christ.

See also *Atonement, Grace*.
2 Corinthians 5:21; Romans 3:24; 5:1, 9

Kingdom of God 'God is King' is one of the constant themes of the Old Testament. And in one sense it was true. But it was only partially true and it was obvious that God would need to act decisively if the evils that man's sin had brought were to be put right. God promised that this would happen.

'The right time has come,' Jesus declared when he began to preach in Galilee, 'and the Kingdom of God is near! Turn away from your sins and believe the Good News.' God had sent Jesus to establish his new rule, to put an end to the evil mess into which the world had fallen, and to make a fresh start, a new age. God's rule is what the 'kingdom' means, rather than a *place* where God rules. The presence of God's rule was seen in Jesus' miracles and in the fact that he could drive out demons. Jesus was putting right both physical and spiritual illnesses to show the power of the new kingdom, in which evil would be completely destroyed.

The life and teaching of Jesus show that the kingdom of God has already arrived. He died for the sins of the old, sinful creation and rose again in the eternal life of the new creation, the life of the kingdom. But it is not yet fully established. This awaits the return of Jesus at the end of the age, when all things will be made new.

Jesus used parable stories to teach about the 'kingdom of God'. The Jews thought that it was going to be deliverance from the Romans. But Jesus made it clear that it was to be a slow growth of something which would eventually affect the whole world. It is worth all we have to enter it. It is not for the proud or self-centred, but for people who humble themselves before God – for sinners who repent.

People who believe in Jesus have his new life already. In the future, they will know the 'new heavens and the new earth', their bodies will be made new, when the new age, the kingdom, is completed. Micah 4:6–7; Mark 1:15; Luke 7:18–23; Matthew 5:1–20; 6:10; 13; Mark 4; 9:45–47; Luke 8; 14:16–24

Law The Old Testament law, the 'Torah' or instruc-tion, was the rule of life given by God (in the first five books of the Bible) to help his people know how to live.

It included the Ten Commandments, the heart of the moral law. It also included social and religious laws, down to detailed matters of hygiene and daily behaviour.

The principles of the law are basic to our understanding of the way man and society have been designed to work. As the 'Maker's manual', the law shows us how God wants us to live. The religious and ceremonial laws no longer apply in detail – for instance, the sacrifices have been fulfilled in the death of Jesus. But the principles hold good.

God first brought his people out from slavery in

Egypt: then he gave them the law. It was not the other way round: they were not expected to obey the law in order to be delivered. But after the return from exile in Babylon many Jews began to see the law as a means of gaining salvation. If a person kept the law, God would accept him.

Jesus himself never rejected the law. But he said quite clearly that its day was past, for its place had now been taken by his own teaching, which fulfilled its deepest meaning. The New Testament completely rejects the false idea that by obeying any law a person can earn salvation. This comes only by the free gift of God ('grace'). The law makes clear what sin is, but this only emphasizes human need, because we are unable to keep the whole law of God. So a true understanding of the law leads a person to Christ, to accept his free forgiveness.

See *Freedom, Grace, Justification.*

Exodus 20 and 21–34; Leviticus; Numbers 2–9; 15; 18–19; 28–30; Deuteronomy; Psalms 1; 9; 119; Matthew 5:17–20; 22:36–40; Luke 10:25–28; Romans 3:31; 8:3–4; John 7:19; Romans 2:25–29; 3:19–21; 7:7–25; Galatians 3:21–24; Hebrews 7:18–19; James 2:8–12

Life Life was 'breathed into man's nostrils' by God and he 'began to live'. God is in all the natural processes that keep us alive; and it is he who determines when life shall end. Life is a person's most valued possession, and one of his greatest desires is for God to bless him with a long life.

But there is more to life than just physical existence. A relationship with God enables people to live life on a new level. This is the full, abundant life that Jesus came to bring. It is 'eternal life', which Jesus offers as a free and permanent gift. Eternal life is life in a new dimension, 'God's life'. 'Whoever has the Son', says John, 'has this life.' It

begins when a person becomes a Christian and survives death. It is an eternal relationship with God.

See also *Death, Resurrection.*
Genesis 2:7; Psalm 104:29; Job 2:4; Psalm 91:16; Deuteronomy 8:3; 30:15–20; John 10:10, 28; 1 John 5:12; John 11:25–26; Romans 6:4–13, 22–23 and many other passages

Light The Bible often uses the contrast of light and darkness to show the absolute difference between God and the forces of evil. 'God is light, and there is no darkness at all in him.' God is altogether good. His holiness is so utterly pure that he is said to 'live in the light that no one can approach'. In contrast to this the forces of evil are called 'the cosmic powers

'I am the vine,' Jesus said, 'and you are the branches.' Those who follow him experience new life, God's own life within them.

of this dark age'. John describes the spiritual battle between 'light' (God and goodness) and 'darkness' (Satan and everything evil). 'The light shines in the darkness, and the darkness has never put it out.' In the life, death and resurrection of Jesus light won its victory over darkness.

Jesus calls himself 'the light of the world' and promises 'the light of life' to all who follow him. Men and women need no longer walk in darkness, ignorant of the truth, cut off from God, and blinded by sin. They can 'live in the light – just as he is in the light'. To become a Christian is to move out of darkness into light. God's people are 'like light for the whole world'. They must let that light shine out to others.

At last, in the new heaven and earth, the light of God's presence will be a constant reality. There will be no darkness, no night, no lamps, not even sunlight. All God's people will be with him, and he will be their light.
1John 1:5; 1 Timothy 6:16; Ephesians 6:12; John 1:4 – 9; 8:12; 1 John 1:7; Matthew 5:14 – 16; Revelation 21:23 – 24; 22:5
Love 'God is love.' This has always been the character of God. It is a mistake to think that the God of the Old Testament could not be described in this way. One of the most moving testimonies to God's love in the whole Bible is by the prophet Hosea. God's love was the reason why he chose and cared for the people of Israel. In return, God's people were expected to love him with their whole being, and show a similar love to their fellow men.

In the New Testament 'love' sometimes translates the usual Greek word for love, *philia*. This means 'intimate affection'. Far more important, however, is the word *agapē*. This is not a sex word, although the Bible regards sex very highly. *Agapē* is used to describe self-giving love, seen above all in Jesus Christ. It is in his death that we see the true depths of this love.

It is far greater than human love. It is the love that unites the Father and the Son. It is the love that

God has for the world, and it becomes part of a Christian's life through the gift of God. It is in fact the mark of God's presence in the life of every Christian. 'If you have love for one another,' Jesus says, 'then everyone will know that you are my disciples.'
1 John 4:8; Hosea 11:1 – 4; 7 – 9; Deuteronomy 7:7 – 8; 6:5; Leviticus 19:18; Romans 5:5, 8; John 3:16, 35; 1 Corinthians 13; Galatians 5:22; John 13:34 – 35; see also John 14:15, 21 – 24; 15:9 – 14; 1 John 4:7 – 5:3
Man and woman Men and women are part of nature. They are 'animals' – yet different from the animals, because God made them to be 'like himself' and to enjoy his friendship. They were the crowning glory of his whole creation on earth.

The story of Adam and Eve in Genesis 2 shows the importance of men and women in God's creation. Adam is put in the Garden of Eden to look after it and to work in it. Work itself is not a necessary evil: it is part of God's original intention. Man was not meant to live alone. God made woman as the ideal partner for Adam, to work alongside him and to share his life. The relationship between man and woman, their sexuality, is part of God's perfect creation.

But when Adam ('man') and Eve ('woman') rebelled against God they lost the open fellowship with God and with one another which they had known. The results of their sin affected every area of their lives. The man's work became burdensome, and the woman's relationship with her husband brought pain as well as pleasure.

The rest of the Bible reflects both the glory and the fallenness of men and women. They are second only to God, crowned with honour. They care for all God has made, sharing his creativity in artistic achievement and caring for the earth's resources. But we see them, too, as spoilers, perverted and degraded, violent and evil.

The New Testament announces the dawn of a new age. Mankind, 'in Adam' is the same as ever. But men and women are 'one in union with

Christ Jesus'. Both are made new and share in the new creation as equal partners, to live life as God originally intended it.
See also *Fall, Future destiny, Life.*
Genesis 1:26 – 28; 2; 3; Deuteronomy 5; 8; Psalm 8; Romans 1 – 3; 5:12 – 19; 8:18 – 25; 2 Corinthians 5:17; 6:16 – 18; Galatians 3:28
Mediator A 'go-between' who brings together (reconciles) two people who are estranged from each other.

When Adam first disobeyed God his sin broke the friendship between them. The Old Testament therefore recognizes the need for a mediator between man and God. The Old Testament prophets spoke in God's name and made God real to their hearers. The priest who offered sacrifices to God represented the people before God. Moses combined both roles as Israel's mediator.

But, important as Moses was, he could never be the perfect mediator between God and the people, because he shared the sinful nature of every human being. Only Jesus, who was both man, but sinless, and the Son of God could be the perfect mediator who arranges a new covenant. This is the main theme of the letter to the Hebrews.
See also *Reconciliation.*
Exodus 32:30 – 32; 33:11; Leviticus 16; Numbers 12:6 – 8; Deuteronomy 5:4 – 5; Galatians 3:19 – 20; 1 Timothy 2:5; Hebrews 7:24 – 25; 8:6; 9:15; 12:24
Mercy The Hebrew word often translated 'mercy' occurs nearly 250 times in the Old Testament. It refers to God's loving patience with the people of Israel, his kindness and readiness to forgive. God had made his covenant-agreement with them, and although they often broke their side of the agreement, he did not disown them. He is faithful and has 'mercy' on them. Some English versions translate the word 'loving kindness'.

In the New Testament, 'mercy' is a loving pity for those in need. God is 'the merciful Father, the God from whom all help comes'. It is because of

his mercy that we are saved. Jesus himself was often moved with pity to respond to the needs of those around him. Christians are expected to show to other people the same mercy which they have experienced from God himself.
Exodus 34:6 – 7; Deuteronomy 7:9; Nehemiah 9:7; 31; Psalms 23:6; 25:6; 40:11; 51:1; 103:4, 8; Daniel 9:9; Jonah 4:2; Micah 6:8; Matthew 5:7; Luke 6:36; 18:13; Romans 9:15; 12:1; 2 Corinthians 1:3; Ephesians 2:4
Messiah 'Messiah' and 'Christ' both mean the 'anointed one' – Messiah is the Hebrew word and Christ is the Greek equivalent.

Throughout the troublesome history of the nation of Israel the hope gradually grew that God would one day send a great Messiah-king to establish his universal and everlasting kingdom. By the time of Jesus many Jews were longing for that day to come. So when they heard of his teaching and miracles they asked, 'Is he the Messiah?'

The New Testament shows plainly that the first Christians identified Jesus as the Messiah. At his baptism, 'God poured out on (anointed) Jesus of Nazareth the Holy Spirit and power.' Afterwards he applied to himself the prophecy of Isaiah that 'the time has come when the Lord will save his people'. But Jesus normally avoided directly calling himself the Messiah because the people understood it in political terms. The Gospels tell of only one occasion on which Jesus claimed to be the Messiah – to a poor, sinful woman at a well. When Peter told Jesus, 'You are the Messiah', he was asked to keep it quiet. Jesus wanted genuine disciples; he was no 'rabble-rouser', out to make a name for himself.

However, when the Jewish authorities began to put the pressure on Jesus, the key question asked by the high priest at his trial was, 'Are you the Messiah, the Son of the Blessed God?' 'I am', answered Jesus, and the high priest, enraged by this 'blasphemy' (insult to

God) secured a unanimous verdict of guilty. Jesus was sentenced to death.

The verdict of the New Testament is that the Jewish court made a mistake. Jesus *was* the Messiah – and God proved this by raising him to life again. As Peter declared on the Day of Pentecost, 'All the people of Israel, then, are to know for sure that this Jesus, whom you crucified, is the one that God has made Lord and Messiah!'

See also *Jesus Christ.*
Deuteronomy 18:15–22; Psalms 2; 45:6–7; 72; 110; Isaiah 9:2–7; 11; 42:1–9; 49:1–6; 52:13 – 53:12; 61:1–3; Jeremiah 23:5–6; 33:14–16; Ezekiel 34:22–25; Daniel 7; Zechariah 9:9–10; Matthew 1:18, 22–23; 16:16, 20; 26:68; Mark 8:27–30; 14:61–64; Luke 2:11, 26; John 4:25–26; 7:26–27, 31, 41–42; 9:22; Acts 2:36; 3:20–21; 4:26–28; 10:38; 18:28; 26:22–23

Miracles One of the striking things about Jesus' life and work is the fact that he did miracles. Even his enemies agreed on this. The miracles described in the Gospels range from curing physical illnesses and casting out devils to calming a storm and bringing the dead back to life.

The miracles are sometimes described as 'mighty works'. They are done through the power of God. The most important display of God's power, the greatest miracle, is the resurrection of Jesus.

Jesus' miracles are also called 'wonders'. They often amazed those who saw them. But Jesus did not want to be seen as a mere wonder-worker. This was why he refused to jump from the highest point of the temple, as the devil suggested in his temptations. Jesus did not want people to follow him just to see his miracles. So he often told the people he cured to tell no one about it.

John's Gospel makes it plain that Jesus' miracles were above all 'signs'. They were signs that he was the Messiah, signs that the new age, the kingdom, had really come. When John the Baptist wanted to know if Jesus

really was the Messiah he was told of the miracles Jesus did and left to draw his own conclusions. By doing miracles Jesus was showing people the kingdom of God. He was giving examples of the fact that in the new age sin and death and sickness would be no more.

Jesus gave his disciples power to do miracles. They continued to heal in the power of Jesus after Pentecost, and miracles remained part of the experience of the early church. One of the 'gifts of the Spirit' mentioned by Paul is the working of miracles, another the gift of healing. But the one who heals is always God himself, never the Christian, or the church.
Mark 10:27; Romans 1:4; Matthew 4:5–7; 11:2–6, 20–21; Luke 9:1; Acts 3:6; Galatians 3:5; 1 Corinthians 12:9–10
Jesus' healings: Matthew 8:2–3, 5–13, 14–15,

When Jesus restored the sight of a man who was blind from birth, he sent him to wash in the Pool of Siloam.

28–34; 9:2–7, 20–22, 27–31, 32–33; 12:10–13, 22; 15:21–28; 17:14–18; 20:29–34; Mark 1:23–26; 7:31–37; 8:22–26; Luke 13:11–13; 14:1–4; 17:11–19; 22:50–51; John 4:46–54; 5:1–9; 9
Jesus' command over the forces of nature: Matthew 8:23–27; 14:25, 15–21; 15:32–38; 17:24–27; 21:18–22; Mark 11:20–26; Luke 5:1–11; John 2:1–11; 21:1–11
Jesus brings the dead to life: Matthew 9:18–19, 23–25; Luke 7:11–15; John 11:1–44
Some Old Testament miracles:
Exodus 14; Joshua 2; 1 Kings 17:17–24; 2 Kings 2; 4–5; Daniel 6 and many other passages
New birth Long before the time of Jesus, the prophet

Jeremiah had seen that men and women need to be completely re-made from within if they are to have a renewed relationship with God. In his discussion with the Jewish leader Nicodemus, Jesus made the same point. He said that only a complete 'new birth' would allow people to make this fresh start.

This fundamental change occurs when a person becomes a Christian. 'When anyone is joined to Christ, he is a new being; the old is gone, the new has come.' Baptism is the outward sign of this new life. The new life is given by the Holy Spirit, the eternal life of God's kingdom, shared with others in the family of the church.

See also *Baptism.*
Psalm 51:10; Jeremiah 31:31–34; John 3:1–21; 2 Corinthians 5:17
Parable A way of teaching spiritual truths by using a

picture or short story. Much of Jesus' teaching was given in parables.

See Part 5: *Religion and Worship in the Bible.*

Peace The Hebrew word for 'peace' has a very broad meaning. It really means 'wholeness' and describes fullness of life in every aspect. It can refer to bodily health, or a long life which ends in a natural death. It is also used to describe safety, and harmony for the individual and for the community. Peace is the most precious of all gifts, and it comes from God himself. 'The Lord is peace.' On the other hand, 'There is no (peace), says the Lord, for the sinners.'

Peace becomes the hallmark of the future age when God will establish his kingdom. God's Messiah, who was to bring in this new age, is called the 'Prince of Peace'. So the New Testament declares that Jesus 'has brought us peace'. He 'came and preached the Good News of peace to all' – a peace bought by his death on the cross. His gift to every Christian is peace with God, and peace with our fellow men. It is also a deep peace of heart and mind unaffected by circumstances. 'Peace,' he told his disciples on his last evening with them, 'is what I leave with you; it is my own peace that I give you. I do not give it as the world does. Do not be worried and upset; do not be afraid.'

See also *Reconciliation.* Genesis 15:15; Psalms 4:8; 85:8–10; Judges 6:24; Isaiah 48:22; 2:2–4; 9:6; Romans 5:1; Ephesians 2:14–18; John 14:27; 2 Thessalonians 3:16

Praise The joy God's people have in him is expressed in 'praise'. They praise him as their Creator and as their Redeemer (Saviour).

One of the Old Testament words for praise comes from a Hebrew word which means 'to make a noise'. It appears in our word 'hallelujah'. Israelite worship included joyful shouting and singing and the sound of many musical instruments. We see this again and again in the psalms (the hymns sung in the temple).

This same note of praise characterizes the Christian church. Christians rejoice above all in the great act of salvation brought about through the life, death and resurrection of Jesus. Angels sang when Jesus was born. Praise is a constant part of Christian prayer – rejoicing, asking God with a thankful heart. Heaven itself continually rings with praise.

See also *Worship.* Psalms 136; 135; 150; 34:3; 35:18 and many other passages; Luke 2:13–14; Philippians 4:4–8; Revelation 4:6–11

Prayer Men and women were made to live in fellowship with God. In this 'sharing', prayer was the normal relationship through which God fulfilled his purposes. It is because of the coming of sin and evil that this relationship is often broken now, and so prayer can seem unnatural or unreal.

But those who trust in God share their life with him in prayer. We pour out our hearts before him. We are open to God in confessing our sin. We ask things of God, confident that God answers prayer. And our prayers always include thanksgiving to God.

The faithful Israelite prayed three times each day. Samuel was so sure of his duty to pray that he considered it a sin if he failed to pray for those in his care. There is no particular pattern laid down for Christians to follow but Paul expects prayer to have a central place in the life of the Christian and the church. It will have a natural place in the restored relationship of God and his people.

Prayer is a Christian family activity. Jesus' model prayer begins 'Our Father . . .' The early church met for prayer, for instance at the house of John Mark's mother where they prayed for the release of Peter. It is the work of the Holy Spirit to help Christians to pray, tuning their minds more and more to the mind of God. 'The Spirit himself pleads with God for us in groans that words cannot express,' wrote Paul to the Romans. Psalm 62:8; 1 John 1:9; Mark 11:24; Philippians 4:6; 1 Samuel 12:23; Colossians 4:2; James

1:5–6; Acts 12:12; Romans 8:26
Jesus' teaching on prayer: Matthew 6:5–15; 7:7–11; 26:41; Mark 12:38–40; 13:33; 14:38; Luke 11:1–13; 18:1–14
Prayers of Jesus: Matthew 6:9–13; 11:25–26; 26:36–44; Mark 14:32–39; Luke 10:21; 11:2–4; 22:46; 23:34, 46; John 11:41–42; 12:27–28; 17
Some other great Bible prayers: Exodus 15; 32; 33; Deuteronomy 32–33; Joshua 17; 10; Judges 5; 6; 1 Samuel 1; 2; 2 Samuel 7; 22; 1 Kings 3; 8; 18; 19; 2 Kings 19; Ezra 9; Nehemiah 1; 9; Job 42; Psalms; Daniel 2; 9; Jonah 2; Habakkuk 3; Luke 1:46–55, 68–79; 2:29–35; Acts 4:24–30, and many prayers in the New Testament letters

Prophecy From an early period in Israel's history prophets played a leading part in the Bible story. It was their responsibility to give God's messages to his people. This often meant declaring God's verdict on the state of the world, showing what God would do now and in the future to put things right.

The prophet spoke with the authority of God and began his message with the statement, 'The Lord says . . .' So the people had to know whether a prophet was truly speaking God's word, or whether he was an impostor. The true prophet was always called to the work by God. 'The Lord took me from my work as a shepherd,' says Amos, 'and ordered me to go and prophesy to his people Israel . . . I am not the kind of prophet who prophesies for pay.'

The prophet was someone to whom God communicated his plans. A 'prophet' who led people away from the God of Israel must be a false prophet. If a person prophesied something that did not come true he was a false prophet. The penalty for such prophets was death, because they were a threat to the faith and security of Israel.

Most prophetic messages referred directly to the situation of the prophet's own time. So it is essential to read them alongside the historical accounts of the same

period. They found fulfilment in the prophet's own age, and also often pointed forward to the day when God would break into world history. So some of the Old Testament prophecies are applied to Christ by the New Testament writers.

With the outpouring of God's Holy Spirit on all believers, everyone, men and women, can proclaim God's message. But there is still a gift of 'prophecy' mentioned in the New Testament. This is one of God's special gifts given to various members of the church in order to build it up.

The prophecies of the Book of Revelation, like those in the Old Testament Book of Daniel, belong to a type of literature called 'apocalyptic'. This contains a special kind of imagery and symbolism which can be understood only if it is applied first to the time in which these books were written. Amos 7:14–15; 3:7; Deuteronomy 13:1–5; 18:20–22; John 5:39; Acts 2:17; 1 Corinthians 11:5; 14:24, 29; Acts 11:17–28; 1 Corinthians 12:10, 29; most of the Old Testament prophecies are contained in the books of the prophets, Isaiah – Malachi

Reconciliation To 'reconcile' two people is to bring them together when they have been enemies. The story of man in the Bible begins with the break in relationships between him and God. It is followed immediately by man's hostility to his fellow man (Cain murders Abel). It is only when the relationship with God is restored that relations between people can be truly healed. This is the effect of the 'reconciliation' which God offers to all.

So it is not surprising that people are often described in the Bible as enemies of God. They are opposed to all that God is and all that he stands for. Mankind is cut off because of sin. It is impossible to reconcile ourselves to God. But, as Paul explained, 'God was making all mankind his friends through Christ.'

This was done in the life, death and resurrection of Jesus himself. It is possible now for people to be friends, in fact children of God, rather than enemies. Sin, the reason for the original estrangement, has been dealt with by Jesus. Yet we are not automatically reconciled to God. It is a gift he offers and which we must accept. But it is a gift that is available for all, and so Christians are expected to explain the 'way of reconciliation' to others.

Reconciliation not only brings peace with God but also peace between one man, or woman, and another. Those who once were enemies find themselves members of the same family when they are reconciled to God. The things that divided them are unimportant compared to the relationship with God which now unites them. This is the solution the New Testament offers to the most bitter racial conflict of Bible times – the split between Jews and non-Jews.

See also *Atonement, Cross, Peace.*
Genesis 3; Romans 5:10–11; 11:15; 2 Corinthians 5:18–20; Ephesians 2:11–18; Colossians 1:19–22

Redemption To 'redeem' something is to buy it back. Jesus said that he came to 'give his life to redeem many people'.

The picture is that of a slave being 'ransomed'. Man is said to be a 'slave to sin'. Even if we want to give up sinning we cannot do so. But by his life, death and resurrection Jesus paid the price that would set us free.

Christians are therefore 'the redeemed', just as the Israelites who had been brought out of slavery in Egypt were 'the redeemed' in the Old Testament. They now belong to God. Paul urges his readers to consider the price that was paid for their redemption and give themselves wholeheartedly in the service of God. A redeemed person is also a free person, so Paul urges his readers not to fall back into the old ways but to allow God to rid them of the marks left by their former slavery to sin. But even the Christian will not experience full freedom immediately. That must wait until the end of the age, when Jesus returns and his people will know the perfect freedom of

living in the presence of God himself.

See *Cross, Freedom, Sons of God.*
Mark 10:45; John 8:34; 1 Peter 1:18–19; Exodus 13:11–16; 1 Corinthians 6:20; Romans 6:12–14; 8:19–23

Regeneration See *New birth.*

Repentance 'Repent sincerely and return to me', God said through Joel, 'with fasting and weeping and mourning. Let your broken heart show your sorrow; tearing your clothes is not enough.'

Jesus called for the same inward change of heart. Repentance means more than saying sorry, or even being sorry, for sin. It involves a decision to leave it behind. Jesus' parable of the Pharisee and the tax collector shows the importance he placed on an inward change of heart.

Jesus' message links repentance and faith. 'Turn away from your sins and believe the Good News.' Repentance is not something which comes naturally to people. It is the gift of God. But when men and women meet Jesus for themselves, they repent. There is no other way into the kingdom of God. God 'commands all (people) everywhere to turn away from their evil ways'.

See also *Forgiveness.*
Joel 2:12–13; Luke 18:9–14; Mark 1:15; Acts 11:18; Luke 19:1–10 (and other examples); Acts 17:30

Resurrection The claim that Jesus rose from the dead is the key fact of the Christian faith. 'If Christ has not been raised, then your faith is a delusion and you are still lost in your sins,' wrote Paul.

There was no doubt, however, in the apostles' minds that Jesus had risen from the dead, as he had said he would. They had seen him on various occasions, and this to them was evidence enough. Paul lists the people who had seen Jesus alive. The disciples were transformed overnight, from being a weak and cowardly bunch into being a fearless group of people who preached and performed miracles in the power of their risen Lord. The grave was

Jesus was raised from death to life. Because of this his followers can be sure that they too can look forward to resurrection life. Death is not the end.

empty, and the Jewish authorities could not produce a body to disprove the claim that Jesus was alive.

Paul teaches that Jesus' followers will share in his resurrection. When a person becomes a Christian he already experiences the life of the risen Jesus working in his own life. And in the future, Christians can look forward with confident expectation to their own resurrection at the end of the age. Believers must face physical death, like everyone else, but they are assured of a future with Christ in a new spiritual existence. Christianity does not look for the immortality of a soul (a Greek idea), but the resurrection of the complete person in a new and more wonderful body.

See also *Heaven.*
Matthew 28; Mark 16; Luke 24; John 20; 1 Corinthians 15; Acts 1:3; 4:10; Romans 1:4; 6:4–13

Revelation Human beings can never know God unless God chooses to 'reveal' himself. In his purity and majesty, he 'lives in the light that no one can approach'. We can know something of God's character through the world he has created (even *this* is revelation) and our own experience of it. But otherwise we can know nothing unless he shows it to us. Moses' encounter with God in the burning bush is a clear example of God revealing to a person what he could never have found out for himself.

In the history of Israel God most often revealed himself through what he did, particularly in delivering people from slavery in Egypt. But time and again they failed to see God at work in their history. So God sent prophets through whom he spoke directly to his people to explain to them what he was doing.

'In the past God spoke to our ancestors many times and in many ways through the prophets, but in these last days he has spoken to us through his Son,' wrote the author of the New Testament letter to the Hebrews. Jesus

Christ himself is the final and complete revelation of God. He is God shown to us in a form we can understand, living as a person on earth.

The Bible itself is 'revelation'. It is the written record of what God did and said in history and through Christ – of his message to his people, from the call of Abraham to the time of the New Testament apostles. Its books were written by people under the guidance of God himself.
Ecclesiastes 5:2; Isaiah 58:8–9; 1 Timothy 6:16; Exodus 3; 6:7; Isaiah 1:3; Amos 3:7; Hebrews 1:1–2; John 1:14; 2 Peter 1:21; 2 Timothy 3:16; John 14:26; 16:13

Saint See *Holiness.*

Salvation God's act of rescue. People are helpless to escape from the situation in which sin has ensnared them. Only God can bring deliverance.

There is a past, present and future tense in the use of 'salvation' in the New Testament. God sent Jesus into the world to 'save his people from their sins'. Sin was dealt with by Jesus in his death and resurrection. By faith in him we can now be 'saved'. This free gift is offered to all, no matter what their religious, racial or social background. 'Everyone who calls out to the Lord for help will be saved.' Christians are already 'saved', because they already have forgiveness and new life. But they will not experience the full meaning of salvation until the end of the age and the return of Jesus Christ. In the meantime they are 'being saved'.

In the Old Testament, salvation is more than just a spiritual deliverance. The major act of salvation was when God freed the Israelites from actual slavery to the Egyptians. The New Testament also teaches that God's salvation affects far more than a person's 'spiritual' life. It concerns the whole person. Nearly a third of the references to salvation in the New Testament are concerned with being set free from specific ills such as imprisonment, disease and demon possession. When a person becomes a

Christian, Christ's salvation affects the whole of life, physical as well as spiritual. But no part of him will be completely whole until he is finally 'saved' at the return of Christ.

See also *Atonement, Freedom, Redemption.*
Matthew 1:21; Ephesians 2:8–9; Romans 10:13; 13:11; 1 Corinthians 1:18; Philippians 2:12; Matthew 9:21–22; Luke 8:36 (where 'saved' is translated 'cured')

Satan Satan is the Hebrew name and Devil the Greek name for the being who personifies all that is evil and opposed to God. Both names mean 'accuser', showing that Satan is the one who tries to tempt people to do wrong so that he can accuse them before God.

The battle between good and evil is not an equally balanced contest. God is all-powerful and eternal; Satan often appears to be in control, but his work is limited by God. He destroys and undermines by tricks and cunning, rather than power. But within the world he holds such power that he can be called its ruler.

Jesus came 'to destroy what the Devil had done', and through his victory over evil in his death and resurrection Satan has been defeated. Although he is still active within the world his defeat.will be total at the end of the age.

We can see clearly how Satan set himself against God's work in the life of Jesus. Jesus was tempted by the Devil in the desert. Peter was used as a tool of Satan and had to be rebuked by Jesus. The betrayal by Judas Iscariot was another part of Satan's work. Jesus had many clashes with evil spirits under Satan's control, but his many exorcisms showed that his power was far greater than that of Satan and the forces of evil.
2 Corinthians 11:14; Ephesians 6:11; John 14:30; 1 John 3:8; John 12:31; 1 Peter 5:8; Revelation 20:10; Matthew 4:1–11; 16:23; Luke 22:3; Matthew 12:22–28

Second coming of Jesus In his first coming to this world Jesus came quietly, lived the life of the humble servant of God and died on the cross. But during

his life he promised that he would return at the end of the world, this time with power and glory for all to see. Many people ignored Jesus when he first came, but when he returns no one will be able to ignore him, and for many it will be a time of grief because it will be the day of judgement. For those who believe, both dead and living, it will be the moment of their final salvation, when Jesus will take them to be with him for ever in a totally re-created world order.

There is no way of finding out when the great day will be. Jesus said that before he comes, the gospel will be preached to all nations. Before he comes, sin will increase and worship will be offered to one who falsely claims to be God. But no one can calculate when he will come, for it will be 'at an hour when you are not expecting him'. The Christian must always be ready, so that he is not caught out and ashamed when Jesus returns.
Matthew 24; 26:64; Mark 13:26; John 14; Acts 1:11; 3:19–21; Philippians 3:20; Colossians 3:4; 1 Thessalonians 1:10; 4:13 – 5:11; 2 Thessalonians 1:5 – 2:12; 2 Peter 3:8–13; Revelation 19–22

Sin The Bible uses many words to describe sin. It is rebellion against God, as the story of Adam and Eve shows. Men and women are therefore enemies of God. Sin is also often described as 'missing the mark' or falling below the standard required by God. A person can be found guilty for *failing* to do what God requires, as much as for deliberately disobeying God's commands. But the essence of all sin is that it is an offence against God. Because of this, men and women are cut off from God and face his anger and judgement. Because of sin, suffering and death came into the world.

The Bible does not concern itself with the thorny problem of where evil comes from. It accepts it as a fact. Satan is its source, but men and women are not allowed to blame Satan for their own downfall, although Adam and Eve tried hard to do so. They are responsible

and held guilty for their own sin. In Jesus Christ God has dealt with the problem of sin, and there will come a day when sin and evil are no more.

See also *Death, Fall, Forgiveness, Hell, Judgement, Suffering.*
Genesis 3; Psalm 51; Isaiah 1:18–20; 59; Romans 1:18 – 2:11; 3:9–26; 5–8; Revelation 20–21

Soul The Bible sees human beings as a unity. It does not speak of an immortal 'soul' locked up in a decaying, sinful body. This was a Greek idea, though it has been held by many Christians through the centuries.

When we read the word 'soul' in the Old Testament it means the whole of a person's being. When the psalmist says, 'Praise the Lord, my soul', he is calling on himself to respond as a whole person to God.

The New Testament uses the word 'soul' in a similar way, meaning 'people'. It is the word used to show that people are more than physical flesh and bone; they have a mind and will and personality. For instance, Jesus said, 'Do not be afraid of those who kill the body but cannot kill the soul; rather be afraid of God, who can destroy both body and soul in hell.'

See also *Body, Flesh.*
Psalm 103:1; Matthew 10:28, and so on

Spiritual gifts When Christ left this earth to go back to his Father, he gave 'gifts' to his followers. These gifts are given by the Holy Spirit to individuals within every local Christian church so that they can continue Christ's work. They show the supernatural nature of the church. As a community of God's people, its work is not limited to its members' natural abilities. The Spirit of God gives those gifts which are needed to build up the church. He gives as he thinks fit.

In Ephesians 4 Paul lists some of the gifts which marked people out as having a special work as leaders of the church – apostles, prophets, evangelists, pastors and teachers. In 1 Corinthians 12 Paul takes other examples, this time emphasizing those which would be found among the members – wisdom, knowledge, faith, healing, miracles, speaking and explaining God's message, speaking in strange tongues and explaining what is said. At the end of the chapter he adds to the list those who have the power to help or direct others. Romans 12 lists some other gifts: service, encouragement, sharing with others and acts of kindness. None of these lists claims to be complete.

Paul believed that in every local church each member should be free to use his God-given gift of ministry. Gifts of the Spirit are not given for private enjoyment but for the good of all, and for this reason Paul deals at some length with the question of speaking in tongues. Paul himself spoke in tongues and was keen for others to have the same gift, but he insisted that there must be someone to interpret. Otherwise no one would understand it, and no one would be helped.
Romans 12; 1 Corinthians 12 and 14, Ephesians 4

Suffering Suffering is seen in the Bible as a *misfortune*. It entered the world because of sin; it is a result of the continuing activity of Satan. Jesus came into the world to free men and women from suffering and death. In his life on earth he showed his love and care by healing many people. And in the new heaven and earth there will be no suffering.

Suffering is also a *problem* in the Bible. As God has total control, suffering must ultimately come from him. Yet how can a God of love allow the innocent to suffer? It is easy to see that sin brings suffering, and not just to the individual but to his whole family. And it is possible to accept that God allows suffering in order to discipline his children. But the Book of Job is an honest attempt to discuss the problem of the suffering of innocent people. Job discards all the theories that are offered him, and in the end accepts his suffering. He does not find a rational explanation, but he sees in God a certainty which can overcome all his doubts

and fears.

In the life and work of Jesus we are shown suffering as a way of life. He lives out the life of the suffering servant outlined in Isaiah 53. He is innocent. He is not suffering for his own sin, but he is suffering because of the hatred of sinful people, and in order to save them from their sin. The Bible does not give us a rational answer to the problem of suffering, but it does give us a practical answer. God took responsibility for it in the death of his Son.
Genesis 3:15 – 19; 2 Corinthians 12:7; Romans 8:21; Revelation 21:4; Amos 3:6; Psalm 39:11; Hebrews 12:3 – 11; Job; Isaiah 53

Temptation God allows his people to be tempted, or tested. Such testing reveals the worth of their love for him. And every test that is overcome strengthens and leads them forward.

The word 'temptation' is more commonly used to refer to the activity of Satan in trying to lead men into sin, as in the temptation of Jesus. The other classic example of temptation is in the story of Adam and Eve. The

serpent gradually leads the woman into doubt and confusion about the will of God; she then sees the fruit, recognizes what it is worth, desires it, realizes what it could do for her, and finally takes it.

Christians are told to be on their guard against temptation. They also have God's promise that he will not allow the testing to become too great to bear. He will provide the power to endure it.

See also *Satan, Sin.*
Genesis 3; Exodus 20:20; Deuteronomy 8:1 – 6; Matthew 4; 6:13; 1 Corinthians 10:12 – 13; Ephesians 6:10 – 18; Hebrews 2:18; James 1:12 – 16; 1 Peter 1:6 – 9; 4:12 – 16

Transfiguration The transfiguration of Jesus came at a turning point in his life. Peter had just recognized Jesus as the Messiah, and Jesus went on to teach his disciples about his coming death and resurrection. Then he went up a mountain (traditionally thought to be Mt Hermon) with Peter, James and John. There they saw Jesus transformed by a heavenly glory, and Elijah and Moses talking with him. The experience ended with

a voice from heaven, similar to that at the time of Jesus' baptism, which said, 'This is my Son, whom I have chosen – listen to him.'

Moses and Elijah represented the two major parts of the Old Testament, the Law and the Prophets. By their presence they showed that all was fulfilled in Jesus. Peter wanted tents to be put up, to make the experience last. But that was not the point. The transfiguration confirmed the rightness of the way Jesus had chosen. It pointed to the glory that would one day be his. But before that time he had to die on the cross. This was the topic of conversation with Moses and Elijah – Jesus' 'exodus'. But the disciples did not understand this until after the resurrection.
Matthew 17:1 – 8; Mark 9:2 – 8; Luke 8:28 – 36

Today Christians around the world find God's word to them in the scriptures. Here is God's revelation of himself on record; here too is almost all we know about Jesus, God's word in person.

Trinity This word is not used in the Bible. It is the name given to the statements about God in the creeds drawn up in the early centuries of the church to explain what is meant by saying that God is Father, Son and Holy Spirit. This is the teaching of Jesus and the New Testament as a whole. From earliest times it was stated at every Christian baptism.

The Jewish teaching was that there is only one God. Nothing and no one must compromise that belief. Yet the New Testament writers clearly show God as the Father who created and sustained everything in his love and power, as the Son who came into this world, and as the Spirit who worked in their own lives.

After the end of the New Testament period the church found it necessary to work out carefully worded statements about three persons in one God, in order to uphold the truth of the New Testament against false beliefs.

See also *God, Holy Spirit, Jesus Christ.* Matthew 28:19; John 5:19–29; 8:23–29, 58; 14–17; Acts 2:32–33; 2 Corinthians 13:14 and so on; Exodus 20:2–6; Deuteronomy 6:4; Isaiah 45:5

Word The 'word of God' is a phrase the Bible often uses when it speaks of God revealing himself to men. Just as we can only know one another well through speech, so God made himself known by his words as well as his acts.

The 'word of the Lord' is God's spoken word. The phrase often occurs in the books of the prophets. This word was not always heard; sometimes it was seen. Jesus, the final and full revelation of God, is also described as the Word. This time God's word could be seen, touched and heard. It is this word or message that the Christian church must make known.

The word of God – his whole 'revelation' of himself – 'endures for ever'. It is powerful and does all that God plans for it to do. And no one is to add anything to it or take anything away from it.

See also *Revelation.*

Jeremiah 1:4; Ezekiel 1:3–28; John 1:1–14; 1 John 1:1–3; 2 Timothy 4:2; Isaiah 40:8; Revelation 22:18–19

World The Greek word *kosmos*, 'world', normally means 'the physical created world'. It is used in this way in the New Testament to describe the world God made.

It is also used to speak of the 'state of the world'. 'The world' is in rebellion against God. So Satan can be called the prince or ruler of 'this world', and the whole world is said to lie in his power. 'World' (represented sometimes by another Greek word, *aion*, meaning 'age' or 'spirit of the age') describes all that is in opposition to God.

The 'world' hated Christ and shows similar hatred to his followers. And yet God loved the world. Christians do not belong to the world but they live in it. They must not share the world's attitudes or conform to its self-centred materialist standards. But they must live with those who are in rebellion, because God loves them and Jesus died for them. John 1:10; 14:30; 1 John 5:19; John 15:18–19; John 17:16–17; Romans 12:2; John 3:16–21

Worship 'I am the Lord your God,' says the first Commandment, 'Worship no god but me.' To worship is to give God the honour due to him. In the psalms God's people worship him for who he is; for what he has done in creation; for what he has done in redemption, rescuing and freeing his people; and for all his good gifts and blessings to individuals.

In the New Testament when Christians met together, they expressed their gladness by 'praising God'. Filled with the Spirit they were to speak to 'one another with the words of psalms, hymns, and sacred songs,' to 'sing hymns and psalms to the Lord' with praise in their hearts. Everyone could take part. 'When you meet for worship one person has a hymn, another a teaching, another a revelation from God, another a message in strange tongues, and still another the explanation of what is said.'

'God is Spirit, and only by the power of his Spirit can people worship him as he really is,' said Jesus. Worship must be real. It must come from the heart. In the Old Testament God spoke sternly against the kind of worship which is only an outward show. True worship is a genuine response to God which shows itself in a life lived to please him. Worship centres on God. His message fills it with content and meaning. As Paul wrote: 'Christ's message in all its richness must live in your hearts. Teach and instruct each other with all wisdom. Sing psalms, hymns, and sacred songs; sing to God with thanksgiving in your hearts.'

Worship is not simply a human activity on earth. In heaven, God's whole creation – humans and angels – praise and worship him.

See also *Praise, Prayer;* and Part 5: *Religion and Worship in the Bible.* Exodus 20:1–3; Psalms 29; 136:4–9, 10–36; 116; Acts 2:43–47; Ephesians 5:18–19; 1 Corinthians 14:26–40; John 4:21–24; Micah 6:6–8; Colossians 3:16; Revelation 4; 5; 7; 15

The Bedouin tent and the town of Bethlehem in the background illustrate the early nomadic life and the later settled lifestyle of Bible times.

7

Home and Family Life in the Bible

It is hard enough to imagine life fifty years ago. How much more difficult, then, to get a true picture of home and family life in Bible times.

For one thing, the land of the Bible is a Mediterranean country, and that, for many of us, means a different climate from our own. In the land of Israel, summer is hot and dry. On days when the desert wind (the sirocco) blows in from Arabia the heat is intense. Winter is wet. The early rains break up the sun-baked ground in October/November. The later rains bring on the crops in March/April.

Modern Israel is a small country, as ancient Israel was, only 150 miles from north to south, and 50 miles from east to west. But it has within it broad and fertile plains, a 9,000ft/2,750m mountain, scorching desert and a tropical valley 1,275ft/390m below sea level. So there is a very varied climate within the same country, and this affects the lives of ordinary people. It can be snowing in Jerusalem in winter, while at the same time, in Jericho, less than twenty miles away, it can be too hot for comfort. The rich used to move down to Jericho for the winter, leaving their poorer neighbours behind in Jerusalem. In this way, money and social class have their effects on family life.

Then, from Abraham (about 1900 BC) to the writing of the last book of the New Testament (about AD 100), the Bible covers about 2,000 years of history. In this time there were many changes. Abraham lived a 'semi-nomadic' life. His descendants settled in Israel (Canaan), built villages and learned the skills of the Canaanite peoples.

The decision to have a king meant other big changes. Instead of village elders there was central control from Jerusalem. Prosperity came, but so did forced labour, taxes, division between rich and poor. Revolution split the country in two. Invasions from Syria, Egypt, Assyria and Babylonia, a 70-year exile, and later the control of the country first by Persia, then by Greece and Rome, brought new customs and outlooks.

All these changes left their mark on home and family life, making it difficult for us to talk about 'life in Bible times' rather than life in a particular Bible time.

Understanding the world of the Bible

Nearly nineteen hundred years have passed since the last Bible book was written. We depend a great deal on the Bible itself for information about how people lived all those centuries ago. But the Bible was not written to tell us these things. It was written to declare God's message: to explain his rescue plan for a lost and unhappy world.

Archaeologists have helped fill the gaps. They have discovered written documents as well as the remains of buildings and the objects people used at home. But often the names of those objects have changed – for example, the words for different musical instruments, precious stones and plants. Sometimes the best we can do is make a good guess at the meaning of a particular word.

Despite the difficulties, it is very important to understand the background of the Bible. God spoke through a number of different people at particular times in history, and through the lives of ordinary people. Jesus himself was born, not into a palace, but into the simple home of an ordinary couple. The closer we get to the people of the Bible and their lives, the better we understand what the Bible has to say.

Threshing the harvest in a village in Israel.

Life Within the Family

The 'family' of Abraham's time was what those of us who live in small family units would call the 'extended family'. It consisted not just of parents and children, but grandparents, aunts, uncles and cousins – and servants, too. It could be very large. Abraham was able to take 318 fighting men with him when he went to rescue Lot from the raiding kings who had taken him prisoner (Genesis 14:14).

In this kind of family group the grandfather had complete authority, not just in practical matters but in religious ones, too. When he died, his eldest son took over by right of birth. The leader's word was law. Abraham's family clan accepted the fact that God had made himself known to Abraham in the silence of the desert. His God was their God, even though they did not always share the kind of faith he had.

God had made a promise to Abraham. He made the same promise again to Abraham's son Isaac and to his grandson Jacob. He would be their God, caring for them and protecting them. In return they must live by his rules. Those rules were spelt out in detail to a later generation, when God gave the 'commandments' to Moses at Mt Sinai. So, from the very beginning, ordinary life in Israel was bound up with religious life. The two were one and could not be separated. Everything the family did was based on God's law. If they treated one another badly, they broke God's law. Things had to be put right between them, and a sacrifice was needed to put them right with God (Leviticus 6:1–6).

Women gather to get water at the spring in Jericho.

Parents and children

Religion and family life were woven together in the way parents brought up their children. Children were encouraged to ask questions and find out about their religion and history (Exodus 13:14). Places where God had done something special for his people were marked with large stones. When the children asked what they were for, the parents would explain (Joshua 4:5–7).

The regular weekly rest-day (the sabbath) was intended also to be a day when God could be remembered and worshipped (Exodus 31:15–17). In early Old Testament times parents and children would visit the local shrine. There they would offer a sacrifice and the priest would teach them. In New Testament times the sabbath day began on the Friday evening with the best meal of the week. Then came a visit to the meeting-house ('synagogue') to hear the scriptures explained by the teacher.

Parents taught their children the laws of God. They also learned by heart other parts of the Bible. David's great poem on the death of Saul and Jonathan was a favourite. In the evenings, members of the family recited many of the stories now written down in the Bible.

☐ **Festivals**
The meaning of the great religious festivals was clearly shown by special ceremonies. At Passover, for example, the eldest child was asked by the father, 'Why do we have this service?' And the child explained how it had come about, as he had been taught.

There was the Day of Atonement, followed by the Festival of Tabernacles at the time of the grape harvest, when everyone lived in tents made of branches to remind them of the way their ancestors lived in the desert. Later in Israel's history the children acted the story of Esther at the Festival of Purim. All the festivals were so full of life and action that children wanted to know what they were about. In this way they learned the history of their nation as the people of God. (See also Part 5: *Religion and Worship in the Bible*.)

☐ **Teaching**
There were no schools as such in Old Testament times. The children were taught at home, first by their mother, then by

their father. In addition to religion and history, which was learned through stories and by question and answer, and memorized, the girls learnt home-making skills – baking, spinning, weaving – from their mother, while the boys learned a manual trade from their father.

The Jews had a saying: 'He who does not teach his son a useful trade, is bringing him up to be a thief.' The father's work, tools and (in later Old Testament times) fellow members of his trade guild, were all important for a boy's education. (See Part 8: *Work and Society in the Bible*.)

Land and animals

Everyone owned some land so both boys and girls had outdoor work to do. There was always plenty to do in looking after the vines, ploughing and threshing.

The children also looked after any animals the family kept – usually sheep and goats. Every family, even the poorest, hoped to be able to buy two lambs at Passover time. One was killed and eaten, but the other became a playmate for the children, giving its wool for their clothing. In a poor home there was no separate shed for the animals, and the lamb often slept with the children and fed from the same dishes (2 Samuel 12:3). At the end of summer it was killed and the meat was preserved in the fat from the sheep's tail. Most families would also have at least one goat which was kept for milk. Some of the milk was allowed to go sour to produce goats'-milk cheese.

Although some households had dogs they were not common and were regarded as scavengers.

The donkey (ass) was the most common form of transport. It could carry heavy loads as well as people. Richer farmers used oxen for farm work and camels for transport.

Nomads and settlers

In the early days of the Old Testament – before the years in Egypt – the people lived in tents. Abraham left a settled, civilized city life in Ur on the far-off River Euphrates to obey God's call. For the rest of his life he was, at least from time to time, on the move. His son Isaac and grandson Jacob also lived in tents – like the Bedouin today.

Water was scarce, particularly in the summer or during a time of drought, and the people who lived in Canaan defended their wells against these wanderers, who took water not only for themselves, but for their animals as well. The dispute between Abraham and Abimelech over the well at Beersheba is one example (Genesis 21:25–31).

Although they had no permanent home, Abraham and his family were settled enough to grow crops. And they never moved far from the big centres of population. After the time of Moses the people of Israel wanted to settle more permanently, and then for some years there was war. When the Israelites had won their land, other groups of nomads wanted to settle there too. So the Israelites in their turn had to learn to deal kindly with these landless strangers, who soon came to form the working class of the population.

The pattern of each day did not vary much. The basic pattern of family life changed little over many centuries. It was interrupted now and then by invading armies, but was otherwise peaceful. The people lived close to the land. Each family looked after its own small farm. There were always some animals to care for. Then there was the daily cleaning, baking, spinning, weaving and dyeing, as well as the work of the farm itself.

Family relationships

Family life grew more important during the course of Israel's history. When the clans began to settle in permanent homes the normal family unit became smaller.

☐ The father
Within this smaller unit, as

In Eastern countries today it is still often the children's job to watch over the sheep.

before, the father had complete authority. He could, if he wished, even sell his daughter into slavery. In early Old Testament days it was possible for a father to have disobedient children put to death. He could divorce his wife without any reason and without providing for her. And he could arrange the marriages of his sons.

☐ Women
The woman was *owned* by her husband, and looked up to him as her master. This attitude was still found even in New Testament times. Though women did much of the hard work, they had a low position both in society and in the family. But the law did protect a divorced woman, and her children were taught to respect her.

Jesus' dealings with women – for example, his readiness to speak to and help the Samaritan woman (see John 4) – contrast strongly with prevailing attitudes. And Christian teaching is clear: "There is no difference . . . between men and women; you are all one in union with Christ Jesus' (Galatians 3:28). There are no second-class citizens in Christ's kingdom.

Some Bible passages on family relationships: Exodus 20:12; 21:7–11; Deuteronomy 21:15–21; 24:1–4 (compare with Matthew 19:8–12)
The teaching in Proverbs on parents and children: 1:8–9; 4 and 5; 6:20ff.; 10:1; 13:1, 24; 17:21, 25; 19:13, 18, 27; 20:11; 22:6, 15; 23:13–16, 19–28; 28:7, 24; 29:15, 17; 30:11, 17
In the New Testament see especially: Ephesians 5:21–33; 6:1–4; Colossians 3:18–21

☐ Inheritance
Normally only sons could inherit – and the eldest son in a family had a special position. He had the right to a double share of his father's property. Only if there were no sons could daughters inherit. If there were no children at all, the property passed to the closest male relative.

☐ Respect and discipline
The book of Proverbs speaks of family relationships more freely and directly than any other Bible book. For their own good, children were expected to respect their parents and pay attention to their teaching and advice. Parents who really love their children will discipline and correct them, especially when they are young.

'A good spanking will teach them how to behave.' 'If a child has his own way, he will make his mother ashamed of him.'

The happiness of parents and children are bound up with one another. And reverence for God is the starting-point.

The New Testament builds on the same foundation. It is the Christian duty of children to obey their parents, and of parents to bring up their children with Christian discipline and teaching – but fathers are not to provoke their children.

Time
Time was not rushed in the Jewish home. Before the Greeks and Romans used candle clocks and water clocks, the usual way of measuring time in small units was by the movement of a shadow (although the Egyptians were using hour glasses much earlier than this). Three different systems seem to have been used in Bible times.

Early in the Old Testament period, when Canaan was under Egypt's influence, the day started at sunrise. There was a twelve-month calendar of thirty days with five extra days at the end of the year. The days of the month were marked by putting a peg into a bone plate which had three rows of ten holes.

Later, perhaps under Babylonian influence, the calendar seems to have changed. The day began at moonrise (1800 hrs) and a whole day became 'an evening and a morning'. The evening was divided into three four-hour watches.

The Romans changed this into four three-hour watches. A new month also began with the moon. The first sign of the new moon was signalled by lighting bonfires on the hills. Months were then only 28/29 days long, so there had to be an extra month at the end of some years to keep the calendar right with the sun. The priests decided when to add this month.

Special Occasions

All over the world, every family has its 'great days', some happy, some sad. They are not the same for all of us, and have changed with the years. Retirement, for example, was not known in Bible times. But we all still share the three most important occasions in the life of a Bible family: the birth of a baby, a wedding, and death.

A new baby

'Children are a gift from the Lord;
they are a real blessing.
The sons of a man when he is young
are like arrows in a soldier's hand.
Happy is the man who has many such arrows.'
These words from Psalm 127 show how the people of Israel felt about children. A big family was a sign of God's blessing. If no children came, people thought God must be displeased – and this could be very hard on a couple who had no children (see for example the story of Hannah in 1 Samuel).

Children were important for a number of reasons. Boys were the most valued. It was so important to have a son that the woman's name was changed to 'Mother of . . .' when her first son was born.

As they grew up boys were able to help work the family's land. Girls were much less important, but still useful workers. A wedding-gift had to be paid to the parents to make up for the loss of the daughter's work when she left to be married.

Sons were also needed to carry on the family name. In the earliest times, before people were sure that there was a life after death, they liked to think they would live on through their children, so without children there was no future. This was why, if a man died without a child, it was the duty of his closest relative to marry the wife. Their first son would then take the dead man's name and inherit his land (the 'Levirate law' – Deuteronomy 25:5–6).

☐ Customs
The new-born baby was washed and rubbed over with salt (it was thought this made the skin firm). Then it was wrapped in 'swaddling cloths'. The mother or her helper placed the baby on a square of cloth. Then she folded the corners over its sides and feet, and wrapped bandages (often embroidered) round the whole bundle to keep the baby's arms straight by its sides. The bandages were loosened several times a day and the skin was rubbed with olive oil and dusted with powdered myrtle leaves. This went on for several months. The wrappings made it easy for the mother to carry her baby in a woollen 'cradle' on her back. At night the cradle was hung from a beam in the house, or between two forked sticks.

Babies were normally breast-fed for two or three years. But there was a very high death-rate amongst babies because of the poor conditions in most houses.

In Old Testament times the baby was named when it was born. The name always had a meaning. It might say something about how the baby was born, his or her character, or the family's feelings towards God. For example, Jacob's wife, Rachel, who had waited so long for her first son, called him Joseph – 'may God add sons'. The name Barak means 'lightning'; Elijah means 'the Lord is God'; Isaiah means 'God is salvation'.

☐ Ceremonies
In New Testament times a baby boy was not named until the eighth day after birth. At the same time he was 'circumcised' (the loose skin was cut off the top of his penis).

In many other nations boys were circumcised when they

A baby is made comfortable in this improvised hammock.

were recognized as adult members of the clan. But as far back as the days of Abraham God had made circumcision on the eighth day after birth the physical sign of the promise he had made to Abraham and his descendants for all time.

This ceremony reminded them that every child in Israel was one of God's own people. Sadly, the real meaning of the ceremony was often forgotten, and by the time of the exile to Babylon it was looked on simply as a sign of being a Jew.

Two other ceremonies sometimes took place at the same time. If the baby boy was the 'firstborn' in the family he belonged to God in a special way and had to be bought back (redeemed). This was because at the time of the exodus, when all the firstborn children of the Egyptians had died, God saved the firstborn sons of Israel. From then on the firstborn belonged to him.

'You must buy back every firstborn male child of yours.' 'This observance will be a reminder . . . it will remind us that the Lord brought us out of Egypt by his great power' (Exodus 13:13ff.).

The first generation after the exodus were redeemed by dedicating the Levites for God's service. After that each family paid five pieces of silver to the priest to buy back their firstborn.

The other ceremony was a sacrifice made by the mother for her 'purification' (see Leviticus 12). According to the law of Moses a person had to be ritually 'clean' to worship God. Certain things – contact with a dead body, for example, or having a baby, or eating forbidden foods which might carry disease – barred people for a time from joining in worship.

To be 'clean' again the mother had to sacrifice first a pigeon and then a lamb. If, like Jesus' parents, Joseph and Mary, they were too poor to afford a lamb, they could offer a second pigeon instead. In

New Testament times money was put into the offering boxes of the temple to pay for the sacrifices, and the women gathered on the steps near the altar for the ceremony.

In New Testament times, too, a boy became a man on his thirteenth birthday. This was marked by a special service called the Bar Mitzvah ('son of the law'). In the months before his birthday he learned to read the passages from the Old Testament Law and Prophets that were to be read in the synagogue that day. He had to recite them at the service. The minister ('rabbi') then spoke to the boy and asked God's blessing on him in the beautiful words of Numbers 6:24–26:

'May the Lord bless you and take care of you;
May the Lord be kind and gracious to you;
May the Lord look on you with favour and give you peace.'

The boy was now a grown-up member of the community. Sometimes his parents took him to watch a service like this the year before his own thirteenth birthday.

Weddings and marriage

The story of creation in Genesis 1 and 2 shows the pattern of marriage – one man to one woman for life – as

A Jewish boy at his 'Bar Mitzvah' service.

God's original design. But it was not long before a code of rules was needed because standards had fallen.

□ Rules and customs

The law-code of King Hammurabi of Babylon (about 1700 BC) implies that:

A man would not take a second wife unless the first was unable to have children. The husband was allowed a secondary wife (a concubine), or his wife might give him a slave-girl, to have children by her. The children of the slave-girl might not be sent away.

It is clear from the story of Abraham that he, too, observed these customs. That is why he was so worried when Sarah insisted on sending away the slave-girl Hagar and her son (Genesis 16:1–6; 21:10–12).

The customs of Jacob's and Esau's time were less strict and allowed more than one wife. This practice grew until, by the time of the Judges and the Kings, a man could have as many wives as he could afford. But having several wives could lead to all kinds of problems. It must have been all too easy to have favourites. Deuteronomy 21:15 seems to recognize

Head of Hammurabi, king of Babylon and 'author' of a famous law-code dating from about 1700 BC.

this problem when it says that man must not take away the inheritance of his firstborn son to give to the child of his favourite wife.

No doubt at first it made good economic sense to have more than one wife: more children meant more workers. But the time came when it cost more to keep several wives than the family gained by having more children.

By New Testament times the usual practice was once again to have only one wife (although at one time King Herod the Great had nine). In this respect the people had returned to the standard set out by Moses and the prophets.

It was very unusual for a man not to marry – there is no Hebrew word for 'bachelor' and people in Israel married very young. The legal ages for marriage were thirteen and over for a boy, and twelve and over for a girl. It was probably because they were so young that marriages were arranged by parents, normally within the same clan in Old Testament times, and ideally with a first cousin.

Marriage to someone from another nation worshipping other gods was forbidden. The law also forbade marriage between close relatives (Leviticus 18:6ff.).

Arranged marriages did not always mean that the young people had no say. Shechem (Genesis 34:4) and Samson (Judges 14:2) both asked their parents to arrange a marriage with a particular girl. It was also possible to marry a slave or a war captive.

Because of the general system of arranged marriages, marriage often came first and love afterwards, in the typically Eastern way. In the East love is understood much more as part of the will, in contrast to the frequent Western emphasis on the emotions. We can therefore be *commanded* to love God, and Western notions of 'falling in love with Christ' are far removed from biblical concepts.

Marriage was a civil rather than a religious affair. At betrothal (engagement) a contract was made in front of two witnesses. Sometimes the couple gave one another a ring or bracelet. The betrothal was as binding as marriage. During the waiting time before the wedding, while the girl was still living at her father's house, the man was excused from going to war (Deuteronomy 20:7).

A sum of money, a bride-price (called the *mohar*), had to be paid to the girl's father. It could sometimes be paid partly in work by the man. The father seems to have been able to use any interest the *mohar* could earn, but he was not allowed to touch the *mohar* itself. It was returned to the daughter on the death of her parents, or if her husband died. Jacob's father-in-law, Laban, seems to have broken with custom and spent his daughter's bride-price (Genesis 31:15).

The girl's father, in return, gave her, or her husband, a 'dowry' (wedding gift). This could be servants (as in the case of Rebekah and Leah), or land or property.

A Yemenite Jewish bride, dressed in traditional finery.

☐ The wedding

This took place when the bridegroom had the new home ready. With his friends, he went to his bride's house in the evening. She was waiting, veiled and in her wedding dress. She wore jewellery which the bridegroom had given her. Sometimes he gave her a headband of coins. (It may have been one of these coins which was lost in the 'lost coin' story told by Jesus – Luke 15:8.) In a simple ceremony, the veil was taken from the bride's face and laid on the bridegroom's shoulder.

The bridegroom, his 'best man' (called a 'companion') and his friends (called the sons of the bridechamber) then took the bride back to his own or his parents' home for a wedding feast to which all their friends were invited. The friends waited at the roadside in their best clothes and went in torchlight procession to the new home, sometimes with music and dancing.

The law of Moses allowed for a man to divorce his wife. But he had to write out divorce papers which gave the woman her freedom before he sent her away. In New Testament times the Jewish teachers often argued about the reasons for divorce. (The Pharisees raised the question with Jesus – see Matthew 19.) Some allowed divorce for anything which displeased the husband – even poor cooking! Others believed there must be a serious moral lapse, such as adultery. But, typically, there was a different standard for women. A wife could never divorce her husband, though under certain circumstances she could force him to divorce her.

A group of professional mourners from Egypt. They are crossing the River Nile with a mummy on its way to burial, in this tomb-painting from Thebes (fifteenth or fourteenth century BC).

Some further Bible passages on marriage, wives and husbands:
Genesis 1:26 – 31; 2:7, 18 – 25; Deuteronomy 24:1 – 4 and Matthew 19:3 – 12; Proverbs 5:15 – 20; 12:4; 18:22; 19:13 – 14; 21:9, 19; 25:24; 31:10 – 31; 1 Corinthians 7; Ephesians 5:22 – 33; 1 Peter 3:1 – 7
Passages reflecting wedding customs: Genesis 24; 29; Judges 14; Matthew 22:2 – 14, 25:1 – 12; Luke 14:7 – 14; John 3:1 – 10; Revelation 21:2

Death

When Paul was facing possible death, he was able to write in his letter to the Philippian Christians: 'What is life? To me, it is Christ. Death then will bring more. I want very much to leave this life and be with Christ.' He knew that for a Christian there is a wonderful life beyond death, made possible by the death and resurrection of Jesus. But the Jewish people had not always believed in life after death.

☐ **Beliefs**
In the early days of the Old Testament, the Israelites believed that when a man died, he went down into a shadowy place under the earth called *sheol*. It was not until much later that people began to ask how a just God could let good people die like this. So they reasoned that *sheol* could not be the end. Surely there would be a resurrection, and a person's final destiny would depend on how he had lived in this life.

The prophet Daniel writes: 'Many of those who have already died will live again: some will enjoy eternal life, and some will suffer eternal disgrace' (Daniel 12:2).

In New Testament times, the Pharisees believed in a resurrection but the Sadducees did not. It was Jesus' victory over death and his promise of resurrection life which finally took away the awful fear of death.

For further Bible passages about death, see Part 6: *Key Teaching of the Bible*, under *Death*.
Passages reflecting customs connected with death: Genesis 23; 48:1 – 12; 49:29 – 50; 14; Deuteronomy 34:5 – 8; 14:1 – 2; 2 Samuel 1:11 – 12; 3:31 – 35; Jeremiah 9:17 – 18; 16:5 – 7; Matthew 9:23; Mark 15:42 – 16:1; Luke 7:11 – 15; John 11:17 – 44

☐ Funeral customs

All through the Old Testament, therefore, death is shown as a tragedy. The funeral arrangements were much the same as they are today. When someone died, his eyes were closed. The body was washed and wrapped in strips of cloth. A quick burial was necessary because of the hot climate. The body was not put in a coffin, but carried on a wooden stretcher (a bier) to the burial-place. Family and friends made a great show of mourning: weeping, wailing, wearing uncomfortable clothes, walking barefoot, putting ashes on their heads, tearing their clothes and shaving off their beards. Sometimes professional mourners were hired to add to the wailing. Mourning normally lasted for seven days, but longer for an important person (seventy days for Joseph; thirty days for Moses). A time of fasting went with the time of mourning. But there was a funeral feast which often took place at the tomb. In countries outside Israel – particularly Egypt – the body was embalmed. The insides and brain were removed and the space filled with a gummy paste.

☐ Burial

The people of Israel often buried their dead in caves. Some caves were large enough for all the members of a family (Genesis 50:13), but if necessary, they could be enlarged to form corridors with shelves cut

A decorated limestone ossuary, in which the bones of the dead were kept. It dates from about the time of Jesus, and was found in the Jerusalem area.

out of the rock on which the bodies could be placed.

Rich people were able to have tombs specially constructed with a stairway leading down through the solid rock to the burial chamber. A slab of stone was put at the entrance with a boulder against it. In New Testament times a large circular stone was sometimes set in a groove and rolled across to cover the opening. But of course the number of caves, even man-made ones, was limited. So the bones were often removed and stored in chests of wood or stone called 'ossuaries'.

The poor were buried in shallow graves in open ground. A row of stones was placed round the body and the spaces in between were filled up with small stones and earth. A slab of stone was then put on the top. All graves were painted white to draw people's attention to them. For they must not be touched: any contact with the dead made a person ritually 'unclean'.

Clothes and Fashion

The Bible covers about 2,000 years of history. But because of the hot climate and the limited number of materials available, dress remained fairly standard in Israel for most of that time.

Dress

The main differences in dress were between the rich and poor. The poor peasant had only the woollen or goats'-hair clothes he stood up in. But rich people had clothes for winter and for summer; clothes for working and clothes for leisure; clothes of different materials – fine linen, or even silk. Some of them spent so much time and money on clothes that they needed Jesus' words to remind them of the really important things in life.

'Why worry about clothes?' he said. 'Look how the wild flowers grow . . . It is God who clothes the wild grass . . . Won't he be all the more sure to clothe you?' (Matthew 6:28 – 30)

Because the names have changed, we do not know which clothes some Hebrew words mean. We have to make careful guesses.

☐ Getting dressed

The first thing a man put on was either a loincloth or a short skirt from waist to knee. This was all he wore when he was doing heavy work.

Over the top of this came a shirt or tunic made of wool or linen. This was like a big sack: a long piece of material folded at the centre and sewn up the sides, with holes for the arms and a slit at the folded end for the head to go through. The shirt was calf-length for a man and coloured, usually red, yellow, black or striped. A woman's tunic came down to her ankles and was often blue. Often it was embroidered on the yoke with a special pattern. Each village had its own traditional pattern of embroidery. Apart from these features a woman's tunic would be very similar to a man's.

The tunic was fastened round the waist with a girdle or belt. This was a piece of cloth, folded into a long strip to make a kind of pocket to hold coins and other belongings. If a man was rich he might have a leather belt with a dagger or an inkhorn pushed into it.

When a man needed to be able to move more freely, to work, he would tuck his tunic into his belt to make it much shorter. This was called 'girding up the loins'. It meant getting ready for action. A woman could lift up the hem of her long dress and use it as a large bag, even for carrying things like corn.

Out of doors, a rich man would wear a light coat over his tunic. This came down to his knees and was often gaily striped or woven in check patterns. Rich people wore lightweight coats indoors as well, perhaps made from imported silk. In Joseph's time, a long-sleeved coat of many pieces was worn by the future leader of the clan (see the story of Joseph, Genesis 37:3).

There was also a thick woollen coat or cloak to keep out the cold, called a *himation* in New Testament times. This was made from two pieces of

Abraham and his family may have dressed like these Semitic people shown in a wall-painting at Beni-Hasan, Egypt, about 1890 BC.

material, often in stripes of light and dark brown, stitched together. The joined material was wrapped round the body, sewn at the shoulders, and slits were then made in the side for the arms to go through.

The shepherd lived in his. It was his blanket when he slept in the open at night. It was also thick enough to make a comfortable seat. A poor man's cloak was so important to him that if it was handed over to guarantee repayment of a debt, it had to be returned to him at sunset.

□ Headgear

In Israel the sun was so hot that some covering was needed to protect the head, neck and eyes. This was usually a square of cloth folded diagonally, with the fold across the forehead. A circle of plaited wool held it in place over the head, and the folds protected the neck. A cap was sometimes worn, and a fine wool shawl or *tallith* over it, especially during prayer. Women put pads on their heads to steady the jars of water and other things they carried.

□ Footwear

Although many poor people probably went barefoot, sandals were the normal footwear. The simplest design was a piece of hide the same size as the foot, with a long leather strap which passed between the big and second toe, and was then tied round the ankle. Sandals were cool to wear, but people's feet got very dusty. Sandals were always taken off before going into someone else's home. It was the lowliest servant's job to take off the visitor's sandals and wash his feet. Sandals also were removed before entering a holy place.

According to custom the right sandal was always put on and taken off before the left. A man selling property took off his sandal and gave it to the buyer as a token that he gave up his right to the property (as Boaz' relative did in the story of Ruth – Ruth 4:7).

Footwear in Bible times

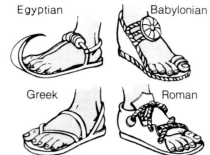

It is interesting that despite the strict rules against all work on the sabbath the Jewish law book allowed for a man to take certain clothes from a burning house on the sabbath day. The list includes underclothes, scarves, stockings and breeches.

Most people had few clothes, and they had to make them last. They were carefully washed with soap made from olive oil, and rinsed in fast-flowing water so that the current could run through the material and loosen the dirt. If someone tore his clothes as a sign of mourning, it was out of real grief!

There were no nightclothes.

At night people simply lay down and loosened their day clothes.

These basic clothes were influenced to some extent by styles from other countries. But fashions did not change much. A painting of Asiatic nomads who visited Egypt can be seen on the wall of a tomb at Beni-Hasan (about 1890 BC). They have cloaks of coloured wool which reach below the knee, with a loose end thrown over the shoulder. This was probably the type of clothing worn by Abraham.

See also Part 9: *Work and Society in the Bible.* under *Clothes-making.*

Different materials

Animal skins were sometimes made into shirts or cloaks. But they were normally worn only by the poorest people. Coarse, rough clothing was also worn by the prophets. It was their distinctive 'uniform'. When the

Israelites and Syrians shown on the Assyrian King Shalmaneser's 'Black Obelisk'. They are wearing pointed caps and shoes, and fringed cloaks.

injured king of Israel heard his men describe a man 'wearing a cloak made of animal skins, tied with a leather belt', he knew at once that it was the prophet Elijah (2 Kings 1). John the Baptist also adopted this style of dress (Mark 1:6).

One of the great arts of Israel was weaving. It was as important as painting and sculpture in other societies.

Clothes have been made from wool from very early times. The wool was often dyed. Some sheep were kept indoors from birth to produce really white wool. Good wool clothes were handed down in the family. (Achan was so tempted by a beautiful Babylonian cloak which he saw in Jericho that he disobeyed God's order to destroy it – Joshua 7:21.)

Camel hair gave a warm but generally coarse cloth. But it could be worked up into a lightweight coat. Goats' hair was brown or black and was used for tent-cloth and cloaks for the poor. Mixed with camel

Egyptian ladies in dresses of fine pleated linen and wearing jewellery. On their heads are cones of sweet-smelling ointment.

hair it produced 'sackcloth' which was coarse and uncomfortable to wear.

Linen was produced from the outer sheath of the flax plant. In Egypt, where a great deal of flax was grown, everyone wore linen clothes, and they made linen so fine it was almost transparent.

Hair
The Israelites in the Old Testament normally grew their hair long. (See for example the stories of Samson and Absalom.) The Asiatic nomads shown as visitors to Egypt on the Beni-Hasan painting have long hair which came over their foreheads and hung down their backs. They also have beards which are neatly trimmed.

Many years later, Assyrian inscriptions show the Israelites wearing beards. (To shave off the beard was a sign of mourning.) But by New Testament times, under the influence of the Greeks and Romans, hair was worn short and many men were clean shaven.

Grey hair was to be respected, as a sign of old age. 'One who had been living for ever' – presumably God himself – is pictured with white hair in Daniel 7:9.

Men sometimes plaited their

An Assyrian hunter. From a relief in the palace of King Sargon II at Khorsabad, eighth century BC.

hair. At other times it was trimmed by the barber. The hair at the sides of the head, by the ears, was never cut. Leviticus 19:27 forbids it, as a pagan practice, a law still observed by orthodox Jews.

Women plaited, braided or curled their hair. It was often kept in place by beautiful ivory combs. In Roman times the hair was piled on top of the head and kept in place by a net. The rich had nets of gold thread.

Make-up
From earliest times women have used beauty aids. In ancient Palestine, Egypt and Mesopotamia women put dark eyeshadow around their eyes.

At first this was to protect their eyes against the strong sunshine. But it soon became a matter of fashion. Minerals were ground up in oil or gum with a small pestle and mortar. The women used their fingers, spatulas made of wood or bronze, or fine brushes to put on their eyeshadow. And they had polished metal mirrors in which to study the effect.

Lead sulphide (*galena*) was used early on, and copper carbonate (*kohl*) gave a greenish tinge. By Roman times, antimony was more often used.

Egyptian women used lip-stick and powderpuffs. Their toe nails and finger nails were painted red with dye from the crushed leaves of the henna plant. Red iron oxide seems to have been used in Egypt as rouge.

Oil, rubbed into the body to soothe the skin, was almost essential in a hot, dry climate. The only time it was not used was during times of mourning. But the oil, like the eye-paint, soon became part of the fashion scene and was per-fumed. A heavy scent helped disguise body odour where there was not much water for washing. 'Good oil' was made from flowers, seeds and fruit, soaked in oil and water. This was then sometimes treated so that the essence could be extracted and strained out.

Other perfumes came from gums or resins and were used either in powdered form, dissolved in oil, or mixed to make ointments. Most of these were imported into Israel and were a luxury. Because of their cost, they were kept in very expensive bottles and containers.

A man and woman in Greek dress.

Jewellery

The people of Israel were not as skilled at making jewellery as some of their neighbours – particularly the Egyptians. But jewellery has been worn from earliest times. Quite apart from its beauty, in the days before banks, a necklace was easier to carry from place to place than a bag of coins. It was certainly less trouble than a herd of cattle. Even before coins, jewels were a form of wealth which could be exchanged for other things – and taken as booty in war.

Bracelets, necklaces, pen-dants, anklets and rings – for ears and noses as well as fingers – were all worn. They were made from gold, silver and other metals, and set with precious or semi-precious stones, or even coloured glass. The stones were smoothed and polished, engraved and sculp-tured. Ivory was beautifully carved. It was often used for panelling and inlay in furniture-making, and also for hair-combs, brooches and plaques, and vases and flasks for cosmetics.

The jewellers and goldsmiths of Egypt were master-crafts-men. They produced some of the most colourful and beautiful jewellery the world has ever seen. Elaborate pendants (pec-torals) hung on bead chains were made from semi-precious stones – deep blue lapis lazuli, turquoise, red carnelian, quartz – and coloured glass in daz-zling blues and reds set in gold and silver. These pectorals were originally intended to give pro-tection against evil spirits. The carved scarab beetles which decorate Egyptian rings and bracelets represent the belief that Re', the sun-god, took the form of a beetle, and are a symbol of eternal life.

When the Israelites left Egypt (the exodus), they took with them gold and silver jewellery as well as clothes. Gold ear-rings were melted down to make a gold bull at Mt Sinai. But the people were soon sorry for this disloyalty to God, and 'both men and women brought decorative pins, ear-rings, rings, necklaces and all kinds of jewellery and dedicated them to the Lord' (Exodus 35:20ff.). Skilled Israelite craftsmen used the gold and jewels to beautify the tent of worship (tabernacle). The sacred breastplate worn by the high priest was set with

A Greek mirror, showing the case, and ivory comb.

A Greek scent-bottle and jug made of glass.

precious stones, one for each of the twelve clans of Israel.

The jeweller's skill was also used in making and engraving personal seals, sometimes worn as rings. These were impressed on lumps of clay to secure and authenticate documents. Poor people had roughly engraved seals of terracotta. But the rich often had beautiful seals cut from carnelian, agate, jasper, rock crystal and other semi-precious stones.

Jewellery was worn in Israel for special occasions – such as a wedding. But to be obsessed with jewels and clothes was wrong and a sign of pride, condemned in both Old and New Testaments (Isaiah 3:16–24; 1 Timothy 2:9).

A signet ring, probably belonging to an Egyptian governor, bearing the name of Pharaoh Tutankhamun.

Persian gold brooches from the Oxus treasure.

Gold ear-rings from New Kingdom Egypt, about 1500–1200 BC.

A Roman gold necklace from the first century AD.

A Persian gold bracelet, part of the Oxus treasure, fifth to second century BC.

A terracotta model of two Greek women chatting. About 100 BC.

Town and City Life

A town on a hill in Israel, fortified with a double wall and towers, shown on an Assyrian relief.

The difference between a town or city and a village in Bible times was not its size but its defences. Villages were un-walled settlements. Towns had walls around them. They were built on top of a hill (or a mound formed by the ruins of earlier towns) for defence. They also needed a good water supply close by. At Megiddo a tunnel was dug from the city to its spring, to bring water inside in case of siege. Towns were usually built in fertile parts of the country, where crops were good and people needed to get together to protect themselves against invaders. They were also often sited at a cross-roads or junction of trade routes.

Towns in early Israel

Towns were very small – often only about 6–10 acres – the size of a modern city square (640 acres make a square mile). There would be about 150–250 houses inside the walls, with 1,000 people living there. From a distance the towns in Canaan looked rather like castles. When the tent-dwelling Israelites first entered the country their spies reported seeing 'cities with walls that reached the sky' (Deuteronomy 1:28). These fortresses first began when nomadic clans decided to settle permanently. The clan chief became a 'king' over his own territory. There was no central government, and the kings of different towns often squabbled and fought.

To begin with the Israelites simply patched up the houses and buildings in the cities they captured from the Canaanites. They had to learn building skills from their neighbours. In times of peace there was a large 'overspill' from the towns, and people camped outside the walls, grazing their cattle and working the land.

Life in the towns was very cramped. Houses were poorly built and joined on house to house. Where the ground sloped, houses were built one above the other. There were no real streets – just spaces bet-ween houses – narrow alleys leading to nowhere in partic-ular. There was no paving. Drains were open channels. Mud and rubbish – garbage, broken pots, old mud-bricks – piled up outside, so that the level of the alleys was often higher than the ground-floor of the houses. Rain turned the whole mess into a swamp.

In winter, people were cooped up in the damp and filth. The summer sun helped, though the smells remained. But by then most of the people had moved away, to live and work in the fields. In peacetime they were country-dwellers for two-thirds of the year, towns-men for one-third.

The fortified gateway was the main open space in each town. In daytime the gates were noisy and crowded, bustling with life – merchants arriving; people buying and selling; elders meet-ing in council; others settling disputes and hearing cases. Beggars, pedlars, workmen, scribes, visitors, traders and shoppers – with their asses, camels and even cattle – all gathered at the city gate.

In the bigger towns there was more space for the shop-keepers. Sometimes each trade had its own area, but there were no specially-built shops. Each tradesman set out his goods on a stall at the side of the street. At night they were packed away. The city gates were closed and barred.

Important buildings

Most towns had one or two larger buildings, as well as houses. From King Solomon's time, when government became more centralized, the town grew more important as an ad-ministrative centre for the dis-trict. At his capital, Jerusalem, Solomon had his 'cabinet' – in-cluding a head of administration, secretary of state, keeper of the palace, chancellor of the ex-chequer and minister of forced labour. He organized twelve tax districts from which he collected food. This involved putting up buildings in which the food could be stored, and providing lodgings for his royal servants and officials in the main towns of each district.

Some of the most important buildings in Israel were connec-ted with religion. There were important religious centres not only at Jerusalem, but also at Dan and Bethel. Most towns had their own small shrine with an altar, very like the Canaanite shrines (the 'high places') which which were supposed to have been destroyed.

Solomon introduced slave and forced labour to carry out a great building plan. At Jerusalem he built the temple, palaces for himself and his queen, and other large halls (one probably to store arms; one as a court of justice). They were impressive stone buildings with cedar beams and panel-ling. The temple was beautiful, with olive-wood doors decor-ated with carved figures, all covered in gold. The Israelites,

MEGIDDO

Because of its position guarding the pass through the Carmel hills Megiddo was the scene of many battles throughout Bible times. It needed to be well fortified.

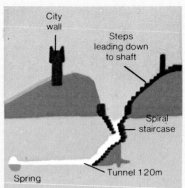

City wall

Steps leading down to shaft

Spiral staircase

Spring

Tunnel 120m

The photograph and diagram are of the water tunnel at Megiddo.

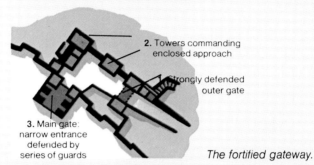

2. Towers commanding enclosed approach

Strongly defended outer gate

3. Main gate: narrow entrance defended by series of guards

An aerial view of Megiddo shows the excavation work.

The fortified gateway.

Governor's house

Pillared building

'Stables'

Grain silo

Water shaft and tunnel

Altar (about 2000 BC)

Temples (about 2500 BC)

'Stables'

City wall

Gateway

taught by skilled craftsmen from Tyre, had come a long way since their nomadic life in the desert (though even then they were able to produce beautiful work, as the making of the tabernacle shows).

Solomon also rebuilt and fortified a number of cities, to strengthen his country's defences. The three most important were Gezer, Megiddo and Hazor. The double walls and massive gateways in all three were built to the same plan. There were also warehouses, and stables for horses and chariots.

When the Jews were in exile in Babylon they could no longer go to the temple at Jerusalem. Instead they met together on the sabbath (Saturday) to listen to the law and hear it explained. When they returned, they built local meeting-houses for this purpose. These were the first 'synagogues' (the Greek word *synagein* means 'to meet together').

New Testament times

With the coming of the Greeks and Romans, towns were planned more carefully. The great cities of New Testament times were very different from the fortress towns of early Israel. Antioch in Syria (the city which was Paul's base) had wide streets, some paved with

marble, baths, theatres, temples and market-places. It even had lights at night. Many towns now had tall buildings, several storeys high, set in narrow streets.

King Herod the Great rebuilt Samaria (renamed Sebaste) and Caesarea in the Roman style, with a main street through the centre of the city, lined with shops, baths and theatres, and crossed at right angles by smaller streets. Houses were built in blocks of four. The Romans built aqueducts to bring piped water into the cities. They built public baths and introduced more efficient drainage works to take away waste water and sewage. Life in the cities, for the rich at least, was now much pleasanter than in earlier times. The poor, and those in more remote places, were less affected by these changes.

In Jesus' day, the most dazzling sight in Jerusalem was the

Part of the extensive remains of Ephesus (in modern Turkey), showing the fine town planning of Greek and Roman times.

great temple being built by the Herods out of white marble, with parts of the walls covered in gold. The temple drew pilgrims from all over the Mediterranean world, especially for the great religious festivals.

There may have been as many as a quarter of a million people living in the city. Its streets were crowded with people buying and selling. The shops and stalls sold everything, from necessities like sandals and cloth, meat, fruit and vegetables, to the luxury goods offered by goldsmiths, jewellers, silk, linen and perfume merchants. There were seven different markets, and two market days each week. Jerusalem had its restaurants and wine shops for ordinary people as well as its grander buildings – the palaces, Roman amphitheatre, and the fortress of Antonia.

This picture of Hebron shows what many Bible towns look like.

Life in the Villages

The 'village' of Old Testament times was simply an unwalled farming settlement. Villages grew up near a stream or spring that would provide water all the year round. As soon as animals were domesticated and people began to grow crops for food, they tended to settle in one place rather than move about. People were farming at Jericho, using picks, axes and digging sticks, as long ago as 6000 BC. At this stage there were only villages and no towns.

The possibility of towns (large settlements) came with the invention of the bronze ploughshare (some time after 4000 BC), when food production increased. Towns (fortified villages) were needed because of the struggle between the settled people and the nomadic people who wanted the same water supplies. Towns were therefore built up as larger, protected centres of civilization (see *Town and City Life*). In peacetime, people lived out in the villages, but when invasion threatened they gathered to the safety of the town. During the summer months, too, the population left the towns for the villages, to work in the fields.

The well was at the centre of village life. Here a Bedouin woman draws water from a well to the south of Jerusalem.

Ownership of land

Abraham and his family lived a partly nomadic, partly settled life. They moved about with their flocks but they also cultivated crops. In Mesopotamia, where Abraham had come from, there had been a 'feudal' system of allocating land. The king provided gifts of land ('fiefs') in return for a promise of personal service, and the land was passed on from father to son. When the Israelites entered Canaan the idea stayed in a new form. God was their king, and he gave them their land. Each family received their land by lot (Joshua 15), just as the fiefs had been given by lot in Mesopotamia.

Because it was God's land, he told them how to make proper use of it and how the produce was to be shared. One plot of land was given to each family, and it seems to have become the family burial-ground as well as the place to grow food. Each person's land was the gift of God (Isaiah 34:17), not to be casually bought and sold. (This was why Naboth would not sell his plot to King Ahab − 1 Kings 21:1−16.) If a family fell on hard times, it was the duty of their nearest relative to buy the land and keep it in the family. As far as we know, the family property went to the eldest son, so it was very important to have a son to carry on the family name and property.

Every fiftieth year was a

The sheep market at Jerusalem: a familiar scene of village and town life down the centuries.

year of Jubilee, when any land which had been mortgaged to pay off a debt was to be returned to the family. This helped keep everyone on the same level and avoided a sharp division between rich land-owners and poor labourers. It also emphasized the import-ance of the family holding.

The land immediately around the village was therefore priv-ate property. The land further outside the villages was looked upon as common land. It was divided into plots, which were distributed by lot to families each year.

Under the kings, beginning with David and Solomon, the old equality began to break down. A new wealthy class of rulers and officials grew up. They oppressed the poor and bought up land. Big estates took the place of small family farms. The people who had lost their land had to hire them-selves out as farm labourers. The poor were very poor, and suffered great hardship. The prophets spoke out against all this (Isaiah 5:8; Micah 2:2).

The change in the owner-ship of land led to a change in housing. In the tenth century BC, all the houses in a town or village were the same size, but by the eighth century BC, some houses were bigger and better and were grouped in a particular part of the town.

Daily work

In early Old Testament times almost everyone in the village was a farmer, growing what was needed for food (see Part 9: *Work and Society in the Bible*). They kept sheep, goats and cattle. These provided food for the family − and also manure for the ground.

The seasons set the pattern of work for the year. The wet season, from October to April, was used for ploughing, sowing (by hand from an open basket), harrowing and weeding. Then the harvesting began − first flax, then barley (April/May), then wheat.

Work on the vines began in the spring, when the plants had to be pruned. As they grew, trailing branches had to be propped up clear of the ground. Grapes were ready for picking from July to October.

Most people also had fig and olive trees. The main crop of figs came in August/September. The olive harvest was last, in October/November, when the grape gathering was over.

Every day the women baked bread. First came the back-breaking effort of grinding the grain into a coarse flour. This was mixed with salt and water to make dough. Usually some of the fermented dough from the day before was mixed in and the bread left to rise before baking.

Another vital job each day was to fetch water from the local spring or well. Only a few houses had their own well or water-storage cistern underground. The women carried the heavy water-pots home on their head or shoulder. There was always plenty to do, from dawn to dark. There might be milk to make into cheese and yoghurt. There was also wool to be spun and woven.

The work in the fields was not all left to the men. Everyone helped with the harvest and with crushing the grapes and olives in the presses. The working day ended at sunset, when the whole family gathered together for the main meal of the day.

Progress and problems

Country life changed very little down the centuries. The plough and other implements improved. But even in New Testament times they were still primitive, the plough cutting one furrow at a time. As time went by there was more specialization on large estates. There were skilled professionals to prune the vines, to drive the teams of oxen and to plough. 'Unskilled' workers weeded the fields, spread manure, and did countless other tasks.

The main problems also remained the same. Water was the first concern in a hot country with no rainfall at all for three or four months in the summer. The village well had to provide drinking water for the family and their animals, and water for the land. Sometimes an endless chain of leather buckets was used to bring the water to the surface and run it along irrigation ditches to the roots of the crops.

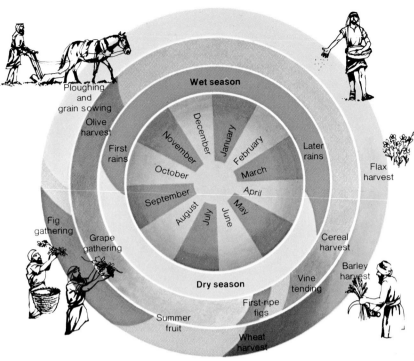

Locusts were another problem. Without warning they could arrive in swarms to eat every bit of living greenery. Wild animals – wolves, jackals, lions – could kill the livestock, too.

A third problem, completely disrupting village life, was a human one. Time and again invading armies attacked or passed through the country, taking prisoners or conscripting young men. If they came at the end of the wet season, the new growing crops were destroyed. If they came at harvest, the crops were taken away as booty or used to feed the army. Either way the villagers were likely to starve.

The changing seasons set the pattern of life for every village farmer.

Shepherds and flocks gather at the entrance of this typical village in Syria.

Housing

In Bible lands there have always been 'nomads' – people who move from place to place – as well as those with settled homes.

Living in tents

Abraham exchanged a settled, civilized city life at Ur in Mesopotamia for a semi-nomadic lifestyle when God called him to leave his home. Like the modern Bedouin, he lived in a goats'-hair tent. The black and brown striped material was woven from goats' hair after shearing time, on a loom pegged out on the ground. Wooden rings were stitched along the edge and in the centre to take nine poles in three rows. The middle row of poles was about 6ft/1.8m high, and the two outer rows a little less.

The tent house was made by propping up a long length of goats'-hair cloth about 6ft/ 1.8m wide, and living in the area underneath it. The women did the hard work, putting up the tent and securing the poles with guy ropes.

The area under the curtain was closed in at the back with a screen made of goats'-hair cloth, or reeds and twigs woven together, and the area was then divided into two 'rooms'. One formed an open porch where visitors could be received, and the remainder was curtained off for the use of the women and for the household stores. The only adult male who could enter this part was the head of the family. Sometimes the ground under the tent was covered with woven matting but more often it was left as bare earth. Tents were pitched in groups for protection. Women very rarely had a tent of their own, unless the family was very rich.

For hundreds of years Abraham's descendants lived in tents: first in Canaan, then in Egypt, then in the desert. When they conquered the Canaanites, they took over the Canaanite cities, patched up the ruins and copied their building style.

House-building

The poorer people in Old Testament times lived in very small houses. There was one square room with an outside yard. Houses were built by groups of neighbours, and by skilled builders who went from place to place.

☐ Building materials

If the house was built on the plain or in a valley, the walls were made of mud brick. Rooms could be added alongside or as another storey as people grew better off, and building skills increased. Mud bricks were quite large – about 21in × 10in × 4in/53cm × 25cm × 10cm – and were made in wooden moulds.

The fathers and grandfathers of the Israelites who settled in Canaan had had plenty of practice at making mud-bricks when they were slaves in Egypt. They began by digging a hole in the ground and filling it with water, chopped straw, palm fibre and bits of shell and charcoal. The workmen then trampled the mixture until they had a soft and pliable mud. Most bricks were laid out to dry in the hot sun. Kilns produced stronger bricks which were used for the foundations. Mud was also used to cement the bricks together and to plaster the finished walls.

It is not surprising that in wet weather the houses tended to leak. They were not very strongly built and it was easy for a thief to break in just by digging a hole through the wall.

In the mountains, where limestone and basalt were ready at

Abraham, his son and grandsons lived in tents, moving from place to place, like these Bedouin.

HOUSES OF THE WELL-TO-DO

Egyptian

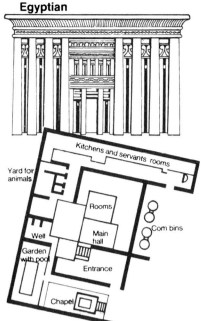

Greek

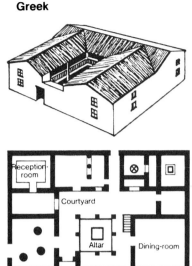

Bedrooms and women s rooms above

Roman

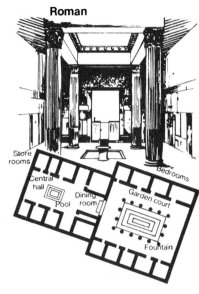

hand, and on the coast where sandstone was found, roughly squared stone was used for the foundations, with rough stone or brick walls nearly 3ft/91cm thick built on top. These thick walls could be hollowed out and alcoves made for storage. In early days the walls were little more than rubble, but as iron tools became available for shaping stone more easily, the stones were roughly squared.

Windows were few and tiny, set high up in the wall for coolness in summer, warmth in winter. There was no glass. Instead, a lattice shutter was put across the hole to keep intruders out. Thick woollen curtains were used in the cold, wet season, to keep the weather out. Doors at first were made of woven twigs. Then, as skills developed, of wood and metal.

☐ The roof

This was made by laying beams across the width of the walls, and smaller beams at right angles across them. The kind of wood depended on how rich you were: sycamore for ordinary homes, cypress and cedar for those who could afford it. Layers of brushwood, earth and clay were then added and

the whole thing made firm by using a stone roller 2ft/60cm long, which was kept on the roof.

After the rain the roof often sprouted grass and the smaller animals might be sent up to graze! Gutters took the precious, but not very clean, water to a storage cistern, waterproofed with a mortar made from ashes, lime, sand and water. To have your own stored water was something of a status symbol in Old Testament times. But it cannot have led to very good health.

The roof was a very important part of the house. Poor people probably climbed up by ladder. The better off had a flight of steps built into the walls, leading from the yard to the roof-space. The roof was used for drying fruit and grain (Rahab hid the spies under the flax which was drying on her roof – Joshua 2:6), and was a cool place on a hot evening. Sometimes the family made a tent of branches and slept out on the roof.

As building skills improved, permanent upper storeys became more common. The rich woman at Shunem built on a special guest-room for the

prophet Elisha (2 Kings 4:10). Sometimes a trellis was put on the roof and vines trained over it. If the house was built into a steep hillside, the roof was sometimes used as a threshing-floor. Householders would shout their news from roof to roof ('from the housetops') above the noise from the streets below. The roof-space was so much part of the life of the house that the law insisted it must have a railing round the edge for safety (Deuteronomy 22:8). Tiled and pitched roofs began to be built shortly before New Testament times.

☐ Inside the house

The floor area was divided into two, like the nomad's tent. The animals were brought into the lower area of the house near the door during winter. This floor area was of beaten earth. The family lived on a raised platform, farthest away from the door. The space underneath may have been used for storing tools and jars – and even keeping small animals. Cooking things, clothes and bedding were kept on the platform.

Sometimes stone chippings were worked into the earth floor. But it was only under

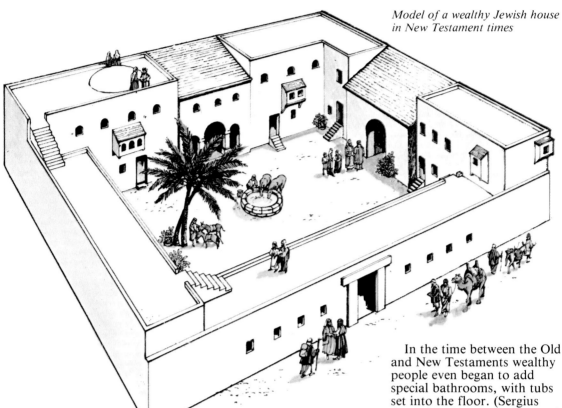

Model of a wealthy Jewish house in New Testament times

Greek influence, after about 300 BC, that the art of making mosaic floors was developed. Even then this was frowned on for religious reasons, and the only mosaic floors found in Israel during Bible times were in the palace of King Herod the Great at Masada and rich houses in Jerusalem.

Life in the home
What was life like for families living in the ordinary small house? During the hot summer, the house was alive with insects. When the weather grew cold, the house was filled with smoke from the fire. There was no real fireplace. The fire smouldered in a hole in the earth floor. If the family was wealthy enough, they warmed themselves around a brazier. But there was no chimney.

When it rained hard and continuously the roof and the walls leaked. The writer of the Old Testament proverb knew

just how miserable that was. 'A nagging wife,' he wrote, 'is like water going drip-drip-drip on a rainy day' (Proverbs 27:15). There were no facilities for bathing, and the house of the ordinary person was so dark that a lamp had always to be kept lit. It was placed on a stand, or in a niche in the wall, in the area farthest from the door.

From the time of Solomon, however, a wealthy class began to emerge, and for them life was very different. Rooms were extended around court-yards and gardens which pro-vided shade and cool currents of air in the summer. In winter it was possible to use rooms in a warmer, sunnier position. The whole house was built on a much larger scale, with pillars to support roof beams. Once pillars were used it was possible to have porches and colon-nades. The prophet Amos talks about the 'winter houses and summer houses' enjoyed by the rich (Amos 3:15).

In the time between the Old and New Testaments wealthy people even began to add special bathrooms, with tubs set into the floor. (Sergius Orata is said to have invented a centrally heated bathroom, with a hot water supply, in about 70 BC!) By New Testa-ment times rich people in Pales-tine had houses built Roman-style, with two rectangular courtyards, one behind the other, each surrounded by rooms.

Furniture
People in the east, even today, have much less furniture than many in western countries. The style, even for the rich, is cool, simple and uncluttered — with just a few mats for the floor, seating, small tables and some kind of heating for winter.

Throughout Bible times the poor possessed very little by way of furniture and furnishings. The 'bed' was a thin wool-filled mattress, spread out each evening on the raised part of the floor. The whole family slept there, under goats'-hair quilts. In the morn-ing they rolled or piled up the bed and bedding and stacked it away. The furniture which the woman at Shunem provided for Elisha was better than average: a bed, a table, a chair and a lamp (2 Kings 4:10). The table was often simply a straw mat laid out on the raised floor. In some homes, but by no means all, there were stools to sit on.

Every house had stone or clay storage bins in which they kept fodder for the animals as well as food stores for the family. There were special jars for storing flour and olive oil, earthenware pots for carrying and storing water. There were cooking pots, too, and bowls for serving food.

☐ Cooking things

One of the most important things in the home was the grinding mill. This was made from two circular stones. The larger, lower stone had a spike which pierced the centre of a smaller one, which was turned round on top of it. Corn was poured through the central hole and as two women turned the top stone with a handle, flour ran out at the edge between the two stones. It was hard work!

A fire for cooking was made simply in the earth floor, or sometimes in an earthenware pot. Charcoal, thorns or dried animal dung provided the fuel. A convex baking-sheet, which could be put over the fire, and a cooking-pot which could stand in the fire, made up the remainder of the basic cooking things.

☐ Lamps

Because the houses were so dark, one of the most important items in any household was the lamp. Throughout the Old Testament period lamps were simply pottery dishes with a lip at one side. Oil was poured into the dish and a wick laid from it to the lip. Such a lamp might stay alight for two or three hours, then need refilling.

By New Testament times potters had learnt how to make lamps in moulds, completely covered over, with a

A simple Jewish oil-lamp, of the kind used from very early times.

small hole for the oil and a spout for the wick. This was safer and more efficient. The wicks were usually strips of flax or rag. Olive oil or animal fat was commonly used, oil from other seeds and vegetables being introduced by New Testament times.

Lamps were small enough for a traveller to carry in his hand. This may have been the picture in the psalmist's mind when he wrote, 'Your word is a lamp to guide me and a light for my path' (Psalm 119:105).

Brooms for cleaning were made of corn stalks. They were kept with the tools the father needed for his trade.

Most of the jars and bowls in everyday use were made by the potter. But in wealthier homes they had things made from metal.

By New Testament times

An oil-lamp from Roman times.

glass, moulded on a core, and produced in Egypt, was used. In about 50 BC, the art of glass blowing was developed in Syria. But although this made glass cheaper, it was still beyond the reach of most people. There were no 'ornaments' as such in the ordinary home. People used their artistic skills in making and decorating the things they used every day.

Pottery from Palestine about 2000 BC.

Food for the Family

A Roman glass jar.

The rich

The rich had a good many extra comforts: high beds, tables, chairs and couches. These were often made of fine wood, carved and inlaid with bone or ivory. There were pillows for their beds, and fine wool blankets. Extra clothes and bedding were stored in chests. In New Testament times wealthy people ate their meals Roman-style, reclining on a three sided couch (*triclinium*) around a square table.

The greatest luxury of all was to be found in the royal palaces, from King Solomon – who built in well-cut stone and lined his walls with cedar – and King Ahab (with a palace at Samaria which boasted beautiful carved ivory inlays and expensive furniture), to Herod the Great. Herod had a summer palace with lovely gardens at Jerusalem, and a winter one at Jericho.

For ordinary people, food and clothing have always been two of the main concerns. 'Don't start worrying,' Jesus said, ' "Where will my food come from? or my drink? or my clothes?" ' He knew how easy it is to worry when there is only just enough to live on. In Bible times this was how most of the people in Israel lived. For this reason their enemies attacked during the growing season. If the crops were destroyed, the people could not survive.

In Gideon's time, 'wherever the Israelites sowed any seed, the Midianites would come . . . and attack them . . . and destroy the crops' (Judges 6:3–4).

Unreliable rainfall, drought, and pests such as locusts, made the crops uncertain. Famines were expected as a normal part of life. It is not surprising that the Israelites saw the golden age of the future as an age of plenty with more than enough for all.

Food

There were a number of sources of food: mainly cereal crops, fruit and vegetables. Bread was the basic item of everyone's diet. The word 'bread' in the Lord's prayer stands for food in general. And Jesus called himself 'the Bread of Life', meaning 'the food of life'.

□ Bread

Barley bread – the bread the boy with the five loaves and two fish gave to Jesus (John 6:9) – was probably the most common. Wheat gave the best flour and was also quite common, and spelt, too, was sometimes used.

The grain was first sorted in a shallow basket, to remove poor grain and any poisonous seeds such as darnel ('tares'), weeds which grew with the corn and looked very similar.

A woman baking flat loaves of bread in a traditional clay oven.

Then it was ground. In early days this was done by rubbing between a small stone and a larger one. Later it was ground between two small millstones. The lower one was fixed; the upper one turned round on top of it.

For each baking, forty litres of flour (Matthew 13:33) were mixed with water (or sometimes olive oil) to form a dough. People seldom had fresh yeast, so a piece of fermented dough ('leaven') from the previous baking was kneaded into the new dough and the whole left

Flat loaves of bread.

to rise. Before it was baked, part of the dough was put aside for the next day's 'leavening'. The bread was baked as a flat cake. This was appetising when fresh, but soon went dry. 'Parched' corn – fresh ears put on a metal sheet over the fire and 'popped' – was a popular alternative. For special occasions cakes and pastries were included in the baking.

☐ Fruit and vegetables
Fruit was another important food. The grape vine did more than produce juice. Many grapes were eaten fresh at harvest time, and many more were dried and used as raisins. Figs, too, were eaten fresh, and also dried and pressed together to make fig cakes. When Abigail gave David supplies for his men they included 'a hundred bunches of raisins and

two hundred cakes of dried figs' (1 Samuel 25:18). They were specially useful for taking on a journey. The prophet Isaiah prescribed a paste made of figs to heal King Hezekiah's painful boil (Isaiah 38:21).

Dates are not mentioned by name in the Bible, but they were certainly grown. The crowd waved date palm branches to welcome Jesus to Jerusalem, the week before he died. Dates were also used in the special sauce (*charoseth*) in which everyone dipped their bread at the Passover meal. The sauce was made from dates, figs, raisins and vinegar.

Olives were also eaten –

Bunches of dates ripen on a date-palm.

some fresh, in October, and others after pickling in salt water. The most important produce of the olive was its oil, which was used in cooking. Pomegranates, almonds and pistachio nuts were also available, and citrus fruits were just coming in in New Testament times.

There were fresh vegetables in season. Beans, lentils and peas were dried and stored in jars. There were also onions and leeks, melons and cucumbers. Vegetables were used to make soups. Esau exchanged his birthright for a bowl of red lentil soup (Genesis 25:29–34). Farm products were also available. Butter was not much used because it would not keep in

Green figs in a basket.

the hot weather. But cheese and yoghurt were popular, and in New Testament times people kept hens and poached the eggs in olive oil.

☐ Meat and fish
Not much meat was eaten. Mutton and meat from the goats was the most common, and birds were caught for food, although the wealthy, even in Old Testament times, fed on lamb, veal and beef. Meat was normally boiled. The lamb roasted for the Passover Festival was an exception. Ordinary people ate meat only on special occasions such as a celebration party, or when entertaining guests at a religious festival, or special sacrifice at the local shrine. On this occasion the family gathered together to eat some of the animal that had been sacrificed at the shrine, as a sign of their renewed friendship with God.

Fish was certainly an important food in New Testament times. (At least seven of Jesus' twelve disciples were fishermen.) Small fish were dried and salted and eaten with bread, as at the feeding of the 5,000. Or they could be cooked over an open fire and eaten fresh, as at the breakfast Jesus prepared for his followers (John 21).

Food laws
Strict laws about diet are laid down in the Old Testament saying what may, and what may not, be eaten. The general rule was that animals which chew their cud and have divided hoofs could be eaten. This ruled out the pig. Fish were allowed, but only those with fins and scales. Many birds were not to be eaten, particularly if they were scavengers. It was also laid down that the blood must be drained from a carcase before it was cooked and that meat and milk dishes were not to be cooked or eaten together.

These two rulings meant that a Jew could not eat at the home of a non-Jew, where these restrictions were not normal. They resulted in a division between Jewish and non-Jewish Christians in New Testament times. Paul needed to teach the Christians at Corinth about their Christian freedom in this respect. In New Testament times, too, a family which followed the teaching of the Pharisees was not allowed to buy or eat food which had been killed in a pagan temple as an offering. For three days before a festival they were not allowed to buy any food at all from a non-Jew.

The reason for these strict laws on diet was never explained. They may have been God's way of protecting the health of the people. They may have been intended to avoid cruelty to animals: for example, the law which forbade the boiling of a kid in its mother's milk; and the draining of the blood, which prevented the practice of cutting a limb off a live animal for meat. Or they may have been given for more strictly 'religious' reasons. This was certainly the reason for forbidding meat which had been offered to an idol. And boiling a kid in its mother's milk may have been a Canaanite religious practice which the Israelites were to avoid. We cannot always be sure in any particular case whether one or all of these reasons holds good.

Some Bible passages about food laws: Leviticus 11; Deuteronomy 14:3ff.; 12:15–24. See also Daniel 1:8ff.; Acts 10:9ff.; 15:28–29; 1 Corinthians 8; 10:18–33

Sweetening and seasoning
The Israelites had no sugar. Honey from wild bees was the main sweetener (see the story of Jonathan in 1 Samuel 14: 25–27 and of Samson in Judges 14:8). But another kind of 'honey' may have been produced by boiling dates and locust beans to make a syrup.

Seasoning was important, too. There was plenty of rock salt on the south-west shores of the Dead Sea. Salt was also obtained by evaporation. The outer layer of rock salt was often impure and hard. It had no flavour and was used to spread on the temple courtyards in wet weather to make them less slippery.

Salt was used for seasoning food, but it was much more important for preserving it. In New Testament times the main industry at Magdala, on the Sea of Galilee, was the salting of fish. Mint, dill (anise), and cummin (seeds like caraway but used in place of pepper) were also used to give food the strong flavouring which everyone liked. They also helped give variety and interest to an otherwise boring diet. Rarer spices, imported from Africa and Asia, were used only by the wealthy.

Drinks
Although water was the basic liquid used in cooking, it was not very good for drinking. Water from the local well or spring was generally safe enough. It was collected in porous earthenware jars in which the water remained cool by a process of slow evaporation. Water from the family cistern, a conical shaped pit in the ground with a waterproof lining, was far from safe. Because the water came from the roof and ran down into the cistern through gutters, it was often dirty and full of germs. In Roman times when water was brought to the towns by aqueduct (as it was to Caesarea and Bethlehem) or by pipeline (as it was to Jerusalem), the water was still not fit to drink. For this reason other liquids made better drinks.

There was milk, often straight from the family goat, or brought to the door by the 'milkman'. But wine was the commonest drink. At the time the grapes were picked, there was fresh grape juice, pressed straight from the bunch into a cup. But most of the juice had to be fermented so that it would keep. The first wine of the year was made from the juice extracted when the grapes were trodden in the press. A second batch was made by squeezing the remainder in a press.

Wine was sometimes mixed with gall or myrrh to relieve pain. (This was offered to Jesus at the crucifixion – Matthew 27:34.) It was also mixed with olive oil to clean and heal wounds. (The Good Samaritan poured oil and wine on the wounds of the injured man – Luke 10:34.)

Although wine was the normal drink – Jesus himself provided wine for the wedding at Cana, and drank enough to be called a 'tippler' ('wine-bibber') by the Pharisees – people under a vow to God, or engaged on special service, sometimes gave up drinking it (Leviticus 10:9; Numbers 6:3). And any drunkenness or excess was always condemned. The Rechabites avoided drinking wine as part of their calling to keep the nomadic way of life. Planting vineyards and producing wine was considered part of a settled life.

Wealthy homes in New Testament times had cellars of fine wines from all over the Mediterranean world. They were kept in narrow jars (*amphorae*) with a pointed end, so that they could be pushed deep into earth or sand to keep the wine cool. But wine was usually stored in leather bottles (wineskins).

Cooking
Food was normally cooked by boiling, in a pot over a fire. Some foods were poached in oil. And bread, of course, was baked. There were several methods of baking bread. The simplest was to scoop out a hole in the ground, make a fire in it, then remove the ash and stick the flat 'pancakes' of dough on the sides of the hole. Sometimes stones were put into the fire, and when the dough was ready for baking, the hot stones were taken out and the

dough placed on them to cook. Or a large shallow earthenware bowl was placed upside down over the fire, and the dough placed on that.

Wealthier homes had a pottery oven. This consisted of a beehive-shaped funnel. The fire was lit in the bottom of the funnel, and the bread was stuck on the inside towards the top. Not until Roman times was a divided oven invented, with the fire separate from the cooking area. None of these methods of baking was very hygienic.

Many vegetables (such as the cucumber), were eaten raw. Lentils and beans were boiled in water or oil. Corn porridge was made with water, salt and butter.

Meals

In the peasant home, meals were very simple. There was no formal breakfast. If anything was eaten at all, it was as a snack carried and eaten on the way to work. The midday meal was usually bread and olives, and perhaps fruit. The evening meal was a vegetable stew, with a piece of bread used as a spoon to dip into the common pot. The whole family ate together for this meal, and if any important guests were present, meat might be added to the cooking-pot. The family sat on the floor to eat.

In a wealthy home it was different. There was more elaborate food with plenty of meat. In New Testament times guests reclined on couches round three sides of a square table. Instead of one dish, there were many.

A Roman, or Roman-style, dinner party followed this pattern: first came the hors d'ocuvres, and wine mixed with honey. Next, three main courses were served on trays. The guests ate with their fingers, though they used a spoon for things like soup! After this course, at a Roman meal, pieces of food were thrown into the fire as a token 'sacrifice' — a kind of 'grace'. Finally pastries and fruit were served as dessert. This was followed by drinks and entertainment. The 'religious' element — the offering to the gods — was one of the reasons why a Jew could never eat with a Gentile. The strict Jewish food-laws was another (see above). But God showed Peter in a vision that the old barriers between Jew and non-Jew must be broken down: Christians, whatever their nationality, belong to one family.

Among the nomadic, tent-dwelling people, a traveller was always welcome to stay — for three days and four hours! — the length of time the hosts believed their food sustained their guest. Flat loaves of bread, and milk, were basic to the meal. For the time of his stay the traveller became one of the clan. Both Old and New Testaments teach the importance of hospitality. As the author of the letter to the Hebrews writes: 'Remember to welcome strangers in your homes' (Hebrews 13:2).

Shopping

The town market was set up in the gateway. People selling the same goods formed groups and normally set up their stalls together. In early Bible times, payment was by barter (exchanging one thing for another). But by Abraham's time, and through most of the Old Testament, people paid with weighed amounts of silver or, more rarely, gold. It was obviously necessary to have standard weights so that everyone knew the value, and this paved the way for coinage.

Vegetables spread out for sale, eastern style, at the Bedouin market, Beersheba.

□ Money

Money as we know it was first used in Bible lands in the eighth century BC, in Lydia (part of modern Turkey). Early coins were made of electrum (an alloy of silver and gold) and the weight of the metal was guaranteed by the stamp on the coin. From this time on the Jewish people rarely had their independence. They were exiled to Babylon, then subject to Persia, Greece and Rome – so not many Jewish coins were minted.

In the Greek period, coins were issued from Acco, on the coast of Israel. Roman coins were used throughout the Empire. The only Jewish coins minted were the small bronze coins first allowed by the Seleucid kings (the Syrian Empire which followed the death of Alexander the Great). The Jewish leaders (Hasmoneans) in Jerusalem coined these to their own designs. At the time of the rebellion against the Romans in AD 66 the Jews minted their first coins in silver. There were so many different coins about, that it was necessary for the buyer and the seller to know their equivalent values. See the chart on money in Part 9: *Work and Society in the Bible*.

□ Measures

There were standard weights and measurements of length,

Grapes ripen on the vine.

dry and liquid capacity, but there was little *exact* measurement. Standard length measurements based on the relative sizes of the human arm and hand arose out of general use. (See Part 9: *Work and Society in the Bible*.) Measurement of distances in Old Testament times were based on a day's journey or even a bowshot.

Olives provided oil for cooking and for lamps.

Foodstuffs were measured by volume rather than by weight. The terms used are often the names of the containers which held the food. (See Part 9: *Work and Society in the Bible*.) A *homer* was an 'ass-load' (perhaps 200 litres) and was the largest measure for cereals. The *ephah* was a container, closed with a lid, holding about one tenth of a *homer*. The *bath* was the same as the *ephah*, but was used for liquids. The *omer* (meaning 'sheaf') was the amount of manna gathered each day. Other measurements were also in use in the market. A *letek* was half a homer. A *hin* was six times the amount a man needs to drink in a day. The *log* was another small unit for liquids.

□ Weights

Precious materials and metals were measured by weight. Small things were weighed on a beam balance with scale pans. The weights were kept in a purse. Merchants sometimes used the fact that they had two sets of weights – one when they were buying, the other when they were selling – to cheat their

customers. But the law of God insisted on strict honesty.

'Do not cheat when you use weights and measures. Use true and honest weights and measures, so that you may live a long time in the land' (Deuteronomy 25:13). 'The Lord hates people who use dishonest scales and weights' (Proverbs 20:23).

The verb 'to weigh' is *shaqal* in Hebrew and the name has been given to the basic unit of weight – the *shekel*.

Social Life

Nowadays we tend to divide life into 'work' and 'leisure' time. The earliest workmen in Israel worked long hours and had no labour-saving tools. So it might seem that there was little time for leisure activities. But this is only partly true. Children have always played games. And slaves and servants enabled the wealthy, at least, to give time to social life and leisure pursuits.

But more than this, God taught his people that they needed rest and leisure. They were to set aside one day in seven as a 'sabbath' in which none of the ordinary work was done. This was for them to rest and relax as well as worship. And there were also special 'holidays' and festivities at the great religious festivals.

Games

Children's games seem to have changed very little. We know that children in Bible times had toys which made a noise – such as rattles and whistles. These have been found in many places by archaeologists. Some rattles were shaped like boxes with small holes in each side, others like dolls and birds, though they were rather heavy to handle.

Girls played with dolls' houses, too. Miniature cooking pots and furniture, made out of pottery, have been found dating from between 900 and 600 BC. Some dolls had jointed arms and legs, and hair of beads and mud. They had holes in their shoulders for puppet strings. But whether these were really used for play, or in religious ceremonies, is not quite certain.

Israelite children, like children everywhere, also played 'imitating' games, copying the grown-ups. Matthew 11:16–17 describes groups of children in the market-place, playing at weddings and funerals.

☐ **Board and dice games**
Draughts was played on boards of twenty or thirty squares. The boards were made of stone, clay, ebony and ivory. Some of those which have been found were cut out at the back to take the 'men'. Chess was played in Babylon before 2,000 BC, and other games such as Ludo and Mancala were also played. What has been called the 'Royal Game' from Ur of the Chaldees seems to have been a form of Ludo. Solitaire

Wooden pullalong toys from ancient Egypt.

Egyptian balls made of painted fabric, spinning tops and a wooden doll.

Girls playing knucklebones.

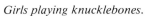

Gaming-boards: from the Royal Graves at Ur (above) and Pharaoh Tutankhamun's gaming-board from Egypt (right).

was also played. Moves were made after throws with two kinds of dice – two-sided discs, or four-sided pyramids called teetotum. The six-sided dice we use today was not known.

People took throwing dice or 'casting lots' very seriously. 'Men cast lots to learn God's will', says the writer of Proverbs, 'but God himself determines the answer' (Proverbs 16:33). The high priest himself used dice to discover God's will. He had two of them – called the 'Urim' and 'Thummim' – contained within a breastplate (a canvas bag embroidered with precious stones which he wore on his chest), which was used as a shaker.

The game played by the soldiers at the trial of Jesus was also a dice game. As a four-sided dice was used, they moved a skittle from a central mark to positions where it could be 'robed', 'crowned' and 'sceptred', and the soldier whose move completed the 'ceremony' called 'king' and collected the stakes which had been put down. In this instance the prisoner was used as a human skittle (Matthew 27:28–29).

Although dice games were so popular amongst the people, the religious leaders strongly disapproved of gambling, and Jewish law disqualified a gambler from testifying before a court of justice.

☐ Ball and target games
Marbles were popular in Egypt. They were rolled through a wall with three archways, to knock down skittles on the other side. Out of doors, hopscotch was known, and there were throwing games with leather balls. Juggling was popular; but there seem to have been no bats or racquets. Sometimes the children made a hole in the ground and had contests to see who could throw the most stones into it from a distance.

Children and grown-ups also practised with slings and stones. A sling was made from a woollen pouch held between two strings about a cubit long. A stone was put into the pouch, and it was whirled round and round. When the slinger let go one of the two strings, the stone flew out at its target. Shooting with bows and arrows was also a pastime. There was target and distance shooting.

☐ Wrestling
Wrestling was also popular. In Babylon they wrestled holding on to the other person's belt. Jacob's wrestling-match, and the expression 'hip and thigh' (Judges 15:8), which was a technical term for a wrestling throw, show that this sport was popular in Israel too.

Public entertainment
As time went on some people began to make a living by entertaining others. This kind of entertainment – what Paul calls a 'spectacle' in 1 Corinthians 4:9 – became very popular in Greek times. It was one of the areas of disagreement between the Sadducees, who enjoyed it, and the Pharisees, who believed it to be wrong.

King Herod built a stadium (for fights between gladiators – who were trained captives taken in war, or criminals – and between men and animals) and an amphitheatre (for chariot-racing) in Jerusalem. He built theatres at Caesarea and Sebaste which can still be seen.

Greek-style athletics were also performed in the stadium and in the gymnasium. The Greeks believed that exercise of this kind was necessary for a healthy body. But Greek athletics were not very popular with the Jewish people. They found it offensive that the athletes competed naked. And the close link with Greek religion was a further obstacle.

The sporting events mentioned in Paul's letters are all linked to the Greek games. He uses the strict training of the athlete as an example (1 Corinthians 9:24–27), and writes of runners competing to win a crown of laurel, pine or olive leaves. He also refers to boxing, with arms and hands bound with studded leather, so that a blow must be avoided rather than parried! Philippians 3:13–14 pictures a race, and Hebrews 12:1–2 reflects the long-distance foot race, where weight has been lost in training and clothes are shed for the race.

Music
Music and dancing have been part of life in all cultures, as far back in history as we can go.

Discus-throwing was one of the events in the Pentathlon, in the Greek games.

This first-century Roman lamp shows a contest between gladiators.

There were three kinds of instruments in Israel – string, wind and percussion. They played together in unison rather than in harmony. And the music seems to have been strongly rhythmic rather than melodic, although there were set tunes to some of the psalms. Because the description of the instruments is rather vague it is not possible to identify them all. But we *do* know something about the following:

☐ **Strings**
The *kinnor* is normally translated 'harp' in the Bible. It may have been a harp or a lyre. It was a small, eight- or ten-stringed instrument with a wooden frame, and could be carried about. We do not know if it was played simply by plucking, or if a plectrum was used. The *kinnor* may be the instrument shown on ancient tomb-paintings at Beni-Hasan in Egypt.

The *nebel*, called a 'psaltery', was another stringed instrument in a wooden frame, played by plucking with the fingers. The word *nebel* means a 'skin bottle' or jar, which suggests a swollen soundbox like a lute.

David was able to play both.

☐ **Wind**
The *halil* (pipe) was the ordinary person's hollow pipe, made of cane, wood or bone. *Halil* means 'to bore', and describes the way the instrument was made. A reed was used in the instrument, and the player carried spare reeds about in a bag.

The *geren* (cornet, horn) was made from the horn of an animal and was used as a trumpet. If the horn used was a ram's horn, the instrument was called a *shofar*, also translated trumpet in some versions of the Bible. It was used on religious and public occasions.

The *hazozra* was a metal trumpet, which in Bible times was made of silver. A continuous call on two silver trumpets was the sign to gather at the tabernacle. One was sounded to call the chiefs together.

☐ **Percussion**
The *menaanim* is a percussion instrument and was probably made of discs rattled along metal rods, suspended in a wooden frame.

Meziltaim are copper cymbals. They were used by Levites in the temple to mark the be-

An Egyptian timbrel made from wood and painted skin.

Two sistrums and a pair of rattles in plaited cane, from Egypt.

ginning, ending, and pauses in the chapters which were sung.

The *tof* was a percussion instrument with a membrane, and is called a 'timbrel' or tambourine in English versions. It was used to accompany singing and dancing. At the time of the exodus Aaron's sister Miriam 'took her tambourine, and all the women followed her, playing tambourines and dancing' (Exodus 15:20).

Unfortunately, because the Israelites were not allowed to portray human figures in their art, we do not know exactly how these instruments were played. But pictures of similar instruments from Egypt, Assyria and Babylonia give us a fair idea. Instruments

Reconstruction of a kinnor, *the harp which David played.*

An Egyptian girl plays a seven-stringed lyre with a plectrum in this tomb-painting at Thebes *(1421–1413 BC).*

were made from a wide variety of materials – cedarwood, sandalwood, leather, gut, ivory, shell, gold and silver.

Music had an important place in the worship at the temple. 1 Chronicles 15:16–24 describes how David organized the temple choir and orchestra 'to sing and to play joyful music'. In the temple the singing was often in parts – one line of a section being sung by one group, and the next sung in response by another. Dancing, too, was often part of the people's joyful expression of worship. When the Ark of the Covenant was brought to Jerusalem 'David and all the people danced with all their might to honour God' (1 Chronicles 13:8).

This first-century AD Roman wall-painting pictures a music lesson.

Right: warned in a dream of King Herod's plan to kill their baby, Joseph and Mary fled with Jesus to safety in Egypt.

8

People of the Bible

Note: Most of the dates given can only be approximate. The overlap in the reigns of some of the kings is because there were times of co-regency.

Aaron Elder brother of Moses and Miriam, born when the Israelites were slaves in Egypt. Moses was not good at speaking, so Aaron spoke for him to the Egyptian Pharaoh, pleading with him to obey God's command and let the people of Israel go. Pharaoh refused, and it was Aaron, with Moses, who warned him of the ten plagues God would send. Aaron gave Moses his loyal backing during the escape from Egypt. But at Mt Sinai Aaron gave way to the people's demands and made them a golden calf-idol to worship. Even so, God forgave him and made him the first high priest of Israel. Aaron was in charge of a special tent used for worship (the tabernacle). There he offered sacrifices to God for the sins of the people and prayed for them to be forgiven. But at times Aaron was jealous of Moses' position as the people's leader. He died before the Israelites entered Canaan and his son Eleazar became high priest after him.
Exodus 4:14; 5 – 12; 28:1; 32:1; Numbers 20:23–29
Abednego The Babylonian name given to one of three Jewish exiles chosen for special service by King Nebuchadnezzer of Bablyon. Shadrach, Meshach and Abednego, led by Daniel, courageously refused to eat the court food because, even in a foreign country, they were determined to obey the food-laws God had given the Jewish people. Later they refused to bow before an idol the king had set up. All three were thrown into a blazing furnace. But God protected them, and they came out unharmed. The king was most impressed. 'No other God can do what this one does', he said.
Daniel 1 – 3
Abel Adam and Eve's second son, brother of Cain. Abel became a shepherd when he grew up, and offered a lamb to God as a sacrifice. This pleased God. But Cain

was jealous because God did not accept his gift of fruit, and he killed his brother. The New Testament explains that it was because of Abel's faith that he, and not his brother, won God's approval.
Genesis 4:1–8; Hebrews 11:4
Abiathar The son of Ahimelech the priest in the days of King Saul. When David became king, Abiathar was made joint high priest with Zadok. But after David's death he conspired to put Adonijah on the throne, instead of Solomon, and was banished.
1 Samuel 22:20ff.; 2 Samuel 8:17; 15:24ff.; 1 Kings 1 and 2
Abihu See *Nadab.*
Abigail The beautiful wife of Nabal, who later married David. (See *Nabal.*)
1 Samuel 25
Abijah The son of King Jeroboam I of Israel. He died as a child.
1 Kings 14
Abijah/Abijam Son of

King Rehoboam of Judah; he reigned for three years, about 913–911 BC.
1 Kings 15; 2 Chronicles 13
Abimelech 1. Because he was afraid for his life, Abraham pretended that his wife, Sarah, was only his sister. Abimelech, king of Gerar, wanted to make her his wife, but God showed him the truth and prevented it.
Genesis 20; 26 (this story may be about another king of the same name who had a similar experience with Isaac)
2. A son of Gideon who killed his brothers to become king.
Judges 8:31ff.; 9
Abiram He joined with Korah and Dathan in leading a rebellion against Moses. (See *Korah.*)
Numbers 16
Abishag The beautiful girl from Shunem who nursed King David in his old age.
1 Kings 1 and 2
Abishai A nephew of King David, brother of Joab, and one of the king's generals.
1 Samuel 26:6–12; 2

Samuel 10:9–10; 16:9, 11–12; 18:2
Abner A first cousin of King Saul and commander of his army. When Saul was killed, Abner put Ishbosheth, Saul's son, on the throne. This led to war between the tribes who accepted Ishbosheth and the tribe of Judah, where David reigned. Abner became angry at the way Ishbosheth treated him and decided to support David as king of the whole of Israel. But he was murdered by David's army commander, Joab, whose brother he had killed.
1 Samuel 14:50; 2 Samuel 3
Abraham/Abram Abram's name was changed to Abraham (father of nations) when God promised to make him the founder of the Hebrew nation. Abraham's original home was the rich and splendid city of Ur on the River Euphrates. He lived there for many years with his father Terah and his three brothers. He married Sarah, his half-sister.

Terah and all his family moved from Ur to Harran, several hundred miles to the north-west. Terah died there, and God called Abraham to move on to Canaan.

Abraham obeyed. He lived as a nomad, moving from place to place with his flocks and herds. Wherever he camped, he built an altar and worshipped God. Famine drove him south to Egypt. But God told him to go back to Canaan. This was the land God promised to give the new nation. Abraham grew old, and still Sarah had no children. Following the custom of his time he had a son by Sarah's servant-woman, Hagar. But this son, Ishmael, was not the child God had promised.

When Abraham and Sarah were both old, God gave them a son – Isaac. The new nation was to come through him. Isaac was still only a boy when God tested Abraham's faith as never before. He was told to take Isaac to a distant mountain and sacrifice him there. With a heavy heart Abraham obeyed, trusting God to keep his promise about his son. Isaac was bound on the altar. The knife was raised ready to strike. Then God's angel called out, 'Do not harm the lad . . . Now I know you will obey God whatever the cost.' A ram, caught in a bush, was offered instead. Then God repeated all his promises to Abraham. 'Your descendants will be as many as the stars in the sky. And all the nations of the earth will be blessed, because you obeyed me.'

After Sarah's death, Abraham sent his trusted servant Eliezer to choose a wife for Isaac from his own family in Harran. Abraham is one of the really outstanding men of the Bible. His faith in God has made him an example for all time.

Abraham was prepared to obey God, even to the point of sacrificing his only son. But at the last moment of testing, God provided a ram caught in a thicket to be offered instead.

Genesis 11:31 – 32; 12:1ff; 17:1 – 8; 21:1 – 3; 22:1 – 14; Romans 4:1 – 3; Hebrews 11:8 – 19; James 2:21 – 23
Absalom Favourite son of King David. He rebelled against his father and plotted to become king. David's men defeated Absalom's army in the forest of Ephraim. Absalom, escaping on a mule, was caught by the head in the branches of an oak. Joab, David's general, killed him – against the king's orders.
2 Samuel 15 – 19
Achan When the Israelites conquered Jericho, Achan disobeyed God's orders and took gold, silver and fine clothes for himself. Because of this the Israelites were defeated at their next battle.
Joshua 7 – 8
Achish A king of Gath. Twice David fled to Achish from King Saul.
1 Samuel 21; 27 – 29
Adam The first man (the word 'adam' means mankind), created by God to be like himself. Adam was put in charge of all the other animal life on earth. He was to live and work in the garden God had planted in Eden, and enjoy its fruits. Only the fruit of one tree was forbidden him – the 'tree that gives knowledge of what is good and what is bad'.

God never intended the man to live alone. He made Eve – the woman – to share his life. Tempted by the thought of being wise like God, Eve took the fruit, and she and Adam both ate it. Knowing they had done wrong, Adam and Eve tried to hide from God. Their friendship with him was spoilt. Because they disobeyed God, from that day to this the whole created world has felt the effects. And every life has ended in death.

Adam and Eve were driven out of Eden. They had children. But their family brought them pain as well as joy.
Genesis 1:26 – 27; 2 – 5:5
Adonijah The fourth son of King David. When David was old, and the elder brothers were dead, Adonijah tried to seize the throne. But David had promised his wife Bathsheba that her son Solomon would succeed him. Adonijah's attempt failed. David forgave him but when Solomon was

king he had Adonijah executed when he seemed once again to be trying to seize the throne.
1 Kings 1 – 2
Agabus A Christian prophet from Jerusalem who told the church at Antioch that a great famine was coming. Later he also warned Paul that he would be imprisoned if he went to Jerusalem.
Acts 11:27 – 30; 21:7 – 14
Agrippa See *Herod*.
Ahab Seventh king of Israel (about 874 – 853 BC). He reigned from the capital city of Samaria. Ahab went to war against Syria three times, and the third time he was killed. He was a successful ruler, but the Old Testament sees him as a wicked king who did more to anger God than all the kings of Israel before him. He married Jezebel, daughter of the king of Sidon, and began worshipping Baal (Melkart), the god of Jezebel's people.

This involved him in a number of clashes with the prophet Elijah. On Mount Carmel Ahab watched Elijah stage a contest with the supporters of Baal, and win a great victory for God. When Ahab had Naboth killed so that he could take his vineyard, Elijah denounced him. Ahab died in battle at Ramoth-gilead. It was God's punishment for his sin.
1 Kings 16:29 – 34; 18; 21; 22
Ahasuerus 1. Hebrew form of the name of a Persian king known to us in its Greek version as Xerxes. Xerxes 1 (486 – 465 BC) divorced Vashti to marry Esther, a Jewish girl, and make her his queen. Ahasuerus is also mentioned in the Book of Ezra. The people of the land complained to him when the returned Jewish exiles began to rebuild Jerusalem.
Esther; Ezra 4:6
2. Father of Darius the Mede.
Daniel 9:1
Ahaz King of Judah about 732 – 716 BC (co-regent from 735 or earlier). He introduced pagan worship and even sacrificed his own son. Ahaz was defeated when Israel and Syria launched a combined attack on Judah. Rejecting the prophet Isaiah's advice, he

appealed to the Assyrian King Tiglath-pileser III for help but by doing so became his subject.
2 Kings 15:38ff.; 2 Chronicles 27:9ff.; Isaiah 7
Ahaziah 1. The son of Ahab and Jezebel. He was king of Israel after Ahab but only for a short time (about 853 – 852 BC). He followed in his father's evil ways and worshipped Baal.
1 Kings 22:40ff.; 2 Kings 1; 2 Chronicles 20:35 – 37
2. A king of Judah, the son of Jehoram (841 BC). He and his uncle, King Jehoram of Israel, with whom he had made an alliance, were murdered by Jehu.
2 Kings 8:24ff.; 2 Chronicles 22:1 – 9
Ahijah A prophet from Shiloh. Ahijah tore his dress into twelve pieces before King Jeroboam I to show how Solomon's kingdom would be divided. He told Jeroboam to take ten of these pieces, because God had chosen him to rule ten of the twelve tribes of Israel.
1 Kings 11:29ff.; 14
Ahimaaz A son of Zadok, the high priest. He risked his life as a spy for King David during Absalom's rebellion.
2 Samuel 17:17ff.; 18
Ahimelech The brave priest at Nob who helped David when he was escaping from King Saul. He gave David bread from the altar and Goliath's sword. When Saul discovered this he had Ahimelech, his fellow priests and everyone at Nob put to death.
1 Samuel 21 – 22
Ahithophel King David's trusted adviser who turned traitor and supported Absalom in his rebellion. When Absalom ignored his advice Ahithophel committed suicide.
2 Samuel 15:12 – 17: 23
Alexander The name of several men (not all necessarily different) in the New Testament.
1. Son of Simon of Cyrene, the man who carried Jesus' cross.
Mark 15:21
2. A member of the high priest's family and one of the Jewish leaders in Jerusalem.
Acts 4:6
3. A Jew who tried to speak to the crowd during the silversmiths' riot at Ephesus (see *Demetrius*).

Acts 19:33

4. A Christian who lost his faith, at least for a time.
1 Timothy 1:20

5. A coppersmith who was bitterly opposed to Paul and the gospel. Paul warned Timothy against him.
2 Timothy 4:14

Amasa King David's nephew, chosen by Absalom to lead his rebel army. After Absalom's defeat, David pardoned Amasa and made him commander of his own army in place of Joab. In revenge Joab murdered him.
2 Samuel 17:25; 20

Amaziah 1. The son of King Joash of Judah, who came to the throne when his father was assassinated. Amaziah (796-782 BC) was a good man, but victory over Edom went to his head. He challenged Israel and lost. He also brought back idols from Edom and refused to listen to God's prophet. The people plotted against him and eventually he was murdered at Lachish.
2 Kings 12:21 – 14:21;
2 Chronicles 24:27ff.

2. A priest at Bethel who opposed the prophet Amos. (See *Amos*.)
Amos 7:10ff.

Amnon The eldest son of King David. He raped Tamar, his half-sister, and in revenge Absalom had him killed.
2 Samuel 3:2; 13

Amon King of Judah after Manasseh, his father (642-640 BC). Amon refused to obey God and worshipped idols instead. After only two years he was murdered by his palace servants.
2 Kings 21:18-26;
2 Chronicles 33:20-25

Amos One of the first of God's prophets to have his messages permanently written down. Amos lived in the eighth century BC. He kept sheep and tended fig-trees at Tekoa, a hill village in Judah. But God sent him north to Bethel in Israel, where King Jeroboam I had set up a golden calf-idol. Here he bravely gave God's message of justice and judgement against oppression and greed. The cheating traders could not make up for their dishonesty simply by offering sacrifices to God.

Amaziah, the priest at Bethel, who was in the pay of the king of Israel, told Amos to pack up and take his message back to Judah. But Amos continued to warn the people of Israel of judgement and exile if they did not repent.
Amos 1:1; 7:10-15

Ananias 1. Ananias and his wife, Sapphira, gave the apostles only part of the money they received from the sale of land, though they pretended to give it all. Because of that lie, both died.
Acts 5:1-11

2. A Christian who lived in Damascus. Just after Saul (Paul) was converted, God told Ananias to go to the house where he was staying. Ananias restored Saul's sight when he had been blind for three days after seeing Jesus on the road to Damascus.
Acts 9:10-19

3. A high priest present when Paul was being questioned by the Jewish council (the Sanhedrin), and who ordered the guard to hit Paul. When Paul was tried by Felix, Ananias was the prosecutor.
Acts 23:2-3; 24:1

Andrew One of the twelve apostles chosen by Jesus. Andrew and his brother Simon Peter were fishermen from Bethsaida on the Lake of Galilee. John the Baptist told Andrew that Jesus was the 'Lamb of God'. Andrew recognized him as the Messiah (Christ) and brought his brother Peter to hear Jesus teach. Later, when they were fishing, Jesus called both brothers to follow him. Andrew brought the boy with the loaves and fishes to Jesus when he fed 5,000 hungry people. When some Greeks who had come to worship at Jerusalem wanted to see Jesus, Andrew and Philip told him about them. Andrew was with the other apostles in Jerusalem after Jesus ascended to heaven.
John 1:35-42; Matthew 4:18-19; 10:2; John 6:6-9; 12:22; Acts 1:13

Anna An old prophetess who was in the temple when Joseph and Mary brought Jesus there as a baby to dedicate him to God. Like Simeon, she recognized Jesus as the Messiah, and told others about him.
Luke 2:36-38

Annas A former high priest, Annas questioned Jesus at the time of his arrest before sending him to Caiaphas.
Luke 3:2; John 18:13-24

Antipas See *Herod*.

Apollos A Jew from Alexandria who went to Ephesus and taught in the synagogue after Paul's visit there. Aquila and Priscilla, friends of Paul, were able to teach him more about Jesus. Apollos then went to Corinth, where he spoke to the Jews with great power about Jesus as the Messiah.
Acts 18:24-28; 19:1;
1 Corinthians 16:12

Aquila A Jewish Christian who was a friend of Paul. Aquila and his wife, Priscilla (or Prisca), were forced to leave Italy when the Emperor Claudius expelled the Jews from Rome (AD 48). Like Paul they were tentmakers and for a time Paul stayed and worked with them in Corinth. When Paul travelled to Ephesus, Aquila and Priscilla went with him (see *Apollos*). Later, Aquila and Priscilla moved back to Rome. In both places Christians met in their home.
Acts 18:1-3, 18-26;
Romans 16:3;
1 Corinthians 16:19;
2 Timothy 4:19

Araunah/Ornan A man from Jerusalem who sold his threshing-floor to King David. Because of David's wrongdoing, Israel was suffering from a plague. David realized he was to blame for the trouble and obeyed God by building an altar on Araunah's threshing-floor. God saw that David was sorry for what he had done and the plague stopped. The temple was later built on this site.
2 Samuel 24:16-25;
1 Chronicles 21:18-30

Archelaus See *Herod*.

Aretas An Arabian king whose capital was Petra (in present-day Jordan). For a time Damascus was part of his territory. When Paul was in Damascus, Areta's governor planned to arrest him, but he escaped by being lowered over the walls in a basket.
2 Corinthians 11:32

Aristarchus A Macedonian Christian, a friend and fellow-worker of Paul. He was with Paul when the Ephesian

silversmiths started a riot. Aristarchus went with Paul to Jerusalem and later set off with him to Rome. When Paul was in prison in Rome he stayed with him.
Acts 19:29ff.; 20:4; 27:2;
Colossians 4:10

Artaxerxes Name of several kings of Persia. Ezra and Nehemiah probably returned to Jerusalem from exile during the reign of Artaxerxes I (464-423 BC).
Ezra 4:6-7

Asa The son of Abijah and third king of Judah. He reigned for forty-one years (about 911-870 BC). When Asa became king he tried to wipe out pagan worship. He won a great victory when a huge Ethiopian army led by Zerar attacked Judah.
1 Kings 15:8ff.;
2 Chronicles 14:1ff.

Asahel A nephew of King David. Asahel was one of David's bravest soldiers and commander of a large division of the army.
2 Samuel 2:18ff.; 23:24

Asaph A Levite who led the singing in King David's reign. His descendants served in the temple choir. Asaph wrote a number of psalms.
1 Chronicles 15:17ff.;
25:1ff.; 2 Chronicles 29:30;
35:15

Athaliah The only woman to rule over Judah (841-835 BC). She was a cruel, evil queen – like Jezebel, her mother – and put to death all the royal children except the baby Joash who was hidden by his aunt. When he was seven there was a coup. Joash was crowned king and Athaliah was killed.
2 Kings 11:1-16;
2 Chronicles 22:10 – 23;
15

Augustus Caesar The first Roman emperor, successor to Julius Caesar. He ruled from 31 BC to AD 14. Augustus ordered the census which brought Mary and Joseph to Bethlehem.
Luke 2:1

Azariah Best-known of several Azariahs is the king of Judah, also called 'Uzziah' (791-740 BC). Azariah was a good king, strong and powerful, who served God. But he still allowed his subjects to worship idols, and fame made him proud. He went into the temple to offer incense, which only the priest was allowed to do.

His punishment was a severe skin disease which forced him to live in isolation and make Jotham, his son, acting king.
2 Kings 14:21ff.; 2 Chronicles 26

Baasha A man from the tribe of Issachar who seized the throne of Israel from Nadab, son of Jeroboam, and ruled from about 909 to 886 BC.
1 Kings 15:16ff.

Balaam A prophet from Mesopotamia who was asked by Balak, king of Moab, to curse the Israelites at the time of their desert wanderings. They had just defeated the Amorites and Balak was afraid his country would suffer the same fate. At first Balaam refused to go and meet the king, but the second time he agreed. On the way, God's angel stopped Balaam's donkey and warned Balaam only to say what God told him. Instead of cursing the Israelites, Balaam blessed them three times. Later he tried to bring about the Israelites' downfall and gain the reward he had been promised by encouraging them to worship Baal. He was killed when the Israelites attacked the Midianites.
Numbers 22 – 24; 31

Balak A king of Moab who reigned at the time when the Israelites were waiting to conquer Canaan. (See *Balaam.*)
Numbers 22:2 – 24:5

Barabbas A robber and murderer accused of rebellion, in prison at the time of Jesus' arrest. The Roman governor, Pilate, knowing that Jesus was innocent of any crime and wishing to set him free, offered to release him. But the religious leaders stirred up the crowd to ask for Barabbas instead. So Barabbas was set free and Jesus was crucified.
Matthew 27:15 – 26

Barak An Israelite from Naphtali chosen by Deborah, the prophetess, to recruit a large army to fight Jabin, a Canaanite king at the time of the Judges. Barak's men won a great victory for Israel which ended twenty years of Canaanite rule.
Judges 4 – 5

Barnabas The nickname ('son of encouragement') of a Jewish Christian, born in Cyprus, who was a member of the church at Jerusalem. He was generous and warm-hearted, and he sold his land to give the money to poor Christians. When Paul came to Jerusalem after his conversion the Christians were still suspicious of him. But Barnabas welcomed him and introduced him to the apostles. The Jerusalem church sent Barnabas to Antioch to help the new Christians there, many of whom were not Jews. He went on to Tarsus to find Paul, and asked him to share in this work.
Barnabas and Paul set out together from Antioch on their first missionary journey and took John Mark, Barnabas' cousin, with them. On their return they reported to an important meeting of church leaders in Jerusalem. The two men later disagreed about asking Mark to come with them a second time. So Barnabas went back to Cyprus with Mark while Paul went on to Asia Minor (Turkey). Barnabas and Paul continued to be good friends and in his letters Paul speaks highly of Barnabas.
Acts 4:36; 9:27; 11:22ff.; 12:25ff.; 15; 1 Corinthians 9:6; Galatians 2

Bartholomew One of the twelve apostles. He was with the other apostles after Jesus ascended into heaven, but we know nothing more of him. It is possible that he was the same person as Nathaniel, the man whom Philip brought to Jesus.
Matthew 10:3; Acts 1:13

Bartimaeus A blind man healed by Jesus.
Mark 10:46 – 52

Baruch A loyal friend of Jeremiah, the prophet, during the last days of Jerusalem, just before the Babylonians captured the city in 586 BC. Baruch wrote down the messages God gave Jeremiah. He stayed with Jeremiah after Jerusalem was destroyed, even when he was forced to go to Egypt. One of the books in the Apocrypha/Deutero-canonicals is named after him.
Jeremiah 36; 43:6

Barzillai A loyal supporter of King David. He fed David and his men at Mahanaim during Absalom's rebellion.
2 Samuel 17:27ff; 19:31 – 39

Bathsheba Wife first of Uriah the Hittite and then of King David. (See *David.*)
2 Samuel 11 – 12; 1 Kings 1 – 2

Belshazzar Ruler of Babylon, killed when Babylon was captured in 539 BC by the Medes and Persians. He had been acting king, ruling in the absence of his father Nabonidus. During a great banquet he was frightened by strange writing on the wall of his dining-hall. Daniel was called to translate the words. He warned Belshazzar that God had judged his kingdom and it had failed. Belshazzar would lose his life and Babylon would be conquered. That very night the Persian army took the city by surprise.
Daniel 5

Belteshazzar This Babylonian name was given to Daniel. (See *Daniel.*)

Benaiah The best-known of several men of this name is the captain of King David's bodyguard who remained loyal when Adonijah tried to seize the throne. Benaiah played a leading part in proclaiming Solomon king, and became commander of his army.
2 Samuel 8:18; 1 Kings 1 – 2

Benhadad Name of three kings of Syria, probably meaning 'son of Hadad' (the Syrian storm-god). Benhadad I (about 900 – 860 BC) helped Asa, king of Judah, against Israel. Benhadad II (about 860 – 843 BC) was an enemy of Ahab, king of Israel. Benhadad III (about 796 – 770 BC) went to war against Israel in the time of Elisha, the prophet. God freed the Israelites from the Syrians several times in answer to Elisha's prayers. He revealed to Elisha that Benhadad would die at the hands of his servant, Hazael.
1 Kings 20; 2 Kings 6 – 8

Benjamin Youngest son of Jacob and Rachel. His mother died when he was born. With his brother Joseph he was the special favourite of his father. Their jealous half-brothers sold Joseph into Egypt. Later, when the brothers were in Joseph's power in Egypt, he tested them to see if they would be equally cruel to Benjamin. But the brothers were changed men. They would not leave Benjamin behind in Egypt, even to save themselves. One of the twelve tribes of Israel was named after Benjamin.
Genesis 35:18 – 20; 43 – 45

Bernice The sister of Herod Agrippa II. (See *Herod Agrippa II.*)
Acts 25:13ff.

Bezalel A skilled craftsman in charge of making the worship tent (tabernacle) when the Israelites were in the desert.
Exodus 35:30ff.

Bildad One of Job's three friends who talked to him in his suffering.
Job 2:11, etc.

Bilhah Rachel's servant, who became the mother of Dan and Naphtali.
Genesis 29:29; 30:3 – 7

Boaz Hero of the Book of Ruth. Boaz was a rich and generous farmer in Bethlehem who married Ruth and became the great-grandfather of King David.
Ruth 2 – 4

Caesar The title of Roman emperors in New Testament times. Augustus reigned when Jesus was born. Tiberius reigned after him. Peter and Paul were probably martyred when Nero was Caesar. Jesus sometimes used the word to mean 'the ruling power'.
Mark 12:14 – 17; Luke 2:1; 3:1; Acts 25

Caiaphas High Priest in Jerusalem AD 18 – 36. At the trial of Jesus he and his father-in-law, Annas, found Jesus guilty of blasphemy and sent him to Pilate for sentence. Caiaphas was the high priest mentioned in Acts, who persecuted the first Christians.
Matthew 26:3, 57ff.; Luke 3:2; John 18:13ff.; Acts 5:17ff.

Cain Eldest son of Adam and Eve. He worked as a farmer. His brother Abel was a shepherd. Because God was pleased with Abel's offering of a lamb, but not with Cain's offering from his harvest, Cain was furious. In a fit of jealous anger he killed Abel, and as punishment lived the rest of his life as a nomad.
Genesis 4; 1 John 3:12

Caleb A spy sent by Moses to find out all he could about Canaan and

the people who lived there. Of the twelve spies who reported on what they had seen, only Caleb and Joshua believed God would make it possible to conquer the land. Because of their confidence in God, Caleb and Joshua were allowed to settle in Canaan – all the other Israelites born in Egypt died in the desert.
Numbers 13 – 14; Joshua 14:6ff.

Canaan Son of Ham. Because of his disrespect, Noah, his grandfather, put a curse on Canaan and his descendants (the Canaanites).
Genesis 9:18–27

Cephas See *Peter*.

Chedorlaomer A king of Elam.
Genesis 14

Claudius The fourth Roman emperor. Claudius reigned AD 41–54. During this time the famine predicted by the Christian prophet Agabus took place. Towards the end of his reign Claudius forced all Jews to leave Rome.
Acts 11:28; 18:2

Claudius Lysias A commander of the Roman garrison at Jerusalem who rescued Paul when an angry crowd of Jews was about to kill him. Claudius Lysias arrested Paul and allowed the Jewish council (the Sanhedrin) to question him, but the session ended in chaos. When he heard about a plot to murder Paul, Claudius Lysias sent him to Caesarea for trial by Felix, the Roman governor.
Acts 21:31 – 23:30

Clement A Philippian Christian who shared in Paul's work.
Philippians 4:3

Cleopas On the day Jesus rose from the dead Cleopas and a friend were walking from Jerusalem to Emmaus. They had thought Jesus was the Messiah and were puzzled about his death and the report that he was alive again. A man joined them. As he explained the Old Testament passages about the Messiah it was as if 'a fire burned within them'. At Emmaus, Cleopas and his friend invited the stranger to join them for a meal. As he asked God's blessing on the food and broke bread they realized it was Jesus. They went to Jerusalem at once to share the news with the other disciples.

Luke 24:13–53

Cornelius A Roman army captain (centurion) stationed at Caesarea. He worshipped God and gave generously to poor people. In a dream, an angel told Cornelius to send for Peter, who was at Joppa (see *Peter*). At Cornelius' house Peter found a crowd of the soldier's friends and relatives eagerly waiting to hear him. They believed and were baptized: the first group of non-Jewish converts to Christianity.
Acts 10

Crescens A friend of Paul. Crescens was with Paul when he was a prisoner in Rome but left him to go and work in Galatia.
2 Timothy 4:10

Crispus Chief official of the Jewish synagogue in Corinth. He and his family were converted and baptized by Paul.
Acts 18:8; 1 Corinthians 1:14

Cushan-Rishathaim A king of Mesopotamia who ruled over the Israelites for eight years during the time of the Judges.
Judges 3:7–10

Cyrus The Persian king who captured Babylon in 539 BC. Cyrus allowed the Jews exiled in Babylon to return to Jerusalem to rebuild the temple. He sent back with them all the treasures taken from the temple by Nebuchadnezzar and gave them a large sum of money to help with the work. Isaiah declared that Cyrus was chosen by God to be king and to free the Jewish captives. The later stories about Daniel took place in the reign of Cyrus.
Ezra 1:1ff. – 6:14; Isaiah 4:28ff.; Daniel 6:28

Daniel Best-known of several Old Testament Daniels is the high-born Jew who was taken captive to Babylon, probably in his teens. At the court of King Nebuchadnezzar Daniel and his three friends, Shadrach, Meshach and Abednego, were trained to be counsellors to the king. Daniel was determined still to obey God. He refused the rich food he was given and instead grew strong on the simple diet allowed by Jewish food-laws.

God gave Daniel great wisdom. Twice he was able to tell Nebuchadnezzar the meaning of strange dreams. Daniel later explained to Belshazzar (who held power after Nebuchadnezzar) the writing that appeared on his wall: the kingdom was about to be over-thrown. That same night Belshazzar was killed and the Persians captured Babylon.

They made Daniel an important official, but the other leaders were jealous of his power and plotted his downfall. Daniel was thrown into the lions' den, but God saved his life.

Daniel also recorded a number of dreams in which God told him of his plans for the future.

Darius 1. Darius the Mede is named in the Book of Daniel as ruler after Belshazzar. Darius is not otherwise known from contemporary records (which give a far from complete picture). Cyrus may have made Darius ruler of Babylon, or may even have used the name Darius himself.
Daniel 5:31ff.
2. Darius I of Persia (522–486 BC), who encouraged the Jews to finish rebuilding the temple.
Ezra 4:5; Haggai 1:1; Zechariah 1:1

This tiny cylinder seal of the Persian King Darius pictures him hunting lions.

3. Darius II of Persia (423–408 BC), mentioned in the Book of Nehemiah.
Nehemiah 12:22

Dathan Joined with Korah and Abiram in leading a rebellion against Moses. (See *Korah*.)
Numbers 16

David Youngest of the eight sons of Jesse, a farmer at Bethlehem. David was a shepherd. He was looking after the flocks when Samuel the prophet came to Bethlehem, sent by God to anoint one of the sons of Jesse as king in place of Saul. When David was chosen his brothers were jealous.

David's skill in playing the harp took him to Saul's court, to soothe the king in his fits of madness. Later, when he was sent to take food to his brothers in the army, David took up the challenge to fight Goliath, the giant champion of the Philistines. He killed him with a stone from his shepherd's sling. After the battle the women came out to meet Saul. 'Saul has killed thousands, but David tens of thousands,' they sang. From then on Saul became very jealous of David and several times tried to kill him. Jonathan, Saul's son and David's close friend, warned him to escape and he became an outlaw. Saul hunted him without mercy, although David twice spared his life.

Saul and Jonathan were killed in battle against the Philistines, and David was crowned in Judah. But it was two years before all Israel accepted him as king. David was a brave soldier and won many victories. He was very popular with the people and ruled them well. When he had captured Jerusalem from the Jebusites David made it his capital. He brought the Covenant Box (the ark) there and planned to build a temple but God forbade it.

David made love to Bathsheba, wife of Uriah, one of his soldiers.When Bathsheba became pregnant David ordered Uriah to the front line and made sure he was killed. David then married Bathsheba. The prophet Nathan denounced his sin and although the king was genuinely sorry and God forgave him, Bathsheba's child died. Their next son, Solomon, was David's heir.

Later there was trouble between David's sons. Absalom, his favourite son, tried to seize the throne. David was forced to leave Jerusalem, but Absalom was defeated and killed, to David's great distress. When he was old, Adonijah, another son, plotted against him.

David was a great king, a great soldier and a great poet, who wrote many beautiful psalms of praise to God. Although he made mistakes and did wrong, he never failed to repent and ask God to forgive him. The Bible describes him as 'a man after God's own heart'.
1 Samuel 16ff. – 1 Kings 2; 1 Chronicles 11 – 29

Deborah The only woman who was a Judge of Israel. Deborah encouraged General Barak to fight against Sisera, commander of the army of Jabin, a Canaanite king. The resulting victory ended twenty years of Canaanite oppression.
Judges 4 – 5

Delilah A beautiful Philistine woman who betrayed Samson. (See *Samson.*)
Judges 16

Demas A Christian who was with Paul when he was a prisoner in Rome. He later deserted Paul and went off to Thessalonica.
Colossians 4:14; 2 Timothy 4:10

Demetrius 1. A silversmith in Ephesus who made souvenirs at the temple of Diana (Artemis) – see below. He was afraid that as a result of Paul's preaching the visitors

would no longer buy these models, and so he encouraged other men in the same business to riot.
Acts 19:24ff.
2. A Christian mentioned in John's third letter, of whom everyone spoke well.
3 John 12

Diana Roman goddess of the moon and hunting, called Artemis by the Greeks. Her magnificent temple at Ephesus was one of the wonders of the ancient world. (See also Part 11: *Nations and Peoples of the Bible,* under *Greek and Roman Religion.*)
Acts 19

Dinah The daughter of Jacob and Leah raped by Shechem, son of a Hivite king. In revenge Dinah's brothers killed Shechem and the men from his city.
Genesis 34

Dionysius A member of the Areopagus, a powerful council at Athens set up to hear religious cases. Dionysius was converted to Christianity when Paul was asked to address the council.
Acts 17:34

Diotrephes A proud and awkward church leader who refused to accept John's authority.
3 John 9–10

Doeg An Edomite who was King Saul's chief herdsman. He was at Nob when Ahimelech the priest fed and armed the escaping David. Doeg betrayed Ahimelech, and then carried out the executions Saul ordered.
1 Samuel 21:7; 22:9ff.

Dorcas/Tabitha A Christian from Joppa who helped the poor by making clothes for them. When she died her friends sent for Peter, and he brought her back to life.
Acts 9:36–41

Drusilla The youngest daughter of Herod Agrippa I and wife of the Roman governor Felix. (See *Felix.*)
Acts 24:24

Ebed-melech An Ethiopian who was one of King Zedekiah's palace officials (sixth century BC). Because he saved Jeremiah's life God promised that Ebed-melech would not be killed when Jerusalem was destroyed.
Jeremiah 38; 39:16–18

Eglon A king of Moab in the time of the Judges. He defeated Israel and captured Jericho, keeping

the Israelites subject for eighteen years. He was murdered by Ehud.
Judges 3:12–26

Ehud A left-handed Israelite from the tribe of Benjamin. Ehud thought up a cunning and daring plot to kill King Eglon of Moab who had oppressed part of Israel, including the eastern section of the land belonging to Ehud's tribe, for eighteen years. With Eglon dead, Ehud gathered an army to defeat the Moabites and free his people.
Judges 3:15–30

Elah Best-known man of this name in the Old Testament is the son of King Baasha. Elah was an evil king who reigned over Israel for less than two years (886–885 BC). While drunk he was killed by Zimri, a general in his army.
1 Kings 16:8–14

Eleazar The most important of several Eleazars was Aaron's third son. Eleazar's two elder brothers were killed, so he became high priest when Aaron died. He was in charge of the Levites and supervised everything to do with the worship tent (tabernacle).
Exodus 6:23; Leviticus 10; Numbers 3ff; Joshua 14, etc.

Eli A Judge and priest in Israel. Samuel's mother (see *Hannah*) took her son to Eli to be trained in the shrine at Shiloh. Eli's two sons, Hophni and Phinehas, were a disgrace. They would not listen to their father, and God warned Eli of their terrible fate. Later, they were both killed in a battle against the Philistines and God's Covenant Box (the ark) was captured. When Eli heard the news he collapsed and died.
1 Samuel 1 – 4

Eliab Jesse's eldest son, the brother of David.
1 Samuel 16:6ff.; 17:13, 28

Eliakim The most important man of this name was the son of Hilkiah, King Hezekiah's chief palace official. When King Sennacherib of Assyria threatened to besiege Jerusalem Hezekiah sent Eliakim, along with Shebna and Joah, to hear the Assyrian spokesmen.
2 Kings 18:18ff.; Isaiah 36 – 37:6

Eliashib A high priest in

the time of Nehemiah who helped rebuild the walls of Jerusalem.
Nehemiah 3:1; 13:4–9

Eliezer Abraham's chief servant. Before Abraham had a son, Eliezer was his heir. It was presumably Eliezer who was trusted with the task of going to Mesopotamia to choose a wife for Isaac.
Genesis 15:2; 24

Elihu The angry young man in the story of Job who wrongly insisted that the reason for Job's suffering must be Job's own sin.
Job 32 – 37

Elijah A prophet who lived in Israel during the reign of King Ahab. Ahab and his foreign queen, Jezebel, sinned against God by worshipping Baal and killing God's prophets. Because of this, Elijah was sent to tell Ahab that God was sending a drought. Then Elijah went into hiding by the Brook Cherith, where ravens brought him food. When the brook dried up, he went to Zarephath in Sidon and stayed with a widow and her household. She shared the last of her food with Elijah, but God renewed her supply of flour and oil until the famine was over. When the widow's son died, God answered Elijah's prayer and brought him back to life.

In the third year of the drought Elijah went back to Ahab. The king accused him of causing Israel's troubles. 'I'm not the troublemaker,' Elijah replied. 'You are – you and your father. You are disobeying the Lord's commands and worshipping the idols of Baal.' He told Ahab to send the prophets of Baal and Asherah to Mt Carmel. There Elijah challenged them to prove that their god was real. If Baal could set fire to their sacrifice then the people would worship him; but if God sent fire to burn up Elijah's sacrifice, that would prove he was the true God. The prophets of Baal danced, prayed, and cut themselves all day, but nothing happened. When Elijah prayed to God the fire fell and burnt his sacrifice. All the people shouted, 'The Lord, he is God.' The priests of Baal were killed – and that same day the drought ended.

Jezebel was furious when she heard her prophets had been killed. Elijah ran away south into the desert to save his life. He felt alone and near to despair. But God spoke to him. He told Elijah there was work still to do. He was to anoint a new king and train Elisha to take over his work.

Later, when Ahab had Naboth killed in order to seize his vineyard, Elijah warned the king that God would punish his whole family. Ahab was killed in battle, but God protected Elijah. When his work was finished, God took him to heaven in a chariot of fire.

The prophet Malachi foretold that Elijah would return: much later he appeared with Moses when the disciples saw Jesus' glory (the transfiguration).
1 Kings 17 – 2 Kings 2; Malachi 4:5 – 6; Luke 9:28ff.

Elimelech See *Naomi.*

Eliphaz One of Job's three friends who came to him in his suffering.
Job 2:11ff.

Elisha Elisha carried on Elijah's work as God's prophet in Israel for more than fifty years. Before Elijah was taken up into heaven, Elisha asked for the share of his power that would make him Elijah's successor. This request was granted. Elisha worked a number of miracles. He brought the Shunammite woman's son back to life and healed Naaman, the Syrian general, of leprosy. Elisha lived through the reigns of six kings of Israel.
1 Kings 19:16ff.; 2 Kings 2 – 9; 13:14ff.

Elizabeth Wife of Zechariah, the priest. Elizabeth had been unable to have children. But to her joy, in old age she became the mother of John the Baptist. Mary, Jesus' mother, was a relative of Elizabeth and visited her before the babies were born. Elizabeth knew at once that Mary's child was the long-awaited 'Lord' (Messiah).
Luke 1

Elkanah Best-known of several men of this name is Samuel's father, the husband of Hannah. (See *Hannah.*)
1 Samuel 1

Elymas/Bar-Jesus A Jewish magician and false prophet at the court of Sergius Paulus, the Roman governor of Cyprus. Elymas was afraid that he would lose his influence if Sergius Paulus became a Christian, so he tried to stop him believing the message preached by Paul and Barnabas. Paul was angry with him for turning God's truths into lies. Elymas was blind for some time as a punishment. When Sergius Paulus saw this, he believed in God.
Acts 13:6 – 12

Enoch A descendant of Adam's son, Seth. He lived in such close friendship with God that the Bible says he did not die. Instead 'God took him away'.
Genesis 5:22; Hebrews 11:5

Epaphras A Christian who founded the church at Colossae. Epaphras visited Paul when he was in prison in Rome and gave him news about the Colossian Christians. As a result Paul wrote his letter to them.
Colossians 1:7 – 8; 4:12; Philemon 23

Epaphroditus A Christian from the church at Philippi. When Paul was in prison in Rome, members of the Philippian church sent Epaphroditus to Rome with a gift.
Philippians 2:25 – 30; 4:18

Ephraim The younger of Joseph's two sons, born in Egypt. Ephraim was adopted by Jacob, his grandfather, and received a greater blessing from him than Manasseh, his elder brother. The tribe which descended from him was an important one. Israel is sometimes called Ephraim by the prophets.
Genesis 41:52; 48

Erastus 1. An assistant of Paul who went with Timothy to work in Macedonia (Greece) while Paul stayed on in Asia Minor (Turkey).
Acts 19:22; 2 Timothy 4:20
2. The city treasurer at Corinth. Erastus was a Christian and sent his greetings to the church in Rome.
Romans 16:23

Esarhaddon Son of Sennacherib. He became king of Assyria (680 – 669 BC) when his father was murdered. Manasseh, king of Judah, was one of many minor kings who were subject to Esarhaddon.
2 Kings 19:37; Ezra 4:2

Esau The (elder) twin brother of Jacob; son of Isaac and Rebekah. He became a hunter, and cared so little about the promises of God that one day when he came in hungry Esau 'sold' Jacob the rights of the elder son in return for food. When Jacob also gained Isaac's blessing by a trick, Esau was angry. Afraid of what he might do, Jacob left home.

In the years that Jacob was away, Esau settled in the area around Mt Seir and became rich. When they met again Esau greeted his brother warmly and accepted his gift of livestock. Esau went back to Seir and founded the nation of Edom, while Jacob went into Canaan. But there was continued trouble between their descendants.
Genesis 25:21ff.; 27 – 28:9; 32 – 33; Hebrews 12:16 – 17

Esther A Jewish girl who became queen of Persia. Esther was an orphan brought up in Susa, capital of Persia, by her cousin Mordecai. After King Ahasuerus (Greek Xerxes) had divorced Vashti he chose Esther as his new queen. Esther kept secret the fact that she was a Jewess. When Haman, the king's chief minister, planned to wipe out all the Jews because he so hated Mordecai, Esther pleaded with the king and uncovered the plot. Instead of being destroyed, the Jews were allowed to kill all their enemies. This event is remembered at the annual Feast of Purim.
Esther

Eunice Mother of Timothy.
Acts 16:1; 2 Timothy 1:5

Eutychus A young man who went to hear Paul preach in Troas. It was late and Eutychus went so sound asleep that he fell to his death from the third-floor window where he was sitting. Paul went down and brought him back to life.
Acts 20:7 – 13

Eve The first woman, and companion to Adam. She and Adam disobeyed God's command not to eat the fruit of the 'tree that gives knowledge'. Because of this, death came into the world and God sent them out of the Garden of Eden. Genesis names three sons of Eve: Cain, Abel and Seth.
Genesis 2:18 – 4:2; 4:25

Evil-Merodach King of Babylon 562 – 560 BC. When he came to the throne he released King Jehoiachin of Judah from prison in Babylon.
2 Kings 25:27 – 30; Jeremiah 52:31 – 34

Ezekiel One of the great Old Testament prophets. Ezekiel was the son of a priest called Buzi and lived in Jerusalem until Nebuchadnezzar invaded the city in 597 BC. Along with King Jehoiachin and other important citizens he was taken captive to Babylon. There he was allowed to have his own house and lived in a settlement of Jewish exiles at Talabib on the River Chebar. After about four years he was called by God to be a prophet. Until Jerusalem was completely destroyed in 586 BC his main message was a call to repentance. The Jews had disobeyed God and must seek forgiveness. After the Babylonians had overthrown Jerusalem Ezekiel looked forward to the day when God would allow the Jews to rebuild the city and God's temple.
Ezekiel 1:1 – 3; 20:33 – 37; 36:26 – 33; 43:1 – 5, etc.

Ezra A priest and teacher of the Law at the time of the exile. Ezra was given permission by King Artaxerxes to lead a large group of Jewish exiles back from Babylon to Jerusalem. The temple had been rebuilt, but when Ezra arrived he was distressed to find that the people no longer obeyed God's laws, even after all that had happened. Many Jews, including priests, had married women from nations that did not worship God. Ezra put an end to these mixed marriages. He taught the people God's laws and they turned to God again with new joy.
Ezra 7 – 10; Nehemiah 8 – 9

Felix The Roman governor before whom Paul was brought for trial at Caesarea. He kept Paul in prison for two years, hoping for a bribe.
Acts 23:24; 24:1 – 27

Festus The Roman governor of Palestine after

Felix. He listened carefully to Paul and called him to defend himself before King Herod Agrippa II and Bernice. He agreed with them that Paul was innocent of any crime. But Paul had appealed to Caesar, and would have to go to Rome for trial.
Acts 25 – 26

Gabriel An angel who was God's special messenger. Gabriel was sent to Daniel twice: once to tell him the meaning of a dream and later to predict what was going to happen to Jerusalem. Gabriel was also sent to announce the birth of John the Baptist to Zechariah, and of Jesus to Mary.
Daniel 8:16; 9:21; Luke 1:11–20, 26–38

Gad Seventh son of Jacob, who gave his name to the tribe of Gad.
Numbers 32

Gaius 1. A Macedonian Christian who was with Paul on his third missionary journey. Gaius was dragged into the amphitheatre during the Ephesian silversmiths' riot (See *Demetrius.*)
Acts 19:29
2. A Christian from Derbe who travelled with Paul to Jerusalem.
Acts 20:4
3. One of the few Christians Paul baptized at Corinth.
1 Corinthians 1:14
4. The Christian friend to whom John addressed his third letter.
3 John 1
These may not all be different people.

Gallio The Roman governor of Achaia, about AD 51–53. Gallio was the Emperor Nero's tutor and the brother of Seneca, the philosopher. While Gallio was governor of Achaia he was based at Corinth. When Paul was in Corinth Jews who were worried about the success of his preaching tried to persuade Gallio to condemn him. However, Gallio refused to get involved with Jewish laws, and as a result Paul was able to continue his work.
Acts 18:12–17

Gamaliel A famous Pharisee, Paul's teacher, and a member of the supreme Jewish council, the Sanhedrin. When the apostles were arrested and questioned, some of the council wanted to put them to death. But

Gamaliel advised caution. 'Leave them alone!' he said. 'If what they have planned and done is of human origin, it will disappear, but if it comes from God, you cannot possibly defeat it.'
Acts 5:34ff.; 22:3

Gedaliah Best-known of several Gedaliahs is the man appointed governor of Judah by King Nebuchadnezzar of Babylon after he had captured Jerusalem. After seven months he was murdered by Ishmael, a member of the royal family. The Jews still living in Judah were afraid that the Babylonians would treat this murder as rebellion, and fled to Egypt.
2 Kings 25:22–26; Jeremiah 39:14 – 41:18

Gehazi Servant of the prophet Elisha. When Naaman came to Elisha to be cured of leprosy, Gehazi took the gift which the prophet refused. He lied to Elisha and as punishment became a leper himself. He continued as Elisha's servant and spoke to King Jehoram about the wonderful things Elisha had done.
2 Kings 4 – 5; 8:4ff.

Gershon Levi's eldest son. Gershon and his descendents formed one of the three groups of Levites.
Exodus 6:16–17; Numbers 3:17ff.

Geshem An influential Arabian who tried to stop Nehemiah rebuilding the walls of Jerusalem.
Nehemiah 2:19; 6:1ff.

Gideon The 'Judge' of Israel who defeated the Midianites, one of Israel's greatest enemies at that time. Gideon was secretly threshing his crop when God's angel messenger called to him to rescue Israel from the Midianites. To make sure that the call was from God he put it to the test. Twice God gave him the sign he asked for.
Gideon chose 300 men from the thousands who followed him. These were divided into three groups. Armed with an empty pitcher, a torch and a trumpet, they surprised the enemy at night with a tremendous shout, 'the sword of the Lord and of Gideon'. Panic broke out in the army of Midian. They turned on each other and

then fled, with the Israelites in hot pursuit. Victory was complete and Gideon gave the land peace for forty years until his death.
Judges 6:11–23, 36–39; 7:1–23

Gog Described in the Book of Ezekiel as the ruler of Magog and the prince of Meshech and Tubal. They invade from the north and Israel wins a great victory over them. In Revelation, Gog and Magog, led by Satan, are totally destroyed by God himself.
Ezekiel 38 – 39; Revelation 20:7–9

Goliath The 9-ft (3-metre) Philistine giant from Gath who was killed by David. The stone from David's sling stunned the giant and he fell to the ground. David then drew Goliath's sword and cut off his head. The Philistine army fled.
1 Samuel 17

Gomer Unfaithful wife of the prophet Hosea. (See *Hosea.*)
Hosea 1 – 3

Habakkuk A prophet to Judah who lived at the end of the seventh century BC, the time of Jeremiah. The Chaldaeans were becoming more and more powerful and Habakkuk found it hard to understand how God could use this wicked nation to punish his people. The answer came that God would one day judge all who were proud and wicked, including Judah's enemies.
Habakkuk

Hadadezer/Hadarezer A king of Zobah in Syria. Three times King David defeated Hadadezer's troops. After the third defeat the people of Zobah became David's subjects.
2 Samuel 8 – 10; 1 Chronicles 18 – 19

Hagar Sarah's servant. Abraham took her as his secondary wife (concubine) when it seemed God's promise that his descendants would become a great nation could not come true because he had no children. Hagar became pregnant and ran away into the desert because Sarah treated her unkindly. An angel told Hagar to return and promised that her son Ishmael would be the founder of a nation.

Ishmael was about fourteen years old when Sarah's son, Isaac, was born. When Ishmael made fun of Isaac Sarah asked Abraham to send Hagar and her son away. Hagar travelled through the desert until all her water was gone. Death seemed near, but instead an angel showed her a well and repeated God's promise about Ishmael.
Genesis 16; 21

Haggai A prophet who probably returned from Babylon to Jerusalem in the party led by Zerubbabel. His message, recorded in the Book of Haggai, was given in 520 BC. Haggai was concerned to find that the people had built houses for themselves and were living in comfort while God's temple was still in ruins. He urged the people to rebuild it.
Haggai

Ham Noah's second son. Ham was the founder of the Egyptian, Ethiopian, Libyan and Canaanite nations.
Genesis 5:32; 6:10; 10:6–20

Haman The chief minister of King Ahasuerus of Persia. He hated the Jew Mordecai for refusing to bow down to him, and plotted to kill Mordecai and all the Jewish people in Persia. Haman was hanged when Queen Esther revealed his plot to the king.
Esther 3 – 9

Hanamel A cousin of Jeremiah. When Jerusalem was about to be captured by the Babylonians Hanamel wanted to sell a field he owned. Jeremiah bought the field to show his belief that one day Judah would no longer be ruled by Babylon and it would be worth owning land again.
Jeremiah 32

Hanani Best-known of several Hananis is the man who travelled to Susa to tell Nehemiah that Jerusalem was still in ruins, even though the Jewish exiles had returned. When Nehemiah had rebuilt the walls of Jerusalem he made Hanani governor.
Nehemiah 1:2; 7:2

Hananiah A false prophet who told people in Judah they would be free of Babylonian rule after two years.
Jeremiah 28

Hannah The wife of Elkanah and mother of Samuel. For several years Hannah had no children. While she was making her annual visit to the shrine at Shiloh Hannah made a vow. She promised God that if he gave her a son, she would give him back to serve God. When Samuel was old enough Hannah took him to Shiloh where he helped Eli, the priest. Mary, the mother of Jesus, echoed Hannah's wonderful prayer of thanks to God before Jesus was born. Hannah became the mother of three other sons and two daughters.
1 Samuel 1 – 2

Hazael An officer at the court of Benhadad II whom God told Elijah to anoint as king of Syria. Elisha wept when God showed him what Hazael would do to the Israelites. Hazael killed Benhadad and seized the throne. He made war against the kings of Israel and Judah.
1 Kings 19:15 – 17; 2 Kings 8ff.

Herod 1. Herod the Great. Son of Antipater, who was made pro-curator of Judea by Julius Caesar in 47 BC. Antipater appointed Herod to be governor of Galilee. After the death of his father and brother Joseph, who was governor of Jerusalem, the Romans gave Herod the title 'king of the Jews'. He reigned from 37 – 4 BC. Herod was hated by the Jews, although he spent large sums of money on the temple. He was not a Jew by birth and murdered members of the Jewish Hasmonaean family whom he saw as a threat to the throne. When the wise men came to worship the baby Jesus he again felt threatened and ordered the murder of all children in Bethlehem under two years old. After his death his kingdom was divided amongst three of his sons: Archelaus, Antipas and Philip.
Matthew 2; Luke 1:5
2. Archelaus, called Herod the Ethnarch, ruled Judea 4 BC – AD 6. When Mary and Joseph returned with Jesus from Egypt and heard that Archelaus was ruler of Judea they decided to settle in Galilee instead. Archelaus treated the Jews and Samaritans so cruelly that they

complained to the Romans, who sent him into exile.
Matthew 2:22
3. Antipas, called Herod the Tetrarch, ruled Galilee 4 BC – AD 39. He imprisoned John the Baptist and as a result of a rash promise agreed to his wife's request to have him beheaded. Pilate handed Jesus over to Antipas for trial because he came from Galilee. Antipas treated Jesus with scorn and then sent him back to Pilate.
Matthew 14; Mark 6; Luke 23:7ff.
4. Agrippa I, called Herod the King, was son of Aristobulus and grandson of Herod the Great. He became ruler of Galilee, Judea and Samaria. To please the Jews he persecuted the Christians. He killed James, the son of Zebedee, and imprisoned Peter. Luke, the writer of Acts, records that Agrippa's death in AD 44 was a result of his pride.
Acts 12
5. Agrippa II was the son of Agrippa I. When he went to Caesarea to visit the Roman governor, Festus, he heard Paul's case. His verdict was that Paul could have been released if he had not appealed to Caesar.
Acts 25:13 – 26:32

Herodias The wife of Herod Antipas. Herod married Herodias while Philip, her first husband, was still alive. Because John the Baptist condemned the marriage, Herodias had him beheaded.
Matthew 14; Mark 6; Luke 3:19

Hezekiah King of Judah 716 – 687 BC (co-regent from 729) after his father, King Ahaz. As soon as he became king, Hezekiah re-opened and repaired the temple. He organized a national campaign to destroy everything to do with idol worship. Hezekiah rebelled against the Assyrians and refused to pay taxes to them. During his reign the northern kingdom of Israel was completely conquered by Assyria. Hezekiah realized that his country was also threatened. He cut a rock tunnel to ensure Jerusalem's water supply in the event of siege. King Sennacherib of Assyria captured several cities in

Judah and surrounded Jerusalem. Judah was saved when death struck the Assyrian army overnight. Soon after this, Hezekiah became very ill but God answered his prayer and gave him another fifteen years to live.
2 Kings 18 – 20; 2 Chronicles 29 – 32; Isaiah 36 – 39

Hilkiah Best-known of several Hilkiahs is the high priest who lived in the reign of King Josiah of Judah. While the temple was being repaired he found an old scroll with God's laws written on it. This discovery led to a great reform in the worship at the temple.
2 Kings 22 – 23; 2 Chronicles 34

Hiram 1. A king of Tyre who was a friend of King David and King Solomon. He sent cedar-wood from Lebanon to Jerusalem for the building of David's palace and later for Solomon's temple.
2 Samuel 5:11; 1 Kings 5; 9 – 10
2. A craftsman sent by King Hiram to help King Solomon build his palace and the temple.
1 Kings 7

Hophni and Phinehas Eli's two sons, priests at Shiloh. Because they showed open contempt for God, he forewarned Eli of their death. Hophni and Phinehas carried God's Covenant Box (the ark) into battle against the Philistines. It was captured and they were both killed.
1 Samuel 2:12ff.; 4

Hosea A prophet in the northern kingdom of Israel, from the time of Jeroboam II until just before the Assyrians captured Samaria in 722 BC. Hosea used his unhappy experience of marriage to an unfaithful wife as a picture of the way God's people had deserted him. Yet despite this, God promised: 'I will bring my people back to me. I will love them with all my heart.' Hosea

Hoshea The last king of Israel. Hoshea made himself king by killing King Pekah. He was defeated by King Shalmaneser V of Assyria and as a result had to pay him tribute. When Hoshea rebelled he was imprisoned by Shalmaneser. Three years later Samaria, the capital

of Israel, was captured and the people taken away to Assyria.
2 Kings 17

Huldah A prophetess who lived in the reign of King Josiah. When Hilkiah the priest found an ancient scroll of God's Law in the temple Josiah asked her advice.
2 Kings 22:14ff.; 2 Chronicles 34:22ff.

Hushai A trusted friend of King David. During Absalom's rebellion Hushai pretended to go over to Absalom's side. His misleading 'advice' won time for David and he enabled him to escape by informing David's spies of Absalom's plans.
2 Samuel 15:32 – 17:15

Hymenaeus A man who was thrown out of the church by Paul because he taught things which were not true and weakened the faith of some Christians.
1 Timothy 1:20; 2 Timothy 2:17

Isaac The son God promised to Abraham and Sarah. He was born when his parents were very old. A few years after Isaac's birth God tested Abraham's faith even more. He told Abraham to sacrifice his son. Just as he was about to kill Isaac, an angel stopped him. God rewarded Abraham and again promised that his descendants would be a great nation.
When Isaac was forty he married Rebekah, a girl chosen for him from Abraham's family in Harran. After many years God answered Isaac's prayer for a son and the twins, Esau and Jacob, were born. God gave Isaac the same blessing he had given Abraham.
When Isaac was old and nearly blind he was tricked into passing the blessing on to Jacob instead of Esau, the older twin. Jacob left home but returned several years later in time to see his father before he died.
Genesis 21 – 22; 24 – 28:9; 35:27 – 29

Isaiah A great prophet who lived in Jerusalem in the reigns of Uzziah, Jotham, Ahaz and Hezekiah. When God called Isaiah to be a prophet he was in the temple. He was given a vision of the glory of God 'the Holy One', and his own sin was forgiven. Now he could speak God's words to the people. Isaiah was married to a prophetess. He had two sons and gave them special names as a sign of what God was going to do.

During Isaiah's time, Judah was in danger of attack from the powerful Assyrian army. When Jerusalem was besieged he encouraged King Hezekiah to trust God and not surrender. After this Hezekiah became very ill. Isaiah prayed and God gave Hezekiah a sign that he would let him live another fifteen years. Isaiah's message gave the people of Judah hope. They could not escape the consequences of their disobedience, but in time God would destroy their enemies and bring them back from exile. Isaiah also looked forward to the time when God's servant, the Messiah, would come.
2 Kings 19 – 20; Isaiah

Ishbosheth/Ishbaal One of King Saul's sons. When Saul was killed by the Philistines, Ishbosheth was crowned by Abner, the commander of Saul's army. He reigned in Israel while David was king of Judah. For two years Judah and Israel were at war. Then Ishbosheth was murdered by two commanders of his army, and David became king of both Israel and Judah.
2 Samuel 2 – 4
Ishmael Son of Abraham and Hagar. (See *Hagar.*)
Genesis 16; 21
Israel The new name God gave to Jacob after he had wrestled all night with the 'man' at the River Jabbok. Israel means 'the man who fights with God'. The twelve tribes descended from Jacob were known as the children of Israel.
Genesis 32:22ff.; 35:9
Issachar Son of Jacob and Leah, who gave his name to one of the twelve tribes of Israel.
Genesis 35:23
Ithamar Aaron's youngest

son. Ithamar was the priest who supervised the making of the worship tent (the tabernacle). He was in charge of two groups of Levites and founded one of the important families of priests. Exodus 6:23; 38:21; Numbers 3ff.; 1 Chronicles 24:1
Ittai A man from Gath who was leader of a band of 600 Philistine soldiers. As a reward for his loyalty, David made Ittai commander of one-third of his army.
2 Samuel 15; 18
Jabin 1. King of Hazor defeated and killed by Joshua.
Joshua 11:1 – 11
2. A Canaanite king, also from Hazor, who oppressed the Israelites for twenty years. His army was defeated by Barak and Deborah. Judges 4
Jacob Son of Isaac and Rebekah; Esau's (younger) twin. When Esau was hungry after hunting, Jacob persuaded him to give up his rights as the

elder son in exchange for a bowl of stew. Later Jacob gained his father's special blessing by pretending to be Esau. After that, Esau hated Jacob and planned to kill him. Jacob escaped north to his Uncle Laban in Harran. On the way he had a dream. He saw a staircase reaching from earth to heaven, with angels moving up and down it. God promised him and his descendants the land where he was sleeping. 'I will not leave you until I have done all that I have promised you.'

Jacob worked for Laban as a shepherd for twenty years. He loved Laban's daughter, Rachel, but was tricked into marrying her sister, Leah, first. While he was in Harran, Jacob became the father of eleven sons and one

Like these Bedouin, Abraham, Isaac and Jacob lived in tents, moving from place to place.

daughter. He waited long years for his first son by Rachel: Joseph. Later Rachel died giving birth to a second son, Benjamin. Laban cheated Jacob but in the end was outwitted. Jacob built up his own large flocks of sheep and goats, and then left for his own country. On the way he had a strange all-night wrestling-match with an unknown 'man', and would not let him go until he had been blessed. God gave him the new name of 'Israel' which means, 'the man who fights with God'

To Jacob's great relief Esau gave him a warm welcome. But afterwards they went their own ways. Jacob lived in the land of Canaan until Joseph invited him to settle in Egypt. Before Jacob died he blessed his sons, the ancestors of the tribes of Israel.
Genesis 25:21 – 34; 27 – 35; 37:1; 42 – 49

Jael A woman from the nomadic Kenite tribe. After Sisera, commander of the Canaanite army, had lost his battle against the Israelites he ran away and hid in Jael's tent. While he was asleep she murdered him. Deborah praised Jael in her victory song.
Judges 4; 5:24 – 27

Jairus The synagogue official at Capernaum who asked Jesus to heal his twelve-year-old daughter. By the time Jesus reached Jairus's house she was dead. But, to the amazement of her parents, Jesus brought her back to life.
Mark 5:22ff.

James 1. The son of Zebedee and a disciple of Jesus. Like his brother John, James was a fisherman. Jesus nicknamed the two stormy brothers 'men of thunder'! When Jesus called him to be one of his special followers James went with him at once. James was present when Jesus brought Jairus's daughter back to life, and at Jesus' glory (the transfiguration). He was killed for his faith by Herod Agrippa I.
Matthew 4:21ff.; 17:1ff.; Mark 5:37; 10:35ff.; Acts 12:2
2. Another apostle, the son of Alphaeus. He was probably the man called 'James the younger'.
Matthew 10:3; Mark 15:40; Acts 1:13

3. One of Jesus' brothers. James did not believe that Jesus was the Messiah until he saw him after the resurrection. He became a leader of the church in Jerusalem and probably wrote the Letter of James. The Jewish historian Josephus records that he was stoned to death in AD 62.
Matthew 13:55; Acts 12:17; 1 Corinthians 15:7; James

Japheth One of Noah's three sons. He survived the flood to become the founder of several nations.
Genesis 5:32; 9:18ff.; 10:1ff.

Jason 1. A Christian with whom Paul and Silas stayed when they were in Thessalonica.
Acts 17:5 – 9
2. A Jewish Christian mentioned by Paul.
Romans 16:21

Jeduthun A Levite who led the singing for worship in the reigns of King David and Solomon.
1 Chronicles 16:41 – 42; 25; 2 Chronicles 5:12

Jehoahaz 1. King of Israel 814 – 798 BC, after Jehu, his father. He led his subjects away from the worship of God and was defeated by Hazael and Benhadad, kings of Syria.
2 Kings 13:1ff.
2. Son of Josiah and king of Judah for three months in 609 BC. He was captured and taken prisoner to Egypt by Pharaoh Neco.
2 Kings 23:31 – 34

Jehoiachin King of Judah for three months in 597 BC. He was taken prisoner to Babylon by Nebuchadnezzar. Many years later a new king of Babylon released Jehoiachin from prison and gave him a place at court.
2 Kings 24:8 – 16; 25:27ff.; 2 Chronicles 36:9 – 10; Jeremiah 52:31ff.

Jehoiada The most important man of this name was chief priest in Jerusalem during the reigns of Ahaziah, Queen Athaliah and Joash. Jehoiada was married to Jehosheba, sister of King Ahaziah. Athaliah, the queen mother, seized the throne when her son died and gave orders for all the royal family to be killed. But Jehoiada hid his nephew Joash, one of Ahaziah's sons. After six years he made Joash king

and Athaliah was killed. Jehoiada ruled as regent until Joash was old enough to govern the country himself.
2 Kings 11 – 12; 2 Chronicles 23 – 24

Jehoiakim Son of Josiah and king of Judah 609 – 597 BC. He was made king by Pharaoh Neco and had to pay taxes to Egypt. Jehoiakim undid all the good of his father's reign and was greedy and cruel. He burnt the scroll of Jeremiah's prophecies. When he rebelled against Babylon Judah was invaded.
2 Kings 24:1 – 7; 2 Chronicles 36:4 – 8; Jeremiah 22:18ff.; 26; 36

Jehoram/Joram 1. Son of King Ahab. Jehoram was king of Israel 852 – 841 BC, after the death of his brother, King Ahaziah. He ended Baal worship but did not wholly reform and was murdered by Jehu, who wiped out all Ahab's descendants.
2 Kings 3; 8 – 9
2. King of Judah 848 – 841 BC (co-regent from 853) after his father Jehoshaphat. Elijah warned that he would die from a terrible disease because he had murdered his six brothers and encouraged his subjects to worship idols.
2 Kings 8:16ff.; 2 Chronicles 21

Jehoshaphat Best-known is the son of King Asa who became king of Judah 870 – 848 BC (co-regent from 873). He was a good king who destroyed idols and made sure his subjects learned God's laws. He improved the legal system and appointed judges in the major towns. But he made the mistake of forming an alliance with King Ahab and became involved in Israel's wars.
1 Kings 22; 2 Kings 3; 2 Chronicles 17 – 21:1

Jehosheba/Jehosha-beath The sister of King Ahaziah of Judah. Jehosheba was married to Jehoiada, the priest. (See *Jehoiada*.)
2 Kings 11:1 – 3; 2 Chronicles 22:11 – 12

Jehu A commander in the army of King Jehoram of Israel. He became king 841 – 814 BC. He was anointed king by Elisha and told to wipe out all King Ahab and Jezebel's descendants as

punishment for their wickedness. This he did. Later in his reign King Hazael of Syria invaded Israel. Shalmaneser III of Assyria includes Jehu in a list of subject kings. Jehu may have asked Assyria to help him defeat Syria.
2 Kings 9 – 10

Jehudi An official at the court of King Jehoiakim who read Jeremiah's scroll to the king.
Jeremiah 36

Jephthah One of the 'Judges' of early Israel. Before he went into battle against the Ammonites Jephthah vowed that if he was successful he would sacrifice whatever came out of his house when he returned. Jephthah returned from defeating the Ammonites to be greeted by his daughter, an only child. Despite his grief Jephthah kept his vow. He ruled as a Judge for six years.
Judges 11 – 12

Jeremiah A great prophet in Judah from about 625 – 585 BC. He was the son of a priest. God called him to be a prophet when he was still young. For years the people of Judah had disobeyed God and disregarded his laws. Jeremiah was sent to warn them that unless they changed their ways their land and city would be captured, and the people taken away to Babylon. But God would forgive them and rebuild their country if they turned back to him. 'I will make a new covenant with the people of Israel . . . I will put my law within them and write it on their hearts.' But the people refused to listen. When Jerusalem was captured, Nebuchadnezzar treated Jeremiah kindly and allowed him to stay in Judah. But his own people forced him to go to Egypt after the murder of the governor of Judah and he probably died there.
2 Chronicles 35:25; 36:12, 21 – 22; Jeremiah

Jeroboam I A man from the tribe of Ephraim who became first king of Israel, the breakaway northern kingdom (931 – 910 BC). During Solomon's reign the prophet Ahijah predicted that Jeroboam would be the ruler of ten tribes. After Solomon's death his son, Rehoboam, succeeded him, but all the tribes

except Benjamin and Judah rebelled against him and made Jeroboam their king. Jeroboam introduced idol worship and ordered two golden calves to be made. He put these in Dan and Bethel to stop his subjects returning to Jerusalem to worship. His bad example was followed by other kings of Israel and led eventually to Israel's total defeat and dispersion by Assyria in 721 BC.
1 Kings 11:26 – 14:20

Jeroboam II Became king of Israel after his father, Joash, and reigned for forty-one years, 793–753 BC. He reconquered land which Israel had lost and during his reign the country became wealthy. Israel grew confident and careless. Neither king nor people took notice of the warnings of the prophets, Hosea and Amos. They continued to worship idols and to disregard God's covenant agreement.
2 Kings 14:23–29;
Amos 7

Jerubbaal Another name for Gideon.

Jesse Grandson of Ruth and Boaz, and father of King David.
1 Samuel 16 – 17

Jesus The name (Old Testament 'Joshua') means 'saviour'. At the time when Herod was king of Judea and the whole country was under Roman occupation the angel Gabriel came to Mary in Nazareth. God had chosen her to be the mother of the promised Messiah. Mary's fiancé, Joseph, was told in a dream that they were to call him Jesus 'because he will save his people from their sins'. A census took Mary and Joseph to Bethlehem, where Jesus was born, in the town of King David, his ancestor. Herod was afraid that Jesus would be a rival king and plotted to kill him, but God guided his parents to take him to Egypt. After Herod died they went back to their home town of Nazareth. Here Jesus grew up and probably worked as a carpenter.

When he was thirty years old, Jesus was baptized by John the Baptist in the River Jordan. He chose twelve followers as his close companions to share his life and work. For three years Jesus taught

the people and worked miracles, healing all kinds of diseases. Crowds followed him. But the Jewish leaders were afraid of his power and of his claim to be the Son of God. They wanted to kill him. Judas, one of the twelve, accepted a bribe and helped Jesus' enemies to capture him without the people's knowledge. Soldiers arrested Jesus in the Garden of Gethsemane, close to Jerusalem. He was tried and condemned by a Jewish court before dawn. Pilate, the Roman governor, had to ratify all death sentences. He found no fault in Jesus, but was afraid of a riot if he let him go free. So Jesus was crucified. He was buried in the tomb of Joseph of Arimathaea, a secret follower.

At dawn on the third day after Jesus' death a group of women found the tomb empty. Angels told them Jesus was alive again. His followers and many other people saw him during the next forty days. Now they knew he really was the Son of God. Then from the Mount of Olives Jesus returned to heaven. While the disciples were still looking at the sky an angel told them that one day Jesus would come back.
Matthew, Mark, Luke, John, Acts 1:1 – 11
(See also Part 6: *Key Teaching of the Bible.*)

Jethro/Reuel A priest in the land of Midian and father-in-law of Moses. When Moses brought the Israelites to Sinai, Jethro came to see him, bringing Moses' wife and sons. He advised Moses to choose capable men to share the burden of leadership.
Exodus 2:16ff.; 3:1;
4:18 – 19; 18

Jezebel The princess from Sidon who married Ahab, king of Israel. Jezebel worshipped the weather and fertility gods Baal and Asherah. (See Part 5: *Religion and Worship in the Bible.*) She persuaded Ahab and forced his subjects to accept her religion. She had God's prophets killed and replaced them with prophets of Baal. But the prophet Elijah escaped to challenge and defeat the prophets of Baal on Mt Carmel. After this Jezebel was determined to kill

Elijah and he was forced to go into hiding. Jezebel signed her own death warrant when she urged Ahab to have Naboth killed so that he could take over Naboth's vineyard. Elijah predicted her violent death, and some time later she was thrown from an upstairs window at the command of Jehu.
1 Kings 16:31; 18:4, 13, 19; 19:1–2; 21; 2 Kings 9:30ff.

Joab King David's nephew and commander of his army. He was fearless but violent. Joab helped David become king of all the tribes of Israel. He remained loyal to David during Absalom's rebellion, but towards the end of David's reign supported Adonijah's revolt. After David's death King Solomon ordered Joab to be executed for taking part in the revolt and for the murders of Abner and Amasa, two other army leaders.
2 Samuel 2 – 3; 10 – 11; 14; 18 – 20; 24; 1 Kings 1 – 2; 1 Chronicles 11ff.

Joanna The wife of an official of Herod Antipas. Joanna was healed by Jesus. She gave money to Jesus and his disciples. On the resurrection morning she was one of the women who found Jesus' tomb empty.
Luke 8:1–3; 24:10

Joash/Jehoash 1. Son of King Ahaziah, made king of Judah when he was seven years old. While he was a baby his life was saved by Jehoiada, the priest. In the early part of his forty-year reign (835–796 BC) he was guided by Jehoiada. He obeyed God's laws and repaired the temple. After Jehoiada's death he introduced idol worship and murdered Zechariah, Jehoiada's son. He stripped gold from the temple to appease the invading Syrians. Joash was murdered by his officials (see *Jehoiada*).
2 Kings 11 – 12;
2 Chronicles 24
2. King of Israel for sixteen years (798–782 BC) after King Jehoahaz, his father.
2 Kings 13 – 14

Job 'Hero' of the Book of Job. Job was a man of outstanding goodness. He lost his wealth, his ten children and his health in a series of disasters. In spite of this he refused to take

his wife's advice and curse God. Three friends who came to visit him were convinced that Job's troubles were his own fault. But he knew that this was untrue. Another friend told Job he must not expect to understand God's ways. Although Job came close to despair and never knew the reason for his suffering God gave him a new understanding of his sovereign power and wisdom. In the end God healed him and restored his fortunes.
Job

Joel A prophet; the son of Pethuel. In his book Joel describes a plague of locusts and a terrible drought. His message was a warning to the Israelites. He called for repentance and spoke of a new age when God would bless those who trusted him.
Joel

Johanan A Jewish leader who stayed in Judah after Jerusalem was captured by King Nebuchadnezzar of Babylon. Johanan warned Gedaliah, governor of Judah, about the plot to murder him. Afterwards, against Jeremiah's advice, he led the people to Egypt.
Jeremiah 40 – 43

John the apostle Like his father, Zebedee, and his brother James, John was a fisherman. He was probably a follower of John the Baptist before Jesus called him to become his disciple. Jesus nicknamed John and James 'sons of thunder' because they were quick-tempered.

Peter, James and John were especially close to Jesus. John was with Jesus when he brought Jairus's daughter back from the dead. He saw Jesus' glory at the transfiguration, and was with him in the Garden of Gethsemane just before his death. John's name is not mentioned in the Gospel of John, but he is almost certainly 'the disciple whom Jesus loved', the one who was close to Jesus at the last supper and to whom Jesus spoke from the cross, and told to look after his mother.

After Jesus had ascended into heaven John, with Peter, became a leader of the church in Jerusalem. He was still in

Jerusalem fourteen years after Paul was converted. There is a tradition that John lived in Ephesus until he was very old. If he is the same John who wrote the Revelation he must also have been exiled to the island of Patmos. The Gospel of John was written to bring men to faith. Three New Testament letters also bear John's name.
Matthew 4:21ff.; 10:2; 17:1ff.; Mark 3:17; 5:37; 10:35ff.; 14:33; Luke 9:49ff.; John 19:26 – 27; Acts 3 – 4; Galatians 2:9

John the Baptist The prophet sent by God to prepare people for the coming of Jesus, the Messiah. In their old age his parents, Zechariah and Elizabeth, were told by an angel that they would have this special son. John was related to Jesus and just a few months older. He lived in the desert of Judea until God called him to be a prophet. Crowds of people came to hear his fiery preaching. 'Turn away from your sins and be baptized,' he said, 'and God will forgive you.' Although Jesus had not sinned, he asked John to baptize him, too, in the River Jordan, to show his obedience to God.

Later John was put in prison by King Herod for his outspoken criticism. From prison he sent some of his disciples to Jesus to ask if he really was the person they were expecting. 'Tell John how I heal the sick and preach Good News to the poor,' Jesus answered. Then he told the crowds, 'John the Baptist is more than a prophet. He is greater than any man who has ever lived.' Not long after this, Herod's wife tricked him into having John beheaded.
Luke 1; 3; 7:18ff.; Matthew 3; 11; 14:1 – 12; Mark 1; 6

Jonah An Israelite prophet who probably lived in the eighth century BC. The Book of Jonah tells his story. God told him to go to Nineveh, capital of Assyria, Israel's enemy. He was to speak out against the wickedness of the people there. Instead he took a ship to Tarshish, in the opposite direction. A storm blew up and Jonah knew it was because he had run away from God. He told the crew to throw him overboard. When

they did this the storm died down. Instead of drowning, Jonah was swallowed by a huge fish which spat him up on a beach.

God gave Jonah a second chance. This time he went to Nineveh and warned the people of God's judgement. Everyone, from the king down, fasted and prayed to God, and the city was spared. But Jonah was angry that God had forgiven Israel's enemy, so God had to teach him a lesson in pity.
Jonah

Jonathan Eldest son of King Saul and a great friend of David. He was a brave warrior and distinguished himself in several battles against the Philistines. Although Jonathan knew David might become king in his place he was a loyal friend and saved him from being killed by Saul. Jonathan and Saul were both killed in battle when the Israelites were defeated by the Philistines. David was deeply grieved and wrote a lament in praise of Jonathan.
1 Samuel 13 – 14; 18 – 20; 23: 16 – 18; 31:2; 2 Samuel 1

Joram See Jehoram.

Joseph 1. Jacob and Rachel's first son after many years of waiting. Joseph was marked out as his father's favourite by the gift of a special coat. Joseph's brothers became jealous of him, especially when he told them his dreams, in which they bowed down to him. They planned to kill him but Reuben persuaded them to delay and Judah suggested that instead they should sell him as a slave. Joseph was taken to Egypt, and the brothers told Jacob he had been killed by wild animals.

In Egypt Joseph was bought by Potiphar, a high official, and put in charge of his household. Potiphar's wife claimed that Joseph had tried to rape her, and he was put in prison. There he was able to tell the butler and baker of the Pharaoh (king) of Egypt the meaning of their dreams. Two years later Pharaoh had dreams he could not understand. The butler remembered Joseph and Pharaoh sent for him.

Joseph told him he must prepare for a long famine. Pharaoh made Joseph his chief minister and put him in charge of the preparations.

Joseph saw his brothers again when they came to Egypt to buy corn during the famine. He pretended to think they were spies and told them to come back with his younger brother, Benjamin, to prove their story. Then he tested them to see if they would be as cruel to Benjamin as they had been to him. When Joseph realized they really cared about Benjamin, he told them who he was.

Joseph invited his father and his brothers' families to live in Egypt. Jacob was overjoyed to see Joseph again. Their descendants lived in Egypt for four centuries.
Genesis 30:24; 37 – 50

2. Husband of Mary and foster-father of Jesus. Although Joseph was not Jesus' father physically, he was his legal father. Before Jesus was born an angel told him that Mary's child was God's Son. Joseph took Mary and the baby to Egypt when he was warned in a dream that King Herod planned to kill Jesus. After Herod's death Joseph brought his family back and they settled in Nazareth, where Joseph worked as a carpenter. When Jesus was twelve Joseph and Mary took him to the temple for the Passover. Nothing more is known about Joseph. He may have died before Jesus was grown up.
Matthew 1 – 2; Luke 1:27; 2

3. Joseph of Arimathaea. A member of the Jewish Sanhedrin council and a secret disciple of Jesus. After the crucifixion he asked Pilate for Jesus' body and placed it in his own unused tomb.
Luke 23:50 – 53; John 19:38 – 42

Joshua 1. Leader of the Israelites after Moses' death. His name means 'God is salvation'. Joshua was chosen to lead the army while the Israelites were in the desert. Of the twelve spies sent by Moses to bring back a report on Canaan, only Joshua and Caleb believed the Israelites could conquer the land

with God's help. God rewarded their faith. Of all the Israelites born in Egypt they were the only ones who lived to occupy Canaan. After Moses' death Joshua led the Israelites into Canaan. When the land had been conquered he divided it up amongst the twelve tribes. Before Joshua died he urged the Israelites to love and obey God. 'As for my family and me,' he said, 'we will serve the Lord.' And the people replied, 'We also will serve the Lord, he is our God.'
Exodus 17:9ff.; Numbers 13 – 14; Joshua

2. High priest immediately after the Jews returned from exile in Babylon. He started rebuilding the temple, but the work ground to a halt. When the prophets Haggai and Zechariah spurred the people into action, Joshua once again took charge.
Haggai; Zechariah 3

Josiah Crowned king of Judah at the age of eight after the assassination of his father, Amon, in 640 BC. Josiah grew to be a strong, good king who led the nation back to God. He ordered the repair of the temple and while this work was being carried out a scroll was found on which were written the laws God gave to Moses. Josiah studied these laws and had them read to the people. Many reforms were made including the keeping of the Passover Festival. When Josiah was thirty-nine years old he was killed in battle against the Egyptians. Jeremiah the prophet mourned Josiah's death.
2 Kings 21:24 – 23:30; 2 Chronicles 33:25 – 35:27; Jeremiah 22:15 – 16

Jotham King of Judah 750 – 732 BC, after his father King Uzziah. He began to reign while his father was still alive but suffering from leprosy. Jotham worshipped God. He fortified Judah and defeated the Ammonites.
2 Kings 15:32 – 38; 2 Chronicles 27:1 – 6

Judah The fourth son of Jacob and Leah. Judah persuaded his brothers to sell Joseph to passing traders on their way to Egypt, instead of killing him. Jacob's last words to Judah promised him a future kingdom.
Genesis 29:35; 37:26 – 27;

38; 49:9–10

Judas/Jude There are several people with this name in the New Testament. Best-known are:
1. Judas, the son of James. He was one of the twelve apostles and was with the others after Jesus' ascension.
Luke 6:16; Acts 1:13
2. One of Jesus' brothers. Judas did not believe Jesus was the Messiah until after his death and resurrection. He may have written the letter of Jude.
Matthew 13:55; John 7:5; Acts 1:14
3. Judas Iscariot. The disciple who betrayed Jesus to the Jewish leaders. He looked after the apostles' money. He probably hoped Jesus would lead a rebellion against the Romans. When Jesus turned out to be a different kind of leader, Judas sold him to his enemies for thirty pieces of silver. Judas led the soldiers to arrest Jesus at night in the Garden of Gethsemane. When he realized how wrong he had been, he returned the money to the priests and committed suicide.
Matthew 10:4; 26:14ff.; 27:3ff.; John 12:4–6; 13:21–30; Acts 1:18–19

Julius The Roman centurion in charge of Paul on his voyage to Rome to be tried before Caesar.
Acts 27:1, 3, 42–44

Keturah Abraham's second wife.
Genesis 25:1ff.

Kish A wealthy man from the tribe of Benjamin; the father of Saul, first king of Israel.
1 Samuel 9:1ff.

Kohath A son of Levi and grandfather of Moses. His descendants were known as the Kohathites and formed one of the three groups of Levites.
Exodus 6:16ff.; Numbers 3:17ff.

Korah 1. A Levite who led a rebellion against Moses and Aaron. He did not see what right they had to be leaders and was angry because the people had not reached Canaan quickly enough. Korah and the others died because they rejected God's chosen leader and rebelled against him.
Numbers 16
2. A son of Levi. His descendants were singers in the temple.

1 Chronicles 6:37; Psalms 44 – 49

Laban The brother of Rebekah, Isaac's wife. He lived in Harran and welcomed his nephew Jacob when he had to leave home. Laban had two daughters – Leah and Rachel. Jacob agreed to work for Laban for seven years to marry Rachel. But Laban tricked him into marrying Leah and he had to work another seven years for Rachel. Jacob in turn outwitted Laban and as a result his flock of sheep and goats became larger and stronger than his uncle's. When Laban discovered that Jacob had secretly left for Canaan he chased after him. God warned Laban in a dream not to harm Jacob. They agreed to go their own ways and Laban returned to Harran.
Genesis 24:29ff., 29 – 31

Lamech 1. A descendant of Cain.
Genesis 4:18ff.
2. Son of Methuselah and father of Noah.
Genesis 5:28–31

Lazarus 1. Brother of Martha and Mary who lived in Bethany. When Lazarus became ill his sisters sent for Jesus. Although he loved them all, Jesus delayed until he knew that Lazarus was dead. (See *Martha.*) Jesus went with the weeping women to the cave tomb – and wept himself. He told people standing by to roll away the stone which blocked the door and then cried, 'Lazarus, come out.' Lazarus came, with the grave clothes still wrapped around him. Jewish leaders who saw this happen believed in Jesus. When the chief priests and Pharisees heard of Jesus' power over death they were afraid the whole nation would follow him, and plotted to kill him and Lazarus, too.
John 11 – 12:11
2. The name of the beggar in Jesus' story of the rich man and the beggar at his gate.
Luke 16:19–31

Leah Elder daughter of Laban, married to Jacob through Laban's trick. She and Jacob had six sons, ancestors of the tribes of Israel, and a daughter.
Genesis 29:16 – 33:7

Levi 1. Third son of Jacob and Leah. His descendants formed the

tribe of Levi. The Levites were chosen to serve God in the tent of worship and, later, the temple.
Genesis 29:34; 34:25ff.; 49:5ff.; Numbers 3:5–20
2. See *Matthew*

Lot Abraham's nephew. He went with Abraham from Harran to Canaan but they parted after their herdsmen quarrelled. Lot went to live at Sodom in the fertile plain. Abraham rescued him from raiding kings. Later, when Sodom was destroyed for its wickedness, Lot just escaped. His wife, stopping to look back at the city, was caught in the disaster.
Genesis 11:31 – 14:16; 19

Luke A Greek-speaking doctor who wrote the Gospel of Luke and the Acts of the Apostles. He was a friend of Paul and travelled with him on some of his journeys, so he was able to describe at first-hand some of the things Paul said and did. On these journeys Luke was also able to learn about Jesus' life and the beginning of the church from the apostles and first Christians. He sailed to Rome with Paul and stayed with him while he was a prisoner there.
Colossians 4:14; 2 Timothy 4:11; Philemon 24

Lydia A 'dealer in purple cloth' who came from Thyatira in Asia Minor (Turkey). She heard Paul preach in Philippi (Greece) and became a Christian.
Acts 16:14–15, 40

Magog See *Gog.*

Malachi The last of the Old Testament prophets (about mid-fifth century BC). The temple had been rebuilt after the return from exile but the people were not serving God wholeheartedly. 'Turn back,' said Malachi. 'Stop cheating God of his dues. Don't test his patience any longer.' Malachi's name means 'my messenger'. As God's messenger he spoke of the coming Messiah and the great day of God's justice and judgement.
Malachi

Manasseh 1. Joseph's elder son who was adopted and blessed by Jacob. His descendants formed the tribe of Manasseh.
Genesis 41:51; 48:1ff.
2. King of Judah for fifty-five years (696–642 BC)

after his father, King Hezekiah. Manasseh led the nation astray, introducing all kinds of idol worship. He was taken prisoner to Babylon by the Assyrians. When he returned to Jerusalem he turned to God and changed his ways.
2 Kings 21:1ff.; 2 Chronicles 33

Manoah Samson's father.
Judges 13; 14:3

Mark (John) The writer of the second Gospel. John Mark lived in Jerusalem. His mother, Mary, allowed the first Christians to meet in her house. Mark later went with Paul and Barnabas, his cousin, to Cyprus on Paul's first missionary journey. He left them halfway through and Paul refused to take him when they set out again. Instead Mark went back to Cyprus with Barnabas. Later Paul and Mark were together in Rome, and Paul wrote of him as a loyal friend and helper. Peter describes him as 'my son Mark' and, by tradition, it was Peter who gave Mark much of the story of Jesus told in Mark's Gospel.
Mark 14:51; Acts 12:12, 25; 13:13; 15:36ff.; Colossians 4:10; 2 Timothy 4:11; Philemon 24; 1 Peter 5:13

Martha The sister of Mary and Lazarus. She lived at the village of Bethany, close to Jerusalem. Jesus often visited their home. When Lazarus was ill the sisters sent for Jesus. Their brother died before Jesus came. Martha went to meet Jesus and said, 'If you had been here, my brother would not have died.' Jesus replied, 'I am the resurrection and I am life . . . Do you believe this?' 'Lord, I do,' Martha answered. And to her great joy, Jesus restored her brother to life.
Luke 10:38–42; John 11:20ff.

Mary 1. Jesus' mother. While she was engaged to Joseph, a carpenter, an angel told her she was to be the mother of Jesus, the Messiah and Son of God. Before Jesus was born, Mary visited her cousin Elizabeth. There Mary spoke the wonderful song of praise to God known as the *Magnificat*. Mary and Joseph went from Nazareth to Bethlehem to register for a

Roman census. There Jesus was born. When the shepherds came, with their story of angels singing, 'Mary remembered all these things and thought deeply about them.' When Jesus was presented at the temple, a few days later, Simeon spoke to Mary about the future: 'Sorrow, like a sharp sword, will break your own heart.' While Jesus was still a baby, Mary and Joseph took him to Egypt because King Herod wanted to kill this rival. After Herod's death they returned to Nazareth.

When Jesus was twelve his parents took him to the temple for the Passover Festival. They were terribly worried when he stayed behind, alone, to talk with the teachers. Mary was with Jesus when he worked his first miracle at the wedding feast in Cana. At his crucifixion she stood by the cross, and Jesus asked one of his disciples (see *John*) to look after her. Mary was with the disciples when they met together to pray after Jesus' ascension.
Matthew 1:18–25; 2:11; 13:55; Luke 1 – 2; John 2:1ff.; 19:25–27; Acts 1:14
2. Sister of Martha. She lived in Bethany with her sister and brother Lazarus and loved to listen to Jesus. Just before Jesus' death she anointed him with precious oil and wiped his feet with her hair. (See also *Martha, Lazarus*.)
Luke 10:38–42; John 11; 12:3ff
3. Mary Magdalene became a disciple of Jesus after he had healed her. She was the first person to see Jesus after the resurrection and ran to tell the apostles.
Mark 16:9; Luke 8:2; 24:10; John 20:1ff.
4. Mary, mother of James and Joseph. She was present at the crucifixion and was one of the group of women who found Jesus' tomb empty on the resurrection morning. This Mary is probably the same person as 'the other Mary' and Mary, wife of Clopas.
Matthew 27:56, 61; 28:1; John 19:25
5. Mary, the mother of John Mark. The first Christians met in her house in Jerusalem.
Acts 12:12
Matthew One of the twelve

apostles, and traditionally writer of the first Gospel. Matthew, also called Levi, was a tax collector before Jesus said to him, 'Follow me.'
Matthew 9:9; 10:3; Luke 5:27–32
Matthias Chosen by the disciples after the death of Judas Iscariot to take the traitor's place as one of the twelve.
Acts 1:21–26
Melchizedek A king and priest of God Most High at Salem (Jerusalem) who met and blessed Abraham after a battle. In the New Testament letter to the Hebrews Jesus is called a high priest 'for ever, in the line of succession to Melchizedek'. Like Melchizedek, Jesus is both king and priest – king of God's kingdom and a priest because he offered the sacrifice of his own life.
Genesis 14:18–20; Psalm 110:4; Hebrews 5:6–10
Menahem One of the last kings of Israel (752–742 BC). When King Shallum had reigned for only one month Menahem killed him and made himself king instead. Menahem was a cruel and wicked king who worshipped idols. During his reign Tiglath-pileser III (Pul) of Assyria invaded Israel. Menahem paid the Assyrians a large sum of money to continue as king.
2 Kings 15:14–22
Mephibosheth The son of Jonathan, David's great friend, and grandson of King Saul. When David was king he gave Mephibosheth a place at the palace and servants to wait on him.
2 Samuel 4:4; 9; 16:1ff.; 19:24–30; 21:7
Merab A daughter of King Saul. Saul promised David he could marry her, but gave her to another man instead.
1 Samuel 14:49; 18:17ff.
Merari One of Levi's sons. His descendants, the Merarites, formed one of the three groups of Levites.
Exodus 6:16ff.; Numbers 3
Merodach-Baladan A king of Babylon (in Babylonian, Mardukapla-iddina II) who sent messengers to King Hezekiah in Jerusalem. Merodach-Baladan hoped to make Hezekiah join with Babylon against Assyria.
Isaiah 39
Meshach See *Abednego.*
Methuselah Remembered as the oldest man who

ever lived. He died, in the year of the flood, 969 years old.
Genesis 5:22–27
Micah/Micaiah 1. A prophet who lived in the eighth century BC. He gave his message at the same time as Isaiah, Amos and Hosea. Micah lived in a village in the lowlands of Judah but his message was for people in Samaria, the capital of Israel, as well as those in Jerusalem. He predicted that both cities would be destroyed because of the evil and harsh treatment of the poor which the leaders allowed to continue. A century later, Jeremiah reminded the people of Micah's words, recorded in the Book of Micah.
Jeremiah 26:18–19; Micah
2. A prophet who lived in the reign of King Ahab. When Ahab planned to fight a battle against the Syrians he asked many prophets if he was going to win. Four hundred prophesied success, and only Micaiah foretold defeat. Ahab was angry at this answer and threw Micaiah into prison, but his prediction came true.
1 Kings 22
Michael An archangel described in Daniel as the guardian of the Jewish people.
Daniel 10:21; 12:1; Jude 9; Revelation 12:7
Michal King Saul's younger daughter and David's wife. She helped David to escape from Saul and saved his life, but Saul gave her to another man.
1 Samuel 14:49; 18:20ff.; 25:44; 2 Samuel 3:13–16; 6:16ff.
Miriam Sister of Moses and Aaron. She watched over her baby brother Moses in the reed basket until he was found by the daughter of Pharaoh. After the Israelites had crossed the Red Sea, Miriam led the women, singing and dancing for joy. Later she quarrelled with Moses, because she was jealous of him as leader. For a short time, as punishment, she suffered a terrible skin disease. But Moses asked God to heal her. Miriam died at Kadesh before the Israelites reached Canaan.
Exodus 2:4, 7–8; 15:20–21; Numbers 12; 20:1
Moab A son of Lot and founder of the nation of Moab.

Genesis 19:36–37
Mordecai Esther's cousin and guardian. Mordecai was a Jew who lived in Susa, capital of Persia. When he heard about a plot to kill all the Jews he persuaded Esther, then queen of Persia, to plead with King Ahasuerus to spare them. Mordecai afterwards became the king's chief minister. (See *Esther*.)
Esther
Moses The great leader who freed the Israelites from slavery in Egypt and led them through the desert to the borders of Canaan. Moses was born in Egypt, brought up by the daughter of the king, and educated as an Egyptian. When he was grown up, Moses was so angry at the cruel way the Israelites were treated that he killed one of the Egyptian overseers. When Pharaoh heard about it, Moses was forced to escape from Egypt. He lived as a shepherd in the desert and married a daughter of Jethro, the man who gave him a home.

After forty years God appeared to Moses. He saw a desert bush which flamed but did not burn up, and knew that God was speaking to him. God told him to go back to Egypt and ask Pharaoh to let his people go. Pharaoh refused, and the Egyptians suffered ten plagues. Then Pharaoh let Moses lead the Israelites out of Egypt. But he quickly changed his mind; the Egyptians pursued the Israelites as far as the Red Sea. The Israelites escaped into the desert but Pharaoh's army was drowned.

After three months the people reached Mt Sinai. Here Moses the leader became Moses the lawgiver. God gave him the Ten Commandments and instructions for building the worship tent (tabernacle). Moses led the people on to the oasis at Kadesh. From there, spies were sent into Canaan. Ten came back with frightening tales. The people shouted and rebelled against Moses, forgetting the power of God. Because they rejected God they were condemned to wander in the desert until all those who rebelled had died.

Moses gave God's law to the new generation before he handed on the leadership to Joshua. When he had blessed the people Moses climbed Mt Nebo so that he could see Canaan, the land he was not allowed to enter because of his own earlier disobedience. Moses was 120 years old when he died in the land of Moab.

At the transfiguration, when they saw Jesus' glory, the disciples also saw Moses and Elijah, the two great Old Testament leaders, talking with Jesus about his coming death.
Exodus 2 – Deuteronomy 34; Luke 9:28ff.

Naaman The Syrian general cured of leprosy by the prophet Elisha.
2 Kings 5

Nabal A rich sheep farmer who lived near Carmel. David, then an outlaw, protected Nabal's land. At sheep-shearing time, when David asked for supplies, Nabal rudely refused. Abigail, Nabal's wife, heard that David's men were about to attack. Without telling her husband she packed up a large amount of food and wine and pleaded with David to spare her husband's life. David called the raid off. When Nabal heard, he collapsed – and died soon afterwards.
1 Samuel 25

Naboth Owner of a vineyard in Jezreel next to King Ahab's palace. Ahab tried to buy the vineyard from Naboth, but he refused to sell. The king sulked at this. Jezebel, his wife, promised Ahab that she would get the vineyard for him. She bribed two informers to say that Naboth had cursed God and the king. Naboth was found guilty and stoned to death. Ahab had the vineyard – but God sent Elijah to tell him that because of this murder his whole family would be wiped out.
1 Kings 21

Nadab Aaron's eldest son. He became a priest but died when he and Abihu, his brother, dishonoured God.
Exodus 6:23; Leviticus 10

Nahor 1. The father of Terah and grandfather of Abraham.
Genesis 11:22–25
2. Abraham's brother.
Genesis 11:26–29;

22:20ff.; 24:10ff.

Nahum A prophet from Elkosh, probably in Judah. His name means 'comforter'. The Book of Nahum records his message given just before Nineveh, capital of Assyria, was captured by Babylon in 612 BC. Nahum said that Nineveh would be destroyed because of its cruelty to other nations.
Nahum

Naomi The mother-in-law of Ruth. Naomi and her husband Elimelech came from Bethlehem. They had two sons, Mahlon and Chilion. The family moved to Moab because of a famine. There Mahlon and Chilion married Moabite girls. After her husband and sons had died, Naomi returned to Bethlehem and Ruth went with her. Naomi arranged for Ruth to marry Boaz. Their son was King David's grandfather. Naomi looked after the child as her own son.
Ruth

Naphtali The fifth son of Jacob; father of the tribe of Naphtali.
Genesis 30:8; 49:21

Nathan Best-known of several Nathans is the prophet who lived in King David's reign. David told Nathan he wanted to build a temple for God. 'God says, not you, but your son will be the one to build,' Nathan answered. After David had taken Bathsheba from her husband and engineered his death, Nathan confronted David with his crime. When David was old, he ordered Nathan and Zadok the priest to anoint Solomon king.
2 Samuel 7; 12; 1 Kings 1; 1 Chronicles 17

Nathanael One of Jesus' twelve apostles. He is mentioned only in John's Gospel but may be the disciple known in the other Gospels as Bartholomew. Nathanael heard about Jesus through Philip.
John 1:45ff.; 21:2

Nebuchadnezzar/Nebuchadrezzar King of Babylon 605–562 BC. He was the son of Nabopolassar who conquered the Assyrian Empire. Nebuchadnezzar led his father's army against the Egyptians and defeated them at Carchemish in 605 BC. Babylon gained control of the countries which had been subject to Egypt,

including Judah. For three years Judah paid tax to Babylon. In 597 BC King Jehoiakim rebelled. Nebuchadnezzar attacked Jerusalem. He took Jehoiachin, who was now king, prisoner to Babylon along with the most important citizens. Nebuchadnezzar made Zedekiah king instead. When Zedekiah rebelled he besieged Jerusalem. The city was destroyed in 586 BC and the leaders of the people taken into exile in Babylon. Daniel was one of an earlier group of Jews taken captive He was trained at Nebuchadnezzar's court. When he was able to explain the meaning of Nebuchadnezzar's dreams, he was made his chief advisor. Nebuchadnezzar's success made him proud. 'Look how great Babylon is. I built it as my capital city to display my power and might.' But God humbled him through a strange madness. When his sanity returned, he was a changed man. 'Now I, Nebuchadnezzar, praise, honour and glorify the King of heaven,' he said.
2 Kings 24 – 25; 2 Chronicles 36; Jeremiah 21:2 – 52:30; Ezekiel 26:7ff.; 29:18ff.; 30:10; Daniel 1 – 4

Nebuzaradan The captain of King Nebuchadnezzar's guard. Nebuzaradan was responsible for sending the Judeans into exile in Babylon after Nebuchadnezzar had captured Jerusalem. He burned down the temple and reduced the city to ruins. However, he carried out Nebuchadnezzar's command to treat Jeremiah kindly and let him stay in Judah.
2 Kings 25; Jeremiah 39ff.

Neco See *Pharaoh*.

Nehemiah Jewish cupbearer to King Artaxerxes I of Persia. In about 445 BC Nehemiah got the king's permission to go to Jerusalem and rebuild the walls destroyed when King Nebuchadnezzar captured the city. He completed the work in fifty-two days, against all kinds of opposition. He was a practical man of action, but also a man of prayer. Nehemiah left Ezra the priest in charge when he went back to Persia. When

he revisited Jerusalem several years later he found that the people had broken God's laws and needed to encourage them to obey God.
Nehemiah

Nicodemus A Pharisee and a member of the supreme Jewish council (the Sanhedrin). He came to talk to Jesus secretly, at night. 'No one can see the Kingdom of God,' Jesus said, 'unless he is born again.' Nicodemus did not understand what he meant then, but later he spoke up for Jesus when the Pharisees wanted to arrest him. After Jesus' crucifixion Nicodemus brought spices to embalm his body.
John 3:1–20; 7:50ff.; 19:39–42

Noah Noah was a good man at a time of great evil and violence. It was so bad, God could no longer tolerate it and sent a terrible flood. Only Noah and his family were saved. Noah followed the instructions God gave him and built a large boat about 430 ft/133 metres long. People saw what he was doing but refused to listen to his warning. When the rains came, Noah, his wife, his three sons and their wives, boarded the ark, with pairs of every kind of living creature. The ark floated until the flood went down. It came to rest on a mountain. After the flood God made a promise to Noah for all time: never again would he send a flood to destroy all living things. The rainbow was the sign of that promise. Noah lived to a great age and his sons became the ancestors of many nations.
Genesis 6 – 9; 1 Peter 3:20

Obadiah 1. A steward in charge of King Ahab's household. When Queen Jezebel gave orders for all God's prophets to be killed, Obadiah hid 100 of them in caves and fed them until the danger was over. He risked his life again when Elijah asked him to arrange a meeting with Ahab.
1 Kings 18
2. A prophet, probably from Judah, who spoke out against the nation of Edom. His message is recorded in the Book of Obadiah. He predicted that Edom would be destroyed for refusing to

help God's people in an emergency. When Jerusalem was destroyed by Babylon in 586 BC, the Edomites were glad and began to invade Judah. Obadiah probably had this event in mind when he spoke. He lived in the sixth or fifth century BC.
Obadiah

Obed The son of Ruth and Boaz and grandfather of King David.
Ruth 4:13ff.

Obed-Edom A Philistine in whose house the sacred Covenant Box (the ark) was placed for a time by King David, after Uzzah's death.
2 Samuel 6; 1 Chronicles 13

Og King of Bashan, a land east of the River Jordan. The Israelites, led by Moses, defeated Og and captured his sixty fortified cities. The land of Bashan was given to the half tribe of Manasseh.
Numbers 21:32ff.; Deuteronomy 3; Joshua 22:7

Omri Commander of the army of King Elah of Israel. His fellow officers made him king when they heard that Zimri had murdered Elah. Omri was a strong and vigorous king. He reigned twelve years (885–874 BC). He chose Samaria as his new capital – well-sited at the top of a steep hill and easily defended. Omri lost some of his cities to Syria but conquered Moab. As a result Moab paid a heavy tax to Israel each year. Omri worshipped idols, and his son, Ahab, followed his example.
1 Kings 16:15–28; 20:34

Onesimus A slave who belonged to Philemon, a Christian friend of Paul living at Colossae. Paul met Onesimus, probably in Rome, after he had run away from his master. While he was with Paul, Onesimus became a Christian. Paul wrote the letter to Philemon asking him to forgive Onesimus and accept him as a brother-Christian. Onesimus travelled back with Tychicus who was taking Paul's letter to the Colossians.
Colossians 4:9; Philemon

Onesiphorus A Christian who helped Paul when he was at Ephesus. He later encouraged Paul by visiting him when he was in prison at Rome.

2 Timothy 1:16ff.; 4:19
Ornan See *Araunah*.
Orpah A Moabite girl who married one of Naomi's sons.
Ruth 1

Othniel The first of the Judges in Israel. Othniel stopped the Israelites worshipping idols. As a result God gave him victory over Cushan-Rishathaim, king of Mesopotamia.
Joshua 15:16–17; Judges 3:7–11

Pashur A priest in charge of the temple in Jeremiah's time. Pashur put Jeremiah in the stocks because he said Jerusalem would be destroyed.
Jeremiah 20:1–6

Paul (Saul) The great apostle and missionary whose letters form a large part of the New Testament. Paul was a Jew, and a Roman citizen. He was born in Tarsus and educated by the Rabbi Gamaliel in Jerusalem. He was a Pharisee opposed to the Christians and present at the stoning of Stephen. Paul was on his way to Damascus to arrest the Christians when he saw a dazzling light and heard Jesus say to him, 'Why do you persecute me?' Blinded by the light, he was led to Damascus. Ananias was sent by God to visit him and restore his sight, and Paul was baptized. At once Paul started preaching about Jesus in Damascus. When the Jews plotted to kill him, he went to Jerusalem. The Christians there were afraid of Paul but Barnabas introduced him to the apostles. After a plot to kill him, Paul returned to Tarsus.

Some years later, Barnabas fetched him to help the church at Antioch in Syria. The two men were later sent to Cyprus and then to Asia Minor (Turkey) to take God's message to many peoples. After the Cyprus visit he was known as Paul, which is the Greek form of the Hebrew name Saul. Paul returned and reported back to the church in Antioch. He also helped the Jewish Christians in Jerusalem to accept the fact that Jesus Christ was the Saviour of all nations, not just the Jews.

On his second journey Paul took Silas as his helper. They visited the

converts in Galatia. At Lystra, Timothy joined them as another helper. From Troas they sailed to Greece where Luke, the writer of the Gospel and Acts, also joined them. A Christian church was started in Philippi, but Paul and Silas were beaten and thrown into prison. After their release, they travelled through Greece. Paul preached in Athens and then stayed in Corinth for eighteen months. Then he returned to Jerusalem with gifts for the poor from Christians in Greece and Asia Minor.

For a while Paul stayed in Syria. Then he set out again for Ephesus. For almost three years he preached to Jews and Greeks there. After visiting Corinth again, Paul returned through Greece and Asia Minor to Jerusalem. He was arrested and sent to Caesarea to be tried by Felix. For two years he was kept in prison, waiting for his case to be heard. By the time he was tried, Festus had replaced Felix as the Roman governor. Paul appealed to Caesar and was sent for trial in Rome. On the way Paul's ship was wrecked just off Malta, but no one drowned. When they reached Rome, Paul was kept under house arrest for more than two years. He was probably set free after his trial and may have preached in Spain. After a second arrest, Paul was executed in Rome by Nero, about AD 67. He had taken Christianity to Europe, left the priceless legacy of his writings to the church for all time, and kept his faith to the end.
Acts 7:58ff.; 9 – 28; the letters of Paul: Romans to Philemon

Pekah A captain in King Pekahiah's army who seized the throne of Israel (740–732 BC). He was an evil king who worshipped idols. Pekah made an alliance with King Rezin of Syria and both countries invaded Judah. King Ahaz of Judah appealed to Tiglath-pileser III of Assyria for help. As a result the Assyrians invaded Israel and captured several cities. Shortly after this Pekah was murdered by Hoshea.
2 Kings 15:25 – 16:5;
2 Chronicles 28:5–6

Pekahiah King of Israel after Menahem, his father, 742–740 BC. Pekahiah allowed the Israelites to continue worshipping idols. He was assassinated in the second year of his reign by Pekah, a captain in his army.
2 Kings 15:22–26

Peter Leader of the apostles and of the early church. Like his father and brother Andrew, Simon Peter was a fisherman. When Jesus called him to be a disciple he changed Peter's name from Simon to Peter, which means 'rock'. Later, Jesus asked his disciples who people thought he was. Peter answered, 'You are the Christ, the Son of the Living God.' Jesus replied, 'You are Peter and on this rock I will build my church.' Peter was one of Jesus' closest disciples. He was with Jesus at his transfiguration and in the Garden of Gethsemane just before his death. After Jesus' arrest Peter was afraid and said three times that he did not know him. But at once he was bitterly sorry. Knowing this, Jesus appeared specially to Peter after his resurrection. At Lake Galilee he told Peter to care for the Christian 'flock' as a shepherd.

On the Day of Pentecost Peter preached boldly about Jesus to the crowds in Jerusalem. About three thousand people became Christians that day. At first Peter preached only to the Jews. But at Joppa God gave him a special dream to show him he must share the Good News with non-Jews, too. King Herod arrested Peter and put him in prison, but the Christians prayed and God set him free. Peter wrote two of the New Testament letters, probably while he was in Rome. Mark probably got some of the story of Jesus for his Gospel from Peter. Peter is said to have died in Rome during the persecution begun by the Emperor Nero – crucified, like Jesus, but upside down.
Matthew 4:18–19; 10:2; 14:28–33; 16:13–23; 17:1–9; 26:30ff.; Mark 1:16–18, 29–31; 5:37; John 1:40–42; 18:10–11; 20:2–10; 21; Acts 1 – 15; Galatians 1 – 2; 1 and 2 Peter

Peter, Andrew, James and John all left their work as fishermen on Lake Galilee to follow Jesus.

Pharaoh Title of the kings of Egypt. Several 'pharaohs' are mentioned in the Old Testament including:
1. The pharaoh visited by Abraham.
Genesis 12:10ff.
2. The pharaoh who made Joseph his prime minister.
Genesis 40ff.
3. The pharaoh who was forced to let Moses lead the Israelites out of Egypt, probably Ramesses II, who built great store cities.
Exodus 5ff.
4. The pharaoh who sheltered Hadad after David defeated the Edomites.
1 Kings 11
5. The pharaoh who gave Solomon his daughter in marriage.
1 Kings 9:16

6. Shishak. He encouraged Jeroboam to lead the ten tribes in revolt against King Solomon's unpopular son, Rehoboam. Later he raided Jerusalem and took away the temple treasure.
1 Kings 11:40; 14:25–26
7. So, who was asked by King Hoshea of Israel to form an alliance against Assyria.
2 Kings 17:4
8. Tirhakah led his army against Assyria during the reign of King Hezekiah. The Assyrian army had to abandon its attack on Jerusalem to meet the Egyptian forces.
2 Kings 19:9; Isaiah 37:9
9. Neco, 610–595 BC. He killed King Josiah of Judah at the Battle of Megiddo. For four years Neco made Judah pay tribute to him, but then he was defeated by Nebuchadnezzar of Babylon at the battle of Carchemish (605 BC). After that Judah was in

Babylon's power. Neco spent his later years defending Egypt and trying to strengthen his country.
2 Kings 23:29ff.; 24:7;
2 Chronicles 35:20 – 36:4
10. Hophra, 587–570 BC. He supported King Zedekiah's rebellion against Nebuchadnezzar of Babylon.
Jeremiah 37:5; 44:30;
Ezekiel 17:15ff.; 29:2
Philemon A Christian friend of Paul who lived in Colossae. Philemon was the master of the runaway slave, Onesimus. (See *Onesimus*.)
Philemon
Philip 1. One of the twelve apostles. He came from the lakeside town of Bethsaida in Galilee, the home town of Peter and Andrew. Philip went straight to Nathanael, told him he had found the Messiah, and introduced him to Jesus. Faced with a crowd of five thousand

hungry people, Jesus tested Philip's faith. 'Where can we buy enough bread to feed all these people?' he asked. Philip was wondering where the money would come from. But Jesus fed them all from five small loaves and two fish. At the last supper, when Jesus said, 'No one goes to the Father except by me,' Philip asked Jesus to show them his father. 'Whoever has seen me,' Jesus answered, 'has seen the Father.'
Matthew 10:3; John 1:43–46; 6:5–7; 12:21–22; 14:8–9; Acts 1:13
2. Son of Herod the Great. His wife, Herodias, left him to marry his half-brother, Herod Antipas. John the Baptist was beheaded because he condemned this marriage.
Mark 6:17
3. Another son of Herod the Great, brother of Antipas and Archelaus. He became ruler of Ituraea.
Luke 3:1
4. Philip the evangelist. One of seven men chosen to help the apostles in the work of the church at Jerusalem. He fled to Samaria when the Christians in Jerusalem were being persecuted by Paul. There he preached and healed many people. An angel sent Philip to meet the Ethiopian chancellor, travelling from Jerusalem to Gaza. This man became a Christian and was baptized. Philip then went and preached in every town along the coast from Ashdod to Caesarea. Philip's four daughters were also involved in making God's message known. About twenty years later Paul stayed at Philip's home in Caesarea.
Acts 6:1–6; 8; 21:8–9
Phinehas 1. The son of Eleazar and grandson of Aaron. When the Israelites were mixing with Midianite women and worshipping their god, Phinehas executed two of the worst offenders. His action stopped an epidemic which had already killed 24,000 people. His faithfulness to God was rewarded with the promise that he and his descendants would always be priests.
Exodus 6:25; Numbers 25; 31:6; Joshua 22:13ff.; Judges 20:28
2. One of Eli's two sons.

(See *Hophni and Phinehas*.)
1 Samuel 2:12ff., 4

Phoebe A Christian woman who was known to Paul. She worked in the church at Cenchreae near Corinth in Greece.
Romans 16:1–2

Pilate Roman governor in Judea AD 26–37. He was cruel and unpopular with the Jews. When Jesus was brought to him to be tried Pilate knew that Jesus was innocent. But he was afraid there would be a riot, and the Emperor would remove him as governor. So he condemned Jesus to death.
Matthew 27; Mark 15; Luke 3:1; 13:1; 23; John 18 – 19

Potiphar Egyptian official who bought Joseph as a slave. (See *Joseph*.)
Genesis 37:36; 39

Priscilla See *Aquila*.

Publius The head man on the island of Malta, when Paul and the others sailing with him to Rome were shipwrecked.
Acts 28:7ff.

Pul See *Tiglath-pileser*.

Quirinius (Cyrenius) Roman governor of Syria at the time of the census which brought Mary and Joseph to Bethlehem.
Luke 2:2

Rabsaris, Rabshakeh, Tartan Titles given to Assyrian officials sent by King Sennacherib to bully King Hezekiah and his subjects into surrendering when Jerusalem was besieged.
2 Kings 18 – 19; Isaiah 36 – 37

Rachel Beautiful daughter of Laban. Jacob worked seven years without pay for Laban because of his love for Rachel; then a further seven, after Laban tricked him into marrying Leah first. For many years Rachel was childless; then Joseph was born. When Jacob left for home, Rachel secretly stole her father's household gods. In Canaan Rachel died giving birth to a second son, Benjamin.
Genesis 29 – 30; 35:18–20

Jacob first saw Rachel when she came to the well to water her father's flock.

Rahab A prostitute who lived in a house on the wall of Jericho. She hid Joshua's two spies because she believed God would give Canaan to the Israelites. In return the spies promised to save Rahab and her family when they captured Jericho. Rahab's name is given as the mother of Boaz in Matthew's list of Jesus' ancestors.
Joshua 2; 6; Matthew 1:5; James 2:25

Rebekah The wife of Isaac and mother of Esau and Jacob. Rebekah grew up in Harran, the city where Abraham lived on his way to Canaan. Her father was Abraham's nephew. When Abraham decided it was time for Isaac to marry he sent Eliezer, his chief steward, back to Harran to find a suitable wife. The first person who came to the well where he was resting his camels was Rebekah. With her family's blessing Rebekah set off for Canaan. Isaac loved her on sight.
For twenty years Isaac and Rebekah prayed for a son. Then twin boys – Esau and Jacob – were born. Home-loving Jacob was Rebekah's favourite; Isaac preferred Esau. When Isaac was old and nearly blind Rebekah helped Jacob to trick his father into giving him the blessing which belonged to Esau, the elder twin. To save him from Isaac's anger, Rebekah sent Jacob to her brother Laban in Harran.
Genesis 24; 25:19 – 26:16; 27

Rehoboam Son of King Solomon. Rehoboam became king after his father's death but was so unwise a leader that the people rebelled. As the prophet Ahijah had predicted, the ten northern tribes made Jeroboam their king. Only Judah and Benjamin stayed loyal to Rehoboam. From this time on, the northern kingdom was known as Israel, and the southern kingdom Judah. Rehoboam was defeated by Egypt and for much of his reign was at war with Jeroboam.
1 Kings 11:43 – 14:31; 2 Chronicles 9:31 – 12:16

Reuben Eldest son of Jacob and Leah. He tried to save Joseph's life when his brothers plotted to kill him. Years later he offered his own two sons as hostages to guarantee Benjamin's safety. Reuben was founder of the tribe named after him.
Genesis 29:32; 37:21 – 22; 42; 49:3

Reuel Another name for Jethro.

Rezin The last king of Syria. Rezin made an alliance with King Pekah of Israel. When Rezin and Pekah attacked Judah, King Ahaz appealed to the Assyrian King Tiglath-pileser III for help. Tiglath-pileser captured Damascus, the capital of Syria, and killed Rezin.
2 Kings 15:37 – 16:9; Isaiah 7:1ff.

Rezon A man from Zobah who became king of Syria. Rezon hated Israel and made trouble for King Solomon throughout his reign.
1 Kings 11:23 – 25

Rhoda Servant girl at the home of John Mark's mother in Jerusalem who answered the door when Peter was released from prison.
Acts 12:12ff.

Rizpah One of King Saul's concubines.
2 Samuel 3:7; 21

Ruth The girl from Moab whose story is told in the Book of Ruth. She married one of Naomi's two sons after the family had gone from Bethlehem to Moab to escape a famine. When Naomi's husband and sons died she decided to go back to Bethlehem. Ruth loved her mother-in-law and went with her. To get food, Ruth gleaned barley in a field belonging to Boaz, a rich relative of Naomi. Boaz treated Ruth well because he knew she had been kind to Naomi. Ruth and Boaz married. Their son, Obed, was the grandfather of King David.
Ruth

Salome One of the women who looked after Jesus and his disciples while they were in Galilee. Salome was present at the crucifixion. On the resurrection morning she was one of the women who took spices to the tomb to embalm the body. Many believe that Salome was the wife of Zebedee and mother of James and John.
(Matthew 27:56) Mark 15:40; 16:1

Samson A Judge in Israel famous for his great strength. Before Samson was born, an angel told his mother he was to be specially dedicated to God as a Nazirite and destined to save Israel from the Philistines. As a sign of this his hair was never to be cut. When Samson grew up he harassed the Philistines singlehanded, although he never fully freed his people. His weakness for women was his undoing. In the end he told a Philistine girl, Delilah, the secret of his strength.
Samson was captured. His hair was cut. He was blinded and put in prison. As his hair grew long again his strength began to return. At a festival Samson was taken to a Philistine temple to amuse the crowd. He grasped the two pillars which supported the temple, prayed and heaved with all his might. The building crashed to the ground, and Samson died with the Philistine leaders and people.
Judges 13 – 16

Samuel The son of Elkanah and Hannah who grew up to be the last great Judge in Israel and one of the first prophets. When Samuel was born, Hannah's heart-felt prayer for a son was answered. In return she kept her promise to God and took Samuel to the shrine at Shiloh to be trained by Eli, the priest. One night Samuel received a message from God that Eli's family would be punished because of his sons' wickedness.
When Eli died, Samuel faced a difficult situation. Israel had been defeated by the Philistines and the people felt God no longer cared about them. Samuel told them to destroy their idols and obey God. Samuel ruled Israel all his life and under his leadership there was peace.
When Samuel was old he made his sons judges and handed his work over to them. But the people were not happy and asked for a king. At first Samuel was against this, but he was guided by God to anoint Saul. After Saul had disobeyed God, Samuel anointed David as the next king. Everyone in Israel mourned when Samuel died.
1 Samuel 1 – 4; 7 – 16; 19:18ff.; 25:1

Sanballat A Samaritan governor who tried to stop Nehemiah rebuilding the walls of Jerusalem.
Nehemiah 2:10, 19; 4; 6; 13:28

Sapphira See *Ananias*.

Sarah Abraham's wife; the mother of Isaac. Abraham married Sarah while he still lived in Ur. Because she was beautiful Abraham twice passed her off as his sister instead of his wife, to protect his own life. When it seemed she would never have any children to inherit the blessing God had promised, Sarah gave her maid Hagar to Abraham, and Ishmael was born. Abraham and Sarah were both old when an angel told Abraham that Sarah would have a son. At first she laughed at the idea, but in due course Isaac was born. He was Abraham's heir. Sarah sent Hagar and her son Ishmael away after Isaac's birth. When Sarah died Abraham bought a cave near Hebron as her burial-place.
Genesis 11 – 12; 16 – 18:15; 20 – 21

Saul First king of Israel. Saul was the son of Kish, a man from the tribe of Benjamin. The Israelites asked their leader, the prophet Samuel, for a king, like other nations. God was their real king but he allowed Samuel to do as they asked. Samuel was guided by God to anoint Saul, the tallest and most handsome man in Israel. Saul was acclaimed as king after he had proved himself in battle.
To begin with he was humble, but he soon became proud and deliberately disobeyed God. Samuel was sent to tell Saul that God had chosen another man to be king. Saul began to suffer from fits of madness. David was known for his skill on the harp and was sent for to soothe the king with his music.
At first Saul treated David kindly, but soon grew jealous of his popularity and tried to kill him. David was forced to escape to the mountains. Saul's power as a leader failed and he was unable to overcome the Philistines. When the Philistine army was preparing to attack Israel again, Saul turned to a

medium for help. In the battle which followed, Saul and Jonathan his son were both killed.
1 Samuel 8 – 31;
2 Samuel 1ff.

Sennacherib King of Assyria, 705–681 BC. He strengthened the Assyrian Empire, sending armies to put down rebel subject nations. After Hezekiah refused to pay tax, Sennacherib attacked Jerusalem. Although he had captured several cities in Judah, Isaiah encouraged Hezekiah not to surrender. Jerusalem was saved. The Egyptian army threatened from the south and death struck the Assyrian army. Sennacherib returned to Nineveh, where he was murdered by two of his sons.
2 Kings 18 – 19;
2 Chronicles 32; Isaiah 36 – 37

Sergius Paulus Roman governor of Cyprus. He was interested in religion and came under the influence of a magician named Elymas. (See *Elymas*.)
Acts 13:7ff.

Seth Third son of Adam and Eve, born after Cain had murdered Abel.
Genesis 4:25ff.

Shadrach See *Abednego*.

Shallum 1. The son of Jabesh; he murdered King Zechariah and made himself king of Israel, 752 BC. Shallum reigned for only one month. He was assassinated by Menahem.
2 Kings 15:10 – 15

2. A son of King Josiah, usually known as Jehoahaz. (See *Jehoahaz*.)
I Chronicles 3:15;
Jeremiah 22:11

Shalmaneser Name of several kings of Assyria. Shalmaneser V (727–722 BC) defeated King Hoshea of Israel and made him pay tax to Assyria every year. When Hoshea rebelled, Shalmaneser besieged Samaria, capital of Israel. After three years Samaria fell and the Israelites were exiled to Assyria.
2 Kings 17

Shamgar One of the Judges in Israel. Shamgar fought off the Philistines.
Judges 3:31; 5:6

Shaphan Best-known of several men of this name is one of King Josiah's important officials. He helped supervise the temple repairs and reported to Josiah the finding of a scroll of God's laws.
2 Kings 22; 2 Chronicles 34

Shebna(h) One of King Hezekiah's most important officials, sent to negotiate with King Sennacherib's spokesmen.
2 Kings 18 – 19; Isaiah 22:15–25; 36 – 37

Shechem The son of King Hamor, a Hivite king. Shechem raped Dinah, Jacob's daughter. (See *Dinah*.)
Genesis 34

Shem Noah's eldest son. He survived the flood and became the ancestor of several 'Semitic' nations, the group of people to which the Hebrews belonged.
Genesis 6 – 10

Sheshbazzar Sheshbazzar led the Jewish exiles back to Jerusalem when King Cyrus of Persia allowed them to return to rebuild the temple. Cyrus handed over to him the treasures Nebuchadnezzar had taken from the temple in Jerusalem before he destroyed it. Sheshbazzar laid the foundations of the new temple.
Ezra 1:8ff.; 5:14ff.

Shimei A man from the tribe of Benjamin who was a relative of King Saul. During Absalom's rebellion Shimei cursed David and accused him of murdering Saul.
2 Samuel 16:5ff.;
19:16–23; 1 Kings 2:8–9

Sihon An Amorite king whose land lay on the east side of the River Jordan. Moses asked Sihon to allow the Israelites to travel through his land to reach Canaan. Sihon refused and attacked Israel. He was defeated.
Numbers 21

Silas A leader of the church at Jerusalem who travelled with Paul on his second missionary journey, in place of Barnabas. At Philippi (in northern Greece) both Paul and Silas were beaten and thrown into prison. After an earthquake shattered the prison they talked to the jailor about Jesus and he became a Christian. Silas stayed in the nearby town of Beroea while Paul went south to Athens, but joined him again in Corinth. He is almost certainly the Christian called Silvanus in some of the New Testament letters. Silvanus helped Peter write his first letter and may well also have helped Paul with his letter-writing. Paul sends greetings from Silvanus in his two letters to the Thessalonians.
Acts 15:22 – 17:15; 18:5;
2 Corinthians 1:19;
1 Thessalonians 1:1;
2 Thessalonians 1:1;
Peter 5:12

Simeon 1. Second son of Jacob and Leah. When Simeon and his brothers went to Egypt to buy corn, he was left behind as a hostage to make sure they brought Benjamin with them next time. Simeon was the ancestor of one of the twelve tribes of Israel.
Genesis 29:33; 34:25ff.; 42:24ff.; 49:5

2. An old man who had been told by God that he would not die until he had seen the Messiah. In the temple he took the baby Jesus in his arms and praised God. His prayer is known as the *Nunc Dimittis*.
Luke 2:22–35

3. A teacher at the church in Antioch. He was probably an African and may well be the Simon of Cyrene who carried Jesus' cross.
Acts 13:1–2

Simon 1. Simon Peter. (See *Peter*.)

2. One of the twelve apostles. He had been a member of the Zealots, an extreme Jewish nationalist group pledged to drive out the Romans.
Matthew 10:4; Acts 1:13

3. A brother of Jesus.
Matthew 13:55

4. A leper who invited Jesus to his house in Bethany. While Jesus was there, a woman anointed his head with expensive perfume.
Matthew 26:6; Mark 14:3

5. A Pharisee who invited Jesus to his house. At dinner a woman wept at the feet of Jesus, dried them with her hair and poured perfume on them.
Luke 7:40ff.

6. Simon of Cyrene, who was ordered to carry Jesus' cross.
Matthew 27:32

7. Simon Magus, a magician at Samaria who tried to buy the apostles' God-given power.
Acts 8:9 – 24

8. A tanner with whom Peter stayed in Joppa.
Acts 9:43ff.

Sisera Captain of the army of Jabin, king of Hazor. He had under his command 900 iron chariots and for twenty years made life unbearable for the Israelites. Sisera was defeated by Deborah and Barak. He escaped on foot, but was killed by Jael when he hid in her tent.
Judges 4 – 5

Solomon The son of King David and Bathsheba. Israel's most famous king. David had fought many wars to create a strong kingdom; Solomon inherited peace. He protected his country by keeping up a strong army and building fortresses. He also made marriage-alliances with the kings of surrounding countries. Israel became a rich country under Solomon's rule. He traded copper and horses for precious cargoes of gold and jewels. Solomon's God-given wisdom made him famous. The Queen of Sheba (south-west Arabia) visited him to test his wisdom.

Solomon built the first temple for God in Jerusalem. The building materials and skilled workmen were provided by Hiram, king of Tyre, in exchange for wheat and oil. It was a magnificent building and stood for 400 years until Nebuchadnezzar destroyed it in 586 BC. He also built palaces for himself and Pharaoh's daughter, one of his wives. Solomon's reign was spoilt by his ill-treatment of his subjects and by his many marriages. He made his subjects angry by demanding free labour and high taxes from them to carry out his building programmes. In the end, Solomon's foreign wives made him turn away from the true God to worship their own gods. When Solomon died, the ten northern tribes rebelled against Rehoboam, his son, and made the rebel leader, Jeroboam, their king.
2 Samuel 12:24; 1 Kings 1 – 11; 1 Chronicles 22:5 – 23:1; 28 – 2 Chronicles 9

Sosthenes 1. Appointed chief official of the synagogue at Corinth when Crispus, the previous ruler, became a Christian. Sosthenes was beaten up after a group of Jews had

failed to persuade Gallio, the roman governor of Achaia, to condemn Paul. If he was later converted, this Sosthenes may be the same as 2 below.
Acts 18:17

2. A Christian known to members of the church at Corinth. The first letter to the Corinthians was sent from Paul and Sosthenes.
1 Corinthians 1:1

Stephanas Stephanas and his family were the first people to become Christians in Achaia (southern Greece). They were amongst the few Christians whom Paul baptized personally at Corinth.
1 Corinthians 1:16; 16:15ff.

Stephen A Greek-speaking Jew who was the first Christian to die for his faith. Stephen was one of seven men chosen by the apostles to arrange care for poor widows in the church at Jerusalem. He had great faith in God. As well as looking after practical matters Stephen preached and worked miracles. He was arrested and brought before the supreme Jewish council (the Sanhedrin). At the end of a brave speech he accused the Jews of killing God's Son. He was stoned to death, but as he died asked God to forgive his murderers. Paul, who was at that time still persecuting the Christians, saw Stephen die.
Acts 6 and 7

Tabitha See *Dorcas*.

Tamar 1. The daughter-in-law of Judah and mother of his twin sons.
Genesis 38

2. David's daughter, raped by Amnon, her half-brother.
2 Samuel l3

Tartan See *Rabsaris*.

Terah Father of Abraham. He set off from Ur with Abraham, intending to go to Canaan. Instead he settled at Harran and died there.
Genesis 11:27–32

Theophilus The person to whom Luke addressed his Gospel and the Acts of the Apostles. He knew something about Christianity but Luke wanted him to have a much fuller explanation. The name 'Theophilus' means 'friend of God'.
Luke 1:3; Acts 1:1

Theudas Leader of a band of 400 rebels. When he was killed, his men

scattered and the movement died out. Gamaliel quoted this example when the apostles were on trial. The movement Jesus had started would similarly come to nothing, unless God was behind it.
Acts 5:34ff.

Thomas One of the twelve apostles. His name means 'twin'. Jesus decided to go to Judea when he heard that Lazarus was ill. Thomas knew that the Jewish leaders there might again try to kill Jesus, but was willing to go and die with him. Thomas's question at the last supper led Jesus to declare, 'I am the way, the truth and the life.' Thomas was not with the disciples when Jesus appeared to them on the first Easter day. He said he would not believe Jesus was alive again unless he saw and touched the scars. A week later, Thomas saw Jesus for himself. 'My Lord and my God,' he said. There is a later tradition that Thomas went as a missionary to India.
John 11:16; 14:5–7; 20:24ff.; 21:1–14; Acts 1:12–14

Tiberius Emperor of Rome in Jesus' lifetime. He ruled AD 14–37. In the Gospels he is simply referred to as 'Caesar'.
Luke 3:1

Tiglath-pileser Tiglath-pileser III (Pul) was king of Assyria, 745–727 BC. He increased Assyrian power by going to war against smaller nations. Israel was one of the countries he invaded. King Menahem paid Tiglath-pileser a large sum of money so that he could remain king of Israel. After King Pekah of Israel and King Rezin of Syria had attacked Jerusalem, Tiglath-pileser responded to King Ahaz's appeal for help by capturing Damascus and several cities in northern Israel. Ahaz became subject to Tiglath-pileser.
2 Kings 15:29; 16:7ff.; 2 Chronicles 28:16ff.

Timothy A Christian from Lystra who was a friend and helper of Paul. His mother was a Jewish Christian; his father Greek. Paul chose Timothy to help him while he was on his second missionary journey. After Paul had left Thessalonica Timothy went back to encourage the

Caesar Augustus ruled Rome at the time of Jesus' birth. Tiberius, pictured here, was emperor during Jesus' adult years.

persecuted Christians there. Later Paul sent him from Ephesus to Corinth to teach the Corinthian Christians. Timothy became leader of the church at Ephesus. He often lacked confidence and needed Paul's encouragement. But he was always loyal and faithful. The two letters which Paul wrote to the younger man are full of wise advice on the leadership of the church.
Acts 16:1–3; 17:13–15; 1 Corinthians 4:17; 1 Thessalonians 1:1; 3:1–6; 1 and 2 Timothy

Tirhakah See *Pharaoh*.

Titus A non-Jewish (Gentile) Christian who was a friend and helper of Paul. Titus was with Paul on one of his visits to Jerusalem and probably travelled with him quite often. For some time Titus worked with the Christians at Corinth. He smoothed over the bad feeling between the Corinthian church and Paul. When Titus rejoined Paul and told him how much better things were, Paul wrote the second letter to the Corinthians. Titus went

back to Corinth with this letter and helped organize a collection there for needy Christians in Judea. He was working in Crete when Paul sent his letter to Titus.
1 Corinthians 16:10; 2 Corinthians 2:13; 7:13ff., 8; 12:18; Galatians 2; 2 Timothy 4:10; Titus

Tobiah An Ammonite who tried to force Nehemiah to stop rebuilding the walls of Jerusalem.
Nehemiah 2:10ff.; 4; 6; 13

Trophimus A Christian from Ephesus who travelled with Paul to Europe and Jerusalem.
Acts 20:4; 21:29; 2 Timothy 4:20

Tychicus A friend and helper of Paul, probably from Ephesus. It is almost certain he travelled with Paul to Jerusalem because he had been chosen by the churches of Asia Minor (Turkey) to take the money they had collected for needy Christians in Judea. Tychicus was with Paul while he was in prison. Paul trusted him and sent him to Colossae and later to Ephesus with the letters he had written. During his last imprisonment in Rome, Paul sent Tychicus to Ephesus to help the Christians there.
Acts 20:4; Ephesians 6:21–22; Colossians 4:7–9; 2 Timothy 4:12; Titus 3:12

Uriah 1. A Hittite soldier in King David's army, and husband of Bathsheba. Because David was in love with Bathsheba, he had Uriah sent to the front line, to get him killed.
2 Samuel 11
2. A priest in Jerusalem. He obeyed King Ahaz's instructions and redesigned the temple to a pattern approved by the Assyrians.
2 Kings 16:10ff.
3. A prophet at the time of Jeremiah; killed by King Jehoiakim because he spoke out against the people of Judah.
Jeremiah 26:20ff.
Uzzah One of the men who helped King David take the Covenant Box (the ark) from Kiriath-jearim to Jerusalem. He drove the cart on which it was placed. When the oxen stumbled, Uzzah put out his hand to steady the ark and died.
2 Samuel 6:3–7
Uzziah See Azariah.
Vashti The queen King Ahasuerus divorced when she refused to obey him.
Esther 1
Zacchaeus A tax collector who lived in Jericho. Because he was a little man, Zacchaeus climbed a tree in order to see Jesus when he came. Jesus looked up and asked if he could visit his house. Zacchaeus was a changed man as a result of his meeting with Jesus.
Luke 19:1–10
Zadok In King David's reign Zadok and Abiathar were the most important priests. At the end of David's reign Abiathar supported Adonijah's claim to the throne. Zadok crowned Solomon as the new king and was rewarded by being made high priest.
2 Samuel 15:24ff.; 17:15; 19:11; 1 Kings 1:7, 32ff.; 2:35
Zebedee A fisherman; the father of James and John, the apostles.
Matthew 4:21–22
Zebulun A son of Jacob and Leah. Father of one of the twelve tribes of Israel.
Genesis 30:19–20; 49:13
Zechariah 1. Zechariah, king of Israel, who reigned for only six months and was murdered by Shallum (752 BC).
2 Kings 14:29; 15:8–12
2. A prophet and priest born during the Jewish exile in Babylon. His first

message was given in 520 BC and is recorded in the Book of Zechariah. By that time the Jews who had returned from exile in Babylon had lost heart and given up rebuilding the temple. Zechariah encouraged them to carry on with this work and promised a bright future.
Ezra 5:1–2; Nehemiah 12:16; Zechariah
3. A priest: the husband of Elizabeth and father of John the Baptist. He was on duty in the temple at Jerusalem when an angel told him he would have a son who would prepare people for the Messiah. Zechariah and Elizabeth were both old. Because he did not believe the angel, Zechariah remained dumb until John was born.
Luke 1
Zedekiah 1. Last king of Judah, 597–586 BC. He was placed on the throne by King Nebuchadnezzar as his subject. When Zedekiah rebelled, Nebuchadnezzar besieged Jerusalem. After several months the Babylonians captured and destroyed the city. Zedekiah was blinded and taken prisoner to the city of Babylon.
2 Kings 24 – 25; 2 Chronicles 36:10ff.; Jeremiah 21, 32, 34; 37 – 39
2. A false prophet who lived in the reign of King Ahab.
1 Kings 22; 2 Chronicles 18
Zephaniah A prophet who lived in Judah in the reign of King Josiah; probably great-great-grandson of King Hezekiah. Zephaniah's message is recorded in the Old Testament book named after him. He warned people in Judah of God's coming judgement if they continued to worship idols and disobey his laws. Injustice would be punished. But for those who returned to God, there would be a bright future.
Zephaniah
Zerah An Ethiopian who led a large army against the troops of King Asa of Judah. Zerah's army was wiped out by the Judeans.
2 Chronicles 14:9–14
Zerubbabel Grandson of King Jehoiachin and a leader of the exiles who returned from Babylon to Judah in 537 BC. He became governor of Judea and worked alongside

Joshua, the high priest. Under their leadership the foundations of the temple were laid. The work ground to a halt until the prophets Haggai and Zechariah encouraged them to spur the people on and finish the task.
Ezra 2:2; 3 – 5; Haggai; Zechariah 4
Ziba Servant of King Saul. After the death of Saul and Jonathan, Ziba told King David that Jonathan's lame son, Mephibosheth, was still alive.
2 Samuel 9; 16:1–4; 19:17ff.
Zilpah Leah's servant and one of Jacob's wives. She was mother of Gad and Asher, two of his twelve sons.
Genesis 29:24; 30:9–13
Zimri Commander in the Israelite army. Zimri killed King Elah and reigned as king of Israel for seven days (885 BC). He was overthrown by Omri.
1 Kings 16
Zipporah Wife of Moses and daughter of Jethro, the man who gave Moses a home when he escaped from Egypt. She was the mother of Moses' two sons.
Exodus 2:16–22; 4:24–26; 18:2–4
Zophar One of Job's three friends who talked to him in his suffering.
Job 2:11

Farming, and selling the produce is at the heart of any non-industrial society.

9

Work and Society in the Bible

The Bible deals with life in many ages and many places. Lifestyles and conditions vary from a semi-nomadic life (part shepherd, part farmer) to the settled life of towns and villages. This in turn changed with the centuries, from the first settlers in Canaan, through the time of the kings of Israel and Judah, and the experience of being captives in a foreign land, to life under Greek and Roman rule. But not everything changed. The lives of ordinary people were not much altered by the great political upheavals. The geography of Israel – with its effect on everyday life – remained the same. And Israel's religion was another constant factor down the ages.

The Bible itself provides much of the information in this section. But this is not its main purpose, and so there are gaps. Archaeology gives much useful information, especially about buildings, tools and other objects discovered in Israel and the surrounding lands. Metal and stone stand the test of time, but wood and leather, cloth and wool, do not last very long in the climate of the Middle East. There are painted pictures from Egypt, and carvings in stone from Assyria to help us picture people of Old Testament times. But the Israelites always avoided picturing people, and not all customs were the same from nation to nation. Then, later, we know a great deal about the Greek and Roman way of life, but cannot be sure how far the Jews in Palestine were influenced by it.

Amateurs, Professionals and Slaves

Throughout the Bible period some of the jobs which would today be the work of 'professionals' were done by each household. Most families owned some land and worked at farming, which often included keeping sheep and goats. Spinning and weaving were done at home by the women of the household. Men built their own homes and were expected to teach the same skills to their children.

Crafts and trades

In Old Testament times Israel had few if any craftsmen who made beautiful things for their own sake. Even when it came to making places of worship, they often had to bring in foreign artists to complete the decoration. It was a poor country and skills were limited to making strictly useful objects. However, certain trades were regarded as skilled from an early period. These were the crafts of certain families, who probably handed down 'trade secrets' from father to son.

Special areas became linked with a particular trade, perhaps because necessary materials were ready to hand. So Succoth became known for the casting of metal utensils. It is likely that some form of trade guilds came into being fairly early, especially in the cities, where the different crafts seem to have had their special quarters. The Bible mentions the carpenters' quarters, the linen workers', the potters', the goldsmiths' and the perfumers' sections.

In New Testament times trade guilds were well known in the Roman Empire. But they had to have a licence from the emperor to make sure they were not simply a cover for undesirable political activities.

Crafts were held in high regard by the Jews at this time. Craftsmen were exempt from the rule that everyone should rise to his feet when a scholar approached. Most of the scribes probably had a trade. The writings of the rabbis mention a nailmaker, a baker, a sandalmaker, a master builder, a tailor. But some trades were despised: among others, tanning, because 'it was dirty'; being a tax collector (publican), because it gave scope for trickery; weaving, because it was women's work. The weavers worked in one of the poorest areas of Jerusalem, close to the Dung Gate.

Slaves and forced labour

Some projects – for example, the building and mining works of the Old Testament kings, and the building works of Herod the Great and his successors – needed enormous numbers of workmen. In Old Testament times slavery was accepted in Israel, but it was not widespread. Men and their families became slaves to better-off households when they were unable to meet their debts. Prisoners-of-war were also made slaves. The Old Testament laws about slaves are remarkably liberal for their time, although people may not always have lived up to these ideals. The Israelites were never allowed to forget that they, too, had once been slaves in Egypt. So they were to free their slaves after six years' service.

King David, however, forced prisoners-of-war to work on his projects. And Solomon organized a system of forced labour using Israelites as well. They were expected to work for the king one month in three. These men, with the slaves, built the roads, fortresses and temples that made Solomon famous. They looked after the king's farms and worked in his factories and mines. Long before, the prophet Samuel had warned the people that having a king would mean compulsory armed service and forced labour. State slavery, if not conscription, probably continued all through the time of the kings of Judah.

In New Testament times there were both Jewish and non-Jewish slaves in Palestine. But they were not forced to do heavy work. For the most part they were servants in the houses of the wealthy and of the court. There do not seem to have been many of them. Workmen for the building projects were more usually hired by the day (as in Jesus' parable of the workers in the vineyard – Matthew 20:1–16). When the temple begun by Herod the Great was completed – AD 62–64 – more than 18,000 men were thrown out of work.

Paul and Peter gave advice to Christian slaves in their letters to various church groups. These men and women lived in the wider Roman Empire, and probably had a much harsher life than that in Palestine.
Deuteronomy 15:12–18; 2 Samuel 12:31; 1 Kings 5: 13–18; 1 Samuel 8:11–18; Ephesians 6:5–9; Colossians 3:22–25; 1 Timothy 6:1–2; Philemon; 1 Peter 2:18–25

Farming

In the main, the people of Palestine have always been farmers, although the nature of the soil, the climate, and other factors made farming a life of constant toil and hardship. A large part of the land was desert and rock, and could not be farmed. When the Israelites first settled in the Promised Land each household was given a plot of land and also, perhaps, grazing rights on land held in common. But, as time passed, those who were well off tried to 'buy out' the small farmers (see Isaiah 5:8), and it was a constant struggle for poor people to hold on to their land.

A typical Israelite farmer did not live on his farm but in a nearby village or town, which was often close to a fortified city. It was important to be within reach of a water supply and protection, in case of enemy invasions. He owned no more land than he and his family could manage by themselves, perhaps with the help of a few servants or hired labourers. Everyone in the farmer's family shared in the work. He might grow arable crops, as well as grapes and olives. He might possess a few

sheep and goats, with one of his sons or a hired shepherd to care for them. Or a farmer might decide to specialize.

The farmer had four main problems: drought; strong winds from the east (the 'sirocco') which could take away his dry soil; locust plagues; and invading armies.

Crops grown
The main crops were grain, grapes (for wine) and olives (for oil). These three are mentioned together over and over again in the Bible (for example, Deuteronomy 7:13; Nehemiah 5:11; Hosea 2:8). But this list of crops can be expanded.

☐ Grain
In the few fertile valleys, the Philistine plain, the Jordan Valley, and the Plain of Jezreel, a valuable crop of

Minding the sheep and goats was work with which the children could help. This modern picture, showing goats being milked, was taken in Turkey.

wheat was grown. Barley was grown more widely, as it needed a shorter growing season and flourished on poorer soil. Spelt and millet were also grown. Bread was the basic item of diet for everyone, and every available valley and lowland area was used for these crops. The many rocks and stones lying about were built into terraces on the hillsides to keep the precious soil from being lost.

□ Vegetables

There were small harvests of vegetables – lentils, peas, beans, onions, cucumbers, garlic and herbs. These were grown near the house or between the vines.

□ Fruit

Wine and raisin cakes were made from grapes. Other fruits included melons, figs, dates, pomegranates and nuts. Many of these provided a useful source of water during the six-month summer drought from May to October. The oil from olives was used for cooking, lighting, medicine and washing. Vines and olives grew on the hillsides.

□ Flax

Some flax was grown for making linen cloth.

Much of the highest land was left for grazing or forestry.

The farmer's year

Some time ago a limestone plaque was discovered dating from about the time of King Solomon, on which was written a kind of schoolboy rhyme. It is called the Gezer calendar.

The two months are (olive) harvest
The two months are planting (grain)
The two months are late planting
The month is hoeing up of flax
The month is harvest of barley
The month is harvest and feasting
The two months are vine tending
The month is summer fruit

Here is the farmer's year at a glance.

□ Olive harvest

From September or October to November there was time for the olives to be picked and pressed for oil. Olive-trees can stand long periods of drought

Sowing.

The farmer's work follows the rhythm of the seasons.

and can grow in very shallow soil. They take two years to mature and, because the fruit ripen slowly, the farmer could pick them whenever he had time.

They were carried in baskets to the vats and, in earlier times, the oil was squeezed out by treading, or pounding with a pestle. Later, a millstone was developed. The olives were placed on a grooved stone wheel, and another stone was turned over them, worked by a beam. The pulp was then pressed under weights.

Large olive presses have been found from the time of David, consisting of a beam which would press on the baskets of olives. The upper end had weights attached, while the lower end was fixed in a hole

Harvesting.

Threshing.

in the wall. The oil ran into stone vats, where it was left for some time to settle and clear.

□ Ploughing and planting

In October/November came the precious 'early rain' after the long summer drought. From then till January was the time for ploughing and planting. The plough was usually a simple wooden stake with a handle and a point of iron (bronze before the time of David). It was attached to a yoke, and drawn by one or two oxen. The farmer could hold the plough with one hand while the other held a stick for beating the oxen. Since

Ploughing.

it was light the plough could easily be lifted over any large stones. It left a furrow 3–4in/80–100cm deep. The seed (wheat, barley, flax) was scattered by hand and then the plough was sometimes used again to cover the seed with earth. Occasionally branches were dragged along to smooth the ground, and a hoe used to remove weeds.

☐ Late planting
From January to March the winter rains fell and planting continued – millet, peas, lentils, melons and cucumbers.

☐ Flax and grain harvests
In March and April the later rains came. These developed the grain to the point where harvesting could begin.

Flax was harvested first, in March and April. The plant was cut with a hoe near to the ground and the stalks were dried, ready to be made into cord and linen cloth.

Then in April, May and June came the harvests of barley and wheat. The stalks were cut with sickles (a small wooden handle with a curved iron or copper blade) and the bundles were tied into sheaves. These were loaded on to donkeys or carts and taken to the 'threshing-floor'. This seems to have been common property and a centre of village life at this time of year. It was usually a rocky outcrop, or clay-covered patch, in a windy spot outside the village. Stones were put around the edge and the sheaves were spread out on the floor about a foot deep.

Sieving grain.

Threshing was done by beating with a stick, or by driving animals round, or by using a threshing-sledge. This was simply a board, or a board on wheels, with bits of stone or iron fixed to it. The stalks were chopped and the grain loosened.

The farmer would then 'winnow', tossing the stalks in the air with a wooden fork or shovel. The straw was blown aside (and in winter used to feed the animals), but the heavy grain fell back on the floor. This was probably then sifted and stored in large earthenware jars, in dry cisterns (silos) dug in the floor, or in 'barns'. There seem to have been large national silos, and the farmer probably paid his 'income tax' (and debts) in grain at this time.

☐ Vines
In June, July and August the vines were pruned and tidied up. Isaiah 5 and Mark 12 provide pictures of how a new vineyard was prepared. A boundary trench was dug, and posts driven in to support a hedge or fence. The young vines were planted in rows and the branches raised up on supports. Then the pruning was done. When the fruit began to form, a shelter of branches or a stone tower was put up, and the household kept

As the grapes ripened, people kept watch over their vineyards from 'watchtowers'.

Winnowing.

The Gezer calendar, which records the months given to different kinds of farm work through the year.

watch against thieves, or raiding foxes or jackals.

☐ Fruit harvest
In August and September the summer fruits were harvested – figs, sycamore figs, pomegranates and grapes. Baskets of grapes were taken to small vats, whose floors sloped towards jars. The grapes were trodden to squeeze out the juice. Great numbers of these vats have been found in the 'Shephelah' (the foothills of Judah).

The picking and the treading of the grapes was all done in holiday mood. The fruit could be eaten at the same time. 'When you walk along a path in someone else's vineyard', says Deuteronomy 23:24, 'you may eat all the grapes you want, but you must not carry any away in a container.' Forty days were needed for the 'lees' or sediment to settle. Then the fermenting wine was stored in new goatskin bags or pottery containers.

In some places wine-making became something of an industry. At Gibeon, fifty-six jar handles have been discovered inscribed with the names of the town and the vineyard owners. In addition there were sixty-three bell-shaped vats used as wine cellars during the time of the kings, together with fermenting-vats and wine presses.

Animals

'Cattle' in Hebrew includes sheep, goats, oxen and asses, but not pigs. Asses were kept for carrying loads, and oxen for ploughing. Only on special occasions were oxen killed for meat. Sheep and goats were always kept together. Sheep mainly provided wool for clothes. They were occasionally eaten as meat – in Israel their distinctive fat tail was considered a rare delicacy. They also provided milk in the form of curds for the very poor. Goats were valuable for meat and milk. Their hair made coarse cloth and their skins made bottles.

Cattle, as well as sheep and goats, were a vital part of the farmer's economy.

The life of the shepherd seems to have altered little from the time of Abraham to that of Jesus. The shepherd led his sheep, knew each one, and watched over them night and day (see John 10:1–6). Despite the rough stone enclosures which served as folds, there was constant danger from thieves and wild beasts – lions, leopards and bears (until they became extinct), wolves and hyenas, jackals, snakes and scorpions. The shepherd carried a staff to catch hold of any sheep which fell, and was armed with a wooden club. If sheep were stolen he had to repay his master. If they were attacked by wild beasts he had to bring back evidence (see Exodus 22:12–13).

New Testament times

Farming changed little in the land of Israel throughout the Bible period, though in other Mediterranean countries notable progress was made. Pharisees often referred to those with no religious education as 'people of the land', which perhaps suggests that the farmer was not held in very high regard. However, the country was being farmed more intensively. A writer of the time described Israel's fruit as being better than that of any other land. Fertile Galilee was producing more flax, and probably some attempts were being made at irrigation. It had, by then, become quite common to keep poultry.

Building, Masons and Carpenters

Materials

The materials available for building were mud, stones and boulders, limestone and wood.

Bricks were widely used where stone was not plentiful. Mud and straw were mixed, shaped – by hand or in wooden moulds – into squares or rectangles, and then dried in the sun. Mud was also used as mortar, sticking loose stones together to make a rubble wall.

The limestone of Palestine is soft and easily cut, but it was not much used for ordinary building work. Sites of old quarries have been found, showing the marks of picks, and unfinished blocks of stone. Hammers, saws, picks, and axes were used as tools. To detach a large block of stone, the rock was split with hammers along the natural faults and wooden wedges hammered in and then soaked. As the wood expanded, the rock cracked.

Skill in building developed slowly in Israel. As slaves in Egypt the Israelites had made bricks for massive building projects. But when they entered the land of Canaan, they showed little interest in building. The spies reported 'large and well fortified' cities in Canaan (Numbers 13:28). But the Israelites destroyed many of these, and the buildings that replaced them were not very impressive.

It was not until the time of David and Solomon that real skill was used, and this must be due mainly to the help and instruction of Phoenician masons and joiners sent by King Hiram of Tyre (see 1 Chronicles 14:1). Buildings put up later, after the alliance with Phoenicia had broken down, reverted to the cruder style. The more elaborate buildings of later times still, owe much to Persian, Greek and Roman influence.

Stones were roughly finished in the quarry, but then sent to the building sites for final trimming. This accounts for the piles of stone chips excavators have found at the palace of Lachish and the later citadel in Jerusalem. But for Solomon's temple, as 1 Kings 6:7 records, the stone was prepared at the quarry, so that there was no sound of hammer, axe or iron tool in the holy place.

Forests were plentiful in

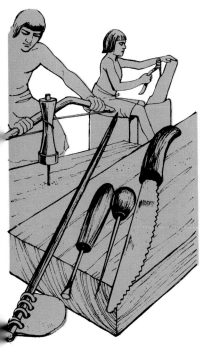

Carpenters at work. The man on the left is using a bow drill; the one on the right an adze. Lying ready: an axe, a chisel, an awl and a saw. These particular tools are Egyptian.

A wooden mallet, bronze chisels and a plumb-bob from Egypt. Tools like these were in use from about 2000 BC.

Israel at that time, particularly in Galilee. For building purposes conifers were often used.

General building work

Building work meant mainly constructing houses and city walls, and digging wells, cisterns, water tunnels and grain silos. These were usually an individual or village community effort. (Compare the building of the walls of Jerusalem by united effort under Nehemiah – Nehemiah 3 – 6.) There was no question of skilled craftsmen doing all the work.

Houses were built on a stone foundation, but the walls were made of brick, plastered on both sides with mud. Sometimes long stones were used as reinforcements and wooden columns were put up on a stone foundation, as supports to extend the reach of the house. Rubble walls were then built between these columns, making small rooms which led off an open court. But normally the house had only one room. Wooden beams were laid across the top of the walls and the roof was made of matting, covered with a plaster of straw, mud and lime. There was usually only one storey, but the roof itself became an extra working-space. A staircase outside the house, or a ladder inside, led up to it. There was a railing round the edge of the roof to prevent accidents.

Town walls were made of rubble or boulder masonry, sometimes plastered and strengthened by towers. The boulders were only roughly shaped, but carefully fitted together. Houses were built along the inside of these walls, but beyond that there was little attempt at town planning. Houses were built wherever there was a space.

As time went on, many houses had a cistern underneath to store rain water. These were

dug out of solid rock, but needed to be lined with slaked lime to stop the water leaking away. Pools for storing water were often cut out of rock and in several cities excavations have revealed tunnels cut to make water more accessible. One at Megiddo is from Israelite times.

Masons and carpenters also made things for everyday use – stone basins, water jars, loom weights, millstones, wooden yokes, ploughs, threshing-boards, carts and furniture.

Special projects

Special building projects of Bible times include David's palace; Solomon's fortifications; the temple and buildings around it in Jerusalem; Ahab's palace at Samaria; Hezekiah's water tunnel in Jerusalem; the rebuilding of Jerusalem after the exile; then the many buildings of Herod the Great and his successors (the temple, Herod's palace, the fortress of Machaerus, the Herodium, Masada, and the harbour at Caesarea). Under Pontius Pilate, an aqueduct was constructed to bring water into Jerusalem.

The temple built by Solomon at Jerusalem must have been the most spectacular early project. Cedar-trees were supplied by Hiram, king of Tyre, who was one of Solomon's allies. Hiram also sent skilled craftsmen. And at this point, for the first time since the Israelites occupied the land, we find finely dressed and shaped stones – ashlar masonry. The corners are well jointed, and bonded; blocks are closely aligned without the use of mortar; and the technique of 'headers' and 'stretchers' is used (stones laid alternately widthwise and lengthwise for extra strength).

The walls of Solomon's temple had three courses of finished stones, surmounted by brick on a row of cedar beams. The wood helped to absorb shock in case of earthquakes. The roof and doors were timber; the floor, walls and ceiling were lined with boards of fir and cedar, decorated with carvings. (See 1 Kings 6.)

The fortifications of Solomon's cities at Hazor, Megiddo and Gezer had city walls of the casemate design (two walls with partitions across, the hollows filled with rubble, or left as store-rooms) and city gates with three guardrooms either side. Under the paved floor of the gate there was a stone drain.

Hezekiah's tunnel was built to bring water from the Gihon spring into the city of Jerusalem. In 1880 an interesting inscription made by the workers was found. It describes two groups of quarrymen, 150ft/45 metres underground, about to meet in the middle after a long (1,750ft/530 metres) and winding route from each end. They can hear one another's picks.

'On the day of the piercing through, the stone-cutters struck through each to meet his fellow, axe against axe. Then ran the water from the spring to the pool . . .'

Because of King Herod's building programme the building trade at the time of Jesus had an important position in Jerusalem. Herod

Women at work plastering the outside walls of their house with mud, as people in Israel did in Old Testament times and for many centuries.

is said to have prepared 1,000 wagons for transporting stones, some of which may have been quarried from the caves under the city itself. Stones 5−10 tons in weight were produced and were moved to the buildings, perhaps on rollers. Arches and vaults were constructed on the Roman pattern.

Jerusalem in Herod's day was also a typical city of the Roman Empire. Excavations of first-century Jerusalem have uncovered large houses built on a lavish scale. There is underfloor heating and piped water. A paved Roman road in a village nearby is flanked by stone holders for torches, to serve as street lights. The houses of the poor continued to be simple, but probably most had more than one storey.

The earliest homes were tents. The picture shows Bedouin sewing together widths of woven goats' hair to make a tent.

Clothes-making

The main materials used for making clothes were linen (from flax), sheep's wool, goats' hair and animal skins (see *Other Jobs: Leatherwork*). Cotton was not used in Israel until they began to import it, probably after the exile. The Israelites loved to decorate their clothes with brightly coloured fringes, borders, and tassels. Gold thread was used to embroider very special clothes – for example, for the high priest (Exodus 39:3).

Linen

In Israel flax grew only on the southern coastal plain, near Jericho, and in Galilee, though in New Testament times the amount grown in Galilee was greatly increased. The Egyptians grew a great deal of flax and, by soaking the flax in running water, were able to produce a very soft kind of linen. The Bible calls this 'fine linen'. It was a 'fine linen robe' that Pharaoh gave to Joseph when he appointed him governor (Genesis 41:42). Linen was used for making clothes and ships' sails. Rahab, in Jericho (Joshua 2:6), hid the spies beneath flax spread out on her roof.

After the flax was cut and dried, the seeds were removed. It was then soaked and dried again in an oven. The fibres were separated and then it was ready for spinning and weaving. Linen was not usually dyed, though occasionally blue threads were woven in. (The blue linen robe which the high priest wore was very special – Exodus 28:31.) So, when the Bible talks about coloured clothes, it usually means woollen ones.

Wool

After being dipped, the sheep were shorn in the spring. The new wool was washed, or sent to the fuller to be cleaned of natural oils. He would do this by treading out the wool on a rock in water. The wool was then spread out to be dried and bleached in the sun. We read of the 'fuller's field' in 2 Kings 18:17, beside a water supply and – as it often was – outside the city because of the smell. The fuller also worked on the newly woven cloth to shrink it, and sometimes he was responsible for dyeing the wool.

Brightly coloured fabric displayed for sale at the Bedouin market, Beersheba.

Dyeing

In Genesis 30:32 Laban's flock included black and white, striped and spotted sheep! This is a reminder that wool can have many natural colours. So the basic dyes will produce a variety of shades. The colours the Bible refers to most often are blue, scarlet, and purple. These may have been the basic dyes. Purple clothes were a sign of royalty and wealth. A poor quality purple may have been produced by dyeing, first with blue, then with red. The best purple came from Tyre and was very expensive. It was made from molluscs (sea snails) found on the east Mediterranean coast. The industry was firmly in the hands of the Phoenicians, and the Israelites probably had to import all their purple clothes.

Certain places in Israel – where there was a good water supply and good grazing for sheep – became centres for dyeing. Among these were Gezer, Bethshemesh, Beth-zur and Debir. At Debir excavations have shown that about thirty homes had rooms specially designed for dyeing. Each contained two stone vats with small openings on top.

Potash and slaked lime were probably put into the vat and dye added later, with more dye in the second vat. The wool was given two baths. The potash and lime fixed the dye, and the wool was laid out to dry. It was then ready for spinning and weaving. Almost every home at Debir also had a loom.

Spinning and weaving

After being combed, the wool was spun into yarn. Spinning was usually the women's work. It was probably done on a simple hand spindle, although only the stone, clay and bone whorls of these have been found. Two main types of loom were used in Israel: a vertical loom and a horizontal loom.

The weaver stood in front of the vertical loom, with the downward threads (warps) attached to a beam across the top (Goliath's spear is said to have been as thick as a weaver's beam – 1 Samuel 17:7) and held down with weights. As the weaver worked, the cross-wise threads were beaten upwards. Five or six warps could be worked on at a time, which made it possible to produce patterns. Because the weaver could move about, he was able to make wide pieces of material. Later a rotating beam was made for the bottom of the loom. The web was begun at the bottom and the finished cloth rolled up. This made it possible to make quite long lengths of cloth.

The horizontal loom was made of two beams, held in place by four pegs in the ground, and the weaver sat in front. The loom could be no wider than the reach of the weaver's arms, although the Egyptians seem to have had a system of two people working this loom. Both wool and linen were woven on this type of loom, and sometimes also the coarser goats' or camels' hair for thick shepherds' cloaks and for tents.

When the Bible talks about embroidered cloth (see Judges 5:30; Ezekiel 26:16) it may refer to different cloths sewn together, or woven patterns, although the Israelites did have embroidery and tapestry.

Shaping clothes

There were two main ways of shaping a garment. If the loom was wide enough, the whole garment could be made in one piece (Jesus had a seamless robe – John 19:23). The weaver started at the sleeve edge and worked across to the other sleeve edge, leaving a hole for the neck.

Sleeves could be as long or short as the person wanted, and the striped pattern was easy to make. When cut off, the free warps were twisted into cords which strengthened the sides. Sometimes they were left as tassels at the bottom corners.

If the loom was narrow, the garment was made in three pieces; the main bodice and sleeves; the front skirt; and the back skirt. The neck opening was given a woven binding to strengthen it.

Sometimes circular garments

A woman spinning outside her tent in the Taurus mountains, Turkey.

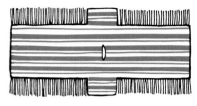

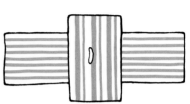

were made. The weaver began in the middle and the web was broadened a warp or two at a time.

Dress styles

(See Part 7: *Home and Family Life in the Bible*, under *Clothes and Fashion*.) It is not easy to

be sure of the details of styles of dress. We have some pictures and we have the Bible's descriptions, but it is sometimes hard to match the two.

At the time of the patriarchs (Abraham to Joseph) there was an ankle-length garment draped over one shoulder and leaving the other bare. It seems unlikely that this was woven, because the top edge is diagonal and the bottom is scalloped. It may have been made of skins and strips of felted wool.

A man might wear a short wrap-round skirt of linen or leather, secured by a belt, with a kind of short-sleeved T-shirt on top. Belts were made of wool and sometimes highly decorated. Proverbs 31:24, describing the 'ideal wife', says that 'she makes clothes and belts, and sells them to merchants'.

A nomad girl working at her loom.

Both men and women often wore an undergarment or tunic of the basic design, sometimes decorated with a sash, and, over the top, a fringed cloak of linen or wool. The main difference between men's and women's clothes was that the women's were more colourful.

In New Testament times, too, the tunic and cloak were the basic dress. The Greek tunic was fuller, though the belt made it possible to shorten it, and it was often sleeveless. Cloaks of many different kinds were worn. But only Roman citizens could wear the Roman toga.

Mining and Metalwork

In Deuteronomy 8:9 Moses promises the Israelites that the land of Canaan will be rich. 'Its rocks have iron in them, and from its hills you can mine copper.' In fact these are the only two metals native to the region of Israel. Gold, silver, tin and lead had to be imported.

Gold and silver

Gold was probably the first metal known to man, because it is found in a pure state and needs no complicated process to cast it. When the Israelites left Egypt, the Egyptians had been using gold for many centuries. They took ornaments of gold and silver with them out of Egypt. And they knew how to work these metals.

To make solid objects the metal was melted and poured into moulds. Exodus 32:4 describes Aaron taking earrings, melting them and pouring the gold into a mould to make a gold bull. Gold could also be beaten into sheets, to cover objects, or beaten into a particular shape. The different Hebrew words for gold in the Old Testament, usually translated 'pure gold', 'fine gold', and 'choice gold', may indicate differences in colour and quality, but the exact meanings are unknown.

When the Israelites entered the land of Canaan, gold and silver formed part of the spoils of war. Craftsmen probably made ornaments and jewellery for those who could afford them and, in times of religious decline, they adopted the practices of the surrounding nations and made idols of silver or overlaid with gold. (This custom was strongly criticized by the prophets.)

Israelite craftsmen cannot have been very experienced. When Solomon needed intricate gold and silver work for the temple and other buildings, he employed experts from Phoenicia. He imported gold from 'Ophir' and is said to have made silver 'as common in Jerusalem as stone'.

The process of refining gold and silver – melting it to separate off the impurities – is often used in the Bible as a picture of the purifying effects of suffering.
Exodus 11:2; 32:4; 25:11, 31; Joshua 6:19; 22:8; Judges 17:1–4; Isaiah 2:20; 40:19; Hosea 8:4; 2 Chronicles 2:7; 1 Kings 10:1–27; Zechariah 13:9; Malachi 3:2–3; 1 Peter 1:7

A copper dagger with a gold hilt from the Royal Graves at Ur, about 2600 BC.

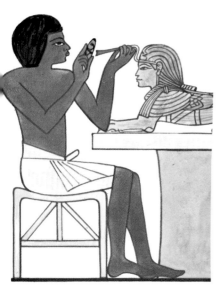

An Egyptian goldsmith shapes and decorates a gold sphinx.

Copper

Copper was the most plentiful metal in early Israel. It was extracted from ore by heating (smelting) and, although the metal was rather spongy, it could be hardened and shaped by cold hammering. At some time before 2000 BC it had been discovered that if up to four per cent of tin was added, the copper was stronger and harder. Its melting-point was also lower, and it could be poured into a mould and cast into shape. The result is bronze. However, the Hebrew words for copper and bronze are the same, so it is not clear when the Israelites began to make bronze. It would certainly have been needed for the finely shaped work of Solomon's temple – the great bronze basin ('sea'), resting on twelve bronze bull-calves, and the bronze pillars whose tops were decorated with lilies and pomegranates.

Copper ore is to be found in the Sinai peninsula and in the Arabah, the desert area between the Dead Sea and the Gulf of Aqaba. Archaeology has shown that this area was being mined while the Israelites were in Egypt, and even much earlier. There is a site at Timnah, fifteen miles north of Elath, where the underground shafts penetrate for hundreds of yards in all directions and at several levels. The deeper workings are hundreds of feet below the surface, and ventilated through air channels.

Job 28 describes the work of mining for silver and, although they did not mine silver in Israel, the picture applies equally to mining for copper and iron. 'They search the depths of the earth and dig for rocks in the darkness. Men dig the shafts of mines. There they work in loneliness, clinging to ropes in the pits.'

Some have suggested that the Israelites learned the art of smelting and working copper from the Kenites (or Midianites), the desert tribe into which Moses married. Another suggestion is that there were travelling tinkers or smiths attached to communities from an early period. An Egyptian tomb-painting shows a group of Asiatics with what seem to be goatskin bellows.

A furnace from the Judges period has been found at Bethshemesh. Here copper was smelted on a small scale, and the heat was intensified, probably through pottery blowpipes or bellows.

Other furnaces dating from the time of Solomon have been found in Israel, some for treating copper, others for iron. The smiths would receive the metal, melt it in a clay pot over the fire and then shape the articles, sometimes using stone moulds. Their main products were for army and home use: arrow-heads, lances and spear-tips, swords, daggers, axes, plough-points, adzes, chisels, needles, safety pins, tweezers, bracelets, bowls and pails.

It is not clear how much mining and smelting activity went on in Solomon's time. At one time archaeologists thought that there had been a minor 'industrial revolution'. They had discovered a number of mining sites and small smelting furnaces in the Arabah. The furnaces were of different shapes – some round, some square and some with two compartments. There were also traces of encampments, where the workers, probably slaves, lived. Brick buildings discovered at a site at the head of the Gulf of Aqaba were identified with the town the Bible calls Ezion-geber. They were thought to belong to a giant smelting-plant to which copper

Assyrian workmen carrying picks and shovels. A relief from Nineveh, about 695 BC.

was sent to be prepared for export, after the initial smelting on the site.

But these proposals are now seriously doubted. More recent excavations have shown that the most impressive mining works were used only at a much earlier period, even before the conquest of Canaan – while the brick buildings may have been a large fortified inn on an important trade-route.

Iron

The use of iron spread very slowly in Israel. It needed to be heated as it was being worked, and so was difficult to produce. When the Israelites entered Canaan, the Canaanites already had chariots with iron fittings and other equipment.

When the Philistines defeated the Israelites in the days of Samuel and Saul, they would not let them have blacksmiths of their own in case they made strong swords and spears. If the Israelites wanted their copper tools sharpened or repaired they had to go to the Philistines, who charged crippling prices. David, however, had great stores of iron. He 'supplied a large amount of iron for making nails and clamps'.

Arrowheads, spearheads and a dagger from the time of the Greek and Persian wars.

And, from this time on, iron objects became more plentiful. Iron ore was also discovered and mined in the Arabah. Joshua 17:16; 1 Samuel 13:19–22; 1 Chronicles 22:3

The New Testament period

In New Testament times there was a smiths' bazaar in Jerusalem. But workers in bronze and iron were not allowed to work on certain religious feast days because of the noise they made. The extravagances of King Herod's court meant an increased trade in luxury goods.

In the temple that Herod built in Jerusalem the double gate, thresholds and lintel were overlaid with gold and silver. The walls inside were covered with gold plating. There were gold and silver lamps and bowls and there were even spikes of gold on the roof to keep the birds away! A thousand priests had to be trained to do much of this work, because no one else was allowed to enter the sacred temple area.

Pottery

By comparison with the products of her neighbours, Israel's pottery seems poor and not very artistic. There is an immense difference between the painted pottery of the Canaanites and Philistines and the limited designs of the Israelites when they eventually occupied the land. But this is because the Israelites were making their pots with a view to usefulness rather than decoration. The forms were good and they were carefully produced.

At the time of King David, craftsmanship improved. There were new shapes and there was some form of decoration. This progress went on and, during the time of the kings, the making of pottery developed into a minor industry with small 'factories', mass production, some standard shapes, and trade marks. Many more pots were made, but the standard was high.

In New Testament times it seems that a good deal of fine pottery was imported.

The potter and his methods

☐ The potters

It is possible, especially during the time of the later kings, that several potters worked together, with their apprentices (often their own sons). There is evidence that potters kept the temple worshippers supplied with pots fit to use for cooking a sacrificial meal in the temple courts.

A Greek vase showing a hunter with his dog. About 550 BC.

There also seems to have been a royal guild of potters 'in the service of the king' (1 Chronicles 4:23). They probably produced large jars for storing produce from the king's private estates. Jars have been found (holding about 10 gallons/45 litres) with a stamp on the handles: 'Belonging to the king'. Underneath is the name of one of four cities: Hebron, Ziph, Socoh, or Memshath. These may have been the sites of royal vineyards, or centres where the people brought their taxes in the form of produce.

The potter's workshop

The whole process of producing pottery was probably carried out on one site. There had to be a handy water supply (a stream or cistern), wheels for shaping the clay, and kilns for firing it. The yard of the potter's house or workshop would be used for preparing the clay and no doubt also became the place where broken pottery or rejects from the kiln (potsherds) would pile up.

Jeremiah 19:2 speaks of the 'Potsherd Gate' near the Valley of Hinnom. Presumably there was a potter's house there. In Nehemiah 3:11 and 12:38 we read of the 'Tower of the Ovens' or 'Tower of the Furnaces' and these expressions may refer to pottery kilns in Jerusalem.

Preparing the clay

Pottery was made from the local red clay. The potter did not alter the quality of the clay, except by mixing it occasionally with ground limestone, which was readily available. This enabled the finished pot to withstand heat (useful in the case of cooking-pots), but it meant that the potter had to fire the clay at a lower temperature, otherwise the limestone would decompose.

The raw clay was exposed to the sun, rain and frost to break it up and remove impurities. Then water was added and it was trampled into mud (see Isaiah 41:25). This needed skill. The water had to be measured and poured on evenly, and the air removed.

Working the clay

When the clay had been prepared, three methods of working it were open to the potter.
● The clay could be pressed down in a mould. Canaanite plaques were made this way, and so also were most of the lamps of New Testament times. Job 38:14 refers to the imprint of a seal on clay.
● The clay could be modelled freehand. In Israel the only things made in this way seem to have been toys, ovens and a few pots.
● Or the clay could be shaped on a wheel – and this was the usual method of working.

The earliest type of potter's wheel known was a circular disc, rotating on a vertical shaft. But about the time of the exodus a different type came into use. This had a second, larger disc, mounted below the first. This speeded the turning and may have been kept moving by the potter's assistants. Potters' wheels were probably used everywhere, but the Bible only mentions one once (when Jeremiah visits the Potter's house – Jeremiah 18:3), and wheels are rarely found. Perhaps they were usually made of wood or clay and so have not survived. Stone wheels have been found at Megiddo, Lachish and Hazor. There is no evidence of a foot-operated wheel before 200 BC, although it was widely used in New Testament times.

When the pot had been shaped, it was allowed to harden. Then it could go back on the wheel and be turned into more delicate forms. At the time of the later kings production was speeded up in various ways. Sometimes a very large lump of clay was put on the wheel and pots were

Inset photographs are of a painted jug from about 1700 BC, a first-century AD Roman lamp showing people treading grapes, and a Roman lamp from Turkey.

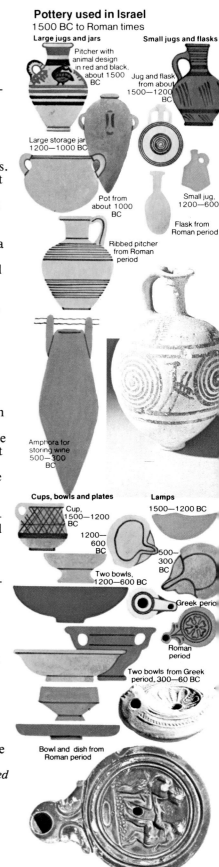

Pottery used in Israel
1500 BC to Roman times

Large jugs and jars

Pitcher with animal design in red and black, about 1500 BC

Large storage jar 1200—1000 BC

Pot from about 1000 BC

Ribbed pitcher from Roman period

Amphora for storing wine 500—300 BC

Small jugs and flasks

Jug and flask from about 1500—1200 BC

Small jug, 1200—600

Flask from Roman period

Cups, bowls and plates

Cup, 1500—1200 BC

1200—600 BC

Two bowls, 1200—600 BC

Bowl and dish from Roman period

Lamps

1500—1200 BC

500—300 BC

Greek period

Roman period

Two bowls from Greek period, 300—60 BC

shaped from the top of it, each one being 'pinched off' as it was completed. Sometimes unskilled workers shaped the clay roughly on the wheel. They used cheap clay and made thick pots, which were then turned into the desired shape and thickness by skilled potters.

☐ **Firing**
The firing of the clay objects in a kiln was the ultimate test of a potter's art. Different clays needed different treatment. But the methods of firing are not known. A number of kilns have been found. Some of them have a U shape, but it is not easy to tell whether they were used for pottery or for copper.

were made. They may have been dipped in milk or olive oil before firing and then lightly polished.

Glazing was used by the Greeks and Romans.

Articles made by the potter
Pottery articles can be divided into two basic designs.

☐ **The bowl**
This could range from a large banquet bowl with four handles, to a small cup (which rarely had handles). Bowls were used for mixing wines, serving food, holding coal, cooking, and so on. The household oven was really an inverted bowl with the

A potter at work in northern Iraq.

uments. And small juglets were specially produced for perfume.

Other objects made of pottery included water bottles for a journey; articles for industry (crucibles, clay moulds, spindle whorls, loom-weights); toys (dolls, horses, camels); and clay objects connected with the Canaanite religion.

If pots were broken, they were sometimes mended with rivets or wires. Sometimes notes or letters were written on pieces of broken pottery. For example, we know of a series of letters (the 'Lachish Letters') written on pieces of pottery (ostraca), from the commander of a smaller garrison to his superior at Lachish during King Nebuchadnezzar's final attack on Judah.

☐ **Decoration**
The Israelites did not glaze their pottery but they had three main ways of decorating it.
● They could use a 'slip'. Fine clay with a rich iron content was thinned with water and then brushed over the parts which the potter wished to decorate.
● Sometimes they painted a line of red or black around the shoulder or middle of the jar or jug.
● They could 'burnish' pots either by hand or on the wheel. To do this, a tool of stone, bone or wood would be rubbed against the clay after drying but before firing. These areas would then shine after firing.

The 'slip' and 'burnish' were sometimes combined.

Some of the perfume jugs which have been found are black. It is not clear how these

A kiln showing pots at various stages. This picture was taken in Israel.

bottom missing. The clay would simply be moulded into shape. It hardened when used as an oven. Broken bits of pot were plastered round the outside to moderate the heat.

Lamps were thrown in the same way as a bowl, and the rims were pinched in while the clay was still soft. Their style changed considerably during the history of Israel, but the basic design was the same. The gradual changes, at different stages, enable the experts to use them as an indication of date.

☐ **The jar or pitcher**
There were jars for wine, for water and for oil. Jars were also used for storing doc-

Other Jobs

Leatherwork

Bible references to articles made with leather (from sheep-and goatskins) include clothes, belts and footwear. The complete hides of small animals were sewn together to make bottles for wine, water and milk. Tents were originally made of leather covering, but later felt or woven goats'-hair was used, as it is today by the Bedouin. Leather was also used as a writing-material. The Isaiah manuscript of the Dead Sea Scrolls, dating from 150 BC, was written on seventeen sheets of leather, the skins sewn together. The details of how leather was processed and worked are not known, but two or three different trades may have been involved.

● There was the job of skinning the animals. Knives have been found which may have been used for this.

● There was the job of tanning. In early times this may simply have been a process of drying the hides in the sun, or perhaps treating them with the juice of certain plants. But tanners were expected to live outside a town because their work was smelly.

● There was the work of shaping and sewing the leather. Paul, Aquila and Priscilla are said to have been 'tentmakers', but some think that this word may mean 'leatherworkers'. Genesis 3:21; 2 Kings 1:8; Ezekiel 16:10; Exodus 26:14; Acts 18:3

Hunting

Esau, we are told, hunted 'venison' (deer). The people of Israel had laws on the subject of hunting – particularly which animals and birds could be eaten and how they were to be

An Assyrian hunting scene. Men trapping deer in a net.

killed. Israelite kings may have hunted for sport, as the Mesopotamians and Egyptians did, since 'deer, gazelles, roebucks and poultry' were brought to the table of Solomon. People hunted when hunger, or the attacks of wild animals on their flocks, drove them to it. But we do not know whether men regularly hunted for a living. The Old Testament references to catching animals are few.

However, the country lies on a main migration route for birds, so it is not surprising to find frequent mentions of the 'fowler' with his nets and snares.
Genesis 25:27; Deuteronomy 14:4–5; Leviticus 17:13; 1 Kings 4:23; Proverbs 1:17; Hosea 7:11–12; Proverbs 6:5; Psalm 124:7

Fishing

In view of all the references in the Gospels, it may seem surprising to include fishing in a section on 'other jobs'. But in fact the Israelites were not much involved in the fishing trade until New Testament times. There is only one Hebrew word for fish – to cover everything from the smallest 'tiddler' to the great fish that swallowed Jonah. The main fishing industry in Old Testament times was in the hands of the Phoenicians, though the presence of a 'Fish Gate' is probably an indication of a market for imported fish in Jerusalem.

By the time of Jesus, however, a flourishing industry seems to have developed on the inland Sea of Galilee. The name of the lakeside town,

A fowling scene from an Egyptian tomb.

Tarichaea ('pickling'), probably indicates that it was a centre for salting and preserving fish. The Gospels describe the fishermen working in family groups, and often using hired helpers. They mended nets and sails, repaired boats and often fished by night. This was dangerous, for storms could quickly blow up on the lake.

An Assyrian catching fish in a pond, using a hook and line. Pictured on a palace relief, from about 700 BC.

Bone or iron fish-hooks were used from early times. Isaiah refers to a hook and line (no rod was used) and Job mentions a spear, but fish were usually netted. There were two kinds of nets. One was a net thrown by hand while the fisherman stood on the shore. The other was a large net (dragnet) used from the boats, with floats and weights attached so that it moved vertically through the water, bringing the fish to the boats or to shallow water in smaller and smaller circles. The fish were brought to the shore and sorted before being sent to market.
Nehemiah 13:16; Mark 1:20; Isaiah 19:8; Job 41:7; Ecclesiastes 9:12; Matthew 13:47-48

Ivory-carving
No list of the crafts in Israel would be complete without a mention of ivory carving, although probably not many craftsmen were involved in it, and those who were may have been mostly foreigners. Ivory was rare. It had to be imported from Africa (or from Syria in the early times). It was a favourite with the kings, but the prophets condemned its use as a symbol of extravagance and idle living.

Solomon probably used ivory carvings and inlay in the temple decorations, but the only detail mentioned in the Old Testament is that he had an ivory throne. King Ahab of Israel built an 'ivory house' in Samaria, his capital. It is at Samaria that the largest Israelite collection of ivory has been found. Excavations have shown that the art flourished among all the Near Eastern nations. Objects found consist mostly of small carvings, inlays and sculptures.
1 Kings 10:22; Ezekiel 27:15; Amos 3:15; 1 Kings 22:39

Gem-cutting
The Israelites used semi-precious stones such as agate, jasper, carnelian and rock-crystal. These were cut and polished to make beads, or engraved with designs, and sometimes the owners' names, to serve as seals. The Bible mentions many different stones, although not all can be identified. Engraving stones and

A carved ivory showing a man holding a lotus. From Nimrud, eighth century BC.

setting them in gold for the high priest's breastplate are described in Exodus 28:9-14.

Glass-making
The art of making articles of glass never seems to have been common in Israel. Long before the Israelites entered Canaan the Egyptians and Babylonians had discovered how to make an opaque form of glass and to shape it over a core of sand. By New Testament times the Romans were making transparent glass and 'blowing' it into shape. Many of the glass articles which have been found in Israel were clearly imported.

Government officials and secretaries
It would be an exaggeration to think in terms of a 'civil service', but throughout Bible history there was always a need for people to serve as administrators, tax collectors and secretaries. In Mesopotamia and Egypt special schools had been instituted to train men for these tasks (see *Education*). Even in the desert, on the way from Egypt, there may have been people appointed by Moses to take the census and receive the contributions for the worship tent (tabernacle).

Solomon organized the country into twelve administrative districts and an officer over each was responsible for collecting tax due to the king. Another department dealt with drafting men for enforced work and this included, among others, two secretaries and a man in charge of records.

The collecting and recording of tax was probably a specialized occupation throughout the time of the kings. In Samaria a storage house has been found containing sixty-three 'ostraca' (pieces of pottery used for writing notes) from the time of Amos. Most of them record receipts for wine and oil deliveries to the king's house.

There were also secretaries to write letters and receive dictation. Jeremiah had a secretary, to whom he dictated his messages. And the same man, Baruch, took charge of the deed of purchase when Jeremiah bought a plot of land.

Tax collectors continued to feature in the Gospels. The Romans sold to Jewish agents the right to collect certain taxes. This was bitterly resented by most of the Jews. Because these collectors worked for the hated Romans and often collected money for themselves, they were regarded as robbers. They were disqualified from holding public or religious office, and were not even allowed to give evidence in the Jewish courts. Exodus 30:11–16; 1 Kings 4:1–6; Jeremiah 36:4; 32:11–12; Luke 19:1–9

Medicine

Diseases

Even where symptoms are described in the Bible, it is not always possible to be sure what diseases were involved. Some form of leprosy was fairly common. Shortage of food in drought, combined with the heat and poor water supply, often led to dysentery, cholera, typhoid and beriberi ('dropsy'). The dust-filled air made blindness very common. Then there were the deaf and the crippled. The number of deaths among children was clearly quite high.

Mental illness was not uncommon. But the Bible often does not make any distinction between this and being possessed by evil spirits. There may also have been a popular belief that 'fits' could be caused by the moon. (In Matthew 4:24, 'epileptic' translates a word which literally means 'moonstruck'.) 2 Samuel 12:15; 2 Kings 4:20; 1 Kings 17:17; 2 Kings 5:1–14; 1 Samuel 19:9; Daniel 4:33

Attitudes to disease

The attitude to illness in Israel was always quite distinct from that of Israel's neighbours. The Mesopotamians and the Egyptians in early times regarded illness as invariably caused by the malice of evil spirits. Treatment was therefore in the hands of exorcist-priests and involved incantations and magic, alongside other methods. Israel also regarded health as a religious matter, but this was because the people firmly believed that God was all-powerful. From him came both good and evil. Health was a divine blessing.

This crippled Egyptian may have had infantile paralysis.

Disease was a sign that the spiritual relationship between a person and God had broken down. Magic was therefore officially forbidden, although no doubt the ordinary people practised it to some extent. The discovery of many small images, probably used as charms, seems to indicate this.

This attitude to illness, however, also had its drawbacks. God was the only true healer. He had given his people a set of rules. If they obeyed, they would enjoy good health. If they disobeyed, they would not. Occasionally God would use his prophets as healers. But this was exceptional and there

was no recognized place for doctors, no reason to explore the physical causes of disease, and little place for medical skills.

The Babylonian king, Hammurabi, had drawn up a code of laws in about 1750 BC. It fixed doctors' fees, and set out penalties for surgeons who were careless in performing operations. The Egyptians were also doing surgery, studying anatomy by dissecting dead bodies, and writing medical and surgical notes on papyrus. But this was unthinkable in Israel. The first reference to doctors in the Bible is critical: 'Asa was crippled by a severe foot disease; but even then he did not turn to the Lord for help, but to doctors.' The book of Job, however, challenges the view that disease is always the direct result of a person's sin.

By the second century BC the prestige of doctors had increased. In Ecclesiasticus it is said that although God is the healer, he has given gifts of healing to men and has provided medicines for the cure of illness. Jesus resisted the view that it is specific sin which always causes illness. He saw disease as evidence of the power of evil in the world as a whole. In healing diseases he was attacking the kingdom of Satan, but this implied no criticism of the work of doctors. General attitudes, however, were hard to change, as certain recorded Jewish sayings show. 'Physician, heal yourself.' 'Live not in a city whose chief is a medical man, for he will attend to public business and neglect his patients.' 'Even the best among doctors is deserving of Gehenna' (hell). Leviticus 26:14−16; Deuteronomy 7:12−15; 2 Chronicles 16:12; John 9:3; Luke 13:16; Mark 2:17; Luke 4:23

Treatment of disease

It is interesting to notice how Israel's laws compensated for their general ignorance about hygiene. To obey these laws was part of their religious duty, but obedience obviously contributed to keeping them healthy as well.
● First there must be one day of complete rest each week for physical and spiritual refreshment.
● Then there were certain foods which must not be eaten. This included pork which, in a sub-tropical climate, carries a high risk of food poisoning. And water must be free from contamination.
● All males must be circumcised − an operation believed to prevent venereal disease.
● A man must not marry members of his own family.
● Careful attention must be paid to cleanliness, in daily personal habits and in sexual relationships.

This is the earliest evidence we have of preventive medicine. The priests were expected to enforce these laws and to take special action in the case of 'leprosy' (though this may not have been the leprosy which we know today).

The prophets occasionally concerned themselves with health. Elisha neutralized poisonous herbs, purified the water of Jericho, and helped to cure Naaman and the Shunammite woman's son. In 2 Kings 20:1−7 Isaiah advises Hezekiah to apply a poultice of figs to a boil − the only real 'prescription' in the Old Testament.

Hippocrates, whose principles many doctors today still swear to follow.

A blind harpist from Egypt.

Various oils and perfumes were used in personal hygiene − myrtle, saffron, myrrh and spikenard. Olive oil and 'balm of Gilead' (a spicy resin) were swallowed or put on wounds and sores. Isaiah's description of Judah throws light on the treatment of wounds: 'You are covered with bruises and sores and open wounds. Your wounds have not been cleaned or bandaged. No ointment has been put on them.' Certain herbs may have been used as painkillers, for example the 'wine mixed with a drug called myrrh' offered to Jesus on the cross. Many effective herbs must have been known, but there must also have been a good deal of superstition. It was widely believed, for example, that mandrake roots would help women to conceive children.

Broken arms and legs were bound up tightly and crutches may have been used. But there is no evidence of radical surgery being done in Old Testament times in Israel, except for the discovery of three skulls in eighth-century Lachish, with holes bored in them. This kind of operation was widespread to relieve pressure (or release demons).

There were, of course,

Israelite midwives from the very earliest times. Even before the exodus they may have formed a kind of guild, with their own code of ethics and recognized leaders (two are named in Exodus 1:15). Mothers sometimes died in childbirth, but often the midwife was very skilled. Tamar successfully gave birth to twins who seem to have been locked in a difficult position (Genesis 38:27–30). Ezekiel, speaking about Jerusalem, throws light on what was normally done after a birth: 'When you were born, no one cut your umbilical cord or rubbed you with salt or wrapped you in cloth.' Midwifery was perhaps the only honourable public duty in which a woman could be employed.
Exodus 20:8; Leviticus 11:13–23; 2 Kings 4:41; 2:19–22; 5; 4:18–37; Jeremiah 8:22; Luke 10:34; Isaiah 1:6; Mark 15:23; Genesis 30:14; Ezekiel 30:21; 16:4

New Testament times
In Greece, medicine and surgery had become a highly developed skill, though still mixed with a certain amount of magic. It was the Greek, Hippocrates, who laid down the principles that the life and welfare of the patient should be the doctor's first consideration; that male doctors should not take advantage of women patients, or procure abortions; and that they should not reveal confidential information. At one time state doctors were employed, paid a salary and had to give free medical attention.

The Romans later adopted some of these practices. Surgical instruments and prescription labels have been found in excavations of Roman cities, and there was a school of medicine at Alexandria in Egypt. Paul's companion, Luke, was a doctor. The language he uses in Luke and Acts sometimes includes technical Greek medical expressions.

A dark stone obelisk inscribed with the Law-Code of King Hammurabi of Babylon, about 1750 BC. The king stands before the sun-god Shamash. Amongst the laws are set fees for doctors, and severe penalties if their treatment fails.

'If a doctor has mended a citizen's broken bone, or has healed an injured muscle, the patient shall pay the doctor five shekels of silver.

'If the patient is a member of the dependent class, he shall pay three shekels of silver.

'If a doctor has made a major incision on a citizen with a bronze lancet, and has caused that man's death, or if he has cut open a citizen's brow and has blinded the man's eye, they shall cut off his hand.'
Paragraphs 221, 222, 218

In Palestine itself the rabbis required that every town should have a physician and preferably a surgeon, too (the woman with the haemorrhage who came to Jesus had been to many doctors). There was always a doctor among the temple officials. His work was to look after the priests, who worked barefoot and were naturally liable to catch certain diseases.

Dentistry was practised even among the ancient Egyptians (some of the mummies have gold-filled teeth!), and the Greek historian, Herodotus, tells us that in 500 BC the Phoenicians were making false teeth. There is no evidence of such a practice in Israel.
Colossians 4:14; Luke 5:12; 13:11; 14:2; Acts 12:23; Mark 5:26

Trade and Commerce

The Old Testament period
□ Sale of land
One of the earliest business deals recorded in the Bible is Abraham's purchase of a field and cave from Ephron the Hittite. From the time when the Israelites settled in Canaan the buying and selling of land was disapproved of. Men held their land in trust from God. They were not the owners. Each family had received a plot of land as its own inheritance. It should therefore remain as part of that family's property.

So there were laws of 're-demption', which provided that, if a man became so poor he had to sell land, a member of his own family must buy it. There were also the laws concerning the 'Jubilee' years, which laid down that every fiftieth year, all land must be returned to its original owner. How far, and at what times in history, these laws actually operated is not known. The system certainly did not operate successfully under the kings. King Ahab of Israel engineered the death of his subject, Naboth, in order to take his property. And rich men bought up the land of those who were unable to pay their debts.

There were ancient customs connected with acquiring land. In the Book of Ruth the seller takes off his shoe and hands it to the buyer. This may have symbolized taking possession by placing one's foot on the land. When Jeremiah bought a field there was a deed of contract and a copy was stored in a clay jar (the Old Testament equivalent of a safe deposit). Genesis 23; Leviticus 25:8–34; 1 Kings 21:1–16; Isaiah 5:8; Ruth 4:7–8; Psalm 60:8; Jeremiah 32:6–15

□ Local trade
Israelite farmers were poor. They generally only produced enough for their family's needs, and there were few things they needed that they could not make themselves – apart from pottery, and metal tools and weapons. Travel and transport were difficult. The ass carried most of their loads, as a pack animal, and carts were small. So, for a long time, local trade was probably very simple. But market-places gradually developed around the gates of towns and cities. Farm produce, sheep and goats were sold there. Potters and smiths made and sold their goods, and visiting foreign merchants set up their stalls.

□ International trade
Three factors led to Israel's involvement in international trade, especially at the time of the kings.
● The first was the growth of 'industries' which needed imported raw materials. Metal-working and clothes-making were the most important of these.
● The second was Israel's con-

quest of new territories which were on the international trade routes.
● Thirdly, the kings themselves had an interest in creating wealth and buying luxury goods.

The fact that traders were popularly called 'Canaanites' probably reflects the fact that for a long time the Israelites were confined to the hills and so were not involved in foreign trade. The prophet Isaiah talks of Tyre 'whose merchant princes were the most honoured men on earth' (23:8). But Hosea declares: 'The people of Israel are as dishonest as the Canaanites; they love to cheat their customers with false scales' (12:8).

□ Trade routes by land
Israel stood at the junction between Asia Minor (Turkey and Syria), Egypt and Arabia. The Israelites made good use of this fact, although it was nomadic desert tribesmen who actually carried the goods by camel caravan.

From Asia Minor they travelled over the Taurus mountains, west of the Syrian desert, through Aleppo, Hamath, and Damascus to Israel.

From Mesopotamia they went north of the Syrian desert via Harran and Aleppo, then south into Israel.

From Arabia their route was

The time of the kings

Israel's exports	Israel's imports
oil and cereals	tin, lead, silver
fruit	(western
honey	Mediterranean)
nuts	copper (Asia Minor)
aromatic gum	timber (Lebanon)
myrrh	linen (Egypt
wool and	and Syria)
woollen cloth	purple dyed cloth
woven	(Phoenicia)
garments	Luxuries:
	by land from the
	East – gems,
	spices, gold
	by sea –
	ivory, apes,
	peacocks,
	precious stones,
	algum wood,
	gold, silver

Extra imports and exports in New Testament times

Exports	Imports
Increased supplies of olive oil to Egypt which had a state monopoly high grade linen	cotton (India) silk (China) other materials from Babylonia Greek wines (Rhodes) salted fish (Tyre) spices (Greece and Mesopotamia) glass bowls (Tyre and Sidon) apples (Crete) cheese (Bithynia) baskets (Egypt) slaves

by the Red Sea shore and at Aqaba, either north to Damascus, via Moab and Gilead, north-west to Jerusalem, or west to the port of Gaza.

☐ Trade routes by sea

Right up to Roman times sea transport was controlled by the Phoenicians. They travelled to the west Mediterranean, perhaps as far as Britain, and operated a coastal route from Lebanon to Egypt, calling at such places as Ugarit, Byblos, Sidon, Tyre, Acco, Caesarea, Jaffa and ports serving the Philistine plain. As time went on, wharves and warehouses were built and extended. There was also a route down the Red Sea and the east coast of Africa, but trade with this area fluctuated.

☐ Royal projects

Some of the kings of Israel formed alliances with neighbouring lands, especially Tyre. This may have been done deliberately to help foster trade, as well as to ensure peace. Tyre at this time became the largest sea power in the Mediterranean, with colonies and ports all around the coast.

Solomon also seems to have acted as a middleman between various countries. It seems he imported horses from Cilicia and chariots from Egypt, and then exported them both to Syria.

When the Queen of Sheba visited Solomon, she may have been part of a trade delegation from South Arabia (where incense was produced). And when Solomon fortified Tadmor (Palmyra), it may have been to make it easier for traders to cross over the Syrian desert.

Solomon enlisted the help of the Phoenicians to build ships at Ezion-geber, at the head of the Gulf of Aqaba. They manned them and sailed to 'Ophir' (probably on the north-east coast of Africa). Later Jehoshaphat, king of Judah,

Reconstruction of a merchant ship of King Solomon's fleet.

had a joint venture with the kings of Israel and Tyre to renew this trade, but the ships were wrecked in a storm.

It seems to have been a practice for kings to try to secure the right to open markets in foreign cities to sell their own produce. King Ahab of Israel had this right in Damascus.

Under some of the kings the nation grew prosperous, and wealth poured into the country. But the prophets viewed this situation with strong disapproval. Prosperity bred pride, corruption, debt and slavery. There was more for the rich, but less and less for the poor. What was worse, imports included not only material goods but also foreign religions.
Ezekiel 27; 1 Kings 5; 9:11; 10:28–29; 2 Chronicles 9:28; 1 Kings 10:1–13 2 Chronicles 20:35–37 1 Kings 22:48–49; 20:34

New Testament times

The 'Roman peace', especially when Pompey had cleared the seas of pirates, provided ample opportunities for trade. In Palestine the profession of merchant was held in great respect, and even the priests engaged in commerce. The range of exports and imports increased. The lists show how they

differed from Old Testament imports and exports.

Trade routes by land had come under the control of the Nabataeans, whose capital was at Petra (in modern Jordan). Camel caravans were often long and there was always danger from robbers. This seems to be particularly true around the area of Jerusalem, although King Herod took measures to suppress it.

Jewish records show that, in spite of Jerusalem's remote highland position, no fewer than 118 different kinds of foreign luxury goods were being sold there. There were seven different markets. Those who brought goods to market paid heavy taxes, and prices were high. There was a busy trade in goods required for worship at the temple, especially animals for sacrifice. Jesus objected to the fact that this trade went on in the temple court, the only place where non-Jews could worship. The temple was probably the most important factor in Jerusalem's commerce. Every Jew had to make payments to the temple treasury, and this no doubt helped Jerusalem to pay for imports.

The Jewish rabbis had strict rules for business deals, and there were market inspectors to see that they were carried out.

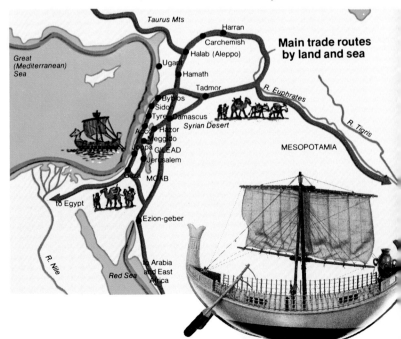

Scales and weights had to be cleaned regularly. Buyers had the right to complain. And no interest was to be charged to fellow-Jews. Personal belongings could be handed over as security against a loan. But essentials such as cloaks, ploughs and millstones were not to be sold in the event of non-payment. These rules clearly have their roots in the Old Testament law, but they were especially emphasized at the time of Jesus.
Luke 10:30–37;
Leviticus 19:35–36;
Deuteronomy 25:13–16

□ **Payment**
In the earliest times trade was by bartering. In Genesis 33:19 and Joshua 24:32 the word used for 'money' means literally 'cattle', which originally no doubt fixed the price of the goods. Gold and silver were soon introduced, but coins were not used until the seventh century BC and after (see the chart on *Money*). A shekel was not a coin, but a weight of gold or silver. So trading involved carrying about large amounts of metal, and merchants were needed to weigh and test the ingots. There is no evidence of any banking systems in Israel before the exile, though these did exist in Mesopotamia.

By New Testament times there were local currencies and a regular system for banking. Trade between countries with different currencies called for the services of money-changers.

Money, Weights and Measures

For many centuries before coins were minted, business deals in the countries of the ancient Near East worked on a kind of barter system: people bought and sold by exchanging goods rather than coins or banknotes. All kinds of things could be exchanged, from foodstuffs to cattle, metals and timber.

A person's wealth was measured in terms of goods: 'Abram was a very rich man, with sheep, goats and cattle, as well as silver and gold.' Job, 'the richest man in the East', owned 'seven thousand sheep, three thousand camels, one thousand head of cattle, and five hundred donkeys'.

In these early days, gold and silver was kept, not in the form of coins, but in the form of jewellery – rings and bracelets – and thin bars. Abraham's servant, arranging a marriage for Isaac, gave Rebecca and her family clothing and silver and gold jewellery. For a long time the 'dowry' – the payment made by a young man to the father of his bride – was given as goods in this way.

But there were several problems with this exchange-of-goods system. One was the difficulty of 'carrying' these things about. Coins in a purse are more manageable than a flock of sheep! It was also difficult to fix the value of one thing against the value of what was offered in exchange.

Gradually metal – silver mainly, but also copper and gold – replaced other goods as the exchange 'currency'. Copper was made into discs, and silver into lumps that could be carried in bags. These were weighed out and standard weights were agreed, at first locally and later more widely. The 'shekels' and 'talents' mentioned in the Old Testament were weights, not coins, until at least the seventh century BC.

The merchants were 'weighers of silver' (and other metals). In order to have some kind of check on them, the purchaser often carried his own weights in a leather bag. The Old Testament laws set high standards: 'The Lord wants weights and measures to be honest and every sale to be fair.'

Assyrians weighing tribute on scales. From Nimrud, about 880–860 BC.

But there were many dishonest merchants, and the prophets spoke out strongly against them: 'They use false measures, a thing that I hate,' God says through the prophet Micah. 'How can I forgive men who use false scales and weights? Your rich men exploit the poor.'

Old Testament liquid measures

Kab = 1.2 litres

Hin = 3.66 litres

Bath = 22 litres

(10 baths = 1 homer = a 'donkey load')

Old Testament dry measures

Log = 0.3 litre

Kab = 1.2 litres

Omer = 2.2 litres

Seah = 7.3 litres

Ephah = 22 litres

10 ephahs = 1 homer = 220 litres

Weights

Bronze weights (140 and 224gm) inlaid with gold, with figures of beetles. They are probably Egyptian, although found at Nimrud.

Hebrew stone weights: 8 shekels/91.4gm; temple shekel; and half-shekel. All are from Lachish, seventh-sixth centuries BC.

A duck-shaped weight carved from agate.

A bronze lion-weight, two thirds of a mina/666gm, from Nimrud, Assyria.

A 1 mina/60 shekel weight. Nebuchadnezzar II of Babylon (605–562 BC) made this copy from a standard fixed about 2000 BC.

A 30 minas/15kg weight carved from black basalt, in the shape of a duck.

Table of Old Testament weights

1 gerah = approx. 0.5gm
10 gerahs = 1 bekah (approx. 6gm)
2 bekahs = 1 shekel (approx. 11gm)
50 shekels = 1 mina (approx. 500gm)
60 minas = 1 talent (approx. 30kg)
The heavy royal shekel weighed 13gm.
The heavy, double standard talent weighed 60kg.

New Testament weights

The litra (pound) = approx. 327gm
The talent = 20 to 40kg

Measurements of length

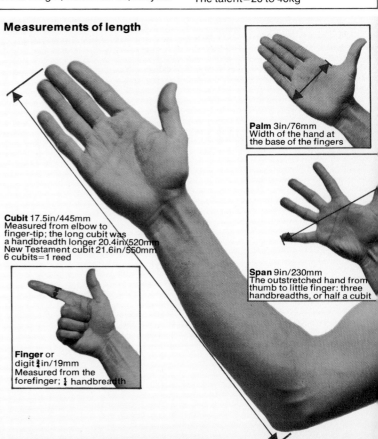

Palm 3in/76mm
Width of the hand at the base of the fingers

Span 9in/230mm
The outstretched hand from thumb to little finger: three handbreadths, or half a cubit

Cubit 17.5in/445mm
Measured from elbow to finger-tip; the long cubit was a handbreadth longer 20.4in/520mm
New Testament cubit 21.6in/550mm
6 cubits = 1 reed

Finger or digit ¾in/19mm
Measured from the forefinger; ¼ handbreadth

Money

Coinage seems to have been introduced in the seventh century BC. Early coins were simply pieces of metal of a standard weight impressed with a seal. The coins were often named after the weights they represented.

Old Testament gold and silver coins

Shekel (approx. 11.4gm)
Mina (approx. 500gm)=50 shekels
Talent (30kg)=60 minas

A silver double shekel minted in Sidon, showing the king of Persia in a chariot. About 400–350 BC.

The earliest known Hebrew coin minted in Judah, fourth century BC.

A gold double daric from Babylon showing the king with sceptre and bow. About 325 BC.

A silver stater minted at Antioch, showing the head of Augustus, 27 BC–AD 14, emperor at the time of Jesus' birth.

A bronze lepton from AD 6–9. Jesus commended a widow who gave two of these small coins – all she had – to the temple treasury.

Bronze coins of the Roman governors (procurators) of Judea. Left, Pontius Pilate, AD 30, who gave the order for Jesus' crucifixion; right, Antonius Felix AD 59, who heard the charges against Paul.

A silver denarius showing the head of Tiberius, emperor AD 14–37, during the lifetime of Jesus.

Distances

New Testament **orgyia** (fathom)=6ft/1.85m

New Testament **stadion** (furlong)=202yd/185m

A sabbath day's journey, the maximum distance allowed by the Jewish law, was fixed at 2,000 cubits/1,000yd/914m

New Testament **milion** (mile)= 1,000 paces (Roman measurement) 1,618yd/1,478m

---

New Testament coins

There were three different currencies used in Palestine in New Testament times. There was the official, imperial money (Roman standard); provincial money minted at Antioch and Tyre (Greek standard); and local Jewish money which may have been minted at Caesarea. Money for the temple (including the half-shekel tax) had to be paid in the Tyrian coinage (the 2-drachma piece), not Roman. It is not surprising that money-changers flourished! Money was coined in gold, silver, copper and bronze or brass. The commonest silver coins mentioned in the New Testament are the Greek *tetradrachma*, and Roman *denarius*, which was a day's wage for the ordinary working man.

Jewish coins
lepton (bronze)
shekel

Greek coins

drachma (silver)
stater (or tetradrachma) (silver)
mina

Roman coins

quadrans
as (bronze)=4 quadrans
denarius (silver)=16 as
aureus (gold)

1 Jewish **shekel**=1 Greek stater (tetradrachma)=4 Roman denarii
30 Jewish **shekels**=1 Greek mina=100 Roman denarii

A shekel minted during the Jewish revolt against Rome, AD 66–70.

'Judea capta': the Emperor Vespasian's coin marking the end of the Jewish revolt, AD 70.

Government and Administration

Israel before the time of the kings

The nation of Israel traces its history back to one man – Abraham – and his family. So, to begin with, the structure of authority was on a family pattern, with the father as the ultimate authority (the 'Patriarch'), under God.

By the time of the exodus, Abraham's 'family' had grown into a nation. But the basic structure was the same. Israel was a nation of twelve family-clans, descendants of the sons of Jacob. Moses became their leader, responsible for over-all 'government', settling disputes. And from the time of the covenant-agreement at Sinai, the people formally accepted God as their King and law-maker.

The Israelites settled in Canaan, and for some time lived as a federation of tribes united by common ancestry and by common worship of one God. There were 'Judges', but they had limited authority, at least until the time of Samuel.

Assyrian scribes. In Old Testament times scribes were part of the government civil service. Some held high positions as secretaries of state.

'There was no king in Israel at that time. Everyone did just as he pleased', and the unfortunate consequences are clear from the stories in the Book of Judges.

Samuel was the last great Judge. 'Every year he would go round to Bethel, Gilgal, and Mizpah, and in these places he would settle disputes.' But the people wanted to have a king, as other nations did. Samuel warned them that it was asking for trouble, but they were determined. And so God sent Samuel to make Saul the first king of Israel.
Exodus 18; 19 – 26; Joshua 7:8–14; Judges 8:22–23; 21:25; 1 Samuel 7:15–17; 8 – 9

The kingdom and its officers

David succeeded Saul, extended the kingdom, and the need grew for a system of administration. The Bible gives three lists of the important people in David's and Solomon's 'civil service'.

Among these was the 'master of the palace', who in the early days of the monarchy may simply have managed the king's property. But he soon

An Egyptian scribe. From a tomb-painting at Thebes, about 1380 BC.

came to be the king's chief minister.

The royal secretary was both the king's personal scribe and secretary of state. He ranked below the 'master of the palace'.

The role of the 'royal herald' (recorder) is not clear, but he was certainly important in the king's court. He may have kept the king aware of public opinion as a kind of royal public relations officer.

There were also military officials. The king had a personal bodyguard of regular troops, in addition to the Israelite army which could call every able-bodied man to arms. The professional troops and the conscripted army had separate commanders; both reported direct to the king.

Solomon divided the land of Israel into twelve areas, each under a district-governor. The governors had to provide food from their districts for the king and his household. They reported to a chief governor. It is possible that Judah may have had its own governor.

Within these divisions each city and the villages around

it appointed its own council of Elders. The exception was the capital, Jerusalem, which probably had a governor who reported direct to the king.
2 Samuel 8:16–18; 20:23–26; 1 Kings 4:1–6; Isaiah 22:15–21; 1 Kings 4:7–19

The divided monarchy
Although the united kingdom of Israel and Judah did not last long, much of the administrative system that David and Solomon set up survived. For example, nearly three centuries later, when Isaiah records how Jerusalem was besieged by the Assyrian king, Sennacherib, the chief officials are still the officials in charge of the palace, the court secretary, and the official in charge of the records.
2 Kings 18:18; Isaiah 36:3

After the exile
After the exile, Israel was under the political control of various foreign powers. But, in religious matters the nation returned to the theory of 'rule by God'. Under foreign supervision, Israel maintained its identity as a religious community with its own religious laws administered by priests and elders.
Ezra 6:7; 7:11 – 12:25

Other nations
☐ Egypt
At the time of Israel's captivity in Egypt the king (pharaoh) was considered to be a god. He owned all the land, although it was leased to citizens.
Administration of the land was delegated to the vizier, the pharaoh's chief minister. It is possible that this is the post that Joseph was given. The vizier was assisted by a treasurer and by another vizier who looked after the northern area of Egypt. There were about forty administrative divisions, called 'nomes', each governed by a 'nomarch', assisted by a panel of judges and sometimes by a 'chief of

police'. All official dealings were carefully recorded by the royal scribes.
The provinces of the Egyptian Empire were ruled by their native princes, as long as they co-operated with their conquerors.
Genesis 41:37–44

☐ Assyria
Tiglath-pileser III, ruler of Assyria just before the Assyrians conquered Israel in 721 BC, reorganized the imperial administration. He established provinces with their own governors. To discourage nationalism in restless defeated lands the Assyrians operated a policy of deporting conquered subjects to other provinces.
2 Kings 17:6

A cast of the seal belonging to Shema, an official under King Jeroboam. Seals were a badge of authority, used on documents.

☐ Babylon
The Babylonian Empire was ruled by a king who had absolute power. The Babylonians continued the Assyrian policy of deporting captives to other parts of the empire and colonizing their lands. Native princes were appointed as governors under Babylonian supervision.
2 Kings 25:18–22

☐ Persia
Under the Persians, some of the people deported by the Assyrians and Babylonians were allowed to return to their

homeland. In the reign of Darius the Great (522–486 BC) the Persian Empire was divided into twenty provinces, called 'satrapies', each governed by an official known as a 'satrap'. Each satrapy also had a secretary and a commander of the garrison, and each kept an eye on the others. There were also travelling inspectors who reported back directly to the king. Generally the Persians allowed local administration and customs to continue, under their over-all control.
2 Chronicles 36:22–23

☐ Greece
The empire of Alexander the Great stretched from his native Macedonia (northern Greece) east to India. His vision was to unite the world under a common culture – Hellenism (from *Hellēn*, meaning Greek) – by intermarriage and by establishing Greek cities, culture and language through all the provinces.
After Alexander's death in 323 BC his empire was divided among his generals. The Jewish people were at first under the control of the Ptolemies who ruled Egypt, but in 199 BC the Syrian Seleucid kings won the territory in battle. They tried to force 'Hellenization', but many Jews fiercely resisted, because they believed it was contrary to their own Jewish faith. This resulted in the Maccabean War of 167 BC. With help from Rome, an 'independent' king-

Two Mede ambassadors shown on a relief at Persepolis, Iran.

dom, ruled by the Jewish Hasmoneans, was established in 143 BC and continued until a dispute between two rival Jewish factions brought in the Roman army. The army's leader, Pompey, captured Jerusalem in 63 BC.

The Roman Empire

Rome had long been a republic, governed by two consuls who were appointed for one year by the governing council (the Senate) and who then returned to the Senate as councillors. The Senate was made up of men who had proved themselves in public office, and it had considerable power. But by 50 BC Julius Caesar had beaten Pompey in a struggle for power, and he became ruler, with absolute power.

Augustus Caesar, the first emperor, tried to make his personal position fit into the existing Roman constitution. But in fact he was above the power of the Senate.

Outside Italy there were two sorts of provinces in the Empire. The Senate kept control of those where peace was established, appointing different governors (proconsuls) each year. The emperor took charge of those which required troops to keep order. He ruled through deputies appointed for four or five years at a time: 'legates' in charge of larger areas; 'prefects' or 'procurators' in charge of smaller and more troublesome ones. Native vassal kings were allowed to rule in some areas, as long as they did as Rome wanted.

In Judea, King Herod the Great was allowed to rule from 40 BC until his death in 4 BC. His kingdom was split into three and each of his three sons ruled over part. Antipas ruled Galilee and Peraea, Philip ruled Ituraea and Trachonitis, and Archelaus ruled Judea (including Samaria and Idumaea). Archelaus was unable to keep order and in AD 6 Judea became a Roman province, governed by a 'prefect' responsible to the emperor, but supervised by the 'legate' of Syria. Pontius Pilate was the fifth 'prefect', or 'procurator' to govern Judea. He remained there from AD 26 to 36.

The Emperor Gaius (Caligula) made Herod Agrippa king over two of the three parts of the country after Philip died and Antipas was deposed. Claudius made him king of Judea as well in AD 41. When Agrippa died in AD 44 his kingdom was once again governed by procurators. But his son (Agrippa II) was made king of Philip's part of the kingdom in AD 48. Acts chapters 23 – 26 illustrate the situation in about AD 57–59. The tribune (military commander) in Jerusalem sent Paul to the procurator Felix who lived at Caesarea. Felix' suc-

A bust of Augustus Caesar, first of the Roman emperors.

cessor Festus was visited by King Herod Agrippa II. But Paul used his right of appeal as Roman citizen and was sent to Rome for the emperor to judge his case.

The emperor's government kept law and order, but it made and maintained some of the best roads ever built – roads along which the first Christians travelled to make the good news of Jesus known far and wide. The Romans provided local government offices, markets, baths and other public amenities. The money for all this came from taxes imposed on the local people: property tax, purchase-

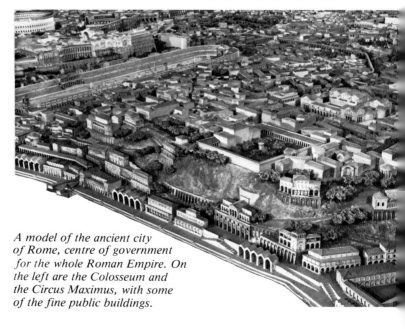

A model of the ancient city of Rome, centre of government for the whole Roman Empire. On the left are the Colosseum and the Circus Maximus, with some of the fine public buildings.

tax, customs duties, even duties on food. The Roman Censor in each area hired tax-collectors to bring the money in, and people were often forced to pay far more than the legal amount.
Luke 3:1; Acts 21:31–36; 22:24–30; 23:12 – 26:32; Luke 3:12–13

☐ Colonies
Many towns in the Empire became Roman colonies. They were regarded as outposts of Rome itself and were governed (like the capital) by two magistrates together. Philippi was one of several colonies featured in the New Testament.
Acts 16:12, 19–40

An inscription recording the fact that Gallio came to Corinth as 'proconsul' in AD 51 or 52. Gallio was magistrate during the time of Paul's stay in Corinth.

☐ City-states
In Greece and other lands certain cities had for many years been self-governing. The Roman authorities allowed some of these – for example Athens and Ephesus – to continue as free cities, although this status held only as long as the peace was kept.

Certain 'holy cities' also retained some control over their own affairs, including Jerusalem, where the high priest and the Jewish council (Sanhedrin) administered local affairs. But their real authority was limited by Rome. The death sentence of the Sanhedrin on Jesus had to be approved by the Roman governor.
Acts 19:35–40; Luke 22:66; 23:1–5, 6–12

Education

Education in the ancient Near East
As far back as Abraham's time certain nations were developing education. In Sumer, Abraham's homeland, there were schools to train future secretaries for work in the temples, palace and business life. This education was voluntary. The pupil's family had to pay and so it was usually only the privilege of the rich. But the range of subjects was wide. Botany, geography, mathematics, grammar and literature were all studied.

Excavations have unearthed many clay tablets containing exercises to be copied, while others record the pupils' attempts and their teachers' corrections. In the palace of Mari, two schoolrooms with benches and desks have been found. School staff included a professor (often called 'the school father', with pupils called the 'school sons'), an assistant who prepared the daily exercises, specialist teachers, and others responsible for discipline (one called 'big brother').

There was a similar system in Egypt, where schools were often attached to the temples. After the beginners' course pupils transferred to a government department where they studied composition, natural science and the duties of office. There was special training in letter-writing and 'model letters' have been found. If they were being trained to be priests, they studied theology and medicine. Discipline was strict: no wine, no music, no women.

Systems like these must have influenced the people of Israel at certain points in their history. Abraham may have been a man of some learning. Joseph would have relied on secretaries for his work as a chief minister of Pharaoh. And Moses had an Egyptian education – so it was a man with a trained mind who was chosen to teach God's law to the people of Israel. But education in Israel itself took a very different course.

Attitudes to education in Israel
The basic idea in Israel and all through the Bible is that all knowledge comes from God. He is the greatest of all teachers. All wisdom and learning should begin with 'the fear of the Lord'. Its aim is to understand the Creator and his work better. So learning leads to praising God (as in Psalm 8). It is not enough simply to satisfy human curiosity. It also helps people to use their God-given abilities to the full. So elementary mathematics was needed for surveying land and calculating the harvest, and for large building works. Studying the movements of the sun, moon and stars helped in working out the calendar. Many of these things were learnt by experience, or, as in other crafts, in an apprenticeship.

At the same time, the education of children was given an

Part of a relief showing teacher and pupils at a Roman school in Gaul.

important place. It was every parent's duty to make sure that his children were taught. But the content of this teaching was almost entirely religious.

● They were to be taught the story of God's dealings with Israel.

● They were to be instructed in God's laws. God is holy and requires holiness from his people. Children must therefore be taught how to 'keep the ways of the Lord'.

● They were to be given instruction in wise dealing. The Book of Proverbs is full of maxims on the subject of 'how to get along with people' and is written for 'sons'. This type of teaching Israel had in common with other nations.
Exodus 20:4; Proverbs 1:7; 9:10; Job 28:28; Deuteronomy 4:9–10; 6:20–21; Exodus 13:8–9; 12:26–27; Joshua 4:21–22; Leviticus 19:2; Genesis 18:19; Proverbs 1:8; 4:1

How education developed in Israel

Education began at home. Abraham was instructed to teach his children. It was important that the truth of God's acts for his people was passed from father to son, from generation to generation. Mothers also probably shared in this when the children were young.

Opinions differ about how many people could read and write in Old Testament times. Some think that only the nobles could. But, on the other hand, Joshua expected written reports on the land of Canaan;

A Roman pen and inkpot.

Gideon expected a young passer-by to be able to read; and in the time of Hezekiah it was presumably a workman who wrote on the wall of the tunnel dug to bring water into Jerusalem (see *Building*). Enough other examples of ancient Hebrew writing have been found to show that there was widespread knowledge of the skill.

It is not known when schools for children started. They are not referred to until 75 BC, when the country came under Greek influence and there was an attempt to enforce elementary education. But there may have been voluntary schools before this. The boy Samuel was handed over to the priest's keeping and was presumably taught by him. This kind of thing may have been a regular practice. The 'Gezer calendar' (see *Farming*) may also be evidence of a more formal type of education. Certainly the young men had the chance to become pupils of the prophets, and probably also of the priests and Levites. Isaiah gave private teaching to a group of disciples and Elisha was very concerned for the welfare of his pupils and their families. But none of this was 'education' either in the modern sense, or in the way we find it in Egypt or ancient Babylon. It was learning about religion in order to serve God better.

After the people returned from exile, a specialized class of Bible scholars, known as 'scribes', came into being. This term had been used earlier to mean secretaries, but some of the Levites were scribes, and even before the exile they were recognized as experts in God's law. According to Jewish tradition, after the exile these scribes were the equivalent of the earlier prophets, and were called 'men of the great synagogue'. They came to be known as 'lawyers', 'doctors of the law' and 'rabbis'. Simon the Just, Shammai, Hillel and Gamaliel were some of the most famous. They taught and explained the written Law of

God, and they applied the Law to contemporary life. These teachings built up into large collections of rules. At first they were taught by word of mouth, but eventually they were written down to form the *Mishnah*, about AD 200. They were regarded as having the same authority as the Old Testament itself.

It was during these last centuries before Christ that the group later known as the Pharisees seem to have organized a school system. Children first went to school in the synagogue, 'the house of the book'. Further education then took place in 'the house of study'. Many of these were under the direction of famous rabbis.

We can only guess at educational methods. Isaiah may throw some light on this. He writes that the people think his message is only for babies: 'He is trying to teach us letter by letter, line by line, lesson by lesson.' This may reflect the practice of teaching a little at a time, or it may represent the first letters of the alphabet being learnt by repetition. Most instruction was given by word of mouth, and various devices were used to make it easy to memorize. Jesus himself used catchwords, repetition, and parables.
Psalm 78:3–6; Proverbs 31:1; 1:8; 6:20; Joshua 18:4, 8–9; Judges 8:14; Isaiah 8:16; Jeremiah 36:26; 1 Chronicles 24:6; Jeremiah 8:8; Mark 7:6–9; Isaiah 28:10; Proverbs 1:8; Mark 9:42–50; Matthew 6:2–18

Adult education

Education in the Bible was not only for children. Abraham was told to teach the whole of his household. Moses taught the people of Israel the Law of God, and the Levites were commanded to pass on this teaching. The kings sent Levites throughout the land to teach, though the prophets complained that this duty was often done badly, and regarded as a way of making money. The custom of regular teaching of the people probably developed only after the exile.

Ezra was a priest and scribe 'with a thorough knowledge of the Law'. He 'devoted his life to studying the Law of the Lord . . . and to teaching all its laws and regulations to the people of Israel.' Nehemiah 8 pictures him standing in a wooden pulpit, with all the people gathered to hear him. Genesis 18:19; Leviticus 10:11; 2 Chronicles 17:7–9; 35:3; Micah 3:11; Malachi 2:7–8; Ezra 7:6, 10

Greek education
By the time of Jesus Greek education had become world-famous. Body, mind and soul, it was thought, needed room for expression. So the syllabus included athletics, philosophy, poetry, drama, music and rhetoric. Boys would attend elementary school between the ages of seven and fifteen. They would then go to a 'gymnasium' for a wider education (not just for athletics). Members of the public were welcome to come and join in the students' discussions. Standards in the gymnasia had declined by the time of Jesus, but these schools still represented the best of Greek culture. They were set up wherever Greeks came to live, and one was started in Jerusalem in 167 BC.

Most Jews thoroughly disapproved of the Greek view of education. The gymnasia were also condemned because Greek athletes practised and competed naked. Foreigners were, however, welcome, and since Paul's home-city of Tarsus was also famous for its gymnasium we may wonder if Paul ever went there. He certainly refers to the Greek games, and shows a knowledge of Greek culture in his letters. 1 Corinthians 9:24–27

War, Weapons and Warriors

War is a dominant theme in the Old Testament, despite the fact that God's law protected life and stood firm against murder. The reason is that God himself was vitally involved with a single nation, Israel. They lived in troubled times. 'The Lord is a warrior,' sang Moses, after the escape from Egypt. Then, when the people of Israel set out to enter Canaan God told them that the battle was his: 'The Lord your God is going with you, and he will give you victory.' The former inhabitants of the land must all be destroyed ('devoted' to God). It was a 'holy war'. But its ultimate goal was peace and well-being. Israel should trust and obey God, otherwise their enemies would win. This is the message of the Book of Judges.

The prophets often continued this theme. When the

The Assyrian army captures a town. This relief from Nimrud, about 730 BC, shows archers providing cover while a battering-ram is used to break down the walls. Other soldiers use scaling-ladders.

kings went to war for political reasons and put their trust in horses, chariots and cavalry, defeat was often seen as God's way of punishing his people for their lack of faith.

But after the exile, when the people came back to their homeland, things changed. The Jews had experienced many defeats and so the idea grew that war was more the work of Satan than of God. They hoped that God would send his own warrior-king to fight a final battle and bring victory and peace to his people, either in this world or in the next. This was the Jewish hope, centred on the coming Messiah.

Jesus himself rejected this view of the Messiah. He came to bring God's peace. There would be division between those who believed and those who did not, but men were not to be regarded as enemies. Only in the visions in the Book of Revelation is Jesus seen as a warrior. But Christians are pictured as soldiers engaged in a spiritual war against evil. Victory in this war is certain, for Jesus by his death and resurrection defeated Satan.

The Egyptian pharaoh standing in his chariot, firing arrows at the enemy.

Physical, historical wars are among the signs that the end of the age is near.
Exodus 15:3; Deuteronomy 20:4; Isaiah 31:1; 5:25−30 and many other passages; Revelation 19:11; Ephesians 6:10−17; John 12:31

The army

From the early days of Israel's history every man was called to be a soldier. He could be summoned by a tribal leader, as Abraham led men out to rescue Lot from his captors. Each of the tribes was responsible for occupying the land assigned to them. They sometimes helped one another in the task, as they rallied under one leader to resist the Canaanites and Philistines, and to defeat the desert tribes who were constantly raiding Israel. Any tribe which did not respond to a call for help was treated with scorn.

Sometimes outlaws would band together as a fighting force, raiding but occasionally protecting the local community. In return for this they expected food and supplies.

There was no standing army until Saul became king. He appointed 3,000 men as a permanent army, under his direct command but with Abner in charge. King David was a military genius. Joab, his commander-in-chief, captured Jerusalem and taught the Israelites new methods of warfare. David was the first king to have a personal bodyguard of great warriors. These men had been with him when he was an outlaw and had proved their loyalty to him.

The Bible speaks of 'fifties' and 'hundreds', with their commanders, but very little is known of the detailed organization of the army. For a long time the army was composed almost entirely of foot-soldiers, some equipped as archers or slingers, others for hand-to-hand combat. The cavalry and chariots used by the Egyptians, Philistines and Canaanites were introduced in Israel under Solomon, but the Israelites fought mainly in the hills where these methods were impractical. 'The gods of Israel', say the officials of King Benhadad of Syria, 'are mountain gods.' The later kings of Judah still sent to Egypt for chariots and horsemen. King Ahab of Israel, however, kept a huge force of chariots, and his stables have been discovered at Megiddo.

After the exile there was no Jewish army except for one short period, when non-Jewish as well as Jewish soldiers were employed and paid a wage. Herod the Great had his own forces. They, too, included foreign mercenaries, and were under Roman command.
Genesis 14; Judges 1; 5:15−17; 1 Samuel 23:1−5; 25; 13:1−2; 17:55; 2 Samuel 23:8−39; 1 Kings 10:26; 20:23−25; 2 Kings 18:24

War in the Old Testament
□ Attack and defence

There were three kinds of weapons used in fighting. In hand-to-hand fighting, clubs, axes, short and long swords were used. There were darts, spears and javelins for throwing. And there were many missiles, from stones and boulders to bows and arrows.

The soldier wore armour to protect himself and carried a shield for defence. The Israelites seem to have used two types of shield. A small round one was carried by the light armed infantry, and a large rectangular one was used by the men at the front, so that the battle line presented a solid

front. The shields were made of a wicker or wooden frame covered with leather, which needed regular oiling. Inside the shield was a handle for holding it. There is little information about the soldiers' armour. Before David's battle with Goliath, King Saul tried to dress him in a helmet and a 'coat of mail' (breastplate). But it was so heavy that he could not walk! There may also have been 'greaves' to protect the legs, and a lower skirt of mail.

The kings built fortresses to protect their land. Saul fortified his capital, Gibeah. David, in addition to work on Jerusalem, built the fortresses of Libnah, Lachish, Gezer and Beth-horon in the foothills as a defence against the Philistines. Solomon strengthened many cities, especially Gezer, Hazor and Megiddo, guarding the strategic pass through the Carmel hills. When the kingdom was divided, border fortresses were established at Geba and Mizpah.
1 Samuel 17:4−7, 37−40

□ Preparations for war

It was important for an invading army to find food close to hand. This was one reason why spring was 'the time of year when kings usually go to war'. (Soldiers in their own land were provided for, by the family or local community.)

Surprise was important, so war was rarely declared. Sometimes nations would provoke war by making impossible demands. Troops were gathered by blowing the ram's horn, by signals set on a hill, or by sending messengers through the land. The king asked God's advice, usually through the prophets and priests. Saul sought advice through dreams and even, once, disobeyed God's plain command by consulting a medium at Endor.

If the response was favourable, the army set out, taking with them priests and sometimes symbols of their faith, such as objects from the

Persian spearmen from a palace wall at Persepolis.

Bronze models of Scythian archers on their horses; about 500 BC.

A bronze helmet from Corinth, early fifth century BC.

tent of worship (tabernacle). When Eli was priest, and again later, they even took the Covenant Box (ark) itself.

Before the battle started, the priest offered a sacrifice. On one occasion King Saul wrongly performed this rite himself. The kings of the surrounding nations sometimes made human sacrifices, but this was regarded with horror in Israel.
2 Samuel 11:1; 1 Samuel 11:1–11; 17:20; 1 Kings 20; 2 Kings 3:11; 1 Samuel 28:6–7; 4; 2 Samuel 11:11; 1 Samuel 13:8–15; 2 Kings 3:27

□ **Fighting methods**
Israel suffered a great deal from raiding bands of desert tribes, especially before the time of the kings. Their attacks were swift and unpredictable. Often they rode in on camels. They plundered the villages, destroyed crops, and took cattle and captives.

Where there was open combat a trumpet gave the signal for attack. And sometimes there was an arranged war-cry, like Gideon's 'a sword for the Lord and for Gideon'. A line of men carrying rectangular shields and long lances would advance, and the archers let fly a volley of arrows to cover them. When the lines met, fighting was hand to hand. Sometimes the issue was decided by contest between two or more champions. Often the army was divided into two companies, to close in on the

An Assyrian soldier, with two Israelite captives.

side and the rear of the enemy. Under King David the general strategy and tactics of open warfare began to be more skilfully planned.

An attack on a city often took place just before dawn to take the defenders completely by surprise. A favourite ruse was to advance with only half the army and then retreat. When the inhabitants joyfully pursued, the other half of the army would enter the city. In David's time the Israelites began to adopt the practice of laying siege to a city. Usually, though, they were the victims, rather than the initiators of this kind of warfare.

The experts in this were the Assyrians. Spies would be sent to discover a city's weaknesses, and, if a succession of towns had already fallen, a delegation was sent to try to frighten the town into submission. All lines of communication were cut off, and they took control of all the water supplies in the neighbourhood. It was to prevent this that King Hezekiah of Judah diverted water into the city by digging a tunnel. The enemy then prepared for a long stay, while conditions in the city gradually grew more horrible. To hasten defeat the Assyrians would construct causeways up to the walls, and wooden machines on

An Assyrian war-chariot, with archers at the ready.

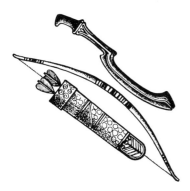

Bow and arrows, and a curved sword from early Israelite times.

wheels. These served as platforms from which arrows could be shot at the defenders, and as battering-rams to weaken the walls. Sometimes they would try to tunnel under the wall. Finally an all-out attack was made. The archers kept up heavy fire, while the rest of the army, protected by shields, scaled the walls with ladders. The defenders meantime hurled down burning arrows, boiling oil and stones in an attempt to keep them off.
Judges 6:1–6, 11; 2 Chronicles 13:12; Judges 7:20; 20:29–36; 2 Samuel 12:27; 2 Kings 18 – 19; 6:24 – 7:20

☐ **The aftermath of battle**
When a city was taken, it was the usual practice to kill, mutilate or enslave all male inhabitants. Women and children were taken captive. The walls were broken down and buildings burnt, and the soldiers were usually free to take whatever plunder they could find, though the more valuable items were claimed by the king. If a city submitted, hostages were taken and a heavy tribute demanded.

The Roman army
In New Testament times the Mediterranean world was at peace under Roman government. No book of the New Testament is written against a background of war, though occasionally the Roman army is present. From time to time Jews rebelled and these rebellions were fiercely crushed by the Romans. The province of Syria, of which Palestine formed a part, being on the border of the Empire, was a potential source of danger. It was therefore under the direct command of the emperor, with detachments of soldiers permanently stationed there.

Roman soldiers often behaved as if the Jews were their servants. But some, especially the officers, won respect from the people. A company of Roman soldiers, detailed to keep the peace in Jerusalem at the time of the Passover Festival, took part in the arrest of Jesus and enjoyed some rough horse-play at the prisoner's expense. In general, however, the Romans had a reputation for justice. Roman soldiers prevented Paul being lynched in Jerusalem, and brought him safely under armed escort to their headquarters at Caesarea, when there were threats against his life.

The emperor had a personal bodyguard, the Praetorian guard, stationed in Rome and some other provincial centres (including Ephesus). When Paul was in prison the 'whole palace guard' knew that he was there because he was 'a servant of Christ'.
Luke 13:1; Matthew 5:41; Luke 7:1–10; Acts 10; John 18:3; Mark 15:16–20; Acts 21:30–36; 23:16–24; Ephesians 6:14–17; Philippians 1:13

A Roman legionary. The soldier carries a javelin and is armed with a short sword. His head and chest are protected with a metal helmet and armour. The large shield provides cover.

Roman warships.

Travel and Transport

The Bible describes many journeys: Abraham moving home from Ur to Canaan; Jacob going down into Egypt; the Israelites journeying through the desert; the Queen of Sheba visiting King Solomon. These are just a few of the journeys recorded in the Old Testament. In the New Testament the travels of Paul and other Christian leaders are recorded in some detail in the Book of Acts, and Jesus himself must have covered very considerable distances during his public ministry.

Pedestrians
In Bible times most journeys were made on foot. Not everybody could afford to keep a pack-animal and, even if a family owned an ass, on a family journey someone would have to walk.

Animals
Although the nomads of the desert kept camels, the main beast of burden throughout Bible times was the ass. The ass was domesticated long before either the horse or the camel, and was always the most popular means of general transport.

Abraham possessed camels, though he probably acquired them after he left Harran. When Jacob settled in Canaan, he seems to have had no further use for them, for they are not mentioned among his property when he went down to Egypt. His son Joseph sent him provisions for the journey on asses. With the development of international trade, particularly the Arabian spice trade, camels were used more and more in Israel from about 1000 BC.

Horses were usually kept for war. They were expensive to feed compared with camels and asses and could not carry as much. But by New Testament times they were often used for civilian purposes, when chariots for transport developed from the basic war-chariot.

'Caravan' convoys
Traders travelled together as a 'caravan' – a convoy of asses and camels – for company, safety and as a protection against thieves. Joseph was sold to one such group of travelling merchants.

The caravan routes crossed Israel in all directions. With the Mediterranean Sea to the west and the Syrian desert to the east, all traffic between Mesopotamia and Arabia, Egypt and the rest of Africa had to pass through a narrow corridor about 75 miles/120km wide.

Great cities grew up at strategic points on these routes. One of these was Palmyra ('Tadmor in the wilderness'), a desert city fortified by King Solomon.

The donkey (ass) was the chief means of transport for ordinary people all through Bible times.

Vehicles
In Old Testament times the use of wheeled transport was limited. Horse-drawn chariots were used by armies and by noblemen – chariots may even have been an indication of rank. (Joseph, for instance, was given a royal chariot to ride in; his family travelled to Egypt in waggons or carts; and the goods were carried by asses.) But without properly made up roads, the condition of the ground restricted the use of chariots. King Ahab had to race back to Jezreel before the rain came and turned the tracks to mud.

Carts drawn by asses or cattle were used on farms. On two occasions it seems that the sacred Covenant Box (ark) was carried in an ordinary farm cart. And the prophet Amos describes the people of Israel groaning 'like a cart loaded with corn'.

Oxen pull this farm-cart with solid wooden wheels. From Roman times.

By New Testament times the Romans had built first-class roads, and chariots of various types were used – from the light chariots raced in the games, to more substantial carriages with room to seat at least two people.

Most streets in towns were very narrow, and those who could afford it travelled in litters. These litters were couches with a framework so that curtains could conceal the traveller. They rested on poles which were carried by men or sometimes by horses.

Genesis 41:43; 45:19; Exodus 14:23–25; 1 Kings 18:44–45; 1 Samuel 6:7–8; 2 Samuel 6:3; Amos 2:13; Acts 8:29–31

A cross-section of a Roman road, showing how it was built. A layer of sand or lime mortar makes a level base. Next comes a hardcore layer of lime concrete and broken stone. The third layer is concrete made with gravel. On top are blocks of stone set in concrete. Water from the surface drains into a ditch on either side.

Roads

There were few paved roads until the Romans began to build a system of fine roads, connecting the provinces of the Empire to Rome, but not with each other. This is why 'all roads led to Rome'.

Before the Romans, conquest, rather than trade, was the usual incentive for roadbuilding. The Romans built roads to keep their empire together, to make it possible to move troops and goods, and to send imperial despatches long distances at speed. A courier on the Roman roads could cover about 75 miles/120km a day.

Roman roads were superbly constructed, and many sections remain intact, even today. They were paved with flat stones or with specially-cut blocks of stone on top of two or three layers of foundation material. The road-builders overcame every obstacle. They built bridges over rivers, causeways through marshes, and tunnelled through rock. Altogether the Romans built more than 50,000 miles/ 80,000km of roads.

Even so, the roads only went where the Romans wanted them to go. There were still many journeys that had to be made on the old 'roads', unsurfaced and worn by travellers over the centuries.

In towns the streets were not very clean, so the Romans provided pedestrians with raised pavements and stepping-stones to allow them to avoid the dirt and mud.

Water transport

In Bible times travel by sea was even more difficult than land travel. The Mediterranean was safe for sailing only in the summer. Between November and March, ships set sail only in an emergency.

The great seafaring nations of the Old Testament period were the Egyptians and the Phoenicians. They built warships and trading vessels, powered by sails and oars. Israel's only successful attempt to develop a navy came during the golden age of Solomon's reign, at a time when the Phoenicians ruled the waves of the Mediterranean Sea.

Israel's border had been extended south to the Red Sea, and Solomon's alliance with Hiram, king of Tyre in Phoenicia, provided him with expert help in constructing a merchant fleet based on the town of Ezion-geber, at the head of the Gulf of Aqaba. Ezion-geber became an important trading-post. (See *Mining and Metalwork*.) From here Solomon's ships carried copper and iron to 'Ophir' (probably southern Arabia, at the other end of the Red Sea) and returned with luxury goods. The round-trip – about 1,250 miles/2,000km each way – took three years.

A century later, in about 850 BC, King Jehoshaphat attempted to revive the trade but his fleet was wrecked by a violent storm, and Israel's brief seafaring history was over.

In the New Testament the Gospel writers record several occasions when Jesus crossed the Sea of Galilee by boat. These journeys were probably made in the fishing boats used on this inland lake, 7½ miles/ 12km wide. The wind funnelling through the surrounding hills can whip the lake into sudden violent storms.

Paul's missionary travels included sea journeys as well as long treks overland. The account of his voyage to Rome given in the Book of Acts reads like a ship's log, with details about weather conditions, seamanship, and even a passenger list. It is one of the most vivid descriptions of a voyage in the whole of ancient literature.

Rome controlled the Mediterranean Sea at the time of Jesus. Corn grown in Egypt and exported from Alexandria on the Nile Delta was vital to the economic stability of the Empire. State-run grain-ships, some as much as 200ft/60 metres long, carried the corn to Italy. During the summer the winds took the ships straight across the sea from Egypt to Italy, but out of season the safer course was by shorter stages, or round the coast. Paul sailed in a corn-ship taking the safer route in late September or early October. When the ship was wrecked, the rest of the cargo and even the ship's tackle were thrown overboard before the valuable grain. It was another ship from Alexandria that took Paul on from Malta to Italy after the shipwreck.

Puteoli, on the Bay of Naples, was the main port of Rome until New Testament times when the harbour at Ostia, nearer to Rome, was improved and eventually became the principal port for the capital city of the Empire.
1 Kings 9:26–28; 10:11–12, 22; 22:48; Mark 4:35–39; Acts 27 – 28:15

Inland waterways

Apart from the Nile, the Tigris and the Euphrates, not many rivers in Bible lands were navigable. Barges (with sails) were used on the Nile, bringing corn to the seaport, but there was no other important river traffic. Although canals were often planned by Roman emperors (Nero, for example, wanted to join the Adriatic and the Aegean Seas by a Corinth canal), few were actually constructed.

Right: Jerusalem is the most famous of all Bible places.

10

Places of the Bible

Note: This section lists places which played a significant part in the Bible books, with the most important Bible references. The final reference indicates where they can be found – on the Old or New Testament Israel maps in this section, or on the maps in Part 12.

Abana Now called Barada, 'cool'. One of two rivers which flow through Damascus in Syria. When Elisha's servant told Naaman to bathe in the River Jordan and be healed, the Syrian general despised the muddy Jordan compared with the clear, fast-flowing waters of Abana and Pharpar.
2 Kings 5:12

Abel-beth-maacah A town in the north of Israel, near Lake Huleh, to which Joab pursued Sheba. Captured by Arameans of Damascus and recaptured more than once.
2 Samuel 20; I KIngs 15:20; 2 Kings 15:29; Map OT/C1

Abel-meholah The place to which the Midianites fled after Gideon's attack. The home-town of Elisha.
Judges 7:22; 1 Kings 19:16; Map OT/C4

Abilene The region north-west of Damascus, governed by Lysanias.
Luke 3:1

Accad Name of a region and a city in ancient Babylonia, founded by Nimrod. See *The Babylonians* in Part 11: *Nations and Peoples of the Bible.* Genesis 10:10

Achaia The Roman province of southern Greece governed from Corinth.
Acts 18:12, etc.; Map p. 342

Achor 'Trouble Valley', near Jericho, where Achan was killed because he disobeyed God's command.
Joshua 7:24

Adam The place where the River Jordan was blocked, allowing the Israelites to cross into the Promised Land. In 1927 earth tremors caused the high clay banks to collapse at the same spot, and the Jordan was dammed for twenty-one hours.
Joshua 3:16; Map OT/C4

Admah One of a group of five cities, of which Sodom and Gomorrah are best-known, now probably

under the southern end of the Dead Sea. The kings of these cities formed an alliance and rebelled against four northern kings in Abraham's day. In the battle that followed, Abraham's nephew Lot was taken captive.
Genesis 10:19; 14:2

Adramyttium A port near Troy and Troas on the west coast of what is now Turkey. A ship from Adramyttium took Paul and his fellow prisoners on the first stage of their journey to Rome. Acts 27:2

Adullam David, on the run from King Saul and fearing King Achish of Gath, took refuge in a 'cave' (probably a fort) near this town. His family and a group of 400 outlaws joined him in hiding. While he was there, three of David's bravest soldiers risked their lives to bring him water from the well at Bethlehem, which was held by the Philistines.
I Samuel 22:1; 2 Samuel 23:13

Aenon near Salim The place where John the Baptist baptized his followers.
John 3:23; Map NT/C3

Ahava The name of a canal and a region in Babylonia where Ezra assembled the second party of returning Jewish exiles. Here they fasted and prayed for God's protection on their 900 mile/1,448 km journey to Jerusalem.
Ezra 8:15, 21, 31

Ai The name means 'the Ruin'. After capturing Jericho, Joshua sent a small force against nearby Ai – and was beaten. The reason was because Achan had defied God's command by taking spoil from Jericho. Achan was punished, and Joshua attacked Ai again. He lured the men of Ai out by pretending to run away, and a hidden ambush force moved in and set fire to the stronghold. See Part 2: *Archaeology and the Bible.*
Joshua 7 and 8; Map OT/B4

Aijalon An Amorite town belonging by right to the tribe of Dan, but given to the Levites. Much later King Rehoboam fortified the city and kept stores and arms there.
Joshua 19:42; 21:24; Judges 1:35; 2 Chronicles 11:10; Map OT/B5

Aijalon A valley through which an important trade-route passed; near to the town of Aijalon. In this valley Joshua fought a great battle against the Amorites, and 'the sun stood still'.
Joshua 10; Map OT/B5

Alexandria A great Egyptian seaport on the Nile Delta founded by Alexander the Great. The famous Pharos light-house tower stood at the harbour entrance. Alexandria was the capital of Egypt under the Ptolemies, and remained a great centre of learning and trade.

In Roman times grain-ships loaded up at Alexandria so that the people of Rome could have cheap bread. The city had a 'museum' of arts and sciences and a famous library containing thousands of papyrus scrolls. There was a strong Jewish community, and it was here that the Old Testament was translated into Greek – the Septuagint version. Apollos, who became an important teacher in the early church, came from Alexandria.
Acts 6:9; 18:24; 27:6; 28:11

Ammon A state on the east of the Jordan whose capital was Rabbah (modern Amman). See *Rabbah*; *Ammonites* and Map in Part 11: *Nations and Peoples of the Bible*

Amphipolis A town on Paul's route through northern Greece on his second missionary journey.
Acts 17:1

Anathoth A town 3 miles/4 km north of Jerusalem belonging to the Levites. The birthplace of Jeremiah.
Joshua 21:18; Jeremiah 1:1; Map OT/B5

Antioch ('Pisidian') A city in the heart of Asia Minor (present-day Turkey) visited by Paul and Barnabas on their first missionary journey. They preached first in the synagogue, but when non-Jews responded to Paul's message the Jews stirred up trouble and threw Paul and Barnabas out of the city. Two or three years later, Paul visited Antioch again, on his second missionary journey, to encourage the Christians in their new faith.
Acts 13:14 – 52; Map p. 345

Antioch in Syria (modern Antakya, on the Syrian border of Turkey). The most famous of sixteen cities with this name, founded by one of Alexander's generals in honour of his father. Antioch, on the River Orontes, had its own sea-port. Under the Romans it became the capital of the province of Syria and third largest city of the Empire, renowned for its culture. It had a large Jewish community. After the death of Stephen, persecuted Christians fled the 300 miles/483 km from Jerusalem to Antioch.

This was the start of one of the largest and most active of the early Christian churches. Many local people were converted, including a large number of Greeks, and it was here that they were first called 'Christians'.

Barnabas, who had been sent from Jerusalem to find out what was happening, set off to find Paul and ask him to help teach the new converts. They taught together in Antioch for over a year. Some time later the church at Antioch sent Paul and Barnabas out to teach in Cyprus and beyond. Antioch remained Paul's base, and for a long time the church there was second only to Jerusalem. The ancient city was levelled by an earthquake in AD 526.
Acts 11:19 – 26; 13:1; 15:35; Map p. 345

Antipatris A town rebuilt by King Herod and named in honour of his father, Antipater. When Paul's life was threatened he was taken under escort from Jerusalem to Caesarea on the coast. On the way they spent the night at Antipatris.
Acts 23:31; Map p. 339

Aphek The Philistines camped at Aphek before the battle in which they captured the Covenant Box (ark) from the Israelites. Eli's sons took the ark to the Israelite camp. Both were killed in the battle, and Eli fell to his death when he heard the news. Much later Aphek became Antipatris.
1 Samuel 4:1; Map OT/B4

Ar Capital of Moab, on the River Arnon. During their time in the desert after leaving Egypt the Israelites

were told to leave this city in peace. God had given it to the Moabites, Lot's descendants.
Numbers 21:15; Deuteronomy 2:9; Isaiah 15:1; Map OT/C6

Arabah The rift valley of the River Jordan, stretching from Lake Galilee in the north to the Dead Sea in the south and continuing on to the Gulf of Aqaba. The 'Sea of Arabah' is the Dead Sea.

Arad A Canaanite city in the Negev captured and occupied by the Israelites. Recent excavations of Tell 'Arad have revealed an Israelite temple and fortresses.
Joshua 12:14; Map OT/B6

Aram A group name for various states in southern Syria, especially Damascus. See *Aramaeans* and Map in Part 11: *Nations and Peoples of the Bible.*

Ararat The mountain country where Noah's ark came to rest when the flood waters drained away. The area, called Urartu in Assyrian inscriptions, is Armenia, on the borders of present-day Turkey and Russia. Mount Ararat itself is an extinct volcano nearly 17,000 ft/5,214 m high.
Genesis 8:4; Jeremiah 51:27; Map p. 315

Areopagus 'Mars hill', north-west of the acropolis in Athens, from which the Council of the Areopagus (which originally met there) took its name.
Acts 17

Argob Part of the kingdom of Og in Bashan, east of the Jordan. It was given to the half tribe of Manasseh, and was a fertile region with many strong towns.
Deuteronomy 3; 1 Kings 4

Arimathea The home of Joseph, a secret disciple of Jesus, in whose new rock-tomb the body of Jesus was placed after he was crucified.
Matthew 27:57; Mark 15:43

Armageddon See *Megiddo.*

Arnon A river which flows into the Dead Sea from the east (now Wadi Mujib). It formed the border between the Amorites and Moabites. The invading Hebrews defeated the Amorites and their land was settled by the tribe of Reuben. The River Arnon remained the southern border.

Numbers 21:13ff.; Isaiah 16:2

Aroer A town on the north bank of the River Arnon, east of Jordan. The southern limit of the Amorite kingdom and later of the tribe of Reuben. Under Moabite rule from the time of Jehu to Jeremiah's day. Also the name of a town in the Negev, south of Beersheba.
Deuteronomy 2:36, etc.; 2 Kings 10:33; Map OT/C6

Ashdod One of five Philistine strongholds in Old Testament times. When the Philistines captured the Covenant Box (ark) they took it to the temple of their god Dagon at Ashdod. Next morning they discovered the statue of Dagon flat on its face; the following day it was broken in pieces. Ashdod fell to King Uzziah of Judah in Isaiah's time. In New Testament times the city (called Azotus) was restored by King Herod.
1 Samuel 5; 2 Chronicles 26:6; Isaiah 20:1, etc.; Acts 8:40; Map OT/A5

Ashkelon An ancient city on the coast of Israel, between Jaffa and Gaza. It became one of the main strongholds of the Philistines. Samson made a raid on Ashkelon, killing thirty men to pay what he owed in a bet. In the centuries that followed, Ashkelon was ruled in turn by Assyria, Babylonia and Tyre. Herod the Great, king at the time Jesus was born, was born at Ashkelon.
Judges 1:18; 14:19; 1 Samuel 6:17; Jeremiah 47:5–7, etc.; Map OT/A5

Ashtaroth/Ashteroth-karnaim A city east of the Jordan, named after the Canaanite mother-goddess. It was captured by Chedorlaomer in Abraham's time and later became a capital of King Og of Bashan. One of the cities given to the Levites.
Genesis 14:5; Deuteronomy 1:4; 1 Chronicles 6:71; Map OT/D2

Asia The western part of Asia Minor (modern Turkey) including a number of important Greek city-states. Later the Roman province of Asia, including the whole west coast, whose most important city was Ephesus. Much of Paul's missionary work took place

in this region.
Acts 2:9; 19:10; Revelation 1:4, 11; Map p. 343

Assos The sea-port in the north-west of modern Turkey from which Paul sailed on his last journey to Jerusalem. Acts 20:13

Assyria An important country in north Mesopotamia. Assyria was a great power from the ninth to the seventh century BC. See *The Assyrians* and Map in Part 11: *Nations and Peoples of the Bible.*

Ataroth A town east of the Jordan, given to the tribe of Reuben.
Numbers 32:3, 34; Map OT/C5

Athens The capital of modern Greece which first became important in the sixth century BC. The city was at the height of its greatness in the fifth century BC when its most famous public buildings, including the Parthenon, were built. Athens was then a model democracy and centre of the arts, attracting playwrights, historians, philosophers and scientists from all over Greece. In 86 BC the city was besieged and stripped by the Romans.
Although it lost its power and wealth as a centre of trade Athens still had a great name for learning about AD 50 when Paul arrived on his second missionary journey, preaching about Jesus and the resurrection. The Athenians loved a discussion and called him to speak before their council. Paul used their altar, dedicated 'To an Unknown God', as his starting-point. He spoke about the God who made the world and is near to each one of us. (Picture page 299.)
Acts 17:15–34; Map p. 342

Attalia Modern Antalya, a port of Pamphylia on the south coast of Turkey, used by Paul on his first missionary journey.
Acts 14:25; Map p. 344

Azekah The town to which Joshua pursued the Amorites; later a fortified border city of Judah.
Joshua 10:10; Jeremiah 34:7

Babel (predecessor of ancient Babylon) After the flood, when people still spoke one language, they planned to build a city on the plain of Shinar (Sumer) in the land of the two rivers

(Mesopotamia) – and a tower that would reach to heaven. God saw their pride and brought the work to a standstill by confusing their language, so that they could not understand one another.
Genesis 10:10; 11:1–9

Babylon A city on the River Euphrates, 50 miles/80 km south of modern Baghdad. Babylon was founded by Nimrod 'the mighty hunter'. It later became the capital of Babylonia and the Babylonian Empire. About 1750 BC, Hammurabi, one of the early kings of Babylon, wrote down on stone a great code of laws which it is interesting to compare with the later laws of Moses.
After the defeat of Assyria in 612 BC Babylon became capital of a powerful empire extending from the Persian Gulf to the Mediterranean. In 597 and 586 BC King Nebuchadnezzar of Babylon conquered rebellious Jerusalem. On each occasion, many of the people of Judah were taken into exile to Babylon – among them the prophets Ezekiel and Daniel.
The city covered a huge area on both banks of the Euphrates. Both inner and outer city were protected by double brick walls 11–25 ft/3–7 m thick. Eight great gates led to the inner city, and there were fifty temples. The 'hanging gardens' of Babylon was one of the wonders of the ancient world. These were terraces on different levels laid out with palms and many other trees and plants, providing colour and shade in a flat land.
In 539 BC the Persians, under Cyrus, took the city. Herodotus, the Greek historian, says they diverted the River Euphrates and marched along the dried-up river bed to enter the city. From that time on, Babylon declined. Nothing remains today but a series of widely scattered mounds, for the archaeologists to work on. See Part 11: *Nations and Peoples of the Bible* under *The Babylonians.*
Genesis 10:10; 2 Kings 24:1; 25:7–13; Isaiah 14:1–23; Daniel 1 – 6; Map p. 315

Bashan A fertile region east of Lake Galilee, famous for its cattle, sheep and strong oak trees. On their way from Egypt to Canaan the Israelites defeated King Og of Bashan, and his land was given to the tribe of Manasseh.
Deuteronomy 3; Psalm 22:12; Isaiah 2:13; Map OT/C2

Beersheba The southernmost town to belong to the Israelites, on the edge of the Negev Desert, and on the trade route to Egypt. The well (be'er) which gave the town its name was dug by Abraham. Hagar came near to death in the desert of Beersheba. It was from this place that Abraham set out to offer up Isaac. Isaac himself was living here when Jacob left for Harran. Beersheba is also mentioned in connection with Elijah and Amos. The phrase 'from Dan to Beersheba' became a common way to speak of the whole land, from north to south. See Part 2: Archaeology and the Bible.
Genesis 21:14, 30–32; 26: 23–33; 1 Kings 19:3; Amos 5:5; Map OT/A6

Beroea A city in northern Greece (Macedonia), 50 miles/80 km from Thessalonica. Paul preached here on his second missionary journey. The Beroeans welcomed him because they studied the Scriptures. But Jews from Thessalonica stirred up the mob against him and he had to leave. But Silas and Timothy stayed behind to teach the Beroeans more about the Christian faith.
Acts 17:10–15; 20:4; Map p. 345

Bethany A village about 2 miles/3 km from Jerusalem on the far side of the Mount of Olives, and on the road to Jericho. Mary, Martha and Lazarus lived here, and Jesus stayed with them when he visited Jerusalem. Jesus raised Lazarus from the grave at Bethany. He ascended to heaven from a place nearby.
Matthew 26:6–13; Luke 10:38–42; 24:50; John 11; 12:1–9; Map NT/B5

Bethel A place 12 miles/19 km north of Jerusalem where Jacob dreamed of a staircase from heaven to earth. God promised to protect him, and said he would give the land to Jacob's descendants. Jacob called the place 'Bethel' (house of God). Centuries later, when the Israelites invaded Canaan, they captured Bethel and settled there.

When the kingdoms of Israel and Judah split up, King Jeroboam of Israel set up an altar and golden calf at Bethel, so that people could worship there instead of at Jerusalem. The prophets condemned this, and when the Israelites were taken into exile Bethel was settled by Assyrians. When the exiles returned, some of them lived in Bethel.
Genesis 28:10–22; Judges 1:22–26; 20:18; 1 Kings 12:26–30; 2 Kings 2; 17:28; Nehemiah 11:31; Map OT/B4

Bethesda/Bethzatha A large pool in Jerusalem. At the time of Jesus it was sheltered by five porches, and it is probably the five-porched pool that has been unearthed by archaeologists in the north-east of the city. The pool was fed by a spring which bubbled up from time to time. Many sick people gathered there, hoping to be healed if they were first into the water after this bubbling. It was here that Jesus healed a man who had been ill for thirty-eight years.
John 5:1–15

Beth-horon (Upper and Lower) These two towns controlled the Valley of Aijalon and the ancient trade-route which passed through it. Many armies took this route in Bible times. Here Joshua pursued the Amorite kings who had attacked the town of Gibeon. Philistines, Egyptians and Syrians also came here.
Joshua 16:3–5; 10:10; 1 Samuel 13:18; Map OT/B4

Bethlehem The city of David, 5 miles/8 km south-west of Jerusalem, in the Judean hills. Rachel, wife of Jacob, was buried nearby. Ruth and Naomi settled here. Bethlehem was David's birth-place, and the place where the prophet Samuel chose him as the future king, to succeed Saul. The prophet Micah foretold the birth of the Messiah at Bethlehem, although it was only a small town.

A modern shepherd looks after his sheep on the hills outside Bethlehem, the town where Jesus was born.

Centuries later the Roman census brought Mary and Joseph to Bethlehem. Shepherds and wise men came to kneel before their baby, Jesus – born in a stable in the 'city of David'. Not long after, jealous King Herod gave orders to kill all the boys in Bethlehem under two years old.
Genesis 35:19; Ruth; 1 Samuel 16; Micah 5:2; Matthew 2; Luke 2; Map NT/B5

Bethphage A village near Bethany, on or near the Mount of Olives, on the east side of Jerusalem. When Jesus came here on his last journey to Jerusalem, he sent two disciples to a nearby village to fetch the young colt on which he rode in triumph into the city.
Matthew 21:1; Mark 11:1; Luke 19:29; Map NT/B5

Bethsaida A fishing town on the north shore of Lake Galilee, near the River Jordan. The home of Jesus' disciples, Philip, Andrew and Peter. Jesus restored the sight of a blind man at Bethsaida, and warned the people of God's judgement. Although they saw his miracles they would not change their ways.
John 1:44; Mark 8:22; Matthew 11:21; Map NT/C2

Beth-shan A very ancient city in northern Palestine where the Valley of Jezreel slopes down to the west bank of the River Jordan. The Israelites failed to drive the Canaanites out of this district. After Saul and Jonathan were killed by the Philistines on Mt Gilboa, their bodies were fixed on the walls of Beth-shan, but later rescued and buried by men from Jabesh-gilead. In New Testament times Beth-shan was known by the Greek name Scythopolis, and became one of the cities of the Decapolis, the only one west of the Jordan (see Decapolis). The modern town of Beisan stands close to the mound of the old site.
Joshua 17:11, 16; Judges 1:27; 1 Samuel 31:10–13; 2 Samuel 21:12; 1 Kings 4:12; Map OT/C3

Beth-shemesh A town about 12 miles/19 km west of Jerusalem, given to the priests. It was near the borders of the Philistines. When the Covenant Box (ark) was returned by the Philistines, it came to Beth-shemesh. But some of the people here were punished for not treating it with respect. Later Jehoash, king of the northern kingdom of Israel, defeated and captured Amaziah, king of Judah, at Beth-shemesh.
Joshua 21:16; 1 Samuel 6:9–21; 1 Kings 4:9; 2 Kings 14:11–13; Map OT/B5

Beth-zur A city of Judah,

4 miles/6 km north of Hebron. Beth-zur was settled by the family of Caleb. Later it was one of fifteen cities fortified by King Rehoboam. Men from here helped to rebuild Jerusalem under Nehemiah's leadership. The place stood on one of the highest hill-tops in the land, and was the scene of one of the great Jewish victories in the Maccabean revolt (*1 Maccabees* 4:26–35).
Joshua 15:58;
1 Chronicles 2:45;
2 Chronicles 11:7;
Nehemiah 3:16; Map OT/B6

Bithynia A Roman province in the north-west of Asia Minor (Turkey). Paul was forbidden 'by the Holy Spirit' to preach here. Yet Bithynia was not forgotten. Peter sent his first letter to Christian believers living in Bithynia, among other places. We know that this area soon became a strong centre of Christianity, for early in the second century the Roman governor Pliny wrote to the Emperor Trajan about the Christians there (see Part 5).
Acts 16:7; 1 Peter 1:1; Map p. 343

Bozrah An ancient city in Edom, south-east of the Dead Sea, about 80 miles/128 km south of modern Amman in Jordan. The prophets foretold that Bozrah would be utterly destroyed.
Genesis 36:33;
1 Chronicles 1:44; Isaiah 34:6; 63:1; Jeremiah 49:13, 22; Amos 1:12; Map OT/C5

Caesarea A Mediterranean port built by Herod the Great. He named the town after the Roman Emperor Augustus Caesar. Statues of the Emperor stood in a huge temple dedicated to him and to Rome. Traders on their way from Tyre to Egypt passed through Caesarea. So it was a centre of inland as well as sea-trade.
Caesarea was the home town of Philip the evangelist. It was also the home of Cornelius, the Roman centurion who sent for Peter, asking him to explain God's message. It was here that Peter learned that 'the Good News of peace through Jesus Christ' was for non-Jews as well as Jews.
Paul several times used

the port on his travels. The Roman governors lived here, rather than at Jerusalem, so it was here that Paul was taken for trial before Felix after his arrest. He spent two further years in prison here. From Caesarea he sailed for Rome after his appeal to Caesar.
Acts 8:40; 21:8; 10; 11; 9:30; 18:22; 23:33 – 26:32; Map NT/A3

Caesarea Philippi A town at the foot of Mt Hermon and close to the main source of the River Jordan. Herod the Great built a marble temple here to Augustus Caesar. And one of his sons, Philip, changed the town's name from Paneas to Caesarea. It was known as Philip's Caesarea to distinguish it from the port.
Jesus had taken his disciples to this part of the country when he asked them, 'Who do you say I am?' The answer came from Peter: 'You are the Messiah, the Son of the living God.'
Matthew 16:13–16; Map NT/C1

Calah A very ancient city of Mesopotamia on the River Tigris, later a leading city of the Assyrian Empire. Excavations at the site, now Nimrud in Iraq, have unearthed inscriptions and ivory-carvings which throw light on the times of the kings of Israel.
Genesis 10:11–12

Cana The village in Galilee where Jesus turned the water into wine at a wedding. During another visit to Cana, Jesus healed the son of an official from Capernaum. Nathanael,

one of Jesus' twelve disciples, came from Cana.
John 2:1–12; 4:46–53; 21–2; Map NT/B2

Canaan The land promised by God to the Israelites. See *Canaanites* and Map in Part 11: *Nations and Peoples of the Bible.*

Capernaum An important town on the north-west shore of Lake Galilee at the time of Jesus. It was Jesus' base while he was teaching in Galilee. Levi (Matthew) the tax-collector lived at Capernaum. So too did a Roman army officer whose servant Jesus healed. There may have been an army post here. Many of Jesus' miracles took place at Capernaum, including the healing of Peter's mother-in-law. Jesus also taught in the local synagogue. But despite all this, the people of the town did not believe God's message, and Jesus had to warn them of coming judgement.
Mark 1:21–34; 2:1–17; Luke 7:1–10; 10:13–16, etc.; Map NT/C2

Cappadocia A Roman province in the east of Asia Minor (Turkey). There were Jews from Cappadocia among those who heard Peter in Jerusalem on the Day of Pentecost. Later the Christians in Cappadocia were among those to whom Peter sent his first letter.
Acts 2:9; 1 Peter 1:1; Map p. 343

Carchemish An important Hittite city from early times,

At Cana in Galilee Jesus went to a wedding – and turned water into wine.

on the River Euphrates. The ruins now lie on the border between Turkey and Syria. When the Egyptian Pharaoh (king) Neco went to attack Carchemish, Josiah, the king of Judah, made a needless attempt to oppose him, and was defeated and killed in the plain of Megiddo. In 605 BC Neco himself was defeated at Carchemish by Nebuchadnezzar, king of Babylon.
2 Chronicles 35:20; Isaiah 10:9; Jeremiah 46:2; Map p. 327

Carmel A mountain range which juts into the Mediterranean Sea close to the modern port of Haifa. The ancient city of Megiddo guarded one of the main passes through the hills some miles inland. It was on Mt Carmel (1,740 ft/535 m at the highest point) that Elijah, God's prophet, challenged the prophets of Baal to a contest. Elisha, who followed Elijah as prophet, also seems to have made a base there.
1 Kings 18:19–46; 2 Kings 2:25; 4:25; Map OT/B3

Cenchreae The eastern port of Corinth in southern Greece, from which Paul sailed to Ephesus.
Acts 18:8; Romans 16:1

Chaldea South Babylonia; Abraham's family home. See Chaldeans and Map in Part 11: *Nations and Peoples of the Bible.*

Chebar A canal running from the River Euphrates in Babylonia (S. Iraq). It was by the Chebar that the prophet Ezekiel, in exile with the Jews in Babylonia, saw some of his great visions of God.

Ezekiel 1; 3; 10; 43

Cherith A desert stream east of the Jordan. Here God provided food and water for Elijah during years of drought and famine, until the stream itself dried up. We do not know exactly where the Cherith was.
1 Kings 17:3–7

Chinnereth The Old Testament name for Lake Galilee, from a place on its western shore. The name is used in descriptions of the boundaries of lands belonging to the tribes of Israel, and of nearby kingdoms. See *Galilee*.
Numbers 34:11; Deuteronomy 3:17; Joshua 11:2, etc.; 1 Kings 15:20

Chorazin A town where Jesus taught, near Capernaum, on a hill above Lake Galilee. Jesus was deeply troubled that these places which heard his teaching did not show any change of heart and life as a result. The site of Chorazin is now a deserted ruin.
Matthew 11:21; Luke 10:13; Map NT/C2

Cilicia A region in south Asia Minor (modern Turkey) which became a province of the Roman Empire in 103 BC. Tarsus, where Paul was born, was the chief town of Cilicia. Behind it, running north-east, lay the wild Taurus mountains, cut through by an impressive pass known as the Cilician Gates.
Acts 21:39; 22:3; 23:34; Map p. 343

Colossae A city in the Lycus Valley, in the Roman province of Asia (now south-west Turkey). It stood just a few miles from Laodicea, on the main road east from Ephesus. The Christian message probably reached Colossae when Paul was staying at Ephesus, though he himself never went there. Paul wrote a letter (Colossians) to the church there.
Colossians 1:2; Map p. 343

Corinth An old Greek city destroyed by the Romans in 146 BC and rebuilt by them a hundred years later. Corinth stood on the narrow neck of land connecting mainland Greece with the southern peninsula, between the Aegean and Adriatic seas. It was a good position for trade.
The town attracted people of many

nationalities. It was dominated by the 'Acro-corinth', the steep rock on which the acropolis and a temple to Aphrodite (goddess of love) was built. Temple prostitutes and a large 'floating' population helped to give Corinth a very bad name for all kinds of immoral behaviour.
Paul stayed in Corinth for eighteen months, on his second missionary journey. During that time he founded a church to which he later wrote at least two letters now in the New Testament (1 and 2 Corinthians).
Acts 18; Map p. 343

Crete A mountainous island in the eastern Mediterranean Sea. The 'Cherethites', who formed part of King David's bodyguard, probably came from Crete. Much earlier, from before 2000 BC until after 1400 BC, the Minoan civilization flourished on the island. It was a home of the Philistines.
In the New Testament, men from Crete were in Jerusalem on the Day of Pentecost. Paul's ship called at the island on its way to Rome. At some stage he had visited Crete and left Titus there to help the newly-formed church. See *Philistines* in Part 11: *Nations and Peoples of the Bible*.
Genesis 10:14; Deuteronomy 2:23; Jeremiah 47:4; Amos 9:7; Acts 2:11; 28:7–14; Titus 1:5, 12–13; Map p. 343

Cush A land in Africa (Sudan) named after the grandson of Noah. The English versions sometimes translate the name as Ethiopia.
Genesis 10:6–8; Isaiah 11:11; 18:11

Cyprus A large island in the eastern Mediterranean Sea. In the Old Testament 'Elishah' may refer to Cyprus, and 'Kittim' to Cypriots.
In the New Testament Cyprus features as the home of Barnabas. It was the first place Paul and Barnabas visited when they set out to take the good news of Jesus to the non-Jewish world. Here they met the governor, Sergius Paulus, and his magician friend. Barnabas later returned to Cyprus with Mark.

Acts 4:36; 13:4–12; 15:39; 27:4; Map p. 343

Cyrene A Greek city on the north coast of Africa, in modern Libya. A man from Cyrene, Simon, was forced to carry Jesus' cross. Jews from Cyrene were among those present in Jerusalem on the Day of Pentecost. Other Cyrenians became involved in the earliest mission to non-Jews, at Antioch.
Matthew 27:32; Mark 15:21; Acts 2:10; 6:9; 11:20; 13:1; Map p. 342

Dalmatia A Roman province on the east coast of the Adriatic Sea, along the coast of modern Yugoslavia. Paul's second letter to Timothy shows him almost alone at the end of his life. His friends have left him for various reasons. Titus has gone to Dalmatia.
2 Timothy 4:10

Damascus The capital of Syria (see *Aramaeans* in Part 1: *Environment of the Bible*). Damascus was already well known in Abraham's day, and is often mentioned in the Old Testament. King David captured the city, but it soon regained its independence. Damascus was the home of Naaman, who came to the prophet Elisha for healing. The prophet later went to Damascus to advise on the king's health.
Isaiah predicted the destruction of Damascus. And after a series of attacks the Assyrians captured the city in 732 BC, carried away its treasures and many of its people, and reduced its power. From 64 BC to AD 33 Damascus was a Roman city.
Paul was on his way to Damascus to persecute the Christians when he met with Jesus himself, and the whole direction of his life was changed. He had to escape from the city later, when the Jews persecuted him.
Genesis 14:15; 15:2; 2 Samuel 8:5; 1 Kings 20:34; 2 Kings 5; 8:7–15; Isaiah 17; Acts 9; Map p. 329

Dan The land belonging to the tribe of Dan, and a town (Laish) in the far north of Israel. Dan was the northernmost city of Israel, and the expression 'from Dan to Beersheba' meant 'from one end of the land to the other'. When

the kingdom was divided, Jeroboam I tried to keep the loyalty of the northern tribes by giving them two golden calves to worship: one was at Dan.
Joshua 19:40–48; 1 Kings 12:25–30; Map OT/C1

Dead Sea See *Salt Sea* and *Arabah*.

Decapolis (the Ten Towns) An association of ten Greek towns gave this region its name. The Decapolis was an area south of Lake Galilee, mostly east of the River Jordan. Many of the people living there were non-Jews, but they joined the crowds that followed Jesus. Jewish Christians fled to Pella, one of these towns, before the war with the Romans in AD 70.
Matthew 4:25; Mark 5:1–20; 7:31–37; Map NT/C3

Dedan See *Dedan* in Part 11: *Nations and Peoples of the Bible*.

Derbe A city in Lycaonia, in southern Asia Minor (modern Turkey), where Paul preached on his first and second journeys.
Acts 14:20–21; 16:1; Map p. 345

Dibon A Moabite town east of the Dead Sea and 4 miles/5.5 km north of the River Arnon. The Israelites captured it at the time of their entry into Canaan. It was given to the tribes of Gad and Reuben, but changed hands several times in the course of its history.
Numbers 21:30; 32:34; Isaiah 15:2; Map OT/C6

Dor A Canaanite town. Dor joined the northern alliance of kings who fought against Joshua and lost. The town was given to the tribe of Manasseh who failed to drive out its inhabitants.
Joshua 11:1–15; Judges 1:27; 1 Kings 4:11; Map OT/B3

Dothan A town on the route from Beth-shan and Gilead to Egypt. Here Joseph's brothers sold him to the Ishmaelite traders. At Dothan, Elisha was rescued from the surrounding Syrian army.
Genesis 37:17–28; 2 Kings 6; Map OT/B3

Ebal A rocky mountain in Samaria, opposite the wooded height of Mt Gerizim, close to ancient Shechem and modern Nablus. Here Joshua carried out a command

Straight Street in Damascus, the place where Paul's sight was restored, is today lined with small shops selling goods of all kinds. Damascus was an important city and centre of trade in Old as well as New Testament times. The inset picture shows a local weaver at his loom.

given him by Moses before the conquest of the land. He built an altar on Mt Ebal and gave the people a choice – to obey God and enjoy his blessing, or to disobey and be punished. Some of the people stood on Mt Ebal, whose bare, scorched height represented God's curse, and others on Mt Gerizim.
Deuteronomy 11:29; 27; Joshua 8:30, 33; Map OT/B4

Eden The garden God made, in the beginning, as a place for his people to live in. After they had disobeyed him, God sent Adam and Eve out of the Garden of Eden. Two of the rivers in it were the Tigris and the Euphrates.
Genesis 2:8 – 14

Edom The mountainous land south of the Dead Sea where Esau's descendants settled.

Edrei The site of a battle where the Israelites destroyed the army of Og, king of Bashan, who fought them before they entered the Promised Land. Edrei is the modern Der'a, on the Syrian frontier with Jordan.
Numbers 21:33; Deuteronomy 1:4; 3:1, 10; Joshua 12:4; 13:12, 31; Map OT/D3

Eglon One of a group of Amorite cities conquered by Joshua in his first vigorous campaign. It was probably Tell el-Hesi near Lachish, in the Shephelah, the low hill-country west of Jerusalem.

Egypt A fertile and powerful land to the south of Israel, prominent throughout the history of the Old Testament, especially at the time of the Exodus. See *Egyptians* in Part 11: *Nations and Peoples of the Bible*.
Genesis 46; Exodus 1 – 14; Map p. 314

Ekron One of the five main cities of the Philistines. It was given to the tribe of Judah in the early years of conquest. But the Philistines on the coastal plain were too strong for them to keep it. When the Philistines defeated Israel and captured the Covenant Box (ark), plague broke out in each of the Philistine cities to which the ark was taken. When the plague reached Ekron, the Philistines finally decided to send the ark back to the

Israelites. Ekron remained a Philistine city. When King Ahaziah turned away from the God of Israel, he sent to consult Baal-zebub, the god of Ekron. 'Beelzebub' was regarded in New Testament times as the prince of evil spirits.
Joshua 15:11, 45–46; Judges 1:18; 1 Samuel 5:10–6:17; 7:14; 17:52; 2 Kings 1:3–6; Amos 1:8, etc.; Map OT/A5

Elah A valley south-west of Jerusalem. The Philistines marched through the Valley of Elah to invade the land of Israel. Here David fought the Philistine champion Goliath.
1 Samuel 17:2

Elam The country east of Babylonia whose capital was Susa. See *Elamites* in Part 11: *Nations and Peoples of the Bible*.

Elath/Ezion-geber A settlement (later a town) at the head of the Gulf of Aqaba on the Red Sea. The Israelites camped there on their way from Egypt to Canaan. King Solomon based a Red Sea trading fleet there. King Jehoshaphat later tried to revive this, but his ships were wrecked. The town eventually came under Edomite control.
Numbers 33:35–36; Deuteronomy 2:8; 1 Kings 9:26–27; 22:48; 2 Kings 16:6; Map p. 323

Emmaus A village within 8 miles/13 km of Jerusalem. It was probably modern El-Qubeibeh. On the day of his resurrection Jesus appeared to two of his followers who were on their way to Emmaus.
Luke 24:13; Map NT/B5

Endor A place in northern Israel, near Mt Tabor. King Saul made a secret journey to Endor on the night before his last battle. He wanted to ask the witch (or medium) there to call up the spirit of the dead prophet Samuel, to advise him. Saul and his son Jonathan were killed next day in the disastrous defeat at nearby Mt Gilboa.
1 Samuel 28; Map OT/B3

Engedi A spring to the west of the Dead Sea where David hid out.
Joshua 15:62; 1 Samuel 23:29, etc.; Map OT/B6

En-rogel A well on the south side of Jerusalem, near where the Hinnom Valley joins the Kidron Valley. Adonijah, one of King David's sons, had himself anointed king here before his father's death. He was trying to prevent the kingdom from going to Solomon.
1 Kings 1:9

Ephesus The most important city in the Roman province of Asia (western Turkey). Ephesus was a bridgehead between East and West. It stood at the end of one of the great caravan trade routes through Asia, at the mouth of the Cayster River. By Paul's day the harbour was beginning to silt up. But the city was magnificent, with streets paved in marble, baths, libraries, a market-place and theatre seating more than 25,000 people. The temple to Diana at Ephesus was one of the seven wonders of the ancient world, four times the size of the Parthenon at Athens.

There had been a settlement at Ephesus since before the twelfth century BC. But by New Testament times the population had grown to something like a third of a million, including a great many Jews.

Ephesus soon became an important centre for the early Christians, too. Paul made a brief visit on his second missionary journey, and his friends Aquila and Prisca stayed on there. On his third journey he spent over two years at Ephesus, and the Christian message spread widely throughout the province. Sales of silver images of Diana began to fall off. People's incomes were threatened and there was a riot.

Paul wrote his letters to Corinth from Ephesus. And some of his letters from prison (Philippians, etc.) are sometimes thought to have been written from Ephesus. Timothy stayed behind to help the church when Paul left. Paul later wrote a letter to the Christians at Ephesus. One of the letters to the seven churches in Revelation was also addressed to them.

There is a tradition that Ephesus became the home of the apostle John.
Acts 18:19; 19; 20:17; 1 Corinthians 15:32; 16:8–9; Ephesians 1:1; 1 Timothy 1:3; Revelation 2:1–7; Map p. 337

Ephraim The land belonging to the tribe of Ephraim.
Joshua 16:4–10, etc.; Map p. 321

Ephrathah Another name for Bethlehem.

Erech One of the great Sumerian cities, in southern Babylonia, about 40 miles/64 km north-west of Ur. It is mentioned in

The Roman Arcadian Way at Ephesus in Turkey leads to the theatre. The inset picture gives a performer's view of the theatre, as he made his entrance into the arena.

Genesis in the list of nations.
Genesis 10:10; Ezra 4:9

Eshcol A valley near Hebron. The name means 'a cluster of grapes'. When Moses sent spies into the Promised Land they brought back samples of the fruit of the country, including a huge bunch of grapes from this valley.
Numbers 13:23–24; 32:9; Deuteronomy 1:24

Eshtaol A place about 10 miles/16km west of Jerusalem, on the borders of the land belonging to the tribe of Dan. This was the home district of Samson. Here he grew up, and the Spirit of God first moved him to go out against the Philistines in the lowlands to the west. In spite of Samson's exploits, the Danites never occupied their inheritance.
Joshua 15:33; 19:41; Judges 13:24–25; 16:31; 18; Map OT/B5

Ethiopia This is Sudan, not modern Ethiopia, and is called Cush in many translations of the Old Testament. See *Cush* in Part 11: *Nations and Peoples of the Bible*.

Euphrates In the Old Testament this great river is often referred to simply as 'the river'. It is 1,200 miles/1,931km long. It rises in eastern Turkey and flows south-east to the Persian Gulf. Its course through the Babylonian plains has moved west, leaving many of the ancient cities which once stood on its banks now 3–4 miles/5–6km to the east. The route to Syria followed the Euphrates north to Carchemish, then turned south towards Damascus, Israel and Egypt. The Euphrates is mentioned as one of the four rivers of Eden.
Genesis 2:14; 15:18, etc.; Revelation 9:14; 16:12; Map p. 315

Ezion-geber See *Elath*.

Fair Havens A small port on the south coast of Crete. Paul's ship called in at Fair Havens on the voyage to Rome. Here Paul conferred with the centurion Julius and the owner·and captain of the ship, who wanted to reach a more attractive harbour in which to spend the winter. In spite of Paul's advice they put out to sea, and were caught in the violent wind which drove them to shipwreck on

Malta.
Acts 27:8–12

Gad The land belonging to the tribe of Gad. Part of the former Amorite kingdom, east of the River Jordan (south Gilead).
Joshua 13:8–13; Map p. 321

Galatia A Roman province in central Asia Minor. Its capital was Ancyra (now Ankara, the capital of modern Turkey). Several cities visited by Paul – Pisidian Antioch, Iconium, Lystra and perhaps Derbe – were in the southern part of Galatia, and Paul's letter to the Galatians was probably addressed to them. Galatia was also one of the areas to which 1 Peter was sent.
Acts 16:6; 18:23; Galatians 1:1; 1 Peter 1:1; Map p. 337

Galilee The name of an area and large lake in northern Israel. The home area of Jesus and a number of his disciples. When his public work began, Jesus spent much of his time here.

Galilee is mentioned occasionally in the Old Testament. It was surrounded on three sides by other nations and strongly influenced by them. Most of Galilee is hilly, but the land falls steeply to 682 ft/210 m below sea level around the lake.

At the time of Jesus several major roads of the Roman Empire crossed Galilee. Farming, trade and the lakeside fisheries were the main industries. Many of the towns and villages mentioned in the Gospels were in Galilee, including Nazareth (where Jesus grew up), Capernaum, Cana and Bethsaida. The lake, which is liable to sudden fierce storms as the wind funnels through the hills that ring it round, is also a focal point in the Gospel stories.
1 Kings 9:11; 2 Kings 15:29; Isaiah 9:1; Luke 4:14; 5:1 and following; 8:22–26; John 21, etc.; Acts 9:31; Map NT/B3

Gath One of five Philistine strongholds in Old Testament times. When the Philistines captured the Covenant Box (ark) it was taken to Gath, but plague followed. Goliath came from Gath, the home of other 'giants', too. Later when David was on the run from King Saul, he

escaped to Gath. Soldiers from Gath helped him when his son Absalom led a rebellion against him. The city was subject to the kingdom of Judah for some time and eventually fell to the Assyrians in the eighth century BC. The site is still not certain.
Joshua 11:22; 1 Samuel 5; 17:4; 21:10 – 22:1; 27; 2 Samuel 15:18; 2 Kings 12:17; 2 Chronicles 11:8; 26:6

Gath-hepher A place in Galilee on the borders of the lands belonging to the tribes of Zebulun and Naphtali. It was the birth-place of the prophet Jonah. It lay close to the later town of Nazareth.
Joshua 19:13; 2 Kings 14:25; Map OT/B2

Gaza One of five Philistine strongholds in Old Testament times, on the coastal plain. Joshua conquered and then lost the city. The town features in the story of Samson. He was put in prison here, and finally died when he brought about the collapse of a great building. Gaza suffered with the other Philistine cities when they captured the Covenant Box (ark).

The town was an important one on the trade route to Egypt. It was conquered by King Hezekiah of Judah, and later by the Assyrian armies and the Egyptian pharaoh.

In the New Testament, Philip was on the road from Jerusalem to Gaza when he met the Ethiopian official and told him the Good News about Jesus.
Joshua 10:41; Judges 16; 1 Samuel 6:17; 2 Kings 18:8; Jeremiah 47; Acts 8:26; Map OT/A6

Geba Modern Jeba', opposite Michmash, 6 miles/10 km north of Jerusalem. A city belonging to the tribe of Benjamin. Saul's army camped here in front of his capital at Gibeah when the Philistines held Michmash. Later Geba became the northern limit of the southern kingdom of Judah, and was fortified by King Asa. Like Michmash, it was on the route of the Assyrian approach to Jerusalem, and was resettled after the exile.
Joshua 18:24; 21:17; 1 Samuel 13:16; 1 Kings 15:22; 2 Kings 23:8;

1 Chronicles 6:60; Isaiah 10:29; Ezra 2:26; Nehemiah 7:30; Zechariah 14:10; Map OT/B5

Gebal A very ancient Phoenician city, often known by its Greek name Byblos. It was on the coast of modern Lebanon, north of Berytus (Beirut). 'There is still much land to be taken,' God told Joshua in his old age. Gebal was one of the areas included on the list. Later, workmen from Gebal helped to prepare the timber and stone for building Solomon's temple. Ezekiel prophesied against Tyre and other Phoenician towns, including Gebal.
Joshua 13:5; 1 Kings 5:18; Psalm 83:9; Ezekiel 27:9

Gennesaret A place on the western shore of Lake Galilee. The name is also used of the lake itself. See also *Galilee, Chinnereth.*
Mark 6:53; Luke 5:1

Gerar A place in the Negev, between Beersheba and Gaza, where both Abraham and Isaac stayed. For safety, Abraham said that his wife Sarah was his sister. Abimelech, king of Gerar, wanted to take Sarah as his wife. But God prevented this.
Genesis 20:26; Map OT/A6

Gerizim The mountain of God's blessing, in Samaria, opposite Mt Ebal (see *Ebal*). Gerizim later became the Samaritans' sacred mountain, the place where they built their temple. It was the mountain which the woman of Samaria mentioned as the place where her ancestors worshipped. The site of the ancient Samaritan temple has recently been found on a spur of Mt Gerizim.
Deuteronomy 11:29 27; Joshua 8:33; John 4:20; Map OT/B4

Geshur A region and town in southern Syria. King David married the king of Geshur's daughter. Their son, Absalom, fled to Geshur after he had killed his half-brother Amnon in revenge for the rape of his sister Tamar.
Joshua 12:5; 2 Samuel 3:3; 13:38, etc.

Gethsemane ('olive press'). A garden across the Kidron Valley from Jerusalem, close to the Mount of Olives. Jesus and his disciples often went there. So Judas knew

where to take the soldiers on the night of the arrest.
Matthew 26:36–56; Mark 14:32–51; Luke 22:39; John 18:1–12

Gezer One of the Canaanite towns Joshua campaigned against. It was in the low hills, on the road from Joppa (on the coast) to Jerusalem. Gezer belonged to Egypt for a while until one of the pharaohs gave it to his daughter, King Solomon's wife. Solomon fortified the town, with Hazor and Megiddo. It is the place where archaeologists discovered the 'Gezer calendar' (see Part 9: *Work and Society in the Bible* under *Farming*).
Joshua 10:33, etc.; 1 Kings 9:15–17; Map OT/B5

Gibeah A hill-top town 3 miles/4 km north of Jerusalem, which became famous as the home and capital city of King Saul. The place had been tragically destroyed as a result of a crime committed by its people during the time of the Judges. The site is at Tell el-Ful, overlooking the suburbs of Jerusalem.
Judges 19:12 – 20:48; 1 Samuel 10:26, etc.; Isaiah 10:29; Map OT/B5

Gibeon A town about 6 miles/10 km north-west of Jerusalem. After the fall of Jericho and Ai the Gibeonites tricked Joshua into a peace treaty. Saul later broke this. David's men fought the supporters of Saul's son Ishbosheth at the pool of Gibeon, to decide which should be king. The tent of worship (tabernacle) was kept at Gibeon, and King Solomon worshipped there. The people of Gibeon helped Nehemiah to rebuild the walls of Jerusalem.
    Archaeologists have discovered a huge pit at Gibeon, with a stairway leading down to water. Inside it there were handles of a great many storage jars, each one inscribed with the name 'Gibeon' and the owner's name. The town seems to have been an important centre for wine-making in the seventh century BC.
Joshua 9; 2 Samuel 2:12–29; 20:8; 21; 1 Kings 3:4; 1 Chronicles 21:29; Nehemiah 3:7; Map OT/B5

Gihon The name of one of the four great rivers which flowed out of the Garden of Eden.
    Gihon was also the name of a spring at the foot of the hill on which the first city of Jerusalem stood. It was then the main source of water for the city. Solomon was anointed king at this spring by the command of his father David, to forestall the attempt of his rival Adonijah to seize the throne. The Gihon spring water was vitally important to the safety of the city and, later, King Hezekiah cut a tunnel to bring the water right through the hill and inside the walls. This tunnel still exists. The water comes out at the Pool of Siloam (see *Siloam*).
Genesis 2:13; 1 Kings 1; 2 Chronicles 32:30; 33:14

Gilboa A mountain and range in the north of Palestine, overlooking the deep Valley of Jezreel which runs down to the River Jordan. King Saul and his army took their last stand against the Philistines on Mt Gilboa. Saul, Jonathan and his other two sons were all killed there.
1 Samuel 28:4; 31:1, 8; 2 Samuel 1; 21:12; 1 Chronicles 10:1, 8; Map OT/B3

Gilead A large area east of the River Jordan, extending north from the Dead Sea. The tribes of Reuben, Gad and Manasseh each occupied part of Gilead. The region was good grazing-land, famous for its flocks and herds. It was also famous for a gum or spice known as the 'balm' of Gilead. This was used to heal wounds, and also as a cosmetic. Jair, Jephthah and the prophet Elijah all came from Gilead.
Genesis 37:25; Joshua 17:1; Judges 10:3; 11; 1 Kings 17:1; Song of Solomon 4:1; Map OT/C3

Gilgal A place between Jericho and the River Jordan. The Israelites camped at Gilgal after crossing the river, and set up stones to mark the event. From Gilgal they set out to conquer Canaan. It became the site of an important shrine, and was on Samuel's circuit as a Judge. Gilgal is mentioned in the stories of Elijah and also of Elisha, who dealt with a pot of 'poisoned' stew there. The prophets Hosea and Amos condemned the worship at Gilgal as empty ritual.
Joshua 4:20; Judges 3:19; 1 Samuel 7:16; 10:8, etc.; 2 Samuel 19:15; 2 Kings 2:1; 4:38–41; Hosea 4:15; Amos 4:4; Map OT/C5

Gomorrah One of five cities probably now beneath the southern end of the Dead Sea. Gomorrah was violently destroyed with Sodom for deliberate, persistent and vicious sin. Throughout the Bible, Sodom and Gomorrah are used as examples to warn God's people of his judgement. Jesus says that any town which refuses to hear his messengers is in a worse situation than Sodom and Gomorrah.
Genesis 14; 19; Isaiah 1:9–10; (Ezekiel 16:48–50); Matthew 10:15

Goshen A fertile area of the eastern Nile Delta in Egypt. When Jacob and his family went to join Joseph, they settled in Goshen. It was a good place for their flocks and herds, and it was close to Pharaoh's court. In the time just before the exodus, the Israelites in Goshen escaped the plagues suffered by the rest of Egypt.
Genesis 45:10; Exodus 8:22, etc.; Map p. 318

Gozan Israelites from Samaria were taken captive to Gozan by the Assyrians. The town is modern Tell Halaf on the River Khabur in north-east Syria.
2 Kings 17:6; 19:12

Great Sea The Bible often uses this name for the Mediterranean Sea.

Greece The conquests of Alexander the Great brought Israel (and the rest of the eastern Mediterranean lands) under Greek control. The influence of Greek civilization, culture and thought was strong in the last centuries before Christ and in New Testament times. See *The Greeks* in Part 11: *Nations and Peoples of the Bible*.
Daniel 11; John 12:20; Acts 6; 17; 18; Map p. 342

Habor The River Khabur in north-east Syria. A tributary of the River Euphrates. The town of Gozan was on the Habor River.
2 Kings 17:6

Hamath Modern Hama, on the River Orontes in Syria. In Old Testament times Hamath was an important town, capital of a small kingdom, and on a main trade-route from Asia Minor (Turkey) south to Israel and Egypt. Hamath Pass, some distance to the south, was the 'ideal' northern limit of Israel. In the reigns of David and Solomon, Israel had a peace treaty with King Toi of Hamath. The town fell to the Assyrians and many of its people were moved into Israel. First Pharaoh Neco (before the Battle of Carchemish) and then King Nebuchadnezzar of Babylon made it their headquarters for a time.
Joshua 13:5; 2 Samuel 8:9–11; 1 Kings 8:65; 2 Chronicles 8:4; 2 Kings 17:24; 18:34, etc.

Harran A town in what is now south-east Turkey, on the River Balikh, a tributary of the River Euphrates. This was the place where Abraham's father, Terah, settled after leaving Ur, and where Jacob worked for Laban. Harran was on the main road linking Nineveh with Aleppo in Syria, and on south to the port of Tyre. It was fortified by the Assyrians as a provincial capital. For three years after the fall of Nineveh it was Assyria's capital city. Then in 609 BC it fell to the Babylonians.
Genesis 11:31; 12:4–5; 29:4, etc.; 2 Kings 19:12; Ezekiel 27:33; Map p. 316

Harod The spring where Gideon chose his fighting-force by watching how the men drank from the stream. The 300 who showed their alertness by stooping and lapping the water were chosen. The place was in northern Palestine, probably by a stream which flows down the Valley of Jezreel.
Judges 7:1–8

Hazor A Canaanite city in the north of Israel. King Jabin of Hazor organized an alliance against Joshua. But he was defeated, and the city was burned. Another king of Hazor was defeated by Deborah and Barak. King Solomon rebuilt and fortified Hazor, with Megiddo and Gezer. In the eighth century BC the Assyrians destroyed the city.
    Archaeologists have uncovered an upper and a lower city, which at its greatest may have housed as many as 40,000

Israel in the Old Testament

A   B   C   D

1   2   3   4   5   6   7

Abel-beth-maacah
Tyre
Dan
Ramah
Kedesh
Maacah
Hazor
Merom
Chinnereth
BASHAN
Ashtaroth
Sea of Chinnereth
GALILEE
River Kishon
Mt Carmel
Plain of Jezreel
Gath-hepher
Mt Tabor
Edrei
Shunem
Endor
Lo-debar
Ramoth-gilead
Dor
Megiddo
Jezreel
GILEAD
Mt Gilboa
Taanach
Beth-shan
Sharon
Ibleam
Dothan
Abel-meholah
Cherith Brook
Samaria
Tirzah
Jabesh-gilead
Plain of Sharon
Mt Ebal
Succoth
Mahanaim
Shechem
Penuel
Mt Gerizim
River Jordan
ISRAEL
Shiloh
Adam
AMMON
Joppa
Timnath-serah
Jazer
Upper/Lower Beth-horon
Bethel
Ai
Michmash
Rabbah
Gibeon
Mizpah
Gilgal
Gezer
Sorek
Gibeah
Geba
Shittim
Ekron
Aijalon
Anathoth
Jericho
Heshbon
Timnah
Kiriath-jearim
Jerusalem
Mt Nebo
Eshtaol
Ashdod
Libnah
Zorah
Bethlehem
Salt Sea (Sea of the Arabah)
PHILISTIA
Makkedah
Wilderness of Judah
Ashkelon
Azekah
Adullam
Tekoa
Ataroth
Valley of Elah
Keilah
Kiriathaim
Mareshah
Hebron
Beth-zur
Dibon
Lachish
Aroer
Eglon
Engedi
Gaza
Maon
Ziklag
JUDAH
MOAB
Gerar
Arad
Beersheba
Ar
Hormah
Ziph
Kir-hareseth
Negev Desert

10   20   30   40 Km
5   10   15   20   25 M

people. The lower part was destroyed in the thirteenth century BC (about the time of Joshua). A city gate and wall from Solomon's time match others of the same design at Megiddo and Gezer. Hazor is mentioned in Egyptian and Babylonian texts, and in the Amarna Letters, as well as in the Bible itself. See Part 2: *Archaeology and the Bible*.
Joshua 11; Judges 4; 1 Kings 9:15; 2 Kings 15:29; Map OT/C2

Hebron A town high in the Judean hills (3,040 ft/ 935 m above sea level). The old name for Hebron was Kiriath-arba. Abraham and his family often camped near Hebron. He bought the cave of Machpelah from the Hittites at Hebron (see *Machpelah*). Moses' twelve spies came to Hebron, and it was later given to Caleb. Hebron was a city of refuge, and one of the Levites' towns. It was David's capital before he captured Jerusalem. Absalom staged his rebellion from Hebron. Much later, after the exile, Jews returned to live there.
Genesis 13:18; 23; 35:27; 37:14; Numbers 13:22; Joshua 14:6–15; 2 Samuel 2:1–4; 15:9–10; Nehemiah 11:25; Map OT/B6

Heliopolis See *On*.

Hermon A mountain on the Lebanon/Syria border. It is over 9,000 ft/2,750 m high. It is also called Sirion in the Bible. It is topped with snow almost all the year round. The melting snow and ice form a major source of the River Jordan. Mt Hermon is close to Caesarea Philippi and may be the 'high mountain' where Jesus' disciples saw him in his glory.
Joshua 12:1, etc.; Psalms 42:6; 133:3; Matthew 17:1, etc.; Map NT/C1

Heshbon A town east of the River Jordan which belonged first to Moab, then to the Amorites, and then to the Israelite tribes of Reuben and Gad. It was prosperous for a while at the time of Isaiah and Jeremiah.
Numbers 21:25–30; 32:37; Isaiah 15:4; Jeremiah 48:2; Map OT/C5

Hierapolis A city in the Roman province of Asia, now in western Turkey. Paul mentions the Christians at Laodicea and

Hierapolis in his letter to nearby Colossae. Over the centuries the hot-water springs at Hierapolis (modern Pamukkale) have 'petrified' to form amazing waterfalls of stone.
Colossians 4:13

Hinnom The name of a valley on the south side of Jerusalem, forming the boundary between the tribes of Judah and Benjamin. Here the kings Ahaz and Manasseh set up a shrine for the god Molech, and children were offered to him in sacrifice. It was destroyed by Josiah. Jeremiah denounced the evil of this place. Later, rubbish from the city was burned in the Valley of Hinnom. So it became a picture of hell. The word 'Gehenna', meaning 'Valley of Hinnom', became a word for 'hell'.
Joshua 15:8; 18:16; 2 Kings 23:10; 2 Chronicles 28:3; 33:6; Jeremiah 7:31; 19:2; 32:35; Map p. 51

Horeb Another name for Mt Sinai.

Hormah The exact site of this town in southern Canaan is not certain. Because of their disobedience, the Israelites were defeated by the Canaanites at Hormah. Later it was conquered and given to the tribe of Judah.
Numbers 14:39–45; 21:3; Joshua 15:30

Ibleam A Canaanite town in the north of Israel, about 10 miles/14 km south-east of Megiddo. Here Jehu killed King Ahaziah of Judah.
Joshua 17:11–12; 2 Kings 9:27; 15:10; Map OT/B3

Iconium Present-day Konya in south-central Turkey. Paul preached at Iconium, then a city in the Roman province of Galatia, on his first missionary journey. He met with violent opposition.
Acts 13:51; 14:1–6, 19–22; 2 Timothy 3:11; Map p. 345

Idumaea The Greek name for the Old Testament Edom. By New Testament times many Idumaeans had settled west of the Jordan, in the dry country in the south of Palestine. This district was then called Idumaea. King Herod was an Idumaean. People came even from this area in the far south to see Jesus in Galilee.

Mark 3:8; Map NT/A7

Illyricum The Roman name of a land stretching along the eastern shore of the Adriatic Sea. It covered much the same area as modern Yugoslavia. The southern part was also called Dalmatia (see *Dalmatia*). When Paul wrote to the Romans, he said he had preached the gospel from Jerusalem as far west as Illyricum. There is no other mention of Paul's work in this land.
Romans 15:19; Map p. 342

Israel The land occupied by the twelve tribes. After King Solomon died and his kingdom was divided, the name Israel referred to the northern part of the land, excluding Judah and Benjamin. See Part 1: *Land of the Bible*.

Issachar The land belonging to the tribe of Issachar, south of Lake Galilee and west of the River Jordan.
Joshua 19:17–23; Map p. 321

Ituraea A name mentioned only in Luke's careful dating of the time when John the Baptist began to preach. Herod Philip was then ruler of Ituraea and Trachonitis. The Ituraeans were probably the descendants of the Old Testament people called Jetur. They were a wild tribal people in the hills west of Damascus, north of the head-waters of the River Jordan. See also *Trachonitis*.
Luke 3:1; compare 1 Chronicles 5:19; Map NT/C1

Jabbok Now the Zerqa, a river that flows into the Jordan from the east, between the Dead Sea and Lake Galilee. Jacob wrestled with an angel beside the Jabbok. Adam – the place where the Jordan was dammed, allowing the Israelites to cross into the Promised Land – stands at the confluence of the Jabbok and the Jordan. The river is also mentioned in the Bible as a boundary.
Genesis 32:22–30; Numbers 21:24; Deuteronomy 3:16; Judges 11:13; Map OT/C4

Jabesh-gilead A town on the east of the Jordan. When the wives of the Benjaminites were killed in a civil war at the time of the Judges, the town of

Jabesh provided replacements. Saul answered an appeal for help when Jabesh was besieged by the Ammonites. Men from Jabesh later risked their lives to remove his body from Bethshan.
Judges 21; 1 Samuel 11; 31:11–13; Map OT/C4

Javan One of the sons of Japheth. Javan is named as the father of a group of peoples, probably including those who lived in Greece and Asia Minor in early times. The name may be connected with the Greek 'Ionia', in western Turkey, and it is used in later parts of the Old Testament for Greece or the Greeks.
Genesis 10:2; 1 Chronicles 1:5; Isaiah 66:19; Ezekiel 27:13

Jazer An Amorite town east of the River Jordan. It was captured by the Israelites and given to the tribe of Gad. Jazer was famous for its vines.
Numbers 21:32; Joshua 13:25; 1 Chronicles 26:31; Isaiah 16:8–9; Map OT/C4

Jebus An early name for Jerusalem.

Jericho A town west of the River Jordan, 820 ft/250 m below sea level, about 5 miles/8 km from the northern end of the Dead Sea. Jericho's fresh-water spring makes it an oasis in the surrounding desert – the 'city of palm trees'. The town guarded the fords of the Jordan, across which Joshua sent his spies. It was well fortified, and the first main obstacle facing the invading Israelites. Joshua gained his first victory in the land when Jericho fell.

At the time of the Judges Ehud killed King Eglon of Moab at Jericho. At the time of Elijah and Elisha it was the home of a large group of prophets. After the return from exile, men from Jericho helped rebuild the walls of Jerusalem.

In the New Testament Jesus gave Bartimaeus his sight, and Zacchaeus became a changed man, at Jericho. The story of the Good Samaritan is set on the road from Jerusalem to Jericho.

Jericho has a very long history covering thousands of years. The first town was built here some time before 6000 BC. At the time of Abraham, Isaac and

Jacob, life in Jericho was a civilized affair. In tombs from about 1600 BC, fine pottery, wooden furniture, basket-work, and boxes with inlaid decoration have been found. Some time after this Jericho was destroyed, but a small settlement remained. See Part 2: *Archaeology and the Bible*.
Joshua 2; 6; Judges 12:13; 2 Kings 2; Nehemiah 3:2; Mark 10:46; Luke 19:1–10; 10:30; Map OT/C5

Jerusalem Capital of Israel's early kings, later of the southern kingdom of Judah, and one of the world's most famous cities. Jerusalem stands high (2,500 ft/770 m) in the Judean hills with no access by sea or river. The ground drops steeply away on all sides except the north. To the east, between Jerusalem (with its temple) and the Mount of Olives, is the Kidron Valley. The Valley of Hinnom curves around the city to the south and west. A third, central valley cuts right into the city, dividing the temple area and city of David from the 'upper', western section.

Jerusalem is probably the 'Salem' of which Melchizedek was king in Abraham's day. It was certainly in existence by 1800 BC. It was a Jebusite stronghold (called Jebus) when King David captured it and made it his capital. He bought the temple site and brought the Covenant Box (ark) to Jerusalem. His son King Solomon built the temple for God, and from that time on Jerusalem has been the 'holy city' – for the Jews, and later for Christians and Muslims, too. Solomon added fine palaces and public buildings. Jerusalem was a political and religious centre, to which the people came for the great annual festivals.

The city declined to some extent after Solomon, when the kingdom became divided. In the reign of King Hezekiah (Isaiah's time) it was besieged by the Assyrians. The king had the Siloam tunnel built, to ensure his water supply (see Part 2: *Archaeology and the Bible*). On several occasions powerful neighbouring kings were pacified with treasures

from the city and its temple. Despite its excellent position and defences King Nebuchadnezzar's Babylonian army besieged Jerusalem in 597 BC and in 586 they captured and destroyed both the city and the temple. The people were taken into exile. Nebuchadnezzar's soldiers tore down the city walls. All the temple treasures were taken away. 'How lonely lies Jerusalem, once so full of people,' wrote the author of Lamentations. 'The Lord rejected his altar and deserted his holy Temple; he allowed the enemy to tear down its walls.' It remained in ruins for fifty years.

In 538 BC the exiles were allowed to return. Under Zerubbabel's leadership the temple was rebuilt. With Nehemiah in charge they rebuilt the city walls.

In 198 BC, as part of the Greek Empire, Jerusalem came under the control of the Syrian Seleucid kings. One of these, Antiochus IV Epiphanes, plundered and desecrated the temple. Judas Maccabaeus led a Jewish revolt and the temple was rededicated (164 BC).

For a time Jerusalem was free. Then, in the middle of the first century BC, the Romans took control. Herod the Great, made king by the Romans, repaired Jerusalem and undertook new building work, including a magnificent new temple.

It was to this temple that Jesus' mother brought him as a baby. His parents brought him again when he was twelve, to attend the annual Passover Festival. When he grew up, Jesus regularly visited Jerusalem – for many of the religious festivals, and to teach and heal. His arrest, trial, crucifixion and resurrection all took place in Jerusalem.

Jesus' followers were still in the city several weeks later, on the Day of Pentecost, when the Holy Spirit made new men of them. So the Christian church began life in Jerusalem – and from there, spread out far and wide. The Christians at Jerusalem played a leading role in the early years. The Council that met to consider the

position of non-Jewish Christians was held at Jerusalem.

In AD 66 the Jews rose in revolt against the Romans. In AD 70 the Romans regained Jerusalem. They destroyed its defences – and the temple. In the fourth century – the reign of Constantine – the city became Christian, and many churches were built.

In 637 the Muslims came – and Jerusalem remained under their control for most of the time until 1948, when the modern state of Israel came into being. Jerusalem was then divided between the Jews and the Arabs – Israel and Jordan. In 1967 the Jews won control of the whole city.

See also Part 2: *Archaeology and the Bible*.
Genesis 14:18; Joshua 15:63; 2 Samuel 5; 1 Kings 6; Psalms 48; 122; 125; 1 Kings 14:25–26; 2 Kings 12:18; 18:13 – 19:36; 20:20; 25; Ezra 5; Nehemiah 3 – 6; Luke 2; 19:28 – 24:49, etc.; John 2:23 – 3:21; 5; 7:10 – 10:42, etc.; Acts 2; 15; Map OT/B5

Jezreel A town in the north of Israel and the plain in which it stood, close to Mt Gilboa. Saul camped at the spring in the Valley of Jezreel before the Battle of Gilboa. King Ahab of Israel had a palace at Jezreel. It was here that the sad story of Naboth's vineyard took place. King Joram of Israel went to Jezreel to recover from his wounds. Queen Jezebel was thrown down from the palace window and died here.
1 Samuel 29:1; 1 Kings 18:45–46; 21; 2 Kings 8:29; 9:30–37; Map OT/B3

Joppa The only natural harbour on the coast of Israel south of the Bay of Acre (Haifa): modern Jaffa, close to Tel Aviv. Joppa was the port for Jerusalem, 35 miles/56 km away. The town has a long history and was mentioned about 1400 BC in the Egyptian Amarna Letters. Jonah set sail for Tarshish (Spain) from Joppa. Dorcas (Tabitha), the woman Peter restored to life, came from Joppa. Peter was there when he had his dream about the 'clean' and 'unclean' animals. He went from Joppa to the house of the Roman officer, Cornelius,

and saw God at work amongst non-Jews.
2 Chronicles 2:16; Jonah 1:3; Acts 9:36–43; 10; Map OT/A4

Jordan The main river of Israel, constantly referred to in the Bible. The Jordan flows from Mt Hermon in the far north, through Lake Huleh and Lake Galilee to the Dead Sea. It is 75 miles/120 km from Lake Huleh to the Dead Sea, but the river winds about so much that it is more than twice that length.

The name 'Jordan' means 'the descender'. It flows through the deepest rift valley on earth. Lake Huleh is 230 ft/71 m above sea level. Lake Galilee is 682 ft/210 m *below* sea level, and the north end of the Dead Sea 1,290 ft/397 m below.

The northern part of the Jordan Valley is fertile; the southern end, approaching the Dead Sea, is desert, but dense jungle grows on the banks. The main tributaries of the Jordan are the Yarmuk and Jabbok rivers, both of which join it from the east. Many smaller tributaries dry up completely through the summer.

Joshua led the people of Israel across the Jordan from the east into the Promised Land near to Jericho. At the time of Absalom's rebellion, David escaped across the Jordan. Elijah and Elisha crossed the Jordan just before Elijah was taken up to heaven. Elisha told the Syrian general Naaman to wash himself in the Jordan and he would be healed. John the Baptist baptized people – including Jesus – in the Jordan.
Joshua 3; 2 Samuel 17:20–22; 2 Kings 2:6–8, 13–14; 5; Jeremiah 12:5; 49:19; Mark 1:5, 9, etc.; Map p. 325

Judah The Judean hills south of Jerusalem and the desert bordering the Dead Sea. The land belonging to the tribe of Judah. Later the name of the southern kingdom, with Jerusalem as its capital.
Joshua 15; 1 Kings 12:21, 23, etc.; Map OT/B6

Judea The Greek and Roman name for Judah. Usually it refers to the southern part of the country, with Jerusalem as capital. But it is sometimes used as a name for the whole land, including

Galilee and Samaria. The 'wilderness of Judea' is the desert west of the Dead Sea.
Luke 3:1; 4:44 ('the whole country' in *Good News Bible*), etc.; Map NT/B5

Kadesh-barnea An oasis and settlement in the desert south of Beersheba. It is mentioned in the campaign of Chedorlaomer and his allies at the time of Abraham. It was near Kadesh that Hagar saw an angel. After the escape from Egypt, most of Israel's years of desert wandering were spent in the area around Kadesh. Miriam died there, and Moses brought water out of the rock. From Kadesh he sent spies into Canaan. It is later mentioned as a point on the southern boundary of Israel.
Genesis 14:7; 16:14; Numbers 20; 13; 33:36; Deuteronomy 1:19–25, 46; Joshua 10:41; 15:23 (Kadesh); Map p. 318

Kedesh A Canaanite town in Galilee conquered by Joshua and given to the tribe of Naphtali. It was the home of Barak. Kedesh was one of the first towns to fall to the Assyrians when Tiglath-pileser III invaded Israel from the north (734–732 BC).
Joshua 12:22; 19:37; Judges 4; 2 Kings 15:29; Map OT/C1

Keilah A town about 8 miles/11 km north-west of Hebron. David saved it from a Philistine attack and stayed there, escaping from Saul.
Joshua 15:44; 1 Samuel 23; Nehemiah 3:17–18; Map OT/B5

Kidron The valley which separates Jerusalem and the temple from the Mount of Olives, on the east. For most of the year the valley is dry. The Gihon Spring, whose water King Hezekiah brought inside the city walls through the Siloam tunnel, is on the west side of the Kidron Valley.
David crossed the Kidron when he left Jerusalem at the time of Absalom's rebellion. Asa, Hezekiah and Josiah, kings who reformed the nation's worship, destroyed idols in the Kidron Valley. Jesus and his disciples crossed it many times on their way to the Garden of Gethsemane.

2 Samuel 15:23; 1 Kings 15:13; 2 Chronicles 29:16; 2 Kings 23:4; John 18:1; Map p. 51

King's Highway The road by which Moses promised to travel peacefully through the land of Edom and the land of Sihon, king of Heshbon. Both refused his request, and so the Israelites were forced to avoid Edom and to fight and defeat Sihon. The King's Highway was probably the main route north to south along the heights east of the Jordan, between Damascus and the Gulf of Aqaba.
Numbers 20:17; 21:22; Deuteronomy 2:27

Kir, Kir-hareseth The name of an unknown place where the Syrians were exiled.
An important fortified town in Moab.
2 Kings 16:9; Amos 1:5; 2 Kings 3; Isaiah 16:7–12; Map OT/C7

Kiriathaim A town east of the Dead Sea given to the tribe of Reuben. It was later taken by the Moabites.
Joshua 13:19; Jeremiah 48:1–25; Ezekiel 25:9; Map OT/C6

Kiriath-arba An earlier name for Hebron.

Kiriath-jearim A hill-town a few miles east of Jerusalem. It was one of the towns of the Gibeonites, who tricked Joshua into a peace treaty. The Covenant Box (ark) was kept at Kiriath-jearim for twenty years before King David took it to Jerusalem.
Joshua 9; 1 Samuel 6:20–7:2; Jeremiah 26:20; Nehemiah 7:29; Map OT/B5

Kishon A small stream which flows across the plain of Megiddo (Esdraelon) and into the Mediterranean Sea just north of Mt Carmel. In the story of Barak heavy rain raised the water level so high that the surrounding ground turned to mud and bogged down Sisera's chariots, giving Israel victory. The prophet Elijah killed the prophets of Baal by the River Kishon after the contest on Mt Carmel.
Judges 4; 5:21; 1 Kings 18:40; Map OT/B2

Kittim One of the sons of Javan in the Genesis 'table of the nations', and so the name of Cyprus and of its early city of Kition (modern Larnaca). See *Cypriotes* in

Part 11: *Nations and Peoples of the Bible*.
Genesis 10:4; 1 Chronicles 1:7; Numbers 24:24; Isaiah 23:1, 12; Jeremiah 2:10; Ezekiel 27:6

Kue/Coa A region from which Solomon obtained horses. It was in the eastern part of Cilicia, in the south of modern Turkey.

Lachish An important fortified town in the low hills about 30 miles/48 km south-west of Jerusalem. Lachish has a long history. It was a military stronghold before the sixteenth century BC.
The king of Lachish joined with four other Amorite kings to fight Joshua. But Joshua won. He attacked and captured Lachish and put everyone there to death. Solomon's son, King Rehoboam, rebuilt Lachish as a defence against the Philistines and Egyptians.
The town had an outer and inner wall, 19 ft/6 m thick. These walls were strengthened with towers. So too was the gateway. A well 144 ft/44 m deep ensured a good supply of water. Lachish had a palace and store-rooms approached by a street lined with shops.
King Amaziah of Judah fled to Lachish for safety. But his enemies followed and killed him there.
When the Assyrian King Sennacherib attacked Judah he besieged Lachish, cutting Jerusalem off from possible help from Egypt. He sent envoys from Lachish to demand Jerusalem's surrender. Lachish fell, and Sennacherib had the siege pictured on the walls of his palace at Nineveh. Archaeologists have also discovered at Lachish a mass grave from this time, holding 1,500 bodies.
The Babylonian army attacked Lachish at the time of the final siege of Jerusalem (589–586 BC). The 'Lachish Letters', written by an army officer to his superior, belong to this period (see Part 2: *Archaeology and the Bible*). Lachish fell and the Babylonians burnt it. After the exile it was resettled, but was never again an important place.
Joshua 10; 2 Chronicles 11:5–12; 2 Kings 14:19; 18:14–21; Isaiah 36 – 37; Jeremiah 34:7; Nehemiah

11:30; Map OT/A6

Laodicea A city in the Lycus Valley of present-day western Turkey (the Roman province of Asia in New Testament times). Laodicea stood at the junction of two important main roads. It grew prosperous from trade and banking. The region produced clothes made of glossy black wool, and also medicines. Water for the town was piped from springs some distance away and arrived lukewarm. A number of these points are reflected in the letter to the church at Laodicea in the Book of Revelation. Paul's letter to the Colossians was intended for Laodicea, too, although he had not been there. The Christian group there may have been started during the time when Paul was staying at Ephesus.
Colossians 2:1; 4:13–16; Revelation 1:11; 3:14–22

Lebanon The modern country of that name and its mountain range. Lebanon in the Old Testament was famous for its forests, especially its great cedar-trees. The Bible refers also to the

snows of Lebanon, and to the country's fertility. All kinds of fruit grow on the coastal plain and lower hill slopes: olives, grapes, apples figs, apricots, dates and all kinds of green vegetables.

The great Phoenician (Canaanite) ports of Tyre, Sidon and Byblos were all on the coast of Lebanon and grew rich exporting its products. See Part 11: *Nations and Peoples of the Bible* under *Canaanites* and *Phoenicians*. King Solomon sent to the king of Tyre for cedar and other wood from Lebanon to build the temple and royal palace at Jerusalem.
1 Kings 5:1–11; Hosea 6:5–7; Ezra 3:7; Psalm 72:16; Isaiah 2:13; 14:8; Ezekiel 31, etc.

Libnah A fortified lowland town not far from Lachish, taken by Joshua. In the reign of King Jehoram of Judah Libnah rebelled. The town survived a siege by the Assyrian King Sennacherib when plague hit his army.
Joshua 10:29–30; 2 Kings 8:22; 19:8, 35; Map OT/A5

Lo-debar A place in Gilead, east of the River Jordan. Mephibosheth,

Jonathan's son, lived there in exile until David brought him to his court.
2 Samuel 9; 17:27; Map OT/C3

Lud Lud, a son of Shem, gave his name to a people known later as the Lydians. They lived in the west of Asia Minor (Turkey) around Sardis. See *Lydians* in Part 11: *Nations and Peoples of the Bible*.

Luz The older name of Bethel.

Lycia A small, mountainous land in the south-west of Asia Minor (Turkey). The ports of Patara and Myra, at which Paul landed, were in Lycia.
Acts 27:5; Map p. 343

Lydda A town about 10 miles/16 km inland from Joppa. Peter healed a lame man, Aeneas, when visiting the first Christians here. The place is now again called by its Old Testament name, Lod.
Acts 9:32–35, 38; Map NT/B5

Lystra A remote city in the Roman province of Galatia (not far from Konya in modern Turkey). Paul and Barnabas went on to Lystra after rough treatment at Iconium, on the first missionary journey. Paul healed a cripple at Lystra, and the people believed him to be Hermes (messenger of the Greek gods) and Barnabas to be Zeus

himself. But Jews from Iconium stirred up trouble, and Paul was stoned and left for dead. Some of the people became Christians, and Paul returned to visit them on his second journey. Lystra (or possibly Derbe) was Timothy's home town.
Acts 14:6–20; 16:1–5; Map p. 345

Maacah A small Aramaean state to the south-east of Mt Hermon. It is mentioned in David's campaigns and one of his warriors came from here.
Joshua 12:5; 2 Samuel 10; 23:34; Map OT/C1

Macedonia A region of northern Greece whose capital was Thessalonica. The Roman province of Macedonia included Philippi and Beroea as well as Thessalonica.

Paul crossed the Aegean Sea from Troas after seeing a vision of a Macedonian man asking him to come over and help them. It was the first stage in bringing the Good News of Jesus to Europe. Three of Paul's letters (Philippians, 1 and 2 Thessalonians) are addressed to Macedonian Christians. They gave generously to his relief fund for Christians in Judea. And several of them became his regular helpers.
Acts 16:8 – 17:15; 20:1–6; 2 Corinthians 8:1–5; 9:1–5, etc.; Map p. 342

Machpelah When Sarah died at Hebron, Abraham still owned no land. So he

bought a plot of land with the cave of Machpelah from Ephron the Hittite. Abraham himself was later buried here, and afterwards Isaac and Rebekah, and then Jacob.

Much later, Herod the Great built a shrine round the place believed to contain the cave and the tombs, and this can still be seen.
Genesis 23; 25:9; 49:30; 50:13

Mahanaim A place in Gilead, east of the River Jordan and near the River Jabbok. Jacob saw God's angels at Mahanaim, before the reunion with his brother Esau. For a short time it was the capital of Saul's son Ishbosheth (Ishbaal). It was King David's headquarters during Absalom's rebellion. One of Solomon's district officers was based at Mahanaim.
Genesis 32:2; 2 Samuel 2:8–10; 17:24–29; 1 Kings 4:14; Map OT/C4

Makkedah Joshua captured this Canaanite town in the south. In a nearby cave he found the five Amorite kings who had fought against him and killed them. The town was given to the tribe of Judah.
Joshua 10:10; 16; 15:41;

A grove of ancient cedars is almost all that remains of the great forests which covered the mountain slopes in Old Testament times. Cedars from Lebanon were used to build the temple in Jerusalem.

Map OT/B5

Malta The modern name of an island in the central Mediterranean Sea, between Sicily and the north coast of Africa. Its ancient name was Melita, and Paul's ship was wrecked here during his voyage as a prisoner to Rome. All the people on board reached land safely and were received kindly by the natives. They spent the winter on Malta before sailing for Italy.
Acts 28:1–10

Mamre A place near Hebron. Abraham, and later Isaac, often camped by the oak-trees at Mamre. It was here that Abraham heard that Lot had been captured. At Mamre God promised him a son, and he pleaded with God to spare Sodom.
Genesis 13:18; 14:13; 18; 23:17; 35:27

Manasseh The land belonging to the tribe of Manasseh. West Manasseh was the hill-country of Samaria as far west as the Mediterranean Sea. East Manasseh was the land east of central Jordan.
Joshua 13:29–31; 17:7–13; Map p. 321

Maon A town in the hills of Judah. Nabal, husband of Abigail, lived here. David stayed here twice when he was an outlaw from King Saul.
Joshua 15:55; 1 Samuel 23:24–25; 25; Map OT/B6

Mareshah A town in the low hills nearly 20 miles/ 32 km south-west of Jerusalem. It was fortified by Rehoboam. Later King Asa destroyed a great army from Sudan here. The prophet Micah foretold disaster for Mareshah.
Joshua 15:44; 1 Chronicles 11:8; 14:9–12; 20:37; Micah 1:15; Map OT/A6

Media North-west Iran. Media came under Assyrian control, but later helped the Babylonians to overthrow the Assyrians. Then Cyrus the Persian brought Media under his control. See *Medes* and Map in Part 11: *Nations and Peoples of the Bible.*

Megiddo An important Old Testament city on the edge of the plain of Jezreel, guarding the main pass through the Carmel hills. About 20 miles/32 km from modern Haifa. So many battles took place here that the New Testament (Revelation 16:16) uses the name symbolically for the site of the great last battle: 'Armageddon', 'the hill of Megiddo'.

Joshua defeated the Canaanite king of Megiddo when the Israelites conquered Canaan. It was given to the tribe of Manasseh. They made the Canaanites who lived at Megiddo work for them, but did not drive them out. King Solomon chose Megiddo, with Hazor and Gezer, to be one of his main fortified cities, with stabling for large numbers of horses and chariots. King Ahaziah of Judah died at Megiddo after being wounded by Jehu's men. So too did King Josiah, attempting to stop the advance of Pharaoh Neco of Egypt.

Archaeologists have discovered twenty main levels of settlement on a mound now 70 ft/21 m high and covering, at the top, an area of more than 10 acres. The earliest settlement goes back to before 3000 BC. Excavation has uncovered, among other things, a Canaanite 'high place'; the city's water supply system; a fortified gateway built to the same pattern as others at Gezer and Hazor; a hoard of carved ivory objects; and a series of stables (probably from King Ahab's time). See Part 2: *Archaeology and the Bible*, also Part 7: *Home and Family Life in the Bible*, under *Town and City Life*.
Joshua 12:21; Judges 1:27–28; 5:19; 1 Kings 9:15; 2 Kings 9:27; 23:29; Map OT/B3

Memphis The ancient capital of Egypt, on the River Nile not far south of modern Cairo. The pyramids at Giza are also near to Memphis. The city remained important for many centuries, up to the time of Alexander the Great. Several of the Old Testament prophets refer to Memphis when they condemn Israel's trust in Egypt.
Isaiah 19:13; Jeremiah 2:16; 46:14; Ezekiel 30:13; Map p. 317

Mesopotamia The land between the Tigris and Euphrates rivers. The centre of some of the earliest civilizations, including the Sumerians, Babylonians and Assyrians, Mesopotamia included such famous cities as Ur, Babylon and Nineveh. Harran and Paddan-aram, where some of Abraham's family settled, are in Mesopotamia. It was the home of Balaam, the prophet who was sent to curse the Israelites, and the country ruled by Cushanrishathaim at the time of the Judges.

People from Mesopotamia were in Jerusalem on the Day of Pentecost and heard Peter and the apostles speak to them in their own languages.
Genesis 24:10; Deuteronomy 23:4 and Numbers 22; Judges 3:8, 10; Acts 2:9; Map p. 315

Michmash A place about 7 miles/11 km north-east of Jerusalem, at a village still called Mukhmas. It was separated from Geba by a deep valley. But an important route, 'the passage of Michmash', crossed an easy part of the valley. The Philistines invaded Israel and camped in force at Michmash, threatening King Saul's capital at Gibeah. Jonathan and his armour-bearer surprised the Philistine garrison by climbing across from Geba at a steep place down the valley, and in the panic which followed Saul defeated the Philistines. Michmash was on the route by which the Assyrians approached Jerusalem from the north. It was reoccupied after the exile.
1 Samuel 13 – 14; Isaiah 10:28; Ezra 2:27; Nehemiah 7:31; 11:31; Map OT/B5

Midian Part of Arabia, east of the Gulf of Aqaba. See *Midianites* and Map in Part 11: *Nations and Peoples of the Bible*. When Moses fled for his life from Egypt after killing an Egyptian overseer, he went to Midian. He married a Midianite wife and stayed there until God sent him back to Egypt to help free the Israelites. At the time of the Judges Gideon defeated a huge force of camel-riding invaders from Midian.
Genesis 25:1–6; Exodus 2:15–21; Judges 6; Map p. 320

Miletus A sea-port on the west coast of present-day Turkey. Paul stayed at Miletus on his way to Jerusalem at the end of his third missionary journey. To save time, the elders from the church at Ephesus came to meet him there and heard his farewell message. At another time Paul, writing to Timothy, says that he had left his helper Trophimus at Miletus because he was ill.
Acts 20:15–38; 2 Timothy 4:20; Map p. 343

Mitylene The most important city and port on the Greek island of Lesbos, off the west coast of Asia Minor (Turkey). Paul stopped there overnight on his last voyage to Jerusalem.
Acts 20:14; Map p. 345

Mizpah/Mizpeh The name (meaning 'watchtower') of a number of different places. When Jacob and Laban made a peace agreement they called the place Mizpah. A Mizpah in Gilead (perhaps the same as Ramoth-gilead) features in the story of Jephthah, at the time of the Judges.

The most important Mizpah is a town a few miles north of Jerusalem. The Israelites met together here at the time of Samuel and the Judges. The town was on Samuel's circuit as a Judge. And at Mizpah he presented Saul to the people as their king. Later, King Asa of Judah fortified the town. After Jerusalem fell to the Babylonians the governor, Gedaliah, lived at Mizpah.
Genesis 31:44–49; Judges 10:17; 11; 20:1; 1 Samuel 7:5–16; 10:17; 1 Kings 15:22; 2 Kings 25:23; Map OT/B5

Moab The country east of the Dead Sea. The land is a 3,000 ft/900 m plateau cut by deep gorges. Moab was the home of Ruth. The country was often at war with Israel, and was denounced again and again by the prophets. See *Moabites* and Map in Part 11: *Nations and Peoples of the Bible*.
Judges 3:12–30; Ruth 1; 2 Samuel 8:2; 2 Kings 3; Isaiah 15, etc.; Map OT/C6

Plains of Moab The place east of the River Jordan opposite Jericho where the Israelites gathered before they crossed into Canaan.
Numbers 22:1; 35:1; Joshua 13:32

Moreh The hill a few miles north-west of Mt Gilboa

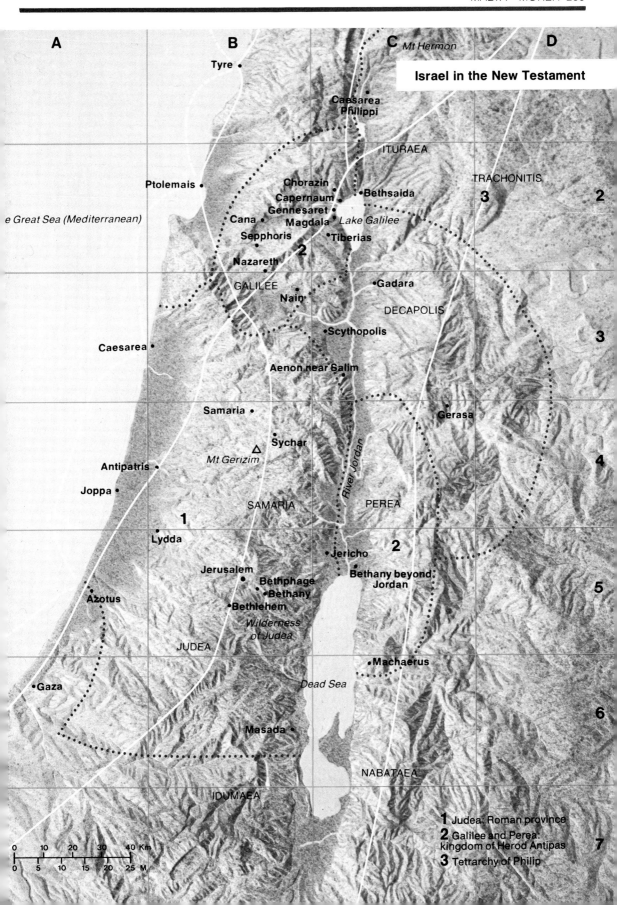

A B C D

Mt Hermon

Israel in the New Testament

Tyre

Caesarea Philippi

ITURAEA

TRACHONITIS

3 2

Ptolemais

Chorazin
Capernaum   Bethsaida
Gennesaret
Cana   Magdala   *Lake Galilee*
Sepphoris   Tiberias

e Great Sea (Mediterranean)

Nazareth

2

GALILEE   Nain   Gadara

DECAPOLIS

Caesarea   Scythopolis   3

Aenon near Salim

Samaria   Gerasa

Sychar
△
Mt Gerizim

River Jordan   4

Antipatris

Joppa   SAMARIA   PEREA

1   2

Lydda   Jericho

Jerusalem   Bethany beyond
Bethphage   Jordan   5
Bethany
Azotus   Bethlehem

*Wilderness
of Judea*

JUDEA

Machaerus

Dead Sea   6

Gaza

Masada

NABATAEA

IDUMAEA   7

0 10 20 30 40 Km
0 5 10 15 20 25 M

1 Judea: Roman province
2 Galilee and Perea:
kingdom of Herod Antipas
3 Tetrarchy of Philip

where the Midianites camped before Gideon's attack.
Judges 7:1; Map OT/B3

Moresheth/Moresheth-gath The home town of the prophet Micah, probably near Mareshah in the low country south-west of Jerusalem.
Jeremiah 26:18; Micah 1:1, 14

Moriah The mountains to which Abraham was told to go for the sacrifice of his son, Isaac. The writer of 2 Chronicles says that the site of Solomon's temple was 'in Jerusalem, on Mount Moriah'. (The Samaritans claimed that the place of Abraham's sacrifice was not Jerusalem, but Mt Gerizim.)
Genesis 22:2; 2 Chronicles 3:1

Mount of Olives/Olivet A 2,700 ft/830 m hill overlooking Jerusalem and its temple area from the east, across the Kidron Valley. In Jesus' day it was planted with olive trees.

King David passed this way when he fled from Jerusalem at the time of Absalom's rebellion. King Solomon built an altar for idols on the Mount of Olives. Later, during the exile, the prophet Ezekiel saw the dazzling light of God's glory leave Jerusalem and move to the Mount of Olives. The prophet Zechariah foresaw God, on the Day of Judgement, standing on the Mount, which would split in two.

When Jesus rode in triumph into Jerusalem he came from the Mount of Olives. Seeing the city from the Mount, he wept over its fate. When he stayed at Bethany on his visits to Jerusalem he must have walked into the city round the shoulder of the Mount of Olives. The Garden of Gethsemane, where he prayed on the night of his arrest, was on its lower slopes. From the Mount of Olives Jesus was taken up to heaven.
2 Samuel 15:30; 2 Kings 23:13; Ezekiel 11:23; Zechariah 14:4; Luke 19:29, 37, 41–44; 21:37; 22:39; Acts 1:12, etc.

Myra A port in Lycia, in the south-west of modern Turkey, where Paul and his party changed ships on his voyage to Rome. Myra was a regular port for the corn-fleet which carried

grain to Rome from Egypt.
Acts 27:5; Map p. 375

Mysia A land in the north-west of Asia Minor (Turkey), forming part of the Roman province of Asia. Paul came to this district during his second missionary journey, but God prevented him from crossing the border from Asia into Bithynia. He passed through Mysia, travelling west, and came to Troas before it became clear where he should go next.
Acts 16:7–8

Nain A town near Nazareth in Galilee where Jesus restored a widow's son to life.
Luke 7:11; Map NT/B3

Naphtali Land belonging to the tribe of Naphtali, in Galilee.
Joshua 19:32–39; Map p. 321

Nazareth A town in Galilee, the home of Jesus' parents, Mary and Joseph. Jesus grew up in Nazareth but made his base in Capernaum when he began his public work. His teaching in the synagogue at Nazareth made the people so angry that they tried to kill him.

Nazareth was close to a number of important trade-routes, and so in contact with the wider world. There are rock-tombs at Nazareth dating from New Testament times, and similar to the Gospels' description of the grave in which Jesus himself was buried.
Luke 1:26; Matthew 2:22–23; Luke 2:39, 51; Mark 1:9; Matthew 4:13; Luke 4:16–30; John 1:45–46, etc.; Map NT/B2

Neapolis The port for Philippi, in Macedonia (northern Greece). This was the place where Paul first set foot in Europe, in answer to a call for help from Macedonia. He later sailed from here on his last voyage to Jerusalem. The place is modern Kavalla.
Acts 16:11; 20:6

Nebo A mountain east of the north end of the Dead Sea, in Moab. Before he died, Moses climbed Mt Nebo and saw the whole of the Promised Land spread out before him. Jebel Osha (3,640 ft/1,120 m high) has a view-point from which it is possible to see as far north as Mt Hermon, as well as the Dead Sea and the Negev. This is probably Mt Nebo.

Deuteronomy 32:48–52; 34:1–5; Map OT/C5

Negev A dry scrubland and desert area in the far south of Israel. The Negev merges with the Sinai Desert on the way to Egypt. Abraham and Isaac camped in various places in the Negev. So too did the Israelites, before they settled in Canaan.
Genesis 20:1; 24:62; Numbers 13:17; 21:1; Isaiah 30:6; Map p. 316

Nile The great river of Egypt on which the country's whole economy depended. The Nile flows from Lake Victoria in the heart of Africa, about 3,500 miles/5,632 km to the Mediterranean Sea. The fertile valley of the Nile (never more than about 12 miles/19 km wide in Upper Egypt) is flanked on either side by desert. Every year the river flooded its banks in spring, leaving behind a layer of fertile mud. Crops would grow wherever the water reached. Too high a flood meant destruction; too low a flood, starvation. The river was also a useful means of transporting goods from one part of the country to another. About 12 miles/19 km north of modern Cairo the Nile divides into a western and an eastern branch. Between them is the flat marshy land known as the Delta.

The Nile features in the dreams of Joseph's pharaoh. The pharaoh at the time of Moses' birth ordered his people to drown all Hebrew boy babies in the Nile. Moses himself was hidden in a basket in the reeds at the river's edge. The Nile also features in the sequence of plagues sent by God when the pharaoh refused to free the Israelites. It is often mentioned by the prophets.
Genesis 41:1–36; Exodus 1:22; 2:3–10; 7:17–25; 8:1–15, etc.; Isaiah 18:2, etc.; Map p. 317

Nineveh An important city in Assyria, notably in King Sennacherib's reign. The Bible says that Nineveh was founded by Nimrod the hunter. The site certainly has a very long history, going back to about 4500 BC. From about 2300 BC the city had a temple to the goddess Ishtar.

Nineveh grew in importance from about

1250 BC, as Assyria's power increased. Several Assyrian kings had palaces there. Sennacherib undertook a great deal of rebuilding and other work.

Reliefs carved on the walls of his new palace show his victories, including the siege of Lachish in Judah. At Nineveh, too, archaeologists discovered a clay prism (the Taylor Prism) which describes how King Hezekiah was 'shut up like a bird' in Jerusalem.

Ashurbanipal, the next king but one, added to Nineveh's greatness. Whole libraries of inscribed tablets, including the *Epic of Gilgamesh* (containing a flood story) and the creation epic (*Enuma elish*), have been discovered at his palace and in the temple of Nabu. Nineveh fell to the Babylonians in 612 BC.

In the Bible, Jonah was sent to save Nineveh; Nahum prophesied against it.
Genesis 10:11; 2 Kings 19:36; Jonah 1:2; 3; Nahum 1:1; Luke 11:30; Map p. 327

Nob When David escaped from King Saul's attempts to kill him, he received help from the priest Ahimelech at Nob. But one of the king's men told Saul, and he had the priests at Nob killed. Isaiah foretold that the Assyrians would camp at Nob and advance on Jerusalem. It seems that Nob was a strong place close to the city, perhaps at Mt Scopus, north of the Mount of Olives. There was still a settlement at Nob when Nehemiah was rebuilding Jerusalem.
1 Samuel 21 – 22; Isaiah 10:32; Nehemiah 11:32; compare Matthew 12:4; Mark 2:26; Luke 6:4; Map OT/B5

Olives See *Mount of Olives*.

On An ancient city in Egypt, famous for its worship of the sun-god Rē. Joseph married the daughter of the priest of On, and they had two sons, Ephraim and Manasseh. On is mentioned later in the prophets, once by its Greek name 'Heliopolis' (city of the sun).
Genesis 41:45, 50; 46:20; Ezekiel 30:17; compare

Isaiah 19:18; Jeremiah 43:13

Ophir A country famous for its gold. It may have been in South Arabia, or East Africa (Somalia), or even India.
1 Kings 9:28, etc.

Paddan-aram The area around Harran in north Mesopotamia (not named in *Good News Bible*). Abraham sent his servant to Paddan-aram to choose a wife for Isaac from the branch of the family which had settled there. Jacob later fled from Esau to his uncle Laban, who was living at Paddan-aram.
Genesis 25:20; 28:2; Map p. 316

Pamphylia A region on the south-west coast of modern Turkey. The town of Perga, visited by Paul, was in Pamphylia. Jews from this region were in Jerusalem and heard Peter

and the apostles on the Day of Pentecost.
Acts 2:10; 13:13; Map p. 343

Paphos A town in the south-west of Cyprus. Paul visited Paphos on his first missionary journey. Here he met the magician Elymas; and the governor of the island, Sergius Paulus, believed God's message.
Acts 13:4–13; Map p. 344

Paran A desert area near Kadesh-barnea, where Hagar's son Ishmael grew up. The Israelites passed through it after the exodus. From here they sent spies into Canaan.
Genesis 21:20; Numbers 10:12; 12:16; 13:1–16, etc.

Patmos An island off the west coast of modern Turkey. The place where John had the visions written down in the Book of

Revelation.
Revelation 1:9

Penuel/Peniel A place near the River Jabbok, east of the Jordan, where Jacob wrestled with the angel.
Genesis 32:22–32; Map OT/C4

Perga A city of Pamphylia just inland from Antalya (Attalia) on the south coast of modern Turkey. Paul visited Perga on arrival from Cyprus on the first missionary journey, and again when he returned to the coast.
Acts 13:13; 14:25; Map p. 344

Pergamum The first administrative capital of the Roman province of

The apostle John saw the visions recorded in the book of Revelation when he was an exile on the island of Patmos.

Asia (west Turkey). The first temple to be dedicated to Rome and the Emperor Augustus was built at Pergamum in 29 BC. Pergamum was also the centre of the pagan cults of Zeus, Athena, and Dionysus. There was a centre of healing connected with the temple of Asclepius (a fourth great pagan cult).

Pergamum was one of the seven churches to which the letters in the Book of Revelation are addressed. The phrase 'where Satan has his throne' may refer to emperor worship.
Revelation 1:11; 2:12–16; Map p. 343

Persia The country which conquered Media and overthrew Babylon to establish an empire which continued until the conquests of Alexander

the Great. See *Persians* and Map in Part 11: *Nations and Peoples of the Bible*.

Daniel was in Babylon when the city was taken by the army of the Medes and Persians. Cyrus, king of Persia, allowed the Jews and other exiles to return to their homelands. The Jewish girl, Esther, became queen to the Persian King Xerxes I (Ahasuerus).
Daniel 5:29–30; 6; 8:20; 10:1; Ezra 1:1–11; Esther 1, etc.; Map p. 332.

Pharpar See *Abana*.

Philadelphia A city in the Roman province of Asia (modern Alaşehir, in western Turkey). Philadelphia was one of the seven churches of Asia to which the letters in the Book of Revelation are addressed.
Revelation 1:11; 3:7–13

Philippi A city 8 miles/ 12 km inland from Neapolis on the coast of Macedonia (northern Greece). It was named after Philip of Macedon. Philippi was annexed by the Romans in 168 BC. It was the site of a famous battle of Antony and Octavian (Augustus) against Brutus and Cassius in 42 BC. Some years later, Octavian made Philippi a Roman colony, which gave its people the same rights and privileges as any town on Italian soil.

Paul visited Philippi on his second missionary journey, after seeing a vision of a Macedonian man appealing to him for help. The first Christian church in Europe was established at Philippi. Paul and Silas were illegally imprisoned here but later released with an apology when they made it known that they were Roman citizens. The letter to the Philippians was written to the church at Philippi.
Acts 16:6–40; 20:6; Philippians 1:1, etc.; 1 Thessalonians 2:2; Map p. 342

Philistia The land of the Philistines, on the coast of Israel. See *Philistines* and Map in Part 11: *Nations and Peoples of the Bible*.

Phoenicia A small state on the coast of Syria, north of Israel. Its chief towns were Tyre, Sidon and Byblos. See *Phoenicians* and Map in Part 11: *Nations and Peoples of the Bible*.

Phoenix Paul's voyage to Rome was delayed by the wrong winds, and the ship was still only at the south coast of Crete when the summer sailing season ended. At a conference at Fair Havens the majority wanted to sail on to Phoenix (modern Finika), the safest harbour on that coast, for the winter. Paul advised them against this, but they sailed, and were caught in a violent storm and shipwrecked.
Acts 27:12

Phrygia A land in the centre of Asia Minor (modern Turkey). Most of it was in the Roman province of Asia, but Paul visited the smaller district which belonged to the province of Galatia. The main cities of this district were 'Pisidian' Antioch and Iconium. Three other Phrygian cities are mentioned by name in the New Testament: Laodicea, Colossae and Hierapolis.
Acts 16:6; 18:23; Colossians 1:1; 4:13; Revelation 3:14–22

Pisgah One of the peaks of Mt Nebo.

Pisidia A mountainous inland area off the south coast of modern Turkey. Paul passed through this remote and dangerous region on his first missionary journey, on his way from Perga to Antioch.
Acts 13:14; 14:24; Map p. 343

Pithom One of Pharaoh's two store-cities, built by Israelite slave labour. It lay east of the Nile Delta in Egypt. See also *Raamses*.
Exodus 11:1; Map p. 318

Pontus The ancient name of the Black Sea, and so of the land along its south coast. This became a Roman province, stretching along most of the northern coast of Asia Minor (Turkey). This was one of the lands to which Peter sent his first letter. The Christian message may have reached Pontus very early, as Jews from there were in Jerusalem on the Day of Pentecost.
Acts 2:9; 18:2; 1 Peter 1:1; Map p. 337

Ptolemais The Greek name of an ancient city on the coast of northern Israel; Old Testament Acco. Paul sailed here from Tyre on his last visit to Jerusalem, and spent a day with the Christians. The city is now again known by its early name Akko (Acre), but has lost much of its importance since the growth of modern Haifa near by.
Judges 1:31; Acts 21:7; (*Acco*); Map NT/B2

Put An African country, probably part of Libya (as in some modern Bible versions).
Genesis 10:6; Jeremiah 46:9; Ezekiel 27:10, etc.

Puteoli The port near Naples in Italy where Paul landed on his way to Rome as a prisoner. The town is now called Pozzuoli.
Acts 28:13; Map p. 345

Raamses/Rameses Egyptian city near the coast on the east side of the Nile Delta. Pharaoh Ramesses II had a palace here. Earlier this was the Hyksos pharaohs' northern capital, Avaris. Exodus records that the Israelites built the cities of Pithom and Raamses as supply centres for the king. It was from Raamses that they set out on their escape from Egypt.
Exodus 1:11; Map p. 318

Rabbah The capital city of the Ammonites (see *Ammon*), sometimes also called Rabbath-Ammon. The Israelites defeated Og, king of Bashan, whose 'iron bed' (or coffin) was preserved in Rabbah. This territory east of the Jordan was given to the tribe of Gad. But it was still occupied by the Ammonites until David's general Joab captured Rabbah. When David fled from his rebellious son Absalom he received help from Rabbah. After Solomon's death Ammon seems to have become independent again, and to have been once more a cruel enemy. The prophets denounce the wickedness of Rabbah and prophesy its destruction.

The city later took the Greek name Philadelphia, and became one of the ten cities of the Decapolis (see *Decapolis*). The name of the ancient people, the Ammonites, is preserved in the modern name, Amman. It is now the capital of Jordan.
Deuteronomy 3:11; Joshua 13:25; 2 Samuel 11:1; 12:26–31; 17:27; 1 Chronicles 20:1–3; Jeremiah 49:2; Ezekiel 21:20; 25:5; Amos 1:14; Map p. 322

Ramah A Hebrew name meaning 'height', and used of several towns on hills. Two of these are important in the Old Testament story.

One was at er-Râm, 5 miles/8 km north of Jerusalem. Near here the prophetess Deborah lived. This Ramah was later close to the border between Judah and Israel. It was captured and fortified by Baasha, king of Israel, and recaptured by Asa of Judah. Isaiah pictures the Assyrians approaching Jerusalem by way of Ramah. Later, when Jerusalem actually fell to the Babylonians, Jeremiah was set free at Ramah. The place was resettled after the exile in Babylon. Rachel's tomb was said to have been near Ramah, and Jeremiah spoke of her weeping for her children. Matthew refers to this prophecy about Ramah in his account of what happened after Jesus' birth.
Judges 4:5; 19:13; 1 Kings 15:17, 22; 2 Chronicles 16:1, 6; Jeremiah 31:15; 40:1; Isaiah 10:29; Ezra 2:26; Nehemiah 11:33; Matthew 2:18; Map OT/B5

The second Ramah was about 12 miles/19 km further north-west. It was probably the birth-place and home of the prophet Samuel, and may have been the same as New Testament Arimathea. It was also called Ramathaim-Zophim.
1 Samuel 1:1; 2:11, etc.; Map OT/B4

Ramoth-gilead A city of refuge east of the Jordan which changed hands several times in the wars between Israel and Syria. It may be the same as Mizpah in Gilead, and so the home of Jephthah at the time of the Judges. One of Solomon's twelve district governors was stationed at Ramoth. Here King Ahab of Israel was killed in battle, and Jehu was anointed king.
Joshua 20:8; Judges 11; 1 Kings 4:13; 22; 2 Kings 9:1–10; Map OT/D3

Red Sea The meaning of the Hebrew word translated Red Sea is 'sea of reeds'. In the story of the exodus it refers to the area of lakes and marshes between the head of the Gulf of Suez and the Mediterranean Sea (the

Philippi, where Paul established the first church in Europe.

Suez Canal area). It is also used for the Gulf of Suez, the Gulf of Aqaba (the northern arms of the Red Sea proper) as some modern Bible versions make plain.
Exodus 13, etc.; Numbers 33:10; Deuteronomy 1:40; Map p. 315

Rephaim The valley south-west of Jerusalem where King David fought and defeated the Philistines. Also the name of one of the peoples who lived in Canaan before the Israelite conquest.
2 Samuel 5:18, etc.

Reuben Land belonging to the tribe of Reuben, east of the Dead Sea.
Joshua 13:15–23; Map p. 321

Rhegium A port on the toe of Italy, on the Strait of Messina opposite Sicily; the modern city of Reggio di Calabria. Paul's ship called here on his voyage to Rome.
Acts 28:13; Map p. 345

Riblah A town in Syria on the River Orontes. King Jehoahaz of Judah was taken prisoner at Riblah by Pharaoh Neco of Egypt. Later, King Nebuchadnezzar of Babylon had his headquarters here. And King Zedekiah, the last king of Judah, was taken to him at Riblah for sentence following rebellion.
2 Kings 23:33; 25:6–7;

Rome Capital of the Roman Empire; on the River Tiber in Italy. The traditional date for the founding of Rome is 753 BC. The city spread over seven hills.
In New Testament times over a million people from all parts of the Empire lived in Rome, most of them in crowded multi-storey housing. The emperor and his government provided subsidies and public entertainments to keep the masses happy. The city attracted wealth, products – and writers and artists – from all over the Empire. Great Roman roads from every part of the Empire led here. There was a busy trade in foodstuffs and in luxury goods through the nearby port of Ostia. In Rome the emperors built some of the most magnificent public buildings any city has ever possessed.
There were Jews from

Rome in Jerusalem on the Day of Pentecost who heard Peter's message. Although Paul did not visit Rome until the time of his imprisonment and appeal to Caesar, there seems to have been a Christian group there quite early. Aquila and Prisca, the Christian couple whom Paul met at Corinth, had come from Rome. They had probably been forced to leave when the Emperor Claudius expelled all the Jews from his capital. The letter to the Romans names a number of Christians in Rome already known to Paul. And there were friends to meet him after his voyage from Caesarea. He was in Rome under guard for two years and during that time may have written a number of his letters to Christians in other places.
Tradition has it that Peter worked in Rome and, with Paul, was martyred here. There were certainly a great many Christians in Rome by AD 64, when the Emperor Nero began a cruel massacre. The evil and corruption of Rome are referred to in Revelation, where the city ('great Babylon') is pictured as a prostitute drunk with the blood of God's people. See *Romans* in Part 11: *Nations and Peoples of the Bible.*
Acts 2:10; 18:2; 19:21; 28:14–30; Romans 1:7, 15; 16; 2 Timothy 1:16–17; Revelation 17:5–18, etc.; Map p. 336

Salamis A commercial centre on the east coast of Cyprus. A number of Jews lived here, and when Paul visited the town he preached in synagogues.
Acts 13:5

Salem See *Jerusalem.*

Salt Sea The Old Testament name for the Dead Sea, given because the water contains very heavy deposits of salt. See *Arabah.*

Samaria Capital of the northern kingdom of Israel. The city was on the main north/south trade-route through Israel and was built on top of a hill so that it could easily be defended. The work of building the city was started about 875 BC by King Omri. It was continued by his son Ahab, who added a new palace. So much carved ivory was used to decorate

the palace that it became known as the 'ivory house'. Over 500 pieces of ivory, some covered with gold leaf, have been discovered by archaeologists in the ruins of the palace.
From the start, the people of Samaria followed pagan religions. Several Old Testament prophets condemned their idol-worship and warned that the city would be destroyed.
The Syrians attacked and besieged Samaria many times, but it was the Assyrians who finally captured the city in 722/1 BC. The people were exiled to Syria, Assyria and Babylonia. They were replaced by colonists from different parts of the Assyrian Empire. When Samaria fell, the kingdom of Israel ceased to exist. The whole area, not just the city, became known as Samaria.
By New Testament times the city of Samaria had been rebuilt by Herod the Great and renamed Sebaste (Greek for Augustus). A few half-caste Jews still remained in Samaria and claimed to worship God there, but these 'Samaritans' were despised and hated by the Jews in Judea. Jesus showed his concern for them by travelling through their land and staying with them. After Jesus' death and resurrection Philip went to Samaria to preach the gospel, and his work was followed up by Peter and John.
A small group of Samaritans still live in Nablus and Jaffa and worship on Mt Gerizim.
1 Kings 16:24, 32; Isaiah 8:4; Amos 3:8; 2 Kings 6:8 – 7:17; Luke 17:11; John 4:1–43; Acts 8:5–25; Map OT/B4

Sardis A city in the Roman province of Asia (in modern Turkey) situated at the point where two main trade-routes met. In Roman times there were thriving dyeing and woollen industries here. One of the seven letters to churches in Asia, in the Book of Revelation, was addressed to the Christians at Sardis. The church had become apathetic. They relied on the past instead of concentrating on the present – an attitude

typical of the city as a whole. It had been the capital of the kingdom of Lydia and at one time ruled by Croesus. His wealth was legendary; gold was easily obtained from a river which flowed close to the city. The first gold and silver coins were minted at Sardis.
Revelation 1:11; 3:1–6

Seir Another name for Edom.

Sela Capital of Edom. The name means 'rock' or 'cliff' and was given to this fortress-city because it was built on a rocky plateau high up in the mountains of Edom. About 300 BC the Nabataeans took Sela and carved the city of Petra (the Greek word for rock) out of the rocky valley at the foot of the original settlement.
2 Kings 14:7; Isaiah 16:1; 42:11

Seleucia (Seleucia Pieria) The port of Antioch in Syria. It was built by, and named after, the first Seleucid king. Paul and Barnabas set sail from here for Cyprus on their first missionary journey.
Acts 13:4

Senir Another name for Mt Hermon. It is also used to describe a nearby peak and sometimes the whole range of mountains.

Sepharvaim A town as yet unidentified, captured by the Assyrians. People from here were brought to Samaria after the Jews had been sent into exile.
2 Kings 17:24, 31; 18:34

Sharon The coastal plain of Israel. It extends from Joppa to Caesarea – about 50 miles/80 km – and is about 10 miles/16 km wide. Today the plain is one of the richest agricultural areas in Israel. In Bible times few people lived here. The land was used as pasture for sheep, but much of it was left in its natural state of thick scrub. The writer of the Song of Solomon (Songs) refers to the 'rose of Sharon', one of the many beautiful wild flowers which grew on the plain.
1 Chronicles 27:29; Song of Solomon (Songs) 2:1; Map p. 13

Sheba A country in south-west Arabia, now the Yemen. Sheba became a wealthy land by trading spices, gold and jewels

Ancient Rome, capital of the Empire.

with the Mediterranean world. In the tenth century BC a queen of Sheba travelled over 1,000 miles/1,600 km by camel caravan to visit King Solomon and test his wisdom. She possibly also wished to arrange a trade agreement. The remains of a great dam and a temple to the moon-god Ilumquh have been discovered at Marib, once the capital of Sheba.
Psalm 72:15; Isaiah 60:6; 1 Kings 10:1–10, 13

Shechem An ancient Canaanite town which became an important religious and political centre for the Israelites; in the hill-country of Ephraim, near Mt Gerizim.

Abraham stopped at Shechem on his journey from Harran to Canaan. While he was here God told him, 'This is the country that I am going to give to your descendants.' Jacob also visited Shechem and set up camp outside the town.

When the Israelites had conquered Canaan Joshua gathered all the tribes together at Shechem. Here they renewed their promise to worship the God who had rescued them from Egypt, and to have nothing to do with foreign gods. But in the time of the Judges Canaanite worship was practised in Shechem. The inhabitants of the town gave Gideon's son Abimelech money from the temple of Baal-berith so that he could pay to have his seventy brothers killed. Abimelech made himself king of Shechem but the people soon turned against him. In revenge he destroyed the town.

After the death of King Solomon ten of the Israelite tribes rejected Solomon's son Rehoboam at Shechem. Jeroboam, the first king of the new northern kingdom, started to rebuild Shechem, and for a short time made it his capital.

Shechem survived the fall of Israel. It became the Samaritans' most important city and they built a temple here. A few Samaritans still live in Nablus, the modern town north-west of the site of Shechem.
Genesis 12:6–7; 33:18 – 35:4; 37:12–18; Joshua 24; Judges 9; 1 Kings 12;

Map OT/B4
Shiloh The town where the worship tent (tabernacle) was set up after the conquest of Canaan. Shiloh became the centre of Israel's worship, and the tent was replaced by a more permanent building. Each year a special festival was held here. Hannah and Elkanah travelled to Shiloh to worship God. On one of these visits Hannah, praying for a son, promised that she would give him back to serve God. When Samuel was born Hannah kept her promise. She brought him back to Shiloh and he grew up in the temple, under the care of Eli the priest.

Archaeological evidence shows that Shiloh was destroyed about 1050 BC, probably by the Philistines. Jeremiah the prophet warned that the temple in Jerusalem would be destroyed just as the place of worship at Shiloh had been. But it seems that some people lived on the site of Shiloh, at least until the time of the exile.
Joshua 18:1; Judges 21:19; 1 Samuel 1 – 4; Jeremiah 7:12; 41:5; Map OT/B4

Shinar Another name for Babylonia. See *Babylon.*

Shittim A place on the plains of Moab, across the Jordan from Jericho, also known as Abel-shittim, 'field of acacias'. The Israelites camped here just before they crossed the River Jordan into Canaan. They were probably at Shittim when the king of Moab tried to persuade Balaam to curse them. Preparations were made here for the conquest of Canaan. A census was taken of men able to fight; Joshua was chosen as Moses' successor; and two men were sent to spy out Jericho.
Numbers 25:1; 22 – 24; 26; 27:12–23; Joshua 2; 3:1; Joel 3:18; Map OT/C5

Shunem A place in the Valley of Jezreel, in northern Israel, modern Sôlem. The Philistines camped here before the battle on Mt Gilboa when Saul and Jonathan were killed. Elisha was the guest of a woman of Shunem, and he restored her child to life. The girl Abishag, who served David in his old age, was also a

Shunnamite. The young woman called a 'Shulammite' in the Song of Solomon (Songs) may have come from the same place.
Joshua 19:18; 1 Samuel 28:4; 1 Kings 1 – 2; 2 Kings 4:8–37; Song of Solomon (Songs) 6:13; Map OT/B3

Shur A desert area in the north-west part of the Sinai peninsula. Traders followed the 'Way of Shur' across the desert towards Egypt. Hagar fled this way after Sarah had treated her unkindly. When the Israelites had crossed the Sea of Reeds after escaping from Egypt they had to travel through this desert, and complained bitterly about the lack of water.
Genesis 16; Exodus 15:22–25

Siddim A valley (probably now submerged at the southern end of the Dead Sea) where Chedorlaomer, king of Elam, fought against the kings of the plain. During the fighting, Lot was taken prisoner, but he was rescued by Abraham.
Genesis 14

Sidon A Phoenician (Canaanite) port on the coast of modern Lebanon. Many skilled craftsmen worked in Sidon. Carved ivory, gold and silver jewellery and beautiful glassware were among its exports. Each Phoenician city was virtually self-governing.

When the Israelites conquered Canaan they failed to take Sidon. In the time of the Judges the people of Sidon attacked and harassed the Israelites. The cultures began to merge and the Israelites were accused of worshipping the gods of Sidon – Baal and Ashtoreth. Jezebel, who promoted Baal worship in Israel, was the daughter of a king of Sidon. Because Sidon was opposed to Israel and the worship of God, the Old Testament prophets predicted the town's downfall. Sidon was captured, in turn, by the Assyrians, the Babylonians and the Persians. Later it came under Greek and Roman control.

In the time of Jesus most of the inhabitants of Sidon were Greek. Many travelled to Galilee to hear him preach. Jesus also

visited Sidon and the neighbouring city of Tyre. He compared Chorazin and Bethsaida, two towns in Galilee, with Tyre and Sidon, saying how much more readily the non-Jewish cities would have responded to him. Paul stopped at Sidon on his journey to Rome and stayed with friends in the city.
Judges 1:31; 10:12, 6; 1 Kings 16:31; Isaiah 23:1–12; Ezekiel 28:20–24; Luke 6:17; Mark 7:24–31; Matthew 11:20–22; Acts 27:3, etc.; Map p. 329

Siloam A pool, originally underground, which was one of Jerusalem's main sources of water. The water in the pool came through a tunnel from the Gihon Spring outside Jerusalem. When the Assyrians threatened to besiege Jerusalem Hezekiah knew that in order to survive the city must have its own water supply, and gave orders for work on the tunnel. It is 1,750 ft/538 m long, cut through solid rock.

When Jesus healed a man who had been blind all his life he first put clay on his eyes and then told him to wash in the Pool of Siloam. The tower of Siloam which collapsed, killing eighteen people, probably stood on the slope of Mt Zion, above the pool.
2 Kings 20:20; John 9:1–12; Luke 13:4

Simeon The land given to the tribe of Simeon, in the Negev, the southernmost part of Israel. It seems that the area was considered an extension of Judah's territory.
Joshua 19:1–9; compare Joshua 15:20–32; Map p. 321

Sinai A mountain in the Sinai peninsula and the area of desert around it. Three months after leaving Egypt the Israelites reached the mountain and set up camp. Here, at Mt Sinai, God gave Moses the Ten Commandments and other laws. The exact identification of Mt Sinai is not known. It was probably one of two peaks – Gebel Musa or Ras es-Safsafeh – in the south of the peninsula.
Exodus 19 – 32; Map p. 318

Smyrna A port serving one of the main trade-

routes across Asia. It is now the city of Izmir in modern Turkey. In New Testament times it was a beautiful city with many splendid public buildings. One of them was the temple built in honour of the Emperor Tiberius, where emperor-worship was practised. One of the letters to the seven churches in the Book of Revelation is addressed to the Christians at Smyrna.
Revelation 1:11; 2:8–11

Sodom The town where Lot settled and which became notorious for its immorality. Sodom was suddenly destroyed, along with Gomorrah. Lot was warned of the impending disaster and escaped. Sodom probably now lies submerged at the southern end of the Dead Sea.
Genesis 13:8–13; 14; 19

Succoth 1. An Egyptian town. The Israelites made their first camp here on their journey out of the country.
Exodus 12:37; 13:20; Numbers 33:5–6; Map p. 318
2. A town in the Jordan Valley which became part of the territory of Gad. Jacob stayed for a while in Succoth after he and his brother Esau agreed to go their separate ways. In the time of the Judges the people of Succoth refused to provide Gideon and his army with food while he was fighting the Midianites. When Gideon was victorious he returned and punished the town officials.
Joshua 13:24, 27; Genesis 33:12–17; Judges 8:4–16; Map OT/C4

Susa Capital of the Elamite Empire until King Ashurbanipal of Assyria destroyed the city in 645 BC and exiled its inhabitants to Samaria. Under the Medes and Persians it once again became an important city. Darius I built a splendid palace here. The ruins, in modern Iran, can still be seen.
The story of Esther, the Jewish girl who became queen of Persia, took place at the royal court in Susa. It was here, too, that Nehemiah acted as royal cup-bearer. The city was later captured by Alexander the Great.
Ezra 4:9–10; Esther 1:2, etc.; Nehemiah 1:1; Map p. 332

Sychar A Samaritan town close to Jacob's well, where Jesus met and talked to a Samaritan woman who had come to draw water. Many people from Sychar believed Jesus was the Messiah when they heard what the woman said about him. The exact site is unknown.
John 4:1–42

Syene A place on the southern border of Egypt; modern Aswan. Isaiah pictures dispersed Jews returning to Jerusalem from as far away as Syene. Papyrus deeds found here record activities of Jewish settlers about 450 BC (the Elephantine Papyri).
Isaiah 49:12; Ezekiel 29:10; 30:6

Syracuse An ancient city in Sicily, where Paul spent three days on the last stage of his voyage to Rome after shipwreck on Malta.
Acts 28:12; Map p. 345

Syria In the Old Testament, Syria is the land occupied by the Aramaeans to the north and north-east of Israel. The capital of Syria was Damascus. See *Aramaeans* and Map in Part 11: *Nations and Peoples of the Bible*. In the New Testament Syria was a Roman province whose capital was Antioch on the Orontes.

Taanach A Canaanite city on the edge of the Valley of Jezreel. Barak fought Sisera near Taanach. It became one of the cities of the Levites.
Joshua 12:21; 21:25; Judges 5:19; 1 Kings 4:12; Map OT/B3

Tabor An 1800ft/550m steep-sided mountain rising from the Plain of Jezreel. The place where Barak gathered his army at the time of the Judges.
Judges 4; Psalm 89:12; Hosea 5:1; Map OT/B3

Tahpanhes An Egyptian town in the east part of the Nile Delta. The prophet Jeremiah was taken to Tahpanhes after the fall of Jerusalem and probably died there.
Jeremiah 43:5–10; Ezekiel 30:18

Tarshish The distant place for which Jonah set sail when he disobeyed God's command to go to Nineveh. A source of silver, tin, iron and lead. It may be Tartessus in Spain.

(Some modern Bible versions translate it as Spain.)
Jonah 1:3; Isaiah 23:6; Jeremiah 10:9; Ezekiel 27:12

Tarsus A town on the Cilician plain 10 miles/16 km inland from the south coast of modern Turkey. An important university city in New Testament times, with a large population, Tarsus was a meeting-place of East and West, of Greek and Oriental. Paul was born at Tarsus and was proud of it. He returned there not long after becoming a Christian. But Barnabas brought him to Antioch to help teach the new Christians.
Acts 9:11; 21:39; 22:3; 9:30; 11:25–26; Map p. 343

Tekoa A town in the Judean hills about 6 miles/10 km south of Bethlehem. A wise woman from Tekoa pleaded with King David to allow his son Absalom to come back to Jerusalem. Tekoa was also the home of the prophet Amos.
2 Samuel 14:2, etc.; Amos 1:1; Map OT/B5

Teman Part of Edom. The people of Teman were famous for their wisdom. It was the home area of Job's friend Eliphaz.
Jeremiah 49:7; Job 2:11

Thebes The ancient capital city of upper Egypt, on the River Nile about 330 miles/531 km south of modern Cairo. Two great temples of the God Amun (Karnak and Luxor) mark the site. From about 1500–1000 BC, when Amun was the official god of the Egyptian Empire, wealth and treasures poured into Thebes. But despite the city's remoteness it fell to the Assyrian King Ashurbanipal in 663 BC. The prophets Jeremiah and Ezekiel pronounced judgement on Thebes (No-Amon) and other Egyptian cities. (Picture under *Succoth*.)
Nahum 3:8–10; Jeremiah 46:25; Ezekiel 30:14–19

Thessalonica The chief city of Macedonia (northern Greece), on the Egnatian Way, the main Roman road to the East. Thessalonica (now Thessaloniki) is still a major city. Paul visited Thessalonica on his second missionary journey. But the anger of

the Jews forced him to move on to Beroea. His two letters to the Thessalonian Christians were written soon after he left.
Acts 17:1–15; 20:4; 27:2; Philippians 4:16; 1 Thessalonians 1:1; 2 Thessalonians 1:1, etc.; 2 Timothy 4:10; Map p. 345

Thyatira A city in the Roman province of Asia (now Akhisar in west Turkey). Thyatira was a manufacturing centre for dyeing, clothes-making, pottery and brasswork. Lydia, the business woman from Thyatira who became a Christian when she met Paul at Philippi, was a 'dealer in purple cloth'. One of the seven letters in the Book of Revelation was addressed to the church at Thyatira.
Acts 16:14–15; Revelation 1:11; 2:18–29

Tiberias A spa town on the west shore of Lake Galilee. It was founded by King Herod Antipas and named after the Roman Emperor Tiberius. It was a non-Jewish town, and there is no record that Jesus ever went there. Tiberias is still a sizeable town today, unlike all the other lakeside places mentioned in the Gospels.
John 6:23; Map NT/C2

Tigris The second great river of Mesopotamia. The Tigris rises in the mountains of eastern Turkey and flows for more than 1,400 miles/2,250 km, joining the River Euphrates 40 miles/64 km from its mouth on the Persian Gulf. The Tigris floods in spring and autumn. The great Assyrian cities of Nineveh, Calah and Assur were all built on the banks of the Tigris. The Bible mentions it as one of the four rivers of Eden.
Genesis 2:14; Daniel 10:4; Map p. 314

Timnah A town on the northern boundary of Judah which fell into Philistine hands. The home of Samson's wife.
Judges 14; Map OT/A5

Timnath-serah, Timnath-heres The town which Joshua received as his own. He was later buried here. The place was in the hill-country of Ephraim, north-west of Jerusalem.
Joshua 19:50; 24:30; Judges 2:9; Map OT/B4

Tirzah A town in northern Israel, noted for its beauty.

It was one of the places captured by Joshua. Later it was the home of Jeroboam I, and the first capital of the northern kingdom of Israel. King Omri later moved the centre of government to his new city of Samaria. The site of Tirzah is Tell el-Far'ah about 7 miles/11 km north-east of Shechem (Nablus).
Joshua 12:24; 1 Kings 14 – 16; 2 Kings 15:14, 16; Songs of Solomon (Songs) 6:4; Map OT/B4

Tishbe The place from which Elijah, 'the Tishbite', presumably came. It was in Gilead, east of the Jordan, but the actual site is unknown.
1 Kings 17:1, etc.

Tob A region south of Damascus. At the time of the Judges Jephthah lived there as an outlaw. The people of Tob helped the Ammonites against David.
Judges 11:3; 2 Samuel 10:6

Topheth The place in the Valley of Hinnom where children were sacrificed. The shrine was destroyed by King Josiah.
2 Kings 23:10; Jeremiah 7:31; 19:6, 11 – 14

Trachonitis A district linked with Ituraea (see *Ituraea*). Together they made up the territory ruled by Herod Philip at the time when John the Baptist began his preaching. Trachonitis was a rocky volcanic area, the haunt of outlaws, east of Galilee and south of Damascus.
Luke 3:1; Map NT/D2

Troas A port about 10 miles/16 km from Troy, in what is now north-west Turkey. Paul used the port a number of times on his travels. It was at Troas that he had his vision of a Macedonian man calling for help, and he sailed from there on his first mission to Europe. On a later visit to Troas he restored Eutychus to life after he had fallen from an upstairs window while Paul was preaching.
Acts 16:8 – 12; 20:5 – 12; 2 Corinthians 2:12; 2 Timothy 4:13; Map p. 345

Tyre An important port and city-state on the coast of Lebanon. Tyre had two harbours, one on the mainland, the other on an off-shore island. In about 1200 BC the Philistines plundered Sidon, the other important Phoenician port

20 miles/32 km or so to the north. From that time on Tyre became the leading city.
Tyre's 'golden age' was the time of David and Solomon. King Hiram of Tyre supplied wood and skilled men to build the temple at Jerusalem. Trade flourished. Tyre's own specialities were glassware and fine-quality purple dye made from local sea-snails.
King Ahab of Israel married the daughter of the king of Tyre. The city is often mentioned in the Psalms and by the prophets, who condemned Tyre's pride and luxury. In the ninth century BC Tyre came under pressure from the Assyrians. The city paid heavy tribute in return for a measure of freedom. In the same year as the fall of Samaria, Sargon II of Assyria captured Tyre. When Assyria lost power Tyre became free and prosperous again. For thirteen years (587 – 574 BC), King Nebuchadnezzar of Babylon besieged the city. In 332 BC Alexander the Great managed to take the island port by building a causeway from the mainland.
In New Testament times Jesus himself visited the area around Tyre and Sidon and spoke to the people. See also *Phoenicians* in Part 11: *Nations and Peoples of the Bible*.
2 Samuel 5:11; 1 Kings 5; 9:10 – 14; 16:31; Psalm 45:12; Isaiah 23; Ezekiel 26; Matthew 15:21; Luke 6:17; Acts 21:3; Map OT/B1

Ur A famous city on the River Euphrates in south Babylonia (modern Iraq); the home of Abraham's family before they moved north to Harran. The site of Ur had been occupied for several thousand years before it was finally abandoned about 300 BC. Excavations have uncovered thousands of inscribed clay tablets describing the city's history and life. The Royal Graves (about 2600 BC) contained many treasures, examples of beautiful craftsmanship: gold weapons, an inlaid mosaic gaming-board, the famous mosaic standard showing scenes of peace and war, and many other things. Ruins of a great stepped

temple tower (ziggurat) still remain. See Part 2: *Archaeology and the Bible*.
Genesis 11:28 – 31, etc.; Map p. 316

Uz The home country of Job, probably in the region of Edom.
Job 1:1

Zarephath/Sarepta A small town that belonged to Sidon, later to Tyre. The prophet Elijah stayed with a widow there during a time of drought. Later he restored the widow's son to life.
1 Kings 17:8 – 24; Luke 4:26

Zeboiim One of a group of five early cities, of which the most famous are Sodom and Gomorrah. See *Admah, Sodom, Gomorrah.*
Zeboiim was also the name of a valley near Michmash, in the desert north-east of Jerusalem, the site of a Philistine raid in the days of Saul.
Genesis 14:2, 8; Deuteronomy 29:23; 1 Samuel 13:18

Zebulun Land belonging to the tribe of Zebulun, in Galilee.
Joshua 19:10 – 16; Map p. 321

Ziklag A town in the south of Judah taken by the Philistine city of Gath. King Achish of Gath gave it to David when he was an outlaw from King Saul. David recovered the captives taken by the Amalekites after they had raided the town.
Joshua 15:31; 1 Samuel 27:6, 30; Map OT/A6

Zin An area of desert near Kadesh-barnea where the Israelites camped after the exodus.
Numbers 13:21; 20:1; 27:14, etc.; Map p. 318

Zion The fortified hill which David captured from the Jebusites to make it his capital, Jerusalem. The name is often used in the Psalms and by the prophets.

Ziph A town belonging to the tribe of Judah, in the hills south-east of Hebron. David hid from Saul in the desert near Ziph, and Jonathan came to encourage him here. But the men of Ziph betrayed him to Saul, and he moved to Maon and Engedi. Later, Ziph was one of the places fortified by King Rehoboam. The site is still called Tell Zif.
Joshua 15:55; 1 Samuel 23:14 – 29; 2 Chronicles

11:9; Map OT/B6

Zoan/Tanis An ancient Egyptian town in the north-east of the Nile Delta. From about 1100 to 660 BC Zoan was used as the capital of Egypt.
Numbers 11:28 – 31; Isaiah 19:11, etc.; Map p. 00

Zoar One of five cities probably at the southern end of the Dea Sea. Lot fled to Zoar at the time when Sodom and the others were destroyed.
Genesis 13:10; 14:2, 8; 19:18 – 30

Zobah An Aramaean kingdom defeated by David; it was between Damascus and Hamath.
2 Samuel 8:3; 10:6; 1 Kings 11:23

Zorah Samson's birthplace.
Judges 13:2; 16:31; Map OT/A5

These Persian archers from King Darius' palace at Susa are portrayed in enamelled brick, almost life-size.

11

Nations and Peoples of the Bible

The Egyptians

The other parts of the country were also important. The deserts and the Sinai peninsula contained valuable metals (copper, gold), and stone that was used for building the giant pyramids and the temples in the Nile Valley.

The land of the Nile

The huge Sahara Desert sweeps across North Africa from the mountains of Morocco in the west to the Red Sea in the east. From the lakes and highlands of tropical East Africa, the River Nile flows north alone across the dry deserts all the way to the Mediterranean Sea. For the last 600 miles to the sea, the river flows through a valley bordered by cliffs on either side. Then, 100 miles from the sea, it splits into two streams. They enclose a great triangle of flat land called the Nile Delta, because its shape is like the Greek letter 'D', *delta*, a triangle.

☐ The Nile flood

Every year, tropical rains in East Africa cause the river to flood its banks, bringing down masses of mud in the flood-waters. Until modern times, that fertile mud was deposited fresh each year along the valley and in the great Delta triangle, which was entirely formed of this mud. This is Egypt: rich green crops on black soil along the narrow ribbon of valley and river, and across the broad Delta. On either side, the yellow-brown deserts stretch away beyond the cliffs. Now-adays, great dams control the Nile floods, and hold back the mud. In ancient times, there was no control. A small flood meant no water for crops, and so nothing to eat. Too big a flood swept away villages and farm animals. To spread the water as far as possible, the ancient Egyptians cut canals and irrigation channels among the fields.

☐ Transport

The Egyptians quickly learned to make boats. At first, they made canoes out of papyrus-reeds, then larger boats of wood. With these they could travel easily on the River Nile along the whole valley, or through the Delta. Going north, they simply rowed with the current. Going south, the north wind would fill their sails to travel against the river's flow. So the Nile has always been Egypt's 'main road'.

Feluccas on the River Nile at Luxor in Egypt. The river has always been the great highway of Egypt.

A land of history

To begin with there were two kingdoms in Egypt: the Nile Valley (Upper Egypt) and the Nile Delta (Lower Egypt). But before 3000 BC a king of the Valley managed to defeat the king of the Delta and become the king of all Egypt. To rule both lands, he built his capital city, Memphis, at the point where the valley widens into the Delta. Menes, this first king of all Egypt, began a line of kings or 'pharaohs'. For the next 3,000 years, thirty such families of kings (dynasties) ruled Egypt, mainly following one after the other. During that long span of time, Egypt enjoyed three periods of greatness.

☐ The Pyramid Age

The first great age in Egypt was the 'Old Kingdom' (about 2600–2200 BC), or 'Pyramid Age', from the huge, pointed stone tombs that the kings built. After the strong kings of the Pyramid Age, Egypt became poorer under less able leaders. Once more rival kings came to power in south and north, until a prince from Thebes again reunited Egypt.

☐ The Middle Kingdom

This prince's family, and the one after it (the 12th Dynasty) were Egypt's 'Middle Kingdom' (about 2060–1786 BC). Its new, strong pharaohs took over the river-valley and deserts of Nubia, south of Egypt, to obtain gold and other African products. By improving the use of the Nile-waters for farming, these kings also increased the crops grown, and the wealth of the people. It was probably about this time that Abraham visited Egypt because of famine in Canaan. Many others like him came from Canaan into Egypt. Some stayed, and were even promoted to important posts in the government of Egypt; others were less fortunate and became servants or slaves.

After the 12th Dynasty, from about 1780–1550 BC weaker kings ruled. This was perhaps the time when Joseph was sold as a slave into Egypt, to be followed some years later by his family. From amongst the foreigners living in the east Delta, princes arose who made themselves kings of all Egypt. They are known as the Hyksos, or 15th Dynasty. But it was not long before Egyptian princes from Thebes in the south again came north, to expel the Hyksos rulers and re-unite Egypt once more.

☐ The Empire
These pharaohs also won control over Canaan, to the north of Egypt, as well as Nubia to the south. This period, the 'New Kingdom', is often called the 'Empire'. It includes the 18th–20th Dynasties, and covers the period from about 1500 to 1070 BC. These kings fought many battles in Canaan and Syria. In Egypt, they built many huge temples, the most important at Memphis (their capital) and Thebes (their sacred city).

In the meantime the Hittites in the far north conquered part of Egypt's empire in Syria. A new line of pharaohs tried to win back the lost provinces, especially kings Sethos I and Ramesses II (19th Dynasty, thirteenth century BC). These kings were great builders. Being a Delta family, they built a new royal city, Pi-Ramesse – the Raamses (Rameses) of Exodus – in the east Delta. This was the climax of the 'oppression' of the Hebrews – who were used as slave-labour by the pharaohs – and the time when Moses was sent to lead the Hebrews out of Egypt (the 'Exodus'). Shortly before 1200 BC another pharaoh, Merenptah, sent soldiers to Canaan and defeated several

groups of people there. One of these was the Israelites, who obviously must have been in Canaan by that date.

Soon after 1200 BC, the ancient world had much trouble. The 'peoples of the sea' and others overthrew the Hittite Empire and most of the kingdoms in Syria and Canaan. Ramesses III pushed the invaders back from Egypt's borders in two fierce battles on land and sea. One of these peoples was the Philistines. After Ramesses III, Egypt's 20th Dynasty and empire lost power under weak kings. They governed badly and low Niles brought famines.

☐ The Late Period
From about 1070 BC to 330 BC, Egypt went through her 'Late Period'. Egypt was never again as powerful as in earlier times. In 925 BC, Shoshenq I (Shishak) subdued King Rehoboam of Judah and King Jeroboam of Israel. The Egyptians recorded this victory in their temple of Karnak. But their power did not last long: 200 years later neither So nor Tirhakah could help the Hebrew kings against Assyria. Nor did Hophra in 588 BC really help Zedekiah against the Babylonians.

From 525 BC Egypt, like her neighbours, was part of the Persian Empire, sometimes rebelling and becoming free again (28th–30th Dynasties), until finally Alexander the Great took over (332–323 BC). After him, the Greek Ptolemies ruled Egypt until the coming of the Roman Empire.
Genesis 12:10–20; 37 – 50; Exodus 1:11 and chapters 1 – 14; 1 Kings 14:25–27; 2 Kings 17:4; 19:9ff.; Jeremiah 37:5–7 and 44:30

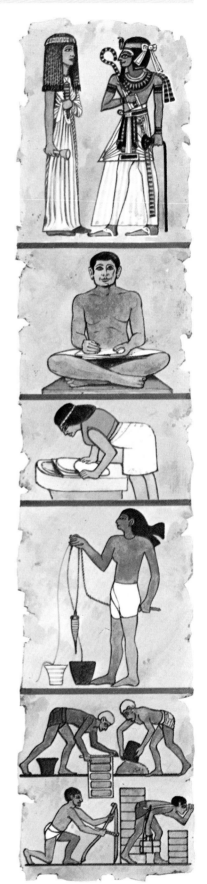

Scenes from everyday life in ancient Egypt. From top to bottom:
A man and woman dressed in the fine linen for which Egypt was famous.
An Egyptian scribe at work.
A woman kneading bread.
A girl, spinning.
Men at work in the brickfields.

Life in ancient Egypt

The pharaoh was supreme ruler of Egypt. He was assisted by his great men, including wise men like those the king sent for to explain his dreams. The land was divided into provinces. Each had its chief city for local government and supplies. Most Egyptians were farmers, growing grain, keeping cattle, depending on the Nile. These are all features of the dreams of Joseph's pharaoh. Dreams mattered to all classes (prisoners as well as kings) and the Egyptians even wrote textbooks to interpret dreams.

Egyptian writing began as pictures ('hieroglyphs'), used to write the sounds of their language. An owl was *m*, a mouth was *r*, and so on. For use on papyrus sheets (an early form of paper), flowing forms of script were used ('hieratic', 'demotic'). The Egyptians wrote stories, poetry, books of wisdom (like the Bible book of Proverbs), as well as everyday things like lists, letters and accounts.

Both Egyptians and foreigners had to work as labourers on building-sites, especially making bricks. For these, straw was needed to mix with the clay to make better bricks. The papyri also mention straw, and fixed work-targets. Like Moses, many young foreigners were brought up at court, were well educated, and had all kinds of jobs. Like Moses and the Hebrews, others, too, tried to escape from Egypt. The papyri mention slaves who ran away to gain their freedom.
Genesis 40 and 41; Exodus 1–14

Egyptian religion

☐ The gods of Egypt

The Egyptians had many gods. Some came from nature: Re, the sun-god; Thoth, Khons, moon-gods; Nut, the sky-goddess; Geb, the earth-god; Hapi, the god of the Nile-flood; and Amun, the god of hidden life-powers in nature. Some stood for ideas: Maat

An Egyptian painting of Hapi, the Nile-god. The picture shows reeds and wild fowl and some of the crops the Nile water made it possible to grow.

was goddess of truth, justice, and right order. Thoth was also the god of learning and wisdom. Ptah was the god of craftsmanship. Most Egyptians turned to Osiris for hope of a life after death. Osiris was said to have been slain by his brother and then made king of the underworld.

Animals noted for special qualities were treated as sacred to particular gods. They could act as 'live images' for their gods. So the Apis-bull was sacred to Ptah, the ibis-birds to Thoth, falcons to Horus, cats to the goddess Bastet. A god was sometimes shown wearing the head of his sacred animal, to make him easier to recognize.

With so many different gods controlling their world, the Egyptians tried to link these to one another. They produced 'myths' (stories about the gods), in which gods were often grouped as 'families'. There would be a chief god and goddess as husband and wife, with a lesser god or goddess as their son or daughter.

In the fourteenth century BC, Pharaoh Akhenaten tried to make all his subjects worship the sun-god only (as seen in the sun's disc – Aten). But

he failed, and after about ten years the Egyptians returned to the gods they had worshipped before.

☐ Worship at the great temples

The life the Egyptians imagined for the gods was modelled on their own daily life. The huge stone temple, hidden behind great brick walls, was the home of the god. The priests were his servants. Each morning, they woke him up with a morning hymn, broke the seal on his shrine, redressed his image, and gave him food and drink offerings for 'breakfast'. These offerings were then placed before statues of Pharaoh's ancestors (earlier kings of Egypt) and the great men of Egypt, before being finally eaten by the priests. At midday, a shorter service and offerings made up the god's 'lunch'. An evening hymn sent him to rest, after a third offering ('supper'). On special festival days, smaller images of the gods were carried in procession from temple to temple. These were days on

The bronze figure of an Egyptian king making an offering.

which the gods 'went visiting', sometimes to celebrate events mentioned in the stories about them. People believed that the 'spirit' of the god lived in his image in the temple.

A worshipper from Egypt.

In theory, Pharaoh himself was high priest of all the gods. In real life, his deputies were high priests in the various temples, assisted by other priests. Only the king, priests and higher officials could go beyond the first sunlit court into dim, pillared halls and the darkness of the sacred inner room of the temple. Akhenaten's sun-god religion worked in the same way, but in open-air temples. There is a famous hymn, praising the Aten as the creator who provides for the world. People have compared it with Psalm 104. But there are no links between the Egyptian hymn and the psalm, or the Hebrew worship of one holy God.

☐ The role of the king
Pharaoh was the go-between for gods and people. Through his deputy priests he made offerings to the gods on behalf of the people in order that, in turn, the gods might shower their gifts on Egypt (good Nile-

floods, rich crops). He also appeared as the representative of the gods to the people. He directed the building and up-keep of the temples which were always built in his name.

☐ The religion of the people
The mass of the ordinary people could not enter the great state temples. They only saw the great gods on festival days, when their veiled images were carried in procession in small sacred boats by the priests. Instead, ordinary people worshipped at small, local shrines, or the chapels at the gateways of the great temples. Their worship was mostly to present offerings, following certain set rituals. The people were allowed to make merry at the great festivals. They also sometimes got time off to worship their own god (this was what Moses asked Pharaoh's permission to do, Exodus 5:1, 3). When troubles such as illness struck them, the Egyptians sometimes thought this was punishment from the gods for wrong-doing. They then confessed their sins and prayed for healing and help. If healing came, they often set up little inscriptions, with a short hymn to the god or goddess, to record their thanks.

Mummies in coffins were buried in tombs with all the belongings the person might need for the after-life in the kingdom of Osiris.

Like most peoples, the ancient Egyptians had a moral sense of right and wrong. Murder or theft were wrong then, as now. But magic was used to grasp at supernatural power. Good or 'white' magic was designed to ward off life's troubles. Harmful or 'black' magic was a crime, and was punished as such. Magic usually meant the exact reciting of spells, often over small images or drawings connected with the subject of the magic. People often wore lucky charms, or amulets. The symbol of life, or the scarab-beetle for renewal, was popular.

☐ Life after death
The early Egyptians buried their dead along the edges of the dry deserts that bordered the Nile Valley. The dry sand and hot sun often dried up and so preserved the bodies of those early people in their shallow graves. The Egyptians came to believe that the body was a home for the soul, and that the soul needed its personal belongings in a life after death something like earthly life. So, when tombs became too big and deep for the sun's heat to dry the body, the Egyptians did this artificially. They packed the body in salt to dry it up, stuffed it and bandaged it (mummification). The mummy was then buried in a coffin in the tomb with the other belongings. Joseph was embalmed in this way, and put

in a coffin in Egypt (Genesis 50:26).

Most Egyptians hoped to have a pleasant after-life in the kingdom of Osiris. They had papyrus-roll books of magical spells to help them pass the judgement of the dead. This by-passed the moral test of that judgement. The most famous collection of spells is the *Book of the Dead*.

Souls of dead kings spent their after-life with the sun-god, crossing the sky in his heavenly boat by day. Then, at night, they passed through the realm of Osiris, providing for their dead subjects. The emphasis on mummification, magic, and richly furnished tombs led to very materialistic views of the after-life.

□ Egyptian religion and the Bible

Egyptian religion was very different from that of the Hebrews. Israel's God dealt with his people in actual history. He required obedience to his just laws more than rituals or sacrifices (1 Samuel 15:22). Ritual without right living was useless. (The Egyptians also admitted this sometimes.) Unlike the gods of Egypt (who needed three meals a day), the God of Israel had no personal need of food or of anything that human hands might provide (see Psalm 50:11–13). Egyptian rituals were symbols, and magical acts. The rites which took place in the Hebrew tabernacle and temple were intended to instruct the people in the nature and purity of their God. Egyptian rites were complicated and for the special few. The Hebrew ones were far simpler, designed mostly for the instruction of people as well as priests.

The Canaanites

Canaan's great legacy to the world is almost certainly the alphabet, invented here between 2000 and 1600 BC (see Part 2). Egyptian influence led to paper (papyrus) becoming the normal writing material. Because this has not survived the centuries in Canaan, examples of the infant alphabet are very rare. They are limited to more durable items – names scratched on cups, for instance.

About 1300 BC 'Canaan' was an Egyptian province covering Lebanon, Syria and what later became the land of Israel. The name may have belonged at first to the coastal plain, then have been extended to include the people of the forested hills – the Amorites (see Numbers 13:29; 35:10; Joshua 5:1). Besides Canaanites and Amorites, there were other groups living in the land. Deuteronomy 7:1 lists five others. So the term 'Canaanites' came to include a mixture of peoples.

Trade

Those living on the coast were traders. In fact, trade was so much a part of Canaanite life that the word Canaanite came to mean 'merchant' in Hebrew (it is used that way, for instance, in Proverbs 31:24). The major ports were Tyre, Sidon, Beirut and Byblos, in the tongue of Canaan that

stretched northwards (the coast of modern Lebanon). From them cedarwood, jars of oil and wine and other goods were exported to Egypt, Crete, and Greece. In return came Egyptian luxuries and writing paper, Greek pottery, and metal ores. Beyond the boundary of Canaan, but sharing many Canaanite characteristics, was the great city of Ugarit (near modern Latakiya). This city, too, was a wealthy commercial centre.

The position of Canaan as a bridge between Asia and Egypt, as well as her trading activities, laid the people open to cultural influences of all sorts. Palaces and temples might be built in Egyptian style for a resident governor or garrison in one city. Syrian styles might be followed in another. Scarabs and other Egyptian jewellery were fashionable – alongside Babylonian cylinder seals and

Wood being unloaded from Canaanite (Phoenician) ships. An eighth-century relief from the palace of King Sargon of Assyria, at Khorsabad. Timber shipped down the coast from Tyre was used to build King Solomon's temple at Jerusalem.

A Canaanite vase from Jericho, fifteenth century BC.

Hittite goldwork from Turkey. These influences are seen most plainly in the way the Canaanites used both Egyptian ('hieroglyphic') and Babylonian ('cuneiform') writing.

Cities and rulers

Canaanite cities were surrounded by defensive walls of earth and stone to keep out raiders and wild animals. Inside, the houses were crowded together, as they are in the old cities of the Near East today. The ordinary people worked for themselves on small patches of land, or at various crafts, or were employed by the king, landowners, and merchants. Beyond the city lay scattered villages of farmers and herdsmen.

The rulers of the cities were constantly quarrelling and fighting with each other. And some were liable to attack by bands of brigands and outlaws who hid in the forests. The Amarna Letters, found in Egypt, describe this state of affairs in about 1360 BC. And the Bible books of Joshua and Judges show that it was much the same a century or two later. This made the conquest easier for the Israelites. A united Canaan would have been much more difficult (see the lists of kings in Joshua 10 and 12).

Canaanites and Israelites

The language of the Canaanites was closely related to Hebrew, perhaps even the same. The life of the Canaanite farmers was not very different from the life of the Israelites in Egypt before they became slaves. So the Israelites were able to settle easily into their Promised Land. It was tempting to fall in with other Canaanite ways, too. But the Canaanite religion was a far cry from the love of God and obedience to his clear, moral laws. So the Israelites were forbidden to mix and marry with these peoples. Everything to do with Canaanite religion must be destroyed (see Deuteronomy 7; 12:1–3).

A Canaanite altar at Byblos.

Canaanite religion

At Mount Sinai God had commanded Israel to have no other gods but him. The Israelites, when they invaded Canaan, must therefore avoid all contact with Canaanite religion. But even before the Israelites invaded Canaan they had begun to worship Baal, the Canaanite god. When they settled in the Promised Land, Baal became a serious rival to Israel's own God. The Book of Judges describes the troubles this caused, and how men like Gideon opposed Baal-worship.

Although little is said about it in the time of King David and King Solomon, later, when Ahab became king of the northern kingdom of Israel, Baal almost ousted the God of Israel. This was the work of Ahab's queen, Jezebel, who came from the Canaanite city of Sidon and brought many priests of Baal with her.
Exodus 20:3; 23:23, 24;
1 Kings 16:29 and the chapters that follow

☐ Canaanite gods

Canaanite gods and goddesses were the powers of nature personified. Baal, which means 'lord', was the title of Hadad, the weather-god (his name probably has the sound of thunder). He controlled the rains, mist, and dew, and so held the key to the good harvests which were essential if the Canaanites were to survive.

Baal's wife was Astarte, also known as Anat, goddess of love and war. His father was El, the chief of the gods, but at the time of the Israelite conquest he had become a shadowy figure. El's wife was Asherah, mother goddess and goddess of the sea. Both Asherah and Astarte were often simply called 'Mistress' (Baalat).

Other leading deities were Shamash, the sun; Reshef, lord of war and of the underworld; Dagon, the corn; and many lesser ones who made up the families and courts of each senior god. This general picture varied from place to place, as each town had its own patron or favourite deity, often called 'Lord' or 'Mistress' of such-and-such a place.

Baal, the Canaanite weather-god.

☐ Stories of the gods

Stories of these gods and goddesses are known from Canaanite (Ugaritic) and foreign sources. They were brutal and bloodthirsty, delighting in battle with each other, and in uncontrolled sexual relationships. They interfered in human affairs simply to satisfy their whims, regardless of the suffering caused. At the same time, they could be kind and generous. They were no more than reflections of their worshippers, dressed up as gods.

Naturally these stories had their effect on the worship of the Canaanites. Religious festivities became a degraded celebration of the animal side of human nature. Even Greek and Roman writers were shocked by the things the Canaanites did in the name of religion. So it is hardly surprising that the Bible totally condemns their wickedness. Deuteronomy 18:9; 1 Kings 14:22–24; Hosea 4:12–14

☐ Temples and priests

The important gods had richly endowed temples in the leading cities, with priests, choirs,

Canaanite 'votive figures' (brought by worshippers making vows) from Byblos.

A Canaanite 'high place' at Megiddo.

and temple servants. On holy days the kings would go in procession to offer sacrifices. Some of these were burnt entirely; some were shared between the god and his worshippers. On occasions of great celebration the ordinary people probably joined the processions and watched the ceremonies from a distance. But the temple buildings were not large, and only the privileged could go into them.

It was a matter of pride for a king to make the temple as grand as he could, covering the statues of the gods and the walls of the shrine with precious metal, and supplying golden dishes for the god's food. As well as a statue of the god, or of an animal that

was his emblem (Baal was represented by a bull, Asherah by a lion), there was also an altar for the sacrifices, an altar for incense, and perhaps a number of stone pillars inside the temple. The pillars were thought to be the homes of gods or spirits. There were also stone pillars, altars, and a wooden pole or tree trunk in simpler open-air shrines ('high places'), where the ordinary people could easily go to make a sacrifice, or to pray. The

A pendant showing the head of Astarte, Baal's wife, goddess of love and war.

pillars sometimes stood for Baal, and the post for Asherah (see Deuteronomy 12:3).

When a sacrifice was offered, the priest often examined the entrails of the animal to forecast the fortune of the worshipper (see *Assyrian and Babylonian Religion*). Other ways of telling the future were by looking at the stars, by making contact with the dead, and by prophetic trances. The priests were also in demand to heal the sick by prayers and incantations.

☐ Sacrifices

The sacrifices offered to the gods were normally animals

A bronze figure of a Canaanite god. The raised right arm probably once brandished a weapon.

and foodstuffs. The fact that Israel was commanded to avoid human sacrifice, and later information from Greek and Roman writings, shows that this was practised, but it is not clear how common it was. Probably it was a rite used in extreme circumstances, when only the greatest sacrifice was thought adequate to persuade the god to act favourably. The god Molech, who is named in connection with this sacrifice, seems to have been a god of the underworld.

The Canaanite and Hebrew languages share several words for sacrifices, priests, and other religious matters. There are some other expressions that are similar, too. There was obviously a common stock of words; but the ideas indicated by them differed from place to place and from faith to faith. Leviticus 18:21; Deuteronomy 12:31; 2 Kings 3:27

☐ Israelite and Canaanite religion
The religion of the Canaanites was totally different from Israelite religion. No evidence for a series of rules of conduct like the Ten Commandments has been found among the Canaanites. There is no known mention of love for any god

and there seems to have been little joy and happiness in Canaanite worship. On the other hand, our information is limited, and it should be noted that kings were expected to care for the poor, the widow and the orphan.

It was a strong temptation for the invading Israelites to respect the gods already in the land, and supposedly responsible for its fertility. As well as this, worship of the Canaanite gods was much less demanding

The Philistines

Long before Israel entered the Promised Land, their ancestors met Philistines in southern Canaan. Many scholars consider that these stories were composed much later, after the Philistines had settled there in the thirteenth century BC. Or the name Philistine may have been used by a later editor to replace an out-of-date name in the story. There are some objects from the Philistine area which show that there were connections with the Greek region as early as 1900 BC. But apart from the documents of the Old Testament, no others have yet been found which specifically mention the people of the district at that time. Genesis 21:32, 34; 26; Judges 16:21ff.; 1 Samuel 5; 13:19–22; 17; 31:9, 10; 1 Kings 1:2

'Sea Peoples'
The Philistines lived in five cities to the south-west of the land of Israel: Ashdod, Ashkelon, Ekron, Gath, and Gaza. They controlled the coast road from Egypt. It was perhaps to avoid them that God did not take his people

than the strict Israelite laws and rituals. Many of God's people gave in to the temptation. The result was the gradual slide towards disaster recounted in the books of Kings. The God of Israel demanded total loyalty.

into the Promised Land 'by the road that goes up the coast to Philistia, although it was the shortest way' (Exodus 13:17).

The Philistines produced their own styles of beautiful, decorated pottery.

Each Philistine city was ruled by a 'lord'. This title (*seren*) is a non-Semitic word, probably belonging to the Indo-European speech of the Aegean area. A word for helmet (*koba'*) found in stories about the Philistines (for example, Goliath in 1 Samuel 17:5) and the names Goliath and Achish may belong to the same family of languages. This evidence from two words and two names can be linked with information from Egypt. There, in the thirteenth and twelfth centuries BC, pharaohs recorded how they beat off invasions by the 'peoples of the sea'. One of these peoples was the Philistines. After defeating them, the Egyptians used some as soldiers to garrison provincial and frontier forts, and allowed others to settle the coast of Canaan, an Egyptian province.

While the Sea Peoples' warriors reached Egypt by ship, and fought the Egyptians on water, their families and household goods trekked down the coast of Syria and Canaan, according to an Egyptian text. These details, and some items in Egyptian pictures of Sea Peoples, point to them as intruders into the Near East. Amos 9:7 states that they came from Crete (Caphtor). Deuteronomy 2:23 says that this was where the men of Gaza came from. 'Philistine' pottery found in Israel is evidence of this link. The pottery belongs to the Mycenean type made in Greece, Crete, and Cyprus. It is found in levels of occupation dating from 1200–1100 BC, especially at sites on the coast.

Model of a Philistine warship, twelfth century BC.

War with the Israelites

In the days of the Judges, and of Samuel, Saul, and David, the Philistines were a constant threat to the Israelites. Both peoples wanted control of the same land. Their military pressure was one factor in Israel's demand for a king. ('We want . . . our own king . . . to lead us out to war' – 1 Samuel 8:20.)

Only after fierce struggles were their attacks finally ended by David, who drove them 'back from Geba all the way to Gezer' (2 Samuel 5:25). Yet the Philistines remained independent, and caused occasional disturbances in later times. They extended their rule northwards along the coast, and inland, whenever they could. Although they were never in control of much of the country for long, it was the Philistines who gave their name – as Palestine – to the whole of the land west of the Jordan.

Religion and culture

The Old Testament gives Philistine gods Semitic names: Dagon, with temples at Gaza and Ashdod; Baalzebub, worshipped at Ekron; and Ashtoreth (Astarte). We know little about Philistine towns, but excavations at Tell Qasile, near Tel Aviv, have uncovered temples with pillars to support the roofs (see Judges 16:21ff). Metal-working, especially in iron, was a Philistine skill.

Philistine soldiers taken captive by Ramesses III of Egypt. They are wearing plumed helmets, and kilts with tassels.

The Assyrians

Assyria is the northern part of modern Iraq, along the Tigris river and eastwards to the foot of the Zagros mountains. The winter rains and the rivers that run into the Tigris provide enough water for farming. Barley and wheat grow on the plains. Grapes, olives, apricots, cherries and other fruit are grown on the hills. The countryside is covered with grass in winter and spring, unlike the land west of the Tigris. There, much of the land is desert, with craggy forested mountains to the north, which in winter are covered with snow. Assyria looked attractive to the wild tribesmen of the desert and mountains. The story of the land is one of constant war with these envious neighbours.

The Assyrians called their capital city, their country, and their national god by one name, Ashur. The city of Ashur is in the south of the country, on the west side of the Tigris. The second city, Nineveh, lies east of the river, opposite modern Mosul, 68 miles/109km north of Ashur. Both cities were prosperous as early as 2500 B and probably long before.

The Assyrian people

First-hand records from Assyria begin soon after 2000 BC. The Assyrian king-list, an important record from a later date, shows that the Assyrians were in their land about 2300 BC. The texts prove that the Assyrians were a Semitic people. They used a language very closely related to Babylonian. They also show, as we would expect from the situation of the country, that the population was very mixed. Many non-Semitic people came in from the east and north. This seems to have happened peacefully, and, in later times, men who were not Assyrians by origin held important government posts.

Assyrians are commonly thought of as cruel imperialists. This picture, which comes partly from their wars with Israel reported in the Old Testament, has to be balanced against the situation of Assyria. Even when the frontiers seemed secure, threats existed, or could be imagined, from foreign rulers a little further away. These threats could only be dealt with by new campaigns. No doubt success encouraged further military adventures. But the Assyrians, like most people, prized peace and prosperity.

A frieze from the palace of King Sennacherib, at the Assyrian capital of Nineveh. Scribes list the booty and the number of dead from a captured town in southern Babylonia.

The Assyrian Empire

Between 1500 and 1100 BC Assyria became a leading state in the Near East, ruling as far west as the River Euphrates. Her kings wrote letters, as equals, to the kings of Egypt. Then Aramaean invaders from the desert completely overran the Assyrian homeland. This began a period of weakness that lasted until about 900 BC.

Then a line of vigorous kings began to regain their lost lands. They also tackled the problems of maintaining control over them. The warrior-kings

The Assyrian king, Tiglath-pileser III, in his state chariot.

Ashurnasirpal II (883–859 BC) and Shalmaneser III (858–824 BC) captured many cities and made their kings vassals. But as soon as the Assyrian army had gone home the subject kings rebelled. Tiglath-pileser III (745–727 BC) was the first to establish an effective system of provincial governors with firm control.

☐ Exile

A common way of trying to break resistance was to take hostages. After a major rebellion large numbers of the population were deported to other parts of the empire and replaced with strangers from far away. (This happened in

King Ashurbanipal of Assyria hunting lions.

Israel when the Assyrians captured Samaria – 2 Kings 17:6, 24ff.; see too 18:31, 32.) The famous emperors Sargon (721–705 BC), Sennacherib (705–681 BC), Esarhaddon (681–669 BC), and Ashurbanipal (669–627 BC) all followed this policy. Under the last two the empire grew too large, covering Egypt, Syria, the land of Israel, north Arabia, parts of Turkey and Persia. The frontiers could not all be defended, nor all rebels defeated. Babylon won independence in 625 BC, and, with help from the Medes, destroyed Nineveh in 612 BC.

□ Works of art
Assyria's great empire brought enormous wealth. Some of it came as tax, some through trade. The kings were able to build great palaces and temples, each aiming to do better than ever before. From those excavated at Nineveh and at Nimrud (ancient Kalah, about 20 miles south) and at other places, we have recovered some fine works of art. Walls were lined with stone slabs carved in low relief to depict the king in religious, military, and sporting life. Furniture was decorated with ivory panels, carved or engraved, often plated with gold. The king lay on a couch and drank from golden goblets shaped like animals' heads. His queen sat beside him. In the palace stores there were vast collections of iron weapons for the army.

Many different influences –

Egyptian, Syrian, Iranian – can be seen in the workmanship of these objects. But the basic culture of Assyria was drawn from the south, from Babylonia (see *The Babylonians*). The most important of all Babylonian customs in Assyria was the cuneiform writing system on clay tablets. Thousands of these tablets have been found in the Assyrian ruins. Some deal with the administration of the empire. Some are diplomatic documents. Some are private legal deeds. Some are the records of the deeds of kings. Most outstanding of all is the library collected by King Ashurbanipal. This library held copies

A reconstruction of the city walls of Nineveh, capital of Assyria (not full size).

of every piece of literature and knowledge that had been handed down from the past. With its recovery, from 1849 onwards, modern study of Assyria and Babylonia began.

The Assyrians and the Bible story
The Assyrians come into the Bible story at the time of the last kings of Israel, when the prophets Amos and Hosea were at work in the north, and Isaiah was coming into prominence in Judah. They were the major world power, and the people of less powerful countries lived under constant threat of invasion.

'I will bring upon you . . . the king of Assyria', says Isaiah. The prophet's prediction to King Ahaz of Judah was terrifying. Ahaz was trying to win Assyrian help against his enemies, the kings of Damascus and Samaria (Israel). But God's messenger was telling him that this, the greatest power of the time, would soon overwhelm his own country. The Assyrian king was Tiglath-pileser III (745–727 BC). He did accept Ahaz and Judah as his vassal. Then he relieved the pressure by conquering Damascus and

most of Israel and making them provinces of his empire.

It was Assyrian practice to make pacts with subject nations all around. If a subject stopped keeping the terms of the pact – if they failed to send an annual tax, or made friends with an enemy of Assyria – the Assyrians would try to change the situation by diplomacy. If that failed, they sent an army.

This happened to Judah. Ahaz kept the treaty, but his son Hezekiah – and King Merodach-Baladan of Babylon – joined a general rebellion when the Assyrian King Sargon died in 705 BC. Hezekiah took control of the Philistine cities which were subject to Assyria. After crushing the trouble in Babylon, Sennacherib, the new Assyrian king, naturally turned to deal with the rebel Hezekiah. His army overran Judah, as Isaiah predicted. Sennacherib's records claim: 'forty-six of (Hezekiah's) strong towns . . . I besieged and conquered, I brought out from them 200,150 people . . . (Hezekiah) I shut up like a bird in a cage in Jerusalem his capital city . . . the awful splendour of my lordship overwhelmed him . . . he sent 30 talents of gold, 300 talents of silver . . . to Nineveh.' Jerusalem, however, remained uncaptured. In fact, the Assyrians never attacked Jerusalem again, although Manasseh, Hezekiah's son, joined an Egyptian-inspired revolt, and was kept captive for a while (about 671 BC).
Isaiah 7:17–25; 2 Kings 15:27 – 16:9, 18:7, 8; 19; 20:12ff.; 2 Chronicles 33:11–13

Assyrian religion
See under *The Babylonians*.

The Babylonians

The southern part of modern Iraq was the ancient kingdom of Babylonia. The city of Babylon first rose to power about 1850 BC for a few generations, then again under Nebuchadnezzar, 1200 years later, for an equally short time. It was the glory of Nebuchadnezzar's city that made Babylon famous in world history.

Civilization began in Babylonia long before Babylon became important. Cities grew up there soon after man learnt how to use the river waters to irrigate the land (see Part 2: *Archaeology and the Bible*). Massive temples of mud brick have been excavated at Uruk (modern Warka, Old Testament Erech – Genesis 10:10). Their freestanding pillars are decorated with coloured mosaics.

□ Writing
Here the oldest known writing was found, the beginning of the Babylonian cuneiform script, in which 800 or more simple pictures stand for common objects or ideas. The pictures quickly changed from representing objects to being used as syllables, for their sound values alone. (For example, drawings of a thin man and a king might mean 'the king is thin' or 'the thin man is king' as pictures; but they could be used as sounds to write the word 'thinking'.) Soon extra signs were included to show grammatical classes, subject, object and so on.

We cannot understand the very earliest clay tablets. But those of the next stage – about 3200 BC – are clearly written in a language we call Sumerian. They include lists of words by groups (stones, animals, professions), and the first

meagre examples of literature, as well as accounts and deeds of sale. From the recognizable pictures, the signs quickly developed into groups of lines (these were easier to inscribe on clay), producing the wedge-shaped cuneiform script. The clay tablets survive well in the soil. They have given us more information about Babylonia than we have about almost any other ancient culture.

A stone tablet showing two figures probably making an exchange of symbols of property ownership. The scratched signs show early Babylonian writing moving from picture-writing to a semi-phonetic system: about 3000 BC.

Sumerians and Akkadians
The Sumerians may not have been the first people to live in Babylonia. But because they have left these documents, they are the first we can identify and name. Their origin is unknown, and we cannot relate their language to any other in the world. Side by side with them in the north lived Akkadian tribes. Their Semitic language was an early form of Babylonian, related to Arabic and Hebrew. The scholars of ancient Babylonia made translations from Sumerian into Akkadian, and these enable modern students to translate Sumerian.

Whoever the Sumerians

A reconstruction of one of the great buildings of Babylon.

□ **Works of art**
Craftsmen in the third millennium (3000–2000) BC made fine jewellery in gold, silver, and semi-precious stones imported from the east and south. Smiths cast copper and bronze for weapons and statues. Stone carvers produced some of the finest pieces of Babylonian art – from great monuments to tiny cylinder seals ¾–2in/2–5cm high which were rolled across clay to leave impressions of the pictures engraved on them. Outstanding examples of these skills were found in the Royal Tombs at Ur (dated at about 2400 BC). The local princes were buried in these tombs with their courtiers, dressed in their finery, and with chariots and waggons.

□ **Inscriptions**
The small tablets which list rations and accounts seem least interesting of all the inscriptions. Yet they are of great value for the names they contain. By careful study we can separate Sumerian, Akkadian,

A reconstruction of the magnificent Ishtar Gate at Babylon.

were, their genius seems to have led to the invention of writing, perhaps of wheeled vehicles, and of city life in Babylonia. Stories copied out about 2000 BC recount the exploits of Sumerian heroes and gods (see below). The most famous of these was Gilgamesh, king of Uruk soon after 3000 BC, who marched to the Lebanon mountains to fetch cedar wood, and perhaps into Turkey, too. His search for eternal life led him to the Babylonian Noah, who told the king how he was given immortality after surviving the flood. Gilgamesh was given two chances of gaining his goal. But he lost both, and returned home. He concluded that only through fame could a man's name live after him. Recent research has shown that some of these stories probably have a factual basis, even though they have mythical episodes (see Part 2: *Archaeology and the Bible*).

About 2300 BC the Semites gained control of Babylonia under King Sargon. His capital was at Akkad, a place we have not yet discovered. His rule extended into north Syria,

where he fought the king of Ebla (see Part 2: *Archaeology and the Bible*). From this time on, the Sumerian language was less important than Akkadian. Sargon's family maintained his empire for about a century until attackers from the east broke their power. From about 2100 to 2000 BC a line of kings based at Ur had a kingdom which was almost as large.

and foreign names. From 2400 BC there are more names of the sort used later by Semites in the west (Canaanites, Hebrews). By 2000 BC large numbers of these 'westerners' (Amorites) were pouring into Babylonia, and they took over the rule of the ancient cities.

□ Hammurabi

The most outstanding of their kings was Hammurabi of Babylon, about 1792–1750 BC. He gained power for his city by war and by diplomacy. During his reign he revised the laws of the land and had them engraved on stone (see Part 9 under *Medicine*). These are 'case laws' like those of Exodus 21 and 22. They begin: 'If a man . . .' In Hammurabi's laws things are not forbidden on moral grounds, as they are in the Ten Commandments. Despite royal authority, these laws soon fell into disuse, but they were copied in schools for another thousand years.

Hammurabi's line (dynasty) collapsed when a Hittite army raided Babylon in 1595 BC. Kassite kings from the east took over, and, although they were not Semites, they quickly adopted Babylonian culture. The land was peaceful for 400 years, then a native dynasty arose.

Nebuchadnezzar and the empire

Chaldaeans and Aramaeans from the west caused turmoil until the Chaldaean King Nabopolassar defeated the Assyrians (612 BC). His new empire contained most of the Assyrian provinces, although his son Nebuchadnezzar (605–562 BC) had to crush rebels in the west, including Judah. The wealth of the empire enabled these two kings to rebuild Babylon on an immense scale, with lavish decoration.

The Book of Daniel describes how Nebuchadnezzar was struck down while boasting of his works (Daniel 4). His son was killed by a General Neriglissar (Nergal-Sharezer,

Jeremiah 39:3), but Nabonidus in turn displaced Neriglissar's son. This king held strong religious convictions. He left Babylon in the care of his son Belshazzar, and lived for ten years in Arabia. After his return, the army of Cyrus the Persian took Babylon. The centre of world history moved away from the city for the last time.

Babylonian contributions to the world at large stem from the period about 3000–1600 BC, when the Babylonian writing system spread throughout the Near East. It took with it the knowledge of astronomy and mathematics (the divisions of the circle, the hour, and the day), which the Greeks borrowed. Other influences are harder to trace, but were undoubtedly strong.

Assyrian and Babylonian religion

Like most peoples in the ancient world, the people of Babylon and Assyria honoured the great powers of the universe, and had favourite gods or goddesses of their own. They told stories about their gods, gave offerings to them in great temples and small shrines, asked for their help, and hoped for their good will. The gods were in control of everything, and their behaviour was unpredictable.

□ The gods

Anu, king of heaven, was the chief of the gods. He was a remote figure. His son, Enlil, ruled over the earth's surface, and was treated as the king of the gods. Enki, or Ea, had charge of the fresh waters that gave life. Each had a wife and family. Ishtar was the wife of Anu, and far more prominent than he was in religious life. She was in charge of war and of love. Enki was given a son – Marduk – who became very important.

Merduk, also known simply as Bel, 'lord', was the patron god of Babylon. His worship began to grow as Babylon's power increased during the period 2000–1000 BC. As time passed he was raised to be king of all the gods (see below). Marduk's son, Nabu, god of Borsippa near Babylon, rose to high honour in turn.

There were other gods separate from these: Shamash, the sun, god of justice; Sin, the moon, worshipped especially at Ur of the Chaldees and at Harran; Adad, the god of rain and storm. Ideas such as fairness, truth, justice, and time, were also given the status of gods from soon after 2000 BC. In Assyria there was also the

King Ashurbanipal pours a drink-offering over dead lions, in front of an offering table and incense stand.

national god, Ashur, whose name was the same as the capital city and the land it ruled. Ashur's origin is unknown. As Assyria grew strong, her theologians identified him with Enlil, as king of the gods.

In Babylonia clay dogs inscribed 'Don't hesitate, bite', 'He barks loudly', and so on were buried under doorsteps to ward off evil.

□ Demons

The Babylonian world was full of shadows. Evil spirits and demons lurked to catch anyone they could. They would slide under the door to attack a man in his sleep, or to snatch a child from its mother's lap, or bring diseases with the wind. Special priests recited prayers and spells over the sick or injured person, calling on the gods for help. Sometimes the affliction would be transferred by a ritual to a goat or some other substitute, which would then be killed or destroyed. People wore charms and amulets to ward off these evils. They also hung them in the doorways and buried them under the doorsteps. These last were sometimes model dogs inscribed with words such as 'Don't wait, bite!'

□ Worship

Each city had a main temple where the patron god of the city was worshipped. Here the people would gather for major festivals at the New Year and on the god's own special day. They lined the streets when the god's statues were carried in procession, taken on tour from one shrine to another. Usually, it seems, ordinary citizens worshipped at small shrines set amongst the houses of a town. There they could ask the god or goddess for a son, pray for success in business, give him 'thank-you presents', or make offerings to win attention, or persuade the deity to rid them of some misfortune. A priest

would perform rites, speak the correct prayers, and accept the animal or goods offered in sacrifice.

□ Divination

The gods had control of everything, according to Babylonian thought, but they did not reveal the future. People could not be certain about anything. So the Babylonians consulted omens. The livers and other parts of sacrificed animals were inspected for unusual symptoms, to see if the gods had 'written a message' in them. They also used other unpredictable things – the flight of birds, or patterns of oil on water.

Astrologers worked out 'omens' from the movements of the stars. The clear night skies made observation easy. And because each star was linked to a god or goddess, it was possible to make all sorts of deductions about the will of the gods. Some of these arts passed to the Greeks, and so to modern astrology. The zodiac is one legacy of the Babylonian astrologers. The 360° circle, and the 60-minute hour, were also first worked out by the Babylonian star-gazers.

□ Myths

Stories about the gods are available to us in Sumerian and

Akkadian (the languages of the early Babylonians). Some tell of their origins. Generally they say that first of all there was an ocean. The dry land and the heavens were born by the ocean, and they, in the form of gods (Anu, heaven, Ki, earth) produced Enlil.

The creation story. In the well-known Babylonian creation story, *Enuma elish*, which was composed not long before 1000 BC (but based on much older stories), the ocean is hostile to her children because they are noisy and disturb her. She decides to destroy them. They learn of her plan and attack her. One after another is defeated until the young Marduk offers himself as the champion of the gods if they will make him their king. They agree, and he sets out, armed with magic spells, to overcome the ocean, Ti'amat.

He succeeds in killing her. Then he splits her corpse in two, in the way you split a fish, and makes one half the earth, the other the sky. The rivers Tigris and Euphrates flow from her eyes. Her lieutenant, Kingu, is also killed.

Figures of the gods, from Assyria. From left to right: the king, the god Asshur, the goddess Ninlil (his wife), Enlil, Sin (the moon god), Shamash (the sun god), Adad (the weather god, holding a bolt of lightning), Ishtar (goddess of love and war), and the king.

Head of the demon Pazazu, modelled in clay. It may have been buried, like the clay dogs, to ward off evil, or hung on the wall of a house.

Marduk takes from him the Tablet of Destinies – the symbol of final authority – which contains the fate of all creatures. He gives this to Anu. Then, at the suggestion of Enki or Ea, his father, he makes man, using the blood of Kingu. This creature is to work the earth, to produce food and drink for the gods, so that they can rest at ease. Then the shrines of the gods are set up. Marduk is hailed as king of the gods at his shrine in Babylon.

This poem was recited during the New Year feast in Babylon, and probably on other occasions. It was used in Assyria with the name of Ashur instead of Marduk.

The Epic of Atrahasis. Another story, copied about 1635 BC and perhaps composed only a little earlier, is the *Epic of Atrahasis.* This tells a differ-

ent story of man's creation, but is clearly one of the sources of the later Babylonian creation story. The gods already exist when this story begins. Most of them are actually at work digging canals and tilling the soil. But the work is too hard, so they go on strike. They march on Enlil's house to burn it down. Enlil sees them coming, and takes advice in heaven. Eventually it is decided to kill the strike leader and to make a substitute worker, man.

Man is made from the leader's flesh and blood, mixed with clay. He then takes over the work, and the gods relax.

The Assyrian king Tukulti-Ninurta I (about 1200 BC) worships before the symbol of the fire-god.

Man multiplies, and the noise people make disturbs the gods. They try to reduce the noise by sending plagues, famines and droughts. Then the gods get together and decide they will have to destroy their creature completely. But the effect of the plagues had been counteracted by the creator god, Enki, who told his favourite, Atrahasis, to direct all prayer and worship to the appropriate god, so that he would withhold his particular plague.

Enki also warns Atrahasis of the plot to destroy mankind through a great flood, and so he is able to escape with his family and animals in a great boat. When the flood is over and Atrahasis once more offers sacrifices, the gods crowd like flies around the smoke, eager for their food. This story of the flood was retold in the *Epic*

of Gilgamesh and is related to the Genesis story.

☐ **Death and the afterlife**
All the dead were thought to inhabit the underworld. There they lived in a land of dust, fed by offerings of food and drink made by their descendants. If no offerings were made, the ghosts of the dead would come back to haunt their families. So, too, would the ghosts of those who were not properly buried. Apparently the wicked had a worse time than the good, for some of the ancient kings served as judges in the underworld. Ideas of life after death were very vague, and offered the Babylonians no hope.

The Persians

The Persians first appear as a nation about 650 BC under King Cyrus I. They were settled east of the Persian Gulf in an area still called Farsistan. Although no one knows where they came from, their language shows they were one of the Indo-European peoples. It is related to Greek, Latin, French, German and English, but more closely to Sanskrit and other Indian languages.

Cyrus the Great

The Persians make a dramatic entrance into the Bible story at the time when Cyrus' grandson, Cyrus II (the Great), marched into Babylon.

In 550 BC Cyrus had taken control of Ecbatana, the capital of the Medes. He conquered what is now Turkey and moved east into north-west India. By 540 BC he was ready to challenge the power of the Babylonian Empire.

The fall of Babylon

The 'Cyrus Cylinder', buried in the foundations of a building in Babylon, contains the king's own account of how he captured the city. It fell without a battle in 539 BC. The course of the Euphrates River had been diverted, allowing the invaders

The remains of the Persian capital, Persepolis, give just a glimpse of past splendour.

to make their way into the city along the dried-up river-bed. There was no destruction. In fact Cyrus restored the temples and buildings.

Policy change

Under Cyrus images of gods which had been collected into Babylon were sent back to the Babylonian cities where they belonged. As part of the policy of peaceful relations throughout the empire, in 538 BC the Jews were allowed to return to Israel. They took with them the treasures which belonged to the Jerusalem temple, which they were given royal permission to rebuild.

The Persian Empire

The setting of the Bible books of Ezra, Nehemiah, Esther and part of Daniel belongs to the time of the Persian Empire under Cyrus and the kings that followed.

The Persian kings extended their borders even further than the earlier empires. Their land stretched east to India; Turkey and Egypt were under their control. King Darius I (522–486 BC), who built a magnificent palace at Persepolis, took Macedonia in northern Greece in 513. After a setback at Marathon, his son, Xerxes I (486–465), pushed south as far as Athens before losing the sea battle of Salamis (480).

Despite attacks from Greeks and revolts in Egypt, the Persians held their empire for 200 years. Then, in 333 BC, Alexander crossed the Hellespont and quickly defeated the Persians, marching as far as India, and spreading the influence of Greek culture.

Enlightened government

Wise government and administration made it possible for Persia to control far-off nations. Cyrus the Great divided the empire into provinces, each with its own ruler or 'satrap'. These were Persian or Median nobles, but

there were nationals under them who retained power locally. The different peoples were encouraged to keep their own customs and religions, and this helped to keep them happy. Darius I (see Ezra 6) made further improvements to the system of government. He also introduced coinage, and a legal system. His new postal system was a vital aid to communication.

A further unifying factor was the use of Aramaic as the diplomatic language of the empire. Aramaic was already known in Judah from Assyrian times: 'Speak Aramaic to us,' King Hezekiah's officials said to the Assyrian messengers, 'we understand it.' Now the royal decrees were often written in Aramaic. The letters in Ezra 4:18 – 6:18 reflect this practice.

Art and culture

The empire created great wealth, and craftsmen flourished. They were brought from every part of the empire to decorate the new palaces at Persepolis, Pasargadae and Susa, whose ruins still show their former magnificence. Quantities of gold plate and jewelry (the famous Oxus Treasure) reveal the craftsmen's skills, and the beauty of luxury goods. The

This delicately worked chariot and horses is just one example of the Persian craftsmen's skill: it is part of the Oxus Treasure.

Book of Esther provides a glimpse of the splendour of palace life in Persia.

Religion

Ancient Persian beliefs were based upon the life of the herdsman: the gods were partly nature-gods, partly ideas like 'contract' (Mitra) and true speech (Varuna). There were sacrifices of animals, and the drinking of *haoma* or *soma* which produced a state of intoxication. At an unknown date the prophet Zoroaster arose in eastern Persia, preaching the worship of Ahura-mazda as the supreme deity worshipped through fire – yet a god to whom men can talk – and the battle between Good and Evil in which man has a part. Zoroaster's ideas influenced the Persian kings, and spread widely, even affecting Jewish thought.

The Greeks

Until modern times the beginnings of Greece were a puzzle. *The Iliad* and *The Odyssey*, two great poems said to have been written by a blind Greek poet called Homer, about 800 BC, give hints of an even older way of life. Now modern discovery has built up a surprising picture of that early civilization. The Minoans in Crete had built great palaces long before, and traded with Egypt. But their empire fell suddenly, to earthquake or invasion. Its last rulers spoke Greek: tablets with the oldest known Greek language have been found in their palace.

The Iliad tells part of the story of the ten-year war when the Greeks attacked the city of Troy. We now know that there was a real Troy, and an early Greek civilization centred on Mycenae on the mainland of southern Greece. Homer echoes memories of what had really taken place long before.

Early history
Greek-speaking people had entered Greece from the north. Greece is a poor and rocky land. The people lived in small towns separated by the mountains. After the great days of Mycenae, the land was never united. Town fought against town. It was often easier to travel by sea than by land. There was too little fertile land to support the people and the Greeks became adventurous sailors. The regular summer winds and the shelter of the many islands helped them to voyage across the Aegean Sea to Asia (modern Turkey). They imported food, and founded new cities on many parts of the Mediterranean coast, especially in Asia Minor. Greeks in Bible times lived over a far larger area than the land we now call Greece.

The 'golden age'
In the fifth century BC the most famous of the Greek cities was Athens. The Athenians took a leading part in defeating two great attacks on Greece by the Persians in 490 and 480 BC. They became rich and powerful, and built many beautiful temples, including the Parthenon, which can still be seen today. Athens also became the home of some remarkable leaders, thinkers, writers and poets. The names of Pericles, Socrates, Plato, Sophocles, Euripides and others are still famous. These

A Greek Theatre

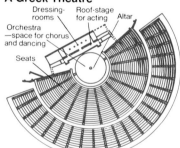

The theatre at Ephesus.

men have had great influence on the world.

Athens was the perfect example of the Greek way of life. It was a 'democracy'. That is a Greek word for a very Greek idea. To an Athenian it meant that every citizen ought to play his part in the affairs of his city. 'Politics' was the business of the 'city' (Greek *polis*). The Greeks were a very gifted people, clever and active, quick to argue, with a great love of freedom, and a feeling for beauty in art and writing. Although they were so divided, they were all very proud of being Greek. They thought of themselves as different from other races, whom they called 'barbarians'. Every four years all the cities met at Olympia in southern Greece for the Olympic Games, and wars between them stopped for that time.

Alexander
Greece was divided and weakened by these bitter local wars. And after 336 BC Alexander the Great, king of Macedon (to the north), conquered the whole country. Alexander's people were Greeks, but had never been important until then. Alexander proved to be a brilliant soldier. He overthrew the great empire of Persia, and made conquests as far east as India. But he was also more than a conqueror. He aimed to spread Greek language and civilization through all this area.

Alexander's hopes were never fulfilled, for he died young, and his generals disputed his empire. It was divided from the start. Ptolemy won Egypt, and founded a line of Greek kings there. Seleucus tried to hold the East, and his line, the Seleucids, made their capital at Antioch in Syria. They struggled for Palestine with the Ptolemies. One of their kings, Antiochus Epiphanes (175–164 BC), became the bitter enemy of the stricter Jews. In Asia Minor, Macedonia and Greece the situation was confused, as rival kings fought for power.

Greek influence

The high point of Greek civilization belongs to the period before Alexander. The later period is known as the Hellenistic age (from *Hellēn*, meaning 'Greek'). During this time Greek became an international language for the eastern Mediterranean and beyond. It was the language of trade, and of education and writing, even for people who still usually spoke their own languages. Even the Jews were influenced by it. In the second century BC the Old Testament

The Parthenon at Athens.

was translated into Greek at Alexandria in Egypt, for the Greek-speaking Jews there.

This translation, called the Septuagint, was the version of the Old Testament best known to the first Christians.

As the power of Rome increased, the Romans became involved in the affairs of Greece. In 146 BC they destroyed Corinth, which had

resisted them. This was the end of Greek political freedom. But their Roman conquerors took over Greek ways of thinking. Greek was established as the official language of the eastern half of the Roman Empire. It was natural for the New Testament to be written in Greek.

The New Testament

The New Testament often mentions Greeks. It sometimes means simply non-Jews (Gentiles), Greek-speaking people of the Roman world. Very little of its story takes place in the land of Greece. Yet Paul, though a strict Jew, wrote in Greek and understood Greek ways of thinking. He knew, for instance, of the Greek interest in athletics, and pictured the Christian life as a race and a boxing match (1 Corinthians 9:24–27). Most of his work was in cities of the Greek kind, especially in Asia Minor (Turkey), which at that time contained some of the largest and richest Greek towns, such as Ephesus. These cities still had their rights, and lived a busy public life. There were meetings, markets, committees, elections, debates, sports, and theatres. They had trade-unions, and even strikes and demonstrations. But the real power belonged to the Roman governor.

Christian meets Greek

The classic meeting of Christian with Greek took place in Athens itself. It was still a university town, though now living on its past glory. Paul found it a city full of religious images. He began to argue with those whom he met in the public square, and was called before the 'Court of the Areopagus' to present his new ideas. Paul spoke in terms they would understand. He quoted their poets. He dealt with the arguments of the Stoics and Epicureans, two leading parties among their thinkers. But he was deeply in earnest, and had more than this to say. For all

A statue of Sophocles, the great Greek playwright.

the cleverness of their scholars they did not know God. He said boldly that God does not 'live in man-made temples' (Acts 17:24) like the beautiful ones that stood all around them. God called all people to change their way of life. He would judge all by Jesus, whom he had raised from the dead.

Most of the Athenians were unwilling to receive these teachings. Greeks, said Paul, looked for 'wisdom', but his message was foolish to them (1 Corinthians 1:22–23). Their thinkers took a different view of life after death. They were proud and did not care to open their minds to the evidence for such a disturbing challenge to their ways.

Greek Religion

See under *The Romans*.

The Romans

The beginnings of the city of Rome are lost in legend. The story was that it had been named after its founder, Romulus, whose ancestors had escaped from the Greek destruction of Troy. The date was said to be 753 BC. That was the year from which the later Romans counted the beginning of their history.

Early history
For centuries Rome was a small and struggling city-state. But it was well placed at a crossing of the River Tiber in the centre of Italy. At first it had kings, and some of them probably belonged to a mysterious and almost forgotten nation, the Etruscans. These kings were at last driven out, and Rome became a 'Republic', headed by two 'consuls' elected for a year and a council called the 'Senate'. After times of strife, poverty and war, Rome slowly won ground, and by 275 BC controlled all Italy.

Rome grew partly by war, but also by a policy of alliances in which Roman citizenship and other rights were freely

A poultry shop. The shops in Rome opened early, closed at midday, and opened again later. They traded in the streets as well as in shops.

granted to allies. Right from the start the Romans were good organizers. They built fine roads and unified the whole of Italy. They were very different in character from the Greeks. They were not very original. But they were practical men, loyal to the state, hard-working and disciplined.

Wars
It was not long before Rome faced a new enemy, Carthage. Carthage was on the coast of modern Tunisia, and controlled the sea-routes and trade of the western Mediterranean. The struggle was to last for over a century. The Carthaginians had a leader of genius, Hannibal. He is best remembered for his bold crossing of the Alps with elephants. He invaded Italy and defeated Rome on her own soil, but he got no support and finally had to retreat. The Romans destroyed Carthage in 146 BC.

By this time Rome had also been drawn into the affairs of the East, where Hannibal had joined Rome's enemies. The Romans defeated Antiochus III of Syria and gave his lands in Asia Minor to their ally Eumenes II of Pergamum.

The Romans built aqueducts as part of a scheme to bring water from the mountains to the cities.

They destroyed Corinth in 146, and began direct rule over Greece. In 133 the last king of Pergamum left his lands to the Romans. Out of them they made the province of 'Asia'.

World power
So Rome became a world power. But there were great changes. The Greeks had a remarkable influence on their conquerors. Romans studied Greek language and thought and copied Greek styles of art and writing. But there were also other changes, for the worse. Asia, in particular, was very rich, and Roman officials began to use their new position to enrich themselves by robbing their subjects. The Senate in Rome was not able to control them. And this was only part of a larger problem. It was not possible to govern a world empire in the same way as a small city. Large armies and regular organization were needed. Ambitious men began to struggle for power. As a result, there were several civil wars in the first century BC.

In 63 BC the Roman general, Pompey, occupied Jerusalem. From that time Rome had a controlling influence on Palestine. Later, Pompey became the Republican champion, against the ambitious Julius

Chariot-racing was one of the popular sports.

Ploughing. The farmer's crops were needed to feed the city-dwellers.

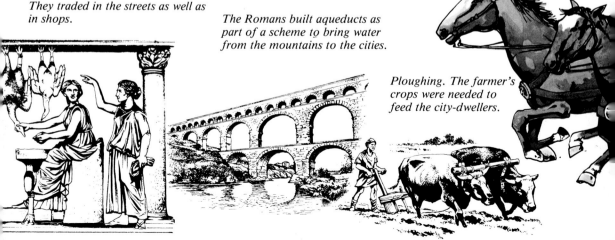

Caesar. But Caesar defeated him and took the title 'dictator', a position which gave him special emergency powers. Caesar was a brilliantly able and vigorous ruler. But he was murdered in 44 by the Republicans Brutus and Cassius. Caesar's friend Antony and his heir Octavian defeated the Republicans in 42 at Philippi in Macedonia, a city well known in the New Testament. Then the two victors quarrelled. Octavian defeated Anthony and his ally Cleopatra, queen of Egypt.

The City of Rome

The Empire and the emperors

People were weary of so many years of war. Octavian gave

Roman coins.

them peace. In 27 BC he received the title 'Augustus'. He claimed to have brought back the Republic and was careful to disguise his real power. He kept control of the army and became, in fact, the first ruler of what we call the 'Empire', though he never used the word. He united the whole Mediterranean world under one peaceful government. It became possible to travel safely by land or sea to every part. There was great thankfulness everywhere for Augustus. He died in AD 14.

Jesus was born in the time of Augustus (Luke 2:1). His teaching, death and resurrection took place in the reign of the next emperor, Tiberius (AD 14–37). Paul travelled during the reigns of Claudius (AD 41–54) and Nero (AD 54–68), the 'Caesar' to whom he appealed at his trial (Acts 25:11).

The Romans and the Jews

Palestine was occupied by the Romans in the time of Jesus. They tried at first to rule there through kings of the Herod family. When this failed in Judea, they sent a Roman governor called a 'procurator'. Although the first emperors were usually careful to respect the feelings of their subjects, they found it difficult to cope with the religion and nationalism of the Jews. Pontius Pilate (AD 26–36) and his successors angered them by their harsh misrule, and in AD 66 there was a desperate rebellion against

Life for ordinary people centred on home and family.

The Colosseum, Rome. This amphitheatre could hold 50,000 spectators.

Rome. When Nero died, rival generals fought for power in Rome. Vespasian, commander of the Syrian frontier army, finally won and became emperor (AD 69–79). It was his son Titus who ended the Jewish rebellion. He destroyed Jerusalem and its temple in AD 70.

Rome had often favoured and protected the Jews in the past. Paul was both a Jew and a Roman citizen. He naturally looked to Rome for justice and protection. Rome had provided

Men at work building the roads for which the Romans are still famous.

the peace and freedom to travel and spread the gospel. When Paul was treated unjustly he used his right as a Roman to appeal to the Emperor. He may not then have known what an evil man Nero was becoming.

Life in Rome

Rome was now the centre of the world, a city of well over a million people. We have vivid pictures of its life: the tall buildings and narrow, congested streets where people lived in fear of fire, and the constant noise of carts kept them awake all night. The emperors and nobles lived in great luxury, but also in fear. There were free men and slaves of many races thronging the streets. The emperors tried to keep the peace by bringing corn from Egypt and organizing bloodthirsty public shows where men or beasts fought to the death. When a great fire broke out in Rome in AD 64, Nero blamed the Christians, and tortured many of them to death.

The good and the bad

For all its achievements there was clearly a bad side to Roman civilization. We can understand how Rome was hated in the occupied country of Palestine. Governors like Pilate, Felix and Festus had no interest in the matters of faith which Jews and Christians debated. Yet Jesus commended a Roman's faith (Luke 7:1ff.) and Peter found another Roman officer, Cornelius, to be a man who sincerely sought God (Acts 10; 11).

After the fall of Jerusalem Christians faced new problems. The Emperor Domitian (81–96) insisted on being worshipped as a god. A faithful Christian could not obey. Rome became an enemy. The Book of Revelation was written when Christians needed strength to meet Roman persecution. Rome on its seven hills (Revelation 17:9) was pictured as a luxury-loving prostitute, like ancient Babylon.

Greek and Roman religion

The Roman Empire covered a very large area, and included peoples with many different beliefs. Those living in the eastern Empire were the ones whom the early Christians first met. They were often influenced by eastern ideas which had been handed down from long before Greek civilization came to them.

The Minoans of Crete and the oldest peoples of Greece worshipped a fertility goddess. Like Baal in the Canaanite myths her consort-god was believed to die and rise again, like the seasons of the year. The details of this kind of religion varied from place to place, but many of these ideas were common throughout the eastern Mediterranean lands. They remained especially strong in country districts, where people's living depended on their herds and crops.

☐ The gods of Greece and Rome

The first Greeks brought with them a new group of gods. Their supreme god was Zeus. He ruled over the other gods who lived on Olympus, the highest mountain in Greece. The Greeks were a logical people, and tried to build complete family histories of the gods and fit all the older beliefs and local stories into the system. So these gods were pictured vividly. They were like people in the way they behaved – often jealous or vengeful, or immoral – but of course they were far more powerful.

Roman religion was really quite different. But when the Romans conquered the Greeks they took over all their gods and gave them Roman names. So Zeus became the Roman god Jupiter. His wife Hera became the Roman Juno, and his brother Poseidon, god of the sea, was given the name Neptune.

Among the other gods were Ares (Mars), god of war; Hermes (Mercury), the messenger of the gods; Hades or

A woman in her home makes the morning offering to the household gods.

Pluto (Dis), god of the dead; Hephaestus (Vulcan), the lame craftsman; and Apollo, god of wisdom.

The best-known of the other goddesses were Artemis (Diana), the huntress and twin sister of Apollo; Athena (Minerva), patroness of art and war; Aphrodite (Venus), goddess of love; and Demeter (Ceres), goddess of the harvest.

These names were remembered long after people ceased to believe in these gods. Some of them are still in use as the names of planets.

☐ Festivals

Greek religion was based on the city. There were great festivals in which everybody took part together, and social events were based on religion. The Olympic Games were first held as a religious event to honour Zeus. The plays in the theatre at Athens, tragedies and comedies, were performed at the festival of the god Dionysus. And the greatest works of Greek art all had a religious meaning.

Yet this religion did not satisfy people. It offered no real answers to the problems of good and evil, life and death. Life was uncertain. These gods had no power to save their cities from sudden disaster. People looked for purpose in life. Why should they live good lives if the gods could not give them justice?

☐ The philosophers

Many thoughtful people turned to philosophy. Plato wrote

down the discussions of his master Socrates, about subjects like justice and life after death, and built up a noble system of thought. Later the Stoics advised people to live in harmony with reason. And the Epicureans believed the world had come about by the chance meeting of atoms. They thought that men should live quietly without fear. Others made new moral lessons from the old stories of the gods. But many were near despair. They worshipped Tyche ('Chance'), and hoped that then the chances of life might favour them. Or they turned to astrology or magic.

New religions

Others found hope in new religions, often from the East,

which promised a personal 'salvation' to the worshipper. This idea was a very important one, but it meant very different things to different people – being saved from evil or death, or from trouble or danger, or being given success in life. It was a fashionable word, rather as people speak of 'security' today. A victorious king was often honoured as the 'saviour' of his people. He was the one who could give them what they needed. It was only a matter of time before some of his less sophisticated subjects began worshipping him as a god.

The Romans

Little is really known about the earliest Roman religion, but it

A Greek temple at Delphi.

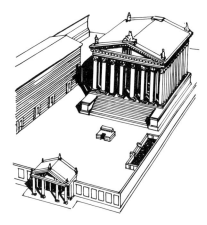

A reconstructed Roman temple at Baalbek, Syria.

was clearly then very different from that of the Greeks. The early Romans felt that a divine power (*numen*) existed in

nature, and they wanted to harness it to their needs. So there were 'gods' for every area of life: gods of the house and of its doorway, of the fields, and so on. Most of these seem to us to have had a vague kind of existence. Only a few of the official gods of the state, like Jupiter, were clearly pictured as persons. But then Greek influence came, and the old Roman gods were fitted into the Greek system. Roman beliefs merged with Greek ideas in such a way that it is hard to separate out what is purely Roman.

□ Religion and the ordinary man

Many things were always common to both Greeks and Romans. Both worshipped many gods, but their religion had little effect on the way the worshipper lived. Neither belief nor behaviour was really important. A person might believe what he wished, as long

as he did what was expected of a good citizen, and remained loyal to the state. There was no great stress on a search for truth, nor was there any powerful body of priests. The gods were distant. They were to be paid due honour. But they were not deeply interested in human affairs.

Educated Romans in the time of Julius Caesar (first century BC) often had little regard for these gods. They would use the forms of religion for their own ends when there was some personal advantage or a political point to gain. But if they thought seriously about life they turned, like the Greeks, to philosophy or new religions.

□ The emperor

Augustus (27 BC–AD 14) tried to revive Roman religion in a more splendid form. His chosen title, 'Augustus', had a sense of religious awe. He wanted to use religion to bind people in loyalty to his own government. In the East he was worshipped as a god in his lifetime, for he had brought peace and good government to a world torn by war. A great temple was built to Rome and Augustus at Pergamum (near the west coast of modern Turkey).

Archaeologists have re-erected one column of the temple of Artemis ('Diana of the Ephesians') at Ephesus – one of the wonders of the ancient world.

□ The mysteries

Those who wanted a more personal faith went to the 'mystery' religions. Here the worshipper was admitted step by step into the secret inner spiritual knowledge of the faith. The mysteries at Eleusis in Greece had been known since early times. But many new foreign cults became popular in the Greek and Roman world of the first century AD. The Egyptian goddess Isis had many priests and an impressive ritual, and was thought to answer prayer. The Persian Mithras was the soldier's god. Men advanced from rank to rank in his service in the fight against evil. For a time Mithraism was one of the most serious rivals of Christianity.

□ Rome and the Christians

Rome usually allowed these different beliefs to flourish. But groups which might not be loyal to the state were always banned. Judaism was specially allowed and, at first, Christianity was too, because it seemed to be a kind of Judaism. But, as time went on, the Romans began to use emperor worship as a test of loyalty. The Emperor Domitian

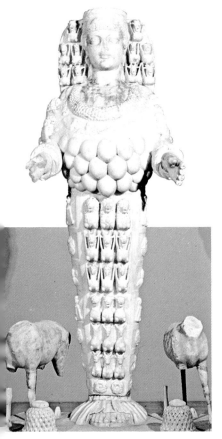

A statue of Diana (Artemis) at Ephesus.

(AD 81–96) required people to worship him as 'lord and god'. So the position of Christians changed and they had to be ready to suffer for their faith. That was the situation when the Book of Revelation was written.

The New Testament accounts of other religions are mostly set in the East (especially in modern Turkey). At Lystra, Paul and Barnabas were mistaken for Hermes and Zeus (Acts 14:12–13). At Ephesus the famous temple of Artemis was one of the 'seven wonders of the world' (Acts 19). She was really an eastern fertility goddess fitted to a Greek name. Paul answered these ideas at Lystra and at Athens: God creates, supplies, loves and judges all men.

☐ **Gnosticism**
Most of these religions easily became mixed. And about the time of the New Testament there arose a kind of thinking called 'Gnosticism'. Gnostics believed that 'spirit' was good and that material things were evil. Gnosticism came to be mixed with Christian and other ideas. But because it put other beings between God and man it denied the special place of Christ. Gnosticism, like the mystery religions, appealed to people who boasted of having a special inner knowledge (*gnōsis*) that was better than the simple 'trust' that Christians talked of. Paul opposed the beginnings of this kind of thinking at Colossae. It became a serious problem for the church in the second century.

Other Nations

NATIONS TO THE NORTH

The great powers to the north in Bible times were Assyria and Babylon (see pages 289–291). But the closest of Israel's northern neighbours was a Canaanite people.

Phoenicians
The Israelites never occupied all of the land God originally promised to them. The Canaanites whose homeland it had been for centuries (see page 284) remained in some areas, particularly on the coast to the north-west – modern Lebanon. One of their towns was the ancient city of Byblos, possibly the place where the alphabet was invented. At any rate the Greeks, who borrowed the alphabet, also borrowed the name of the city as their word for book (*biblos*).

☐ **Trade**
Byblos had a flourishing merchant shipping trade from at least the eighteenth century BC. But it is two nearby ports that are most often mentioned in the Bible. The power of Tyre and Sidon increased and overtook Byblos after 1000 BC. It was about this time that David and Solomon formed trade alliances with King Hiram of Tyre. He supplied fine wood, and gold, and skilled craftsmen for building the temple and palaces at Jerusalem, in return for twenty towns in Galilee (1 Kings 9:10ff.). Hiram and Solomon also combined in operating a fleet on the Red Sea. The ships brought back gold and jewels.

The chief exports of Tyre and Sidon were cedarwood from the mountains of

Lebanon and purple dye from cuttle-fish. But the people built their empire on trade. They were middlemen, dealing in linen from Egypt, silver, iron and tin from Spain, ivory and ebony from the coastlands (Ezekiel 27 gives a very full description).

They spread their colonies across the Mediterranean, to North Africa, Italy, and Spain, where they were known as the Phoenicians. Their language was a form of Canaanite, similar to Hebrew, but their literature is known only at second-hand. Their religion, too, continued Canaanite ideas (see Part 5: *Religion and Worship in the Bible*). It was brought into Israel by the marriage of King Ahab to Jezebel, daughter of the king of Sidon. Ahab built a temple to Baal at his capital and Jezebel and the prophets of

Figures in bronze with gold decoration left by worshippers in a Canaanite temple at Byblos, eighteenth century BC.

Baal threatened Elijah's life (1 Kings 18).

Aramaeans and Chaldaeans

Inland from Phoenicia, other related (Semitic) tribes had settled at the time when Israel was moving into Canaan. These were the Aramaeans (Syrians in the Authorized/ King James' Version). We know some of their history from Hebrew and Assyrian records, and a few inscriptions written in Aramaic. There were several tribes, each centred on one city. They were scattered throughout Syria, across to Assyria, and down the River Euphrates into Babylonia where one branch became the nation of the Chaldaeans. Smaller kingdoms north of Galilee were soon absorbed by Israel and by the major Aramaean kingdom, Damascus.

In the reign of Solomon Damascus won independence from Israel, and a strong line of kings built up power there (see 1 Kings 11:23; 15:18). Until the Assyrians made Damascus a province in 732 BC its kings (including Ben-Hadad and Hazael who feature in the Bible stories) were often at war with Israel and Judah, trying to control the roads to Egypt and Arabia. From time to time they were able to dominate their fellow Aramaean rulers to the north, and in the seaports.

□ Aramaic

Because they were so widespread (this increased even more when Assyrian kings conquered and deported many of them to Assyria and Persia), their language – Aramaic – became the common language for diplomats and traders all over the Near East from about 750 BC. When King Sennacherib's Assyrian officials came to threaten Jerusalem, King Hezekiah's men begged them to speak in Aramaic. The decrees of the Persian kings were written in Aramaic. When the people living in the land had complaints against the Jews who returned with Zerubbabel, they wrote to the king in Aramaic. Part of the Book of Daniel is also in Aramaic.

After Alexander brought Greek to the Near East, Aramaic took second place for official purposes. But it remained the common language over a wide area and was spoken by the Jews in Israel in New Testament times. The New Testament contains several Aramaic phrases, for example: *talitha koum (cumi), abba* (the everyday word for 'father'), and *Eli, eli lama sabachthani* (Jesus' words from the cross).
2 Kings 18:26; Ezra 7:12–26; 4:7 – 6:18; Daniel 2:4 – 7:28; Mark 5:41; 14:36; Matthew 27:46

Hittites

Before the time of the Israelites and Aramaeans, Syria was controlled by the Hittites from Turkey. They were an Indo-European race who built up an empire which was very powerful from about 1600–1300 BC. Their capital city was Hattusha (now Bogazköy), near Ankara, the modern capital of Turkey. In its ruins the royal archives have been found. They are written in the Babylonian cuneiform script on clay tablets, but in the Hittite languages. Amongst the important documents are many treaties made with subject states. These follow a set pattern – the same pattern followed in Exodus and Deuteronomy, where God's treaties with his people, Israel, are set down.

The Hittites also developed a hieroglyphic writing of their

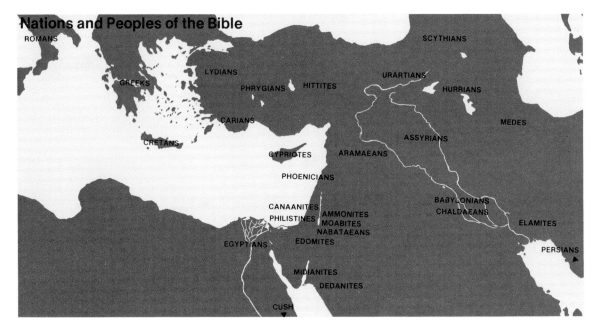

Nations and Peoples of the Bible

ROMANS
SCYTHIANS
LYDIANS
GREEKS
PHRYGIANS HITTITES
URARTIANS
HURRIANS
CARIANS
MEDES
CRETANS
ASSYRIANS
CYPRIOTES
ARAMAEANS
PHOENICIANS
BABYLONIANS
CHALDAEANS
CANAANITES
PHILISTINES AMMONITES
MOABITES
NABATAEANS
EDOMITES
EGYPTIANS
ELAMITES
PERSIANS
MIDIANITES
DEDANITES
CUSH

Jbail in Lebanon, the Phoenician harbour of Byblos.

own. In 1286 BC the Hittites fought the Egyptians at the Battle of Qadesh. Neither side won, so they drew up a treaty to agree a border. This was roughly the line followed by the northern boundary of Israel's Promised Land (see Joshua 1:4). About 1200 BC the Hittite Empire disappeared under the attacks of the Sea Peoples (see *Philistines*). Their culture was lost, except in a few outposts. These included some places in northern Syria (Carchemish, Hamath), where descendants of the Hittites mingled with other peoples. Hittite kings and Hittite women are still mentioned in the time of Solomon and even of Elisha – 1 Kings 10:28ff.; 11:1; 2 Kings 7:6. (The Hittites living in Canaan very much earlier – at the time of Abraham, Genesis 23 – may have been migrants from the north, or a separate group.)

Hurrians
One group which became part of the Hittite Empire was the Hurrian people. They are known from 2500 BC in Babylonia. But their origin is uncertain and their language – recorded in cuneiform texts – is not properly understood. Groups of them settled throughout the Fertile Crescent. They appear in Edom (the Horites, Genesis 14:6), in Shechem and in Gilgal (the Hivites, Genesis 34:2;

Joshua 9:3–7). Hurrian names occur on cuneiform tablets of about 1400 BC found in Canaan, and Egyptian texts refer to Canaan as 'Huru'. At that time there was an important Hurrian state in upper Mesopotamia (Mitanni). These kings wrote letters to the pharaohs of Egypt. Among their gods they worshipped Mithra and others well known in India. The Hurrians had a strong influence on the Hittites, and they carried Babylonian culture wherever they went.

Smaller states
After the fall of the Hittites, smaller states appeared in Turkey.

☐ Carians
In the south-west was Caria. The Indo-European Carians remain virtually unknown. We are not yet able to read their alphabet. They served as mercenary soldiers in Egypt, where their inscribed gravestones have been discovered, and in Judah.
2 Kings 11:4, 19

☐ Lydians
On the west coast lived another Indo-European people, the Lydians. Inscriptions and objects unearthed in their capital, Sardis, are beginning to reveal their culture and history. Gyges (Gog), who was king about 650 BC, was used by the prophet Ezekiel as a figure standing for a distant ruler. Obadiah refers to Sardis (Sepharad) as one of many places of exile. Lydia had rich deposits of gold. It was here that coinage began and the wealthy Croesus ruled. He was defeated by Cyrus the Persian in 546 BC. Lydia (Lud) is named as an ally of Tyre and Egypt in Ezekiel. From 133 BC it was part of the Roman province of Asia.
Ezekiel 38:2; Obadiah 20; Ezekiel 27:10; 30:5

☐ Phrygians
East of Lydia was Phrygia, the home of another Indo-

European group. In Assyrian records and the Old Testament it is called Meshech. According to Ezekiel it was a warlike nation, trading in copper and slaves. Several of the rulers were named Midas (though this may be a title, like 'pharaoh') and were buried in richly furnished tombs around Gordium, the capital, which has recently been excavated. After the middle of the seventh century BC, Phrygia came under Lydian rule (an event reflected in Ezekiel 38 and 39). In 116 BC it became part of Roman Asia. From 25 BC the eastern part was counted as being in Galatia.
Ezekiel 32:26; 38:2, 3; 39:1; 27:13; 38; 39

☐ Urartians
Still further to the east lay the kingdom of the Urartians. This was a very different race, which may be linked to the Hurrians and the Armenians. Its name was given to the mountains in their land. The highest of all is now called Mount Ararat. It was on one of the mountains of the Ararat range that Noah's ark came to rest. About 750–650 BC strong Urartian kings tried to dominate northern Syria and check the Assyrians. They gave sanctuary to the sons who murdered King Sennacherib. Their temples and palaces show distinctive designs and decoration. But they used the cuneiform script to write their language. The Urartians worshipped a god called Haldi, and called themselves the children of Haldi.
Genesis 8:4; 2 Kings 19:37

☐ Scythians
The horse-riding Scythians ('Ashkenaz') came from central Asia in the seventh century BC. Some groups of Scythians burst into the Near East. They destroyed Urartu, and joined with the Medes, in alliance with Babylon, to overthrow Assyria. In due course they provided men for the Persian army. One Scythian troop marched through Syria to raid

Egypt, reaching Ashkelon about 630 BC.
Jeremiah 51:17

TO THE EAST

Away to the east, beyond Assyria and Babylonia, the Israelites knew that there were other peoples. But they had little contact with any of them until late in their history, after their own state had collapsed.

Elamites
The oldest of these were Elamites, an isolated nation whose chief city was Susa. They had lived there from prehistoric times. Their culture shared with the Sumerians (see *Babylonians*) in the earliest cities and writing. Their king, Chedorlaomer, joined the attack on cities in the Jordan Valley, and was defeated by Abram. The Elamites were often under the thumb of their western neighbours. The Assyrians sent some of the citizens of Samaria to Elam and Elamites were sent to Israel to replace them. Elam became part of the Persian kingdom.
Jews from 'Elam', the semi-independent kingdom called Elymais in Greek, heard Peter in Jerusalem on the Day of Pentecost.
Genesis 14:1; Ezra 4:9; Isaiah 11:11; 21:2; Jeremiah 25:25; Acts 2:9

Medes
In north-west Persia, Assyrian kings met Median tribes from the ninth century BC onwards. They were on fairly good terms for two hundred years. Then the Medes joined with the Scythians, in alliance with Babylon, to bring about the downfall of Assyria (612 BC). The Medes had already been under Scythian pressure for

A bearded sphinx which decorates a palace staircase at Persepolis, Persia.

some decades. But this time the Median king, Cyaxares, had built up his own strength, and was able to extend his rule as far as the Lydian frontier in Turkey, and over the Persians to his south.
Astyages, next king of the Medes, was overthrown by his son-in-law, Cyrus the Persian, in 549 BC. Media then became a province of the new Persian Empire. They played their part in the fall of Babylon. Media's capital, Ecbatana (modern Hamadan), became the Persian capital. Median officers held high positions in the Persian court, and Median words were adopted into Persian. Median influence was so strong in the Persian Empire that we find the joint phrase 'Medes and Persians' being used. And the Greeks called their great Persian war 'the war with the Medes'.
One tribe of Medes, the Magi, had a special religious position (like that of the Levites in Israel).
Jeremiah 25:25; 51:11, 28; Daniel 5:28

ACROSS THE JORDAN

Three nations settled on the east of the River Jordan about the same time as Israel occupied their land. Their history is known only from references in the Old Testament, in Assyrian inscriptions, and from archaeological discoveries.

Ammonites
North of the Dead Sea, between the Arnon and Jabbok rivers, lived the Ammonites. They were related to the Israelites through Lot, and did not stand in their way on the march to the Promised Land. But they did attack later, during the days of the Judges and of Saul. King Nahash made peace with David. But his son insulted David's messengers and hired men from Aram to fight for him. David's generals captured his capital, modern Amman, and took control of the land. In the reigns of later kings, Ammonites often raided across the Jordan, and were again made subject when Judah was strong. After the exile, the Ammonite Tobiah interfered with Nehemiah's work.
The Ammonite kingdom was protected from raiders by a series of stone watch-towers. Excavation done in Ammon reveals ruined houses and tombs with pottery like that of the Israelites, stone statues, seals engraved with their owners' names, and a few brief inscriptions, which show that their language was similar to Hebrew. The main road east of the Jordan – the King's Highway – brought traders through the Ammonite kingdom on their way from Damascus to the Gulf of Aqaba. These were a source of wealth and a strong cultural and religious influence.
Genesis 19:38; Judges 3:13; 10; 11; 1 Samuel 11; 12:12; 14:47; 2 Samuel 10; 12:26–31; 2 Chronicles 20:1–30; 26:8; 27:5; Nehemiah 2:10, 19; 4:3, 7

Moabites
South of the River Arnon was Moabite country. These people, related to Israel and Ammon – again through Lot, Genesis 19:37 – would not let Israel pass through their land to Canaan. And they constantly harassed the Israelites for much of the Old Testament period. Moab is listed among the countries attacked by Ramesses II of Egypt (about

1283 BC). The city of Dibon was taken. Here, much later, King Mesha recorded his triumph over Israel on a famous stone (the Moabite Stone). The inscription shows that his language was similar to Hebrew. His belief that his god (Chemosh) acted in history was also very much like Israel's belief.
Numbers 21; Judges 11:17; 3:12–30; 1 Samuel 14:47; 2 Samuel 8:2, 12; 2 Kings 13:20; 24:2; 1:1; 3:4–27

Edomites

Another people related to Israel who also refused to let the Israelites pass through their land were the Edomites. The land of Edom lay south of Moab, stretching down to the Gulf of Aqaba. The Edomites lived here, ruled by kings, from

an early date. Some Edomites travelled as traders; others worked at copper mining and farming. Like their neighbours they were hostile to Israel. They were conquered more than once, but often broke free again. Their Red Sea port, Ezion-geber (Elath), was used by Solomon and later kings. Many Hebrew prophets spoke bitter words against Edom. The Edomites took advantage of the exile to occupy much of southern Judah. This area, known later as Idumaea, was

In this frieze at Persepolis, ancient capital of Persia, a Mede leads pointed-capped Scythians, bringing gold bracelets and cloth.

the home of the Herod family who ruled Judea in New Testament times.
Genesis 36:1–19, 36–39; 1 Kings 9:26; 22:48; 2 Kings 14:22; Amos 1:11–12; Jeremiah 49:7–22; Obadiah

Amalekites

These people were related to Edom and Israel (like the Edomites they were descendants of Esau). They were a nomadic tribe and at the time of the exodus attacked Israel in the Sinai desert and further north. In the days of the Judges they often raided Israel. They were bitter enemies of Israel for many centuries.
Genesis 36:12, 16; Exodus 17:8–13; Numbers 14:43, 45; Judges 3:13; 6; 7:12; Deuteronomy 25:19; 1 Samuel 15; 30:1–20; 1 Chronicles 4:43

Arabian tribes

Arabia was the home of several tribes who make brief appearances in Israelite history.

☐ Midianites

The Midianites lived south of Edom along the Red Sea coast, engaging in trade and riding in on camels to raid the settled lands. Moses met them in the Sinai Desert and married a

The treasury, Petra (in modern Jordan). The beautiful rock-cut city of Petra was the capital of the Nabataean kingdom.

Midianite wife. The Midianites were descendants of Abraham through his second wife, Keturah.
Genesis 37:28; Judges 6 – 8; Exodus 2:16ff.; 3:1; Genesis 25:1–6

☐ Dedan

Within the general area of Midian the city of Dedan (now Al-'Ula) later grew up. This major trading centre was known even to the Babylonians.
Isaiah 21:13; Jeremiah 25:23; 49:8; Ezekiel 27:20

☐ Nabataeans

After the time of Alexander the Great, another Arab tribe, the Nabataeans, made their home in Edomite and Midianite territory, building up a strong kingdom by controlling the trade which brought incense from southern Arabia to Damascus and across to Gaza. For a few years they ruled Damascus (2 Corinthians 11:32) but were conquered by Trajan of Rome in AD 106. Their chief city was Petra.

Ararat (in eastern Turkey), the highest mountain in the kingdom of the ancient Urartians.

TO THE SOUTH

Cush (Sudan)

To the south of Egypt lies the Sudan (Old Testament 'Cush'). Pharaoh Tirhakah (see above) came from Cush. But usually Egypt dominated, and Cushite soldiers served in her armies. Ebedmelech, who rescued Jeremiah, was a Sudanese. An independent kingdom existed there in Hellenistic and Roman times, with its capital at Meröe. Queens, entitled Candace, often ruled this state and it was the chancellor of one of these whom Philip met going home from Jerusalem. 2 Kings 19:9; Jeremiah 38:7; Acts 8:27

THE ISLANDS

The Israelites had no good seaport and never gained much knowledge of the Mediterranean. They were only vaguely aware of the existence of the peoples of Cyprus and Crete.

☐ Cypriotes

The Cypriotes had close links with Syria and Israel/Judah through trade ('purple from the island of Cyprus', Ezekiel 27:7). In early times the island was known as Elisha or Alashiya, and was a major source of copper. Flourishing cities with colonies of Myceneans from Greece were destroyed by the Sea Peoples (see *Philistines*) about 1200 BC. One city that revived afterwards was Kition, modern Larnaca (Old Testament 'Kittim'), whose name was sometimes used for the whole island, and even for the opposite coasts. As a distant place, the name was used to stand for Rome in Daniel 11:30. Cyprus came under the rule of Rome in 58 BC, and was governed by a proconsul from 27 BC. It was a natural stopping-place for ships passing from the eastern Mediterranean coast to Turkey or Rome.

☐ Cretans

Crete is known in the Old Testament and other ancient texts as Caphtor. The Minoan civilization flourished there from 2000 BC, merging with the Mycenaean. It fell in the twelfth century BC. The Cretan scripts Linear A and Linear B represent a local form of writing. Linear B was adopted for an early form of Greek. Caphtor was one of the places from which the Philistines came. Later inhabitants probably supplied David's bodyguard of Cherethites. One Cretan poet — Epimenides — had some strong words to say about the Cretans. But some responded to the Christian message. Jeremiah 47:4; Acts 18:28; Titus 1:12

Here, from Egypt through the lands of the eastern Mediterranean to the Tigris–Euphrates basin, is the arena of Bible history.

12

Atlas of Bible History

Beginnings: Creation to the Flood and After

The first eleven chapters of Genesis, the first book of the Bible, look back to the very beginning. Our world and everything in it – sun, moon, land and water, birds, animals and every living creature – was made by God. Everything God made was good. And the high point of God's creation was the making of people to take charge of the world and to enjoy God's friendship.

Sadly this perfect world was soon shattered. The first humans, prompted by evil, chose to disobey God. Sin, suffering and death became a permanent part of the pattern of life. The free and open relationship with God was a thing of the past. Already a new creation was needed.

The scene grew darker as evil actions multiplied, until God's judgement became inevitable. The flood was his response. But God had not entirely given up on his world: one good man, Noah, and his family, together with a pair of each bird, animal and reptile, was saved.

God gave Noah the plan for a gigantic boat (the ark) which would float on the rising waters. The measurements given are enormous: about $450 \times 76 \times 45$ ft/$137 \times 23 \times 14$ m (more than half the length of a modern Atlantic liner). It had a wooden framework bound with reeds and sealed with a thick layer of tar.

For five months the rain fell and the flood rose to cover the

The eleventh tablet of the Assyrian version of the Epic of Gilgamesh, *which tells the Babylonian story of the flood (seventh century BC).*

earth. It took a further seven and a half months before the ground dried and Noah and his family were able to leave.

God promised that while seed-time and harvest last he will never again destroy the earth by flood: the rainbow is the lasting sign of a promise he will never break.

□ Setting
The story of mankind begins in Eden, placed somewhere in Mesopotamia, the region which became (with Egypt) one of the two great centres of civilization in the Near East before 3000 BC. The story of Noah, too, belongs here, in the land of the two great rivers,

In the beginning, the Bible says, God created everything that exists – and it was good.

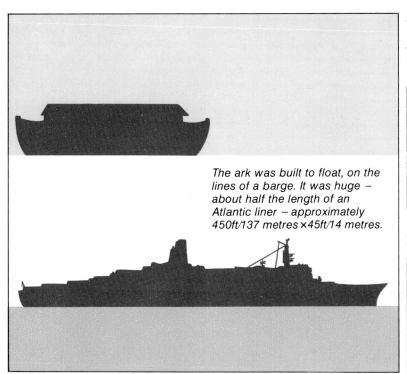

The ark was built to float, on the lines of a barge. It was huge – about half the length of an Atlantic liner – approximately 450ft/137 metres×45ft/14 metres.

Mt Ararat, in eastern Turkey. The Bible says that Noah's ark grounded on the Ararat range of mountains after the great flood.

Tigris and Euphrates (modern Iran). The ark came to rest, the Bible says, among the mountains of Ararat (in what is now eastern Turkey).

☐ **Other stories**
There are other stories besides the Bible account of both the creation and the great flood. Of special interest are the Assyrian and Babylonian stories, also set against a Mesopotamian background. See Part 2, under *Archaeology and the Old Testament* and Part 11, under *Assyrian and Babylonian religion.*

The World of the Old Testament

The story of ancient Israel, the major theme of the Old Testament begins around 2000 BC. Genesis 11 to the end tells the stories of the Patriarchs, Abraham to Joseph, fathers of the

nation, called to be God's people in a special sense.

In the Book of Exodus, God rescues his people from slavery in Egypt, under the leadership of Moses. He gives them his

laws at Mt Sinai and establishes the pattern of worship, focussed on the tabernacle – his special tent.

The people's disobedience leads to forty years of camping in the desert before God fulfils his promise to lead them into a new land of their own.

The Book of Joshua describes the conquest of the land and its division amongst the family-clans of Israel.

Judges records a low-point of national life: disobedience to God, invasions, and the heroes

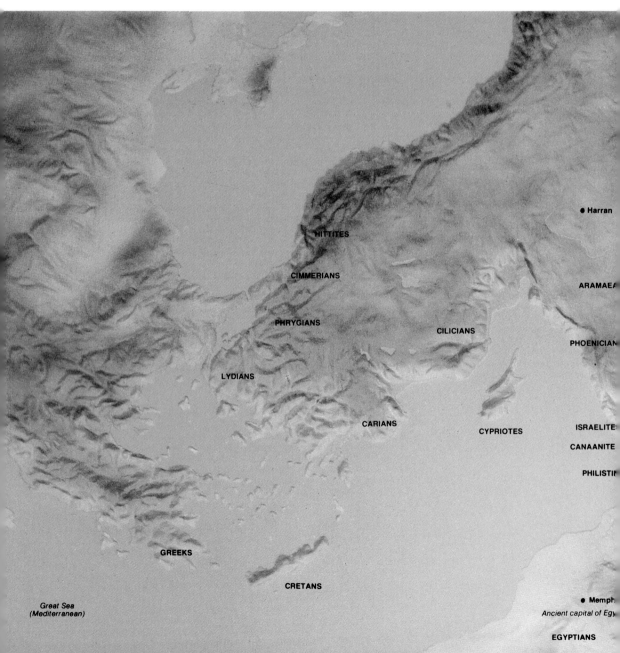

HITTITES

CIMMERIANS

PHRYGIANS

CILICIANS

● Harran

ARAMAEA

PHOENICIAN

LYDIANS

CARIANS

CYPRIOTES

ISRAELITE

CANAANITE

PHILISTIN

GREEKS

CRETANS

Great Sea
(Mediterranean)

● Memph
Ancient capital of Egy

EGYPTIANS

God sent to the rescue.

The prophet Samuel heralds the beginning of the monarchy – Israel's first kings, Saul, David and Solomon. The golden age of Solomon, when the temple was built in Jerusalem, ends and the nation splits in two: ten northern breakaway tribes form Israel and two southern tribes with Jerusalem as their capital form Judah.

Great powers rise to the north: Assyria in the ninth century BC and Babylon a century later. Greedy for empire, they swallow up the smaller nations. Israel falls to Assyria, Judah to Babylon – her people taken into exile. God has brought judgement on his people for their constant disobedience and failure to listen to his message through the prophets.

Persia conquers Babylon and the exiled Jews return to rebuild Jerusalem and its temple and re-establish God's worship. Here the Old Testament narrative ends, with the books of Ezra, Nehemiah and Esther.

The events in this 1,500-year saga are played out against the background of a world centred on the eastern Mediterranean, stretching south to include Egypt and east through Persia (Iran).

(See too the nations map in Part 11.)

(Information about the nations shown on the map can be found in Part 11: *Nations and Peoples of the Bible*.)

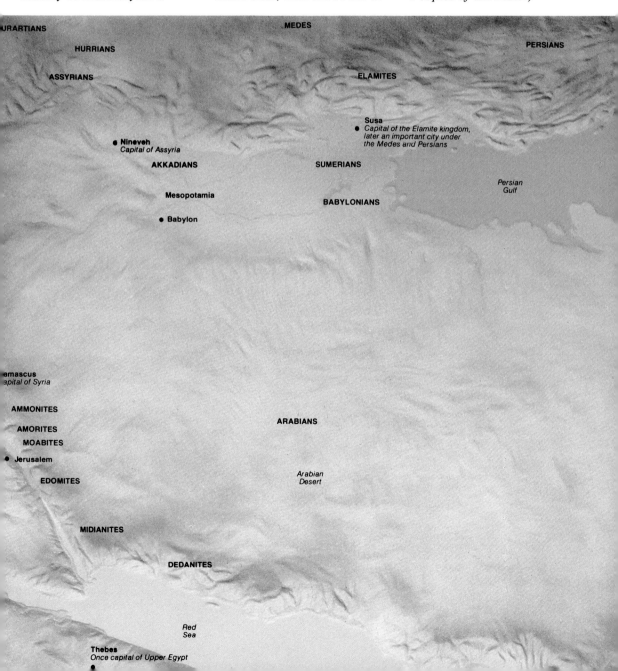

URARTIANS

HURRIANS

ASSYRIANS

MEDES

PERSIANS

ELAMITES

Susa
Capital of the Elamite kingdom, later an important city under the Medes and Persians

Nineveh
Capital of Assyria

AKKADIANS

SUMERIANS

Mesopotamia

Persian Gulf

BABYLONIANS

Babylon

Damascus
Capital of Syria

AMMONITES

AMORITES

MOABITES

Jerusalem

EDOMITES

ARABIANS

Arabian Desert

MIDIANITES

DEDANITES

Red Sea

Thebes
Once capital of Upper Egypt

The Patriarchs: Abraham to Joseph

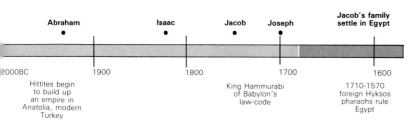

Abraham	Isaac	Jacob	Joseph	Jacob's family settle in Egypt
•	•	•	•	

2000BC	1900	1800	1700	1600

Hittites begin to build up an empire in Anatolia, modern Turkey

King Hammurabi of Babylon's law-code

1710-1570 foreign Hyksos pharaohs rule Egypt

Abraham, whom God called to be the ancestor of a great nation, came from the south Mesopotamian city of Ur. Some of his family settled at Harran in the north while he went on to Canaan, in obedience to God's command.

The world of Israel's early ancestors was one of rich and powerful kingdoms in the river valleys of Egypt and Mesopotamia. In the lands between were many walled cities and tiny kingdoms. These strongholds protected the settlers who farmed the country around. But there were also nomadic tribes who moved from place to place in search of good grazing for their flocks and herds. Abraham and his family were just one group among many on the move in the area.

This was the pattern in Canaan when Abraham arrived to set up camp at Shechem. The coastal plain and the Jordan Valley, where there was good farm land, were already settled. This looked attractive to Abraham's nephew Lot, who moved down from the hills to camp near Sodom. But life there had its dangers. Lot was only one of many who suffered when rebel kings tried to throw off the control of their distant overlords (Genesis 14).

☐ Abraham

Abraham spent most of his life in Canaan (the land God promised to give to him and his descendants), based near Hebron, apart from a brief visit to Egypt at a time of famine. At long last the promised son, Isaac, was born. But Abraham never owned the land. When his wife Sarah died he had to buy ground from a Hittite to bury her. **(Map 1)**

☐ Jacob

Abraham's grandson Jacob, having cheated his brother Esau out of his inheritance, left on a hurried visit to relations in Paddan-aram, the district around Harran. For twenty years he worked for his wily uncle Laban. Then he took his two wives and their children, his flocks and herds, and returned home. Jacob was still very much afraid of Esau's anger and at Mahanaim he

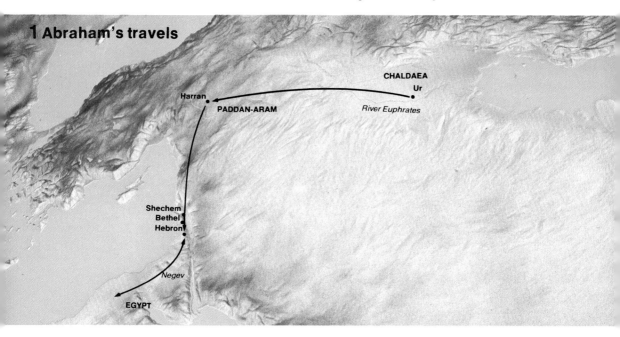

1 Abraham's travels

CHALDAEA
Ur

Harran
PADDAN-ARAM   River Euphrates

Shechem
Bethel
Hebron

Negev

EGYPT

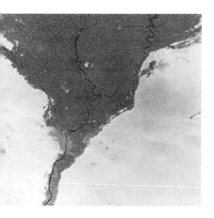

This satellite picture of the Nile Delta, Egypt (photographed on infra-red film) shows as red the crops, trees and plants of the fertile area. Suburban areas, with sparse vegetation, appear as light pink, the desert as light grey, cities dark grey, the waters of the River Nile as blue-black.

prayed desperately for God's help. Reassurance came and the reunion was a friendly one. The rest of Jacob's life was spent in Canaan until in his old age he joined Joseph in Egypt. **(Map 2)**

☐ **Joseph**
Joseph's position as Jacob's favourite son, and his boasting, earned his brothers' hatred. When the opportunity came,

they sold him into slavery. In Egypt Joseph rose to high position. He was imprisoned on a false charge, but eventually became one of the king of Egypt's chief ministers.

Drought and famine often struck Canaan. In Egypt Joseph ensured that grain was stored. His brothers came to buy corn, and the whole family eventually settled in Goshen, in the eastern Nile Delta, near to the court. This is where the Book of Genesis ends. **(Map 3)**

Two pictures of Harran today. Here, over 600 miles/960 km north-west of Ur, Abraham broke his journey and some of the family settled.

2 Jacob's journey, and his return home

3 Joseph and his family go to Egypt

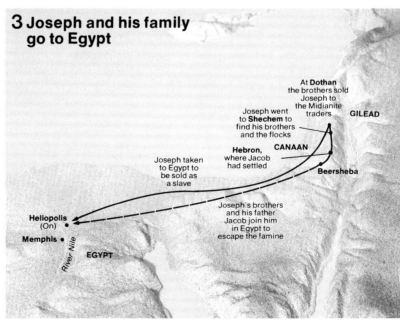

From Egypt to the Promised Land

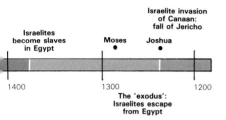

Israelites
become slaves
in Egypt

Moses
●

Israelite invasion
of Canaan:
fall of Jericho

Joshua
●

1400   1300   1200

The 'exodus':
Israelites escape
from Egypt

Pharaoh Ramesses II is generally thought to have been the pharaoh of the exodus.

For nearly 400 years Jacob's people remained in Egypt. During that time they had grown into a nation – the nation of Israel. The Egyptians, now ruled by a less friendly dynasty of kings, began to see these people as a threat. They tightened their control, forcing the Israelites to work as slaves in the brickfields. To reduce their growing numbers, new-born Hebrew babies were drowned in the Nile. The people cried out to God – and he sent them a leader: Moses (see Part 8: *People of the Bible*). The date was probably early in the thirteenth century BC, about the time when Ramesses II was king of Egypt.

It took a series of terrible plagues before the king of Egypt would agree to let the Israelites leave his country. Time and again he refused. It was the tenth plague that gained Israel's freedom, and this was something different.

'All through Egypt,' Moses announced, 'on a certain night, the firstborn sons in every household will die.' The first-born sons of the Hebrews would be safe if the people carefully followed the instruc-tions Moses gave them. They must mark their doorposts with the blood of a lamb killed in sacrifice. They must cook the lamb (again as instructed) and eat it that night, with bitter herbs and bread made without yeast. They must pack their belongings and get dressed, ready for a journey. It all happened as God said.

Every year afterwards the people of Israel kept the anniversary of this event as the Festival of the Passover: for after this (when death 'passed

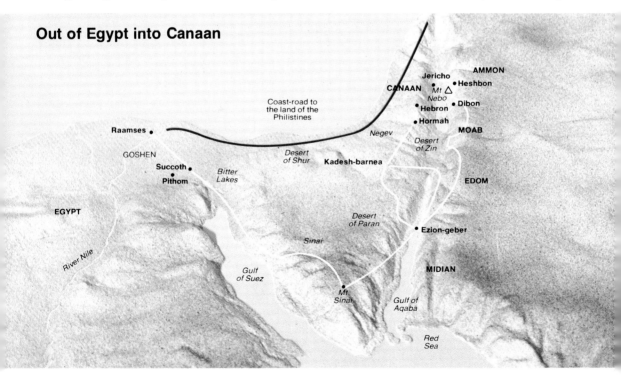

Out of Egypt into Canaan

AMMON
Jericho
• Heshbon
CANAAN   Mt △
Nebo
• Hebron   • Dibon
• Hormah
Coast-road to
the land of the
Philistines
Negev   MOAB
Raamses •
Desert
of Zin
GOSHEN   Desert
of Shur   Kadesh-barnea
Succoth •   Bitter
Pithom •   Lakes   EDOM
EGYPT
Desert
of Paran
• Ezion-geber
Sinai
River Nile   MIDIAN
Gulf
of Suez
Mt
Sinai   Gulf of
Aqaba
Red
Sea

over' the families of Israel) Pharaoh let them go.

Even so, at the last minute he changed his mind and sent his army in pursuit – but the Israelites escaped across the 'sea of reeds' to Sinai. The 'exodus' had begun. The word means simply a going out or departure. But this 'going out' of Egypt, *the* exodus, was the key event in the history of Old Testament Israel. All future generations were to look back to it. Annual religious festivals commemorated it. Parents were to make sure their children learned what it meant.
Exodus 1–15

☐ The commandments at Mt Sinai

After travelling for nearly three months the refugees camped before Mt Sinai, one of the mountain peaks in the south of the Sinai peninsula. There, in an awe-inspiring setting, God completed what he had begun when he rescued the people

The Judean hills seen from the foothills of Moab: the promised land on which Moses gazed from Mount Nebo.

from Egypt. He made his agreement (covenant) with them. He formally declared that the rabble of ex-slaves were his people, the nation of Israel.

For their part they must listen to him and obey his laws, summed up in the Ten Commandments which he gave to Moses on two stone tablets. They set out the basic principles that would govern the people's lives. Their promise to obey was confirmed in a solemn ceremony. Animal sacrifices were offered and the blood was sprinkled on the people and on the altar. So the agreement was sealed.

God then told them how to build a special tent (the tabernacle) that would be the sign of his presence with them all the rest of their journey.

See Part 5, under *The Commandments, Fasts and Festivals, Tabernacle and Temples.*
Exodus 16–40

☐ Which way?

We cannot be certain of the Israelites' route through the Sinai Desert. Numbers 33 lists

many places we cannot now locate. But most probably the people travelled south, close to the coast for some way, then inland to the region of Mt Sinai.

They moved on to Kadesh and sent spies to explore the land of Canaan. The report came back: the land was rich and fertile, but it was a land of walled cities and giant people.

When they heard this, the Israelites refused point-blank to obey God and go forward. As punishment they spent forty years in the harsh conditions of the desert. Then they took the road on the east side of the Arabah Valley, skirting Edom, to fight their first battles with the Amorites and Moabites. They camped on the plains of Moab across the Jordan from Jericho. Moses died, and Joshua became their new leader.
Numbers; Deuteronomy

Joshua, the Conquest and the Judges

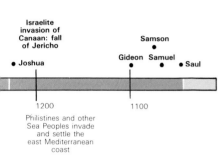

Israelite invasion of Canaan: fall of Jericho

• Joshua

Samson
•
Gideon Samuel
• • • Saul

1200   1100

Philistines and other Sea Peoples invade and settle the east Mediterranean coast

Joshua took over leadership of the people when at last (about 1230 BC) they crossed the River Jordan to enter Canaan from the west. In front of them was the walled town of Jericho. The whole land God had promised them was waiting to be possessed.

Canaan at this time was divided into a large number of small independent states, each centred on a fortified town with its own ruler.

☐ The fall of Jericho
Joshua's first aim was to take Jericho, a strategic walled town which was ancient even then, as modern excavations have shown. It fell after a remarkable siege. The Bible describes how each day for six days the whole army marched round the town without a sound except for their tramping feet and the blast of trumpets. On the seventh day they marched round seven times and then gave a tremendous shout. The walls collapsed. The men moved in and completely destroyed the town.

☐ Victory in the south
After an initial setback Joshua took nearby Ai and then marched on to establish himself at Shechem, a key town on the road through the centre of the country. This gave him a good foothold in Canaan. Enemies remained to the south and north. They were alarmed by his successes and attacked from the south.

The men of Gibeon tricked Joshua into making an alliance with them, so the kings of Jerusalem, Hebron and neighbouring cities made war on them. Joshua came to help his allies and defeated their enemies at the battle of Beth-horon. He executed the kings. Then one after another he took and destroyed the cities of Makkedah, Libnah, Lachish, Eglon and Debir. When he went back to Gilgal, the south of the country was in his hands.

☐ The northern alliance
News of the Israelite victories travelled fast. In the north, the king of Hazor gathered his allies and they marched out to deal with the invaders. Joshua took them by surprise in their camp by the spring waters of Merom and won another victory. He captured the important city of Hazor and burned it down. (Hazor is another city which has been extensively excavated by archaeologists.)

1. **Othniel** of Judah defeated Cushan-rishathaim
2. **Ehud** of Benjamin killed King Eglon of Moab
3. **Shamgar** defeated the Philistines
4. **Deborah** (from Ephraim) and Barak (from Naphtali) defeated Jabin and Sisera
5. **Gideon** of Manasseh defeated the Midianites and Amalekites
6. **Tola** of Issachar
7. **Jair** of Gilead
8. **Jephthah** of Gilead defeated the Ammonites
9. **Ibzan** of Bethlehem
10. **Elon** of Zebulun
11. **Abdon** of Ephraim
12. **Samson** of Dan fought the Philistines

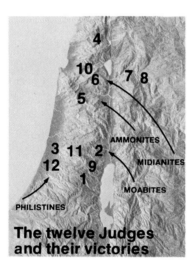

The twelve Judges and their victories

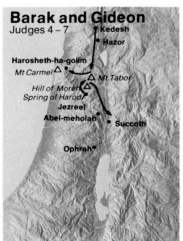

Barak and Gideon
Judges 4 – 7

Kedesh
Hazor
Harosheth-ha-goiim
Mt Carmel△
△ Mt Tabor
Hill of Moreh
Spring of Harod
Jezreel
Abel-meholah
• Succoth
Ophrah•

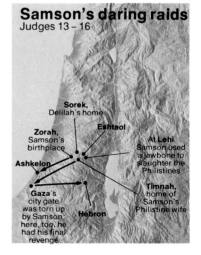

Samson's daring raids
Judges 13 – 16

Sorek, Delilah's home
Zorah, Samson's birthplace
Eshtaol
At Lehi Samson used a jawbone to slaughter the Philistines
Ashkelon
Timnah, home of Samson's Philistine wife
Gaza's city gate was torn up by Samson; here, too, he had his final revenge
Hebron

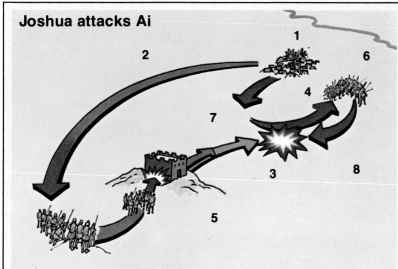

Joshua attacks Ai

1. Joshua sets up camp

2. Joshua sends his ambush force west of the city

3. Men of Ai advance into the valley towards the Israelites

4. Joshua's main force retreats

5. The ambush force enters and fires the city

6. Joshua sees the fire and signals about turn

7. The ambush force advances

8. Ai troops are caught between the two forces and routed

He killed the kings who opposed him but left the other cities standing.

Settling the land

Joshua had defeated the kings of Canaan, destroyed many key cities – and with them many Canaanite religious centres. The conquest was not complete, but Joshua had done enough for the people to begin settling in the land. Different parts were allocated to the various tribes, and each tribe had to take possession of its own area.

They never succeeded completely. Enemies remained to harass them, and all too often the Israelites simply adopted the Canaanite way of life and worshipped Canaanite gods. But there were some outstanding victories (like those won by Judah: Judges 1) and everywhere the Israelites established themselves in the land. Canaan became the land of Israel. Joshua

Archaeology

See Part 2: *Archaeology and the Bible*, under *The Conquest of Canaan*.

The Judges

The tribes settled into the areas allotted to them. They were scattered now, and surrounded by hostile neighbours. Joshua was dead. It began to seem

impossible to gain full control of the land. Gradually the Israelites lost sight of the fact that God was fighting for them. They began to compromise with the nations around, and with their gods, for the sake of peace. Their enemies took advantage of their evident weakness. The Book of Judges relates the sad story.

The surrounding nations returned to the attack: the king of Mesopotamia from the north: Moabites and

Ammonites from across the Jordan; Midianites from the east. The Canaanites at Hazor grew strong enough to make a second attack on the settlers. And from the coastlands the Philistines pushed the Israelites further and further into the hills.

As at so many times in their history, the Israelites cried to God for help in their need. The 'Judges' won at least a temporary respite. The most famous of these freedom-fighters are Deborah and Barak, Gideon, Jephthah and Samson.

The Israelites conquer and occupy Canaan

Israel's First Kings: Saul, David and Solomon

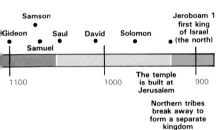

Samson
Gideon • Saul David Solomon Samuel
• •

Jeroboam 1
first king
of Israel
• (the north)

1100   1000   The temple is built at Jerusalem   900

Northern tribes break away to form a separate kingdom

The last and greatest of the Judges was Samuel – prophet and king-maker. When Samuel grew old, the people asked for a king to rule them, like the other nations. Samuel warned them that a king would mean conscription to the army, forced labour and oppression. But the Israelites insisted. And at last Samuel did as they asked.

☐ Saul
The first king was a tall, handsome Benjaminite called Saul. No sooner had he become king than Saul was faced with a challenge from the Ammonites who moved from the east to besiege Jabesh. He gathered an army and launched a three-pronged attack which drove them off. Following this, and all through his life, there was war with the Philistines. Power soon went to Saul's head and he began to disregard God's clear instructions. Because of Saul's disobedience, his son Jonathan did not inherit the throne. Instead, during Saul's lifetime, God sent Samuel to anoint David as Israel's next king.

☐ David
While still just a shepherd-boy, David killed the Philistine champion, Goliath. His popularity made Saul jealous, and for a number of years David was forced to live as an outlaw, in danger of his life. Then Saul and Jonathan were killed in battle against the Philistines on Mt Gilboa. David was made

PHILISTINES

David defeats the Philistines and ends their control over the land

Saul's campaigns

Aphek
Philistines gather

Endor
Saul consults a medium

Beth-shan
Saul's body nailed to the city wall; rescued by men from Jabesh

Mt Gilboa, where Saul and his son Jonathan died.

Battle of Gilboa.
Saul and Jonathan killed
Mt Gilboa
Israelite camp

Shunem

Valley of Jezreel

Philistines camp at Michmash; raids to Ophrah, Beth-horon, Zeboiim

Bezek
Saul sets out from Gibeah, gathers an army at Bezek, and routs the Ammonites

Jabesh-gilead

AMMON
King Nahash of Ammon sets out to attack Jabesh

Campaign against the Ammonites
1 Samuel 11

Rabbah

Saul's last campaign
1 Samuel 28; 31

Aijalon

Jonathan defends the pass at Michmash

Michmash

Gilgal
Saul proclaimed king again

Mizpah
Saul proclaimed king

Gibeah

Geba
Jonathan kills Philistine commander

Saul wins further victories against the people of Edom, Ammon, Moab and Amalek

Philistine troops move north to camp near Shunem

War against the Philistines
1 Samuel 13 – 14

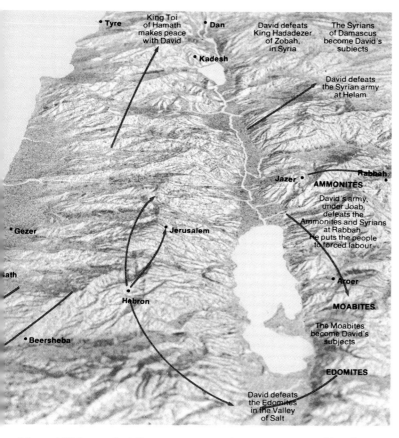

Tyre

King Toi
of Hamath
makes peace
with David

Dan

Kadesh

David defeats
King Hadadezer
of Zobah,
in Syria

The Syrians
of Damascus
become David's
subjects

David defeats
the Syrian army
at Helam

Jazer

AMMONITES

Rabbah

David's army,
under Joab,
defeats the
Ammonites and Syrians
at Rabbah.
He puts the people
to forced labour

Gezer

Jerusalem

Aroer

MOABITES

The Moabites
become David's
subjects

iath

Hebron

Beersheba

EDOMITES

David defeats
the Edomites
in the Valley
of Salt

David was made king at Hebron, but for two years he was king only of Judah. At the pool of Gibeon he met the Israelites supporting Saul's family and defeated them. Gradually he won control of the whole country. Then he began to wage war on enemies round about, extending the land in all directions.

king at Hebron, but for two years he was king only of Judah. Gradually he won control of the whole country.

David united the kingdom, captured Jerusalem, the Jebusite stronghold, and made it his capital. He was a soldier-king. During his lifetime he expanded the kingdom and drove off old enemies. His legacy to his son Solomon was peace and security.

☐ Solomon

David wanted to build a temple for God in Jerusalem, but he had to be content with getting materials together. It was Solomon who built the temple, and many other fine buildings.

'Solomon's kingdom included all the nations from the River Euphrates to Philistia and the Egyptian border. They paid him taxes and were subject to him all his life.' Peace and security freed the king to attend to other affairs, among them government and administration.

A strong, secure kingdom made it possible for Solomon to prosper through trade alliances. His wisdom was legendary. At Solomon's court there was leisure for culture and beauty. His reign was Israel's golden age.

But there was another side to the picture. The introduction of heavy taxes, forced labour and foreign gods sowed the seeds that were to divide the kingdom after his death.
1 Samuel 8 – 1 Kings 11

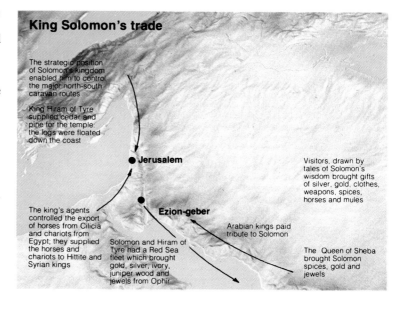

King Solomon's trade

The strategic position of Solomon's kingdom enabled him to control the major north-south caravan routes

King Hiram of Tyre supplied cedar and pine for the temple: the logs were floated down the coast

The king's agents controlled the export of horses from Cilicia and chariots from Egypt; they supplied the horses and chariots to Hittite and Syrian kings

Jerusalem

Ezion-geber

Solomon and Hiram of Tyre had a Red Sea fleet which brought gold, silver, ivory, juniper wood and jewels from Ophir

Arabian kings paid tribute to Solomon

Visitors, drawn by tales of Solomon's wisdom brought gifts of silver, gold, clothes, weapons, spices, horses and mules

The Queen of Sheba brought Solomon spices, gold and jewels

The Two Kingdoms

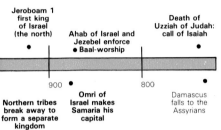

Jeroboam 1 first king of Israel (the north)	Ahab of Israel and Jezebel enforce ● Baal-worship	Death of Uzziah of Judah: call of Isaiah

900 ● — 800 ●

Northern tribes break away to form a separate kingdom

Omri of Israel makes Samaria his capital

Damascus falls to the Assyrians

Judah. King Ahab of Israel had one of the worst records. He and his foreign wife Jezebel supported the worship of Baal, opposed the prophet Elijah and persecuted those who worshipped God. The remains of Ahab's 'ivory house' at Samaria can be seen today (see Part 2: *Archaeology and the Bible*). Assyrian annals record that he brought 10,000 men and 2,000 chariots to the Battle of Qarqar, where he joined forces with the Egyptians to resist the Assyrian King Shalmaneser (853 BC).

Under King Solomon Israel became a rich and powerful kingdom, but the people were oppressed and burdened with heavy taxes and forced labour. When Solomon's son Rehoboam came to the throne they appealed to him to lighten their burdens. He refused. The ten northern tribes rebelled. They set up a new kingdom, the kingdom of Israel, with Jeroboam I ruling as king from his capital at Shechem. In the south, Rehoboam ruled the kingdom of Judah (the tribes of Judah and Benjamin) from Jerusalem.

Jeroboam also had to set up a new centre of worship for the northern kingdom, now cut off from Jerusalem. He chose Dan, in the north, and Bethel, an important centre when Samuel was alive. But pagan practices quickly became part of the worship. The historians who wrote Kings and Chronicles classified the kings as 'good' or 'bad' depending on whether they reformed religion or let the pagan practices continue.

Uzziah and Hezekiah were two of the reforming kings of

Elisha

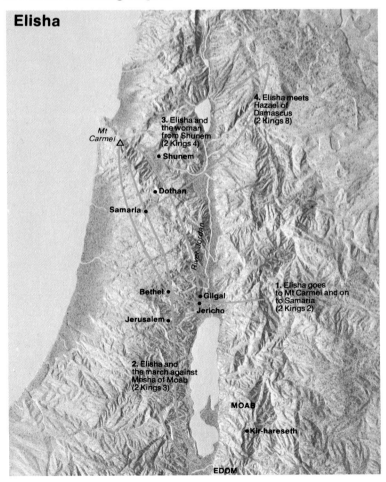

4. Elisha meets Hazael of Damascus (2 Kings 8)

Mt Carmel

3. Elisha and the woman from Shunem (2 Kings 4)

● Shunem

● Dothan

Samaria ●

River Jordan

Bethel ●

● Gilgal

Jericho

1. Elisha goes to Mt Carmel and on to Samaria (2 Kings 2)

Jerusalem ●

2. Elisha and the march against Mesha of Moab (2 Kings 3)

MOAB

● Kir-haroseth

EDOM

Elijah

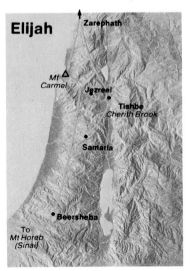

Zarephath

Mt Carmel

Jezreel ●

Tishbe
Cherith Brook

● Samaria

● Beersheba

To Mt Horeb (Sinai)

The kingdoms of Israel and Judah

Tyre
Queen Jezebel's home

Abel-beth-maacah

SYRIA

Dan
Israel's cult centre in the north

Kedesh

Combined armies of Egypt, Israel and Syria march to Qarqar to fight the Assyrians

Syrian attack

Hazor

Intermittent attacks from Syria
900-800 BC (1 Kings 15; 2 Kings 6 – 7)

Acco

Chinnereth

Mt Carmel
Scene of Elijah's contest with the prophets of Baal

River Kishon

Shunem
Elisha stayed here

Ramoth-gilead

Dor

Megiddo

Jezreel
Jezebel died here

Mt Gilboa

Taanach

Beth-shan

Ahab (Israel) and Jehoshaphat (Judah) set out to re-capture Ramoth-gilead from the Syrians but are defeated
(1 Kings 22)

ISRAEL

Ibleam

Dothan

Samaria
Capital of Israel

Tirzah

Jabesh-gilead

Penuel

Succoth

Mahanaim

Shechem
Israel's first capital

River Jordan

Joppa

Aphek

Bethel
Israel's southern cult centre

Shiloh

AMMON

Gezer

Mizpah

Ramah

Gibeon

Geba

Gilgal

Ekron

Aijalon

Gibeah

Jericho

Jerusalem
Capital of Judah

Ashdod

Bethlehem

Beth-shemesh
Here Jehoash of Israel defeated Amaziah of Judah

Ashkelon

PHILISTIA

Gath

Tekoa

River Arnon

Lachish
Here Amaziah of Judah died

Mareshah

Hebron

Gaza

Ziph

En-gedi

JUDAH

MOAB

Gerar

Joram (Israel) and Jehoshaphat (Judah) march against Mesha of Moab
(2 Kings 3)

Beersheba

Zerah the Ethiopian attacks Judah; King Asa defeats him at Mareshah
(2 Chronicles 14)

Shishak of Egypt attacks Jerusalem
(1 Kings 14.25)

Kir-hareseth

EDOM

The Rise of Assyria

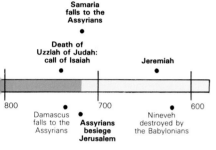

Samaria
falls to the
Assyrians

Death of
Uzziah of Judah:
call of Isaiah

Jeremiah

800

700

600

Damascus
falls to the
Assyrians

Assyrians
besiege
Jerusalem

Nineveh
destroyed by
the Babylonians

Israel and Judah, in their strategic position between Egypt and the Mesopotamian powers, were very vulnerable to aggression. David and Solomon were successful partly because none of the larger nations were powerful enough to attack during their reigns. But after the division of the kingdom the nations immediately around – Syria, Ammon, Moab – gave the subsequent kings of Israel and Judah increasing trouble. However, it was the growth of the major powers farther north-east that proved decisive.

The Assyrian Empire had an earlier period of power under Tiglath-pileser I about 1100 BC. But the ruthless aggression for which Assyria was so much feared reached its peak in the period between 880 BC and 612 BC. The empire was based on three great cities: Asshur, Calah and Nineveh.

From the mid-ninth century BC, the time of Ahab in Israel, the kings of Assyria repeatedly attacked Israel. Soon King Jehu of Israel was paying tribute to Shalmaneser III of Assyria. A hundred years later Ahaz of Judah asked Tiglath-pileser III of Assyria to help him fight Syria and Israel (Isaiah 7; 2 Kings 16). He did so and defeated them both, but Judah had to become a subject kingdom of the Assyrians in return for their help.

When Israel refused to pay their yearly tribute, the next king of Assyria took Samaria, exiled the people and destroyed the northern kingdom (722/1 BC; 2 Kings 17). Soon after this, Egypt was defeated by the Assyrians. In 701 BC the powerful King Sennacherib besieged Jerusalem, because King Hezekiah had stopped paying tribute and joined a rebellion, but Hezekiah trusted in God and the city was saved (2 Kings 19).

The Assyrians had to fight many battles to defend their empire. In the next century several provinces regained their freedom. The empire lasted until Asshur fell to the Medes in 614 and Nineveh was destroyed by the Medes and Babylonians in 612.
See also *The Assyrians* in Part 11.

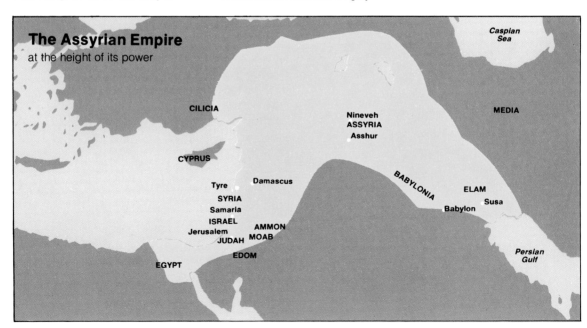

The Assyrian Empire
at the height of its power

Caspian
Sea

CILICIA

Nineveh
ASSYRIA
Asshur

MEDIA

CYPRUS

Tyre

Damascus

BABYLONIA

ELAM

Susa

SYRIA

Samaria

ISRAEL

Jerusalem

JUDAH

AMMON

MOAB

Babylon

EDOM

EGYPT

Persian
Gulf

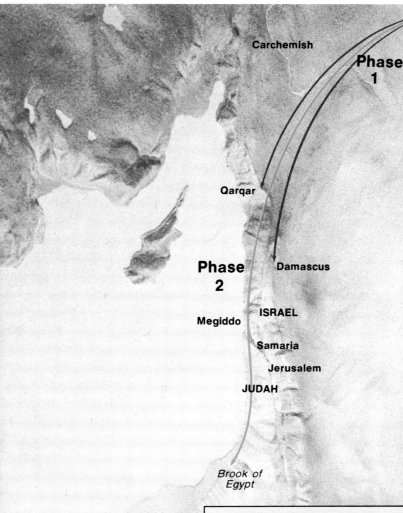

Nineveh ASSYRIA

Carchemish

Phase 1

Qarqar

Phase 2

Damascus

Megiddo

ISRAEL

Samaria

Jerusalem

JUDAH

Brook of Egypt

EGYPT

The Assyrian invasions

Phase 1
- In 853 BC Shalmaneser's army was confronted at Qarqar by twelve kings who had come together to oppose him: one was Ahab of Israel.
- In 841 BC Shalmaneser again marched on the area, laying siege to Damascus. Jehu of Israel paid him tribute. Shalmaneser then had to secure his northern borders against attack, and Damascus seized the opportunity of attacking Israel and Judah.

Phase 2
- A century later Assyria regained power. King Tiglath-pileser III invaded the area in 743 BC and frequently after that. King Azariah of Judah paid him tribute. The Assyrians increasingly adopted the policy of taking subject people into exile.
- Tiglath-pileser campaigned as far as 'the brook of Egypt' in 734 BC. Then in 733 BC he attacked Israel, destroying Megiddo and Hazor and turning the coastal plain, Galilee and the area beyond the Jordan into Assyrian provinces.
- In 732 BC Samaria was spared only because their rebellious King Pekah was assassinated (2 Kings 15:27–31).
- Shalmaneser V captured Hoshea, king of Israel in 724 BC, and laid siege to Samaria (2 Kings 17:4). He took it in 722 BC.
- In 722/1 BC Sargon II despoiled the city of Samaria, carried off the cream of the population into exile, and so destroyed the northern kingdom of Israel (2 Kings 17:5).

PROPHETS OF THE ASSYRIAN PERIOD

Jonah
Sent to warn the inhabitants of Nineveh (capital of Assyria) of God's judgement. As a result, the people changed their ways and God spared the city.

Amos
Born in Judah but prophesied in Israel during reign of Jeroboam II. Condemned Israel's neighbouring countries for their cruelty, but mostly Israel for breaking God's laws. Warned that the Israelites would be taken captive by the Assyrians.

Hosea
In the years leading up to the fall of Samaria, Hosea warned that the people would become slaves in Assyria because they had forgotten God. They had even turned to Assyria and Egypt for help.

Isaiah
Lived in Jerusalem at the time when Judah was threatened by the Assyrians. Looked ahead not only to the deliverance of Jerusalem from the Assyrians but also to its conquest by the Babylonians and to a future age of peace.

Micah
Warned of the Assyrian and Babylonian invasions; predicted the fall of both Samaria and Jerusalem.

Zephaniah
Lived during Josiah's reign. Condemned the worship of Canaanite and Assyrian gods. Predicted disaster for the pagan nations around. Foretold the destruction and restoration of Jerusalem.

Nahum
Predicted the destruction of Nineveh as a judgement on the Assyrians for their cruel treatment of other nations.

The Babylonian Invasion

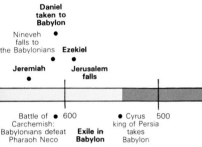

Daniel
taken to
Babylon

Nineveh
falls to
the Babylonians   Ezekiel

Jeremiah   Jerusalem
                   falls

Battle of   ● 600   ● Cyrus   500
Carchemish: king of Persia
Babylonians defeat   Exile in   takes
Pharaoh Neco   Babylon   Babylon

If Assyria in the Bible meant
oppression, Babylon meant
power. Nabopolassar, governor
of the area around the Persian
Gulf, freed Babylon from the
Assyrians and in 626 BC was
made king. He continued to
gain victories over the
Assyrians and in 612 BC the
Babylonians and Medes captured the Assyrian capital
of Nineveh. They were not
content with taking over
Assyria itself but set out to
conquer the whole Assyrian
Empire.

The Assyrians retreated to
Harran but were soon driven
out. The Egyptians, realizing
that their own country might
be in danger, marched north to
support them. King Josiah of
Judah intercepted the Egyptian
army at Megiddo. In the resulting battle he was killed and
Judah became subject to Egypt
(2 Kings 23:29). Four years
later, in 605 BC, the Babylonian
army led by the new king of
Babylon, Nebuchadnezzar,
defeated the Egyptians at
Carchemish (Jeremiah 46:1–2).
The Babylonian Empire was
spreading. Jehoiakim of Judah
was one of the many kings who
now had to pay tribute to
Nebuchadnezzar.

After a fierce battle with
the Babylonians in 601 BC the
Egyptians encouraged Judah
to rebel. Nebuchadnezzar sent
troops to crush the rebellion

and in 597 BC, shortly after
Jehoiachin had become king,
Judah submitted. The king and
many of the country's leaders
were taken into exile in Babylon. The policy of the
invaders was not just to
plunder and destroy, but also
to weaken the subject nations
and prevent further rebellions
by deporting their leading
citizens (2 Kings 24:10–17).

Despite this, ten years later
Zedekiah, a puppet king placed
on the throne of Judah by
Nebuchadnezzar, appealed to
the Egyptians for help. The
Babylonians invaded Judah
and laid siege to Jerusalem.
The siege lasted eighteen
months. Finally, a breach was
made in the walls. In 586 BC
the city was taken. King
Zedekiah was captured and
blinded. Valuable objects
including the temple treasure
were taken to Babylon. Jerusalem and its temple was
destroyed and the citizens
deported. Only the very poor
were left to cultivate the land
(2 Kings 25:1–21).

See also *The Babylonians* in
Part 11.

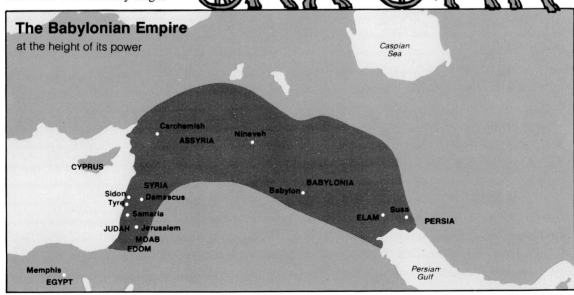

The Babylonian Empire
at the height of its power

Caspian
Sea

Carchemish
ASSYRIA   Nineveh

CYPRUS

SYRIA   BABYLONIA
Sidon   Damascus   Babylon
Tyre
Samaria
JUDAH   Jerusalem   ELAM   Susa   PERSIA
MOAB
EDOM

Memphis   Persian
EGYPT   Gulf

Nineveh
ASSYRIA
MEDIA

Carchemish

ELAM

River Tigris
Susa

River Euphrates
Babylon
BABYLONIA
PER

The Babylonian attacks

SYRIA

CYPRUS

Damascus

Sidon
Tyre

Megiddo

Samaria

AMMON

Jerusalem

JUDAH MOAB

EDOM

Memphis

EGYPT

- In 609 BC King Josiah of Judah was killed at Megiddo. He was opposing the Egyptian army which was marching in support of Assyria against the increasing threat of the Babylonians and Medes.

- Nebuchadnezzar of Babylon, having defeated the Egyptians at Carchemish, made Judah a subject state in 605 BC, and occupied the coastal plain.

- Jehoiakim of Judah tried to enlist the help of Egypt against Babylon in 601 BC following the battle between Pharaoh Neco and King Nebuchadnezzar.

- Jerusalem was forced to surrender to Nebuchadnezzar in 597 BC, and leading citizens were exiled to Babylon.

- Ten years later Nebuchadnezzar again marched on Jerusalem following a rebellion. In 586 BC the city was taken and destroyed, and the citizens were taken into exile.

PROPHETS OF THE BABYLONIAN PERIOD

Jeremiah
Continually warned that Jerusalem would be captured and the inhabitants exiled to Babylon. Prophesied against the pagan nations around. Promised that after seventy years the Jews would return. After the destruction of Jerusalem in 586 BC Jeremiah was forced to live in Egypt.

Habakkuk
Habakkuk questioned how God could allow the cruel Babylonians to defeat his own people.

Ezekiel
One of the Jews taken captive to Babylon. He predicted the downfall of nations hostile to Judah and encouraged the exiles with the hope of returning to their own land.

Obadiah
Prophesied against Edom for attacking Judah at the time of the Babylonian invasion.

Daniel
Taken captive during Nebuchadnezzar's attack on Jerusalem in 605 BC, Daniel became a chief minister at the royal court in Babylon. He prophesied the downfall of the Babylonian and succeeding empires.

The Exile

For 200 years the prophets had been warning that judgement would fall on the people if they refused to listen to God and to keep his laws. In the eighth century BC Amos and Hosea told the northern kingdom of Israel how they would suffer if they did not keep their promise to obey God. They ignored the warning and in 721 BC the Assyrians captured Samaria, their capital city. The people were deported and scattered in other provinces of the empire. Foreigners were settled in the land and it became the Assyrian province of Samaria. The ten tribes of Israel were never heard of again.

In the south, Judah too was threatened, but King Hezekiah trusted God and listened to his prophet Isaiah, and Jerusalem was spared. But the people of Judah only half learned the lesson. The idea grew that Jerusalem, the city of God, was unconquerable. They were safe. It did not matter what they did.

When a new danger loomed – from Babylon – no one listened to Jeremiah's warnings. In 605 BC, when the Babylonians took control of Syria, King Jehoiakim of Judah had to pay tribute. And the Babylonian King Nebuchadnezzar took hostages back to Babylon.

Rebellion resulted in the siege and capture of Jerusalem in 597 BC. The king and many leading citizens were taken to Babylon. The exile had begun.

King Zedekiah's rebellion ten years later resulted in the destruction of Jerusalem and the temple. Those who were not killed were deported to Babylon, leaving only a handful of people. Very little remained of the kingdom of Judah. Settlers from Edom were already taking over the land south of Hebron and Beth-zur. Nebuchadnezzar appointed a governor, Gedaliah, to rule the rest of the country in the name of Babylon. The Book of Lamentations describes the horror of it all. The cities were in ruins. Apart from the thousands exiled to Babylon many people had died in the fighting. Many more died of starvation and disease in the siege. Now few remained to farm the land the invaders had ruined.

Gedaliah made his headquarters at Mizpah and tried to rule well. But some still refused to accept the Babylonian rulers. They plotted against Gedaliah and murdered him. His supporters were afraid and fled to Egypt, taking the prophet Jeremiah with them. The Babylonians carried off still more of the people in 582 BC, and joined the land to the province of Samaria.

Jeremiah 27 – 28; Lamentations; 2 Kings 25:22–26; Jeremiah 40 – 43

Great Babylon with its temples and grand processional way, approached through the Ishtar Gate.

Because of their disobedience to God the whole nation suffered transportation and exile.

☐ The exiles

In Babylon the Jews lived in their own settlements in the capital and other towns. They were free to build houses, earn a living and keep their own customs and religion. They could not go back home but they were not ill-treated. King Jehoiachin and his family were hostages in the king's household. Some Jews, like Daniel, rose to high positions in government service. Skilled Jewish craftsmen were among the workmen Nebuchadnezzar employed. Many became so much at home in Babylon that when the opportunity came to rebuild Jerusalem they did not want to go. But some Jews longed to return to Judah and in exile they clung to their religion and their way of life.

Ever since Solomon had built the temple it had been the centre of Jewish faith and worship. Now it was gone. There was nowhere to offer the temple sacrifices. So the people began to lay new stress on those parts of their religion that they could observe. Keeping the day of rest, the sabbath, became very important. So also did circumcision, the sign of God's covenant with them, and the laws about what was clean and unclean. And they began

to value the written records of God's message as never before. Some of the priests, such as Ezra, began to study the law of God in every detail (they were called 'scribes'). Many of the books that make up our Old Testament were given their present form during the time of the exile.

☐ The prophets

Their defeat and the fall of Jerusalem was a shattering blow to the Jews. A heathen king had beaten them. They had lost the land God gave them. Their king, the true descendant of David, was exiled. The temple of God lay in ruins. They faced bitter questions. Could God not save them? Had he broken his promise? Had he given them up? They were forced to look again at all their ideas about God and about themselves, his people. It led to a new understanding.

The answer was there in the words of the prophets. Ezekiel was with the exiles in Babylon telling the people, even before Jerusalem fell, what God was doing. Jeremiah had said the same back in Jerusalem. The disaster was God's judgement on his people for their disobedience. They had not kept their part of the agreement made at Mt Sinai. But this calamity was not the end. God had not deserted them. He

would rescue them from exile and restore them to their land. Their suffering was helping to prepare them for the new things God was going to do.

See further *The Return to Jerusalem.*
Isaiah 40; Jeremiah 30; Ezekiel 11:14–21 and so on.

The Return to Jerusalem

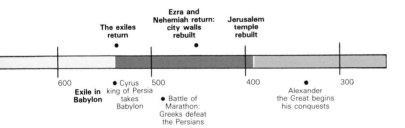

The exiles return

Ezra and Nehemiah return: city walls rebuilt

Jerusalem temple rebuilt

600   ● Cyrus   500   400   ●   300

Exile in king of Persia
Babylon takes
Babylon

● Battle of
Marathon:
Greeks defeat
the Persians

Alexander
the Great begins
his conquests

In the first half of the sixth century BC Babylon appeared all-powerful. But the prophets spoke of a God to whom kings were as puppets, and who could use even pagan powers to fulfil his purposes.

Cyrus the Persian united the two kingdoms of Media and Persia to the east of Babylon. He conquered lands as far east as India. Then he attacked Babylon. In 539 BC, nearly fifty years after King Nebuchadnezzar had captured Jerusalem, Cyrus conquered Babylon and took over the whole empire.

The Persian kings extended their borders even further than the earlier empires. They took Egypt and all of what is now Turkey. When Babylon fell, Cyrus began to reorganize the empire. He divided it into provinces, each with its own ruler, called a 'satrap'. These were mainly Persians, but under them were local rulers who retained some power. The different peoples were encouraged to keep their own customs and religions.

As part of this policy, in 538 BC Cyrus issued a decree saying that the Jews could 'go to Jerusalem and rebuild the Temple of the Lord, the God of Israel'. They were to be given money and all the supplies they needed. Cyrus gave them back the gold and silver bowls and other things that Nebuchadnezzar had taken from the temple. The first party of exiles made the long journey back home.

☐ Rebuilding the temple

In Jerusalem Zerubbabel (a descendant of the last king of Judah) and the priest, Jeshua, took charge. Work began on rebuilding the temple. But conditions were difficult. The people had first to build homes and make a living for themselves. Their enemies harassed them. Soon they grew discouraged and work on the temple came to a standstill – for fifteen years.

Then the prophets Haggai and Zechariah spoke out, stirring the people to action. Word came from the new Persian king, Darius, confirming Cyrus's decree and ordering the governor of the province to give the Jews whatever help they needed. Four years later the temple was finished and dedicated with a joyful festival.

The returned exiles were still only a small and struggling community, and their city had no walls to protect it. In the reign of King Artaxerxes (464–423 BC) two new leaders came to Jerusalem. Ezra was probably the first to arrive. He was a priest and he brought with him another group of return-

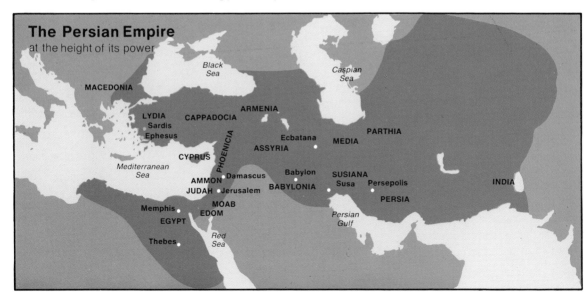

The Persian Empire
at the height of its power

MACEDONIA

Black Sea

Caspian Sea

ARMENIA

LYDIA
Sardis
Ephesus

CAPPADOCIA

PARTHIA

PHOENICIA

Ecbatana

MEDIA

ASSYRIA

CYPRUS

Mediterranean Sea

Damascus

Babylon

SUSIANA

AMMON

BABYLONIA

Susa

Persepolis

INDIA

JUDAH Jerusalem

PERSIA

MOAB

Memphis

EDOM

EGYPT

Persian Gulf

Thebes

Red Sea

ing exiles. He was naturally interested to see how the law of God was being kept. He found that many, even the leaders, had married wives from the surrounding peoples and were worshipping their gods. Ezra called on them to give up their foreign wives and obey the Lord their God.
Haggai, Zechariah, Ezra

☐ **Nehemiah and the city walls**
Not long after, Nehemiah, another Jew, who was Artaxerxes' wine steward in Susa, heard how things were in Jerusalem and was very concerned. He fasted and prayed, asking God's help. Then he raised the matter with the king, who gave him permission to go to Jerusalem and rebuild the walls.

Nehemiah first surveyed the ruins, and then organized the work of rebuilding the walls. He made certain families responsible for building particular sections.

Enemies from all round Judah did their best to stop the work. They planned an attack on the builders; they plotted to discredit or kill Nehemiah. But the work went on, with some of the men always armed and standing guard. After fifty-two days, 'with God's help', the work on the wall was finished and it was dedicated with thanksgiving.

For twelve years Nehemiah was Governor of Judah, appointed by the Persians. Together he and Ezra guided the community in obedience to God. They made a number of reforms. Nehemiah stopped wealthy Jews charging their poorer neighbours so much for food that they were having to mortgage their land and sell their daughters as slaves. Ezra read the law of God to the people and explained it. They were moved to tears as they realized they had not kept it. In a written document signed in their name by their leaders, the people made a solemn promise that in future they would obey all God's commands and keep his laws.
Nehemiah

☐ **The 'dispersion'**
Many Jews did not return, but remained settled in other parts of the Persian empire. The book of Esther tells how King Xerxes I even made a Jewess his queen.

The 'dispersion', as Jews living in other lands came to be called, was significant later in New Testament times. Because they were away from the temple, these Jews developed the local synagogue as a centre of teaching and worship. And this laid the basis for the later rapid spread of the Christian churches which were formed on this model.
Esther

See also *The Persians* in Part 11.

The Jews who returned to Jerusalem determined to study and keep God's laws.

PROPHETS OF THE PERSIAN PERIOD

Haggai
In 520 BC, eighteen years after the Jews had returned from exile in Babylon, Haggai urged them to forget their own interests and finish rebuilding the temple.

Zechariah
Prophesied to the returned Jewish exiles between 520 and 518 BC; predicted the destruction of nations which had oppressed the Jews; and foresaw a time when people would come from every part of the world to worship in Jerusalem.

Joel
Warned of devastation which would sweep across the land like a plague of locusts, and gave hope of great blessing to follow.

Malachi
A prophet who lived in the fifth century BC. By this time the Jews had become disillusioned and apathetic. Malachi reminded them of God's demands and of the coming Messiah.

The Greek Empire and Culture

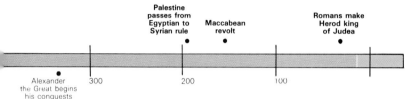

Palestine
passes from
Egyptian to   Maccabean
Syrian rule   revolt

Romans make
Herod king
of Judea

300   200   100

Alexander
the Great begins
his conquests

King Darius I of Persia (522–486 BC), builder of the great new capital, Persepolis, and conqueror of western India, also pushed the empire westwards. In 513 he took Macedonia in northern Greece and planned to conquer all of Greece.

In 490 the Persians were defeated by the Greeks at Marathon, and the stage was set for some of the greatest stories of Greek classical antiquity.

Xerxes I (486–465) invaded Greece, even occupying Athens, but was defeated in the sea-battle of Salamis. Artaxerxes, Darius II, and the kings that

followed, took up the struggles. The fortunes of Persia and Greece, Media and Egypt ebbed and flowed until finally, in 333 BC, the Greek soldier Alexander of Macedon crossed the Hellespont to begin his meteoric career.

Alexander was only twenty-two when he set out on a campaign which swept across the ancient world. He 'liberated' Egypt from the Persians (founding the port of Alexandria), then marched east, to the heart of the Persian Empire. He pressed on as far as India, conquering all who stood in his way and founding Greek city-states wherever he went. His

title 'Alexander the Great' was well earned. He died, when only thirty-three, in 323 BC.

Following his death, the great Greek Empire was divided up among his four generals. The Seleucid rulers, based in Antioch in Syria, controlled Palestine. The Ptolemies, based in Alexandria, ruled Egypt. Culturally, however, the Greek or 'hellenistic' world continued as a unity, with Greek as a common language and with a common pattern of civilization.

☐ The Greek ideal
Alexander's ambition was not simply one of conquest. He believed in Greek ideals and wanted to spread Greek culture and thought. He encouraged army veterans to settle in distant places and build up societies based on the Greek way of life. He was remarkably successful. Greek became the international language. More than 300 years later, when the New Testament came to be written, it was in common language Greek rather than the Aramaic which Jesus spoke.

City-states were built and organized on the Greek pattern, with a strong and lasting impact in Syria and Palestine. Everywhere there was evidence of Greek town-

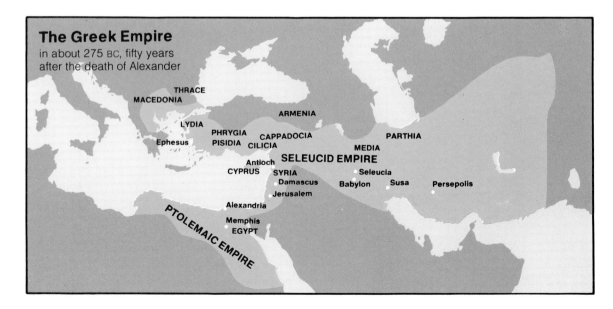

The Greek Empire
in about 275 BC, fifty years after the death of Alexander

THRACE
MACEDONIA
ARMENIA
LYDIA
PHRYGIA
PISIDIA   CAPPADOCIA
Ephesus   CILICIA   PARTHIA
MEDIA
Antioch   **SELEUCID EMPIRE**
CYPRUS   SYRIA   Seleucia
Damascus   Babylon   Susa   Persepolis
Jerusalem
Alexandria
Memphis
EGYPT
PTOLEMAIC EMPIRE

planning (still to be seen to-day in many remarkable ruins throughout the Middle East, from Palmyra in the Syrian desert to Ephesus on the west coast of Turkey). Each city had its market-place and public buildings, temple(s) and theatre built in Greek architectural style. The Romans, when they came to power, adopted the Greek patterns which were there already.

Greek thought was as powerful an influence for change as Greek building. Greek plays performed in the theatres were linked with Greek religious festivals. Paul, a Jew born in Tarsus on the south coast of Turkey in the first century AD, was able to quote the Greek philosophers and poets. Just a few miles from Bethlehem, where Jesus was born, was an area known as the ten towns, the Decapolis: these were Greek city-states.

In the period between the Old and New Testaments Greek culture and thought penetrated deep into Jewish society, even though the Maccabean freedom war won some measure of independence from the Greek kings of Syria who ruled the land. Coins were struck with Hebrew on one side, Greek on the other.

The background of the hellenistic world played a vital part in events which were to follow: the events of the New Testament.

See also *The Greeks* in Part 11.

Palmyra, a Greek city out in the Syrian Desert.

Rome — and the World of the New Testament

straight roads, aqueducts, plumbing and central heating, and the baths. To the Greek Games were added Roman spectator sports and contests.

The Romans brought law, order and stability to the countries they ruled. The peace was forcibly maintained by garrisons of soldiers whose presence was not generally

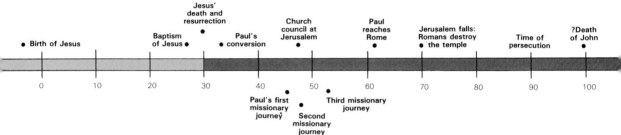

- Birth of Jesus
- Baptism of Jesus
- Jesus' death and resurrection
- Paul's conversion
- Church council at Jerusalem
- Paul reaches Rome
- Jerusalem falls: Romans destroy the temple
- Time of persecution
- ?Death of John

0   10   20   30   40   50   60   70   80   90   100

- Paul's first missionary journey
- Second missionary journey
- Third missionary journey

The spread of Greek culture (hellenism) and the fact that many Jews were dispersed in other lands had set the scene for the New Testament. The final key factor was Roman rule, which unified the ancient world politically, just as hellenism unified it culturally.

☐ **The Roman Empire**
The Romans gradually took control of the former Greek Empire. Corinth fell in 146 BC; Athens in 86. In the first century BC Julius Caesar conquered Gaul and Pompey brought Syria and Palestine under Roman control. He occupied Jerusalem in 63 BC. The Romans absorbed Greek ideas, language and culture. Their legacy to the world was essentially practical: fine

appreciated. Four legions were stationed in Palestine, and there were heavy taxes to pay. The atmosphere was highly charged and revolt — especially where the Jewish religion was concerned — was a constant danger.

In 27 BC Octavian became in effect the first ruler of the Roman Empire. He adopted the title Augustus, and during

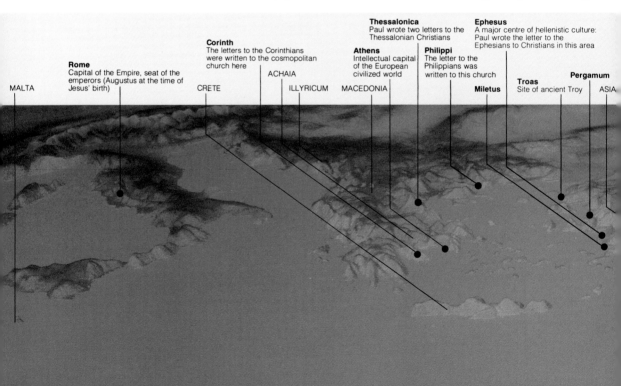

Thessalonica
Paul wrote two letters to the Thessalonian Christians

Ephesus
A major centre of hellenistic culture: Paul wrote the letter to the Ephesians to Christians in this area

Corinth
The letters to the Corinthians were written to the cosmopolitan church here

Athens
Intellectual capital of the European civilized world

Philippi
The letter to the Philippians was written to this church

Rome
Capital of the Empire, seat of the emperors (Augustus at the time of Jesus' birth)

Troas
Site of ancient Troy

Pergamum

MALTA   CRETE   ACHAIA   ILLYRICUM   MACEDONIA   Miletus   ASIA

his reign Jesus Christ was born.

☐ **When the time was ripe**
The time was ripe for the coming of Jesus.

The religions of classical antiquity had become bankrupt. The old gods of Greece and Rome had merged with the mystery religions, the traditional pagan religions of the rural areas (the worship of earth and fertility gods) and a general awareness of a world of spirits. After the philosophy of the Greeks and the materialism of the Romans, people were searching for more 'spiritual' answers: but all too often they simply lapsed into superstition.

In an age of degenerate religion, many non-Jews were attracted to the Jewish faith and became 'God-fearers'.

Because of Roman roads and the Roman peace, the good news could travel quickly throughout the Roman Empire.

See also *The Romans* in Part 11.

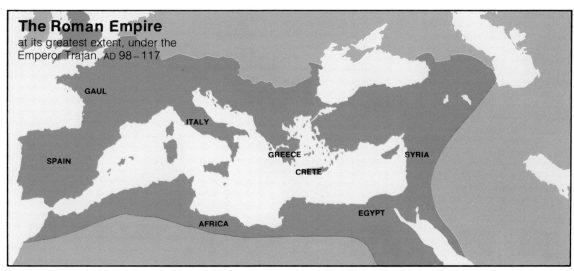

The Roman Empire
at its greatest extent, under the Emperor Trajan, AD 98–117

GAUL

ITALY

SPAIN

GREECE

SYRIA

CRETE

AFRICA

EGYPT

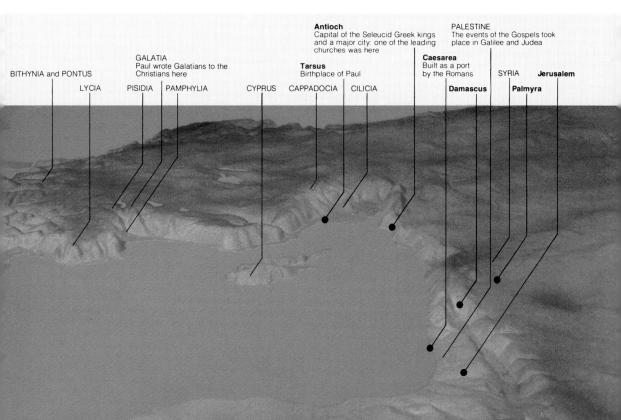

Antioch
Capital of the Seleucid Greek kings and a major city: one of the leading churches was here

PALESTINE
The events of the Gospels took place in Galilee and Judea

GALATIA
Paul wrote Galatians to the Christians here

Tarsus
Birthplace of Paul

Caesarea
Built as a port by the Romans

BITHYNIA and PONTUS

LYCIA

PISIDIA

PAMPHYLIA

CYPRUS

CAPPADOCIA

CILICIA

Damascus

SYRIA

Palmyra

Jerusalem

The Jewish Hope

Herod's kingdom

ITURAEA
GALILEE TRACHONITIS
DECAPOLIS
SAMARIA
PEREA
JUDEA
IDUMAEA
NABATAEA

The Jewish people had lived under foreign occupation for some 500 years since returning to their own land. Under Greek rule they had paid tribute to Ptolemy of Egypt and adopted Greek as the language of the empire. In 198 BC the Seleucid Greek ruler of Syria, Antiochus the Great, defeated the Ptolemies and took Palestine. But he in turn was defeated by the Romans at Magnesia in 190 BC.

The Romans taxed the Seleucid Empire harshly, and they in turn took any opportunity to loot cities and temples. Antiochus Epiphanes used the opposition of loyal Jews, the 'Hasidim' or 'pious ones', as an excuse to plunder the Jerusalem temple. Later he built a pagan Greek centre in the heart of the city and in the temple an altar to Zeus on which pigs (forbidden under Jewish food laws) were sacrificed.

This final affront resulted in the Maccabean Revolt. The Jews succeeded in freeing themselves for a time and were able to cleanse and rededicate the temple in 165 BC. The high priest Aristobolus, a later member of the Hasmonean family who had led the revolt, declared himself king in 104 BC. But before long, rivalries among the Jews gave the Romans the chance to intervene. The last high-priest king was executed in 37 BC.

□ **The Herod family**
Judea became subject to Rome under the governor of the province of Syria. But the Jews kept the freedom to practise their religion and had their own ruler: from 37 to 4 BC an Idumean Jew named Herod. Despite his ambitious building projects – including a new temple in Jerusalem – the Jews hated Herod the Great, and he is chiefly remembered for his tyranny and cruelty. (Jesus was born while Herod was still king and it was Herod the Great

King Herod's fortress at Herodium.

who ordered the killing of the children in Bethlehem.)

When Herod died, the kingdom was divided among three of his sons. Archelaus inherited Judea and Samaria but was such a repressive ruler that in AD 6 the Romans removed him and appointed a Roman governor or 'procurator' instead. (From AD 26 to 36 this was Pontius Pilate.) Herod Antipas ruled Galilee and Perea. And Philip ruled Iturea, Trachonitis and the land to the north-east.

☐ **Religious ferment**
The Jews had to accept the authority of Rome and of King Herod's family, but their loyalty was to the priests. The High Priest had great power. There were also a number of religious parties or factions at the time of Christ. Many priests and a large part of the Jewish Council (the Sanhedrin) were Sadducees – very conservative in religious matters and inclined to political compromise to safeguard their high positions. The Pharisees were religious purists, delighting to keep every detail of the law, but tending to a holier-than-thou attitude.

☐ **Revolutionaries**
While the Pharisees and Sadducees tried to make the best of Roman rule, the Zealots were committed to the overthrow of the foreign forces. They were the freedom fighters, and at least one of the apostles, 'Simon the Patriot', was a former Zealot.

☐ **The Messiah**
Although some, such as the hated tax collectors, profiteered under the Roman occupation, many were thrown back on their hope of a Messiah, the Deliverer whom the prophets had promised God would send to set them free. They tended to interpret the promise in political terms. But even so, there were many, like Simeon in the temple when Jesus' parents came to present their baby, who were 'waiting for Israel to be saved'.

It was in this time of ferment, unrest and expectation that Jesus was born.

See also Part 5: *Religion and Worship in the Bible*, under *Between the Testaments* and *Jewish Religion: New Testament Times*

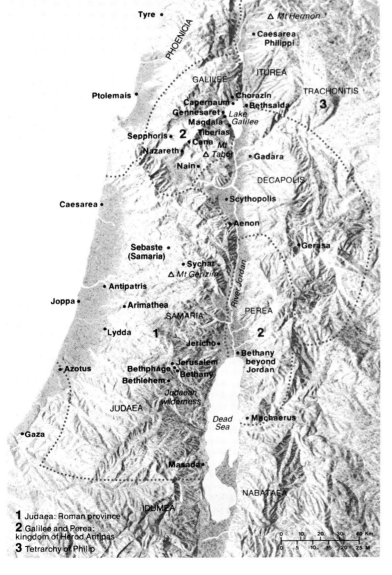

1 Judaea: Roman province
2 Galilee and Perea: kingdom of Herod Antipas
3 Tetrarchy of Philip

Palestine in New Testament times.

In the Steps of Jesus

Jesus was born, Luke's Gospel tells us, at the time when the Roman Emperor Augustus had ordered a census throughout the Empire. It was near the end of the reign of King Herod the Great. Although Mary, his mother, and Joseph came from Nazareth, Jesus was born in Bethlehem, the birthplace of his illustrious ancestor, King David.

The Gospels make it plain that this baby, born into an ordinary family, was the Messiah, or 'Christ' – the one God had long promised would save his people. Many Jews were ready and waiting for him – though he was not to be the kind of king they imagined.

Jesus' infant years were spent in Egypt, out of reach of cruel King Herod. On the king's death the family returned to Nazareth and a quiet life whose annual highlight was the visit to Jerusalem for Passover. When Jesus was twelve Mary and Joseph took him with them for the first time.

☐ A public figure
It was about AD 27, in the fifteenth year of the Emperor Tiberius, that Jesus' public work began. He joined the crowds that flocked to John the Baptist beside the River Jordan and, despite having no sin to confess, was baptized by John, identifying himself with his people.

Forty days of fasting and testing in the desert prepared Jesus for his return to Galilee and the start of a new life as a travelling teacher. Quickly gathering a following of his own, Jesus soon chose twelve to go with him on his travels. From this time until his death (probably about three years later) Jesus was a public figure.

Much of his time was spent in the area around Lake Galilee. But there were frequent visits to Jerusalem, especially for major festivals. Once at least he chose to go through (rather than round) Samaritan country. And he travelled to the far north, to the district of Caesarea Philippi, close under Mt Hermon. The Gospels name many of the places Jesus went to, although it is not possible to work out a precise sequence (see map).

☐ The last week
Probably in the spring of AD 30 Jesus went to Jerusalem for the last time, to celebrate Passover with his twelve friends. He had made a name for himself as a great teacher, one who cared about ordinary people. And he constantly astonished the crowds who followed him with miracles of healing. His twelve friends watched and listened. Three of them saw him transfigured with glory on a mountain in Galilee. They became

Here on the east side of Lake Galilee the Gadarene swine rushed into the lake. In the distance is the place where Jesus fed a crowd of more than 5,000 people.

convinced that Jesus really was God's Messiah.

But there was opposition which grew stronger and stronger. Jesus offended the religious teachers by his plain speaking. They realized that his claims went far beyond those of a great teacher: Jesus was making himself out to be God. Didn't he claim to forgive sins? Hadn't he said that he and God his Father were one?

In Jerusalem that week the opposition came to a head and boiled over. Judas, one of Jesus' twelve friends, arranged to betray him. He was arrested at night and tried by the Jewish Council, with false charges laid by 'witnesses'. First thing in the morning the Roman governor Pontius Pilate was brow-beaten by threat of revolt into ratifying the sentence of death.

On a hill outside the city wall Jesus died as a common criminal on a cross (like the two who died with him).

A hasty burial followed, in order not to break the sabbath laws.

But at daybreak on the Sunday morning, women coming to observe the last rites found the tomb empty, the body gone. And before the day was out many of Jesus' followers had seen him alive.

See also Part 8: *People of the Bible*, under *Jesus*; Part 5: *Religion and Worship in the Bible*, under *The Teaching of Jesus*; and Part 6: *Key Teaching of the Bible*, under *Atonement, Cross, Jesus Christ*, etc.

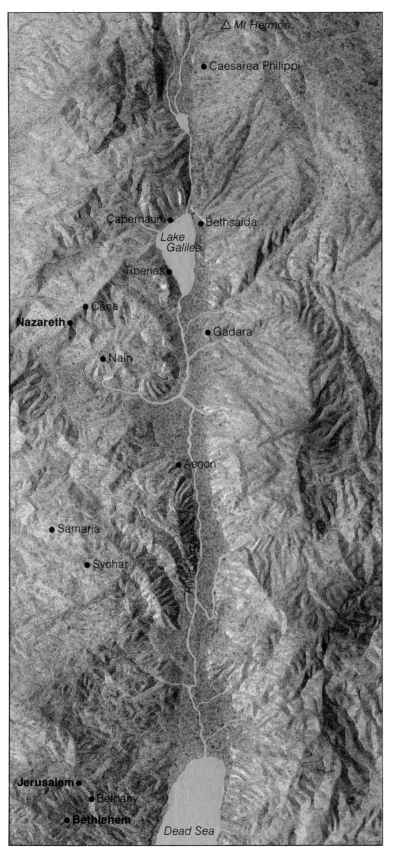

Lake Galilee: four of Jesus' disciples were Galilee fishermen and much of his ministry took place around the lake

Nazareth, Jesus' home town

Pentecost and After: the Spread of the Church

Six weeks after his resurrection, during which time he was seen often by his followers, Jesus returned to God his Father. The disciples were instructed to wait in Jerusalem: they needed the special power of God's Holy Spirit if they were to carry out Jesus' command to make him known. On the Day of Pentecost that power came, transforming the disciples.

The church grew rapidly in Jerusalem under the apostles' leadership. Then the Jews stoned Stephen and persecuted the Christians. Believers scattered all over Judea and Samaria; in towns and villages new Christian groups were founded (Acts 8). At this time (about AD 34) two important events occurred. Saul (Paul) the Pharisee, a fierce opponent of the new sect, was converted as he went to arrest believers in Damascus (Acts 9). And in Caesarea Peter preached to a Roman centurion, Cornelius, who was baptized into the

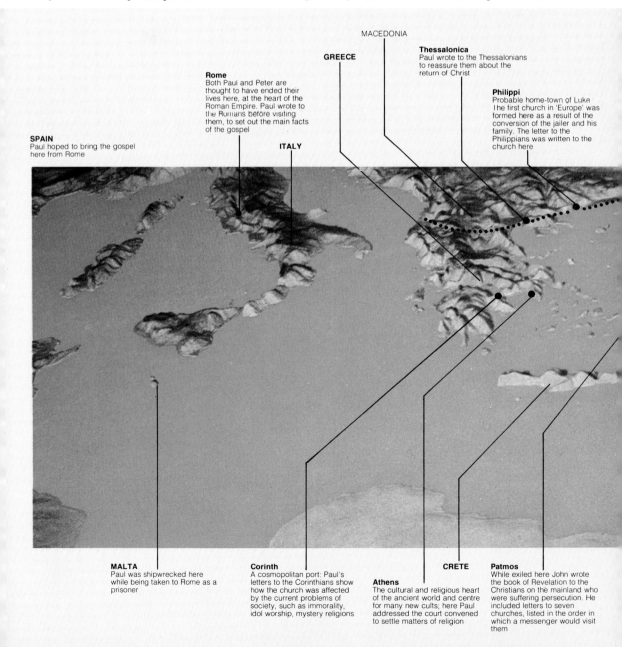

MACEDONIA

GREECE

Thessalonica
Paul wrote to the Thessalonians to reassure them about the return of Christ

Rome
Both Paul and Peter are thought to have ended their lives here, at the heart of the Roman Empire. Paul wrote to the Romans before visiting them, to set out the main facts of the gospel

Philippi
Probable home-town of Luke. The first church in 'Europe' was formed here as a result of the conversion of the jailer and his family. The letter to the Philippians was written to the church here

SPAIN
Paul hoped to bring the gospel here from Rome

ITALY

MALTA
Paul was shipwrecked here while being taken to Rome as a prisoner

Corinth
A cosmopolitan port: Paul's letters to the Corinthians show how the church was affected by the current problems of society, such as immorality, idol worship, mystery religions

Athens
The cultural and religious heart of the ancient world and centre for many new cults; here Paul addressed the court convened to settle matters of religion

CRETE

Patmos
While exiled here John wrote the book of Revelation to the Christians on the mainland who were suffering persecution. He included letters to seven churches, listed in the order in which a messenger would visit them

church – the first non-Jewish convert.

In Antioch, the capital of the province of Syria, Christians preached not only to Greek-speaking Jews ('hellenists') but to non-Jews ('Greeks') who had no connection with the Jewish religion. Many became believers; they were nicknamed 'Christians' (Acts 11:19–26). The church in Antioch sent out the first missionaries – Paul and Barnabas. They preached in Cyprus and what is now Turkey (Acts 13 – 14). Non-Jews as well as Jews became

Christians. This led to a major problem. Could 'Gentiles' become Christians without first becoming Jews? The conference held at Jerusalem in AD 49 decided that they could (Acts 15). It was a crucial step forward for the church.

Missionary activity increased. On his second journey Paul took the gospel into Europe (Acts 16), about AD 50. His third journey ended in his arrest, but he finally reached Rome in AD 62 and although he was a prisoner, he was able to preach freely (Acts 28).

Many others were preaching the gospel and helping the churches. By AD 64, when the Book of Acts ends, there were churches in all the main centres of the Empire, and from these the gospel was spreading out to surrounding areas.

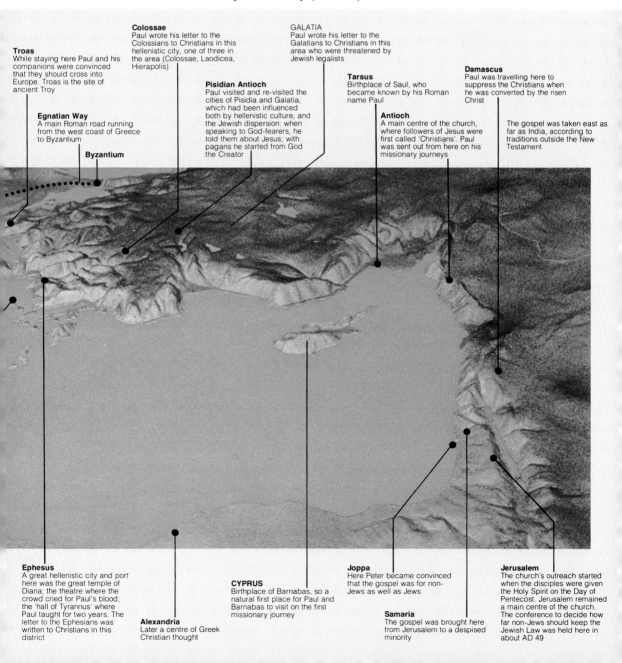

Colossae Paul wrote his letter to the Colossians to Christians in this hellenistic city, one of three in the area (Colossae, Laodicea, Hierapolis)

GALATIA Paul wrote his letter to the Galatians to Christians in this area who were threatened by Jewish legalists

Troas While staying here Paul and his companions were convinced that they should cross into Europe. Troas is the site of ancient Troy

Egnatian Way A main Roman road running from the west coast of Greece to Byzantium

Byzantium

Pisidian Antioch Paul visited and re-visited the cities of Pisidia and Galatia, which had been influenced both by hellenistic culture, and the Jewish dispersion: when speaking to God-fearers, he told them about Jesus; with pagans he started from God the Creator

Tarsus Birthplace of Saul, who became known by his Roman name Paul

Damascus Paul was travelling here to suppress the Christians when he was converted by the risen Christ

Antioch A main centre of the church, where followers of Jesus were first called 'Christians'. Paul was sent out from here on his missionary journeys

The gospel was taken east as far as India, according to traditions outside the New Testament

Ephesus A great hellenistic city and port here was the great temple of Diana; the theatre where the crowd cried for Paul's blood; the 'hall of Tyrannus' where Paul taught for two years. The letter to the Ephesians was written to Christians in this district

Alexandria Later a centre of Greek Christian thought

CYPRUS Birthplace of Barnabas, so a natural first place for Paul and Barnabas to visit on the first missionary journey

Joppa Here Peter became convinced that the gospel was for non-Jews as well as Jews

Samaria The gospel was brought here from Jerusalem to a despised minority

Jerusalem The church's outreach started when the disciples were given the Holy Spirit on the Day of Pentecost. Jerusalem remained a main centre of the church. The conference to decide how far non-Jews should keep the Jewish Law was held here in about AD 49

Paul's Journeys

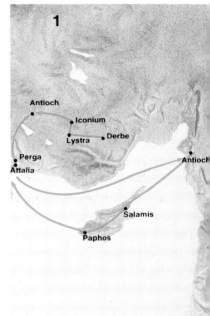

Following the remarkable encounter with the risen Jesus on the Damascus road which turned his life around, Paul became the key figure in the spread of Christianity to the west. In the letters to church groups which form a large part of the New Testament Paul refers to his frequent journeys and to the constant dangers he faced. Three of those missionary journeys are fully recorded by his companion, Luke, in the book of Acts – and there was a fourth journey as a prisoner sent for trial in Rome.

□ Journey 1
The first journey took Paul and Barnabas from their base at Antioch in Syria by ship to Cyprus, and from there to present-day Turkey: Attalia, Perga, Pisidian Antioch, Iconium, Derbe and Lystra. They returned by the same route and took ship to go back to Antioch. John Mark, who had set out with them, returned home from Perga. The date was about AD 45 or 46.

□ Journey 2
The second journey, a year or two later (AD 48–51), included an 18-month stay at Corinth. This time Paul took Silas with him, after a disagreement with Barnabas about John Mark.

Crossing from Asia Minor to Greece, bringing the gospel to Europe, Paul and his companions landed at Neapolis.

The Egnatian Way, the great east–west Roman highway, brought Paul to Philippi with the good news of Jesus.

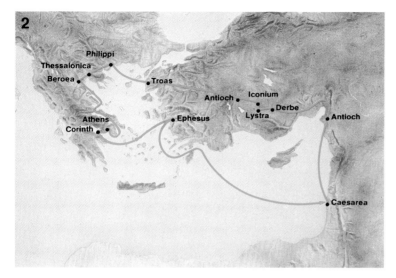

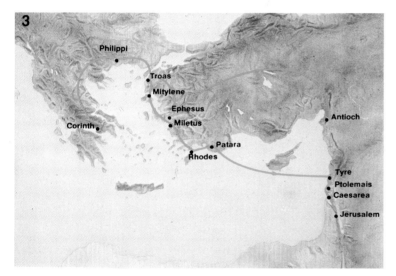

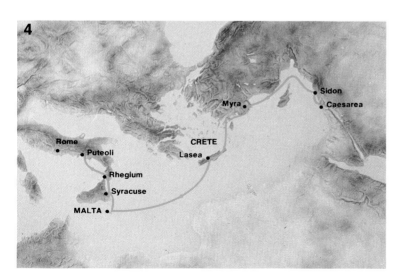

They went overland from Antioch revisiting the churches established on the first journey, and joined by Timothy at Lystra. From this region they went to Troas on the coast and crossed to northern Greece: from Philippi to Thessalonica, Berea, Athens and Corinth (where they stayed), returning by ship from Corinth via Ephesus and Caesarea to Antioch.

☐ **Journey 3**
On the third journey (beginning AD 53) Paul and his companions again went overland through Galatia and Phrygia (Turkey) 'strengthening all the believers'. They stayed for over two years at Ephesus where the response to the good news about Jesus was so great that the silversmiths lost their trade in statuettes of the goddess Diana and started a riot. From Ephesus Paul went to Philippi, Corinth and back, taking ship around the coast from Troas to Assos, Mitylene, Miletus, Rhodes, Patara, then Tyre to Ptolemais and Caesarea en route for Jerusalem.

☐ **Voyage to Rome**
In Jerusalem Paul was arrested and the next two years were spent in prison (AD 58–60) before he finally appealed to be heard by Caesar (his right as a Roman citizen) and set sail for Rome. This fourth voyage, in the autumn, was very different from the rest. Although Paul had Luke with him he was under guard. The ship set out unwisely from Crete, was caught in a fierce gale and wrecked off Malta, where the whole party, having escaped with their lives, over-wintered before completing the journey to Rome. Christians came out to meet Paul as he entered the capital and for the next two years he continued to spread the good news of Christ, though under house-arrest and awaiting trial.

Index

Please note that people and places which appear only in the A to Z sections are not included in this index.

Numbers in italics refer to photographs and illustrations or material in picture captions. Bold numerals indicate major entries.

ACKNOWLEDGMENTS

PHOTOGRAPHS

Alitalia: p.301
J. M. Allegro: p.64 (centre left)
Barnaby's Picture Library: p.66 (top left)
BBC Hulton Picture Library: pp.30, 43, 64, 74, 76 (top and bottom)
Bible Society: p.78
British Library: pp.71 (all), 73
British Museum: pp.33 (centre right), 34, 53, 55, 56, 57 (letter, arrowheads and slingstones), 172, 173 (centre bottom), 189, 191, 192 (bottom), 198, 228, 228–29, 232 (top), 239, 241, 247, 249 (top right, centre, bottom), 283, 287 (top left), 291, 293, 294, 297, 308, 312 (top right)
Cairo Museum: p.48
Camera Press: pp.32, 132, 248 (top left), 309 (bottom left)
Church Missionary Society: p.81 (centre left and right, bottom)
Maurice Chuzeville/Louvre Museum: p.279
Colorific!: p.177
Tony Deane: pp.312 (bottom, all three), 313 (left)
Douglas Dickins: p.162
École Française d'Archéologie, Athens: p.245
Margaret Embry: p.130
Ermine Street Guard: p.250
Mary Evans Picture Library: p.29 (top right, both)
Haifa Maritime Museum: p.288
Sonia Halliday Photographs: F. H. C. Birch p.304 (top right); Prue Grice p.222; Sonia Halliday cover pp.27, 51 (bottom), 64 (bottom left), 79, 159 (and title page), 164, 175 (bottom), 185 (centre), 194, 215, 219, 226, 227 (left), 251, 253, 260, 275, 280, 341 (top right); Laura Lushington p.9; Barrie Searle pp.68, 114; Jamie Simson p.211; Jane Taylor pp.43 (centre and bottom left), 50 (bottom), 57 (bottom), 70, 317 (top right and bottom), 319 (and endpapers), 335, 338
Robert Harding Picture Library: pp.45, 296
Andre Held: p.139 (top)
Michael Holford: pp.57 (centre left), 283 (bottom)
Israel Museum: pp.52 (top right), 64 (centre right)
Keystone Press: p.303
Lateran Museum, Rome: p.248 (bottom)
Duncan Leighton: p.141
Lion Publishing/David Alexander: pp.23, 24 (all), 25, 26 (right), 35, 36, 40, 41, 43, 44, 47, 49, 50 (centre), 51 (top and centre right), 52 (bottom), 59 (both), 60, 77, 83 (top), 85, 90, 93, 115, 117, 123, 124 (both), 125 (all), 126, 127, 136 (left), 137 (both), 144, 149, 151, 155, 160, 173 (ring, bracelet, brooch, earrings), 175 (top), 176 (both), 178, 179, 183 (top left), 184 (top left), 185 (loaves and figs), 187, 188 (both), 190 (top), 192 (top), 203, 212, 217, 221 (both), 225, 227 (right), 231 (both), 232 (bottom), 233, 242, 243, 256, 257, 259, 260 (inset), 266–67, 273, 285 (centre), 286 (top), 298, 299, 304 (bottom left), 322, 323, 340, 341 (top left and bottom right), 344 (both)

Phil Manning, with the help of CMJ: p.139 (bottom right and left)
Mansell Collection: pp.29 (bottom left), 236, 248 (top right), 282 (bottom)
Middle East Photographic Archive: pp.161, 193, 318
Alan Millard: pp.66, 183 (top right), 184 (bottom right), 224 (top)
NASA: p.317 (top left)
Richard Nowitz: pp.67, 113, 119, 122 (both), 165
Pictor: pp.134, 224 (bottom), 292 (top)
Picturepoint: pp.69, 88, 153, 180, 271, 290, 310, 313
Jean-Luc Ray: pp.83 (bottom), 157, 333
Rex Features: p.136 (right)
John Rylands University Library, Manchester: p.63
Ronald Sheridan: pp.23 (bottom), 31, 46, 183 (bottom), 190 (bottom), 285 (top), 286 (centre right and bottom left), 287 (bottom right), 305, 307
Transworld Feature Syndicate: p.166 (bottom right)
Wycliffe Bible Translators: pp.81 (top right and top left), 84
ZEFA UK: pp.28, 33 (top, centre left and bottom), 62, 64 (top right), 118, 121 (top right and bottom left), 128, 135, 292 (bottom)

DRAWINGS

All the drawings in this book, apart from the models and plans acknowledged under photographs, have been specially commissioned. Much of the research and reference material for these has come from Lion Publishing's other titles and photo-library, especially *The Lion Handbook to the Bible*, *Photo-Guide to the Old Testament* and *Photo-Guide to the New Testament*.

We are indebted to numerous reference books, whose help we gratefully acknowledge. Amongst these we would like to make special mention of the following: Brockhampton Press, *Picture Reference* series; Carousel books, *Everyday Life* series; Cambridge Bible Commentary, *Old Testament Illustrations* and *New Testament Illustrations*; Elsevier/Phaidon, *Making of the Past* series; Inter-Varsity Press, *New Bible Dictionary*; Macdonald, *Peoples of the Past* series; Marshall Cavendish, *Bible Today*; Nelson, *Atlas of the Bible* and *Shorter Atlas of the Bible* by L. H. Grollenberg; Oxford University Press, *Oxford Bible Atlas*; Princeton University Press, *The Ancient Near East in Pictures* by J. B. Pritchard.